HISTORY OF THE
HARVARD LAW SCHOOL

And Of Early Legal Conditions
in America

Volume I

Da Capo Press Reprints in

AMERICAN CONSTITUTIONAL AND LEGAL HISTORY

GENERAL EDITOR: LEONARD W. LEVY

Brandeis University

HISTORY OF THE
HARVARD LAW SCHOOL

And Of Early Legal Conditions
in America

BY CHARLES WARREN

Volume I

DA CAPO PRESS • NEW YORK • 1970

A Da Capo Press Reprint Edition

This Da Capo Press edition of
History of the Harvard Law School
is an unabridged republication of the first
edition published in New York in 1908.

Library of Congress Catalog Card Number 72-112311
SBN 306-71913-4
Copyright, 1908, by Charles Warren

Published by Da Capo Press
A Division of Plenum Publishing Corporation
227 West 17th Street, New York, N. Y. 10011

HISTORY OF THE
HARVARD LAW SCHOOL

And Of Early Legal Conditions
in America

Volume I

Joseph Story

HISTORY

OF THE

HARVARD LAW SCHOOL

AND OF

EARLY LEGAL CONDITIONS

IN AMERICA

By

CHARLES WARREN

OF THE SUFFOLK BAR

VOLUME I.

ILLUSTRATED

NEW YORK
LEWIS PUBLISHING COMPANY
1908

INSCRIBED
TO
A. B. W.

but for whom, this book would
never have been undertaken.

Preface

Justinian, in his directions to the compilers of his *Pandects,* wrote:

Begin, then, to instruct, with the guidance of God, your scholars in the science of the Law . . . to the end that they may be made worthy ministers of justice and of the Republic.

Such instruction and such end have been the aim of Harvard Law School since its foundation. If less than this were true, there would be no occasion for this book.

In the preface to the first volume of his *Reports,* Coke said:

It is therefore necessary that memorable things should be committed to writing (the witness of times, the light and life of truth) and not wholly be taken to slippery memory, which seldom yieldeth a certain reckoning.

"Memorable things" and memorable men have impinged upon the past of the Harvard Law School, and it has been my task to fix in writing some impressions, hitherto unpublished, of that past from men who formed a part of it, and to gather together from the disjointed writings of others their records of that past.

When I first began to write this history, I deemed it necessary to describe the legal conditions existing in Massachusetts at the date of the founding of the Law School. To do this, it became requisite to show the difference between the Bar of that State and of other States. This led me to a consideration of the history of the early American Bar—how it was created, how it was educated, and what were the influences which promoted or retarded its growth. So arose the addendum to my title "And of Early Legal Conditions in America."

If further excuse is needed for thus developing the scope of this book, I might say that no consecutive summary of the early history of lawyers in this country has ever yet been made, so far as I am aware, and there seems a real vacancy in legal literature to be filled, however insufficiently. This portion of my work does not claim to be a deep historical research among original records, but rather the collation, for convenient reference and from hundreds of scattered sources, of the scanty, available information as to the rise of the American Bar.

The reader who wishes to concern himself merely with the Law School and not with early American legal history is therefore advised to begin at Chapter XII.

In recording the history of the Law School itself, I have had three things especially in view; first, to set forth events, facts, and conditions in the language of the contemporary actors, if possible; second, to keep constantly before the reader the legal and political conditions contemporaneous with the various stages of the life of the School—though John Cotton, the old Puritan, may have believed that "the more any law smells of man, the more unprofitable", the writer of to-day knows that unless his law history is redolent of man and man's deeds, it will be a dry and unsavory work.—Third, I have accumulated, as far as possible, purely statistical and routine matters in chapters by themselves, so that by judicious skipping of these chapters the reader may, I hope, find an interest in the others, only slightly obstructed by bald facts and figures.

Volume III, containing the Alumni Roll, has not been written by me, but has been compiled by the publishers, subject to my editorial suggestions. While it is impossible to make such a roll absolutely complete, requests for biographical data have been sent to all living graduates; and as to deceased graduates, the mass of facts collected by the Law School Librarian, John H. Arnold, at the time of making the Law School Catalogue, as well as biographical dictionaries, etc., have been largely used.

I have been hampered in describing the Law School between the years 1817 and 1870, owing to the non-existence of any Law Faculty or other official Law School records covering that period, so that I have had to search for the official facts through the mass of papers, letters, reports and records in the Harvard Archives pertaining to the College in general. I wish to acknowledge my indebtedness to the courteous and ready assistance and suggestions given me in this work by the officials of the Harvard College Library and by Mr. John H. Arnold and Professor James Barr Ames of the Law School. My grateful acknowledgements are also due to William Kent, Artemas H. Holmes and James G. Croswell, all of New York, William V. Kellen and Ezra R. Thayer of Boston; Charles P. Greenough of Brookline, Mass.;

Edward H. Daveis of Portland, Maine; the Misses Parsons of Cambridge, Mass.; Miss Harriet G. Loring of Washington, D. C.; Mrs. Charles Bradley of Providence, R. I.; Mrs. Alexander S. Porter of Boston; the officials of the Massachusetts Historical Society and the Massachusetts State Libraries; and to many others, graduates of the School and relatives of the Professors, who have kindly loaned to me autographs, letters and pictures, and who have sent to me their reminiscences.

While I cannot hope that this history is free from errors, I can only say, that in writing it I have at times been obliged to conform to Lord Eldon's description of the life of a student of the law, and to "live like a hermit and work like a horse". The labor will be more than repaid, however, if the results shall prove to be of any service to Harvard, or shall (in the words of Coke) "tend to some discharge of that great obligation of duty wherein I am bound to my profession.

Accipe, quo semper finitur epistola verbo,
Et vigeant jura et (lector amice) Vale."

CHARLES WARREN.

Boston, Mass., October 27, 1908.

Errata and Addenda

Volume I.

Page 17, line 12.—"June 2" instead of "Jan. 18".

Page 17, line 13.—"October 13" instead of "June 21".

Page 18, line 18.—"New England" instead of "American".

Page 22, line 9.—Insert after "1647" the words "the Governor and four assistants and".

Page 22, last line.—Insert; "That alone was declared to be law which was made such by the Assembly. This meant the exclusion of English law when unconfirmed by the Assembly."

Page 24, line 12.—Insert after "laymen" the words "the President and Council acting as the Court, with the General Assembly as a Court of Appeal."

Chapter I end.—Insert "The American Colonies in the Seventeenth Century", by Herbert L. Osgood (1904-07).

Page 33, last line.—"1731" instead of "1733".

Page 36, line 1.—"About 1307" instead of "in 1327".

Page 40, line 23.—Should read, "Dialogus de Scaccario written in 1178".

Page 40, line 26.—"About 1290" instead of "1275".

Page 40, line 30.—"About 1307" instead of "1327".

Page 40, line 34.—"1472" instead of "1742".

Page 40, Note.—Add, *"The Sources of English Law,* by H. Brunner; *Materials for the History of English Law,* by F. W. Maitland, *Pol. Sci. Qu.,* Vol. IV (1889)".

Page 41, last line.—"1628" instead of "1633".

Page 60, line 37.—"Associate" instead of "Assistant".

Page 85, line 8.—Note reference (9) instead of (5).

Page 88, last line.—Insert; "The early courts were the local or Courts of Sessions, and the Court of Assizes consisting of the Governor and Council. In 1683, the Governor and Council were made a Supreme Court and distinct Courts of Sessions were constituted for each county."

Page 94, line 24.—"Twelve" instead of "six".

Page 94, line 33.—"1757" instead of "1751".

Page 95, Note 6.—Should read "Judge of the Supreme Court 1790, Chief Justice 1798".

Page 95, Note 4.—Should read "Chancellor 1777-1801".

Page 96, line 2.—Should read "Daniel D. Tompkins".

Page 109, line 19.—Insert: "Up to 1683, all judicial business was done by the Governor and Council. In that year, a Provincial Court was established, and the Governor and Council became a Court of Appeal."

Page 112. line 22.—"Up to 1702" instead of "At first".
Page 114, line 32.—Insert after "reports in" the date "1799".
Page 131, line 14.—"Selden" instead of "Seldon".
Page 142, Note 1.—Strike out "Solicitor General to his Majesty".
Page 188, line 20.—Strike out "who".
Page 207, line 32.—"1805" instead of "1806".
Page 235, line 4.—"Johnson's dissenting" instead of "Marshall's".
Page 238, line 10.—"1807" instead of "1907."
Page 247, line 27.—"1805" instead of "1806".
Page 264, Notes.—Renumber notes 1-6 as 7-12, and notes 7-12 as 1-6.
Page 307, line 11.—Insert "were" before "referred".
Page 327, lines 32-33.—Strike out all words after "improve it".
Page 328, line 22.—Note reference (2) instead of (1) ; same in note.
Page 344, line 18.—Note reference (2), instead of (1) ; same in note.
Page 360, line 5.—"One of the first" instead of "the first".
Page 366, line 29.—Note reference (2) instead of (1) ; same in note.
Page 371, line 15.—"Barrington's" instead of "Barnington's".
Page 378, line 28.—Insert "Richard S." before "Coxe".
Page 397, line 26.—"Sullivan" instead of "Livingston".
Page 431, line 30.—Insert "he" before "wrote".
Page 448, line 8.—"forty-nine" instead of "thirty-nine".
Page 448, Note, last line.—"49" instead of "39".
Page 505, line 1.—"Gardiner" instead of "Gardner".

Volume II.

Page 114, line 22.—"The Columbian Law School in Washington" instead of "that College".
Page 124, line 17.—"fifty-one" instead of "fifty".
Page 132, line 15.—"Company" instead of "Corporation".
Page 201, last line.—Note reference (2) instead of (1) ; same in note.
Page 226, line 5.—"O'Conor" instead of "O'Connor".
Page 240, Note 3.—"(1860)" instead of "(1866)".
Page 259, line 37.—"Arphaxed" instead of "Asphaxed".
Page 274, line 27.—"L. S. 1861-62" instead of "U. S. 1861-62."
Page 331, Note.—"Harvard" instead of "Howard".
Page 432.—See Appendix I, page 515.
Page 443.—See Appendix I, page 515.
Page 463.—See Appendix I, page 515.
Page 476.—See Appendix I, page 515.
Page 502, line 10.—"result" instead of "results".

Table of Contents

VOLUME I.

VOLUME II.

Illustrations

Volume I.

INTRODUCTORY CHAPTER.

The Harvard Law School, the first collegiate school of law now in existence, was founded in Massachusetts in 1817. The first private school of law, the Litchfield Law School, was opened in Connecticut thirty-three years earlier, in 1784. The first American professorship of law was established at the College of William and Mary in Virginia in 1779.

For one hundred and fifty years prior to 1779, lawyers were obliged to rely upon their own exertions for a legal education.

The early lawyers were few in number, lacking in education, and weak in influence.

It was sixty-six years from the landing of the Pilgrims and fifty years from the foundation of Harvard College before Harvard sent out, in the Class of 1686, her first graduate destined to be trained for the bar, Benjamin Lynde. It was one hundred and ten years after the establishment of Massachusetts Bay Colony before a lawyer sat in her General Court as a legislator—John Read, in 1738.

It was one hundred and thirty-five years before a regular Bar Association existed in the Province of Massachusetts.

Harvard College was one hundred and forty-eight years old before she admitted a lawyer to her councils as a member of the Corporation—John Lowell, in 1784.

This lack of lawyers in the early days of American history, and the lateness of the establishment of any adequate means of legal education cannot properly be understood without some knowledge of the conditions surrounding the practice of law and its development in the American Colonies and in the early years of the United States.

The real facts in the history of any institution cannot be fully appreciated, if looked at as disconnected and isolated.

As Maitland says, "Such is the unity of all history that anyone who endeavors to tell a piece of it must feel that his first sentence tears a seamless web—a statute of limitations must be set; but it must be arbitrary. The web must be rent; but as we rend it we may watch the whence and whither of a few of the ravelling threads which have been making a pattern too large for any man's eye."(1)

And as John Morley says, "I want to know what men did in the thirteenth century, not out of antiquarian curiosity, but because the thirteenth century is at the root of what men think and do in the nineteenth."(2) The state of legal education at the present time therefore can be best understood by an understanding of its past.

No attempt has hitherto been made, so far as is known, to bring together from the innumerable scattered sources the scanty information existing in relation to the early Bar of the American Colonies, Provinces, and States.

The first eleven chapters of this book therefore are devoted to an effort to give some idea of the lawyers, the practice of law, the legal conditions of the times, both in America and England, and the development of legal education prior to 1817—the year of the foundation of the Harvard Law School.

If the results of this effort, in chapters two and five, shall appear to repeat only well known and trite facts, the excuse may be offered that, though a twice-told tale, it may become a newly-lighted tale in the juxtaposition in which it is presented. And if the narrative of the early Bar, in chapters one, three, and four, shall seem to consist of a mere marshalling, in wearisome rank, of bare names and dates, the reader must remember that frequently little more is known of famous lawyers than their names and the titles of their cases; and that the lack of posthumous impression has long been reckoned one of the misfortunes attending the practice of the legal profession.(3)

---

(1) *Prologue to a History of English Law—Law Quarterly Review* Vol. XIV (1898).

(2) *The Problems of To-day for the History of the Common Law,* by J. H. Wigmore.

(3) "The fame of the great lawyers, so far as it is built up in the active labors of the forum, rests proverbially upon a most slippery basis. No man has yet earned a reputation that has outlived the generation who witnessed his triumphs, upon the mere faith of a reporter's notes. We have an indistinct rumor, an imperfect tradition of the glories of an old forensic renown, in some remembered name of the last century. We turn to the reports to find some picture of that rich and glowing mind which is said to have wrought effects almost miraculous upon the auditors of the courts in the past time, and to have swayed the multitude, in its day, with a command which none could resist. How "shrunken and wooden" do we find the carved image of that fame in these dusty crypts of the law! We look elsewhere in vain. The overlabored actor himself has had no time or no inclination to embody and preserve the brilliant thoughts or the learned reasons which, in the utterance, so dazzled and

Six facts stand out prominently in the history of the development of early law practice in the American Colonies and Provinces.

First, the rigid state of the Common Law itself at the time.

As has been well said, "It is not altogether strange that our law at that time should seem to a plain Puritan to be a dark and knavish business; for it was still heavily encumbered with the formalism of the Middle Ages. It was, indeed, already, like Milton's lion, 'pawing to get free its hinder parts;' and there was a sort of truth in Coke's dithyrambic praise of it, then but recently published, that 'reason is the life of the law—nay, the common law itself is nothing else but reason;' but it was the truth of prophecy, and not the truth of fact. The law also was then mainly hidden away from laymen and wrapped in a foreign tongue; and it was taught at the Inns of Court in the rudest way— ' hanc rigidam Minervam,' said Sir Henry Spelman, a contemporary of our founders, 'ferreis amplexibus coercendam.' 'My mother,' said Spelman, 'sent me to London to begin upon our law,' (1570) 'Cujus vestibulum salutassem reperissemque linguam peregrinam, dialectum barbarum, methodum inconcinnam, molem non ingentem solum sed perpetuis humeris sustinendam, excidit mihi (fateor) animus.' "(1)

Second, the unpopularity of lawyers as a class. In all the Colonies, he was a character of disrepute. In many of them, persons acting as attorneys were forbidden to receive any fee; in some, all paid attorneys were barred from the courts; in all, they were subjected to the most rigid restrictions as to fees and procedure. Even in England, the lawyer's reputation may be estimated to a certain extent by the titles of frequent tracts which were printed in London, like *The Downfall of Unjust Lawyers; Doomsday Drawing Near with Thunder and Lightning for Lawyers,* (1645); *A Rod for Lawyers Who are Hereby declared Robbers and Deceivers of the Nation; Essay Wherein is Described the Lawyers, Smugglers and Officers Frauds,* (1675);(2) And in the minds of many Englishmen the lawyer

---

charmed the hearers. The finer essences have fled—the dead skeleton only remains."—*Memoirs of the Life of William Wirt,* by John P. Kennedy, Vol. II.

(1) Speech of James B. Thayer at the 250th Commemoration of Harvard College, Nov. 5, 1886.

(2) See *Lawyer and Client,* by William Allen Butler (1871).

So John Milton said in 1640:

was synonymous with the cringing Attorney Generals and Solicitor Generals of the Crown and the arbitrary Justices of the
King's Court, all bent on the conviction of those who opposed
the King's prerogatives, and twisting the law to secure convic-
tions.

Third, the scanty materials at hand in the Colonies for the
study of law, and the scarcity of printed law books and reports,
even in England.

Fourth, the supremacy of the clergy in the magistracy and in
the courts of New England. "During the period from 1620 to
1692," said a writer in the *North American Review* in 1829, "no
trace can be found of law as a science or profession. The clergy
possessed, as in England, much of the legal knowledge of the community."(1) It was to their clergyman that the colonists looked
to guide their new governments, and in their clergymen, they
believed, lay all that was necessary and proper for their lawful
and righteous government. It followed, therefore, that the "Word
of God" played a greater part in the progress and practice of
the law than the words of Bracton, Littleton or Coke. Where
such was the condition, there was more need of clever clergymen than of trained lawyers.

Fifth, the participation and interference of the royal Governors
in the judicial system of the Colonies.

As early as 1747, Dr. W. Douglass, in his *Summary of the
Present State of the British Settlements in North America,*
wrote that "it is said that a Governor and such of the council as
he thinks proper to consult with, dispense with such provincial
laws as are troublesome or stand in their way of procedure of
their court of equity so called." In New York, a royal Governor
found it necessary to remove a Chief Justice who failed to decide in his favor, in order "to discourage advocates of Boston
principles." In Maryland, the Bar was at constant war with
the Governor in order to preserve the legal rights of the Colony
from the arbitrary dictates and proclamations of the executive.
In South Carolina, the lawyers were forced to petition the pro-

----

"Most men are allured to the trade of law, grounding their purposes
not on the prudent and heavenly contemplation of justice and equity
which was never taught them, but on the promising and pleasing thoughts
of litigious terms, fat contentions and flowing fees."

(1) See review of *American Jurist,* Vol. I in *North American Review,*
Vol. XXIX (Oct. 1829).

prietary in complaint of the Governor holding all the judicial offices.(1)

Sixth, the ignorance of the judges and their lack of legal education. In 1764, Thomas Pownall, "late Gov. Capt. Gen. Commander in Chief and Vice Admiral of His Majesty's Provinces Massachusetts Bay and South Carolina and then Gov. of New Jersey," wrote(2) :

I cannot in one view better describe the defects of the provincial courts in these infant governments than by that very description which my Lord Chief Justice Hale gives of our county courts in the infancy of our own government; wherein he mentions,

"First, the ignorance of the judges, who were the freeholders of the county.

Secondly, that these various courts bred variety of law, especially in the several counties; for the decisions or judgments being made by divers courts and several independent judges and judiciaries who had no common interest amongst them in their several judicatories; thereby in process of time every several county would have several laws, customs, rules and forms of proceedings."

Upon the first article of this parallel it would be no dishonour to many gentlemen sitting on the benches of the courts of law in the colonies to say that they are not and cannot be expected to be lawyers or learned in the law.

As will be shown in greater detail in the first seven chapters of this book, all these six factors served to retard the rise of the American lawyer in the 17th and early 18th Centuries.

As the struggle for Independence grew nearer, the colonists began to maintain more and more earnestly their absolute rights to the privileges of the English Common Law. Their lawyers made the Common Law more and more the object of study. It became the custom in some of the Colonies to send the young lawyer to England to complete his legal education.

As the Colonies became more wealthy and commercially prosperous, law books were imported from England and sold in increasing quantities, especially after the publication of Blackstone in 1765. When the Revolution broke out and the Colonies were thrown absolutely upon their own resources, a movement

---

(1) See especially Chapter VII in *The Provincial Governor,* by Evarts B. Greene (1898).
(2) *The Administration of the British Colonies,* by Thomas Pownall (1764).

began in several of their educational institutions to introduce the
study of law as a part of the general system of education; and
various law professorships were established during the last
twenty years of the 18th Century, though with small success.

Then came a period of reaction. The old prejudices of the
early 17th Century were revived against lawyers in the closing
years of the 18th. A violent opposition to anything English,
and especially to the English Common Law doctrines, swept over
the United States—which lasted with varying force until after
1810. Then came the War of 1812 and the ensuing commercial
distress and panics, diverting attention from all forms of education. Meanwhile, the early years of the 19th Century were the
great formative period of American law; American law reports were being introduced, and American law books written.
And it was under the spur of the desire to teach young men
American law systematically and more thoroughly than they
could be taught in law offices that the American Law Schools
arose.

Such in brief is the history of the legal conditions out of which
the Harvard Law School had its origin in 1817, and which will
be described more fully in the succeeding chapters.

CHAPTER I.

New England Law and Lawyers in the 17th Century.

MASSACHUSETTS.

Sixty-five men landed at Plymouth in 1620, no one of whom was a lawyer.

Among the founders of the Massachusetts Bay Colony, 1628-1634, there was not an actual practising lawyer, although John Winthrop, its Governor, and Emmanuel Downing, the father of George Downing whose name stands number two on the roll of the first class of Harvard graduates, (Harv. 1642.), had been admitted to the Inner Temple in London.(1)

Richard Bellingham, Simon Bradstreet, Herbert Pelham, John Humphreys, and Thomas Dudley and a few others had doubtless been students of law or university men but they were not engaged in the practise of the profession.

At the beginning of this period of "Law without lawyers" in the Plymouth Colony, the whole community acted as the court. Thus in the first recorded offence against the law, in March 1621, "John Billington is convented, before the whole company for the contempt of the captain's lawful commands with opprobrious speeches; for which he is adjudged to have his neck and heels tied together." The second offence was, as Governor Bradford informs us, the first duel fought in New England upon a challenge at single combat with sword and dagger between Edward Doty and Edward Lester, servants of Mr. Hopkins. "They are adjudged by the whole company to have their head and feet tied together and so to lie for twenty-four hours without meat or drink." Later the Governor and Assistants constituted the Court.

In Massachusetts Bay Colony, from 1629 to 1635, the Governor and Assistants acted both as magistrates, legislators and judges; and their proceedings as such "Court of Assistants" are

---

(1) *Proc. Mass. Hist. Soc.* 1878, p. 3.

to be found entered in the same book and intermixed with the records of the General Court or Legislature. (1)

After 1635 and up to 1684 the General Court acted for some time both as a legislature and as a judicial court of appeals. It met, not only to pass laws, but also "for the imposition of lawful fines, mulcts, imprisonments and other lawful correction."

In 1636, the General Court by resolve asked the Governor to make a draft of law "agreeable to the word of God," to be the fundamental law. In the meantime, the magistrates were to proceed in the courts to determine all causes according to the laws of the General Court, and where there was no law, "then as near the law of God as they can." (2)

Gradually, however, the Court of Assistants became a separate judicial body, and by the law of 1660 their terms of sitting and their powers were definitely prescribed as a Superior court. Inferior courts were established in 1639.

In modes of procedure, the Magistrates and the Court followed somewhat the general proceedings of English law; but in their decisions, they were practically uncontrolled by any system of law. They were inclined to believe, as Winthrop said, that "such laws would be fittest for us which should arise pro re nata upon occasions."

This was quite in accordance with the desires of the clergy, who then formed the prevailing power in the Colonies.

The ministers advise in making of laws, especially ecclesiasticall, and are present in courts and advise in some speciall causes annual and in framing of Fundamental Lawes. Matters of debt, trespass and upon the case, equity, yea and of heresy also are tryed by a jury.

So said Thomas Lechford; (3) and as another contemporary writer said:

The preachers by their power with the people made all the magistrates and kept them so entirely under obedience that they durst not act without them. Soe that whenever anything strange

---

(1)   Preface by John Noble to *Records of the Courts of Assistants,* (1901).
Early Court Files of Suffolk County, by John Noble—*Publications of the Colonial Society of Massachusetts,* Vol. III (1895-97).
(2)   *Mass. Colonial Records,* Vol. I.
(3)   *Plaine Dealing, or News from New England,* by Thomas Lechford (1642).

or unusual was brought before them, they would not determine the matter without consulting their preachers.(1)

As an example of the intermingling of the clergy, it may be noted that in 1635 it was ordered that "none among us shall sue at the lawe before Mr. Henry Vane and the two Elders have had the hearing and desyding of the cause if they cann."

But while so much power lay in the discretion of the magistrates, the people felt themselves unsafe. As John Winthrop wrote:(2)

The deputies having conceived great danger to our State in regard that our magistrates for want of positive law in any cases might proceed according to their discretion, it was agreed that some men should be appointed to frame a body of grounds of laws, in resemblance to a magna charta, which being allowed by some of the ministers and the general court, should be received for fundamental laws.

It was natural, and characteristic of the times, that this matter of framing a code should have been entrusted by the magistrates to two clergymen, each of whom framed a separate model. Rev. John Cotton, a Fellow of Emmanuel College, Cambridge, England, prepared a code called by Governor Winthrop, "A copy of Moses, his judicials, compiled in an exact method." It was founded on the Scripture throughout, with references thereto, and established a pure theocracy. The other was compiled by Rev. Nathaniel Ward, a minister at Ipswich, and the author of a curious book entitled, *The Simple Cobbler of Agawam.* He had been a barrister of Lincoln's Inn in England in 1615,(3) had entered the ministry in 1618 and been suspended for Puritanism in 1633 by Archbishop Laud. This great work of his, called, *The Body of Lib-*

---

(1) *An Account of the Colonies,* Lambeth MSS., Perry's *Historical Collection* III., 48.
(2) *History of New England,* by John Winthrop, Vol. I., p. 194. The record reads as follows: "At the General Court, May 25, 1636, it was ordered that the Governor (Henry Vane), the Deputy Governor (John Winthrop), Thomas Dudley, John Haynes, Richard Bellingham, Esquires, Mr. (John) Cotton, Mr. (Hugh) Peters and Mr. Shepherd are entreated to make a draught of laws agreeable to the word of God which may be the Fundamentals of this Commonwealth and to present the same to the next General Court."
See Cotton's *Moses, His Judicials,* in *Mass. Hist. Soc. Proc.* (2nd Series,) Vol. XVI. (1902).
(3) See Gray, C. J. in *Jackson v. Phillips,* 14 Allen (Mass.) p. 599 (1867).

erties, consisting of one hundred fundamental laws, is entitled to the fame of being the first American Law Book.(1)   It was accepted by the people in 1641, as better suited to the times than Cotton's Code.(2)   Still, even in Ward's Code it is to be noted that in cases not therein provided for, it was the "word of God" which was to guide the courts, and not the English Common Law.   Thus Liberty Number I. provided:

I.   No man's life shall be taken away, no man's honour or good name shall be stayned, no man's person shall be arrested restrayned, banished, dismembered, nor any wayes punished, no man shall be deprived of his wife or children, no man's goods or estates shall be taken away from him nor any way indammaged under colour of law or Countenance of Authority, unless it be by virtue or equitie of some expresse law of the Country warranting the same established by a generall court and sufficiently published, or in case of the defect of a law in any particular case by the word of God.   And in Capitall cases, or in cases concerning dismembering or banishment, according to that word to be judged by the Generall Court.(3)

Many other enactments about this time were far different from the English Common Law of the day, as for instance, that there should be no monopolies except such as were profitable to the country, and those for a short time only; that all deeds of conveyance, whether absolute or conditional, should be recorded; that instead of the right of primogeniture the elder son should have a double portion of his parent's real and personal estate; that no injunction should be laid on any church, church officer, or member, in point of doctrine, worship or discipline, whether for substance or circumstance, besides the institutions of the Lord.

This *Body of Liberties* was probably not printed in full, or

---

(1)   No copy of this was discovered until 1843 when Mr. Francis C. Gray found it in the Boston Athenæum.   See *Mass. Hist. Soc. Coll.* Vol. VIII (3rd Series) p. 196.
See also *Colonial Laws of Massachusetts* by W. H. Whitmore (1890).

(2)   In 1641 there was published in London *An Abstract of the Lawes of New England As they are now Established,* which is probably Cotton's Code.   See *Mass. Hist. Soc. Proc.* (2nd Series) Vol. XVI (1902).

(3)   *The General Laws and Liberties of New Plimouth Colony* also provided (1671) that "no person shall be endamaged in respect of Life, Limb,. Liberty, Good name or Estate, under colour of Law or countenance of authority, but by virtue or equity of some express Law of the General Court of this Colony, the known Law of God, or the good and equitable Laws of our Nation suitable for us."

published at the time; but in 1649 a revision of all the laws then in existence was published, known as the *Laws and Liberties,* a similar revision was made in 1660, (the earliest, of which any copy is extant), and another, in 1672.(1)

In 1644, the General Court requested the opinion of the elders as to whether the magistrates should be guided by the word of God in cases not covered by statute, and the elders replied in the following terms:

We do not find that by the patent they are expressly directed to proceed according to the word of God; but we understand that by a law or liberty of the country, they may act in cases wherein as yet there is no express law, so that in such acts they proceed according to the word of God.

In 1645, the General Court itself stated, in substance:

The laws of the colony are not diametrically opposed to the laws of England for then they must be contrary to the laws of God on which the common law, so far as it is law, is also founded. Anything that is otherwise established is not law but an error.(2)

It is evident that with such a basis for the decisions of the courts, there was little need of lawyers learned in the English Common Law. "When the holy Scriptures were considered as

---

(1)   See *The Body of Liberties of* 1641, by H. H. Edes, *Publications of the Massachusetts Colonial Society,* Vol. VII. (1900-1902).

(2)   The foundation of the law upon the Word of God was even at this time a familiar doctrine even in Common Law England.
Thus as late as 1650, Lord Chief Justice Keble said in 5 *How. St. Trials* that the law of England was "the very consequence of the very decalogue itself—as really and truly the law of God as any Scriptural phrase. . . . Whatever was not consonant to the law of God in Scripture . . . . was not the law of England but the error of the party which did pronounce it."
So John Milton in his *Defence of the People of England* in 1651 appealed "to that fundamental maxim in our law by which nothing is to be counted as law that is contrary to the law of God or of reason."
In a book entitled, *Quaternio or a Fourfold way to a Happy Life. Set forth in a Discourse between a Countryman and a citizen, a divine and a lawyer, wherein the Commodities of the Countrey and the Citie; together with the excellency of Divinitie and the Law are set forth,* published in 1636 by Thomas Nash of the Inner Temple, it is said "Now because it is a hard thing, yea indeede impossible almost, for a man to observe these lawes which he knoweth not; therefore I did desire to know the Lawes of the Kingdome wherein I lived and thereby as a rule to frame and fashion all my actions by . . . . . I had often heard and upon Inquiry I have found it to be true that all Lawes politicall are meere derivatives out of the primitive Law of God and Nature."

a proper guide in all cases of doubt, and the parties spoke for themselves, there was no place for an order of lawyers."(1)

The important trials early in the Century were conducted with entire disregard of the fundamental principles of the Common Law. Thus, in the trial of Anne Hutchinson before the General Court in 1637, her plea that, "I am called to answer before you, but I hear no things laid to my charge," was disregarded; and her demand that the witnesses against her be sworn, was complied with only partially. So in the trials of the Quakers, in 1661, before the Court of Assistants, their appeals to the "law of England" and their denial of the right of the Colony to "make laws repugnant to the laws of England," were swept aside by the answer, "You have broken our law, and we shall try you."(2) It seems to be a fact that the English Common Law was used in deciding cases merely as an illustration. Thus, an account is given in the Hutchinson papers(3) of a case before one Symonds, a magistrate, involving the right of taxation to pay for a dwelling house voted by a town to its minister. The magistrate found for the plaintiff, saying that the "fundamental law which God and nature has given to the people cannot be infringed;" and although he quoted writers like Finch and Dalton, saying, "Let us not despise the rules of the learned in the law of England who have every experience," the precedents on which he relied were colonial, and the Common Law was regarded as binding, only so far as it was expressive of the Law of God.

The early court records themselves show the constant citation of scriptural authority. "The reasons of Appeal and the Answers make much use of quotations from Scripture—a pertinent quotation seemed sometimes decisive in settling a disputed point. Possibly there was sometimes a readier acquiescence in an opinion of Moses that in one of the Lord High Chancellor."(4)

There can be little wonder therefore that "for more than the ten first years," as Hutchinson says, "the parties spake for themselves for the most part; sometimes, when it was thought the cause required it, they were assisted by a patron, or man of su-

---

(1) Address before the Suffolk Bar on *Origin and History of the Legal Profession in Massachusetts*, by William Sullivan, in 1825.

(2) See *American Criminal Trials*, by P. W. Chandler (1841).

(3) *Hutchinson Papers*, Vol. II p. 1.

(4) *Early Court Files of Suffolk County*, by John Noble—*Publications of the Massachusetts Colonial Society*, Vol. III. (1895-97).

perior abilities without fee or reward."(1) And though Ward, in a sermon preached at the annual election in 1641, had declared, that the magistrates "ought not to give private advice and take knowledge of any main cause before it came to public hearing," his proposition was rejected on the ground that its adoption would render it necessary to provide lawyers to direct men in their causes.

Probably the first lawyer in the Colonies was Thomas Morton, described by Governor Bradford as "a kind of pettie-fogger of Furnewells Inne," although set forth by himself on the title page of his book, *The New British Canaan* (1637), as "of Clifford's Inn Gent."(2) Governor Dudley spoke of him as "a proud, insolent man," who had been "an attorney in the West Countries while he lived in England." He came to Massachusetts in 1624 or 1625 with Captain Wollaston and settled in what is now Quincy. At his place named Merry Mount, he opened, as the old chronicler says, "a school of atheisme, set up a maypole and did quaff strong waters and act as they had anew revived and celebrated the feast of ye Roman Goddess Flora or the beastly products of ye madd Bacchanalians." The patience of the rulers being exhausted, he was imprisoned and then shipped out of the Colony.

The first educated lawyer who practised in the Colony appeared on the horizon in 1637 or 1638, when Thomas Lechford, "of Clement's Inn in the County of Middlesex, Gentleman"(3) landed in Boston. For three years he was, so Washburn calls him, "the Embodied Bar of Massachusetts Bay."(4) Under the conditions prevalent, he found the practice of law in Boston far from

---

(1) *History of Massachusetts Bay Colony,* by Thomas Hutchinson, Vol. I.

(2) Clifford's Inn and Furnewell's Inn were Inns of Chancery. The Inns of Chancery were so called, "probably because they were appropriated to such clerks as chiefly studied the forming of writs which was the province of the cursitors who were officers of Chancery, such as belong to the Courts of Common Pleas and King's Bench, and in Stowe's time were chiefly filled with attorneys, solicitors and clerks." They were inferior in rank to the Inns of Court, at which only those who were studying to be called as barristers were admitted. See Chapter II. *Infra.*

(3) Mr. Justice Shallow—"By yea or nay, sir, I dare say my cousin William is become a good scholar. He is at Oxford, still, is he not?"
Silence—"Indeed, sir, to my cost."
Shallow—"He must then to the inns of court shortly. I was once of Clement's Inn, where, I think, they will talk of mad Shallow yet."
King Henry IV, Part II, Act III, Scene 2—(Printed in 1600).

(4) *Judicial History of Massachusetts,* by Emory Washburn, (1840).

lucrative; and he described himself as being supported largely as a scrivener "in writing petty things." Little is known of him; but it is certain that his legal knowledge was of value in the Colony, for it was at his suggestion that a law was passed in 1639, by which it was ordered, that in order that the records should "bee of good use for president to posterity. . . . every judgment with all the evidence bee recorded in a book, to bee kept to posterity."(1)

In 1639, his habits brought him into such trouble with the authorities, that at a Quarter Court in September, it was ordered, that "Mr. Thomas Lechford for going to the Jewry and pleading with them out of court is debarred from pleading any main cause hereafter unless his own and admonished not to presume to meddle beyond what he shall be called to by the court." In 1640, he was "convented" before the Quarter Court, and, according to the record, "acknowledged he had overshot himself, and was sorry for it, promised to attend to his calling, and not to meddle with controversies, and was dismissed." In 1642, after his return to England, he published his *Plaine Dealing or News from New England,* from which it appears that his trouble with the courts was due to the fact that he tried to set up the Common Law, while the Puritan courts cared nothing at all for the Common Law, but were trying to set up, especially in criminal matters, the Mosaic Law.(2) The foreman, he wrote, gave the charge to the grand juries, "under the heads of the ten commandments," and this was his warning:

I fear it is not a little degree of pride and dangerous improvidence to slight all former laws of the church and state, cases of experience and precedents, to hammer out new, according to several exigencies, upon pretence that the Word of God is sufficient to rule us.

It has been said that it was because of their experience with Lechford that the colonists adopted Article No. 26 of the *Body of Liberties,* providing that, "Every man that findeth himself unfit to plead his own cause in any court shall have the liberty to employ any man against whom the court doth not except to

(1) *Mass. Colony Records,* Vol. I, p. 275. To him therefore is owed the *Records of the Court of Assistants,* (published first in print in Massachusetts in 1901).

(2) *The First Lawyer in Boston,—Amer. Law Rev.* Vol. XIX. See also *Mass. Col. Rec.,* Vol. I., p. 270.

help him, *provided he give him no fee or reward for his pains."*
This statute remained in force, however, only a few years.

Forty years passed on after Lechford's disgusted return to
London, and still no educated lawyer appeared in Massachusetts.
There were, however, attorneys of some kind, as they are mentioned in the records of the General Court in 1649, and elsewhere. Little, however, is known of them, and they were doubtless what Governor Winthrop would call, "mean men," of but
little or no legal education. They appeared, probably by special
powers, and by judicial requisition.(1)

In 1654, an act was passed prohibiting every person who was
a "usual or common attorney in any Inferior Court" from sitting
as a deputy in the General Court;(2) and in 1656, an act was
passed, providing that:

---

(1) See *Address to Worcester County Bar, October 2, 1829,* by Joseph
Willard. Thus in 1652, in Middlesex, Mr. Coggan appeared as attorney
to Stephen Day, the first printer: in 1654, in the case of Ridgway against
Jordan, the defendant appeared by his attorney, Amos Richardson: and
in 1656, in the case of John Glover against Henry Dunster, who had been
president of Harvard College, Edmund Goffe and Thomas Danforth appeared for the plaintiff. This Amos Richardson was a tailor, and Coggan (John) was in the mercantile business and kept the first shop in
Boston. Goffe, then an old man, was for several years the representative
from Cambridge, and Danforth also; and the latter, besides, filled the
office of assistant and deputy governor; but neither of them was of the
legal profession.

(2) This provision of law is strangely suggestive of the famous "Dunces'
Parliament" held in 1404 at the order of Henry IV, and described by Sir Edward Coke as follows: "At a parliament holden at
Coventry Anno 6 H 4 the parliament was summoned by writ and by colour
of the said ordinance it was forbidden that no lawyer should be chosen
knight, citizen, or burgess, by reason whereof this parliament was fruitless
and never a good law made thereat, and therefore called indoctum parlia-
mentum or lack learning parliament, and seeing these writs were against
law, lawyers ever since (for the great and good service of the Commonwealth) have been eligible; for as it hath been said the writs of parliament cannot be altered without an act of parliament; and albeit the prohibitory clause had been inserted in the writ, yet being against law,
lawyers were of right eligible and might have been elected knights, citizens, or burgesses in that parliament of 6 Hen 4."
And Sir Bulstrode Whitelock in the reign of Charles II in a book entitled *Notes on King's Writ for choosing members of Parliament,* described
this parliament as follows: "In 5 H 4 the King being in great want of
money and fearing that if the lawyers were parliament men they would
oppose his excessive demands and hinder his illegal purposes (according
to their knowledge and learning in the lawes and publique affayres); to
prevent this the King issued forth writs of summons with a clause of
'nolumus' to this effect: 'we will not that you or any other sherife of
our kingdome or any other man of lawe by any means be chosen.' This
parliament was held 6 Hen. 4 and was called the lacke-learning parliament; either (saith our historian) for the unlearnedness of the persons
or for their malice to learned men. It is stiled by Sir Thomas Walsing-

This court taking into consideration the great charge resting upon the colony by reason of the many and tedious discourses and pleadings in courts, both of plaintiff and defendant, as also the readiness of many to prosecute suits in law for small matters: it is therefore ordered by this court and the authority thereof that when any plaintiff or defendant shall plead by himself or his attorney for a longer time than one hour, the party that is sentenced or condemned shall pay twenty shillings for every hour so pleading more than the common fees appointed by the court for the entrance of actions to be added to the execution for the use of the country.

It was not until 1647 that any English law books were to be found in the Colony, when the Governor and Assistants ordered the importation of two copies each of Sir Edward Coke on *Littleton;* the *Books of Entries;* Sir Edward Coke on *Magna Charta;* the *New Terms of Law;* Dalton's *Justices of the Peace;* Sir Edward Coke's *Reports,* "to the end that we may have better light for making and proceeding about laws." And in 1650, it was ordered, that "whereas this Commonwealth is much defective for want of maritime affairs and for as much as there are already many good laws made and published by our own land and the French Nation and other kingdoms and commonwealths, . . . the said laws printed and published in a book called *Lex Mercatoria* shall be perused and duly considered and such of them as are approved by this court shall be declared and published to be in force in this jurisdiction."

In 1684, the Colony itself began to feel the need of lawyers; as it found itself summoned into the court of King's Bench at Westminster, and its own legal rights in gravest peril. For while its charter of 1628, allowed the Massachusetts Bay Colony to make laws and ordinances, "so as such laws and ordinances be not contrary or repugnant to the laws and statutes of this our realm of England." the colonists, having more regard for the laws of God than for those of the King, had not proceeded in very strict compliance with it. In 1665, the English Royal

---

ham in his *Margent* 'the parliament of unlearned men,' and from them, thus packed, the king (saith our author) obtained a grant of an unusual taxe and to the people 'full of trouble and very grievous'—They who will have a 'nolumus' of learned senators must be contented with a 'volumus' of uncouth lawes which I hope will never be the fate of England."
See *New York Bar Assn. Proc.* Vol. XIII.
James I issued a proclamation to voters for members of Parliament directing them "not to choose curious and wrangling lawyers who seek reputation by stirring needless questions." See *Green Bag,* Vol. V (1893).

Commissioners, on examination of the Colony statute books, reported to the General Court 26 criticisms or censures upon the laws. The General Court refused to yield in most particulars, and as a result, there were several years of constant conflict between it and the Crown authorities in England.

In June, 1683, a writ of quo warranto was issued from the Court of King's Bench to oust the holders of the charter. Massachusetts, having no lawyer of distinction within its own bounds, retained Mr. Robert Humphreys of London, a barrister of the Inner Temple, to interpose delay. The writ, being abandoned later for technicalities, a writ of scire facias was issued out of the High Court of Chancery on Jan. 18, 1684, and judgment was entered by default, June 21, 1684, by Lord Keeper Francis North, Lord Guilford, whereby the charter of 1628 was declared forfeited, because of usurpations by the Colony. (1) With the forfeiture of the charter, all the old laws of the Colony were annulled; (2) all its courts disappeared; and a legal chaos seemed existent.

On July 26, 1686, a new court, the Superior Court, was created under the new Governor, Sir Edmund Andros, composed of a majority of the councillors. Three judges were appointed, no one of whom was a lawyer—William Stoughton Chief Justice, John Richardson and Simon Lynde. Benjamin Bullivant, a physician and apothecary, was appointed Attorney General—a man of "considerable eloquence and knowledge of laws."

At the same time, a table of attorney's fees was established, and attorneys were obliged, upon admission to the Bar, to take oath, not only that they would not charge larger fees than those established by law, but that they would be "contented with such fees" as were allowed by the Council, or by the judges of the Superior Court.

Giles Masters, Capt. Nathaniel Thomas, Anthony Checkley, a merchant and military man, Christopher Webb, a merchant, and John Watson, a merchant, were admitted and sworn as attorneys. (3)

---

(1) For the best account of these legal proceedings see *Edward Randolph* in the *Publications of the Prince Society*. It may be noted that one of these usurpations alleged was the chartering of Harvard College.

(2) See Parsons C. J. in *Storer v. Freeman*, 6 Mass., 438, (1810); and Shaw C. J. in *Commonwealth v. Alger*. 7 Cush 53.

(3) Of Watson, John Dunton an English bookseller in Boston in 1686, in his *Life and Error*, speaks as "formerly a merchant in London, but not

At this time, Randolph, Secretary for Sir Edmund Andros during his tyrannical reign as Royal Governor, wrote to a correspondent in England, Jan. 24, 1689:

I have wrote you the want we have of two, or three, honest attorneys, (if any such thing in nature.) We have but two; one is West's creature,—came with him from New York, and drives all before him. He also takes extravagant fees, and for want of more, the country cannot avoid coming to him so that we had better be quite without them than not to have more. I have wrote Mr. Blackthwaite the great necessity of judges from England.

But the necessity of procuring judges and lawyers from England was soon to pass away.

For in 1686, Benjamin Lynde graduated from Harvard College, and "was admitted," his diary says, "for the study of the law (as my father had advised) into the Honorable Society of the Middle Temple as by the admission of October 18, 1692." From Harvard thus appeared in history the first American Barrister and later the first legally educated judge.(1)

A new royal charter for Massachusetts was granted by King William in 1691; and with it began a new era for the law—for that charter "effected as perfect and thorough a revolution as ever was produced by a similar act in any state or nation; . . . by making freehold and property, instead of church membership, the qualification of the right of electing and being elected to office, religion became no longer the end and object of civil government."(2)

The courts became a separate and distinct institution from the magistrates. The judges, however, held their commissions at the King's pleasure, and were chosen by the royal governors, still largely influenced by the clergy, who preferred men with no legal training.

In 1696, an act was passed, approved by the King in 1699,

---

thriving there he left the Exchange for Westminster Hall, and in Boston has become as dextrous at splitting of causes as if he had been bred to it. He is full of fancy, and knows the quirks of the law: But, to do him justice, he proves as honest as the best lawyer of them all."

(1) Benjamin Lynde was made Judge of the Superior Court in Massachusetts in 1712 and Chief Justice in 1728.

On the occasion of publishing Judge Lynde's commission, Judge Sewall, in an address to the jury, remarked, "that they would hereafter have the benefit of Inns of Court education, superadded to that of Harvard College."

(2) *History of Harvard University*, by Josiah Quincy, Vol. I, p. 55.

which established a Superior Court of Judicature and inferior courts; at the same time, forms of writs were directed, and the courts were empowered to make rules for the regulation of practice. No one of the judges appointed, however, was a lawyer.

A similar condition prevailed in the Court of Special Oyer and Terminer, which was appointed in 1692 to try the witchcraft cases. Of this court, Chief Justice William Stoughton and Judge Samuel Sewall were educated for the ministry, Judges Nathaniel Saltonstall and Peter Sergeant were gentlemen without a profession, Judges Wait Winthrop and Corwin, and Anthony Checkley, the Attorney General, were merchants or military men. It may be noted however that this absence of legal training was not confined, to the Colonies, for several of the Lord Chief Justices of England in this Century were men of little education at the bar; and of Sir John Kelynge, who was at the head of the King's Bench under Charles II., it was said, that "however fit he might have been to charge the Roundheads under Prince Rupert, he was very unfit to charge a jury in Westminster Hall."[1] And while the witchcraft court has been criticised for its reckless disregard of rules of evidence, and also for condemning the defendants unheard, it is to be remembered that no defendant at this time, even in England, was allowed to have counsel to plead for him in a criminal trial for felony or treason. It was not until 1696 (7-8 William III., c. 3.), that this privilege was granted to persons accused of treason, and not until 1836 (6-7 William IV., c. 114), in cases of felony. It is to be noted also that the modern forms of trial had not then been very long established, even in England; for Sir Nicholas Throckmorton's case, in 1557 (only one hundred and forty years previous), is the first trial reported in State Trials which was conducted substantially in accordance with the forms familiar at the present day.[2]

---

(1) An interesting defence of the legal ability of this court is made by Abner E. Goodell in a paper on *Witch Trials in Massachusetts, Mass. Hist. Soc. Proc.* Vol. XX. (1883) in which he says: "The regret which some, in consequence of the representations of late writers upon the witch trials, may have been led to feel, that those trials had not been conducted by lawyers, is not warranted by the disclosure of the records of the tribunals of England or her colonies if it springs from the belief that a more humane and rational course of procedure might, in that case, have been expected. . . . . Lawyers and laymen, as well as clergymen, were equally under the influence of the superstitious terrors of that day of darkness and delusion."

(2) See *General View of the Criminal Law of England,* by Sir James Fitzjames Stephen (1863).

CONNECTICUT.

The condition of the courts and of the legal profession existing in Massachusetts in the 17th Century was practically the same in Connecticut.

A few of the leaders in its settlement in 1637 were men educated in the law—Roger Ludlow, an Oxford graduate, a student in the Inner Temple in 1612, a member of the Court of Assistants in Massachusetts; Governor John Haynes, a man "very learned in the laws of England"; and Governor John Winthrop the younger, a barrister of the Inner Temple in 1624. But with these exceptions there are no records of the existence of any trained lawyers in Connecticut for a century.

The first American written constitution was prepared by Ludlow in 1639; and in 1650, he drafted at the request of the General Assembly a *Body of Lawes* in 77 sections, 14 of which were taken from the Massachusetts *Body of Liberties,* the rest being the fruit of his own learning. This code, which showed great ability, originality and research, became the foundation of all law in Connecticut.

For ninety years, there was in Connecticut no court separate from the Magistrates. At first, the General Court or Assembly sat as a High Court. It consisted of the Governor, Deputy Governors, the twelve Assistants (or Councillors) elected at large, and the Representatives. After 1665, the Governor, Deputy Governor, and, at least six of the twelve Assistants exercised all the judicial powers of the General Court, and were called the Court of Assistants. It was not until 1710 that a separate Superior Court was constituted, with a Chief Justice and four justices (usually elected from the Assistants). The General Assembly still continued as a final Court of Appeal. (1)

As in Massachusetts, practically none of the judges were trained lawyers—the natural result of the system of framing the courts.

There was no printed revision of the laws until 1702; and the printing of the laws annually in pamphlet form did not begin until 1727, the custom having previously been to send a manuscript copy to each town.

There was little pleading of any kind in law suits, and no acts were passed prescribing forms, until 1709, 1720 and 1731.

(1) See the famous case of *Winthrop v. Lechmere*, in which the King in Council in 1728 reversed the Connecticut court's decisions.

Under all these circumstances, the Bar developed even later than in Massachusetts.

In 1667, the General Court prohibited "all persons from pleading as attorneys in behalf of any person that is charged or prosecuted for delinquency (except he speak directly to matter of law and with leave from the authority present)" under fine of ten shillings, or the stocks for one hour.

In 1708, an act was passed, regulating the admissions of attorneys to practise, and providing that:

No person except in his own case, shall be admitted to make any plea at the Bar without being first approved of by the court before whom the plea is to be made, nor until he shall take in said court the following oath, viz.: "You shall do no falsehood, nor consent to any being done in the court, and if you know of any to be done, you shall give knowledge thereof to the justices of the court, or some of them, that it may be reformed. You shall not wittingly and willingly promote, sue or procure to be sued, any false or unlawful suit, nor give aid or consent to the same. You shall delay no man for lucre or malice, but you shall use yourself in the office of an attorney within the court according to the best of your learning and discretion, and with all good fidelity, as well to the court as to the client. So help you God."(1)

This law required authority from the court in each particular case; and no statute providing for the general admission of attorneys existed until 1750.

In 1725, an act was passed, taxing all persons practising as attorneys in the Colony, "for their faculty," by which those who were "the least practitioners" were to be set in the list for 50 pounds, and others "according to their practise."

In 1730, the number of attorneys was limited as follows:

Whereas many persons of late have taken upon themselves to be attorneys at the Bar so that quarrels and lawsuits are multiplied and the King's good subjects disturbed; to the end that said mischief may be prevented and only proper persons allowed to plead at the Bar, Ordered: that there shall be allowed in the colony 11 attorneys and no more . . . . which attorneys shall be nominated and appointed from time to time as there shall be occasion by the county courts.

---

(1) This form of oath is substantially the same as that in use in Massachusetts and was derived from that in use in England in 1649.

And in actions as to land titles involving ten pounds or less, a party was allowed one attorney to plead, and over ten pounds, two attorneys.

It is not surprising, therefore, that in the statistics of the Connecticut Bar, prepared by the noted Judge Thomas Day, there appear the names of no lawyers practising in the 17th Century.

RHODE ISLAND.

In Rhode Island, before its first charter, the General Court assumed all the judicial powers. Under the charter of 1647, the ruling town magistrates composed the courts. Under the royal charter of 1663, and up to 1729, the Governor, Deputy Governor and his ten (elected) Assistants, exercised the judicial powers.

It was not until 1729 that criminal and civil courts were established separate from the executive magistrates, and not until 1747 that the judiciary was recognized by act of the General Assembly, as a separate branch of the Colonial government. The Court so formed, consisted of a Chief Justice and "four judicious and skilful persons," chosen by the General Assembly.(1)

At no time was knowledge of the law considered essential to the members of the Court; and the judge, probably because of his ignorance, did not even charge the jury.(2)

In 1699, the Earl of Bellomont, in his report to the Lords of Trade, said:

Thus courts of justice are held by the governor and assistants who sit as judges therein, more for constituting the court than for searching out the right of the causes coming before them or delivering their opinion on points of law (whereof it is said they know very little). They give no directions to the jury nor sum up the evidences to them, pointing out the issue which they are to try. Their proceedings are very unmethodical, no ways agreeable to the course and practice of the courts in England and many times arbitrary and contrary to the laws of the place; as is affirmed by the attorneys at law that have sometimes practiced in their court.

A full code of law was adopted in 1647, embodying an elaborate classification of crimes, and providing that "in all other matters not forbidden by the code, all men may walk as their conscience persuades them."

---

(1) *Judicial System in Rhode Island*, by Amasa M. Eaton, *Yale Law Journal* Vol. XIV.
(2) This custom remained unchanged in Rhode Island until 1833.

It appears that in this same year a text-book of maritime law was known in the Colony, for the Assembly resolved in 1647, that the *Laws of Oleron* should be in force for the benefit of seamen.(1)

As early as 1680, and again in 1686, a committee was appointed to make a digest of the laws, "that they may be putt in print;" but the earliest known printed copy of laws was made in 1719.

The first Record Book of the courts is still preserved, covering the years 1671-1685, from which it appears, that civil cases did not average over fifteen a year, and were almost exclusively in debt, trespass, detainer and slander. Of the early Bar, little or nothing is known.

The earliest statutory reference to lawyers was in 1668-9, when it was enacted, that any person who was indicted might employ an attorney to plead in his behalf.

In 1718, an act was passed, limiting the number of lawyers to be permitted to argue in any case to two, one of them to be a free holder of the Colony. In 1729, lawyers were forbidden to be deputies, their presence in the assembly sitting as a court of Appeal being "found to be of ill consequence." This act was repealed, however, in 1731.

The office of Attorney General was created in 1650, by an act which quaintly declared that "because envy, the cut throat of all prosperitie will not fail to gallop with its full career, let the sayd attorney be faithfully engaged and authorized and encouraged." Henry Bull, who was born in 1689, and elected Attorney General in 1721, tells an anecdote of himself, which seems to fairly illustrate the conditions of early law practice:

When he made up his mind to practice law he went into the garden to exercise his talents in addressing the court and jury. He selected five cabbages in one row for judges, and twelve in another row for jurors; after trying his hand thus awhile, he went boldly into court and took upon himself the duties of an advocate, and a little observation and experience there convinced him that the same cabbages were in the court house which he thought he had left in the garden, five in one row and twelve in another.

MAINE AND NEW HAMPSHIRE.

In Maine, Thomas Gorges, the head of the Colonial Government, was an English barrister of the Inns of Court—a practising

---

(1) Kent's *Com.,* Vol. III, p. 13, note.

lawyer, and the only one during the whole first century of the Colony.

The General Court at first tried all criminal and civil cases; later it established two inferior courts which existed until 1692, when the Colony was incorporated into the royal Province of Massachusetts, and came under its judicial system.

It was not until 1720 that there was a resident lawyer practising in the Maine courts—Noah Emery of Kittery, brought up as a cooper, but who later studied law.

In New Hampshire, as in Massachusetts and the other Colonies, the courts were for a long time composed, largely, if not wholly, of laymen. Richard Martyn, Chief Justice in 1693-94, was a merchant. In 1699, when a separate Superior Court of Judicature was established (consisting of John Hinckes, Chief Justice, Peter Coffin, John Gerrish and John Plaisted), all the judges were laymen.

The earliest, and practically the only, trained lawyer of the 17th Century in the Colony, was John Pickering, of Portsmouth. In 1696, Charles Story, an English barrister, was sent to the Colony as Judge of Admiralty.

THE REASONS FOR THE SCARCITY OF LAWYERS.

A close study of legal conditions in the early history of the New England Colonies forces one to the conclusion that the lack of educated lawyers in the 17th Century in those Colonies was largely due to the absence of respect for the English Common Law. And one is inevitably driven to the further conclusion that the courts of the early 19th Century were far from historically accurate in the theory which they framed as to the existence of Common Law doctrines in this country, a theory which was stated by Chief Justice Parsons in 1807 as follows:

Our ancestors when they came into this new world claimed the common law as their birthright and brought it with them, except such parts as were judged inapplicable to their new state and condition—the common law of their native country as it was amended or altered by English statutes in force at the time of their immigration. (1)

(1)   Parsons C. J. in *Commonwealth v Knowlton*, 2 Mass., p. 354 (1807.) See Shaw, C. J. in *Young v. Emery*, 16 Pick. p. 110 (1833).
And see Judge Story in his *Commentaries on the Constitution* and in *Van Ness v. Packard*, 2 Peters 144 (1829).

As has been seen, it was not historically true that either in Massachusetts, Connecticut or Rhode Island, the colonists of the 17th Century brought with them the English Common Law, or governed themselves by it. So far from being proud of it "as their birthright," they were in fact decidedly anxious to escape from it and from the ideas connected with it in their mind.

The Common Law was neither popular nor a source of pride at this time, even in England. (1) It was a period when Sir Edward Coke had been removed as Chief Justice of King's Bench by James I, in 1616. The judges held office only at the King's pleasure. The Star Chamber Court had flourished under Charles I. The Chancellors were endeavoring to mitigate some of the harshness and irrationality and technicality of the Common Law courts. The old feudal tenures were extant, with all their follies and burdens.

The fact is, that the English Common Law, 1620-1700, was in force in New England only so far as it was specifically adopted by statute—or so far as the colonists, by custom, had assented to its binding force.

Thus, in a case in Massachusetts, as late as 1687, the defendant pleaded that the Magna Charta of England and the statute law, "secure the subjects' properties and estates . . . . To which was replied by one of the judges, the rest by silence assenting, 'We must not think the laws of England follow us to the ends of the earth or whither we went.' "(2)

Chief Justice Atwood, who visited Boston in 1700, in his report to the Lords of Trade, states that he had "publicly exposed the argument of one of the Boston clergy that they were not bound in conscience to obey the laws of England;"(3) and he

---

(1) Signs of the dissatisfaction with the state of the law in England may be seen from the flood of pamphlets demanding its reform, such as; *Reformation Proceedings at Law,* by Thomas Felds in 1645; *Survey of the English Laws, their Unsoundness and Corruption Discovered,* by F. W. in 1652; *England's Balme, or Proposals by way of Grievance and Remedy towards the Regulation of Law and Better Administration of Justice,* by William Sheppard in 1657; *Certain Proposals for Regulating the Law,* by John Shepheard in 1651; *Perspicuous Compendium of Several Irregularities and Abuses in Present Practice of Common Laws of England,* by D. W., in 1656; Warr's *The Corruption and Deficiency of the Laws of England;* Jones' *An Experimental Essay touching the reformation of the Laws of England.*

(2) *Judicial History of Massachusetts,* by Emory Washburn, p. 106.

(3) *Documents relative to Colonial History of New York,* Vol. IV. p. 929.

notes that the methods of the courts were "abhorent from the
Laws of England and all other nations."

John Adams in his *Novanglus* said, even in 1774:

How then do we New Englanders derive our laws. I say not
from Parliament, not from the common law; but from the law of
nature and the compact made with the King in our charter. Our
ancestors were entitled to the common law of England when
they emigrated; that is to say to as much of it as they pleased to
adopt and no more. They were not bound or obliged to submit
to it unless they chose.(1)

As already seen, Connecticut was extremely independent of
the Common Law; and as Robert Quary reported to the Board of
Trade in England, "the people are of a very turbulent, factious
and uneasy temper. I cannot give their character better than by
telling your Lordships that they have made a body of laws for
their government which are printed; the first of which is that
no law of England shall be in force in their government till made
so by act of their own."(2)   In the famous case of *Winthrop v.
Lechmere,* in 1728, the Colony's agent in London was instructed
to argue that English Common Law could be binding beyond the
sea, only in case it had been accepted by the colonists' own choice.
"The common law always hath its limits environ'd by the sea."(3)

In fact, Connecticut never adopted the Common Law, even by
statute. Its recognition at all grew up through usage and custom
only, and was coincident with the first professional education of
lawyers and judges. As the Bar grew to be composed of men
familiar with the law of England, and its reported cases and
commentaries, the legal character of the bench improved, and
the rules of Common Law gradually became, by judicial application, the law of Connecticut. But Judge Jesse Root, in the

---

(1) *Adams' Life and Works,* Vol. IV., p. 122.

Thomas Jefferson said in a letter to Attorney General Rodney Sept. 25,
1810, speaking of Levi Lincoln of Massachusetts as a possible successor
to Cushing as Chief Justice of the United States Supreme Court: "He
is not thought to be an able common lawyer, but there is not and never
was an able one in the New England States. Their system is sui generis,
in which the common law is little attended to."

See *Jefferson's Complete Works,* Vol. V., p. 546. As to Common Law in
Massachusetts Colony, see *Tucker's Blackstone* Appendix, Vol. I., p.
397 *et seq.*

(2) Quoted in *The Connecticut Intestacy Law,* by Charles M. Andrews,
Yale Law Journal, Vol. III.

(3) *Governor Talcott Papers,* Vol. II. appendix. These instructions
were drawn up by John Read, afterwards the leader of the Bar in Boston,
in the early 18th Century.

Preface to the first volume of his Reports, as late as 1798, denied that English law had ever been applicable, per se:

Our ancestors who emigrated from England to America were possessed of the knowledge of the laws and jurisprudence of that country; but were free from any obligations of subjection to them. The laws of England had no authority over them to bind their persons, nor were they in any measure applicable to their condition and circumstances here . . . . In every respect their laws were inapplicable to an infant country or state, where the government was in the people, and which had virtue for its principle and the public good for its object and end; where the tenure of land was free and absolute, the objects of trade few, and the commission of crimes rare. (1)

In Rhode Island, it was not until 1770 that by statute the Common Law was formally adopted, as follows:

In all actions, matters, causes, and things whatsoever where no particular law of the colony is made to decide and determine the same, then in all such cases the law of England shall be put in force to issue, determine and decide the same, any usage, custom or law to the contrary notwithstanding.

The real fact is, that during these years, 1620-1700, the colonists were making a Common Law for themselves; and their usages and customs, and the expedients to which they were forced, in order to adapt their rules of life to the surroundings and the time, gradually hardened into positive rules of law.(2)

---

(1) See Zephaniah Swift's *System of Laws of Connecticut;* Peter's *History of Connecticut.*

(2) See Parsons, C. J. in *Com. v. Knowlton,* 2 Mass., p. 534 (1805).

Shaw, C. J., in *Com. v. Chapman,* 13 Metc., p. 68 (1847).

In England, in 1600, Lord Coke was deriving Common Law from usages and precedents three, four, and five hundred years old; but in Massachusetts in 1810, customs only one hundred and fifty years old had crystallized into a part of its Common Law.

For example, a practice of the court in early days, of proceeding with the suit against one debtor, when the other lived out of the Colony—"a practice originated from necessity" in the early seventeenth century, was held in 1809 a Common Law rule. (*Tappan v. Bruen,* 15 Mass. 19).

In *Campbell v. Johnson,* 11 Mass. p. 187 (1814), it was held that "Immemorial usage, (i. e. usage since 1620), has a force equally binding as statutes;" and see Parker, C. J., in *Puter v. Hall,* 3 Pick. p. 373 (1825). So "the immemorial usage of Massachusetts, founded on necessity," of a wife conveying her dower by joining in the deed, had become Common Law in Massachusetts early in the eighteenth century. "The celebrated Mr. Read, the first lawyer in his time, resolved this usage into New England Common Law," said Parsons, C. J., in *Fowler v. Shearer,* 7 Mass. 21.

So the statute as to low water mark ownership of Massachusetts Bay Colony, being a usage and practice all over Massachusetts, had become a common law rule in 1832; see Shaw, C. J., in *Barker v. Bates,* 13 Pick. 258.

An interesting commentary on this growth of an American Common Law is to be found in the diary of Ezra Stiles, President of Yale College. (1)

Jan. 6, 1773—Dined with Judge (Peter) Oliver (Chief Justice of Massachusetts) and spent the afternoon together. We discoursed on the extending of the English Law to America, whether Statute or Common. He said all the English statutes before the Colonies had Existence were to be extended here—(a singular opinion)—all made since with extending clauses reached us—those made without, etc., did not extend here. This I see is Court Law. He considered the Descent of Inheritance in Massachusetts as being neither according to England in general or Co. of Kent, but Mosaic. He said by Common Law the Estates of Felons went to the King, in Kent to the children, in New England to the children; so that the Common Law he said would not apply to New England in this Case. In England and Massachusetts no Quaker evidence by affirmation can convict capitally—Judge (Frederick) Smyth (Chief Justice of New Jersey) told Judge Oliver that when he came to Jersies he objected this but they all cried out their usage to admit Quaker Testimony in capital cases and that he was obliged to give way to it, tho' different from the Laws of England. We also discussed on Slavery of Negroes in Virginia, etc.; that of necessity the American Public Law must differ and vary from the Public Law of England.

The absence of lawyers in the 17th Century is, therefore, easily understood, when once the conditions described above are appreciated. When English precedents were not followed or used as a guide in the courts, and the courts were composed of clergymen and merchants, of Governors and their Deputies or Assistants, of politicians appointed or elected, rather than of trained lawyers, there was no real need or scope for men trained in English law; and no real lawyers appeared until the call arose for them.

This call came early in the 18th Century. Prior to 1700, the law had been a layman's law, a popular equitable system, which worked well enough under the simple conditions of the times. As the practice of the law became more extended and disciplined however, and as contingencies unprovided for by statute constantly arose, Judges grew more and more into the habit of borrowing from the provisions of the English Common Law. The precedents springing from local customs became more numerous

---

(1) *Literary Diary of Ezra Stiles*, Vol. I., p. 331 (1901).

and complicated; and by 1720, a regular trained Bar began to arise in New England.

And while it was the subordination of the Common Law to the Law of God and of the clergy which had been largely accountable for the non-existence of lawyers in the Colonies in the 17th Century, it was on the other hand through the advent of the American lawyer that the English Common Law was later developed in the Colonial courts.

NOTE.

For authorities in general, see:

Courts of Justice in the Province of Massachusetts Bay, 1630-84—Amer. Law Rev., Vol. XXXIV, 1902.

Judicial Action by the Provincial Legislature of Mass. Bay,—Columbia Law Review, Vol. II, 1902.

Local Law in Massachusetts and Connecticut, by W. C. Fowler.

The Colonial Laws of Massachusetts, by W. H. Whitmore (1890).

Judicial History of Massachusetts, by Emory Washburn (1840).

Plymouth Colony Laws.

Massachusetts Colonial Records.

Records of the Courts of Assistants, edited by John Noble (1901).

Plaine Dealing, or News from New England, by Thomas Lechford (1642).

Emancipation of Massachusetts, by Brooks Adams (1887).

History of New England, by John Winthrop.

History of New England, by John G. Palfrey (1858).

Address on Origin of the Legal Profession in Massachusetts, by William Sullivan (1826).

Three Episodes of Massachusetts History, by C. F. Adams (1892).

Judicial History of New England, by Conrad Reno (1900).

History of the Judiciary of Massachusetts, by William T. Davis (1900).

Address to Worcester County Bar, Oct. 2, 1829, by Joseph Willard.

Judicial History of Massachusetts, by Albert Mason, in *The New England States,* (1897).

Attorneys and their Admission to the Bar in Massachusetts, by Hollis R. Bailey (1907).

Connecticut, Origin of Her Courts and Laws, by William Hamersley in *The New England States,* (1897).

Judicial History of Rhode Island, by Thomas Durfee in *The New England States,* (1897).

History of New Hampshire, by Jeremy Belknap (1792).

Bench and Bar of New Hampshire, by C. H. Bell (1894).

History of Rhode Island, by S. G. Arnold (1859).

The Judicial System in Rhode Island, by Amasa M. Eaton, *Yale Law Journal,* Vol. XIV.

The Law, the Courts and Lawyers of Maine, by William Willis (1863).

Roger Ludlow, by John M. Taylor (1900).

Judicial and Civil History of Connecticut, by Dwight Loomis and G. E. Calhoun (1895).

English Common Law in the Early American Colonies, by Paul F. Reinsch (1899).

CHAPTER II.

English Law, Lawyers, and Law Books and Reports in the 17th Century.

In the year 1692, when the first New England lawyer was admitted into the Temple in London, the Common Law, as a system to be studied from reported decisions, was only about a century old.

Those cases which are to the modern student almost his earliest landmarks, were then to be found in reports published only a few years before the Pilgrims landed at Plymouth.

Shelley's case (1 Coke 93) had been decided in 1579-1581; *Thorogood's case* (2 Coke 9), on fraud in the execution of a deed, in 1582; *Slade's case* (4 Coke 91), which established the use of the action on the case upon assumpsit in place of debt, in 1596; *Twyne's case* (3 Coke 50), on gifts in fraud of creditors, had been decided in 1585; *Spencer's case* (5 Coke 16), in 1583; *Calye's case* (8 Coke 32), on the liability of innkeepers, in 1584; *Lopus v. Chandelor* (Cro. Jac. 1), the Bezoar Stone case on warranties, in 1603; *Dumpor's case* (4 Coke 119), on waiver of forfeiture, in 1603; *Semayne's case* (5 Coke 91), on sheriff's liability, in 1605; the Six Carpenters case or *Vaux v. Newman* (8 Coke 146), on trespass ab initio, in 1611; *Sutton Hospital case* (10 Coke 1), on corporations, in 1612; *Lamplaugh v. Braithwait* (Hobart 105), on consideration in assumpsit, in 1616; *Manby v. Scott* (1 Lev. 4), on a wife's contract, in 1659.

While the Common Law on its civil side had begun, by 1620, to provide fairly complete and even-handed justice as between one private citizen and another, (as the reports of Chief Justice Dyer, Chief Justice Anderson and Sergeant Plowden during the reign of Queen Elizabeth show)(1), on its criminal side it was a source of horror to lovers of liberty and right, throughout the 17th Century. Great judges, as a rule, were hardly possible under the arbitrary rule of the Stuarts or of Cromwell; the State Trials were trials only in name, though the complete disregard of the

---

(1) *The Five Ages of the Bench and Bar of England,* by John M. Zane.

rules of law and evidence by the justices presiding over them resulted in bringing about the new era of the English Common Law.

In 1636, about the time when Connecticut was being settled, and a code of laws framed by Ludlow, John Hampden was being tried in England for refusing to pay ship money.

In 1641, the year when Massachusetts had adopted the *Body of Liberties,* occurred the trial for treason of the Earl of Strafford, and two years later the trial of William Laud, Archbishop of Canterbury.

Eight years later, in 1649, Chief Justice Rolle refused to preside over a court to try Charles I, and the King was tried before Lord President Bradshaw at a Special High Court of Justice, his line of defence having been laid out by Sir Mathew Hale.

In 1660, the regicides were tried for treason at Old Bailey before Sir Orlando Bridgman, Chief Baron of the Court of Exchequer.

In 1662, the trial of Sir Henry Vane the younger occurred before Chief Justice Foster.

In 1683, came the trial for treason of Lord Russell (the Ryehouse Plot Case) before Sir Francis Pemberton, Chief Justice of Common Pleas, and of Algernon Sydney before the infamous Lord Chief Justice Jeffreys.

In 1685, Lady Alice Lisle had been tried and executed by Jeffreys; and Titus Oates had been tried for perjury and pilloried; in 1688, occurred the trial of the Seven Bishops for libel, before Lord Chief Justice Wright.

Two trials of especial interest to the American Colonies were those of William Penn for "tumultuous assembly" in 1670, and Capt. William Kidd for murder and piracy in 1701.

In the midst of these dark times of the law, however, two clear lights had shone out in the persons of the great Lord Chief Justices—Sir Edward Coke and Sir Mathew Hale. The former had been deposed by James I, in 1616, before the settlement of New England. The latter had been head of the Court of King's Bench from 1671 to 1676. He presided in 1665 as Chief Baron of the Exchequer at the witch trials in Suffolk, which were the prototype of those occurring twenty-seven years later in

Salem, Massachusetts; (1) and in 1676 over the trial of John Bunyan, the tinker, to the long sentence imposed on whom, the world owes *Pilgrim's Progress.*

Mathew Hale's services to the development of law during this Century were, however, not confined to his opinions from the bench. Although Francis Bacon, in 1592, at the age of thirty-one, had proposed in the House of Commons a plan to amend and consolidate the whole body of English Law, Hale was the first to conceive the opinion that the law of England was capable of being reduced to a system and created scientifically. (2) Since the reign of Edward I, there had been slight change in the laws or in the mode of administering justice in England, and they had become quite unsuited to the altered circumstances of the country. In 1653, therefore, Hale was made chairman of a committee on Law Reform of which Cromwell, Sir Algernon Sydney and Sir Anthony Ashley Cooper were members. He drew up a plan for legal reforms, including a scheme for the recording of deeds; but it was not adopted, "because," as Sir Edward Ludlow in his *Memoirs* says, "of the opposition of the lawyers who desired to possess in their own hands the laws, liberties and estates of the nation." Whether or not this was the real reason, it is plain that England was not ready for most of these innovations; and though the public registry of deeds had already been adopted in some of the American Colonies, this, with many of Hale's other suggestions, failed in the more conservative country. To Hale, however, was largely due the action of Parliament, in 1649, in requiring the use of the English language in law books and proceedings,—a reform which lasted only until the Restoration of Charles II and which was not put permanently in force until nearly one hundred years later, in 1733. (3)

---

(1) Chandler in his *American Criminal Trials* says, that "the account of the trial of witches in Suffolk was published in 1684. All these books were in New England and the conformity between the behaviour of Goodwin's children and most of the supposed bewitched at Salem and the behaviour of those in England, is so exact as to leave no room to doubt the stories had been read by the New England persons themselves or had been told to them by others who had read them."

(2) See Lecture on *The System of Law,* in *Life of Nathaniel Chipman,* by Daniel Chipman (1846).

(3) Campbell's *Lives of the Chief Justices,* Vol. II., p. 185. As early as 1609 King James had said in a speech when the *Revised Version of the Bible* was nearly ready for publication, "I wish the law written in one vulgar language; for now it is an old mixt and corrupt language only understood by lawyers."

The 17th Century, though not prolific in great lawyers or judges until its close, was a period of great changes in the courts of England.

The old special courts for the trial of cases on the Law Merchant—the Staple (or Market) courts, the Courts Prepoudrous—had disappeared, and such cases had gradually come into the Courts of Chancery and the Admiral's Court, and in some instances into the Common Law Courts, where the law merchant was proved, like foreign law, as a question of fact.(1)

The Court of Star Chamber—so inveighed against by the Puritans and feared by all English subjects—had been abolished in 1641.

The establishment of the High Court of Chancery as a body co-ordinate in power with the Common Law Courts, had been finally brought about. For many years the Lord Chancellors, especially Thomas Egerton, Lord Ellesmere, had, with the aid of Sir Francis Bacon, the King's Attorney General, been waging a bitter fight against Chief Justice Coke in behalf of the right of the Chancery to issue writs of injunction against the other Courts.(2)

And in 1616, a case in King's Bench, of slight importance in its facts, had brought the downfall of Lord Coke and of the exclusive pretentions of the Courts of Common Law.(3)

The abolition of the incidents of feudal tenure and the establishment of new systems of conveyancing had also thrown more and more cases into the Equity Courts through their jurisdiction over trusts, mortgages, and specific performance. And with the Chancellorship of Sir Heneage Finch, (Lord Nottingham), in

---

(1) See *What is the Law Merchant,* by F. M. Burdick, *Columbia Law Review,* Vol. II.

(2) See case of *Throckmorton v. Finch,* 3 Coke Inst., 124; Cro. Jac., 344. *The Expansion of the Common Law,* by Sir Frederick Pollock.

See especially *Falstaff on Equity,* by Charles E. Phelps—a commentary on Falstaff's remark in *Henry IV.,* Part I., Act 2, Scene 2.

(3) The quaint facts were that an agent of the defendant had taken one of the plaintiff's witnesses to a tavern, and calling for a pot of sack, left the room as soon as the man had raised it to his mouth. When the cause came on and the witness was called, the court was informed that he could not come and the agent deposed "that he left him in such a condition that if he continued in it but for a quarter of an hour, he was a dead man." The verdict was for the defendant, and to be relieved from such a verdict, application was made to the Court of Chancery. Johnson's *Life of Coke,* Vol. I., p. 287 (1845).

1673-82,(1) and that of his successor Sir Francis North, (Lord Guilford), the modern law of equity began.

By the end of the 17th Century, the stability of the Common Law Courts had also been established; for, by the Bill of Rights of 1688, the judges were no longer to hold office at the King's pleasure but "quam diu se bene gesserint." It was no longer possible for the King to say, like James II, "I am determined to have twelve lawyers for judges who will be all of my mind as to this matter;" bringing forth the reply of Chief Justice Jones of the Common Pleas, "Your Majesty may find twelve *judges* of your mind, but hardly twelve lawyers."(2)

THE LAWYERS.

For two hundred years after the Norman Conquest, legal proceedings had been almost entirely in the hands of the clergy. They were the scholars, the students of canon and civil law, almost the only class possessing a knowledge of reading.(3)

The first learned lay lawyers appeared in the reign of King John. Gradually the judges were appointed more and more as lawyers and less as priests; and finally, in Henry III's reign, the Pope forbade his clergy to study temporal law or to sit in lay courts. Of the clerical lawyers one of the last, and greatest, was Bracton, who died in 1267.(4)

The Year Books, begun under Edward I, show the legal profession in full bloom, most of the cases, however, being tried at the bar by the Serjeants.

In 1292, Edward I ordered that the justices of the Court of Common Pleas should decide as to what attorneys and apprentices should be chosen from each county.(5)

---

(1) "Emphatically called the Father of Equity." See Story's *Equity Jurisprudence*, Vol. I., p. 46.
It has been said that Nottingham drew his own portrait when he wrote of Hale, "He looked upon equity as a part of the common law and one of the grounds of it; and therefore, as near as he could he did always reduce to certain rules and principles, that men might study it as a science and not think the administration of it had anything arbitrary about it."
(2) Campbell's *Lives of the Chief Justices*, Vol. II., p. 337.
(3) *Legal Profession in England—Amer. Law Review*, Vol. XIX, 677. It is curious to find this history reproduced in the early days of Massachusetts when the clergy again were the preponderating factor in the law.
(4) See *The Golden Age of the Common Law*, by John N. Zane, *Illinois Law Rev.* (1907).
(5) Pollock and Maitland, *History of English Law*, Vol. I., p. 199.
The Courts and Admissions to the Bar—Harv. Law Rev., Vol. XII.

In the *Miroir des Justices* (written by Andrew Horne in 1327 in the reign of Edward II), it was laid down that:

Every pleader is to be charged by oath that he will not maintain nor defend what is wrong or false to his knowledge, but will fight for his client to the utmost of his ability; thirdly, he to put on before the court no false delays; nor false evidence, nor move nor offer any corruptions, deceits, tricks, or false lies, nor consent to any such, but truly maintain the right of his client, so that it fail not through any folly, negligence, or default in him.

In 1381, the popular hatred of attorneys was shown in the outcry against them in Wat Tyler's rebellion(1), an outcry which was reproduced in almost every particular 400 years later, in the Shay's rebellion in Massachusetts, in 1787.

In 1403, the attorneys had increased to 2,000, and by an act in that year it was ordered that all attorneys be examined "and none admitted but such as were virtuous, learned, and sworn to do their duty."

In 1413, the undersheriffs, clerks, receivers and bailiffs had been excluded from practising as attorneys, because "the King's liege people dare not pursue or complain of the extortions and of the oppressions to them done by the officers or sheriffs."(2)

In 1606, by statute, none were to be admitted as attorneys in the courts except those brought up in the Inns "well practised and skilled and of an honest disposition."

As gradually from the time of King John to Edward I the Courts had become localized at Westminster Hall, that "lock and key of the common law" as Coke called it, the lawyers gathering also in London from all parts of the kingdom, formed there a kind of University of their own in certain buildings called "Inns," where instruction was given in the principles of English Common and statute law exclusively.

Gradually "Inns of Court" came to signify the four Hon-

---

(1)   See Shakespeare *Henry VI*, Part II., Act 4, Scene 2.

"Dick the Butcher—The first thing we do, let's kill all the lawyers.

Cade—Nay, that I mean to do. Is not this a lamentable thing, that of the skin of an innocent lamb should be made parchment; that parchment being scribbled o'er should undo a man. Some say: the bee stings; but I say, tis the bee's wax; for I did but seal once to a thing, and I was never mine own man since."

(2)   It is interesting to find this legislation reproduced three hundred years later in many of the American Colonies, 1700 to 1750.

ourable Societies of Lincoln's Inn, Gray's Inn, The Inner Temple, and the Middle Temple.(1.)

The exact origin of these Inns of Court is unknown; but they probably existed in their present form in the reign of Edward III in 1327. Henry III had taken them under his special protection, and in 1235 prohibited the study of law in any other place in London than the Inns of Court. Little satisfactory information however is to be had about them until the time of Henry VI (1422-1461) when Sir John Fortescue, the Chancellor, sketched them in detail in his *De Laudibus Legum Angliae.*

He described them as composed of four large Inns of about 200 students each, and ten lesser Inns of Chancery having about 100 students each. The students were chiefly young men of birth; and in 1586, the number in the various Inns of Court and Chancery was 1703.(2)

The severance between the two branches of the profession dates from an order of the Inns of Court in the reign of Philip and Mary, in 1557, as follows: "In all admissions henceforth this condition implied that if he that is admitted practice any attorneyship ipso facto be dismissed, and to have liberty to repair to the Inns of Chancery whence he came." The only persons entitled and admitted to practise in the courts were those who had been "called" as barristers by the "benchers" or officers of one of the four Inns of Court. Attorneys (officers of the Common Law Courts) and solicitors (officers of the Courts of Chancery) could only draw writs and papers and instruct the barristers as to the matter in litigation and were generally graduates of the Inns of Chancery. Many men famous in English history had been connected with the Inns. Lord Bacon had written his essays from his "chamber in Graie's Inn" and had ridden forth from there in 1617 to be installed as Lord Keeper of the Great Seal. Sir Philip Sidney was of Gray's Inn. John Hamp-

---

(1) The term "Inn or "Inne" was the Saxon equivalent for the French "hostel," signifying, not a public place of entertainment, but the private city or town mansion of a person of rank or wealth; thus, "Lincoln's Inn" was the hostel of the Earl of Lincoln and leased to lawyers and students of law, and the Inner and Middle Temple was the home of the Knights Templar.

(2) See especially *Laws and Jurisprudence of England and America,* by John F. Dillon, Chapters II., III. and IV., for much information about the Inns of Court.

See also *Education for the English Bar in the Inns of Court, Green Bag,* Vol. XV; and for elaborate accounts see *Introductory Lecture,* by David Hoffman (1823).

den, the patriot, had been in the Inner Temple in 1613, and other of its barristers were Manwood, Anderson, and Heneage Finch. Sir Thomas More and Fortescue and Mathew Hale had been members of Lincoln's Inn. In the Middle Temple there had been Plowden, Dyer, Doddridge, and Popham.

The principal method of instruction in these Inns in the 17th Century was the exercises of reading, bolting, and mooting of cases. There were no prescribed attendance, no lectures and no regular course of study, however, a student being simply obliged to eat three dinners, (six, in case of a non-University man) in the Hall of the Inn, in each of the four terms, Hilary, Easter, Trinity and Michaelmas; and after "keeping" a certain number of terms (at different periods, 7, 10 and 5 years) he was called by the "benchers" as a barrister. The mooting of cases consisted of arguments by barristers who had been called to the bar or by students who had become expert "bolters," generally at meal time in the Hall in the presence of the students. Bolting consisted of conversational discussions upon cases put to the student by a bencher or two barristers sitting as judges in private chambers. The readings were performed by two Readers appointed yearly from among the oldest and most distinguished barristers. The Reader generally chose as his topic some statute, and for three weeks elaborated on it with much form and solemnity, giving out cases to be argued by the barristers in his presence.

These readings were often cited as authority; thus Littleton's was on the Statute De Donis, Bacon's was on the Statute of Uses, Dyer's was upon the Statute of Wills, and Coke's upon the Statute of Fines. As it was a high honor to be selected as a Reader, the expense of the feasts given by him in return became very great; and finally the high festival into which the reading developed quite overbalanced the serious portion of the exercises. (1)

By the beginning of the 18th Century, even the very moderate amount of instruction given through the readings and moots had been gradually discontinued, or had failed, because of inattendance by the barristers and students; and the legal education received became almost nominal. The student could, if he chose, carry on independent study, but no assistance was given to him and no examination required.

(1) See *The Five Ages of the Bench and Bar of England,* by John M. Zane.

In fact the Inns were legal societies or clubs rather than Law Schools.

In spite of the poor facilities for acquiring a knowledge of the law, it is interesting to note what course of reading a law student of the 17th Century was expected to pursue. Thus Rolle, in his *Abridgment* in 1668, gives the following advice to students :

Spend two or three years in the diligent reading of *Littleton, Perkins, Doctor and Student,* Fitzherbert's *Natura Brevium* and especially my Lord Coke's *Commentaries* and possibly his *Reports*—After two or three years so spent, let him have a large commonplace book, afterwards it might be fit to read the *Year Book;* because many of the elder *Year Books* are filled with law not so much in use ; he may single out for his constant reading such as are most useful, as the last part of *Edward III,* the *Book of Assizes,* the second part of *Henry VI, Edward IV, Henry VII,* and so come down in order and succession of time to the latter law, viz. : *Plowden, Dyer, Coke's Reports,* the *Second Term* and those other *Reports* lately printed.

Lord Hale and Lord Roger North both recommended :

Littleton's Tenures, Perkins, Doctor and Student, Fitzherbert's *Natura Brevium, Coke's Reports,* the *Year Book* mentioned as *Henry VII, Plowden, Dyer* and *Rastal's Entries.*

And Lord Coke in the third volume of his *reports* says :

Right profitable are the ancient books of the common law yet extant as *Glanville, Bracton, Britton, Fleta, Ingham* and *Novae Narrationes;* and those also of later times as the old *Tenures;* old *Natura Brevium, Littleton, Doctor and Student, Perkins, Fitzherbert, Natura Brevium* and *Stamford.* If the Reader, after the diligent reading of the case shall observe how the case is abridged in those two great abridgments of Justice Fitzherbert and Sir Robert Brooke, it will both illustrate the case and delight the Reader ; and yet neither that of Statham nor that of the *Book of Assizes* is to be rejected; and for pleading, the great *Book of Entries* is of similar use and utility. To the former Reports you may add the exquisite and elaborate commentaries at large of Master Plowden . . .   and the summary and fruitful observations of . . .   Sir James Dyer . . .   and mine own simple labours; then have you fifteen books or treatises and as many volumes of the Reports besides the abridgments of the common law.

The one indisputable knowledge needed was that of special pleading, as Rastall said in 1564 :

This book entituled a *Collection of Entrees* contayneth the forme and maner of good pleading which is a great part of the cunning of the law of England, as the Right Worshipfull and great learned man Syr Thomas Littleton Knight, sometime one of the justices of the Common Pleas, in his third book of *Tenures* in the chapter of confirmation saith to his sonne.

LAW BOOKS AND REPORTS.

The absence of a legal profession in America at this time can be better understood, perhaps, if one bears in mind the extremely limited resources on which the student and the practitioner of law in England had at this time to depend.

In the year 1692, at the time of the establishment of the first system of separate courts in Massachusetts, the first printed law book in England was only about two hundred years old—Littleton's *Tenures* printed in 1481 in the reign of Henry VI, only a few years after the introduction of the printing press into England.

Before the beginning of the 17th Century hardly twenty-five law books had been printed.(1)

The following are those which were at all commonly known.

Glanville's *Treatise on the Laws and Customs of England,* written in 1187, printed in 1557.
Dialogues de Scaccario, written in 1157.
Henry Bracton on *Laws and Customs of England,* 1262, printed 1569.
John Britton's *Abridgment,* 1275, printed 1580. (The first law book composed in French, *Bracton and Fleta* being in Latin).
Fleta's *Commentary,* 1285, printed 1647.
Ralph de Hengham's *Register of Writs,* 1300, printed 1616.
Andrew Horne's *Miroir des Justices,* 1327, printed 1642.
Old Tenures, 1328.
Natura Brevium—writs, 1328-1376, printed 1572.
Novae Narrationes—pleadings, 1448, printed 1599.
Littleton's *Tenures,* 1742, printed 1481.
Nicholas Statham's *Abridgment,* 1473.
Anthony Fitzherbert's *Grand Abridgment of the Law,* 1514-1516.
Rastall's *Abridgment of the Statutes,* 1527.
Rastall's *Register Original,* 1531.

---

(1) See Dugdale's *Origines Juridiciales* (1666) as to law books of this period, also Reeve's *History of the English Law;* also *Law and Lawyers* by W. L. Willis in *American Quarterly Review,* Vol. XIII-XIV; *The Common Law* by Charles P. Daly (1894).

Saint Germain's *Doctor and Student,* 1530, printed 1598.

Rastall's *Entries,* 1566.

Rastall's *Terms of Law,* 1572, printed 1598.

John Perkins' *Profitable Book of Conveyancing,* 1532, printed 1609.

Office of the Justice of the Peace, 1547.

William Staunforde's *Pleas of the Crown,* 1556.

Brooke's *Grand Abridgment of the Law,* 1568, printed 1573.

Lombard's *Archaiomea,* 1568.

Pulton's *Abstract of the Penal Statutes,* 1577.

Theloal's *Digest of Original Writs,* 1579.

Kitchen's *Courts,* 1580.

Lombard's *Eisenachia,* 1581.

Crompton on *Office and Authority of a Justice of the Peace,* 1583.

Manwood's *Forest Law,* 1598.

And at the end of the 17th Century, the first law book written in the English language was only about 160 years old, Rastall's *Abridgment of the Statutes* (1527).

Until the decree of Parliament of 1649, requiring all reports to be in English, almost all law books had been in Norman French or Latin, for the reason, as Coke says in the Preface to the third volume of his *Reports*:

that it was not thought fit nor convenient to publish either those or any of the statutes enacted in these days in the vulgar tongue lest the unlearned by bare reading without understanding might suck out errors and trusting to their own conceit might endanger themselves and some times fall into destruction.

During the 17th Century, few law books of importance had been published.

West's *Symboleography* was printed in 1605. In the same year Cowell's *Institutes* had appeared; in 1606, Cowell's *Interpreter,* and in 1607, Cowell's *Dictionary;* (1) Swinborne on *Wills and Testaments,* in 1611; Dalton's *Justice of the Peace,* in 1612; Finch's *Common Law of England,* in 1613.(2)

Lord Bacon's great work (though small in size) on *Elements of the Common Laws of England,* was published in 1630. And just about the same time Lord Coke put forth his famous *Institutes*—the first volume *Commentary on Littleton,* in 1633, the

---

(1) These three books were largely used by law students and passed into many editions down to as late as 1727. Cowell's *Institutes* received the compliment of being translated into English by direct of order of Parliament in 1651.

(2) Regarded as the best elementary book for students until the publication of *Blackstone* in 1765.

Exposition of Magna Charta, in 1642, *Pleas of the Crown,* in 1644, and *Jurisdiction of Courts,* in 1648. In 1631, came Dodd-ridge's *English Lawyer;* in 1646, March on *Slander;* in 1653, Brownlow's *Declarations and Pleadings.*

In 1641, was published Sheppard's *Touchstone of Common Assurance;* in 1656, William Sheppard wrote his *Abridgment;* and in 1659, the first English law book on Corporations entitled *Of Corporations, Fraternities and Guilds.*(1)

In 1668, appeared Chief Justice Rolle's *Abridgment.*(2)

In 1666, Sir William Dugdale wrote his famous *Origines Juridiciales,* the mine from which comes a large part of our information as to English laws, writs, judges, attorneys and sergeants.

The earliest reports of cases had been, of course, the *Year Books* which first began to be printed about 1481 and covered cases from about 1280 in Edward I's reign to 1537 in Henry VIII's.(3)

During the next one hundred years down to the time of the Commonwealth there had only been a few volumes of reports—those of *Plowden, Dyer, Keilway, Benlow, Dalison, Davies, Hobart, Bellewe* and *Coke,* about fifteen in all.(4)

---

(1)   See especially as to this *The First Book in English on the Law of Corporations,* by Amasa M. Eaton—*Yale Law Journal,* Vol. XIV, (1903.)

(2)   There were also a few books on the law merchant and admiralty law such as Malynes' *Lex Mercatoria or Ancient Law Merchant* (1622); Davies on *Impositions* (1656); Godolphus' *View of Admiralty* (1686); Prynne's *Animadversions* (1669); Zouch's *Jurisdiction of the Admiralty* (1686).

(3)   For full account of these see *Year Book Bibliography, Harvard Law Review,* Vol. XIV.

(4)   The first volume of the *The Commentaries or Reports of Edward Plowden of the Inner Temple, An Apprentice of the Common Law* had been published in 1571; the volumes covering roughly the times of Edward III to Elizabeth (1350-1580), and their value consisting largely in the fact that while many of the early reports and year books contained the off hand opinions of the judges upon motions, all of Plowden's cases were "upon points of law tried and debated." Sir James Dyer's *Notes* (Chief Justice of Common Pleas) had been the next cases printed as *Reports,* a posthumous work, in 1585; and Keilway and Bellewe had also come out in Elizabeth's reign. Lord Coke's *Reports* (which were really Commentaries), had been published from 1601 to 1616, when he was Attorney General and Chief Justice of the Common Pleas and of the King's Bench, and covered nearly completely the law of the reigns of Elizabeth and James I; each case generally containing the full pleadings and often a treatise on the point at issue. Of them Lord Bacon had said "Had it not been for Sir Edward Coke's *Reports* . . . . the law by this time had been almost like a ship without ballast for that the cases of modern experience are fled from those that are adjudged and ruled in former time."

These few reports, together with a small number of authoritative reports published in the reign of Charles II., such as *Croke* (1657), *Yelverton* (1661), *Rolle* (1675), *Vaughan* (1677), *W. Jones* (1675), *Leonard* (1658) and *Saunders* (1686), were practically the only reports known in the American Colonies, and substantially the only ones having any weight in England as law.

Nevertheless during the time of the Commonwealth and the later Stuarts (1649-1689), a flood of other reports had burst from the press,—nearly fifty volumes.(1)

Parliament's order requiring law publications to be in English had aroused all kinds of law writers and publishers from their former lethargy. It was a period when the Press was tremendously stimulated in all directions. Printing ran riot—the "age of pamphlets" so Dr. Johnson termed it.

Of this raking up of old cases and precedents Wallace in his book on the *Reporters* says:

"It was the mistake of Charles I, that for nearly the whole of his arbitrary measures he endeavored to obtain the sanction of the common law. Noy, his Attorney General, had found in the recesses of his recondite lore some precedents which relieved the King of most of his difficulties. . . . for they gave to the Crown the powers of the people . . . . and Charles . . . . assumed them as authority. This brought the law into unnatural prominence."

Most of these Reports were worthless as law, and in general it may be said that they completely disregarded Bulstrode's advice, given in the preface of his second volume: "That as the laws are the anchor of the Republic, so the Judicial Reports are as anchors of the laws and therefore ought to be well weighed before put out."(2)

---

(1) See Wallace's *The Reporters* (1845); *The English Law Reporters* —*Harvard Law Review*, Vol. XV.

In 1662 the act was passed requiring the licensing of printed publications; and under this, until 1692, all law books were required to bear the imprimatur of the Lord Chancellor, the Lord Chief Justice or the Lord Chief Baron.

(2) Many were simply copies, often unauthorized, of MSS. notes by a lawyer or judge of cases merely heard of by him; others are copies of students' notes. Most of them were posthumous, the cases in a single volume sometimes extending over a period of one hundred years. Thus *Anderson* and *New Benloe* cover 130 years, *Owen* 100, *Savile* 95, *Goldsboro* 83. Many were translations or transcriptions several times removed from the original; thus *Croke, Winch, Popham, Owen, Leonard, Hetley, J.*

Few, if any, of these reports were known in the American Colonies.

As to the Chancery reports at this time (1692), scarcely any existed. In fact the decrees of Lord Ellesmere, who had been Lord Chancellor from 1596-1617, were practically the first to be recorded to any extent. The decrees of the early chancellors—politicians and ecclesiastics as they were—as well as the decrees of the later lawyer chancellors, headed by Sir Thomas More, had been, as Blackstone said, "rather in the nature of awards formed on the sudden . . . . with more probity of intention than knowledge of the subject founded on no settled principles, as being never designed, and therefore never used for precedents." And as Whitelock said, "A keeper of the seal has nothing but his own conscience to direct him, and that is sometimes deceitful." This was the "Roguish Equity," of which Selden spoke in his *Table Talk,* "which varied with the length of the Chancellor's foot."(1)

Bridgman were originally written in Latin or French and first appear in English.

Some often report only a portion of a case. Thus the leading case of *Manby v. Scott* is partially reported in 1 *Siderfin* 109 and 1 *Levinz* 4, the opinion by Sir Orlando Bridgman is in Bridgman's *Collection,* Justice Hyde's opinion in 1 *Modern,* Chief Baron Hale's in Bacon's *Abridgement,* and parts of the case are in *Keble* and *Modern Reports.*

Wallace says that in the great case of *Vidal v. Girard's Exors,* in the Supreme Court of the United States (2 How., 127) "Mr. Binney (p. 88) showed at the bar that as to the principal authority cited by the chief justice (*Baptist Association v. Owen's Exors,* 4 Wheat. 1) . . . . there were no less than four different reports of it, all variant from each other. That as to one of the reporters the case had been decided 30 years before the time of his report . . . . that another reporter gave two versions of the case entirely different, not only from that of his co-reporter, but likewise from another of his own; that a fourth account by a yet distinct reporter was different from all the rest."

Some report the same case under different names. Thus *Clark v. Day* is found in 1 *Croke Eliz.* 313, *Owen* 148, *Moore,* 593, *Rolle,* and inaccurately in all, it is stated.

Most of the reports were well described in 1657 by Sir Harbottle Grimstone (later Master of the Rolls), "a multitude of flying reports, whose authors were as uncertain as the times when taken, have of late surreptitiously crept forth. We have been entertained with barren and unwarranted products which not only tends to the depriving of the first grounds and reasoning of the young practitioner who by such false lights are misled, but also to the contempt of divers of our former grave and learned justices."

Chief Justice Holt in later days also complained bitterly of his reporters, saying that the "skimblescamble stuff which they published would make posterity think ill of his understanding."

(1) Wallace says that "Though the binding nature of precedent in equity is said to have been acknowledged a good while ago by Bridgman (1 *Mod.,* 307) and Lord C. J. Trehy (3 *Chanc. Cas.,* 95) it is yet true

There was therefore no scope or reason for reports of their decisions; and the only Chancery reports covering this time were hardly more than brief notes on procedure, "reports shadowy, obscure and flickering," as Judge Story called them.(1)

Such was the meagre list of Common Law and Chancery reports, less than 100 in all, from which English students and lawyers of the 17th Century were obliged to extract the law, and out of which English judges had built and were building the fabric of the Common Law of England.

Yet to such an extent had this Century increased the roll of law books as compared with the previous 16th Century that the writer of the preface of 5 *Modern* (1711), describing 80 volumes of the Common Law said:

Thus I have given an historical account of our reports which a country lawyer (who was afterwards advanced to a seat of justice) told the bar were too voluminous, for when he was a student he could carry a complete library of books in a wheelbarrow, but they were so wonderfully increased in a few years they could not then be drawn in a waggon.

---

as a general thing at any rate that until the time of Lord Hardwicke equity was administered pretty much according to what appeared to be good conscience applied to the case."

Chief Justice Vaughn says in 1671 "I wonder to hear of citing precedents in matters of equity; for if there be equity in a case, that equity is an universal truth and there can be no precedent in it."

(1) *Carey* (1557-1604), *Choyce Cases in Chancery* (1557-1606), *Tothill* (1559-1646), *Reports in Chancery* (1616-1710), *Nelson* (1625-93), *Cases in Chancery* (1660-90), *Freeman* (1676-1706), *Finch* (1673-80), *Swanston, Vernon* (1681-1720); See *Vidal v. City of Philadelphia* (2 Howard, 193).

CHAPTER III.

New England Law and Lawyers in the 18th Century.

After the passing of the troublous times of James II and the revocation of most of the colonial charters, and after the Treaty of Utrecht, when peace was established on two continents, the American Colonies rapidly grew in wealth and influence.

Means of education increased. William and Mary College was founded in Virginia in 1692, Yale College in 1700, Kings College (Columbia) in New York, in 1754, College of New Jersey (Princeton), at Newark, in 1746, Brown at Providence, in 1764. The first public library was established in New York in 1729, consisting of 1600 volumes. While the first printing press had been brought into Massachusetts in 1629 and set up at Cambridge, being owned partially by Henry Dunster, President of Harvard College, there were nine printers in Massachusetts prior to 1692; and the first paper in all the Colonies was published in 1704, the *Boston News Letter.*(1)

In January, 1673, the first monthly postman began his trip between New York and Boston. In 1693, the first act was passed, encouraging "A general Letter Office in Boston." In 1704, the office of "Deputy Postmaster General for the Colonies," located in New York, was established by Act of Parliament. In 1753, Benjamin Franklin, then filling this office, established a penny post.

There was, at the same time, a very rapid extension of commerce, of export trade, of shipbuilding, fisheries, and slavetrading. A class of rich merchants began to control in the community. Questions as to business contracts and business paper began to arise. Land grew more valuable, and the legal determination and stability of landed rights become more necessary. Though

---

(1) Then followed the *Boston Gazette,* and the *American Magazine,* at Philadelphia, in 1719; the *New England Courant* in 1721, the *New York Gazette* in 1725, the *Maryland Gazette,* at Annapolis, in 1728, the *South Carolina Gazette,* at Charleston, and the *Rhode Island Gazette,* at Newport, in 1732, the *Weekly Journal,* at New York, in 1733, the *Virginia Gazette,* at Williamsburg, in 1736, the *Connecticut Gazette,* at New Haven, in 1755, the *American Magazine,* at Philadelphia, in 1741, the *Pennsylvania Journal* in 1742, the *North Carolina Gazette,* at New Berne, in 1755, the *New Hampshire Gazette,* at Portsmouth in 1756.

less encumbered with elaborate trusts and settlements than in England, wills grew more complicated. Important questions arose between the government of the various Colonies. The political liberties guaranteed by the principles of the English Common Law became increasingly more vital to the colonists, as the Royal Governors attempted to enlarge their own powers, and the King and Parliament began to trespass on what the Colonies regarded as their own prerogatives.

Thus arose the need for lawyers trained in English law. The need, supplied at first by barristers from England, was soon filled by native lawyers, educated in the colleges and in law offices of the Colonies.

MASSACHUSETTS.

While the Bar in Massachusetts developed rapidly in legal training, the bench still lagged behind; and for many years was composed chiefly of laymen.

Of the Chief Justices of the Superior Court of Judicature in Massachusetts, the first, William Stoughton (Chief Justice 1692-1701) was a clergyman (1); his successor, Waite Winthrop, (Chief Justice 1701, and 1708-1717) was a physician (2); Isaac Addington (1702-1703), was a physician (3); Samuel Sewall (1718-1728), was a clergyman (4); Benjamin Lynde (1728-1749), was a barrister of the Middle Temple (5); his successor, Paul Dudley, (1749-1751), was a barrister of the Inner Temple (6); Stephen Sewall (1752-1760), was a tutor in Harvard College (7); Thomas Hutchinson (1760-1771), was a wealthy merchant (8); Benjamin Lynde, the younger, (1771-1772), had a legal education in the Colony (9); Peter Oliver (1772-1776), was a literary man (10).

Of the twenty-three associate judges, Edmund Trowbridge, Chambers Russell (11) and William Cushing, were the only ones

(1) Born 1631, Harvard graduate of 1650.
(2) Born 1642, grandson of John Winthrop, Judge of Admirality, 1699.
(3) Born 1645.
(4) Born 1652, Harvard, 1671, Judge of Probate, 1715-1728.
(5) Born 1666, Harvard, 1686, Advocate General of the Court of Admirality, 1697.
(6) Born 1675, Harvard, 1690, Attorney General, 1702.
(7) Born 1702, Harvard, 1721.
(8) Born 1711, Harvard, 1727, 1752 Judge of Probate, 1758 Lieut. Gov.
(9 Born 1700, Harvard, 1718.
(10) Born 1712, Harvard, Harvard, 1730.
(11) Born 1713, Harvard, 1731, Judge of Probate, 1752.

who had any regular legal education, the rest being laymen or men trained for the ministry. Roger Mompesson and Robert Auchmuty, Judges of Admirality, had been English barristers. No other trained lawyers appeared on the Bench.

Notwithstanding their lack of systematic legal training, however, many of these judges were men of great learning and some of them had read considerable law. Thus it has been said of William Stoughton that(1):

He had extraordinary attainments in legal learning . . . . It is true that he as well as Dudley and Sewall was bred a clergyman; but those who imagine that the study of divinity unfits the student for forensic, legislative or magisterial duties are to be reminded that the legal is but a lay branch of the clerical profession from which it sprung; and that the secularizing of jurisprudence is a work of modern times. . . . . I think the three magistrates I have named, each of whom acceptably held the post, either in Massachusetts or New York, of chief justice of the highest judicial court will compare favorably in respect to all those acquirements necessary to the proper conduct of trials and the administering of forensic justice, with, at least, the average benchers of the Inns of Court in the days of William and Anne.

So too of Samuel Sewall, Washburn says:

From a perusal of his journal it is apparent that he had a natural taste for legal science which he had cultivated by a very respectable course of study—He must have been altogether better read in the principles of the common law than any other judge upon the bench.

And Sewall's address to the Grand Jury at the opening of the first court in the new Town House in Boston, April 27, 1793, contains most enlightened views:

Let never any judge debauch this bench by abiding on it when his own cause comes under trial. May the judges always discern justice with a most stable, permanent impartiality.—Let the attorneys remember they are to advise the court as well as plead for their clients.

Thomas Hutchinson being a man of liberal culture had devoted much time to the reading of law though he had never practised

---

(1) See *Witch Trials in Massachusetts* by Abner E. Goodell—*Mass. Hist. Soc. Proc.*, Vol. XX (1883).

law. In his diary he remarks, that "Though it was an eyesore to some of the bar to have a person at the head of the law who had not been bred to it, he had reason to think the lawyers in general at no time desired his removal."(1)

That the lawyers were restive under the Chief Justice's lack of legal knowledge, is shown, however, in a letter written by John Adams to William Tudor (March 8, 1817), regarding a controversy between the Governor and the General Court in which he had appeared as counsel:

Mr. Hutchinson had wholly misunderstood the legal doctrine of allegiance. . . . . I had quoted largely from a law authority which no man in Massachusetts had ever read. Hutchinson and all his law counsels were in fault; . . . They dared not deny it lest the book should be produced to their confusion. It was humorous enough to see how Hutchinson wriggled to evade it. He found nothing better to say than that it was 'the artificial reasoning of Lord Coke.' The book was *Moore's Reports*. . . . . It had been Mr. Gridley's.(2)

It is a noticeable fact, however, that 20 out of 33 of the Superior Court Judges, though without legal training, were graduates of Harvard College. And even of the judges of the lower Courts of Common Pleas in Suffolk County, 12 out of 25 were graduates of Harvard; in Middlesex, 7 out of 20; in Essex, 12 out of 30; in Plymouth, 8 out of 19.(3)

Of the ten Attorney-Generals, Thomas Newton, (who came over in 1688), was the only English barrister; although Addington Davenport had received a Master's Degree at Oxford, and seven of the others had studied law in the Province, six being Harvard graduates.

It was not until June 20, 1701-2, that practice of the law became first dignified as a regular profession, through the requirement by statute of an oath for all attorneys practicing in the courts, as follows:

---

(1) An interesting sidelight is thrown on this, by an entry in his diary under date of July 22, 1774, when he was in England visiting Sir Francis Bernard.

"Sir Francis mentioned among other things that he apologized to Lord Mansfield for appointing me Chief Justice, not having been bred to the law; adding that he had no cause to repent it. Lord Chief Justice Wilmot being by, broke out with an oath "By ――――, he did not make a worse chief justice for that!" See *Diary of Thomas Hutchinson*, p. 195.

(2) *Life of Thomas Hutchinson*, by James K. Hosmer (1896).

(3) See biographies in *Judicial History of Massachusetts*, by Emory Washburn.

You shall do no falsehood, nor consent to any to be done in
the court, and if you know of any to be done you shall give
knowledge thereof to the justices of the court, or some of them,
that it may be reformed. You shall not wittingly and willingly
promote, sue or procure to be sued any false or unlawful suit,
nor give aid or consent to the same. You shall delay no man
for lucre or malice, but you shall use yourself in the office of an
attorney within the court according to the best of your learning
and discretion, and with all good fidelity as well to the courts
as to your clients.(1)

The scarcity of lawyers and the fear of parties retaining the
whole Bar is shown by the passage of the Act of June 16, 1708,
providing that "no person shall entertain more than two of the
sworn allowed attorneys at law, that the adverse party may have
liberty to retain others of them to assist him, upon his tender of
the established fee which they may not refuse.(2)

At first the native lawyers were, in general, men of little distinction, or reputation; and the lawsuits were of small import.

During the first half of the 18th Century, New England was
crippled by foolish financial management, through the unlimited issue of paper money, and from 1704 to 1741, the depreciation
of the currency produced innumerable troubles. These conditions
gave rise to much litigation; and William Shirley reported to the
Board of Trade, in 1743, that "it was not infrequent for persons
of some circumstances and character to suffer judgments to be
given against them by default in open court for such debts, and
to appeal from one court to another merely for delay; whereby
lawsuits were scandalously multiplied and a litigious, trickish
spirit promoted among the lower sort of people."(3)

Even as late as 1758, John Adams, soon after he was admitted to the Bar, stated, that he "found the practice of law was
grasped into the hands of deputy sheriffs, pettifoggers, and
even constables, who filled all the writs upon bonds, promissory
notes and accounts, and received the fees established for lawyers, and stirred up many unnecessary suits."

In 1747, Dr. Douglas wrote in his *Summary,* "Generally in all

---

(1) This oath followed almost exactly the form set forth in England
in *The Book of Oaths* (1649); and see also *The Practick Part of the
Law* (1676).
(2) This provision appeared again in 1785; and as late as 1836, (*Rev.
St. Ch.* 88, Sect. 26) it was provided, that no more than two persons
for each party should, without permission of the court, be allowed to manage any case.
(3) *Life of Thomas Hutchinson,* by James K. Hosmer, p. 20 (1896).

our colonies, particularly in New England, people are much addicted to quirks of the law. A very ordinary countryman in New England is almost qualified for a country attorney in England."(1)

Contemporary with these conditions, however, a small Bar of native lawyers of really great ability was growing up.

The Nestor of them was John Read, who, born in 1679, graduated from Harvard in 1697, studied in Connecticut and was admitted to the Bar in New Haven in 1708. Before his death in 1749, he acquired the reputation of being "the greatest common lawyer that ever lived in New England." Of him, Adams said later, "He had as great a genius and became as eminent as any man." To him is due many of the forms of writs, actions, declarations and conveyancing, later in use. He was retained by the Colony of Connecticut, and also by Massachusetts, in important boundary dispute cases with New York, New Hampshire and Rhode Island; also for the town of Boston in many cases, one of particular importance involving the title to Dock square, tried for six years and appealed to the King in Council, where he won.(2)

After Read, came Jeremiah Gridley, who, born in 1702, a Harvard graduate of 1723, studied first for the ministry and later became "the father of the Boston Bar," Attorney General in 1742, and the great legal scholar of the Century. His office was the training school for James Otis, Jr., and John Adams, of whom Gridley used to observe, that "he had reared two young eagles who were one day to peck out his eyes." Oxenbridge Thacher, Benjamin Pratt (later Chief Justice of New York), and William Cushing, (later Chief Justice of the Supreme Court of Massachusetts and Justice and Chief Justice of the Supreme Court of the United States), were also his pupils.

Judge Edmund Trowbridge, born in 1699, a Harvard graduate of 1728, was the great "real estate" lawyer of the time, termed by Chief Justice Isaac Parker, in 1813, "perhaps the most profound common lawyer of New England before the Revolution." His opinions and his essay on the law of mortgages were considered of such value as to be annexed (after his death in 1793, at the age of

---

(1) *A Summary, Historical and Political, of the First Planting, Progressive Improvements and Present State of the British Settlements in North America,* by William Douglas (London 1747).

(2) *Life of John Read,* by George B. Read (1903).

94) to Volume 8 of the *Massachusetts Reports;* and such was his
learning and ability, that it is said by John Adams, that he had the
entire command of the practice in Middlesex, Worcester, and
several other counties, and had the power to crush any young
lawyer by a frown or nod.   In his office in Cambridge studied
Francis Dana and Theophilus Parsons (both of whom became
Chief Justices of the Supreme Court of the State of Massachusetts), James Putnam, Royall Tyler, (Chief Justice of Vermont), Rufus King, Christopher Gore and Harrison Gray
Otis.

Contemporary with Gridley, were William Shirley, Robert
Auchmuty, and William Bollan who were native English lawyers,
Richard Dana(1), Benjamin Kent(2), James Otis, Sr.(3),
Timothy Ruggles (4), and Benjamin Pratt (5).

About two decades later, another group of lawyers added distinction to the Bar—James Otis, Jr.(6), Oxenbridge Thacher
(7), Samuel Adams (8), Jonathan Sewall (9), Robert Treat
Paine (10), John Worthington (11), and Joseph Hawley (12),
the two latter being the most prominent of the few lawyers practising in the western part of the Province.

About 1765, just prior to the Revolution, a third group of
eminent young lawyers of considerable law learning began to
distinguish themselves—John Adams(13), Josiah Quincy, Jr.
(14), Samuel Quincy (15), Sampson Salters Blowers (16),

---

(1)   Born in 1700, Harvard graduate of 1718.
(2)   Born about 1705, Harvard 1727, educated as a clergyman.
(3)   Born in 1702, father of James Otis, Jr.
(4)   Born in 1711, Harvard 1732.
(5)   Born in 1709, Harvard 1737, Chief Justice of New York in 1761.
(6)   Born in 1725, Harvard 1743, studied with J. Gridley.
(7)   Born in 1720, Harvard 1738, studied for the ministry, later studied
law with J. Gridley.
(8)   Born in 1722, Harvard 1740.
(9)   Born in 1728, Harvard 1748, a school teacher, later studied law
with Judge Chambers Russell, admitted to practice 1758, Attorney General
1767.
(10)   Born in 1731, Harvard 1749, became a minister, later admitted
to the Bar in 1759.
(11)   Born in 1719, Yale 1740, studied law with Gen. Phinehas Lyman.
(12)   Born in 1724, Yale 1742, studied for the ministry, later studied
law with Gen. Lyman.
(13)   Born 1735, Harvard 1755, studied law with Judge James Putnam,
admitted to the Bar in 1758, called as Barrister 1761.
(14)   Born in 1744, Harvard 1763.
(15)   Born in 1735, Harvard 1754, studied with Benjamin Pratt.
Solicitor General 1767.
(16)   Born in 1742, Harvard 1763, studied law under Gov. Hutchinson.

Theophilus Bradbury(1), William Cushing(2), Daniel Leonard(3), Theodore Sedgwick(4), and Caleb Strong(5).

At first no special qualifications and no definite term of study had been required for admission to the Bar. But, in reality, in order to master the profession, a student in the Colonies had to acquire far more knowledge than a student at the Inns of Court in London; for as Gridley said to Adams in 1758:(6)

A lawyer in this country must study common law and civil law and natural law and admiralty law and must do the duty of a counsellor, a lawyer, an attorney, a solicitor and even of a scrivener; so that the difficulties of the profession are much greater here than in England.

Notwithstanding this outlook, the students of law increased in number, so that in 1756, John Adams, who had begun to study in the office of Judge James Putnam of Worcester (Harvard 1746), wrote, that they were "very numerous."(7)

Gradually, under the influence of the able lawyers mentioned above, a regular Bar began to establish itself; and out of it grew rules regulating practice, course of study and legal etiquette. By 1757, when John Adams was meditating the opening of an office in the country part of the then county of Suffolk, he was told "that the town of Boston was then full of lawyers, and many of them of established character for long experience, great abilities, and extensive fame, who might be jealous of such a novelty and might be induced to obstruct me."

That these lawyers were men of importance to their juniors, is amusingly shown by Adams, in a further entry in his diary. Oct. 24, 1758; "Went into the court house and sat down by Mr. Paine at the lawyers' table. I felt shy under awe and concern; for Mr. Gridley, Mr. Pratt, Mr. Otis, Mr. Kent and Mr. Thacher

---

(1) Born in 1732, Harvard 1757, practiced law in Maine 1761-1779, one of the earliest lawyers there.

(2) Born in 1732, Harvard 1751, studied law with J. Gridley, was the first regular educated lawyer to settle in Maine, 1755, Chief Justice of Massachusetts 1776.

(3) Born in 1740, Harvard 1760.

(4) Born in 1746, left Yale without graduating in 1765, studied for the ministry, admitted to the Bar in 1766.

(5) Born in 1745, Harvard 1764, admitted to the Bar in 1772.

(6) *John Adams' Life and Works*, Vol. II., p. 46.

(7) General Gage later denounced "this country where every man studies law"; and in 1768 the British Attorney General said, "Look into the papers and see how well these Americans are versed in Crown Law".

were all present and looked sour. I had no acquaintance with anybody but Paine and Quincy and they took but little notice."

As early as 1761 the Bar had formed a regular association; and had prescribed seven years of probation—three of preliminary study, two of practice as attorney in the Inferior Court, and two of practice as attorney in the Superior Court.(1) John Adams, noting in his diary July 28, 1766, the Bar meeting for the admission of three young gentlemen, Mr. Oliver, Mr. Quincy and Mr. Blowers, consoled himself for the "swarming and multiplying" of lawyers, by the reflection that four years must elapse before they could assume the gown. Adams describes as follows the admission to practice of himself and Samuel Quincy, Nov. 6, 1758, their sponsor before the Court being Gridley, the Attorney General:

I began to grow uneasy, expecting that Quincy would be sworn and I have no patron, when Mr. Gridley made his appearance, and, on sight of me, whispered to Mr. Pratt, Dana, Kent, Thacher, about me. Mr. Pratt said nobody knew me. "Yes," says Gridley, "I have tried him and he is a very sensible fellow!" At last he rose up and bowed to his right hand and said, "Mr. Quincy," when Quincy rose up; then he bowed to me, "Mr. Adams," when I walked out.

After being presented to the bench with a few complimentary remarks, "the clerk was ordered to swear us; after the oath, Mr. Gridley took me by the hand, wished me much joy, and recommended me to the bar. I shook hands with the bar and received their congratulations, and invited them over to Stone's to drink some punch, where most of us resorted, and had a very cheerful chat."

This genial relationship between the seniors and juniors of the Bar on days of admission was preserved for some time later. Thus, Prentiss Mellen (Harvard 1784), and later Chief Justice of Maine, who studied with Shearjashub Bourne at Barnstable and was admitted to the Plymouth Bar, says, that "according to the fashion of that day on the great occasion I treated the judges and all the lawyers with about half a pail of punch, which treating aforesaid was commonly called the colt's tail."

In 1763, Adams writes in his diary, that the Bar had agreed "that nobody should answer to a suit but the plaintiff himself or some sworn attorney, and that a general power should not be

(1) *Adams' Life and Works*, Vol. II., p. 197. G. Dexter, *Mass. Hist. Soc. Coll.* Vol. VI., p.145.

admitted;" also that "no attorney should be allowed to practice in the Superior or Inferior Courts unless duly sworn."

About 1760, Chief Justice Hutchinson, by a rule of court, introduced the distinction between barristers and attorneys, and provided that none but barristers could argue in the Superior Court. This rule was not always enforced; for Josiah Quincy, Jr., who was refused to admission as a barrister, being obnoxious in his politics to the ruling powers, says in his *Reports* in Aug., 1769:

At the last sitting of the Superior Court in Charlestown I argued (for the first time in this court) to the Jury though not admitted to Gown, the legality and propriety of which some have pretended to doubt; but as no scruples of that kind disturbed me, I proceeded (maugre any) at this court to manage all my own Business, (for the first time in this country) though unsanctified and uninspired by the pomp and magic of the long robe.

By rule of court, three years of practice was required before admission as a barrister. This was later increased to seven years, with a regular grade of promotion,—similar to the custom of England, where five years' residence in the Inns of Court was required, and three years, of a graduate of Oxford or Cambridge.

At the same time Hutchinson also introduced a costume for the judges, consisting of a black silk gown, worn over a full black suit, white bands, and a silk bag for the hair. This was worn by the judges in civil causes, and criminal trials, excepting those for capital offenses, in which trials they wore scarlet robes, (1) with black velvet collars and cuffs to their large sleeves, and black velvet facings to their robes.

Of such importance was this costume that Hutchinson deemed it worthy of record to note in his diary, after describing the riot in Boston on the night of the 26th of August, 1765, when all his plate, family pictures, furniture, wearing apparel and the books and manuscripts, which he had been thirty years collecting, were destroyed by the mob, that: "The Superior Court was to be held the next morning in Boston. The Chief Justice who was deprived of his robes and all other apparel, except an undress he was in when the mob came, appeared in that undress and an

(1) The color of the robes may remind one of Cromwell's remark, "Well, if I cannot rule by red gowns, I will rule by redcoats." Campbell's *Lives of the Chief Justices*, Vol. II., p. 187.

ordinary great coat over it which he borrowed."(1). Soon after the Revolution this costume was laid aside, it is supposed, because it was not suited to the simplicity of the form of government, and the last appearance of the judges in gowns was at the funeral of Governor Hancock in October 1793, when they wore black silk.(2)

John Adams, writing to his pupil, William Tudor, says of these innovations:

I pass over that scenery which he introduced so showy and so shallow, so theatrical and so ecclesiastical of scarlet and sable robes, of broad bands and enormous tie wigs more resembling fleeces of painted merino wool than anything natural to man and that could breathe with him. I pass over also the question whether he or his court had legal authority to establish a distinction between barristers and attorneys. Innovations, though often necessary, are always dangerous.(3)

It appears from the court records for the August term 1762, that 26 gentlemen had been called by the court to be barristers at law, and that twelve of them had appeared in barristers habits —black silk gown, bands and bag wigs.(4)

By 1768, the order of barristers was so well recognized that it is known that there were then 25(5). In 1770, a new Bar Association was formed in Boston; and several of the other counties, notably Essex, had similar associations, of great ability.

---

(1) *Diary and Letters of Thomas Hutchinson*, pp. 67, 69. See also *Life of Thomas Hutchinson* by James K. Hosmer, p. 95. "So strict was Lord Eldon (on matters of dress) that I remember Wetherell, when Attorney General, having forgot the full bottom wig and appeared in a tie, Lord Eldon 'regretted that his Majesty's Attorney General was not present at the bar, as the interests of the Crown were concerned.'" *Life of Lord Campbell*, Vol. I., p. 793.
(2) William Sullivan in his *Familiar Letters on Public Characters* (1847), says that "the judges had up to this time (1793), worn robes of scarlet faced with black velvet in winter, and black silk gowns in summer."
(3) *Adams' Life and Works*, Vol. X., p. 233, Vol. II., p. 133. G. Dexter in *Mass. Hist. Soc., Proc.*, Vol. XIX, p. 144.
(4) See *Life of James Otis, Amer. Law Rev.*, Vol. I, 541.
(5) Of these 25, eleven were in Suffolk, Richard Dana, Benjamin Kent, James Otis, Jr., Samuel Fitch, William Read, Samuel Swift, Benjamin Gridley, Samuel Quincy, Robert Auchmuty, and Andrew Cazneau, of Boston, and Jonathan Adams, of Braintree; five were in Essex, Daniel Farnham and John Lowell, of Newburyport, William Pynchon, of Salem, John Chipman, of Marblehead, and Nathaniel Peaselee Sergeant, of Haverhill; one was in Middlesex, Jonathan Sewall; two in Worcester, James Putnam, of Worcester, and Abel Willard, of Lancaster; three in Bristol, Samuel White and Robert Treat Paine, of Taunton, and Daniel Leonard, of Norton; in Hampshire, John Worthington, of Springfield;

At the time of the Revolution, there were in the whole Province 36 barristers and 12 attorneys practising in the courts.(1)

In February, 1781, the following rule was made by the Superior Court of Judicature:—the first order relating to lawyers made by the Court after Massachusetts became a State:

Whereas learning and literary accomplishments are necessary as well to promote the happiness as to preserve the freedom of the people, and the learning of the law when duly encouraged and rightly directed, being as well peculiarly subservient to the great and good purpose aforesaid, as promotive of public and private justice; and this court being at all times ready to bestow peculiar marks of approbation upon the gentlemen of the Bar, who, by a close application to the study of the science they profess, by a mode of conduct which gives a conviction of the rectitude of their minds, and a fairness of practice that does honour to the profession of the law, shall distinguish themselves as men of science, honour and integrity: Do order that no gentlemen shall be called to the degree of Barrister until he shall merit the same, by his conspicuous learning, ability and honesty; and that the Court will, of their own mere motion call to the Bar such persons as shall render themselves worthy as aforesaid; and that the manner of calling barristers shall be as follows: The gentleman who shall be a candidate shall stand within the bar. The Chief Justice, or in his absence the senior justice, shall, in the name of the Court, repeat to him the qualifications necessary for a Barrister of the Law; shall let him know that it is a conviction in the mind of the Court of his being possessed of these qualifications that induces them to confer this honour upon him; and shall solemnly charge him so to conduct himself as to be of singular service to his country by exerting his abilities for the defence of her constitu-

---

in Plymouth, James Hovey and Pelham Winslow. After 1768, these barristers were called: Joseph Hawley, of Northampton, David Sewall, of York, Moses Bliss, of Springfield, Zephaniah Leonard, of Taunton, Theophilus Bradbury, of Falmouth (Portland), David Wyer, of Falmouth, Mark Hopkins, of Great Barrington, Simeon Strong, of Amherst, John Sullivan, of Durham, Daniel Oliver, of Hardwick, Francis Dana, of Cambridge, Sampson Salter Blowers, of Boston, Daniel Bliss, of Concord, Samuel Porter, of Salem, Joshua Upham, of Brookfield, Shearjashub Bourne, of Barnstable, James Sullivan, of Biddeford, Jeremiah D. Rogers, of Littleton, Oaks Angier, of Bridgewater, John Sprague, of Lancaster, Caleb Strong, of Northampton, Elisha Porter, of Hadley, Theodore Sedgwick, of Sheffield, Benjamin Hichborn, of Boston, Theophilus Parsons, of Newburyport, Jonathan Bliss, of Springfield, William Tudor, Perez Morton and William Wetmore of Boston, and Levi Lincoln, of Worcester.

(1) Of the 31 barristers mentioned by Washburn in his *Judicial History of Massachusetts* from 1700 to 1776, 17 were Harvard graduates. 1 from Yale, 4 from English Colleges and 9 non-graduates.

tional freedom; and so to demean himself as to do honour to the Court and Bar.

Not only was the Bar an able, brilliant and educated one from 1760 to 1775; but the cases tried demanded talents of high order.

In 1761, arose probably the most famous colonial case of the 18th Century, that of the Writs of Assistance *Paxton's Case* (Quincy Reports, p. 51), graphically described by John Adams. The trial took place in the Council Chamber, in the building now known as "The Old State House" in Boston.

In this chamber near the fire, were seated five judges with Lieut. Governor Hutchinson at their head, as Chief Justice, all in their new fresh robes of scarlet English cloth, in their broad bands and immense judicial wigs. In this chamber were seated at a long table all the barristers of Boston, and its neighboring County of Middlesex, in their gowns, bands and tye-wigs. They were not seated on ivory chairs, but their dress was more solemn and more pompous than of the Roman Senate when the Gauls broke in upon them. Two portraits at more than full length of King Charles the Second in splendid golden frames were hung upon the most conspicuous sides of the apartment. In a corner of the room must be placed, wit, sense, imagination, genius, pathos, reason, prudence, eloquence, learning, science and immense reading hung by the shoulders on two crutches covered with a cloth great coat, in the person of Mr. Pratt, who had been solicited on both sides, but would engage on neither, being about to leave Boston forever, as chief justice of New York.

The court which sat on this august occasion, consisted of Chief Justice Hutchinson, Benjamin Lynde, John Cushing, Peter Oliver and Chambers Russell. The counsel engaged were Jeremiah Gridley in favor of, and Oxenbridge Thacher and James Otis, Jr. against, the application. "Then and there was the first scene of the first act of opposition to the arbitrary claims of Great Britain. Then and there the child, Independence, was born. Every man of an immense crowded audience appeared to me to go away, as I did, ready to take up arms against writs of assistance."

In 1762, the important case of *Dudley v. Dudley* arose, involving the question whether a devise under Governor Dudley's will was a fee simple or an entailment. "In the first argument," says William Sullivan (in 1825), "Otis and Gridley contended, that it was the former; Kent (a very inferior man) and Trowbridge, that it was the latter. In the second argument, Auchmuty was substituted for Kent. The argument was a very able one, even in comparison with those of modern times. The court decided the devise to be a fee simple. But as none of its members were lawyers, they wisely forbore to give any reasons for their opinion."

In November, 1770, came the trial of Captain Preston and the British Soldiers for murder, "the Boston Massacre." It was the high test of the honor and independence of the American Bar that John Adams, and Josiah Quincy, Jr., then only seven years out of college, and not yet a barrister, and his classmate Sampson Salters Blowers (Harvard 1763), were willing to undertake the defence of the unpopular side.(1)

The trial lasted eight days before Benjamin Lynde, John Cushing, Peter Oliver and Edmund Trowbridge. The counsel for the crown were Robert Treat Paine, and Samuel Quincy, Jonathan Sewall, Attorney General, signed the indictments. Of the defendants, Preston and six of the others, were acquitted; two were found guilty of manslaughter, but praying the benefit of clergy, were "each of them burnt in the hand in open court and discharged."(2)

NEW HAMPSHIRE.

For the first fifty years of New Hampshire history, no practising attorney was made a judge, although George Jaffrey, the Chief Justice from 1726 to 1732, was a Harvard graduate.(3)

In 1754, Theodore Atkinson, who had been a clerk of the Court of Common Pleas in Massachusetts, and had been admitted to the Bar in 1731, became the first Chief Justice with any legal training.(4)

---

(1) John Adams wrote in his diary March 5, 1773, "The part I took in defense of Capt. Preston and the soldiers, procured me anxiety and obloquy enough. It was, however, one of the most gallant, generous, manly and disinterested acts of my whole life, and one of the best pieces of service I ever rendered my country. Judgment of death against those soldiers would have been as foul a stain upon this country as the execution of the Quakers or witches anciently."

(2) At this time in England, all persons capable of taking holy orders, i. e., who could read, who had committed a felony other than wilful murder, might claim "benefit of clergy," and thus escape punishment other than imprisonment for one year and burning in the hand. See *Criminal Laws of England*, by Sir James Fitzjames Stephen, p. 71 (1863).

(3) Born in 1682, Harvard 1702, Chief Justice 1726-32. There were 13 Chief Justices from 1693 to 1776.

(4) Born in 1697, Harvard 1716, Chief Justice 1754-75.

Prior to the Revolution, only two other judges had been lawyers, Leverett Hubbard (Harvard 1742), who had studied law in Rhode Island, appointed Judge in 1763, and William Parker, appointed in 1771, "a well read and accurate lawyer"(1) and the head of the Bar.

From 1776 to 1782, the Chief Justice was Meschech Weare, who had studied theology but did not preach(2); Mathew Thornton, a physician, and John Wentworth, a lawyer of little distinction, being his associates.

From 1782 to 1790, Samuel Livermore was Chief Justice. He was a trained lawyer, born in 1732 in Massachusetts, a graduate of Princeton in 1752, a student in the office of Judge Edmund Trowbridge, in 1769 King's Attorney in New Hampshire, Attorney General of the State in 1776. He sat on the bench however with three associates who were not lawyers, and he himself was intolerant of legal precedent. It is said that in charging the jury, he used to caution them "against paying too much attention to the niceties of the law to the prejudice of Justice"; and when reminded of previous rulings of his own, contrary to his present ruling, he would reply that "every tub must stand on its own bottom."

Jeremiah Mason says, in his autobiography, that Benjamin West, "by far the best lawyer in this region of the country", told him this anecdote of Livermore, as illustrating the uselessness of citing precedents. "Judge Livermore, having no law learning himself, did not like to be pestered with it at his courts. When West attempted to read law books in a law argument, the Chief Justice asked him why he read them; 'if he thought that he and his brethren did not know as much as those musty old worm-eaten books'? Mr. West answered, 'These books contain the wisdom of the ancient sages of the law'. The reply was, 'Well do you think we do not understand the principles of justice as well as the old wigged lawyers of the dark ages did?' "

Josiah Bartlett, a physician, was Livermore's associate, of whom it was said, that "when the law was with the plaintiff, and equity seemed to him on the other side, he was sure to pronounce in favor of equity." John Dudley, the most prominent of the assistant judges from 1785 to 1797, was a farmer and trader; and his style of charging the jury has been quoted as follows:

---

(1)   Born in 1703.

(2)   Born in 1713, Harvard 1735, Chief Justice 1776-82.

Gentlemen of the jury, the lawyers have talked to you of law. It is not the law we want, but justice. They would govern us by the common law of England. Trust me, gentlemen, common sense is a much safer guide for us, the common sense of Raymond, Exeter and the other towns which have sent us here to try this case between two of our neighbors. It is our business to do justice between the parties not by any quirks of the law out of Coke or Blackstone—books that I never read and never will—but by common sense as between man and man.

In one case, in which Jeremiah Mason had filed a demurrer, Judge Dudley said that "demurrers were no doubt an invention of the bar to prevent justice, a part of the common law procedure," but that he had always "thought them a cursed cheat". "Let me advise you, young man," he added, "not to come here with your new fangled law—you must try your cases as others do, by the court and jury".

William Plumer thus describes the condition of the Courts:

Under the colonial government, causes of importance were carried up, for decision in the last resort, to the governor and council, with the right, in certain cases—a right seldom claimed—of appeal to the king in council. As the executive functionaries were not generally lawyers, and the titular judges were often from other professions than the legal, they were not much influenced in their decisions by any known principles of established law. So much, indeed, was the result supposed to depend upon the favor or aversion of the court, that presents from suitors to the judges were not uncommon, nor, perhaps, unexpected. On one occasion, the chief justice, who was also a member of the council, is said to have inquired, rather impatiently of his servant, what cattle those were that had waked him so unseasonably in the morning by their lowing under his window; and to have been somewhat mollified by the answer that they were a yoke of six-feet cattle, which Col. ——— had sent as a present to His Honor. "Has he?" said the judge; "I must look into his case—it has been in court long enough."

Under date of June 24, 1771, John Adams says:

Mr. Lowell, who practised much in New Hampshire, gave me an account of many strange judgments of the Superior Court at Portsmouth. . . . . During the revolution, the same practice of going beyond the courts of law for redress was continued; and the form which it took, under the constitution of 1784, was that of a special act of the Legislature, restoring the party to his law, as it was called, that is, giving him a new trial in the Superior Court, after his case had come to its final decision in the ordinary course of the law. . . . . The supposed interest of lawyers in the multiplication of suits, the litigious spirit of parties, ever eager to grasp at new chances of success, and the love of power, natural to legislative bodies, all combined to render this irregularity in the administration of justice not unacceptable to the public.

Belknap, in his history, written in 1792, thus describes the legal conditions:

In the administration of justice, frequent complaints were made of partiality. Parties were sometimes heard out of court, and the practice of watering the jury was familiarly known to those persons who had much business in the law.

While the rude decisions of the courts, based on common sense, were, not wholly without value in their influence on the development of the law,(1) nevertheless before a Bench so little addicted to legal methods, there was small need or opportunity for trained lawyers; and the Bar of New Hampshire, during the whole 18th Century, was consequently few in number. Two lawyers however may be noted.

Mathew Livermore, born in 1703, a Harvard graduate of 1722, was regularly admitted to the Bar in Portsmouth in 1731, at which time, says John Adams, "there was no regularly educated lawyer in the town." He became Attorney General in 1755 and died in 1776.

Wiseman Claggett, one of the quaintest geniuses of the whole colonial Bar, arrived in Portsmouth in 1758, and was then admitted to the bar of the Superior Court. He had been a barrister in the Inns of Court, and later a practising attorney in Antigua in the West Indies. Until the Revolution, he divided the business of New Hampshire with Samuel Livermore (later the Chief Justice), Claggett receiving most of the criminal business, Livermore the civil.

In 1758, at the time of the chartering of Dartmouth College, there were only eight trained lawyers in New Hampshire; and none of them were of such ability as to be retained by President

---

(1) As Judge Bell said, in *B. C. & M. R. R. v. State,* (32 N. H. 231): "We regard the ignorance of the first colonists of the technicalities of the common law as one of the most fortunate things in the history of the law, since while the substance of the common law was preserved we happily lost a great mass of antiquated and useless rubbish and gained in its stead a course of practice of admirable simplicity."

Wheelock, he engaging as his counsel, William Smith and William Smith, Jr., of New York and John Ledyard, of Connecticut; the head of the Bar, William Parker being legal adviser of Governor Wentworth.(1)

There was no regular Bar Association until after the Revolution.(2) And to 1785, the Bar continued small, not exceeding twenty-nine in number; after that date a new era began.

In 1786, Jeremiah Smith began practice in New Hampshire. He was born in 1759, after having entered at Harvard in 1777, and remained for two years, he graduated from Queens (now Rutgers College), and studied law at Barnstable, Mass., with Shearjashub Bourne. The great Jeremiah Mason, who, born in 1768, had graduated from Yale in 1788 and studied law in Judge Simeon Baldwin's office at New Haven, was admitted to practise in 1791, and removed to Portsmouth in 1798. Nine years later, his only rival, Danial Webster arrived at Portsmouth. Webster was born in 1782, graduated at Dartmouth in 1801, studied in New Hampshire, and with Christopher Gore in Boston in 1804, admitted to the Bar in 1805. With them may be mentioned Arthur Livermore(3), John Prentice(4), George Sullivan(5), Ichabod Bartlett(6), John Sullivan(7), Benjamin West(8), William King Atkinson(9), William Plumer(10) and John Pickering(11).

---

(1) See *Dartmouth College Cases* by John M. Shirley.
(2) The etiquette of the early lawyers was rather loose. A story is told of Claggett, which illustrates the rude condition of the times. Samuel Livermore, having advertised in the New Hampshire *Gazette* the fact of moving his office, also the fact that he had Newmarket Lottery tickets for sale, Claggett wrote and published:

> "Pray is it not a thing surprising
> To see a lawyer advertising
> Tho' Law's the plea and the intent
> Yet lawyers should quote precedent
> To me it is there's no dispute on't
> A tree's known best by the fruit on't
> So he that sells the choicest wine
> Need have no bush (that is) no sign
> But with the lawyer we agree
> The end of law's a lottery."

(3) Born in 1766, studied with his brother Edward St. Loe Livermore, Judge of Superior Court 1798, Chief Justice in 1809.
(4) Born in 1747, Harvard graduate of 1766, studied with Samuel Livermore, Attorney General 1787-1793.
(5) Born in 1771, Harvard graduate of 1790, studied with his father Gen. John Sullivan.
(6) Born in 1768, Dartmouth graduate of 1808, studied with Moses Eastman and Parker Noyes, admitted in 1812.
(7) Born in 1740, studied with Samuel Livermore, 1782-85 Attorney General, 1789 Judge of U. S. District Court.

By the beginning of the 19th Century, the Bar was one of great lustre, so that even Judge Story used to speak of its "vast law learning and prodigious intellectual power." (1) In 1805 it contained 106 lawyers, of whom 91 were admitted to practice in the Superior Court, 77 of whom were college graduates—from Harvard 35, Dartmouth 34, Yale 6, Brown 2.

As professional education spread, and as the science of jurisprudence came to be studied, and precedent and authority insisted upon, the unprofessional judges disappeared; and Richard Evans, appointed in 1809 and removed in 1813, was the last judge not a lawyer.

At the same time, with the appointment of John Pickering as Chief Justice from 1790 to 1795, and of Jeremiah Smith as Chief Justice in 1802, there arose a new order of things; and the practice of law was reduced to a practical science; and as the court said in *Lisbon v. Lyman*, 49 N. H., "Chief Justice Smith found the law of New Hampshire, in practice and administration, a chaos, and left it comparatively an organized and scientific system."

---

(8) Born in 1746, Harvard graduate of 1768, studied for the ministry, admitted 1773.

(9) Born 1765, Harvard graduate of 1783, studied with John Pickering, Judge of Superior Court 1803, Atty. Gen. 1807.

(10) Born 1759, studied with Joshua Atherton, admitted 1787.

(11) Born 1737, Harvard graduate of 1761, Chief Justice 1790-95, U. S. District Judge 1795-1801.

(1) "There were giants in the land in those days. It was customary for the advocates whose professional aid was in most request at that time to attend the courts from county to county through the state, as the leading barristers ride the circuit in England. Every important trial was a tournament in which these celebrated celebrities were matched against each other. * * * In the ratio of her population New Hampshire has contributed more mental and more moral strength to the bar, to the Senate and to the Cabinet of the country than any other state in the Union. That was the season of her intellectual greatness. Ichabod Bartlett, the Randolph of the north, the brilliant flashes of whose wit, keen sarcasm and pungent irony gave life and spirit to the dry judicial discussions—Sullivan, the fascination of whose happy eloquence still lingers—Fletcher, whose legal acumen, clear, distinct and precise statement, closely reasoned argument and conscious mastery of his subject adorn no less the bench than formerly the bar. Jeremiah Mason, that counsellor of marvelous sagacity, unrivalled in his knowledge of human nature, and Daniel Webster. The collision of such minds invigorated and sharpened the facilities whose native temper was competent to sustain the shock. * * * It was in this school—that Judge Woodbury formed and fixed that habit which he ever afterwards retained—which is the first need though the rarest accomplishment of an American statesman, to think continentally."

Eulogy on Justice Levi Woodbury, by Robert Rantoul, Oct. 16, 1851, XIV *Law Reporter* (1851).

VERMONT.

The settlers in the New Hampshire Grants (later the State of Vermont), were chiefly men who had come thither from Connecticut, Massachusetts and Rhode Island, for the purpose of enjoying greater religious freedom; and they had an instinctive prejudice against the institution of courts, which they conceived as controlled by the clerical and government interests in the Colonies from which they had emigrated. To such an extent was this feeling carried, that the Legislature of Vermont, in the first seven years of its existence, constituted itself a court of chancery; and passed frequent acts, vacating and commuting judgments of the courts, and forbidding prosecutions of real or possessory actions or actions on contracts; and while this was done to a less extent after the constitution of 1786, it still kept up the practice of granting new trials, over the heads of the courts.

It is not surprising that, under these conditions, neither great lawyers nor judges were produced in Vermont at this time, and that, as Mason says in his autobiography:

The courts of Vermont then were badly organized and usually filled with incompetent men (except C. J. Nathaniel Chipman). Most of the members of the bar were poorly educated and some of vulgar manners and indifferent morals.

There were, however, in 1790, a few men of great ability at the Bar, like Charles Marsh(1), Stephen R. Bradley(2), Stephen Jacob, Royall Tyler (later Chief Justice)(3), and Elijah Paine (later U. S. District Judge).(4)

---

(1) Born 1765, graduate of Dartmouth in 1786, student at Litchfield Law School, U. S. Dist. Atty. 1797.

(2) Born 1754, Yale graduate of 1775.

(3) Born 1757, studied with John Adams, 1797 Judge of Supreme Court, 1800 Chief Justice.

(4) Born 1757, Harvard graduate 1781, admitted to the Bar in 1784, Judge of Supreme Court 1791-95, U. S. District Judge 1801-42.

NOTE. See, for authorities in general.

History of New Hampshire, by Jeremy Belknap (1792).

Judicial History of New Hampshire before the Revolution, Law Reporter, Vol. XVIII 301.

Bench and Bar of New Hampshire, by C. H. Bell (1894).

Life of Jeremiah Mason, by George S. Hillard (1873).

Life of Jeremiah Smith, by John H. Morison (1845).

Review of Life of Jeremiah Smith, Law Reporter, Vol. VIII.

Life of Charles Marsh, by James Barret (1871).

Address by David Cross in *Southern New Hampshire, Bar Assn. Proc.,* Vol. I.

RHODE ISLAND.

The first Chief Justice of Rhode Island, Gideon Cowell, in 1747, was not a lawyer; the second, Joshua Babcock (a Yale graduate of 1724), was a physician; and for one hundred and seventy-five years, few of the judges were educated lawyers. Even as late as 1819, a farmer was chosen Chief Justice.

Little is known of the Bar in the 18th Century. The best known lawyers were the Attorney Generals, Daniel Updike, in 1722; James Honeyman, about 1732; Oliver Arnold in 1766; Henry Marchant, in 1770, who studied law with the learned Judge Trowbridge of Massachusetts; William Channing, born in 1727, a graduate of Harvard in 1747, a leading lawyer at the time of the Revolution, and one of the signers of the Declaration of Independence, Attorney General in 1777. Most of the able lawyers at the Bar at that time became Tories—James Brenton, Robert Lightfoot, a barrister of the Inner Temple, Mathew Robinson, W. G. Simpson, John Usher.

The real Bar of Rhode Island hardly arose until the time of James Burrill, (1) and of Tristam Burgess, (2) in the beginning of the 19th Century.

The one reported case of any historical interest was as late as 1786, that of *Trevett v. Weeden,* involving the paper money and stay laws, and distinctive as one of the first cases in which an American State Court held a legislative act to be unconstitutional. It was tried before Chief Justice Paul Mumford, Gen.

Samuel Livermore by Charles R. Corning. *Grafton & Coos Co. Bar Assn. Proc.* 1888.

Arthur Livermore, by Ezra S. Stearns. *Grafton & Coos Co. Bar Assn. Proc.,* (1893).

Life of William Plumer, by William Plumer, Jr., (1856).

Parker, J. in 13 *New Hampshire Reports,* 536, 557, 558, 560.

Preface to Chipman's *Reports* (Vermont) Vol. I.

(1) Born 1772, graduate of Brown College in 1788, studied in office of Theodore Foster and later of David Howell (afterwards U. S. District Judge) admitted to practice in 1791, Chief Justice 1816-17.

(2) Born 1770, studied at Brown College 1793-1797, admitted to the Bar in 1799, Chief Justice 1817-18.

In his *Memoirs of Tristam Burgess* (1835) Henry L. Bowen says "Burrill had no superior in his native state and few in any section of the Union."

Contemporary with Burrill and Burgess were Asher Robbins, William Hunter, and Benjamin Hazard.

James M. Varnum and Henry Marchant for the defendant, and Henry Goodwin (later Attorney General), for the plaintiff. (1)

In Connecticut, a Superior Court was established in 1711, consisting of the Chief Justice and four other distinguished members of the Council (the higher branch of the Legislature).

The early judges were seldom trained lawyers. Roger Wolcott, who was judge in 1732 and Chief Justice in 1741, was a weaver; Roger Sherman, judge of the Superior Court 1766-1789, was in his early days a shoemaker; Jonathan Trumbull, Chief Justice, 1766-1769, began as a minister, and became a merchant, incidentally studying law, but never regularly trained.(2) Oliver Ellsworth, judge of the Superior Court in 1784, studied first for the ministry, and so did Jesse Root, Chief Justice in 1796.

Of 18th Century lawyers before the Revolutionary war, there were comparatively few of distinction or legal training. One of the earliest was Thomas Fitch, born in 1699, a graduate of Yale in 1721, who codified the laws, became Chief Justice and later Governor; "Probably the most learned lawyer who had ever been an inhabitant of the Colony", said the first President Dwight of Yale.

Jared Ingersoll, the elder, born in 1722, a Yale graduate of 1742, was a trained lawyer and acted as the Colony's agent in England. Phineas Lyman, born in 1716, Yale 1738, was also eminent about the middle of the Century.

Nothing illustrates the smallness of the Bar better than the fact that when the famous case of *Winthrop v. Lechmere* 1724-1728,

---

(1) *Note.* For authorities in general, see:
Gleanings from Judicial History of Rhode Island, by Thomas Durfee, *R. I. Hist. Soc. Coll.,* No. 18.
History of Rhode Island, by Samuel G. Arnold.
Memoirs of the Rhode Island Bar, by Wilkins Updike (1842).
Robert Lightfoot, in *Loyalists of American Revolution,* by Lorenzo Sabine.
The Judicial System in Rhode Island, by Amasa M. Eaton—*Yale Law Journal,* Vol. XIV.
The Supreme Court of Rhode Island—Green Bag, Vol. II.
The Supreme Court of Rhode Island, by W. P. Sheffield.
(2) Born 1710, a graduate of Harvard in 1727. So great was his sagacity and ability, that during his long Governorship of the State (1769-1784), Washington's constant reliance on his advice, taking the form of "we must consult Brother Jonathan," became the foundation of that nickname for the United States.

arose—the case of an appeal from the decision of the Probate
Judge and of the Superior Court, by a brother claiming the whole
of the estate of an intestate, in conformity with the Common Law
of England, and denying the validity of the Connecticut statute of
descent, which was absolutely inconsistent with the English Common Law, no counsel were sent from Connecticut to argue the
case before the King in Council in London; but both sides relied
on English lawyers, Sir Philip Yorke, Attorney General of England (later Lord Chancellor) appearing for the appellant; and
for the appellee Sir John Willes (later Attorney General and
Chief Justice of Common Pleas), and a Mr. Booth (of whom
nothing is known).(1)

One of the first American lawyers to argue before the King in
Council, was William Samuel Johnson, who appeared there in
the famous Mohegan case, involving important landed interests
in Connecticut. Born in 1727, a Yale graduate of 1744, and
a doctor of Civil Law at Oxford, he was one of the leaders of
the Bar in the middle of the Century, and for a long time was
Colonial Agent in London. Two other lawyers were especially
prominent in Connecticut before the Revolution.

Mathew Griswold, born in 1714, who was quaintly described by
President Stiles of Yale College in 1790, as follows: "Fitted for
college, settled a farmer, studied law proprio Marte bo't him
the first considerable Law library, took atty oath and began
practice 1743—a great reader of law", and who became Chief
Justice in 1769, succeeding Jonathan Trumbull; and Roger Sherman, born in Massachusetts in 1721, admitted to practice in 1754,
made a judge of the Court of Common Pleas in 1759, a member of
the Council or Upper House in 1766 and also Judge of the Superior Court, which latter position he held until 1789, the last four
years being a colleague of Oliver Ellsworth. He was counsel for
Connecticut in the great struggle, 1770-1782, over Pennsylvania
lands. In 1783, he was appointed with Richard Law to digest the

---

(1) Nine years later, in 1737, when the similar Massachusetts case of
Phillips v. Savage was argued before the King in Council, only one
colonial lawyer appeared in the case, Jonathan Belcher of Boston, with
whom was Sir John Strange (Later Master of the Rolls); Sir Dudley
Ryder (later Lord Mansfield's predecessor as Lord Chief Justice), and
John Brown, (of whom nothing is known), appearing for the other
side. See *Mass. Hist. Soc. Proc.*, Vol. V. (1860).
    Mass. Hist. Soc. Proc., Vol. VIII., 2d Series (1893).
    The Talcott Papers, Conn. Hist. Soc. Coll., Vol. IV.
    Mass. Hist. Soc. Coll., 6th Series, Vol. V.

statutes. He was head and front of the Revolutionary move-ment and one of the Signers. Contemporary with him were, James A. Hillhouse(1), Samuel Huntington(2), Eliphalet Dyer (3), Richard Law (4), Amos Botsford, Samuel Holden Parsons (5), Charles Chauncey (6) and Jesse Root (7).

During the latter part of the Century the number of lawyers greatly increased, as the inhabitants of the State were somewhat noted for their litigious character; and Noah Webster stated that the docket of Oliver Ellsworth, in whose office he was a student, frequently numbered from 1000 to 1500 cases, and that during the sessions of the court there was scarcely a case tried in which he was not of counsel. These cases were small and brought in little fees. Jeremiah Mason, of New Hampshire, who graduated from Yale in 1788, describes conditions as follows:

I spent a year in Mr. (Simeon) Baldwin's office in New Haven. He married a daughter of the then celebrated Roger Sherman—His reputation (Mr. S's) was then at the zenith. His manners, without apparent arrogance, were excessively reserved and aristocratic.

When I commenced the study of the law was a period of ex-treme depression and poverty throughout the country.—The pro-fession of law felt this depression severely. The State of Con-necticut was overstocked with lawyers. Most of them had but little business, with fees and compensation measurably small.

The professional income of Pierpont Edwards, supposed to be the largest in the State, was said not to amount to $2000.

Many of those engaged in the law followed also other occupa-tions, such as farming, resuming their practice when the court arrived in the county on circuit.

Among the more prominent Connecticut lawyers after the Rev-olution were Noah Webster(8), Zephaniah Swift(9), Simeon

---

(1) Born in 1730, a Yale Graduate of 1749.
(2) Born in 1732, judge of the Superior Court in 1774, one of the Signers, of whom it is said "few lawyers enjoyed a more extensive prac-tice".
(3) Born in 1721, a Yale graduate of 1740, Chief Justice, 1789-93.
(4) Born in 1733, a Yale graduate of 1751, Chief Justice 1786-89.
(5) Born in 1737, a student with Governor Mathew Griswold, the last royal Attorney General.
(6) Born in 1747, Judge of the Superior Court 1789-93, "for 40 years a lecturer on jurisprudence."
(7) Born in 1736, Princeton graduate of 1756, Chief Justice 1796-1807, author of *Root's Reports*.
(8) The author of the famous dictionary, born in 1758, graduate of Yale in 1778, a student in the office of Oliver Ellsworth, and admitted to the Bar in 1781.

Baldwin(1), Oliver Wolcott(2), Thomas S. Williams(3), David Daggett(4), Roger Griswold(5), Chauncy Goodrich(6), Pierrepont Edwards(7).

The greatest Connecticut lawyer of the early 19th Century was Roger Minott Sherman, who was born in 1773, graduated from Yale in 1792, studied in Judge Ellsworth's office and also attended lectures of Judge Reeve at his law school in Litchfield, admitted to the Bar in 1796.

MAINE.

As late as 1770, the only educated lawyers residing in Maine were, David Sewall (Harvard 1755), Theophilus Bradbury, (Harvard 1757), John Sullivan, James Sullivan (later Atty. General and Governor of Massachusetts), William Cushing,

---

(9)   Born in 1759, Yale 1778; the author in 1795 of the *System of Laws of Connecticut*, and in 1822 of the *Digest of Laws of Connecticut,* which has the distinction of being the first comprehensive view of the English Common Law published in America, practically an American digest, Chief Justice in 1806-19.

(1)   Born in 1761, a graduate of Yale in 1781, and Judge of the Superior Court in 1806.

(2)   Born in 1760, a graduate of Yale 1778.

(3)   Born in 1777, a graduate of Yale in 1794, Chief Justice in 1834.

(4)   Born in 1764, a Yale graduate of 1783, and United States Senator in 1813, Chief Justice 1834.

(5)   Born in 1762, a Yale graduate of 1780.

(6)   Born in 1759, Yale graduate of 1776, and United States Senator in 1794.

(7)   Born in 1750, Princeton graduate of 1768.

NOTE.   See for authorities in general:

Roger Ludlow, by John M. Taylor (1900).

History of the Judicial System of New England, by Conrad Reno. (1900).

Oliver Ellsworth, by William G. Brown (1905).

Judicial and Civil History of Conn., by Dwight Loomis and J. G. Calhoun (1895).

Preface to *Kirby's Reports.*

Preface to *Root's Reports.*

Lives of the Chief Justices of the U. S., by H. Flanders.

Roger Sherman, by Lewis Henry Boutelle (1896).

Phineas Lyman, in *Loyalists of the American Revolution,* by Lorenzo Sabine (1864).

Roger Minott Sherman, by William A. Beers (1882).

Sanderson's *Lives of the Signers,* (2d Edition 1882).

Yale Men as Writers on Law and Government, by S. E. Baldwin, *Yale Law Journal,* Vol. XI.

Yale in its Relation to Law, by Thomas Thacher, *Yale Law Journal,* Vol. XI.

The Supreme Court of Connecticut, by S. E. Baldwin in *The Supreme Courts of the States and Provinces* (1897).

Life of Jonathan Trumbull, by J. W. Stuart (1859).

(Harvard 1751), and David Wyer (Harvard 1758), who studied with James Otis, Jr., and later became a Tory refugee.

There were, however, in Portland (then Falmouth), several persons of education and clerical habits, who attended the Court of Common Pleas to assist parties in their suits—Jabez Fox, Enoch Freeman the elder, Stephen Longfellow, and Samuel Freeman—all Harvard graduates. Later, rigid rules adopted by the Bar put an end to this practice.

Although native lawyers were few, the Portland court was frequently attended by lawyers from other Colonies, Jeremiah Gridley, James Otis, Jonathan Sewall, John Adams, John Lowell, Daniel Farnham and John Chipman, from Massachusetts; and Mathew Livermore, Samuel Livermore, William Parker and John Sullivan, from New Hampshire.

CHAPTER IV.

LAW AND LAWYERS IN THE 18TH CENTURY, IN MARYLAND, VIRGINIA, NEW YORK, PENNSYLVANIA, NEW JERSEY, AND THE SOUTHERN STATES.

The history of the law and lawyers in the Colonies outside of New England is much the same as in Massachusetts and Connecticut.

At first the General Assembly or Legislature constituted the court; later the Governor and his Deputies, and in most Colonies, it was not until a half century after settlement that a separate and independent court was established.

In all the Colonies, for nearly a century, the courts were made up of merchants or of men of property, with occasionally a lawyer as Chief Justice.

In all the Colonies, except Maryland, the Bar failed to develop any strength before the middle of the 18th Century; and in all the Colonies, a decided prejudice existed for many years against lawyers and attorneys as a class. It is to be noticed, however, that, while in New England this feeling is traceable largely to the control exercised by the clergy in administrative matters, in the other Colonies it was due chiefly to the jealousy of the merchants and wealthy planters at the exercise of power by any other class.

Thus these three factors—the ignorance of the judges, the control of the courts by the royal governors, and the strong feeling against the legal profession in the mind of the public, served to retard the growth of the Bar, and its training by any systematic methods.

Towards the beginning of the American Revolution, however, the influence of lawyers from Maryland, Pennsylvania, Virginia and South Carolina who had received an education in the Inns of Court in England produced a great change in the standards of ability and knowledge among the members of the Bar in those Colonies, and undoubtedly acted as a spur to the development of more adequate modes of legal instruction in America. In fact a collegiate education was so general among those who made their mark at the Bar that it may be said without exaggeration, that the American lawyer of the late 18th Century and of the early 19th Century was the product of the colleges—Harvard, Yale, Princeton, Brown, Columbia, and the College of William and Mary,—and of the Inner and Middle Temple in London.

MARYLAND.

Maryland, in 1646, about twelve years after its settlement, adopted the following "Act for Rule of Judicature":

Right and just in all civil causes shall be determined according to the law or most general usage of the Province since its plantation or former presid'ts of the same or like nature to be determined by the judge. And in defect of such law, usage, or president, then right and just shall be determined according to equity and good conscience, not neglecting, so far as the judge of judges shall be informed thereof and shall find no inconvenience in the application to this Province, the rules by which right and just useth and ought to be determined in England in the same or the like case. And all crimes and offences shall be judged and determined according to the law of the Province or in defect of certain law then they may be determined according to the best discretion of the judge or judges judging as near as conveniently may be to the laudable law of usage of England in the same or like offences.

As early as 1662, an act was passed, declaring that when the laws of the Province were silent, justice was to be administered according to the laws and statutes of England, and that "all courts shall judge of the right pleading and the inconsistency of the said laws with the good of the province according to the best of their judgment." And in 1678, there is a record of a vote in the General Assembly to purchase Keble's *Abridgement of the English Statutes* and Dalton's *Justice of the Peace,* for the use of the County Courts.

It is perhaps due to this very early recognition of the Common Law that the law and the legal profession seem to have reached a higher stage of development in the 17th Century in Maryland than in any other American Colony.

Almost from the beginning, the Province had a series of courts based on the English system—Courts of Pupowder (Pypoudry) or market courts, Courts Baron and Leet, incident to the landed estates, County Courts, the Provincial Court, and a Court of Appeals.

Although, in 1638, the General Assembly tried many cases, the

Provincial Court gradually absorbed all superior jurisdiction. It consisted of the Governor and his Council, all appointed by the Proprietor or his deputy, and therefore "dependent on the mere breath of his nostrils".(1) Its members also composed the Upper House of the General Assembly and the Court of Appeals.

The records of the proceedings of this Court are extant, in the first two volumes of Maryland Archives up to 1657, and in cases to be found in volumes one and four of Harris and McHenry's Reports, covering cases from 1658 to 1776, (these being the most ancient of American judicial decisions, with the exception of the records of the Massachusetts Court of Assistants.)

The lack of lawyers in the composition of the Courts, even as late as 1767, is shown in an opinion of Daniel Dulany:

On perusing the record I am strongly of the opinion that the judgment of the Provincial Court ought to be reversed; but what may be the opinion of the court of appeals I should be more confident in predicting if the judges were lawyers by profession, than I am on the consideration that they are not.(2)

The first lawyer of record, and "father of the Maryland Bar," was John Lewger, Attorney for the Lord Proprietary, who landed in 1637, three years after the settlement of the Province, and whose name appears as counsel in a case that same year. He became a member of the Provincial Court, Secretary of the Province, and died in 1648.

The next attorney of record was James Cauther, in 1637, who appeared in a confession of debt. He was a planter as well as attorney, and died in 1643. In 1638, Cyprian Thoroughgood appeared as attorney in a suit for damages for refusal to furnish lumber under a contract. Cuthbert Fenwick (termed in the writ for the General Assembly in 1640, "Gent. Attorney") appeared, in 1644, to collect a claim for tobacco for a Virginian client.

Between the years 1634 and 1660 the names of many other attorneys appear of record.(3)

At this time there appeared also the first American woman lawyer, Mrs. Margaret Brent. Not only did she plead in court, but

(1) See *Calvert v. Eden* 2 Harris and McHenry 345, 360.
(2) See Opinion of Daniel Dulaney on the Judgment of the Provincial Court in *West v. Stegar* 1 H. & McH. 247 (1767).
(3) Thomas Gerrard, Thomas Notley (later Governor), Peter Draper, Thomas Mathews, William Harditch, John Weyville, George Manners, and most distinguished of all, Giles Brent (later Attorney General).

she insisted on her right to take part in the General Assembly, as appears from the following quaint record of that body:

Jan. 21, 1647-8—came Mrs. Margret Brent in the house for herselfe and voyce also, for that att the last court 3rd Jan: it was ordered that Mrs. Brent was to be looked uppon and received as his Lps (Lordship's) attorney. The Gov'r denyed that the sd. Mrs. Brent should have any vote in the howse. And the sd. Mrs. Brent protested agst all proceedings in this first Assembly unless shee may be pst and have vote as aforesaid.

In 1659, it was enacted that "the attorneys on both sides speak distinctly to one error first before they proceed to the next, without disturbing each other."

In 1662, an act was passed forbidding sheriffs, commissioners, clerks, and deputy sheriffs, and officers of the court, from practising as attorneys in their respective courts.

By the year 1669, the attorneys had so increased as to occasion a report by a Committee of the Lower House of the Assembly "that the privileged attornies are one of the great grievances of the country." Charges of impeachment were preferred against one John Morecraft for having taken fees on both sides of a case and also for "that he is retayned as attorney for some, with unreasonable fees, for a whole year's space, so that by that means it causes several suits to the utter ruin of people." The Upper House, however, dismissed the charges, expressing its wonder that "attornies of ability and sworn to be diligent and faithful in their places and offices" should be "called a grievance, nay the grand grievance of the country."

In 1674, an act was passed declaring

the abuse of severall persons in this Province practising as attorneys and solicitors at Law by taking and exciting excessive fees for their clients, whereby the good people of this province are much burthened and their causes much delayed, and by the great number of attorneys whereby many and unnecessary and troublesome suits are raysed and fomented;

and providing that thereafter only a "certain number of honest and able attorneys be admitted, nominated and sworn" by the Captain General to be attorneys and councillors, and all others to be forbidden to practice. Fees were regulated, the highest being 800 pounds of tobacco in the Court of Chancery, 400 pounds in the Provincial Court, and 200 pounds in the County

Courts. Heavy fines and the penalty of disbarment were imposed for demanding or receiving more than the legal fees.

And in 1715, a comprehensive act was passed "for rectifying the ill practices of attorneys of this province and ascertaining fees", providing that no person should practise law without being admitted thereto by the justices of the court, establishing rates of fees, and providing against neglect of duty. At the same time court rules required gowns to be worn by both lawyers and judges.

In 1721 and 1722, laws were passed to punish attorneys who by neglect of their duties caused loss to their clients.

The natural jealousy against lawyers, entertained by all agricultural communities, culminated in 1725, in an act regulating lawyers' fees with extreme strictness, and giving an option to the planter to pay in tobacco or in currency at a fixed rate. Against this act, a petition was presented in the Upper House by Daniel Dulany Senior, Thomas Bordley, Joshua George and Michael Howard, "late practitioners of the law", alleging the act to be destructive of their privileges as British subjects.

This petition is of vital interest as being one of the first of the series of struggles by the colonists to maintain their rights under the English Laws and Constitution; it was followed by the publication by Dulany, in 1728, at Annapolis, of his famous pamphlet, *The right of the Inhabitants of Maryland to the Benefit of the English Laws.*

In 1729, when the act was extended for three years, the lawyers petitioned the Proprietor in London against it, employing John Sharpe, a barrister of Lincoln's Inn, as their counsel. The Proprietor gave his dissent, on the ground that such a law "was not agreeable to any known law here", and to his dissent was appended the opinion of the then Attorney General of Great Britain, Philip Yorke (later the great Lord Chancellor Hardwicke).

Of the Bar of the early 18th Century, this Daniel Dulany the elder stood at the head, born about 1680, educated at the University of Dublin, admitted to the Bar of the Provincial Court in 1710, barrister of Gray's Inn in 1716, later Attorney General of the Province.

Others of prominence were Charles Carroll, born in 1660, educated at the University of Douai in France and in the Inner Temple in London, who came to Maryland in 1688, as Attorney General vigorously resisted the attempt to overthrow Lord Baltimore's Government, was arrested for high misdemeanor by the Royal Governor, and died in 1720; Robert Ridgely; Col. Henry Jowles, a barrister, and Chancellor of the Province in 1697; Griffith Jones and Stephen Bordley. (1)

The greatest of Maryland's lawyers before the American Revolution was undoubtedly Daniel Dulany the younger, born in 1721, educated in the Temple, and admitted to the Bar in 1747. So extended became his reputation that he was consulted on questions of jurisprudence by eminent lawyers in England; and cases were frequently withdrawn from Maryland courts, and on one occasion even from the Chancellor of England, to submit to him and abide by his award. His opinions, like those of his father, were deemed of such weight that many of them were included with reports of decided cases, when law reports were first printed in Maryland in 1809. (2)

At the time of the Stamp Act agitation, he was hailed as the William Pitt of Maryland, because of his famous pamphlet on *Considerations on the Propriety of imposing taxes on the British Colonies for the purpose of raising a revenue by Act of Parliament*, published at Annapolis, Oct. 14, 1765.

Of Dulany, William Pinkney said, a few years after the Revolution, "Even amongst such men as Fox, Pitt and Sheridan, he had not found his superior".

Noted also among the Maryland lawyers who opposed the Stamp Act was Samuel Chase, "the torch that lighted up the revolutionary flame in Maryland". He was born in 1741, studied at Annapolis, admitted to the Bar in 1763, Signer of the Declaration of Independence and later Judge of the United States Supreme Court. Prominent also was the Scotch lawyer, George Chalmers, who came to Baltimore in 1763 from Edinburgh, and who, after his return to England in 1775, became noted as a law

---

(1) In 1692, it is recorded that on the assembling of the Provincial Court after the Protestant Revolution, George Plates, Griffith Jones, William Dent, Samuel Watkins and Philip Clark took the new test oath and on motion the court limited the number of attorneys to be allowed to practice.

(2) Samuel Tyler in his *Memoirs of Roger Brooke Taney* (1872) says "The opinions of Daniel Dulany had almost as much weight in court in Maryland, and hardly less with the court lawyers of England, than the opinions of the great Roman jurists that were made authority by edict of the Emperor, had in Roman court. This was due, in some degree, to the fact that there were no reports of Maryland decisions until 1809. . . . . The high reputation of this great lawyer stimulated the ambition of the Maryland bar, while his opinions were models of legal discussion for their imitation."

writer, his *Opinions of Eminent Lawyers on various points of English jurisprudence concerning the Colonies, Fisheries and Commerce of Great Britain* being of especial interest to students of Colonial law.

In 1773, the Royal Governor Eden's attempt to fix the fees of state officials by proclamation aroused all defenders of the sole right of the people to legislate. In the bitter struggle which arose the full strength of the ante-Revolutionary Bar of Maryland was engaged, Daniel Dulany, Charles Gordon, John Hammond taking the side of the Crown, and Charles Carroll (1), Samuel Chase, Thomas Johnson (2), Thomas Stone (3), and William Paca (4) being prominent in behalf of the Colony's rights.

The lawyers of Maryland after the Revolution will be mentioned later in this book.

NOTE.

For authorities in general see:

Glance at our Colonial Bar, Green Bag, Vol. XI.

Adoption of English Law in Maryland, Yale Law Journal, Vol. VIII.

Bar of Early Maryland, Green Bag, Vol. XII.

Studies in the Civil, Social and Ecclesiastical History of Early Maryland, by Theodore C. Gambrall, (1893).

Historical View of the Government of Maryland, by John Van L. McMahon, (1831.)

Maryland Jurisprudence, American Jurist, Vol. XV.

Maryland Archives, Procedings and Acts of the General Assembly.

Some Characteristics of the Provincial Judiciary, by Charles F. Phelps, *Maryland Bar Association Report,* Vol. II (1897.)

The Founders of the Bar of Maryland, by Elihu S. Riley, *Maryland Bar Assn. Report,* Vol. II, (1897.)

The Courts and Bench of Colonial Maryland, Maryland Bar Assn. Report, Vol. III, (1898.)

Development of the Legal Profession 1669-1715, by Elihu S. Riley, *Maryland Bar Assn. Report,* Vol. IV, (1899.)

---

(1) Born in 1737, studied in the Temple in London, later in Paris and returned to reside at Carrollton in 1764, Signer of the Declaration.

(2) Born in 1732, later first governor of the State of Maryland, and judge of the U. S. Supreme Court in 1791.

(3) Born in 1743, studied law under Johnson, Signer of the Declaration.

(4) Born in 1740, graduate of the College of Phila. in 1759, studied law for four years under Stephen Bordley, admitted to the bar in 1764, Chief Justice in 1778, Governor in 1782, Judge of the U. S. District Court in 1789, Signer of the Declaration.

Luther Martin as a Lawyer and Lover, by Robert F. Brent, *Maryland Bar Assn. Report,* Vol. IV, (1891.)

Luther Martin by Henry P. Goddard, *Maryland Hist. Soc. Proc.,* (1887).

Economics and Politics in Maryland, 1720-1750, *and Public Service of Daniel Dulany the Elder,* by St. George Leakin Sioussat in *Johns Hopkins Univ. Studies in Historical and Political Science Series,* Vol. XXI (1903).

Beginnings of Maryland, by Bernard A. Steiner in *Johns Hopkins Univ. Studies in Historical and Political Science Series,* Vol. XXI, (1903).

The English Statutes in Maryland, in *Johns Hopkins Univ. Studies in Historical and Political Science Series,* Vol. XXI, (1903).

Life of George Chalmers in *Loyalists of American Revolution,* by Lorenzo Sabine (1864).

Life of William Pinkney, by Rev. William Pinkney (1863).

VIRGINIA.

Of all the Colonies, Virginia was the most truly British in its institutions and modes of life. The presence of what was practically a landed aristocracy tended towards conservatism.

As one old writer has quaintly said:

If New England be called a Receptacle of Dissenters and an Amsterdam of Religion, Pennsylvania the nursery of Quakers, Maryland the Retirement of Roman Catholics, North Carolina the refuge of Runaways and South Carolina the Delight of Buccaneers and Pyrates, Virginia may be justly esteemed the happy retreat of true Britons and true Churchmen for the most part neither soaring too high nor drooping too low; consequently should merit the greater esteem and encouragement.

Story in his *Commentaries on the Constitution* remarks that:

The laws of Virginia during its colonial state do not exhibit as many marked deviations in the general structure of its institutions and civil polity from those of the parent country as those in the northern colonies. The common law was recognized as the general basis of its jurisprudence—and expressly provided for in all the charters—and was—in its leading features very acceptable to the colonists.

Sir William Berkeley in 1671, in his answer to the Lord Commissioners, said:

Contrary to the laws of England we never did, nor dare, to make any (law), only this, that no sale of land is good and legal unless within three months after the conveyance it be recorded.

Hugh Jones, in his *Present State of Virginia,* wrote in 1724 that the Province was

ruled by the Laws customs and constitution of Great Britain which it strictly observes, only where the circumstance and occasion of the country by an absolute necessity requires some small alteration which nevertheless must not be contrary (though different from and subservient) to the Laws of England.

A collection of laws containing 61 acts was made as early as 1632; in 1643 a new code was passed; in 1656-58 there was a second revision containing 131 acts, and a third revision in 1662. The preamble to this last act was the first legislative recognition of the Common Law:

We have endeavored in all things (as near as the capacity and constitution of this country would admit) to adhere to these excellent and often refined laws of England to which we profess and acknowledge all our obedience and reverence.

For a long period the laws existed only in manuscript; and in 1671, Sir William Berkeley, the staunch, conservative, royal governor, wrote:

But I thank God there are no free schools nor printing and I hope we shall not have these hundred years; for learning has brought disobedience and heresy and sects into the world, and printing has divulged them and libels against the best governments. God keep us from both.

The earliest surviving evidence of printing done in Virginia is the edition of *Revised Laws* in 1733, three years before the establishment in 1736 of the first Virginia newspaper, the *Gazette*.

The only court of law for some years was the General Assembly. This body, composed of twenty-two elected burgesses and the Governor and Council, convened at Jamestown July 30, 1619, the first English legislative body in America; and on the second day of its sitting constituted itself a Court to try one Thomas Garret for indecent behavior. In 1643, a judicial system was established, much resembling that of Massachusetts, consisting of County Courts, (begun in 1623-24) composed of local wealthy planters, and the Quarter Courts (or General Court as they were termed, after 1662) composed of the Governor and his Councillors (thirteen in number at first, later nineteen, and still later sixteen). There was also an appeal in some matters to the General Assembly.

Jefferson, in the preface to his Reports, states that the General Court was "chosen from among the gentlemen of the country for their wealth and standing without any regard to legal knowledge"; and as late as 1781, Lord Culpepper, in his statistical account of Virginia said (1) :

There was much confusion in the laws and it was difficult to know what the laws were. All causes were decided in the County Court or in the General Court. The County Court consisted of 8 or 10 gentlemen appointed by the Governor, annually. They had no education and fell into many mistakes.

Campbell in his history of Virginia says:

The insufficiency of these courts was now growing more apparent than formerly, since the old stock of gentry who were educated in England were better acquainted with law and with the business of the world than their sons and grandsons who were brought up in Virginia and commonly knew only reading, writing and arithmetic, and were not very proficient in them.

Anthony Stokes, Chief Justice of Georgia, in 1783, in his *View of the Constitution of the British Colonies of North America and the West Indies,* states that in the Colonies where a system of County Courts prevailed and where there were a large number of judges in general unacquainted with the law, little decorum was observed; in Colonies where judges went on circuit there was more impartial administration of justice.

As early as 1661-2, an act was passed regulating very precisely the proceedings of the courts, the forms of opening and closing, and requiring all declarations, answers and evidence to be preserved.

In the 17th Century the problem of how to deal with attorneys appears to have perplexed Virginia more than any other Colony.

As early as 1642-43, under an act "for the better regulating of attorneys and the great fees exacted by them", fees were confined to 20 pounds of tobacco in the County Court and 40 pounds in the Quarter Court; they were forbidden license to plead in more courts than the "Quarter Court and one County Court"; and they could not refuse to be "entertayned in any cause" under heavy fines to be paid in tobacco. This act, however, did not

---

(1)   See *Mass. Hist. Soc. Coll., 1st Series,* Vol. V.

apply to "such as shall be made special attorneys nor to such as shall have letters of procuration out of England."

In 1645, it was provided that "whereas many troublesome suits are multiplied by the unskillfulness and covetousness of Attorneys who have more intended their own profit and their inordinate lucre than the good and benefit of their clients be it therefore enacted that all Mercenary Attorneys(1) be wholly expelled from such offices"; and in 1647, the Courts, if "they perceived that either party was like to lose his cause by his weakness" were themselves to "open the case" or "to appoint some fitt man out of the people to plead the cause—and not allow any other attorneys in private causes betwixt man and man in the country"; and attorneys were forbidden to "take any recompence either directly or indirectly." This Mercenary Attorney Act was repealed in 1657 and provision made for licensing attorneys; the next year, however, trouble apparently having again arisen, all fees were taken away from attorneys. "Since these mercenary attorneys maintain suits in law to the great prejudice and charge of the inhabitants of this colony", they were forbidden "to plead in any court or give counsel in any cause or controversy, for any kind of reward or profit", on penalty of 5000 pounds of tobacco, and were required to swear, when they appeared in any cause, that they had not violated this Act, "because the breakers thereof through their subtility cannot easily be discerned."

In 1680, a law was passed allowing attorneys to practise under rigid restrictions. Fees were fixed at 500 pounds of tobacco (about $15—$20) in the General Court, and 150 pounds in the County Court.

In 1686, it was enacted that no person should appear in any court as attorney, without first obtaining a license from the governor:

Inasmuch as all courts in the country are many times hindered and troubled in their judicial proceedings by the impertinent discourses of many busy and ignorant men who will pretend to assist their friend in his business and to clear the matter more plainly to the court, although never desired nor requested thereunto by the person whom they pretend to assist and many times to the destruction of his cause and the great trouble and hindrance of the court.

---

(1) The word "Mercenary" here meant only "serving for pay or fees". It did not have the opprobrious definition later given to the word.

This act, being found "inconvenient", was repealed the next year; but the repealing act was itself repealed by royal proclamation.

In 1742, an act was passed to prevent lawyers from exacting or receiving exorbitant fees.

All this legislation was directed probably not so much against the legal profession itself, as against the character of the men who composed it. Most of the attorneys were mere charlatans, men of no character or influence. As Judge Minor said in his *Institutes*, (1) "for fully a century, the lawyer seems to fortune and to fame unknown", not one of them having attained a notoriety or distinction worthy of a biographer. John Fiske says that "they were frequently recruited by white freedmen, whose career of rascality as attorneys in England had suddenly ended in penal servitude". Although this statement is unqualifiedly denied by a Virginia lawyer, claiming that there are no records to sustain it,(2) there is record in 1736 of one, Henry Justice, an English barrister of the Middle Temple, who was convicted of stealing a Bible and other books from Trinity College Library in Cambridge and sentenced to transportation to Virginia.(3)

The fact undoubtedly is that the business in the courts was so simple and so exclusively confined to commercial matters (actions of debt and on bonds), that litigation was entrusted to the prominent officials and wealthy merchants and planters(4). The business was not lucrative enough to attract educated English lawyers. Moreover, Virginia was a rural community, and like all such, was jealous of special classes of men.

In the 17th Century, Nathaniel Bacon, the leader of Bacon's Rebellion in 1675, who had studied law in the Temple, William Byrd, Receiver General of the Royal Revenue, and Benjamin

---

(1)   Minor's *Institutes*, Vol. IV., p. 168. (1875).

(2)   *Lawyers of the 17th Century, William & Mary College Quarterly*, Vol. VIII.

(3)   *Old Virginia*, Vol. II., by John Fiske.

(4)   Thus in York County Records, of the names of 13 men who appeared on the docket as attorneys between 1640 and 1675, with the exception of William Sherwood (who was a trained lawyer) and John Holdcraft and William Swinnerton, all were either planters or merchants prominent in the community; Francis Willis, James Bray, Thomas Bullard, John Page, and Daniel Parke becoming members of the Virginia Council; William Hockaday, Thomas Bushrod, Dr. Robert Ellyson, Gideon Macon being at different times members of the House of Burgesses and Karbry Kiggars. (See *William & Mary College Quarterly* Vol. VIII.

Harrison, Speaker of the House of Burgesses, appear to have been the only trained lawyers with the exception of the King's Attorney Generals.

In the early 18th Century, many of the Virginia lawyers had received an Inns of Court education. Prominent among them were William Byrd of Westover, who, born in 1674, studied law in the Middle Temple, collected the finest library in the American Colonies, and died in 1743; Edward Barradale, who had been Judge of Admiralty and a member of the Council and Attorney General, and died in 1743; William Hopkins, a well educated lawyer who practised in Virginia for twelve years; Sir John Randolph, born in 1692, who graduated at the college of William and Mary, became a barrister of Gray's Inn at London, was made Attorney General for the Colony, argued the cause of the Colony in England in 1752 and ranked as one of the greatest practitioners in America; Stevens Thomson, one of the early Attorney Generals, and John Ambler, who practised between 1735 and 1766, both of whom had studied in the Middle Temple.

The lawyer of largest general reputation in these early times was probably John Holloway, who had been an attorney of the Marshalsea Court in London. For thirty years he practised with great success in Virginia; and for fourteen years was Speaker of the House of Burgesses. He was described by Sir John Randolph as distinguished more for learning and as relying more upon the subtle artifice of an attorney than the solid reasoning of a lawyer. His opinions, however, were looked upon as authoritative, and his fees were exorbitant. He died in 1734.

The years 1750-1775 witnessed a marked growth in the size and ability of the Virginia Bar; and there arose a group of lawyers, most of whom were educated either at Princeton, William and Mary, or in the English Universities or Inns of Court, and whose political and legal talents placed Virginia in the forefront of the American Colonies. Among these were Peyton Randolph(1), John Randolph(2), Edmund Pendleton(3), John Blair(4), John

---

(1) Born in 1721, a graduate of Oxford, of the Inner Temple, King's Attorney General in Virginia, in 1748, President of the first Congress in 1774.

(2) Brother of Peyton, born in 1728, educated at William and Mary and the Inner Temple, Attorney General in 1766, "One of the most splendid monuments of the Bar" says Wirt, "A polite scholar as well as a profound lawyer", and who left Virginia in 1775 as a Tory refugee.

Lewis(1), George Wythe(2), Robert Carter Nicholas(3),
Thomas Jefferson(4), John Tyler(5), Dabney Carr(6), Peter
Lyons, George Johnson, Paul Carrington, George Mason(7),
and Richard Henry Lee(8).

The most noted of all the early lawyers was, admittedly, Patrick Henry, who, born in 1736, and admitted to the Bar in 1760,
leaped into instant fame by winning, in 1764, the famous *Parsons Case.* (5)

This Virginia Bar was thus interestingly summed up by St.
George Tucker in a letter to William Wirt in 1813:

Literary characters may leave their works behind them,

---

(3) Born in 1721, was examined and licensed to practise law "by the
eminent lawyer Barradale" in 1744, Chief Justice of Virginia Court of
Appeals in 1779.

(4) Born in 1732, a student in the Temple, in 1779 Chief Justice Virginia General Court, in 1789 Judge of the United States Supreme Court.

(1) In whose office the eminent George Wythe studied.

(2) Born in 1726, admitted to the Bar in 1756, Professor of Law in
1780 in the College of William and Mary, sole chancellor of the Court
of Equity in 1788, the legal teacher of Jefferson, who called him "my
faithful and beloved mentor in youth and my most affectionate friend
through life", instructor also of Marshall, Madison and Monroe, of whom
Wythe once remarked that "all three would at least become 'Minent.'"

(3) Born in 1715, and later Judge of Court of Appeals and Attorney
General.

(4) Born in 1743, admitted to the bar in 1767, after nearly five years
study and preparation in the office of George Wythe and others.

(5) Born in 1747, studied law in office of R. C. Nicholas, later Governor of Virginia and United States District Judge.

(6) Born in 1743.

(7) Born in 1725, the author in 1776 of the Virginia Constitution,
the first written constitution of a free commonwealth, pronounced by Madison in the debates on the Federal Constitution, "the ablest man in debate
he had ever seen."

(8) Born in 1732, a student in the Temple, returned to Virginia in 1752,
never actively practised.

(9) This case is interesting as an illustration of the fact that practically all the cases in which American lawyers in the 18th Century
gained distinction, were of a political nature. The facts were, that as
far back as 1696, each minister of a parish had been provided with an
annual stipend of 16,000 pounds of tobacco, at ten shillings eight pence
per 100 pounds. In 1755, the tobacco crop fell short; and the Legislature passed an act, to continue for ten months, allowing persons from
whom any tobacco was due, to pay in tobacco or in money at the rate of
sixteen shillings eight pence per 100 pounds, at the option of the debtor.
Rich planters benefited by paying their debts at this rate and getting from
fifty to sixty shillings for their tobacco.

In 1758, on a surmise of a short crop, a similar act was passed. The
price rose to fifty shillings. The King in Council denounced the act as
a usurpation. The Clergy resolved to test the question, and suit was begun by Rev. James Maury against the Collector of the County, in 1762
with Peter Lyons for the Plaintiff and the able and widely known John
Lewis for the Defendant. The first trial resulted in a victory for the
plaintiff; the second was won by Patrick Henry for the defendant.

as memorials of what they were; soldiers may obtain a niche in the temple of Fame, by some brilliant exploit; orators, whose speeches have been preserved, will be remembered through that medium; judges, whose opinions have been reported, may possibly be known to future judges, and members of the bar; but the world cares little about them; and if they leave no reports, or meet with no reporter to record their opinions, etc., they sink into immediate oblivion. I very much doubt if a single speech of Richard H. Lee's can be produced at this day. Nevertheless, he was the most mellifluous orator that ever I listened to. Who knows any thing of Peyton Randolph, once the most popular man in Virginia, Speaker of the House of Burgesses, and President of Congress, from its first assembling, to the day of his death? Who remembers Thompson Mason,—esteemed the first lawyer at the bar? Or his brother, George Mason, of whom I have heard Mr. Madison, (the present President), say, that he possessed the greatest talents for debate of any man he had ever seen, or heard speak. What is known of Dabney Carr, but that he made the motion for appointing committees of correspondence in 1773? Virginia has produced few men of finer talents, as I have repeatedly heard. I might name a number of others, highly respected and influential men in their day. The Delegates to the first Congress, in 1774, were Peyton Randolph, Edmund Pendleton, Patrick Henry, George Washington, Richard H. Lee, Richard Bland and Benjamin Harrison. Jefferson, Wythe and Madison did not come in till afterwards. This alone may show what estimation the former were held in: yet, how little is known of one-half of them at this day? The truth is, that Socrates himself would pass unnoticed and forgotten in Virginia, if he were not a public character, and some of his speeches preserved in a newspaper: the latter might keep his memory alive for a year or two, but not much longer.(1)

Perhaps the most important contribution to legal science made by the Virginia Bar was in the Revision of the Statutes, by a Commission, consisting of Jefferson, Pendleton, Wythe and George Mason (T. L. Lee not being a lawyer withdrawing), on whose report, and, largely by the efforts of James Madison, a complete new code, the first thorough revision of the whole law ever made in America, was established for Virginia in 1785.

Of the Virginia Bar after the Revolution, besides those already mentioned, five men stand out pre-eminently: John Marshall, who was born in 1755, attended the law lectures of Chancellor Wythe at William and Mary College in 1779, and was admitted to the Bar in 1780; Edmund Randolph, born in 1743, son of John

(1) *Memoirs of William Wirt*, by John P. Kennedy (1849).

Randolph, and nephew of Peyton Randolph, in 1789 the first Attorney General of the United States, and undoubtedly the head of the Southern Bar; St. George Tucker, who came to Virginia in 1770, studied law at William and Mary College, in 1788 Judge of the Court of Appeals, and afterwards Professor of Law in William and Mary College; John Tyler, father of President John Tyler, born in 1747, who studied with Robert Carter Nicholas and became United States District Judge; and Spencer Roane, born in 1762 and educated at the College of William and Mary under Chancellor Wythe, one of John Marshall's chief rivals at the Bar, and Judge of the Court of Errors of Virginia in 1794.

During the latter years of the Century, a sixth eminent Virginian lawyer came to the Bar—Henry Clay, who, born in 1777, became, at the age of fifteen, a small clerk in the High Court of Chancery, where he attracted the attention of Chancellor George Wythe, for whom he acted four years as amanuensis, and after a year's study of law in the office of Governor Brooke, Attorney General of Virginia, was licensed to practice, in 1797.

NOTE.

For authorities in general see:

History of the Colony and Ancient Dominion of Virginia, by Charles Campbell, (1860).
History of Virginia, by R. R. Howison, (1846).
History of Virginia Codification, — *Virginia Law Register,* Vol XI.
Hildreth's *History of the United States,* Vols. I and II.
Court and Bar of Colonial Virginia, — *Green Bag,* Vol. X.
Old Virginia, by John Fiske, Vol. II, (1897).
Virginia Lawyers, — *Green Bag,* Vol. X.
Lawyers in Virginia between 1704 and 1737, —, *Virg. Law Reg.,* Vol. I, (1877).
Virginia Historical Register, Vol. I, p. 119 et seq.
Speech of Charles M. Blackford in *Proceedings of Virginia Bar Association,* Vol. VII (1898).
Glance at Our Colonial Bar, — *Green Bag,* Vol. XIII.
Thomas Jefferson as a Lawyer, — *Green Bag,* Vol. XV.
Patrick Henry as a Lawyer, — *Green Bag,* Vol. XVI.
Virginia Lawyers, — *Green Bag,* Vol. X, Nos. 1, 2, 3.
Sketches of the Life and Character of Patrick Henry, by William Wirt (1817).
Edmund Randolph, by Moncure D. Conway (1888).
John Randolph of Roanoke, by Hugh A. Garland (1851).

Henry Clay as a Lawyer, Law Reporter, Vol. XV (1852).

Local Institutions of Virginia, Johns Hopkins University Studies in Historical and Political Science, 3d series (1885).

Our Judicial System, by Benjamin Watkins Leigh. *Proc. Virginia Bar Association,* Vol. I (1889).

County Courts in Virginia, Proc. Virginia Bar Association, Vol. VI (1894).

The General Court of Virginia, Proc. Virginia Bar Association, Vol. VII (1895).

Life of Chancellor Wythe in *Wythe's Cases in Chancery,* (1852 edition).

Letters and Times of the Tylers, by Leon G. Tyler (1884).

Discourse on the Life and Character of Hon. Littleton Waller Tazewell, by Hugh Blair Grigsby (1860).

Preface to *Virginia Statutes,* by William Waller Henings (1809).

NEW YORK.

Under the Dutch rule in New York, 1653-1664, the judicial functions were exercised by the Burgomasters and Schepens of New Amsterdam, in much the same way as in Massachusetts by the Great and General Court.

In 1664, when New Amsterdam became "New Yorck", the Court of Mayor and Aldermen for the City of New York was substituted. A code of law and practice commonly known as the "Duke's Law," was at once promulgated, in October, 1664. It was largely prepared by Mathias Nichols, an English barrister of Lincoln's Inn, and Secretary of the Province, from suggestions made by Lord Chancellor Clarendon and was compiled from the Common Law, the Dutch Colonial Law, and the local laws in force in the New England Colonies, fixing very precisely and elaborately the details of the courts, land tenure, police regulations, taxes, and religious liberty.

In 1673, the Dutch again conquered New York, and reverted at once to their old laws. In 1674, however, Sir Edmund Andros returned to reclaim the English rule, and as Governor, restored to New York, by proclamation, the "known books of laws formerly establisht".

No digest of the Colony laws was made until that of William Livingstone and William Smith, Jr., in 1752, comprising all the statutes passed between 1691 and 1751. A second edition was compiled by Peter Von Schaack in 1773.

In 1691, a Superior Court was constituted, consisting of a

Chief Justice, Joseph Dudley of Massachusetts, and four assistant judges, all appointed by the Royal Governor, and holding office "during his pleasure".

In addition there were Courts of Justice of the Peace, of Sessions, and of Common Pleas, and curiously, just at this time, when Courts of Pypowdry (Market Courts) were dying out in England, they were revived in New York in 1692, and as late as 1773 were extended to the new counties. The privilege of a Court Leet and Court Baron also was attached to many of the old manor holding families, such as the Livingstones, Van Renselaers, Courtlandts, Philips and Beekmans.

As in other Colonies, none of the judges were men of legal training except the Chief Justices; and of the latter the only lawyers of distinction were Colonel Lewis Morris, who was Chief Justice in 1720, of whom it was said that "no man in the Colony equalled him in the knowledge of the law"; Lieutenant Governor James Delancey, Chief Justice in 1733, a barrister of the Inner Temple of whom it was said, "His knowledge of law, history, and husbandry excepted, the rest of his learning consisted only of that small share of classical scholarship which he had acquired at Cambridge and by a good memory retained. He was too indolent for profound researches in the law"; Benjamin Pratt, who came from Massachusetts as Delancey's successor, in 1761; and William Smith, Jr., a Yale graduate, who was Chief Justice for a short time in 1763.

Jurists could not be found in New York to accept places on the bench (except for temporary purposes) "during his Majesty's pleasure": and though the Assembly many times sought to compel the appointment of judges during good behavior, Governor Colden and the other royal Governors vetoed all such measures.

The first lawyer of New Amsterdam was Dirck Van Schelluyne, in 1653. He had obtained in Holland a license to practice, but, there being no other lawyers in the new city to fight, and consequently no suits, he performed the duties of notary, kept a grocery store, and finally, becoming discouraged, left the city. In the early days of the English occupation, the estimation in which lawyers were held will appear from the following entry on the Minutes of the Council, held at the Stadt Huys on May 16, 1677:

Query? Whether attorneys are thought to be useful to plead

in courts or not. Answer. It is thought not. Whereupon resolved and ordered, That pleading attorneys be no longer allowed to practise in ye Government, but for ye pending cases.

This was later modified, and the court in Sept. 1677 made a rule that:

No one be admitted to plead for any other person or as attorney in court without hee first have his admittance of the court or have a warrant of attorney for his so doing from his clyent.

In 1683, the office of Recorder of the City of New York was created; and James Graham, a Scotch lawyer, who held the position from 1683 to 1701, as well as that of Attorney General of the Province, appears to have been the only trained lawyer in the Province at that time.

From an early date the power of appointment of attorneys was exercised by the Governor, and the first license to an attorney bears date of 1709. W. Smith Jr., in his contemporary history, laments that the Governors at times licensed all applicants, "however indifferently soever recommended", though sometimes they took advice of the Chief Justices.

The only lawyers of distinction in the early 18th Century were James Alexander(1), William Smith(2), John Tuder, David Jamieson, Francis Harrison, James Emott, Joseph Murray, John Chambers, Abraham Lodge, William Nichol(3), and Daniel Horsmanden(4).

The history of the early Bar, however, is notable for the trial of three famous cases. The first was that of *Col. Nicholas Bayard* in 1702 indicted for high treason, in which William Nichol and James Emott appeared as his counsel. (24 *Howell State Trials*). This trial as reported gives evidence of great learning and research.

The second was the famous *Zenger* or *Liberty* case. In 1733, John Peter Zenger had started, in New York City, the *Weekly*

---

(1) Born about 1690, came to New York in 1715, studied law after his arrival, attorney general 1721-23, and "though no speaker, was at the head of his profession; for sagacity and business penetration and in application to business no man could surpass him."

(2) Born in 1697, a Yale graduate of 1719, "of first reputation as a speaker", Justice of the Superior Court of New York in 1763.

(3) Born in 1657, came to New York in 1688, attorney for the prosecution of Jacob Leisler in 1691, and for the defense of Rev. Francis Makemie in 1707.

(4) Born in 1691, Chief Justice in 1763-1776.

Journal. The comments published on the Royal Governor Cosby had caused the paper to be pronounced as "seditious", and in 1735, Zenger was arrested for libel. James Alexander and William Smith at once offered their services as his counsel. They began his defence by a hot attack on the commissions of the judges, as unconstitutional, because appointed "during pleasure". For this they were summarily debarred, the Chief Justice saying, "The matter has come to the point that we must leave the bench or you the bar." Their names were not restored to the rolls until two years later. In this plight, Zenger engaged the services of Andrew Hamilton of Philadelphia, then the greatest lawyer in the Colonies, and the only one who had a continental reputation. Hamilton, although eighty years old, undertook the case with ardor. Of him, William Smith Jr. wrote in 1757: "He had art, eloquence, vivacity, and humour and was ambitious of fame, negligent of nothing to ensure success, and possessed a confidence which no terrors could awe". He at once set up the defence of truth and powerfully urged the rights of the jury to decide all the facts. But at this time the law of England was, as Lord Mansfield a few years later proclaimed it, "the greater truth, the greater libel", and the jury were only to decide on the fact in publication. As Fiske says, "In the history of freedom of the press, Hamilton's name is beside the great names of Erskine and Fox. It should in fact surmount theirs, for his argument preceded theirs." Gouverneur Morris termed Hamilton "the Day Star of the American Revolution".

"The question before this court and you gentlemen of the jury", argued Hamilton, "may in its consequences affect every freeman that lives under a British Government on the Main of America. It is the best cause, it is the cause of liberty—the liberty both of exposing and opposing arbitrary power—by speaking and writing truth." . . . "What a strange doctrine it is, to press everything for law which is in England", he boldly urged. The jury at once acquitted Zenger. The pamphlet report of this case published in 1735 and republished several times is one of the earliest law books in the American Colonies. (1)

The third famous case was that of persons concerned in the alleged negro plot in 1741, the account of which was printed in 1744, by Daniel Horsmanden, City Recorder. He states that in

_____

(1) See infra, Chapter VI.

the terror over the supposed conspiracy the whole Bar of the city, consisting of seven members only, besides the Attorney General Bradley, Messrs. Murray, Alexander, Smith, Chambers, Nichols, Lodge, and Jameson offered their services to the prosecution "as a matter affecting not only the city but the whole province."

Though small in numbers, a regular Bar Association was in existence as early as 1748; and was active in opposing the claim of the Royal Governors to appoint judges during their pleasure. In 1763, it opposed Gov. Colden's attempt to extend the royal prerogative by imposing his authority on the courts in an important matter of practice; and two years later it largely organized the determined and successful resistance to the Stamp Act; (1) and in the same year, a Committee of the Bar sent in a petition to Parliament against internal taxation and the extension of the admiralty jurisdiction. In 1765, Governor Colden, writing to the Earl of Halifax of the "dangerous influence which the profession of the law had obtained in this province more than in any other", expressed a wish that "the people were freed from the domination of lawyers". Shortly after this, however, the Bar Association went out of existence.

During the middle of the 18th Century, as Chancellor Kent, in his address before the Law Association of the City of New York, in 1836, said, "The New York bar contained a constellation of learned and accomplished men". Chief of these were William Livingston, who was born in 1723, a Yale graduate of 1741, studied law with James Alexander, in 1745, later with William Smith, and in 1752, collected and published the first digest of Colony laws; and William Smith, Jr., from whose personal recollections most of New York's early history is now known, born in 1728, a Yale graduate of 1745. Among others were Whitehead Hicks(2), John Tabor Kempe, the last Royal Attorney General; Benjamin Kissam; Peter Van Schaack, Recorder of New York and Editor of the Revision of the Statutes in 1774(3); John Morin Scott(4); Samuel Jones, Recorder, and Benjamin Nicoll.

The number of lawyers even at the beginning of the Revolution

---

(1)   Sir William Johnson wrote to England from New York that the lawyers' opposition to the Stamp Act was for fear that "business must decrease from the duties on Law Proceedings."
(2)   Born in 1728, Judge of Supreme Court 1776-80.
(3)   Born in 1747, a Columbia graduate of 1768, studied with W. Smith, Jr.
(4)   Born in 1730, a Yale graduate of 1746.

was still comparatively small, for in the sixty-eight years between 1709 and 1776 only 136 had been licensed as attorneys by the Governor. (1)

Valentine, in his history of the City of New York, gives a list of only 41 lawyers practicing in the city between 1697 and 1769.(2)

---

(1) It is interesting to note that the last license in the *Book of Commissions,* signed by the Royal Governor Tryon, is under date of March 11, 1776, and that on the very next page the "People of the State of New York, by the Grace of God free and independent", make their first appointment of a Secretary of State. See *In the matter of Cooper,* 22 N. Y. 67.

(2) *History of the City of New York,* by David T. Valentine, 1853. Clerk of Common Council.

Names of Attorneys practicing in the City of New York between the year 1695 and the Revolutionary War.

  1697 David Jamison, Gent.
  1698 James Emott, Gent. Atty at Law
  1701 Thomas Weaver Esq.
  1702 John Bridges
       Robert Milwood
  1708 May Bickley
       Jacob Regnier
       Roger Mompesson
  1718 Tobias Boel
  1728 Joseph Murray
       John Chambers
  1730 Abraham Lodge
       Richard Nicholls
       James Alexander
       William Smith
  1740 Daniel Horsmanden
  1743 Lancaster Graen
  1745 Elisha Parker
       John Burnet
       Samuel Clowes
  1746 William Searle
  1747 John McEvers Jr.
       John Van Cortlandt
  1748 Bartholomew Crannell
       William Livingston
  1749 John Alsop
  1751 Augustus Van Cortlandt
       Lambert Moore
  1763 Whitehead Hicks
  1768 Benjamin Kissam
       Benjamin Helme
       Rudolphus Ritzema
       John McKesson
  1769 Richard Harrison
       Philip Livingston Jr.
       Thomas Jones
       Philip J. Livingston
       John William Smith
       John D. Crimshire
       David Mathews
       Samuel Jones.

Professional practice at this time, outside of political matters, was scanty, and as Sedgwick said, in his *Life of Livingston,* "the great number of cases were collection of debts owed by English merchants and suits in ejectment—which does much to diminish any regret which may be felt for the want of colonial reports".

The State Constitution of 1777 provided that all attorneys, solicitors and counsellors should be appointed by license from the courts.

After the Revolution, the profession was called into most active business. The courts were crowded with cases, largely of marine, insurance, and mercantile law. Many of the Tory lawyers had left the Province. In 1779, the Legislature suspended all licenses to plead or practise law granted before April 21, 1777, subject to restoration provided that the lawyer should give satisfactory proof before a sheriff's jury that he had been true to the American cause; and as many of those lawyers who had not become refugees were unable to take this oath, a great opportunity was thus opened for the younger men at the Bar.(1)

Even in 1785, the roll of the New York City Bar numbered only 40. A brief sketch of six of the more prominent will give some idea of their legal education. It is to be noted that, with very few exceptions, all the noted lawyers were college graduates.

John Jay, born in 1745, six years Hamilton's senior, and eleven years older than Burr, graduated from Columbia (then King's college) in 1764, and studied law under Benjamin Kissam. Admitted to the Bar in 1768, he became, in 1776, Chief Justice of New York; and in 1789 he was appointed the first Chief Justice of the United States Supreme Court.

Gouverneur Morris, born in 1752, graduated from Columbia College in 1768, studied law with William Smith, Jr., and was admitted to practice in 1771.

Alexander Hamilton, born in 1751, in the West Indies, came to America in 1772, graduated at Columbia College and in July, 1782, was admitted as attorney after four months' study. Even before admission, he had composed a manual on the practice of law so valuable that lawyers copied it in manuscript.

---

(1) A graphic summing up of a few of the leaders at the close of the 18th Century is given in the *Discourse on the Life, Character and Public Services of Ambrose Spencer,* by Daniel D. Barnard, (1849).

Only two years after his admission he established his fame as a lawyer, in the case of *Rutgers v. Waddington,* tried in 1784.

Aaron Burr was born in 1756, graduated at Princeton in 1772, studied law in the office of Thomas Smith for six months, confining himself entirely to an acquaintance with forms, and trusting to gain a knowledge of principles later. Although by rule of court a three years' course of study was required, the court dispensed with the rule in his case, owing to his military service, and admitted him to practice in 1782, the same year with Hamilton.

Three years later James Kent was admitted to practice. Born in 1763, he graduated at Yale in 1781, "and stood as well as any in my class", he wrote, "but the test of scholarship at that day was very contemptible. I was only a very inferior classical scholar". He studied law in the office of Egbert Benson, Attorney General of New York, and from 1786 to 1793, practised at Poughkeepsie. In 1797 be became Recorder of the City of New York, in 1798 Judge of the Supreme Court, in 1804 Chief Justice, in 1814 Chancellor.

In the same year that Kent graduated from Yale, Edward Livingston (born in 1764) graduated from Princeton. He studied in the office of John Lansing, and he, Kent, Burr and Hamilton were all in the habit of meeting at Albany for discussion of legal terms and methods of study. Admitted to the Bar in 1785, in 1803, Livingston went to Louisiana where he became in 1805 the author of the first American Code of Procedure.

Besides these there were in practice, or soon coming to practice, James Duane(1), George Clinton(2), Egbert Benson(3), Robert R. Livingston(4), Richard Morris Smith, Richard Varick(5), John Lansing(6), Morgan Lewis(7), Robert Troup(8), Edward

---

(1) Born in 1733, first Mayor of New York, 1784-1789 U. S. District Judge.

(2) Born in 1739, studied in office of W. Smith.

(3) Born in 1746, graduate of Columbia 1765, Atty. Gen. 1777-89, Judge of Supreme Court 1794.

(4) Born in 1746, graduate of Columbia 1765, student with W. Smith, and W. Livingston, Chancellor 1789-1801.

(5) Born in 1750, Recorder 1783, Reviser of Laws of New York with S. Jones 1789.

(6) Born in 1754, student in office of James Duane, Judge of the Supreme Court 1776-1790, Chief Justice 1790-1798, and Chancellor in 1801.

(7) Born in 1754, Princeton graduate 1773, student in office of John Jay, Chief Justice in 1801.

(8) Born in 1757, Columbia graduate 1774, studied law with John Jay and in New Jersey under William Patterson, U. S. District Judge in 1789.

Livingston, Richard Harrison, John Lawrence, DeWitt Clinton (9), Daniel O. Tompkins(10), Josiah Ogden Hoffman, William Brockholst Livingston(1), William W. Van Ness(2), Abraham Van Vechten(3), and Robert Yates(4).

No better idea of the New York Bar at the close of the 18th century can be obtained than from the description by Ex-Chancellor Kent of his personal impressions.

After the peace of 1783, a few gentlemen of the colonial school resumed their ancient practice; but the Bar was chiefly supplied by a number of ambitious and high spirited young men, who had returned from the field of arms with honorable distinction, and by extraordinary application they soon became qualified to commence their career at the Bar with distinguished reputation . . . . Colonel Burr was acute, quick, terse, polished, sententious, and sometimes sarcastic in his forensic discussions. He seemed to disdain illustration and expansion, and confined himself with stringency to the point in debate. But among all his brethren Colonel Hamilton was indisputably preeminent. This was universally conceded. He rose at once to the loftiest heights of professional eminence by his profound penetration, his power of analysis, the comprehensive grasp and strength of his understanding, and the firmness, frankness and superiority of his character. . . .

At that day everything in law seemed to be new. Our judges were not remarkable for law learning. We had no precedents of our own to guide us. . . . . Nothing was settled in our courts. Every point of practice had to be investigated, and its application to our courts and institutions questioned and tested. . . . . There were no decisions of any of the courts published. There were none that contained any investigation. In the city of New York, Hamilton, Harrison, Burr, Cozine and perhaps John Lawrence and old Samuel Jones (then deemed and known as the oracle of the law) began to introduce the knowledge and cultivation of the law which was confined of course to Coke, Littleton, and the reporters down to Burrow.

Hamilton brought a writ of right in a Waddell case in this city which made quite a sensation and created much puzzle in the

---

(9) Born in 1769, Columbia graduate 1786, studied in office of Samuel Jones.

(10) Born in 1774, Columbia graduate 1795, Judge of Supreme Court in 1805.

(1) Born in 1757, Princeton graduate 1774, Judge of Supreme Court 1802, Judge of U. S. Supreme Court 1807.

(2) Born in 1776, Judge of Supreme Court 1807-22.

(3) Born in 1762, studied with John Lansing, termed "the father of the New York Bar," being the first lawyer admitted under the State Constitution, Attorney General 1810, 1813-15.

(4) Born in 1738, studied with W. Livingston, Judge of the Supreme Court 1776, Chief Justice 1790-98.

court. The judges of the Supreme Court (Norris, Yates and Lansing) were very illiterate as lawyers. . . . The country circuit courts were chiefly occupied in plain ejectment suits and in trying criminals. In short, our jurisprudence was a blank when Hamilton and Harrison first began by their forensic discussions to introduce principles and to pour light and learning upon the science of law. . . .

Mr. Hamilton returned to private life and to the practice of the law in New York in the spring of 1795. . . .

Between the years 1795 and 1798 he took his station as the leading counsel at the Bar. He was employed in every important and especially in every commercial case. He was a very great favorite with the merchants of New York, and he most justly deserved to be, for he had uniformly shown himself to be one of the most enlightened, intrepid, and persevering friends to the commercial prosperity of this country. Insurance questions, both upon the law and the fact, constituted a large portion of the litigated business in the courts, and much of the intense study and discussion at the Bar. The business of insurance was carried on principally by private underwriters, and as the law had not been defined and settled in this country by a course of judicial decisions, and was open to numerous perplexed questions arising out of our neutral trade, and was left, under a complicated mixture of law and fact, very much at large to a jury, the litigation of that kind was immense. Mr. Hamilton had an overwhelming share of it, and though the New York Bar could at that time boast of the clear intellect, the candor, the simplicity, and black-letter learning of the elder Jones, the profound and richly varied learning of Harrison, the classical taste and elegant accomplishments of Brockholst Livingston, the solid and accurate, but unpretending common law learning of Troup, the chivalrous feelings and dignified address of Pendleton, yet the mighty mind of Hamilton would at times bear down all opposition by its comprehensive grasp and the strength of his reasoning powers.

He taught us all how to probe deeply into the hidden recesses of the science, or to follow up principles to their far distant sources. He was not content with the modern reports, abridgments, or translations. He ransacked cases and precedents to their very foundations; and we learned from him to carry our inquiries into the commercial codes of the nations of the European continent, and in a special manner to illustrate the law of insurance by the severe judgment of Emerigon and the luminous commentaries of Valin. If I were to select any two cases in which his varied powers were most strikingly displayed, it would be the case of *Le Guen v. Gouverneur and Kemble,* argued before the Court of Errors in the winter of 1800, and the case of the *Croswell v. The People,* argued before the Supreme

Court in February term, 1804, and involving a libel on Thomas Jefferson.

NOTE.

For authorities in general see:

Allegiance and Laws of Colonial New York, Harv. Law Rev. Vol. XV.

History of New York, by William Dunlap, (1840).

History of New York, by William Smith, (Vol. I, pub. in London in 1757; Vol. II in N. Y. in 1826).

History of New York, by Ellis H. Roberts (1887).

Lives and Times of the Chief Justices, by Henry Flanders (1881).

Dutch and Quaker Colonies in America, by John Fiske (1899).

American Law Review, Vol. V, p. 445.

Rufus King, Life and Correspondence, by Charles R. King, (1894).

Address by George Shea in *New York Bar Association, Proc.* Vol. II.

New York Bar Assn. Proc. Vol. XII, p. 127.

Address of James Kent before Law Association of City of New York, Oct. 21, 1836.

Memoir of Alexander Hamilton, a letter by James Kent (1832).

Life of James Kent, by William Kent, (1898).

Memoirs of the Life of William Livingston, by Theodore Sedgwick, Jr., (1833).

Aaron Burr, by Samuel L. Knapp (1835).

Aaron Burr, Life and Times, by James Parton (1882).

Diary and Letters of Gouverneur Morris, by Anne Carey Morris, (1888).

Gouverneur Morris, by Jared Sparks (1832).

Alexander Hamilton, by John T. Morse, Jr. (1876).

Lives of William Smith, Jr., Lindley Murray, and Beverley Robinson, in *Loyalists of American Revolution,* by Lorenzo Sabine, (1864).

American Criminal Trials, by Peleg W. Chandler, (1847).

Life of Edward Livingston, by Charles H. Hunt, (1864).

Lives of the Governors of the State of New York, by John S. Jenkins, (1851).

PENNSYLVANIA.

The first courts in Pennsylvania were constituted under the Duke of York's Government in 1673, County Courts, the records of at least one of which (Upland or Chester County) from November 1676, to June 1681, are still extant. The judges were for many years exclusively Swedes and of no legal training. No attorney was allowed to practice for pay before them. They exercised legislative as well as judicial powers, hearing suits for debts, approving indentures of apprentices, imposing taxes and fines, punishing misdemeanors, granting lands, adjusting title disputes, and directing uses of the revenue.

In 1682-3, the Governor and Council exercised judicial power.

In 1684, under Penn's charter a Supreme Court was constituted composed of five judges, of which Nicholas More, a physician, was Chief Justice. Of the first six Chief Justices only one was a trained lawyer—John Guest, an English barrister, who became Chief Justice in 1706. In the same year (1706) Roger Mompesson, who had been an educated lawyer, the Recorder of Southampton and twice a member of Parliament in England, was appointed Chief Justice, at the instance of William Penn, who wrote to James Logan, advising "the people to lay hold of such an opportunity as no government in America ever had of procuring the services of an English lawyer."

After him came three Chief Justices of little legal note, then came David Lloyd, a noted English lawyer, who was Chief Justice, 1719-1731. James Logan, a man of little legal training followed, 1731-1739; then Jeremiah Langhorne, a preacher, 1739-1743. John Kinsey (1743-50)(1), William Allen (1751-74), and Benjamin Chew (1774-79), were all trained lawyers (the last two being English barristers).

The associate judges were invariably laymen, usually merchants, and, as William Rawle said in 1826, it was practically true that "before the Revolution the Bench was rarely graced by professional characters."

No records of the Supreme Court are extant; and David Lloyd says that in his time (the end of the 17th Century) they were written "on a quire of paper". A few of the decided cases, however, are reported in Dallas' *Reports;* and in 1892 a volume of Colonial cases, the earliest dating back to 1683—seventy years before the earliest case reported in Dallas—was published by Judge Pennypacker.

Although the court decisions were based largely on rough

---

(1) The records of the Provincial Council, April 5, 1743, state: "His Honour told the council that as the place of chief justice was vacant by the death of Mr. Langhorne and it would be of very great advantage to the province that one of the profession of the law preside in the Supreme Court, he had made an offer of it to Mr. Kinsey, a gentleman well known to them."

and businesslike notions of equity, and with little regard to precedents, the Colony had a full and well settled code of law from the beginning—consisting of the "Frame of Law" agreed upon in England in 1682, the Great Law or Body of Law enacted at Chester in the same year, the Act of Settlement passed in Philadelphia in 1683, and eighty chapters of statutes enacted the same year, the Frame of Government in 1683 and 1696, and the laws of 1701. These codes embodied a complete system and rendered more elaborate legislation unnecessary for a long time.

Upon the settlement of the Province by Penn and his Quakers, there was an instinctive antipathy to lawyers as a class, as being men of strife and of barratrous tendencies, and therefore opposed to the fundamental religious views of the new settlers.

To avoid the necessity of courts and lawsuits, provision was made in 1683, for the appointment of three "common peacemakers" in every precinct, their arbitration to be valid and final as a judgment.

In the "Laws agreed upon" in England May 5, 1682, it was provided:

> that in all courts all persons of all persuasions may freely appear in their own way and according to their own manner and there personally plead their own case themselves and if unable, by their friends; that all pleadings, processes, and records in court shall be short and in English and in an ordinary and plain character that they may be understood and justice speedily administered.

In 1686 and in 1690, the Provincial Council attempted, but without success, to pass a bill preventing any person pleading in any civil causes of another, before he

> be solemnlye attested in open court that he neither directly nor indirectly hath in any wise taken or received or will take or receive to his use or benefit any reward whatsoever for his soe pleading.

In 1698, Gabriel Thomas wrote, (1) "Of Lawyers and Physicians I shall say nothing, because this country is very peaceable and healthy: Long may it so continue and never have occasion for the tongue of the one nor the pen of the other—both equally destructive of men's estates and lives."

---

(1) *An Historical and Geographical Account of the Province and Country of Pennsylvania and of West Jersey in America*, by Gabriel Thomas (London 1698).

At the end of the 17th Century, while there were a few lay lawyers, such as Abraham Man, John White (Attorney General in 1683), Charles Pickering, Samuel Hersnet (Attorney General in 1685), Patrick Robinson, and Samuel Jennings, there were only three or four trained English lawyers in the Province.

Of these, by far the most famous, possibly the greatest lawyer in all the American Colonies, was Andrew Hamilton, a barrister and bencher of Grays Inn. He came to Philadelphia in 1682, and was successively Recorder of Philadelphia, Vice Admiralty Judge, Speaker of the Assembly, and Attorney General. David Lloyd, a noted Welsh jurist, was sent out from England as Attorney General in 1686 and held many offices of trust in the Province, being looked upon as the great advocate of the people's rights. He became Chief Justice in 1718, and was described by James Logan, his successor as Chief Justice in 1731, in a letter to Penn as "a man very stiff in all his undertakings, of a sound judgment and a good lawyer, but extremely pertinacious and somewhat revengeful."

The paucity of lawyers was well illustrated by Penn in 1700, in replying to the charges made by Robert Quary, Judge of Admiralty, of failing to prosecute William Smith Jr. for a heinous crime. In his answer Penn stated that the defendant had subsequently

married ye only material witness against him, which in the opinion of ye only two lawyers of the place (and one of them ye King's advocate of ye Admiralty and ye attorney general of the county) has rendered her incompetent to testify against him.

McCall states that, in 1706, the whole Bar of Philadelphia consisted of G. Lowther, David Lloyd, Robert Assheton and Thomas Clark. At all events, it was so small that there are records of cases in which the plaintiff complained that the defendant had cornered all the lawyers in the Province. Thus in 1708, there was a petition to the Council from one complaining that he had been sued in trover by Joseph Growden and that the latter had retained all the lawyers in the county, wherefore he prayed the Council to assign him counsel. So too, in 1709, one Francis D. Pastorius complained that one Spogell had got a writ of ejectment and had feed and retained the four known lawyers of the Province "in order to deprive the Petitioner of all advice in law," and the petitioner being too poor to "fetch lawyers from New York or remote places, prays that Spogell's proceedings may be enjoined."

Shortly before this, Lord Peterborough had written:

I took a trip once with Penn to his colony of Pennsylvania; the laws there are contained in a small volume and are so extremely good that there has been no alteration wanted in any one of them ever since Sir William made them. They have no lawyers. Everyone is to tell his own case, or some friend for him.

Early in the 18th Century, other English lawyers came into the Province, as business increased—William Assheton, John Moland, and Tench Francis. The latter, who succeeded Andrew Hamilton as Attorney General in 1744, is stated to have been the "first of the lawyers of that province to master the technical difficulties of the profession." He was the brother of Richard Francis, the well known English author of *Maxims of Equity,* and came from Ireland in 1740. Secretary Peters wrote, at this time, of the lawyers "all of whom except Francis and Moland are persons of no knowledge and I had almost said, no principle."

The first Statute as to the admission of lawyers was enacted in 1722, providing that "there may be a competent number of persons of an honest disposition and learned in the law admitted by the justices . . . to practice as attorneys." A form of oath was also prescribed.

Although Governor Keith, in 1723, complained of the great increase of lawsuits—431 writs being issued in 1715-16 and 847 in 1721-22; it would seem that the Quaker population was, as a rule, a non-litigious one, and this fact partially accounted for the lack of lawyers.

So strong were the Quakers in every branch of life, that even the courts were obliged to take notice of their religious forms. Thus in 1725, when John Kinsey, a prominent Quaker lawyer (later Chief Justice) was compelled by Sir William Keith, the Governor, to take off his hat before being allowed to address the court, so great consternation was caused in the Province, that the Society of Friends appointed a committee to address the Governor, and to demand of him the free exercise of the privilege of appearing in courts or otherwise, in their own way and according to their religious persuasion. A Rule of Court later assured full liberty in this point of conscience.

Horace Binney, (the leader of the Philadelphia Bar in the early 19th Century) thus sums up the conditions:

Of the primitive Bar of the Province of Pennsylvania we know nothing, and next to nothing of the men who appeared at it from time to time up to the termination of the Colonial Government.

The statement of C. J. Tilghman in the Bush Hill case (*Lyle v. Richards,* 9 *Serg and Rawle*) reveals to us all we know and all that probably we can ever know in regard to this subject; for as the grandson of Tench Francis who was attorney general in 1745 and connected by marriage association with the most eminent families of the Bar, he knew as much of the former Bar as any of his contemporaries and they have all long since departed without adding anything to what he left.

From what I have been able to learn, said the C. J., of the early history of Pennsylvania, it was a long time before she possessed any lawyers of eminence. There were never wanting men of strong minds very well able to conduct the business of the courts without much regard to form.

In the lists given by Martin, in his *Bench and Bar of Philadelphia,* it appears that there were 23 lawyers before 1700 and 51 between 1700 and 1785, in the Province of Philadelphia. Of the practising attorneys between 1683 and 1742, only ten had had any legal training. Seventy-six lawyers were admitted to practice in the Supreme Court between 1742 and 1776.

Just before the War of the Revolution, a considerable group of distinguished and educated lawyers composed the Bar. Chief among them were Benjamin Chew, a Maryland lawyer, born in 1718, a barrister of the Middle Temple, who succeeded Tench Francis as Attorney General in 1755, and became Chief Justice in 1774; Thomas McKean, who was born in 1734, admitted to practice in 1757, and studied in the Middle Temple in 1758 and became Chief Justice in 1777; Edward Shippen, who was born in 1729, studied in the office of Tench Francis, admitted in 1748, studied in the Middle Temple in 1750 and became Chief Justice in 1799. Others of note were Joseph Galloway (1), John Dickinson (2), Francis Hopkinson (3), George Read (4), Joseph

---

(1) Born in Maryland, in 1731, acquired an immense real property practice, was a favorite pleader; at the Revolution he became a Tory and left this country, his estate amounting to 400,000 pounds being confiscated.

(2) Born in Maryland, in 1732, studied in the office of William Killen (afterwards Chief Justice of Delaware), and in Philadelphia in the office

Read(1), and Alexander Wilcocks. The chief characteristic of the Philadelphia Bar of this period was the large number who had received education in the English Inns of Court.

After the Revolution, the Bar attained great and distinguished development, so that in 1785, it appears from White's Directory that there were then 34 Counsellors at law. Of these, the most notable were, William Lewis, the "Senior of the Bar," who (says Binney) "loomed large like Theophilus Parsons at Boston and Luther Martin at Baltimore"(2); Edward Tilghman(3); William Tilghman(4); James Wilson, probably the leader among advocates at the Bar(5); Jared Ingersoll(6); Alexander J. Dallas(7; Willaim Rawle(8); William Bradford(9); Jasper Yeates(10); and Richard Peters.(11)

---

of John Moland, who was the most conspicuous member of the Bar after 1741, later he attended the Middle Temple.

(3) Born in 1737, studied under Chew, and was one of the signers of the Declaration of Independence, later Judge of Admiralty, and of the United States District Court 1790-91.

(4) Born in Maryland, in 1734, admitted to the Bar in 1753, like Dickinson a student in the Middle Temple and like him a King's Attorney General. "A deep read lawyer, versed in special pleading," later Chief Justice of Delaware, a signer of the Declaration of Independence.

(1) Born in 1741, a graduate of Princeton and of the Temple, one of the most distinguished of the students in Richard Stockton's office in New Jersey.

(2) Born in 1748 and studied law in the offices of Nicholas Waln and George Ross, was admitted to the Bar in 1776, and became the great criminal lawyer of his day. He was the fearless counsel for John Fries in the case which led to the impeachment in 1805 of Judge Chase, of the United States Supreme Court.

(3) A grandson of Tench Francis, born in Maryland in 1750, studied in the Middle Temple, and was admitted to the Bar in 1774. He was the consummate Pennsylvania authority on all points connected with estates, tenures, uses, and remainders.

(4) Born in 1759, studied law with Kemp in New York, admitted to practice in 1783, and became Chief Justice of the State in 1806. He was a master of Equity Jurisprudence.

(5) Born in Scotland in 1745, educated at the University of Glasgow, St. Andrews, and Edinburgh, came to Philadelphia in 1766, and studied in office of John Dickinson. He was one of the signers, one of the most important members of the Constitutional Convention and was retained in almost every important case. Appointed judge of the U. S. Supreme Court in 1789, it was said that his "ability as a judge did not equal his eminence off the bench."

At a Philadelphia dinner a wit gave the following toast. "To the memory of three great Philadelphians—Benjamin Franklin, of Boston; Albert Gallatin, of Geneva; James Wilson, of Edinburgh!"

(6) Born in 1752, in Connecticut, graduated at Yale in 1766, and educated in the Middle Temple, 1774-1778; admitted to the Bar in 1779.

(7) Born in Jamaica in 1759, studied in the Temple, came to the United States in 1787, and was admitted to the Bar in Philadelphia in 1785. He published the first volume of *Dallas' Reports,* in 1790.

(8) Born in 1759, studied law with Kemp in New York, and in the

It is interesting to note, that the first American novelist, Charles Brockden Brown, was a student of law in Philadelphia in 1790, but regarded the law as a "tissue of shreds and remnants of a barbarous antiquity, patched by the stupidity of modern workmen into new deformity."

Of the lawyers who made the beginning of the 19th Century brilliant, the leaders were, Horace Binney(1); Charles Jared Ingersoll(2); Charles Chauncey(3); Jasper Moylan; John Sergeant(4); Richard Peters(5); Peter S. Du Ponceau(6); Thomas Sergeant(7); and Joseph Hopkinson(8).

NOTE.

See for authorities in general:

Dutch and Quaker Colonies, by John Fiske (1899).

A Glance at our Colonial Bar, Green Bag. Vol. XI.

Pennsylvania Colonial and Federal, by Howard McJenkins (1903).

English Common Law in the Early American Colonies, by Paul S. Reinsch.

Bench and Bar of Old Philadelphia, by John H. Harris (1883).

Discourse Before the Law Academy, Sept. 15, 1838, by P. McCall (1838).

An Essay on Equity in Pennsylvania, by Anthony Laussat (1825) in *Penn. Bar Assn. Rep.,* Vol. I (1895).

Middle Temple in 1781, and became United States District Attorney in 1791, being prosecutor in the whiskey Insurrection and in the famous John Fries case. "Between 1793 and 1813 his practice was as large as any lawyer at the bar."

(9) Born in 1755, a Princeton graduate in 1772, was judge of the Pennsylvania Supreme Court in 1791 and the second attorney general of the United States, succeeding Edmund Randolph, of Virginia, in 1794.

(10) Born in 1745, graduate in 1761 of the College of Philadelphia, a student in the Temple, Judge of the Supreme Court in 1791.

(11) Born in 1744, graduate of College of Philadelphia in 1761, United States District Judge 1792.

(1) Born in 1780, a graduate of Harvard in 1797, studied in office of Jared Ingersoll, admitted to the Bar in 1800.

(2) Born in 1782, student of Princeton 1796-1799, admitted to the Bar in 1802.

(3) Born in 1777, Yale graduate of 1792, studied with Jared Ingersoll, admitted in 1799.

(4) Born in 1779, Princeton graduate of 1795, admitted in 1799.

(5) Born in 1780, admitted in 1800, Reporter of United States Supreme Court.

(6) Born in 1760.

(7) Born in 1782, Princeton graduate of 1798, studied with Jared Ingersoll, Judge of Supreme Court 1834-46.

(8) Born in 1770, Univ. of Penn. graduate of 1786, admitted to practice 1791, United States District Attorney in 1828.

Pennsylvania Jurisprudence, by John W. Simonton, *Penn. Bar Assn.* Vol. I.

Bar of Pennsylvania and its Influence, by J. Levering Jones, *Penn. Bar Assn.* Vol. X.

Courts of Pennsylvania in the 17th Century, by Lawrence Lewis, Jr. (1881) *Penn. Bar Assn.* Vol. I.

The Common Law of Pennsylvania, by George Sharswood (1855) *Penn. Bar Assn.* Vol. I.

The District Court, by James T. Mitchell in *Penn. Bar Assn.* Vol. V, (1885).

Joseph Galloway, by Ernest H. Baldwin (1902).

Life of Joseph Galloway and Edward Shippen in *Loyalists of the American Revolution,* by Lorenzo Sabine.

Remarks to Bar on Death of Charles Chauncey and John Sergeant, by Horace Binney (1853).

The McKean Family, by Roberdeau Buchanan (1890).

William Tilghman, by Horace Binney (1827).

Life of Horace Binney, by Charles C. Binney (1903).

Horace Binney, Green Bag, Vol. V.

The Supreme Court of Pennsylvania, by Judge F. Carroll Brewster in *The Supreme Court of the States and Provinces,* Vol. I, *Series* 3, (1895).

Life of Thomas McKean, by Judge James T. Mitchell in *The Supreme Court of the States and Provinces,* Vol. I, *Series* 3, (1895).

Life and Times of John Dickinson, by Charles J. Stillé (1891).

Memoir of William Rawle, by T. J. Wharton, *Penn. Hist. Assn. Proc.* Vol. IV, (1837).

Memoir of William Bradford, by Horace Binney Wallace (1856).

The Republican Court, or American Society in the Days of Washington, by Rufus W. Griswold (1855).

Life of George Read, by William T. Read (1870).

Life of Charles Jared Ingersoll, by William M. Meigs (1897).

Scharf and Westcott's *History of Philadelphia* (1884).

The Supreme Court of Pennsylvania, by Owen Wister, *Green Bag.* Vol. III.

Life and Writings of Alexander James Dallas, by George M. Dallas (1871).

Pennsylvania Colonial Cases, by Samuel W. Pennypacker (1892).

The Law Association of Philadelphia, 1802-1902, (1906).

The Courts of Pennsylvania Prior to the Revolution, Univ. of Penn. Law Rev. Vol. LVI, (1908).

Judicial Memoranda in the History of Pennsylvania in *The Journal of Jurisprudence,* Vol. I (1821).

NEW JERSEY.

In the Judicial and Civil History of New Jersey, by John Whitehead (1897), no names of any lawyers practising in the

17th Century are given; and it is said, "the courts of New Jersey were not established upon any settled plan nor upon any perfected system, until about the beginning of the 18th Century." From the time of the conquest of the Colony of East Jersey from the Dutch, in 1664, the judicial power lay in the Governor, and on appeal from the small local courts to the Governor and Council.

The Supreme Court was established in 1704, (two years after the consolidation of East and West New Jersey); and presided over by an English lawyer, Roger Mompesson, who arrived in Philadelphia in 1703 and who was also Chief Justice of New York.

Out of eight of his successors down to the Revolution, three only, Thomas Gordon, in 1709, David Jamison, in 1710, and Robert Hunter Morris, 1738-44, were educated lawyers. Of the latter it was said, that "he reduced the pleadings to precision and method and possessed the great perfection of his office, knowledge and integrity, in more perfection than had often been known before in the colonies." Few of the other judges before the Revolution had legal training.

In 1682, the Legislature of East New Jersey enacted that "in all courts, all persons of all persuasions may freely appear in their own way and according to their own manner, and there personally plead their own cause, and if unable, by their friends or attorneys."

Of the early lawyers little is known; and it was not until the founding of Princeton in 1746 that a trained Bar began.

In 1740, an act was passed regulating in detail the practice of law and establishing fees. In 1769-70, a storm of attacks centered around lawyers, arising from the cost, abuses, and multiplicity of suits. Charges were preferred in the Assembly against even the leaders of the Bar; and mobs attempted to prevent the lawyers from entering the court houses. With the passing, however, of the financial crisis then prevailing, these attacks gradually died out.(1)

It is a well known fact that in its administration of justice, New Jersey has always, even to the present day, followed more closely the old English precedents than any other American State.

(1) *The Provincial Court of New Jersey with Sketches of the Bench and Bar*, by Richard F. Field (1849), N. J. Hist. Soc. Coll., Vol. III.
Constitution and Government of New Jersey with Reminiscences of the Bench and Bar, by L. Q. C. Elmer (1872), N. J. Hist. Soc. Coll., Vol. VII.

As an example, in 1755, the Supreme Court instituted the order of Sergeants, in imitation of the ancient English degree of Sergeant at Law; and in 1763, it was ordered that "no person for the future shall practise as a sergeant in this court but those that are recommended by the judges to the governor for the time being and duly called up by writ and sworn agreeably to the practice in England."(1)　Later the number of Sergeants was fixed at twelve; and they conducted examinations for admission to the Bar. They were not abolished until as late as 1839.

In 1767, a distinction was made (as in Massachusetts) between attorney and barrister (or counsellor as it was termed in New Jersey); and it was provided that no man should practice as counsellor until he had been an attorney for three years and duly examined in court for the advanced status.

By the time of the Revolution, an organized Bar had grown up; and there is a record of the call of a meeting of the State Bar, in September, 1765, to discuss the Stamp Act, at which meeting it was unanimously resolved to use no stamps for any purpose.

Of lawyers of prominence, prior to the Revolution, two stand forth pre-eminent. David Ogden, born in 1707, a Yale graduate of 1728, judge of the Supreme Court in 1772, of whom it was said that as a lawyer, he had no equal in New York or New Jersey; and his pupil, Richard Stockton, born in 1730, a Princeton graduate of 1748, who was admitted to the Bar in 1754, as counsellor in 1758, and as Sergeant at law in 1763, in 1774 made Judge of the Supreme Court. His practice was very large both in New Jersey, and in Pennsylvania, where he was the frequent opponent at the Bar of Dickinson, Shippen, and Chew. His reputation was such that a legal education in New Jersey was hardly considered complete unless it included a course of study in his office, and he had frequent applications besides from students of other States. Among his pupils were Elias Boudinot, William Paterson (later Judge of the United States Supreme Court), Joseph Read, Jonathan D. Sergeant, and William Davie and John Rutherford of Virginia.(2).

---

(1)　*History of the Supreme Court of New Jersey,* by Francis B Lee, Vol. I (1896).

(2)　Sanderson's *Lives of the Signers.*
Many of the prominent lawyers became Tories—Isaac Allen, William Taylor, Henry Waddell, Cortlandt Skinner the last Royal Attorney General, Frederick Smyth the last Royal Chief Justice, William Franklin.
See *Lives in Loyalists of the American Revolution,* by Lorenzo Sabine.

SOUTH CAROLINA.

The fundamental constitution of South Carolina was adopted at the time of its settlement, in 1670-71, under its charter of 1663.

As early as 1712, by a special act, the Assembly adopted the English Common Law as a rule of adjudicature, and also 126 English statutes which had been selected by Chief Justice Trott as applicable to the condition of the Colony. Before that, there had been doubt as to how far the English Law was applicable; and in 1692, the Assembly, in an address to Governor Ludwell, had complained because the court had "assumed to put in force such English laws as they deemed adapted to the province; but the Assembly conceived that either such laws were valid of their own force or could only be made so by an act of the Assembly."

No law passed prior to 1682 is to be found on record. The first authority for printing the laws was given in 1712. There is no regular record of any judicial proceedings, prior to 1703, nor any record entered in any bound books, prior to 1710. Regular court records are extant from 1716.

The first compilation of the law was made by Chief Justice Trott in 1734, the second by Judge Grimke in 1789.

For many years the Chief Justice of the Colony constituted the whole court; and there were no assistant judges prior to 1736.

For nearly 100 years Charleston was the sole source and centre of all judicial proceedings.(1) This condition, however, became so intolerable, owing to the expense of attending court and the delays in obtaining justice, that in 1769, Circuit Courts were established in the various counties. The amount of business transacted in the courts was not large; as it is said that in the seven years before the War of the Revolution, the average number of judgments yearly in the whole Colony was only 236.

The first Chief Justice of record was Edmund Bohun, in 1698, a man of no legal training; the next, in 1702, Nicholas Trott, an English lawyer of distinction. He remained in office for many years, finally becoming so arbitrary and so obnoxious that, in 1717, articles of complaint were brought by "Richard Allein, Richard Whittaker and other practitioners of law," alleging that he had "contrived many ways to multiply and increase his fees—"

---

(1) It is curious to note that the old English Courts of Pipowder (or Market Courts) were revived in South Carolina from 1723 to 1738. See *Pipowder Courts, Green Bag,* Vol. V.

that he gave advice in causes depending in his courts, and not only acted as counsellor in these cases, but had drawn deeds between party and party, and that the whole judicial power of the province was lodged in his hands, he being, at the same time, sole judge of the Court of Common Pleas, Kings Bench, Vice Admiralty, also member of the Council and hence Judge of the Court of Chancery. The Governor, Council and Assembly joined in an address to the Proprietary for his removal, which request was not, however, granted.

From 1698 to 1776, there were fourteen Chief Justices, and from 1736 to 1776 twenty-seven associate judges; but scarcely anything is known concerning them, except that they had little legal training.

As William Henry Drayton, (later Chief Justice), writing about the time of the Revolution, says, "A few years ago, the bench of justice in this Colony was filled with men of property, and if all of them were not learned in the law, there were some among them who taught their brethren to administer justice with public approbation; and one in particular, (Rawlins Lowndes) had so well digested his reading, although he had never eat commons at the Temple, that he was without dispute, at least, equal to the law learning of the present bench."(1)

At the beginning of the Revolution the only native American on the bench was Drayton.

Of the early lawyers little is known. In the twenty-seven years prior to the Revolution, the whole number admitted to the Bar was 58; in the twenty-five years after the Revolution, 238 were admitted in Charleston alone.

In 1761, at the time when John Rutledge, the earliest of South Carolina's great lawyers, began to practice, the Bar consisted of probably not more than twenty. But though small in numbers, it was more highly educated than any Bar in America, for a considerable proportion of its members had received their legal training in England. Thus, William Wragg, one of the earliest lawyers, born in 1741, was an English barrister; Peter Manigault, born in 1731, was a barrister of the Inner Temple, and returned to practice in South Carolina in 1754. John Rutledge, born in 1739, studied in the office of James Parsons, at Charleston, and

_____

(1) *Life and Times of William Lowndes,* by Mrs. St. J. Ravenel.

became a barrister of the Inner Temple in 1761. Returning to Charleston, he at once took rank as the ablest lawyer of the Province, headed the Stamp Act opposition, was one of the Signers, and became Chief Justice of the State Court in 1791, and of the United States Supreme Court in 1798. William Henry Drayton, "the Sam Adams of the South", born in 1742, was educated at Oxford. Thomas Heyward, born in 1746, became a barrister of the Middle Temple, and was one of the Signers. Thomas Lynch, Jr., born in 1749, a barrister of the Middle Temple, was the third Signer from South Carolina.

Of the generation of lawyers who came into practice at the time of the Revolution who studied in the Inner Temple were John Laurens, born in 1755; John Julian Pringle, born in 1753; Edward Rutledge, born in 1749; Charles Cotesworth Pinckney, born in 1746; Thomas Pinckney, born in 1750; William H. Gibbes, born in 1754; and Hugh Rutledge, born in 1741. John F. Grimke, Theodore Gaillard and Arthur Middleton received their education in English universities. Aedanus Burke, born in 1743, was educated as a priest in the College of St. Omer in France. Richard Hutson, born in 1747, and later Chancellor, was a graduate of Princeton.

After the Revolution almost all the lawyers of distinction were college graduates.(1)

NOTE.

For authorities in general see:
History of South Carolina, by David Ramsay (1808).
Sketch of History of South Carolina, by W. J. Revers (1856).

(1) From Princeton graduated Timothy Ford; William Johnson, (born in 1771 later Judge of United States Supreme Court); John Taylor, Charles J. Colcott, Daniel E. Huger, John McCrady.

From Yale graduated Abraham Nott, Isaac Griggs, Enoch Hanford, John Gadsen.

From Litchfield Law School graduated William D. Martin, John C. Calhoun, Benjamin C. Yancey, Edmund Bacon.

From Brown graduated John Dick Witherspoon, Abraham Blanding.

Among those who received no collegiate education outside of South Carolina were the famous chancellor Henry William De Saussure, the "Kent of South Carolina," (born in 1763, studied law with Jared Ingersoll and admitted to Philadelphia Bar in 1789); Elihu H. Bay, Judge and reporter of decisions, (born in 1754); Henry Pendleton, Keating Lewis Simons, Charles Pinckney, Thomas Lee, (born in 1769), Robert Y. Hayne, (born in 1791), Hugh Swinton Legaré, (born in 1797), William Lowndes, (born in 1782).

The principal offices for study were those of Charles Cotesworth Pickney, (who numbered among his students William Johnson, John Taylor, John McCrady) and of John and Edward Rutledge.

View of the Constitution of the British Colonies in North America and the West Indies, by Anthony Stokes (1783).

Glance at our Colonial Bar, Green Bag. Vol. XI.

Willis on *Law and Lawyers, Amer. Quarterly Review.* Vol. XIV and Vol. XV.

Bench and Bar of South Carolina, by John B. O'Neall (1859).

Old Virginia and her Neighbors, by John Fiske (1897).

Life and Times of William Lowndes, by Mrs. St. J. Ravenel (1901).

NORTH CAROLINA.

In North Carolina, John Locke's Constitution, framed in 1669, called the *Grand Model,* prescribed a form of government and an institution of law and law procedure, differing from anything in America. Proving too impracticable and chimerical, it was abrogated in 1693; and, 1715, an act was passed, providing that the Common Law should be in force, "so far as shall be compatible with our way of living and trade", and certain specific English statutes were also adopted. No compilation of laws was made until 1732. A Commission was appointed to revise the laws in 1746, and again in 1776; and the first printed collection of laws was in 1751.

At first the Governor and Council acted as the Court. Later a General Court, consisting of a Chief Justice, and two to ten assistant judges, was established. The earliest Chief Justice named in the Records was the famous Anthony Ashley Cooper, Lord Shaftesbury, who exercised the duties of his post through a deputy. Only a few of the Chief Justices prior to 1746 were trained lawyers, and when such, they were English barristers sent from England, the first barrister coming in 1731; but in 1746, a Superior Court was constituted, the judges of which were required by statute to be lawyers.

Under Locke's Constitution, the prejudice against lawyers was shown by the provisions in the 10th article, that "it shall be a base and vile thing to plead for money or reward", and that no one but a near kinsman should plead another's cause, until he had taken an oath in open court that he had not "directly or indirectly bargained for money or other reward." It was also provided, that "since multiplicity of comments as well as of laws have great inconveniences and serve only to obscure and perplex, all manner of comments and expositions on any part of these fundamental constitutions or on any part of the common or statute law of Carolina, are absolutely prohibited."

Early in the 18th Century, however, attorneys and advocates were allowed to practice; but the Court ordered that they must be licensed by the Chief Justice and Judges; and that no sheriff, undersheriff, or clerk should plead as attorney at law.

In 1743, attorneys were made liable for double damages to clients suffering from neglience in the management of a cause.

Of North Carolina lawyers little is recorded; but the condition of education in the Colony was unfavorable to the development of native talent.

One of the earliest lawyers of note was Thomas Barker, one of the commissioners appointed to revise the Statutes in 1746, the early friend and instructor of Samuel Johnston. The latter was born in Scotland in 1733, and was "pre-eminent in the province for ability, learning, wealth, and character." He was Governor of the State in 1782, and a Judge of the Superior Court in 1800.

Other early lawyers were Henry Eustace McCulloch, a barrister of the Inner Temple, who practised in the Province from 1761 to 1767; Thomas Jones and Alexander Elmsly, both English lawyers; John Dawson, a Virginian; William Avery, born in Connecticut, a Princeton graduate, and Attorney General in 1777; Jasper Charlton; William Cumming and Robert Smith.

Undoubtedly the most prominent of all the North Carolina Bar was James Iredell, who was born in England in 1751, and who came to the Province in 1768, where he studied law under Samuel Johnston, and in 1770, "with the approbation and recommendation of Chief Justice Howard, received from Governor Tryon a license to practise law in all the Inferior Courts." In 1771, he was licensed by the Governor to practise in the Superior Courts.

Of the conditions of the legal profession in North Carolina in those days the following graphic account is given(1):

Upon horseback, often alone, through the dense forests and across the almost trackless Savannahs . . . the lawyer of that day travelled his weary circuit. . . . Accommodations by the way were generally despicably vile; inns or taverns in the true sense had no existence. After the fatigue of a long day's

---

(1) *Life and Correspondence of James Iredell,* by Griffith J. McRee (1857).

journey the wayworn traveller was often content with a bench
by the hearth of some primitive log cabin—Books he had not,
save a volume or two stuffed into his saddle-bags with a scanty
supply of apparel.   At this period, too, in what was then
called the "back country", now the interior of North Carolina, the gentlemen of the bar were objects of obloquy and
denunciation to a generally poor and illiterate people, and frequently experienced at their hands the grossest outrages. . . . .
The people justly complained of the burden of their taxes—a
burden augmented by the extortion of illegal fees by the officers
of the courts; but with a blind prejudice, many of them only
saw in the profession, those who defended their oppressors, and
who prosecuted them when their opposition broke out into acts
of violence. Uncultivated settlers who subdue the wilderness are
apt to look with suspicion upon the proprietor of the soil when
he demands rent for his land or its value;—and the attorneys
employed to bring ejectments or sue for use, as the venal instruments of tyranny, bandits hired by gold to despoil them of
the fruits of their honest industry.

In 1777, Iredell became Judge of the Superior Court, resigning
the next year.   In 1789, he was appointed Judge of the Supreme
Court of the United States.

Contemporary with him, after the Revolution, were Abner
Maurice Moore; Archibald McClaine; Alfred Moore, who, born
in 1755, a student at Harvard but not a graduate, succeeded Iredell in the United States Supreme Court; William R. Davie, born
in England in 1756, a Princeton graduate of 1776, admitted to
practise in North Carolina in 1780, and of whom it was said "if
he had superiors in legal learning and close reasoning, he as an
orator was inferior to none in the State;" John Hayward, who
was born in 1753, became Attorney General in 1791 and published his reports in   .

Both of the signers of the Declaration of Independence from
North Carolina, were lawyers.   One, William Hooper, was born
in Boston in 1742, a graduate of Harvard in 1760, and a student
under James Otis in 1761, the same year in which Otis argued
the Writs of Assistance.   He came to North Carolina in 1767,
and within six years became a leading member of the Bar.   The
other, John Penn, was born in Virginia in 1741, a student under
Edmund Pendleton, and removed to North Carolina in 1774.

The early courts after the Revolution under the State Judiciary
Act of 1777 were composed of men of very inferior learning and
personality;   and Iredell's resignation in 1778 from the court

was due to the fact that "unable to determine the opinions of the court, he was unwilling to share the discredit of ignorance or participate in the odium of illegal decisions."

NOTE.

For authorities in general, see:

History of North Carolina, by F. L. Hawke (1889).

English Common Law in the early American Colonies, by Paul F. Reinsch.

Sanderson's *Lives of the Signers.*

Life and Correspondence of James Iredell, by Griffith J. Mc-Ree (1857).

Address on the Life of William Hooper, by Edward A. Alderman (1894).

Life of William R. Davie, in *Spark's American Biography.*

The Supreme Court of North Carolina, by Walter Clark, *Green Bag,* Vol. IV.

Alfred Moore, Green Bag, Vol. XII.

A Masterpiece of Constitutional Folly, Green Bag, Vol. XII.

GEORGIA.

No laws were passed by the General Assembly of Georgia until 1755, the Colony having previously been under the arbitrary rule of the Proprietor.

In 1762, an act was passed to encourage a printer to set up a printing press and to print the laws, and in 1779 the first digest of laws was made.

The first court of Georgia, held at Savannah in 1733, was lawyerless; but when Georgia became a Crown Colony in 1752, the Chief Justice was required to be an English barrister. The three assistant judges were usually laymen of high standing in the community, and received no salaries.

In 1789, the Superior Court of the State was established. The native Bar of the early 18th Century was small; but a few English barristers practised in Savannah. George Walton, one of the Signers, who was born in Virginia in 1740, admitted to the Bar there in 1774, and removed to Georgia, is one of the few American lawyers of the State whose name survives.

Of the Bar, Stokes wrote in 1783:

The practical part has so employed the attention of colonial advocates that few have leisure to attain to any considerable degree of knowledge and the advocate who has the greatest fluency may sometimes be considered as the ablest lawyer. . . . Most of the questions which arise in the colonies are founded in litigation and not in intricacy.

Of Georgia's lawyers of the later years of the 18th Century, four have taken places well at the front of the American Bar: Abraham Baldwin(1), John McPherson Berrien(2), William H. Crawford(3) and James M. Wayne(4).

The Bar, though small, contained, however, like that of South Carolina, a large proportion of educated men. In Miller's *Bench and Bar of Georgia,* published in 1858, thirty-three lawyers are mentioned, of whom nineteen were born prior to 1800. Of these, one was a graduate of Yale, Abraham Baldwin; five of Princeton, Berrien, Wayne, John Forsythe, Peter Early and Walter T. Colquitt; and four of Litchfield Law School (to which institution, it is said, Georgia sent more students than any State outside of New England and New York)—Lucius Q. C. Lamar, William C. Dawson, Thomas F. Foster and Robert Rutherford.

NOTE.

For authorities in general see:
Bench and Bar of Georgia, by Stephen F. Miller (1858).
Glance at our Colonial Bar, Green Bag, Vol. XI.
History of Georgia, by Charles C. Jones (1883).
History of Augusta, by Salem Dutcher (1890).
Georgia Law Books, by Joseph R. Lamar in *Georgia Bar Assn. Proc.* Vol. XV.
A Lawyerless Court, by Walter G. Charlton in *Georgia Bar Assn. Proc.* Vol. XVIII.
Georgia Lawyers Viewed by a Woman, in *Georgia Bar Assn. Proc.* Vol. XVIII.

(1)   Born in Connecticut in 1754, a Yale graduate of 1772, U. S. Senator 1799-1807.
(2)   Born in 1781, Princeton graduate of 1796, Judge U. S. District Court 1810-21, U. S. Senator 1825-9, 1840-52, Atty. Gen. of United States 1829-31.
(3)   Born in 1772, U. S. Senator 1807-16.
(4)   Born in 1790, Princeton graduate of 1808, Judge of Georgia Superior Court 1824-29, Judge of U. S. Supreme Court 1835.

CHAPTER V.

The 18th Century in England was a period in which the law itself was being rapidly made, and great judges were making it.

In 1700, Chief Justice Holt came upon the King's Bench; and in 1704, (a year before the birth of Lord Mansfield) gave forth his epochal decision in *Coggs v. Barnard* (2 Lord Raym. 909). This was eighteen years before the first legally trained lawyer took his place on the Massachusetts Bench, three years after the first lawyer sat on the Pennsylvania Bench, and eleven years before the first educated lawyers appeared at the New York Bar.

In 1756, Sir William Murray, Lord Mansfield, became Lord Chief Justice of England. This was the year when John Adams began to study law,—four years before Patrick Henry was admitted to the Bar, and while John Rutledge was studying in the Temple.

The *Leading Cases,* (so called by the text book writers of the 19th Century) were, between 1700 to 1785, coming fresh from the printing press each year. Cases now familiar to law students as historical landmarks were then of vivid interest to the practising lawyers of the American Colonies.

Thus in 1711 came the first case on restraint of trade, *Mitchell v. Reynolds* (1 P. Wms.); in 1719, the case of *Cumber v. Wane* (1 Strange 426), involving the doctrine of consideration, was decided; in 1722, *Armory v. Delamire* (1 Strange 504), the chimney sweep and the jeweler case; in 1750, *Penn v. Baltimore* (1 Ves. 444); in 1773, *Scott v. Shepard* (2 W. Bl. 892), the *Squib case,* as to actions of trespass; in 1774, *Fabrigas v. Mostyn* (Camp. 161), on transitory actions; in 1789, *Palsey v. Freeman* (3 T. R. 51), establishing the law of deceit; and many others whose names are like old friends to the lawyer and student of today.

In these years too occurred the great State trials, like those of the Jacobites, Lord Kilmarnock, Lord Balmerino, and Lord Lovat for treason, before Lord Hardwicke in the House of Lords in 1746; the trial of John Wilkes for seditious libel, before Lord Camden in the Court of Common Pleas, in 1763; *Rex v. Woodfall,* in 1770, as to the publication of the Junius letters, the trial of Lord George Gordon in 1781; the famous legal battle on the law of libel, in the trial of the dean of St. Asaphs, in 1783; the beginning of the impeachment trial of Warren Hastings, in 1787.

The status of Common Law in England, as it was when Lord Mansfield came on the bench, is thus described by Lord Campbell:

This system was not at all badly adapted to the condition of England in the Norman and early Plantagenet reigns, when it sprang up,—land being then the only property worth considering, and the wants of society only requiring rules to be laid down by public authority for ascertaining the different rights and interests arising out of land, and determining how they should be enjoyed, alienated, and transmitted from one generation to another. In the Reign of George II, England had grown into the greatest manufacturing and commercial country in the world, while her jurisprudence had by no means been expanded or developed in the same proportion. The legislature had literally done nothing to supply the insufficiency of feudal law to regulate the concerns of a trading population; and the Common Law Judges had, generally speaking, been too unenlightened and too timorous to be of much service in improving our code by judicial decisions. Hence, when questions necessarily arose respecting the buying and selling of goods,—respecting the affreightment of ships, respecting marine insurances,—and respecting bills of exchange and promissory notes, no one knew how they were to be determined. Not a treatise had been published upon any of these subjects, and no cases respecting them were to be found in our books of reports,—which swarmed with decisions about lords and villeins,—about marshaling the champions upon the trial of a writ of right by battle,—and about the customs of manors, whereby an unchaste widow might save the forfeiture of her dower by riding on a black ram and in plain language confessing her offense. Lord Hardwicke had done much to improve and systematize Equity—but proceedings were still carried on in the courts of Common Law much in the same style as in the days of Sir Robert Tresilian and Sir William Gascoigne. Mercantile questions were so ignorantly treated when they came into Westminster Hall, that they were usually settled by private arbitration among the merchants themselves. If an action turning upon a mercantile question was brought in a court of law, the judge submitted it to the jury, who determined it according to their own notions of what was fair, and no general rule was laid down which could afterwards be referred to for the purpose of settling similar disputes.(1)

With the latter half of the Century, however, began the modern common law of business and personal relations, as distinguished from the old feudal common law, confined as it was to questions of realty and pleading. The wide range of contract law began to be opened out. The doctrines of the laws of bills and notes, insurance, and maritime commerce became fixed. The law of evidence, none of the present rules of which, except that excluding hearsay, were well established prior to 1688, was becoming well developed. On the other hand, the law of torts was hardly in existence before 1800; there were no negligence cases; the great contests of Erskine and Fox on the law of libel had not begun. The law of business corporations did not exist.

It was not until 1733, that Sir Peter King, Lord Chancellor, finally prevailed upon Parliament to provide that the English language should thenceforth be used in all law proceedings, although Lord Chief Justice Raymond and all other judges had opposed the change.

Coincident with the opinions on modern Common Law had been the advent of the first law reports of anything like modern accuracy—*Lord Raymond's Reports, Salkeld* and *Comyns* (of indifferent worth but covering Lord Holt's career); *Burrow's Reports* (1757-1771), *Cowper* (1774-1778) and *Douglas* (1778-1784) covering Lord Mansfield's decisions; and *Term Reports* (1785-1800) covering the term of Chief Justice Kenyon.

Of Chancery Reports, those of *Peere Williams* (1695-1736) were the chief source of study in the early part of the Century; while *Atkyns, Vesey Sr.* and *Ambler* included the decisions of the greatest of all the Chancellors, Philip Yorke, (Lord Hardwicke) (1737-1756); and *Cox* and *Vesey Jr.* reported the decisions of Charles Pratt, (Earl Camden) and of Lord Thurlow.

Nevertheless, even as late as 1776, hardly more than one hundred and fifty volumes of reports were in existence in England. And probably not one half of these, had crossed the Atlantic; while hardly thirty were in familiar use in America.

Of law books of importance, the following were published during this Century. Hawkins *Pleas of the Crown* was published first in 1716, Hale's *Pleas of the Crown* in 1736, and Foster's

(1) Campbell's *Lives of the Chief Justices,* Vol. III., p. 299.

in 1763. Wood's *Institutes* appeared in 1722. Bacon's *Abridgment* was published in 1736; Jacob's *Law Dictionary* in 1729; Fonblanque's *Equity* in 1737;(1) Viner's *Digest* from 1742 to 1753; Comyn's *Digest* appeared between 1762 and 1767; Bohun's *Declaration* in 1743; Lilly's *Register* in 1745; Rutherforth's *Institutes of Natural Law* from 1754-56; Fearne's *Contingent Remainders* in 1772; Reeves' *History of English Law to the time of Elizabeth* in 1787. Of Blackstone's *Commentaries,* in 1765, mention will be made later. At the very end of the Century appeared Woodeson's *Elements of Jurisprudence* in 1783, Park's *Marine Insurance* in 1786, Jones' *Bailments* in 1790, Powell's *Contracts* in 1790, Bayley's *Bills and Notes* in 1789, Chitty's *Bills and Notes,* and Tidd's *Practice* in 1799.

This list after all is a scanty one; but in America few of these text books were known, and fewer still were to be obtained.

The education of a law student in England during this Century was of the most meagre description. The old mootings and readings in the Inns of Courts had practically died out.

Roger North wrote some years before his death (which occurred in 1733) a *Discourse on the Study of the Law* in which he said(2):

Of all the professions in the world that pretend to book learning, none is so destitute of institution as that of the Common Law. Academick studies which take in that of the civil law, have tutors and professors to aid them, and the students are entertained in colleges under a discipline, in the midst of societies, that are, or should be, devoted to study; which encourages, as well as demonstrates, such methods in general as everyone may easily apply to his own particular use. But for the Common Law, however, there are societies which have the outward show or pretense of Collegiate Institution, yet in reality nothing of that sort is now to be found in them; and whereas in more ancient times there were exercises used in the Hall, they were more for probation than for institution; now even those are shrunk into mere form, and that preserved only for conformity to rules, that gentlemen by tale of appearances in exercises rather than by any sort of performances might be entitled to be called to the Bar.

(1)   Up to the publication of Joseph Story's books on *Equity*, Fonblanque's *Equity* was for one hundred years the best elementary book on equity in use in America. "It finally expired under the weight of its own notes" says J. C. Marvin in his *Legal Bibliography.*
(2)   This discourse was not published until 1824. See *Early History of Legal Studies in England,* by Joseph Walton, *Amer. Bar Assn. Proc.* Vol. XXII (1899).

And it has been recently said:

There was really no legal education at the Inns of Court in the year 1800. In the days of Queen Elizabeth and James I regular courses of study were prescribed, attendance at moots and in hall was insisted on and discipline was vigorously maintained. But that had all fallen into misuse or lingered only in a few antiquated forms. There were still a few so called exercises. A student after dining in hall was provided with a printed form of questions. Armed with this he would trembling approach the dais and say to the first good natured looking bencher whose eyes he could catch, "If I were seized in fee of Blackacre"—The bencher smiled and bowed. The student continuing the enunciation of the problem concluding boldly with these words which were not on the paper "I maintain the widow shall have her dower." The bencher bowed again and the student retired having "kept his exercise." Any student who had eaten the prescribed number of dinners and paid his fees was made a counsellor at law; the ceremony was conducted like the return of stolen goods "without any questions being asked"; he need never have read a single page of any law book. S. Ireland in his historical account of the Inns of Court published in 1800 adverts to the "ceremony of mootyng" as "a custom long since in disuse except in New Inn for the benefit of students of the Middle Temple where about a year and a half since we are informed a mootyng took place to the no small diversion of the passers by."

The students had in fact to teach each other. There was in Tidd's office a society which met once a week exclusively for the discussion of legal questions. It was modelled upon the plan of the Court at Westminster with a Chief Justice and counsel.(1)

Students of the 18th Century gave their time largely to the pleasures of London. The *Spectator* of March 24, 1710, speaks of that "numberless branch of peaceable lawyers—those young men who being placed in the Inns of Court in order to study the laws of their country frequent the playhouse more than Westminster Hall and are seen in all public assemblies except in a court of justice."

As stated above, no qualifications were required by the Benchers of the Inns of those whom they were supposed to examine to be called as barristers, except the proof that they had kept twelve terms by eating the requisite number of dinners in the Inn.

Some few students, like Lord Thurlow about 1750, were placed in the office of a solicitor where they learned how actions were commenced and conducted, together with the practice of the courts.

---

(1) *A Century of Law Reform,* Chap. I., by W. B. Odgers (1901).

It was not, however, until the latter part of the 18th Century that the regular practice began of studying in the office of some distinguished special pleader. This "pupilizing system" was introduced by the special pleaders Thomas Warren and Mr. (later Mr. Justice) Buller; and in their offices and in those of George Wood, Tindal and Tidd were educated many of England's most famous judges; Erskine, Copley (Lord Lyndhurst), Cottenham, Campbell, Brougham, Parke (Lord Wenleysdale), Abbott (Lord Tenterden), and Denman.

The life of a student in such an office is well described by Lord Campbell in 1803:

I got a letter from Mackintosh to Tidd the most eminent special pleader in England. With him I begin my studies in arte placitandi next week. He has six or a dozen pupils besides, dashing young fellows. . . . The terms of all special pleaders are the same, viz: 100 guineas for one year or 200 guineas for three years. Tidd is by far the first man in this line. He has constantly from 10 to 15 pupils . . . . It is impossible for you to form any conception of the idleness of most of the nascent plea drawers. They drop into the office for half an hour on their way to Bond Street. For weeks and months they remain away altogether. When they are assembled the subjects discussed are not cases and precedents but the particulars of a new fashion in dress or the respective merits of the Young Chicken and Signora Crassini . . . . Nothing but the irresistible motives which spur me on could enable me to combat the disgust inspired by special pleading. It is founded upon reason but rude, rude is the superstructure. This however is now a necessary post in carrying on your professional advances. The four judges who preside in the court of King's Bench all practised as special pleaders . . . . I continue to go regularly at eleven and stay till four . . . . In Tidd's office there was a society which met weekly for the discussion of juridical questions. This consisted of his pupils for the time being (among them Pepys) and any former pupils who chose to attend (among them Denman and Copley) . . . . Special pleaders in general are not at the Bar. One or two who remain pleaders permanently are considered as something between attorneys and barristers but the common way is for a young man to plead a few years under the bar as they call it before being called. It is easier to get this kind of business than briefs in court and you thus gradually form and extend your connections.—Tidd is a man of very low origin— He was clerk to an eminent man in this line and his master dying he set up for himself—He published a *Practice of the Court of King's Bench* which has passed through several editions and gained him high celebrity. He makes between 2000 and 3000 pounds a year . . . . He takes very little pains with his pupils. He comes about one o'clock, saying "How d'ye do" as he passes into his own room, remains there until four or five correcting what has been drawn, nods to any straggler who is still remaining and returns to Vauxhall for the day. His office however for a man really desirous and determined to improve himself is in my mind far the best in London. You see here such a quantity and such a variety of business that you may learn more in six months than by reading or hearing lectures for seven years.(1)

Of the course pursued by a student who could not enter a special pleader's office, Campbell's account of the student days of John Scott (Lord Eldon) gives the best idea:(2)

The custom having been introduced for law students to become pupils of a special pleader or equity draughtsman, Mr. Scott would have been glad to have conformed to it if the state of his finances would have enabled him to pay the usual fee of a hundred guineas. . . . . Mr. Duane, an eminent Catholic conveyancer agreed to let him have the run of his chambers for six months without a fee. (Conveyancing was chiefly in the hands of Roman Catholics, being prevented from being called to the Bar they practiced successfully in Chambers.)—To supply the deficiency arising from his not having been with a special pleader or equity drafts-man he copied all the MSS forms he could lay his hands upon.

He went through a systematic course of reports and coming down to a Reporter of such low credit as Vernon he could tell the names of most of the cases reported with the volume and page where they could be found.

We are not told that he ever dipped into the *Code,* the *Pandects,* or the *Institutes of Justinian;* or that he found any pleasure in *Puffendorf* or *Grotius* or that he ever formed the slightest acquaintance with *D'Agnesseau* or *Pothier.* Nor in any of his arguments at the Bar or judgments from the Bench does he as far as I am aware ever refer to the civil law or any foreign writer as authority or by way of illustration.

The course of reading advisable for a student either in his own or a special pleader's chambers was stated by Lord Chief Justice Reeves in 1787 as follows:

Read Wood's *Institutes* cursorily and for explanation of the same, Jacob's *Dictionary.* Next strike out what lights you can from Bohun's *Institutio Legalis,* and Jacob's *Practising Attor-*

---

(1) *Life of Lord Campbell,* Vol. I.
(2) Campbell's *Lives of the Lord Chancellors,* Vol. IX.

ney's Companion, and the like, helping yourself by Indexes. Then read and consider Littleton's *Tenures* without notes and abridge it. Then venture on Coke's *Commentaries.* After reading it once, read it again, for it will require many readings. Abridge it. Commonplace it. Make it your own, applying to it the faculties of your mind. Then read Sergeant Hawkins to throw light on Lord Coke. Then read Wood again to throw light on Sergeant Hawkins. And then read the statutes at large to throw light on Mr. Wood.

In spite of this elaborate course for law students, the *Bibliotheca Legum Angliae* by John Worrall and Edward Brooke, published in 1788, mentions as the only books expressly intended for students; *Blackstone, Eunomus or Dialogues upon the Law and Constitution of England;* and the *Elements of Jurisprudence* by Dr. Wooddeson, (Blackstone's successor as Vinerian Professor at Oxford). To these may be added Francis S. Sullivan's *Lectures on the Constitution and Laws of England,* published in 1776.

Undoubtedly the real education gained by a law student in the 18th Century was through attendance at the various courts.

Dr. Johnson said to Boswell "you must take care to attend constantly in Westminster Hall, both to mind your business, as it is almost all learnt there, (for nobody reads now), and to show that you want to have business."

Thus, it is said that Lord Mansfield's chief resource, in 1730 when studying at Lincoln's Inn, was in listening to the judgments of Lord Chief Justice Raymond in King's Bench. To such an extent was he influenced by this method of gaining a liberal knowledge of the law that later, when he became a judge himself, he was in the habit, in giving his judgments, of explaining the intricacies of the cases before him and the reasons of his judgments "for the sake of the students."(1) He even caused a box in the court of King's Bench to be set apart for students to which students and barristers "flock by scores."

So too, it was said of John Scott (Lord Eldon), that "he diligently attended the courts in Westminster Hall (1775) with his note book in his hand. Lord Bathurst presiding in the court of Chancery, from whom little was to be learned, he took his place in the students box in the court of King's Bench, where Lord Mansfield shone in the zenith of his fame."

---

(1)   Campbell's *Lives of the Lord Chief Justices. Life of Lord Campbell.*

This practice of Lord Mansfield was followed also by Lord Kenyon; and, as Campbell writes in his diary, "our box being near the bench at Guildhall, Lord Kenyon, while the counsel were speaking, would bring the record to us and explain the issue joined upon it which the jury were to try."

Nothwithstanding the uselessness of the Inns of Courts as places of education, the 18th Century saw most of England's great lawyers called as barristers by these Inns; thus in the Inner Temple were, Thurlow, Comyns, Wedderburn (Lord Loughborough), Burrow, Lord Bathurst, Charles Talbot, George Grenville, Pratt (Lord Camden), and Abbott (Lord Tenterden); in the Middle Temple—Kenyon, Dunning, Scott (Lord Eldon); in Lincoln's Inn—Murray (Lord Mansfield), Charles Yorke, Law (Lord Ellenborough), Erskine, Copley (Lord Lyndhurst); Campbell in 1800, Denman in 1801, and Brougham in 1803.

CHAPTER VI.

A Colonial Lawyer's Education in the 18th Century.

Acquisition of the law is difficult without ready means of access to the books of the law and these were sadly lacking in the American Provinces.

Of the reports published in England by the time of the American Revolution (not over one hundred and fifty in number) hardly more than thirty were in familiar use on this side of the Atlantic; and the number of text books accessible was even smaller. Practically all the law books used in the Colonies were imported from England.

Although printing had begun in the Colonies as early as 1638-9, when Stephen Daye printed, at Cambridge, *The Oath of a Freeman*, the vast proportion of all books printed, from that date down to the American Revolution, was of a religious or historical nature. A careful examination of elaborate *American Bibliographies* discloses only thirty-three law books printed in America prior to 1776, including in this number at least eight repeated editions of the same book. (1)

Most of these books were manuals for use of Justices of the Peace, Sheriffs and other petty officers, and treatises on the general rights of Englishmen, and especially of Juries.

The first seven law books printed fairly illustrate the whole list.

1680—*Reasons for Indictment of the Duke of York, Presented to the Grand Jury of Middlesex Saturday June 26, 1680* (Boston).

1693—*The Englishman's Right, A Dialogue between a Barrister at Law and a Juryman, plainly setting forth the antiquity, the excellent designed use and office and just privileges of juries by the laws of England*, by Sir John Hawles (Boston).

1705—*Lex Mercatoria Or the Just Rules of Commerce Declared. And Offences against the Rules of Justice in the Dealings of men with one another selected*, by Cotton Mather (Boston).

---

(1) See the monumental work of Charles Evans, *American Bibliography*, Volumes I, II, III, (1893) and Isaiah Thomas *History of Printing in America*, published in Vol. VI of *American Antiquarian Society Proceedings* (1874).

1710—*The Constable's Pocket Book: Or a Dialogue between an old Constable and a new, being a guide in their keeping the peace*, by Nicholas Boone (Boston).

1716—*Lex Parliamentaria or a Treatise on the Law and Custom of the Parliaments of England*, by George Petyt (London, printed and reprinted in N. Y. and sold by William and Andrew Bradford in N. Y. and Phila.).

1720—*The Security of Englishmen's Lives or the Trust, Power, and Duty of the Grand Jurys of England*, by John Somers.

1721—*English liberties or the Freeborn Subjects' Inheritance, containing Magna Charta, Charta de Foresta, the Statute De Tallagio non Concedendo, the Habeas Corpus Act and several other statutes with comments on each of them.*

Likewise the Proceedings in Appeals of Murder; of Ship Money; of Tonnage and Poundage; of Parliaments and the qualification and choice of members; of the three estates and of the settlement of the Crown by Parliament. Together with a short history of the succession not by any hereditary right; Also a declaration of the liberties of the subject; and of the oath of allegiance and supremacy. The Petition of Right with a short but impartial relation of the difference between King Charles I and the Long Parliament concerning the Prerogative of the King, the Liberties of the Subject and the rise of the Civil Wars. Of trials by Jury and of the qualifications of Jurors; their punishment for misbehaviour and of challenges to them. Lastly of Justices of the Peace, Coroners, Constables, Churchwardens, Overseers of the Poor, Surveyors of the Highway, etc. with many law cases throughout the whole and Compiled first by Henry Care and continued with large additions by W. N. of the Middle Temple Esq. The fifth edition.

There was no law book written by an American until 1736, when George Webb of Virginia published:

The Office and Authority of a Justice of the Peace. And also the duty of Sheriffs, Constables, Coroners, Church Wardens, Surveyors of Highways, Constables & Officers of Militia. Together with precedents of warrants, judgments, executions and other legal process, issuable by magistrates within their respective jurisdictions, civil or criminal, and the method of judicial proceedings before justices of peace in matters within their cognisance out of sessions, collected from the common and statute laws of England and acts of assembly now in force; and adapted to the Constitution and practice of Virginia. By George Webb Gent. one of his Majesty's Justices of Peace of the County of New Kent (Williamsburg, Va., printed by William Parks 1736).

There were also printed about thirty-five or forty books or pamphlets giving reports of famous cases, of which all but

five or six were of criminal trials, murder, burglary and piracy.
The first of these was the trial of Thomas Southerland for murder
in West Jersey, printed in 1692; the next, the trial of Col. Nicholas
Bayard in New York for high treason, published in 1702. A report
of a case in Chancery in New York was printed in 1727. In 1736,
John Zenger printed a report of his famous trial for libel in New
York in 1735. Two years later, another report of this trial was
printed in Philadelphia, with comments by English barristers of
the Barbadoes.

In 1753, a report of the case of *William Fletcher v. William
Vassall* for defamation, tried in the Massachusetts Superior Court
and pending on appeal to the King in Council, was printed. A
report of the trial of Admiral Byng by Court martial in England
was printed in 1757. A full account was printed in 1763 of the
famous proceedings against John Wilkes in England, to which
was appended *"An Abstract of that Precious Jewel of an Englishman, the Habeas Corpus Act, also the North Briton No. 45 being
the paper for which Mr. Wilkes was sent to the Tower—Addressed to All Lovers of Liberty."*

In 1770, a full report of the trial of the British soldiers in Boston for murder was published.

In 1774, was printed *Arguments against Slavery in the case
of James Somerset, a negro, lately determined in the Court of
King's Bench; wherein is attempted to demonstrate the unlaw-
fulness of Domestic Slavery in England,* by Francis Hargrave.

No reprint was made in America, prior to 1776, of Coke, or of
any standard English law writer, except Blackstone. There was
no reprint of any English Law Reports.

It is not surprising therefore that scant references are found
to English cases, or law reports in the Colonial Court records;
or that as a rule, the early cases contained citations of only the
most elementary books, writers and principles. (1)

---

(1) Thus Wood's *Institutes* and Hale's *Analysis of the Law* seem to
have been favorite citations of Chief Justice Sewall in the early part of
the 18th Century in Massachusetts. As early as 1730, in a printed argument in the Superior Court in Massachusetts, citations are found of 1
Coke, 2 Coke Rep., 1 *Modern, Hobart* and *Chancery Cases.*
   In the Zenger libel case in New York in 1735 counsel quoted freely
from Coke's *Inst.* 5 *Coke Rep. Vaughn's Reports,* Hawkins *Pleas of the
Crown,* decisions of Lord Holt.
   Some of the lawyers who came over from England brought with them
their acquired knowledge of English cases. Thus in South Carolina in
a trial of pirates in 1718 the Chief Justice Trott (an English barrister)
quotes *Spelman, Godolphin,* Coke's *First Institute,* Selden's *Notes on
Fortescue, Laws of Oleron, Digests* and *Pandects of Justinian.*

The early Colonial lawyers were hampered not only by this scant supply of law books and reports, but their difficulties in studying and determining the statutory law of the Colonies were even more serious. While Massachusetts and Connecticut printed their statutes reasonably early, the other colonies were late in doing so; thus the first collection of Colonial Laws of New York was published in 1710; the Acts and Laws of Rhode Island were first printed in 1730; those of New Jersey in 1732; those of Virginia in 1733; South Carolina in 1736; the first collection of Charters and other Public Acts relating to Pennsylvania in 1740 and all its laws in 1742; the laws, statutes, ordinances, and Constitution of the City of New York in 1749; Bacon's *Compilation of Laws,* in Maryland in 1765.

So few copies were printed however that it was unusual for any lawyer to possess a full set of the local laws of his colony.

"Even partial editions of Colonial laws (at least in Virginia) were extremely difficult to be obtained. Few gentlemen, even of the profession in this country, have ever been able to boast of possessing a complete collection of its laws," said St. George Tucker in 1803 in the preface to his edition of *Blackstone.*

The few law books and reports that existed in America were to be found almost entirely in the libraries of the richer lawyers, (1) and sometimes among the books of the local clergymen. "Fifty or one hundred volumes were considered a very considerable collection of books for a lawyer's library."(2) The following examples give some idea of the prevalent conditions. Even the largest library in the Colonies in the middle of the 18th Century, that of William Byrd the younger, in Virginia, contained only 350 volumes of law and statutes out of a total of 3625(3). And in the library of the wealthy Ralph Wormeley of Rosequill, Virginia, who died in 1701, a graduate of Oriel College, Oxford, and a trustee of William and Mary College, the only legal works were *Coke's Reports,* and *Coke's Institutes,* a collection of Virginia and of Massachusetts laws, a treatise on Maritime Law, and *The office of the Justice of the Peace.*

Judge Edmund Trowbridge of Massachusetts possessed what Theophilus Parsons called "not only the best but probably the

---

(1) George Bliss in his address to the Bar of Hampshire County Sept. 26, 1826, says John Worthington, Joseph Hawley and Jonathan Bliss had the only law libraries in all Western Massachusetts.

(2) *Biographical Sketches of Eminent Lawyers,* by S. L. Knapp, (1821).

(3) *Old Virginia,* by John Fiske.

only thoroughly good one (law library) then in New England and even in America". It contained all the valuable books on English law then in existence. (1) John Adams complained of impoverishing himself in order to provide himself with an adequate law library.

President Stiles of Yale writes, in 1790, of Governor Griswold, who was Chief Justice in 1769, that "he bought him the first considerable law library in Connecticut, took Att. oath an began practice in 1743—a great reader of law. Has a fine library of well chosen books—about 550 volumes, now left in his study, besides a part of his library given to his son in Norwich—about 200 Law Books, the rest history and divinity".(2)

The Philogrammatican Society of Connecticut, of which Jonathan Trumbull was Secretary, purchased for its library in 1738, ninety-four works of which the following were the only law books—Coke's *Institute's,* Lilly's *Abridgment,* Coke's *Reports,* Bohun's *Declarations and Pleadings,* Jacob's *Introduction to Common Civil and Canon law.*(3)

In the famous library of Rev. Thomas Prince of Boston, who died in 1758, out of about 1500 volumes, there were but five on the Common Law—*Britton* (1640), *English Liberties with Magna Charta etc.* (1721), Cowell's *Institutes of English Law* (1664), *The Exact Constable, Church Warden, etc.* (1682), Spelman's *Archaeologus* (1626). There was also a copy of the *General Laws and Liberties* (1672), Bacon's *Novum Organum,* Grotius on *War and Peace* (1680) and five books on civil and canon law.(4)

The inventory of the library of Patrick Henry in 1799 disclosed only 63 volumes of law books.

In the Colonies outside of Massachusetts, Virginia, and Connecticut, there were few law libraries of any size; although, towards the time of the Revolution, the Pennsylvania lawyers who pursued their studies in the Inns of Courts in England accumulated considerable numbers of English books.

---

(1) For interesting account of Judge Trowbridge and his libraries see *Memoirs of Theophilus Parsons,* by T. Parsons Jr.

(2) See MSS. *Itinerary of a Journey from New London to New Haven in 1790.*

(3) *Journal of American History,* Vol. I., No. 1—It is interesting to note that there were 13 books on medicine, a half dozen or so on history, Milton's *Paradise Lost,* a few volumes of the *Spectator,* and all the rest of the library consisted of religious works.

(4) See *Catalogue of Library of Rev. Thomas Prince* (1846).

Even the scanty supply of libraries which the Colonies possessed was depleted at the time of the Revolution by the flight of Tory lawyers, most of whom were wealthy and carried their books away with them.(1)

Some of these law libraries of refugees were confiscated however, or were purchased for the Judges and lawyers by legislative resolves. Thus a resolve of the Massachusetts Legislature, in 1779, authorized the sale to Hon. James Sullivan of the *Modern Entries, Pleas of the Crown, Foster,* and *Hawkins* and the Reports of *Strange, Keyling* and *Burrow* which had belonged to Benjamin Gridley who had become a royalist.(2)

The College Libraries of the time contained practically no law books. In the first catalogue of the Harvard College Library (1723) works of Lord Bacon, Seldon, Grotius and seven volumes of Common Law—Spelman's *Glossary,* Pulton's *Statutes,* Keble's *Statutes,* Coke's *First and Second Institutes* and two volumes of the *Year Books* were the only books on legal subjects. After the burning of the library in 1764, the following seven volumes, presented by Thomas Hollis constituted for many years the sole law library of the College:(3)

Bacon's Historical Discourse (1647). Burns' *Ecclesiastical Law* (1763). Carpenter D. P. *Glossarium etc.* (1766). *Codex Theodosianus.* Glanvill R. *Tractatus de Legibus etc.* (1604) Horne's *Mirror* (1642). Prynne's *Sovereigne Power of Parliaments* (1643)

There were no public libraries in which books of law could be found.

And as there were in the Colonies no collegiate law lectures before 1780, and no law schools before 1784, the young man who aspired to be a lawyer had two courses open to him.

The first was, to pick up such scraps of knowledge of practice,

---

(1) Peter S. DuPonceau who studied in Philadelphia in 1784 under William Lewis writes in 1837 (*Penn. Hist. Soc. Proc.* Vol. IV).

"I had gone through Blackstone's *Commentaries* and Wood's *Institutes* and was advised to enter upon the study of *Coke upon Littleton.* I wanted to have a copy of the work all to myself to read it at my ease; but it was not easy to be procured. After many fruitless applications I bethought myself of putting an advertisement in the papers in which I offered to give a set of Valin's *Commentary on the French Marine Ordinances* in exchange. To my great astonishment and delight I received a note from Mr. Rawle then unknown to me, accepting the offer."

(2) See *Life and Writings of James Sullivan,* by T. G. Amory.

(3) See Preface to the first official *Catalogue of Library of the Harvard Law School,* by Charles Sumner (1833); also edition of 1846.

as he could, by serving as a copyist or assistant in the clerk's office of some inferior or higher court, and by reading such books, Coke chiefly, as he could borrow.

This was the exiguous training which many eminent lawyers received who could not afford the time or the money to adopt the second course. They are well described by Hugh Blair Grigsby in his picture of the venerable James Nimmo of the Norfolk (Virginia) Bar in 1802: "He was of that substantial class of lawyers who, having received an elementary grounding in Latin and mathematics in the schools of the time, entered the clerk's office and served a term of duty within its precincts. He was thus well versed in the ordinary forms of the law and with the decision of the courts in leading cases. With such men as a class there was no great intimacy with the law as a science. As long as the case lay in the old routine, this class of lawyers would get along very well; but novelties were unpleasant to them; they hated the subleties of Special Pleading, and they turned pale at a demurrer." (1)

Some few young men of pre-eminent native ability achieved distinction without training even in a clerk's office. Thus Patrick Henry was admitted to the Bar in Sept. 1760 at the age of 24, after but six weeks' solitary study of *Coke upon Littleton* and the Virginia Statutes, although one of the three examiners, George Wythe, refused to sign his license, leaving it to Peyton and John Randolph to admit him. The latter said they "perceived him to be a young man of genius, very ignorant of law but did not doubt he would soon qualify himself." Wirt states, however, in his life of Henry,(2) that "in spite of his talents he never conquered his aversion to systematic study of the law and could rarely see the bearing of reported cases", this failing standing often in the way of success.

The second course open to a law student was the familiar one of entering the office of some leading member of the Bar, preferably one of the few who had good law libraries, and there absorbing, by study, observation, and occasionally by direct teaching from his senior, the principles of the law.

For the privilege of entering such an office a student was obliged to pay a sum of money, usually $100 to $200, sometimes

---

(1) *Discourse on life and Character of Hon. Littleton Waller Tazewell,* by Hugh Blair Grigsby (1860).
(2) *Life of Patrick Henry,* by William Wirt.

James Wilson

as much as $500, if admission was desired to the office of some pre-eminent celebrity. An interesting illustration of the value set on these privileges is found in a promissory note (still extant) as follows:

Phila. March 22, 1782. I promise to pay James Wilson Esq. or order on demand one hundred guineas, his fee for receiving my nephew Bushrod Washington as a student of law in his office. G. Washington. (1)

In the office, the student had access to all his senior's law books for study. He pored over the MSS. volumes of forms, and the abstracts, commonplace books, and MSS. notes of cases, which each lawyer of those days made for himself. (2) He was expected to copy out pleadings and other documents for his senior, and to draft briefs. In return the lawyer gave to his student such advice, information, or instruction as his time or his whim permitted.

As a rule, the lawyer was too busy a man to pay much attention to his students; and the chief advantage gained by them was in personal association with the able lawyers against whom he tried his cases, and in the general influence which great characters have on younger men who come in contact with them.

Thus even so learned a lawyer as James Wilson was said to have been of slight advantage to his students, as an instructor:

Mr. Wilson devoted little of his time to his students in his office (among whom were Judge Washington and Samuel Sitgreaves) and rarely entered it except for the purpose of consulting books. Hence his intercourse with them was rare, distant, and reserved. As an instructor he was almost useless to those who were under his direction. He would never engage with them in professional discussions; to a direct question he gave the shortest possible answer and a general request for information was always evaded.(3)

An interesting sidelight on this lack of sympathy in the relations between lawyer and student is found in an essay written by William Livingston,(4) while a student, in 1745, in the office

---

(1) See *Letters and Times of the Tylers*, by Leon G. Tyler.
(2) For interesting description of a student's life, see *Life of James Sullivan*, by T. G. Amory.
(3) Sanderson's *Lives of the Signers*.
(4) *Life of William Livingston*, by Theodore Sedgwick Jr. (1833). This essay appeared in print in Parker's *New York Weekly Post Boy* for Aug. 19, 1745, signed Tyro Philolegis.

of the great Scotch lawyer James Alexander, then the leading lawyer of New York,—an invective against the mode of studying law as then practised, and against the drudgery to which clerks were subjected.

The following extracts show the general feeling of the writer.

There is perhaps no set of men that bear so ill a character in the estimation of the vulgar, as the Gentleman of the Long Robe: Whether the disadvantageous idea they commonly entertain of their integrity, be founded upon solid reason, is not my design to enquire; but if they deserve the imputation of injustice and dishonesty, it is in no instance more visible and notorious, than in their conduct towards their apprentices. That a young fellow should be bound to an attorney for 4, 6 or 7 years, to serve him part of the time for the consideration that his master shall instruct in the mystery of the law the remainder of the term; and that notwithstanding this solemn compact (which is binding on either side, is reciprocally obligatory) the attorney shall either employ him in writing during the whole term of his apprenticeship, or, if he allows him a small portion of the time for reading, shall leave him to pore on a book without any instruction to smooth and facilitate his progress in his study, or the least examination of what proficiency he makes in that perplexed science; is an outrage upon common honesty, a conduct scandalous, horrid, base, and infamous to the last degree!

These gentlemen must either have no manner of concern for their clerk's future welfare and prosperity, or must imagine, that he will attain to a competent knowledge in the Law, by gazing on a number of books, which he has neither time nor opportunity to read; or that he is to be metamorphos'd into an attorney by virtue of Hocus Pocus. Is it the father's intention, when he puts his son to an attorney, and gives a large sum into the bargain, that he shall only learn to write a good hand? But whoever attentively considers how these apprentices are used, and forms a judgment from the treatment they meet with, would certainly imagine, that the youth was sent to the lawyer on purpose to write for him, because his father could find him no employment; and if his master, out of the exuberance of his humility, graciously condescends to instruct him, it's only by the bye, in order to enable him to be a more profitable servant. . . . I averr, that 'tis a monstrous absurdity to suppose, that the law is to be learnt by a perpetual copying of precedents. These gentlemen may indeed plead custom, and in pleading that, they admit my assertions; . . . It does not want any great measure of knowledge to see the ridicule of this monstrous practice; but what makes it the more astonishing, is its being practised by men of learning and unquestioned honesty: . . . It is therefore an affront to common sense to multiply arguments for the proof of a thing which none but a lawyer and a madman will pretend to deny. And if no logick can convince them of the injustice of such a practice, I believe no reasonable person would blame an apprentice for discharging at them the argumentum basilinum, or what the English call Club-law, with full force and virtue? This is an argument of mighty energy, and was much in vogue in the Protector's time, when a man, unable to convince his antagonist by syllogysm, knocked him down. And in no case can this coercive way of reasoning more justly be made use of, than in the case under consideration, as nothing whatsoever can be a greater provocation, or demand a more forcible kind of logick.

As an offset to the above, an interesting view of the more helpful relations between a lawyer and his student is found in John Quincy Adams' diary, in his description of his senior, Theophilus Parsons(1).

Nov. 27, 1787. It is of great advantage to us to have Mr. Parsons in the office. He is in himself a law library, and a proficient in every useful branch of service; but his chief excellency is, that no student can be more fond of proposing questions than he is of solving them. He is never at a loss, and always gives a full and ample account, not only of the subject proposed, but of all matters which have any intimate connection with it. I am persuaded that the advantage of having such an instructor is very great, and I hope I shall not misimprove it as some of his pupils have done.

The best idea of the scanty sources of information, open to a student of those days, can be gained by a citation of the studies of a few of the prominent men of the time.

Thus Col. James Otis, father of the famous James Otis Jr., who studied law, prior to 1750, at Barnstable, Massachusetts, found as the only books obtainable, Coke's *Institutes,* Brownlow's *Entries,* and Plowden's *Commentaries* and *Reports.*(2)

Rhode Island law students, said Wilkins Updike(3), prior to the Revolution, were brought up on *Coke upon Littleton, Doctor and Student, Bacon's* and *Sheppard's Grand Abridgment, Croke, Vaughan, Salkeld, Hardwick* and *Strange Reports;* and *Cowell's* and *Jacob's* law dictionaries. "A Lawyer's Library then, like Petrarch's, could be transported in his saddle bags".

---

(1)   See *Mass. Hist. Soc. Proc. 2nd Series,* Vol. XVI (1902).
(2)   *Address before the Bristol County Bar,* by Abraham Holmes (1834).
(3)   *Memoirs of the Rhode Island Bar,* by Wilkins Updike, (1842).

Oliver Ellsworth, of Connecticut, (later Chief Justice of the United States Supreme Court) had as his only text books, Bacon's *Abridgment* and Jacobs' *Law Dictionary.*(1)

Of William Wirt, of Maryland, who was admitted to the Bar of Virginia, in 1792, after a year and five months study of law, Kennedy says, "he had travelled along the flinty highway of *Coke*—and his whole magazine of intellectual artillery at this time comprised no other ammunition than a copy of *Blackstone,* two volumes of *Don Quixote* and a volume of *Tristram Shandy.*(2)

The following is the course of study recommended by William Smith, one of the early leaders of the Bar of New York, to a young friend of John Jay, about 1760.

But now I bring our student home to the studies of his profession of law and I would advise these books in the following order.

First, for the knowledge of the law in General.

1   The treatise of law in Wood's *Institute,* on the civil law, or in *Domat,* which are both the same.

2   *Puffendorf de officio Hominis.*

General study of the elements of the common law in the following order.

Hale's *History of the Common Law.*

Fortescue's *Practice of the Laws of England.*

Sir Thomas Smith's *De Republica Anglorum.*

First Book of *Doctor and Student.*

Second part of Bacon's *Elements.*

Wood's *Institutes of the Common Law.*

Then to fill up and enlarge your ideas you may read Bacon's *Abridgment of the Law* which it is presumed will all be soon published.

In reading the *Abridgment,* which is contrived so as to read pleasantly, I would advise that you constantly refer from the *Abridgment* to Wood, and from Wood to the *Abridgment.*(3)

John Adams, at the age of 25, records in his diary a course of study which probably exceeds that of any other law student of the time, especially noticeable being his study of the civil law, of which he writes as early as 1758:

---

(1)   *Lives and Times of the Chief Justices,* by Henry Flanders (1881).
(2)   *Life of William Wirt,* by John P. Kennedy, (1849).
(3)   *Lives of the Chief Justices,* by George Van Santvord, (1882).
It will be noticed how closely this follows the course for study given in England by Chief Justice Reeve.

Few of my contemporary beginners in the study of the law have the resolution to aim at much knowledge in the civil law. See me distinguish myself from them by the study of the civil law in its native languages. I shall gain the consideration and perhaps the favor of Mr. Gridley and Mr. Pratt by this means.

and in November 1760, he records:

I have read a multitude of law books—mastered but few— *Wood, Coke,* two volumes Lillie's *Abridgment,* two volumes *Salkeld's Reports, Swinburne,* Hawkin's *Pleas of the Crown, Fortescue, Fitzgibbon.* Ten volumes in folio I read at Worcester quite through, besides octavos and lesser volumes of all sizes that I consulted occasionally without reading in course, as dictionaries, reporters, entries, and abridgments. During the last two years, Justinian's *Institutes* I have read through in Latin with Vinnius' *Perpetual Notes.* Van Muyden's *Tractatio Institutionum Justiniani* I read through and translated mostly into English from the same language. Wood's *Institutes of the Civil Law* I read through. These on Civil Law. On the law of England I read Cowell's *Institute of the Laws of England, Doctor and Student,* Finch's *Discourse of Law,* Hale's *History* and some reporters, *Cases in Chancery, Andrews, etc.*—also a *General Treatise of Naval Trade and Commerce*—All this series of reading has left but faint impressions and a very imperfect system of law in my head. I must form a serious resolution of beginning and pressing quite through the plans of my Lords Hale and Reeve. Wood's *Institutes of Common Law* I never read but once and my Lord Coke's *Commentary on Littleton* I never read but once. These two authors I must get and read over and over again. And I will get them too and break through, as Mr. Gridley expressed it, all obstructions.

Besides I am but a novice in natural law and civil law. There are multitudes of excellent authors on natural law that I have never read; and indeed I never read any part of the best authors *Puffendorf* and *Grotius.* In the civil law there are *Hoppius* and *Vinnius,* commentators on *Justinian, Domat,* etc., besides institutes of Canon and feudal law that I have read. Much may be done in two years I have found already; and let it be my care that at the end of the next two years I be better able to show that no time has been lost than I ever have been.

Resources however, such as Adams could have access to, in Boston, were not available for the country practitioner. And the office of the average country lawyer, even towards the end of the 18th Century, contained little more than *Coke on Littleton,* Comyn's *Digest,* Bacon's *Abridgment,* Hale's or Hawkin's *Pleas*

of the Crown, Blackstone, Lillie's *Entries, Saunders Reports*
and some brief book on Pleading and on Practice. (1)

Probably a copy of *Blackstone* was not to be found in Hampshire County before the year 1770. They had *Hale* and *Gilbert,* and, a short time before the Revolution, Bacon's *Abridgment,* but there was not in the county a copy of Comyn's *Abridgment.* They had *Coke* and *Littleton* as well as *Rastell, Fitzherbert, Bracton, Britton* and *Fleta.* (2)

said George Bliss in his address to the Hampshire Bar in 1826.

Partly because of the lack of books, partly because of the undeveloped state of the law of business and personal relations, a student spent most of his time on the subjects of real property and pleadings as found in the rigorous pages of *Coke on Littleton,* and often in the still more refractory volumes of *Bracton, Britton, Fleta* and *Glanville.*

John Adams says that when, as an applicant for admission to the Bar, he sought Gridley's aid:

I have a few pieces of advice to give you, Mr. Adams, said Gridley. One is, to pursue the study of the law, rather than the gain of it; pursue the gain of it enough to keep out of it, enough to keep out of the briers, but give your main attention to the study of it. The next is, not to marry early; for an early marriage will obstruct your improvement; and, in the next place, it will involve you in expense. Another thing is, not to keep much company, for the application of a man who aims to be a lawyer must be incessant; his attention to his books must be constant, which is inconsistent with keeping much company. In the study of the law, the common law, be sure deserves your first and last attention; and he has conquered all the difficulties of this law, who is master of the Institutes. You must conquer the Institutes. The road of science is much easier now than it was when I set out; I began with *Coke-Littleton,* and broke through. (3)

It was on *Coke on Littleton* that Chief Justice Jay was brought up. (4) Littleton's *Tenures* (5) were the main study of James Iredell, in 1770.

(1)   *Life of Charles Marsh of Vermont,* by James Barret (1871).
(2)   *Address of George Bliss to Hampshire County Bar,* Sept. 26, 1826.
(3)   Adams' *Life and Letters,* Vol. II.
(4)   *Lives of the Chief Justices,* by Henry Flanders.
(5)   McRee, in his *Life of James Iredell,* gives the following account of his study; and the extracts from his diary show the difficulty with which the "Tenures" retained his attention.
He was a diligent student, he copied Mr. Johnston's arguments and

Of Chief Justice Theophilus Parsons, who studied with Theophilus Bradbury, his son writes that William Pinkney (the leader of the American Bar of the first decade of the 19th Century) said to him "Do you know one point in which your father surpassed all the lawyers of the country? It was in his thorough study and comprehension of *Coke Littleton.* I have read that book more perhaps than anyone among us now, and I know what it can do for a lawyer." (1)

Coke and *Bracton* were the chief studies of Thomas Jefferson (1762-1767). (2)

When I was a student of the law after getting through *Coke Lyttleton* whose matter cannot be abridged, I was in the habit of abridging and commonplacing what I read meriting it, and of course sometimes making my own reflections on the subject.

Coke Lyttleton was the universal elementary book of law students and a sounder Whig never wrote nor profounder learning in the orthodox doctrines of British liberties. Our lawyers were then all Whigs. But when his black letter text and uncouth but cunning learning got out of fashion, and the honeyed Mansfieldism of *Blackstone* became the student's book, from that moment, that profession (the nursery of our Congress) began to slide into Toryism and nearly all the young brood of lawyers are now of that line. They suppose themselves indeed to be Whigs because they no longer know what whiggism or republicanism means.

The older American lawyers agreed with Lord Eldon's views, who, in advising a young friend in 1800 to read *Coke* again and again, wrote:

If it be toil and labour to you, and it will be so, think as I do when I am climbing up to Swyer or to Westhill, that the world will be before you when the toil is over; for so the law world will

---

pleas in interesting cases. He read carefully and attentively the text books, referring to the authorities quoted, and collating and digesting kindred passages from all the writers within reach; he attended the courts, returned to his chamber and wrote out the arguments of his own applicable to the cases. . . . In his diary Aug. 23, 1770, he writes: "I have not done as much as I ought to have done, read a little in Littleton's Tenures and stopt in the middle of his chapter on Rents, whereas, if I had gone through it, it would have been better and more agreeable than losing three or four games of billiards."

"August 24—This morning pretty well employed; read a good deal in Littleton's Tenures, and afterwards a little in the Edinburgh Magazine for 1758.

August 29—Read a little in Littleton's Tenures, not much though, being interrupted."

(1) *Memoirs of Theophilus Parsons,* by T. Parsons, Jr.
(2) *Thomas Jefferson as a Lawyer, Green Bag* 153, Vol. X.

be, if you make yourself complete master of that book. At present, lawyers are made good, cheap, by learning law from *Blackstone* and less elegant compilers. Depend upon it, men so bred will never be lawyers, (though they may be barristers), whatever they call themselves. I read *Coke on Littleton* through, when I was the other day out of the office, and when I was a student I abridged it. (1)

Later 18th Century lawyers, however, though still immersed in *Coke* by their instructors, did not share this profound admiration. Thus Mr. Justice Story wrote of his entry upon the study of law in 1798 as follows:

I confess my heart sunk within me. . . . Then the student, after reading that most elegant of all commentaries, Mr. Justice Blackstone's work, was hurried at once into the intricate, crabbed, and obsolete learning of *Coke on Littleton*. . . . You may judge how I was surprised and startled on opening works where nothing was presented but dry and technical principles, the dark and mysterious elements of the feudal system, the subtle refinements and intricacies of the middle ages of the common law, and the repulsive and almost unintelligible forms of processes and pleadings. . . . Soon after Mr. Sewall's departure to Washington I took it (*Coke*) up, and after trying it day after day with very little success I set myself down and wept bitterly. . . .
I went on and on and began at last to see daylight, ay, and to feel that I could comprehend and reason upon the text and the comments. When I had completed the reading of this most formidable work, I felt that I breathed a purer air and that I had acquired a new power. . . . I pressed on to the severe study of special pleadings and by repeated perusals of *Saunders Reports* acquired such a decided relish for this branch of my profession that it became for several years afterwards my fa-

---

(1) Twiss' *Life of Lord Eldon.*
Lord Campbell also writes in 1849 in his diary:
"I have taken to my old favorite *Co. Litt.* It certainly is very pleasant reading. I am more than ever struck by its unmethodical and rambling character, but one must admire the author's stupendous familiarity with all parts of the law of England; he is uniformly perspicuous, he gives amusing glimpses of history and manners and his etymologies and other quaint absurdities are as good for a laugh as *Joe Miller* or *Punch.* * * * No man can thoroughly understand the law as it is without knowing the changes it has undergone, and no man can be acquainted with its history without being familiar with the writings of Lord Coke. Nor is he by any means so dry and forbidding as is generally supposed. He is certainly unmethodical, but he is singularly perspicuous, he fixes the attention, his quaintness is often amusing and he excites our admiration by the inexhaustible stores of erudition which without any effort he seems spontaneously to pour forth. Thus were our genuine lawyers trained. Lord Eldon read *Coke upon Littleton* once, twice and thrice and made an abstract of the whole work as a useful exercise."

vorite pursuit. . . . I also read through that deep and admirable work. . . . *Fearne on Contingent Remainders and Executory Devises* and I made a MSS. abstract of all its principles. (1)

And Daniel Webster (2) who studied first in 1801 in the office of Thomas W. Thompson at Salisbury, N. H., said:

I was put to study in the old way, that is, the hardest books first, and lost much time. I read *Coke-Littleton* through without understanding a quarter part of it. . . .
A boy of twenty, with no previous knowledge of such subjects, cannot understand *Coke*. It is folly to set him upon such an author. There are propositions in *Coke* so abstract, and distinctions so nice, and doctrines embracing so many distinctions and qualifications, that it required an effort not only of a mature mind, but of a mind both strong and mature, to understand him. Why disgust and discourage a young man by telling him he must break into his profession through such a wall as this? I really often despaired. I thought I never could make myself a lawyer and was almost going back to the business of school teaching.

John Quincy Adams records in his diary(3):

March, 1788 I this day got through my folio of Lord Coke which has been hanging heavily upon me these ten weeks. It contains a vast mass of law learning, but heaped up in such an incoherent mass that I have derived very little benefit from it—indeed I think it a very improper book to put into the hands of a student just entering upon the acquisition of the profession.
. . . The addition of Wood's *Institutes* and more especially of Blackstone's *Commentaries* has been an inestimable advantage to the late students in the profession.

It was the advent of Blackstone which opened the eyes of American scholars to the broader field of learning in the law. He taught them, for the first time, the continuity, the unity, and the reason of the Common Law—and just at a time when the need of a unified system both in law and politics was beginning to be felt in the Colonies.

---

(1) In a letter to his son W. W. Story, Feb. 9, 1841, Judge Story says, "It reminds me strongly of my own case when escaping from the walls of college, I found myself in a lawyer's office, among the dusty rubbish of former ages; for at that time there were few elementary works to smooth the passage, and from reading the classical work of Blackstone, I had immediately to plunge into the dark page of Coke upon Littleton. I could say, with Spelman, that my heart sank within me."
(2) *Autobiography of Daniel Webster* (1829).
(3) See *Mass. Hist. Soc. Proc., 2nd Series,* Vol. XVI, (1902).

Up to this time, wrote Blackstone, the student has been "expected to sequester himself from the world, and by a tedious, lonely process to extract the theory of law from a mass of undigested learning. How little therefore is it to be wondered at, that we hear of so frequent miscarriages, that so many gentlemen of bright inaugurations grow weary of so unpromising a search; and that so many persons of moderate capacity confuse themselves at first setting out and continue ever dark and puzzled during the remainder of their lives."(1)

The publication of Vol. I of the *Commentaries* was made in England in 1765 and Vol. IV in 1769; and as early as 1771-72 an American Edition of the full work was published in Philadelphia in four volumes at $2 per volume, 1400 copies being ordered in advance. The list of subscribers was headed by four governors and three lieutenant governors; and the first name among private citizens was "John Adams, Barrister at law, Boston". The booksellers of Boston subscribed for 239 copies, of Charleston 89, of Philadelphia 84, of New York 60, of Norfolk, Williamsburgh and Winchester in Virginia 97. In addition there had previously been imported into the Colonies at least 1000 copies of the English edition, at ten pounds per set.(2)

Even prior to their publication in book form, Blackstone's lectures had been known in America; for in September, 1759, Jonathan Sewall wrote to John Adams "Your account of Mr. Blackstone's lectures is entirely new to me. I am greatly pleased with it"; and Adams records in 1765 a conversation with Mr. Gridley on Blackstone. The title page of a book entitled *Con-*

---

(1) It was to Mansfield that the credit was due of discovering and turning to public usefulness the genius of Blackstone as a jurist. A vacancy occurring in the Professorship of Civil Law at Oxford, Blackstone had been promised the appointment by the Duke of Newcastle; but the latter finding him unwilling to bestir himself for the Government in political agitation appointed another man. Mansfield then advised Blackstone to settle at Oxford and to read law lectures to such students as chose to attend.

These lectures in 1753 had attracted the attention of Charles Viner who had made a fortune from the proceeds of his *Abridgment* (published 1742 to 1753). And when Viner died, in 1756, he bequeathed a considerable sum for the maintenance of a professor at Oxford at a salary of 200 pounds—who should give a course of sixty lectures per year *"On the Law of England"* in the English Language."

To fill this first professorship of law in any English speaking college William Blackstone Esq. Solicitor General to his Majesty was appointed in 1758.

(2) See Preface to Hammond's *Blackstone's Commentaries.*

ductor Generalis, published in 1764 in New Jersey—a manual for justices and petty officers—contains the following—

"To which is added a treatise on the *Law of Descent in Fee Simple,* by William Blackstone Esq., Barrister at Law, Vinerian Professor of the Law of England."(1)

The popularity of the *Commentaries* gave an impetus to the importation of other law books; so that, by 1775, Edmund Burke said in the House of Commons:(2)

In no country perhaps in the world is the law so general a study. The profession itself is numerous and powerful; and in most provinces it takes the lead. The greater number of the deputies sent to the Congress were lawyers. But all who read, and most do read, endeavour to obtain some smattering in that science. I have been told by an eminent bookseller, that in no branch of his business, after tracts of popular devotion, were so many books as those of the law exported to the plantations. The colonists have now fallen into the way of printing them for their own use. I hear that they have sold nearly as many of Blackstone's *Commentaries* in America as in England. General Gage marks out this disposition very particularly in a letter on your table. He states that all the people in his government are lawyers, or smatterers in law; and that in Boston they have been enabled, by successful chicane, wholly to evade many parts of one of your capital penal institutions. . . . . This study renders men acute, inquisitive, dexterous, prompt in attack, ready in defence, full of resources. In other countries, the people, more simple, and of a less mercurial cast, judge of an ill principle in government only by an actual grievance; here they anticipate the evil, and judge of the pressure of the grievance by the badness of the principle.

(1) James Iredell wrote from Edenton, North Carolina, July 31, 1771, to his father in London:

"Will you be so obliging as to procure Dr. Blackstone's Commentaries on the Laws of England for me, and send them by the first opportunity. I have indeed read them through by the favor of Mr. Johnston who lent them to me; but it is proper I should read them frequently and with great attention. They are books admirably calculated for a young student, and indeed may interest the. most learned. The law there is not merely considered as a profession but as a science. The principles are deduced from their source, and we are not only taught in the clearest manner the general rules of law, but the reasons upon which they are founded. By this means we can more satisfactorily study, and more easily remember them, than when they are only laid down in a dictatorial, often an obscure manner.

Pleasure and instruction go hand in hand."

See *Life and Letters of James Iredell,* by Griffith J. McRee (1857).

(2) Speech on Moving Resolutions for Conciliation with the American Colonies, March 22, 1776.

They augur misgovernment at a distance; and snuff the approach
of tyranny in every tainted breeze.

Whether the change is to be attributed to the influence of
Blackstone, or to the increased facilities for obtaining books, or
to the freer ideas brought about by the American Revolution,
the broadening of the study of the law, after 1780, is a striking
and remarkable feature in the history of law in this country.

The young lawyer was now expected to know something of
the general principles of public law, and to approach jurisprudence in a spirit of scientific inquiry.   He was taught general
views in addition to particular rules.

Knowledge of technical details of feudal tenure, of obscure
customs and bewildering pleadings, was no longer enough to
qualify the best students.

A law course of reading prescribed in Judge Parker's office
in Portsmouth, New Hampshire, and in Charles Chauncey's
office in New Haven, Conn. for Ezra Stiles, Jr. (Harv. 1778)
was as follows:(1)

Burlamaqui's *Principes de Droit Naturel;* Montesquieu, *l' Esprit
des Lois;* Lord Kames' *History of Law; Blackstone;* Wood's
Maxims; Wood's *Institutes; Co. Litt;* Bacon's *Abr.;* Hawkins'
Pleas of the Crown; Gilbert's *Evidence, Devises,* and *Tenures;
Law of Bills of Exchange;* Molloy *De Jure Maritimo;* Hale's
Abridgment; Lex Testamentorum; Sullivan's *Lectures;* Bohun's
Institutes and Declarations; Boot on *Suits at Law; Offic. Cler.
Pac.;* Burns' *Justice;* Dalrymple's *Institutions of the Laws of
Scotland, etc.; Institutes of Tribonian* and part of the *Pandects;
Puffendorf;* Poulton's *Crim. Law; Salkeld's Rep.;* 1 and 2 *Bur-
row;* part of *Lord Raymond's, Holt's* and *Shower's Reports,*
Godolphin's *Legacy Orph.,* 40 volumes.

A similar course was assigned to John Quincy Adams who
studied in the office of Theophilus Parsons in 1788, first, Robertson's *History of Charles V,* Vattel's *Law of Nature and Nations,*
Gibbon's *Rome* and Hume's *England;* next, Sullivan's *Lectures,*
Wright's *Tenures, Co. Litt.;* Wood's *Institutes;* Gilbert's *Evidence;* Foster's and Hawkins' *Pleas of the Crown;* Bacon's *Pleas
and Pleadings;* Buller's *Nisi Prius;* Barrington's *Observations on
the Statutes; The Institutes of Justinian.*(2)

(1) *Literary Diary of Ezra Stiles* Vol. II; *The Study of Elementary
Law* by S. E. Baldwin *Yale Law Jour.,* Vol. XIII.
(2) *Study of Elementary Law,* by S. E. Baldwin, *Yale Law Journal,*
Vol. XIII; *Proc. Mass. Hist. Soc.* Vol. XVI, *2nd Series.*

A very extensive foundation for a course of legal study is described by John Randolph, who wrote in 1795 on the fly leaf of a volume of Hume's *Treatise of Human Nature*—"I was sent to Philadelphia in Jan., 1790, to study law with the then Attorney General of the United States (Edmund Randolph). This book was the first he put into my hands, telling me that he had planned a system of study and wished me to go through a course of metaphysical reading. After I returned the book, he gave me *Shakespeare* to read, then *Beattie on Truth,* after that Kaine's *Elements of Criticism* and fifthly Gillie's *History of Greece.* What an admirable system of study!—Risum teneatis!"

So too the broader course of study in the latter part of the 18th Century can be seen from Chancellor Kent's description of his legal education:(1)

When the college (Yale) was broken up and dispersed in July 1779 by the British, I retired to a country village and finding Blackstone's *Commentaries* I read the fourth volume. Parts of the work struck my taste and the work inspired me, at the age of sixteen with awe and I fondly determined to be a lawyer. In Nov. 1781, I was placed by my father with Mr. (now called Judge) Benson who was then attorney general, at Poughkeepsie. There I entered on law and was the most modest, steady, industrious student that such place ever saw. I read the following winter, *Grotius* and *Puffendorff* in large folios and made copious extracts. My fellow students who were gay and gallant thought me very odd and dull in my taste; but out of five of them four died in middle life drunkards . . . In 1782, I read Smollett's *History of England,* and procured at a farmer's house where I boarded *Rapin's History* (a large folio) and read it through, and I found during the course of the last summer among my papers my MSS. abridgment of Rapin's *Dissertations on the Laws and Customs of the Anglo Saxons.* I abridged Hale's *History of the Common Law* and the old books of practice and read parts of *Blackstone* again and again. The same year I procured Hume's *History* and his profound reflections and admirable eloquence struck most deeply on my youthful mind. I extracted the most admired part, made several volumes of MSS.

Horace Binney, who studied in the office of Jared Ingersoll in Philadelphia in 1799, thus described his legal course:(2)

---

(1) *Life of James Kent,* by William Kent (1898). See letter to Thomas Washington of Tennessee, written October 6, 1828.
(2) *Life of Horace Binney,* by Charles C. Binney (1903).

A methodical study of the general system of law and of its grounds and reasons, beginning with the fundamental law of estates and tenures, and pursuing the derivative branches in logical succession, and the collateral subjects in due order, by which the student acquires a knowledge of principles that rule in all departments of the science and learns to feel as much as to know what is in harmony with the system and what is not.
. . . The Profession knows this by its fruits to be the most effectual way of making a great lawyer.

Judge James M. Wayne of Georgia summarized his twenty months in Judge Channing's office in New Haven, about 1808, as follows :(1)

First he gave to me several lectures upon the ethics of the profession, illustrating them by narratives and ancedotes from the lives of eminent lawyers. These were not conversations, but precisely written chapters upon the practice of the profession in the different relations of law and client, lawyer with lawyer, and lawyer with the court and jury, in which were traced their obligations to each other with exactness and truth. I was then lectured for 3 or 4 months upon the Roman Law. First, historically as to its source and its reception in modern Europe, and then in its sub-division concerning persons, things, rights, the modes of prosecuting them, and in all of those analogies in relation to contracts which exist between it and the English common law. In connection with this course I was carried through the history of the English common law, before I was permitted to take up any of the works ordinarily first used in getting a knowledge of the law. Hale's *History of the Common Law* was his text, and Edward I his hero. Every Statute of that prince's reign and of each succeeding reign in any way bearing upon the improvement of the law, I was made to know something of, in contrast with the antecedent defective condition of English law.

A more old fashioned course of studies was pursued by Chief Justice Roger B. Taney who thus describes his legal education in his Memoirs :

In the spring of 1796 I read law in the office of Jeremiah Thurly Chase at Annapolis, Judge of General Court.
From the character of the judges of the General Court, of the bar who attended it, and the business transacted in it, Annapolis was considered the place of all others in the State where a man should study law, if he expected to attain eminence in his profession.

---

(1) *Biographical Sketches of Eminent American Lawyers Now Living,* by John Livingston, (1852).

My reading in the office of a judge, instead of a practising lawyer, had some advantages; but upon the whole was I think a disadvantage to me. It is true, it gave me more time for uninterrupted study, but it gave me no instruction in the ordinary routine of practice, nor any information as to the forms and manner of pleading. In that day, strict and nice technical pleading was the pride of the bar and I might almost say of the court. And every disputed suit was a trial of skill in pleading between the counsel, and a victory achieved in that mode was much more valued than one obtained on the merits of the case . . . .Nor was it so easy in that day for an inexperienced young lawyer to satisfy himself upon a question of special pleading. *Chitty* had not made his appearance, and you were obliged to look for the rule in Comyn's *Digest* or Bacon's *Abridgment* or Viner's *Abridgment* and the cases to which they referred; and I have sometimes gone back to Lilly's *Entries* and *Doctrina Placitandi* in searching for a precedent. . . . We had no moot court. My preceptor, Mr. Chase, did not encourage them, and in this he agreed, I believe, with the leaders of the Bar in Annapolis in whose offices there were students. He thought that discussions of law questions by students was apt to give them the habit of speaking upon questions which they did not understand or of which they had but an imperfect and superficial knowledge —that its tendency therefore was to accustom them to loose arguments and to lay down principles without proper qualifications. He advised me to attend regularly the sittings of the General Court, to observe how the eminent men at that bar examined the witnesses and brought out their cases, and raised and argued the questions of law, and afterwards to write a report of it for my own use. . . . All the lawyers of Maryland who had risen to eminence and leadership were trained in the manner described and advised by Mr. Chase.

"Taney studied law," says his biographer, "in the old way, beginning with the fundamental law of estates and tenures, and pursuing the derivative branches in logical succession, and the collateral subjects in due order, considering the grounds and reasons of everything as he proceeded. Pleading and evidence and the rules of practice, he had thoroughly mastered. The old law treatises like *Coke upon Littleton* had not been superseded by Indexes, Digests and Treatises, which supply thoughts without cultivating the power of thinking. The *Entries, Brooke,* and *Coke,* and *Levinz,* and *Rastall* had not yet made their exit." (1)

A final and perhaps the best illustration of the average legal education is William Plumer, Jr.'s, account of his father, Will-

---

(1) *Memoir of Roger Brooke Taney* by Samuel Tyler (1872).

iam Plumer, Sr., who was a contemporary of Jeremiah Mason, Jeremiah Smith, Daniel Webster, and Ichabod Bartlett in New Hampshire, and who studied law in 1784, in the office of Joshua Atherton.

Atherton gave him *Coke upon Littleton,* as his first initiation into the mysteries of the law; and it is not strange that the ardor of the young aspirant was somewhat cooled by this selection of masters, so quaint, austere and forbidding. After digging for some three or four weeks, in the rugged soil of the feudal tenures, and beginning, as he thought, to get some glimpses of its hidden treasures, he was told by his instructor that he must suspend his legal studies and commence with the Latin Grammar. He must read *Virgil* and *Cicero* before he could understand *Coke* and *Littleton.* This was a new and, to him, most unwelcome labor. He, however, laid aside his law, and took up Lilly's *Latin Grammar,* probably the first grammar he had ever seen, certainly the first he had ever attempted to study. . . .

In 1785 his new instructor, John Prentice, a graduate of Harvard College, though probably not a well-read lawyer, possessed a respectable standing at the bar; and, like Atherton, was afterwards Attorney General. His law library consisted at this time of Blackstone's *Commentaries;* Wood's *Institutes of the Laws of England;* Hawkins' *Pleas of the Crown;* Jacob's *Law Dictionary; Salkeld; Raymond* and *Strange's Reports;* the *New Hampshire Statutes,* and a manuscript volume of Pleas and Declarations. . . . He read the whole of *Blackstone* rapidly through, in the first instance, to acquire, in this way, a general idea of its contents; and then went over it, more carefully, a second time, with a view to its more thorough comprehension. He devoted at least ten hours a day to this study, though he seldom read more than forty or fifty pages in that time. But these were carefully studied, or, if not fully understood, at least, examined with his best care and attention. His instructor was not much inclined, nor indeed always able, to answer the questions which he asked; and the few books within his reach often failed to furnish the desired information. Under these circumstances his practice was, after reading a portion of *Blackstone,* to trace the subject through other books; and then, taking a walk in some retired place, to review in his mind the substance of what he had read, examining the relations of one part with another, and of the whole with what he had learned before, till he felt himself master of the lesson, and prepared to go farther. .

On the important subject of Pleas and Pleading, Prentice had no books, except a manuscript volume of forms, said to have been collected by Theophilus Parsons. This the student copied, and added to it in the course of his practice, such other pleas and declarations as he thought worthy of preservation, whether drawn by himself, or derived from other sources. He, at the same time, took copious notes of his reading, and formed abstracts and digests of the law under separate heads, thus reducing his knowledge to a regular system.

Daniel Webster's own account of his course of study in the office of Christopher Gore, in 1804, is a typical example of the course followed in the early years of the 19th Century.

Before coming to Boston he had studied about two years in Salisbury, N. H.—the first works which he read being *Vattel, Burlamaqui* and *Montesquieu* on the Law of Nations; then *Blackstone* and *Coke;* and the histories of *Hume* and *Robertson;* and "happening to take up *Espinasse's Nisi Prius"*, he wrote, "I found I could understand it and arguing that the object of reading was to understand what was written, I laid down the venerable *Coke* et alios similes reverendos and kept company for a time with *Mr Espinasse* and others, the most plain, easy and intelligent writers."

Mr. Gore had just then returned from England, and renewed the practice of the law. He had rooms in Scollay's Building, and, as yet, had no clerk. A young man, as little known to Gore as myself, undertook to introduce me to him. In logic, this would have been bad. Ignotum per ignotum. Nevertheless, it succeeded here. We ventured into Mr. Gore's rooms, and my name was pronounced. I was shockingly embarrassed, but Mr. Gore's habitual courtesy of manner gave me courage to speak. . . . He talked to me pleasantly for a quarter of an hour; and, when I rose to depart, he said: "My young friend, you look as though you might be trusted. You say you came to study, and not to waste time. I will take you at your word. You may as well hang up your hat at once; go into the other room; take your book, and sit down to reading it, and write at your convenience to New Hampshire for your letters." . . . It was a situation which offered to me the means of studying books and men and things. It was on the 20th day of July, 1804, that I first made myself known to Mr. Gore; and, although I remained in his office only till March following, and that with considerable intervening absences, I made, as I think, some respectable progress.

In August the Supreme Court sat. I attended it constantly, and reported every one of its decisions. I did the same in the Circuit Court of the United States. I kept a little journal at that time, which still survives. It contains little besides a list of books read.

In addition to books on the common and municipal law, I

find I read *Vattel* for the third time in my life, as is stated in the journal, Ward's *Law of Nations,* Lord Bacon's *Elements,* Puffendorff's *Latin History of England,* Gifford's *Juvenal,* Boswell's *Tour to the Hebrides,* Moore's *Travels,* and many other miscellaneous things.

But my main study was the common law, and especially the parts of it which relate to special pleading. Whatever was in *Viner, Bacon,* and other books then usually studied on that part of the science, I paid my respects to. Among other things I went through *Saunders' Reports,* the old folio edition, and abstracted, and put into English, out of Latin and Norman-French, the pleadings in all his Reports. It was an edifying work. From that day to this the forms and language of special pleas have been quite familiar with me. I believe I have my little abstract yet.

When all is said, however, as to the meagreness of a lawyer's education, one fact must be strongly emphasized—that this very meagreness was a source of strength. *Multum in parvo* was particularly applicable to the training for the Bar of that era.

There was truth in the reply of a great lawyer, when asked how the lawyers who formed the United States Constitution had such a mastery of legal principles,—"Why they had so few books"(1). "Many other students," wrote Webster, "read more than I did, but so much as I read, I made my own."

And Chancellor Kent's remark "that he owed his reputation to the fact that, when studying law during the war, he had but one book, Blackstone's *Commentaries,* but that one book he mastered,"(2) sums up very concisely the cause of the greatness of many an early American jurist.

---

(1) See *How Successful Lawyers were Educated,* by G. C. Macdonald (1896).
Sir Edward Sugden in England once said "I resolved, when beginning to read law, to make everything I acquired perfectly my own, and never to go to a second thing until I had entirely accomplished the first. Many of my competitors read as much in a day as I read in a week; but at the end of the twelve months, my knowledge was as fresh as on the day it was acquired, while theirs had glided away from their recollections."
(2) See *Magazine of American History,* Vol. XIII (1885).

CHAPTER VII.

EARLY AMERICAN BARRISTERS, AND BAR ASSOCIATIONS.

The local law office does not account, however, for all the educated American lawyers of the 18th Century.

A far greater number than is generally known, received their legal education in London in the Inns of Court; and the influence, on the American Bar, of these English-bred lawyers, especially in the more southerly Colonies, was most potent. The training which they received in the Inns, in exclusively English Statutory and Common Law, based as it was on historical precedent and customary law, the habits which they formed there of solving all legal questions by the standards of English liberties and of rights of the English subject, proved of immense value to them when they became later (as so many did become) leaders of the American Revolution.

It has been stated that 115 Americans were admitted to the Inns, from 1760 to the close of the Revolution(1); from South Carolina 47, from Virginia 21, from Maryland 16, from Pennsylvania 11, from New York 5, and from each of the other Colonies 1 or 2. And probably twenty-five or fifty American-born lawyers had been educated in England prior to 1760.(2)

Among the more distinguished may be named John Rutledge, Charles Cotesworth Pinckney, Thomas Heyward, Thomas Lynch, John Julian Pringle, and John Laurens, from South Carolina; John Randolph, Richard Henry Lee and Arthur Lee, from Virginia; Charles Carroll, from Maryland; Joseph Read, from New Jersey; and Thomas McKean, Edward Tilghman and William Tilghman, Jared Ingersoll, Benjamin Chew, William Rawle, and John Dickinson, from Pennsylvania.

The breadth of education to be sought in England may be gathered from the following letter written, from Charleston, July 30, 1769, by John Rutledge, to his brother in London:

---

(1) *Life and Times of John Dickinson,* by Charles J. Stillé (1891).
(2) See Chapters I, III and IV supra.

The very first thing with which you should be thoroughly acquainted is the writing shorthand. . . . Be constant in attending the sittings in Chancery out of terms, and when there are no sittings at Nisi Prius in London or Westminster; for I would prefer attending the King's Bench and Sittings of the Chief Justice of that court at Nisi Prius when they are held. And remember what I hinted to you of attending alternately in the different courts by agreement between you and some of your intimate fellow students, and then of comparing and exchanging notes every evening. . . . But you must exert yourself to the utmost in being able by some means or other to attend the House of Commons constantly . . . I would not have this make you a dabbler in politics. What I intend by it is that you may have opportunities of seeing and hearing the best speakers, and of acquiring a good manner and proper address. . . . I believe Sheridan is the only lecturer in England upon oratory, and I think it would be advisable to attend him and mark well his observations. . . . And now in regard to particular law books—Coke's *Institutes* seem to be almost the foundation of our law. These you must read over and over with the greatest attention, and not quit him until you understand him thoroughly and have made your own everything in him which is worth taking out. A good deal of his law is now obsolete and altered by acts of Parliament; however, it is necessary to know what the law was before so altered. *Blackstone* I think useful.(1) The reports are too tedious to be all read through; at least whilst you are in England, I would give the preference to the most modern. . . . I look upon it that if you go through all the cases reported since the Revolution, when the Constitution seems to have been re-established upon its true and proper principles, and since which time by the alteration of the Judges' commission and their increasing independence, to what it is at this day, the law has been in its greatest perfection, and not encroaching either upon the people's liberties or the prerogative; I say, if you do this, you will have a collection of the very best cases. . . . I would read every case reported from that time to the present. Distinguish between your reading of law and equity, and don't confound the two matters. . . . They are kept very distinct in the courts of England, though here blended together very often and very ridiculously. . . . I would have you also read the statute laws throughout. . . . Vast numbers of them you will find of no manner of use, except indeed as matter of history; but this thing I think in the main will be of vast service to you . . . . Stock yourself with a good collection of law maxims both Latin and English—they are of great use . . . Make your

(1) It is to be noted that this letter was written before *Blackstone* had been republished in the Colonies.

self thoroughly acquainted with all the terms of the law. . . . The little book called *Termes de la Ley,* will help you. *Doctor and Student* is a good book, though a little one, and good authority. *Bacon* you know is my favorite, and where authors seem to differ I think he will best reconcile them. Be well acquainted with Crown Law, Hale's, Hawkin's and Judge Foster's, and what other Crown Law books there are, read carefully.

The facilities for legal study supplied by the Inns of Court were, however, the least of the opportunities open to young American barristers in London at this time. For these years, 1750 to 1775, formed a period of remarkable brilliance in English history. Students of law were not only studying at the Inns side by side with the future Chief Justices, Kenyon and Ellenborough, and the future Chancellors, Thurlow, Eldon and Erskine; but they were also listening to the luminous judgments of Lord Mansfield on King's Bench, to the commanding eloquence of Pitt, (Lord Chatham) and the oratory of Charles Pratt, (Lord Camden); they were elbowing, in the Inns themselves, the burly frame of Samuel Johnson the autocrat of literature; and they were witnessing David Garrick's "powers of acting vast and unconfined."(1)

In forming an idea of the colonial lawyer's education, one further factor must be borne in mind,—the remarkable extent to which 18th Century lawyers, especially those of New England, Virginia, and South Carolina were college-bred men. Practically all the early lawyers in Massachusetts were Harvard graduates; and of the lawyers admitted to practice in Boston at the Suffolk Bar, in later years, from 1780 to 1817, 139 were Harvard graduates; 7 were from Brown, 6 from Dartmouth, 1 from Williams, 3 non-graduates.(2)

---

(1) Of Jared Ingersoll who was in the Middle Temple in 1774, his son Charles J. Ingersoll wrote, that "Mansfield, Blackstone, Chatham and Garrick and other luminaries of that period were objects of his constant attention, and of his correspondence, and ever after among the pleasures of his memory."

See *Life of Charles Jared Ingersoll,* by William M. Meigs (1897).

(2) Of the lawyers, other than the Judges and Attorney Generals, mentioned by Washburn in his *Judicial History of Massachusetts,* 17 were Harvard graduates, 4 English bred lawyers, 4 non-graduates and 1 from Yale.

Of the members of the Worcester Bar, in Massachusetts, admitted prior to 1800, 45 graduated from Harvard, 5 from Brown, 3 from Dartmouth, 2 from Yale, 1 non-graduate. Of those admitted between 1800 and 1817, 28 graduated from Harvard, 11 from Brown, 12 from Dartmouth, 3 each from Yale and Williams, 2 from Union and 6 non-graduates.

See *Address before the Worcester Bar,* by Joseph Willard, Oct. 2, 1829.

In New Hampshire, in 1805, of the 106 members of the Bar, 77 were college graduates—from Harvard 35, Dartmouth 34, Yale 6, Brown 2.

In Maine, in 1770, of the six trained lawyers, four were Harvard graduates.

In Connecticut, practically all the lawyers of distinction were Yale graduates.

In New Jersey, the prominent lawyers were almost exclusively college men, either from Yale, like David Ogden, or from Princeton, like Richard Stockton.

In Pennsylvania as already noted, a large proportion of the Bar was educated in England or the College of Philadelphia and the University of Pennsylvania.

The records of William and Mary College and of Princeton contained the names of many of Virginia's prominent lawyers.

In South Carolina, almost all of distinction at the Bar after the Revolution graduated from Princeton, Yale, or the College of South Carolina.

New York alone seems the exception in the matter of liberal training for her Bar; for in the early 18th Century, men of education were rare in that Province. There were no college graduates on the Bench, except James Delancey, and none at the Bar, except William Smith. It seems that commerce engrossed the attention of the principal families, and their sons were sent from the writing school to the counting house, and thence to the West Indies.(1)

In 1741, when William Livingston graduated from Yale, there were but six other lawyers in the Province who were college graduates, three of whom were his own brothers.

And as the historian William Smith, Jr. (born in 1728) writes of his own time:

To the disgrace of our first planters, who beyond conparison surpassed their eastern neighbors in opulence, Mr. James Delancy, a graduate of the University of Cambridge, and Mr. Smith were for many years the only academics in the Province except such as were in holy orders—and, so late as 1746, the author did not recall above thirteen more.

In the later part of the 18th Century, however, New York recruited her Bar very largely from graduates of King's College (Columbia).

---

(1) *Life of William Livingston,* by Theodore Sedgwick Jr. (1833).

THE BAR ASSOCIATIONS.

After 1770, as the course of legal study became liberalized, and the Bar became more compact in its organization, and assured of its power, it gradually established very rigid rules, fixing requirements for office study by students desiring admission as lawyers. These rules paved the way for the establishment of regular law schools. They also tended to constitute lawyers as more and more of an educated guild.

Nothing gives a better view of the educational condition of the law student at the end of the 18th Century than the *Bar Book Suffolk County* 1770, containing the records of its proceedings up to 1805.(1)

Mention has been made(2), of the rule, first adopted by the Essex Bar in 1768, and later generally by other Massachusetts County Bars that:

It is agreed that we will not take any young gentleman to study with us, without previously having the consent of the Bar of this County; that we will not recommend any persons to be admitted to the Inferior Court, as attorneys, who have not studied with some barrister three years at least, nor as attorneys to the Superior Court, who have not studied as aforesaid, and been admitted at the Inferior Court, two years at least; nor recommend them as barristers till they have been through the preceding degrees, and been attorneys at the Superior Court two years at the least,—except those gentlemen who are already admitted in this County as attorneys at the Superior and Inferior Courts, and that these must be subject to this rule so far as is yet to come.

In 1800, the term of years was extended so that "students of college out of the State be not admissible to the Bar until they shall have studied one year longer than those educated at Harvard University;" and "gentlemen admitted to the Bar of other States who have practised thereat less than four years must have a term of study within this county of at least one year."

In 1771, the Suffolk Bar required that "consent of the Bar shall not be given to any young gentleman who has not had an education at college, or a liberal education equivalent in the judgment of the Bar." This at once established a very high

---

(1) See *Mass. Hist. Soc. Proc.*, (1882), and *Historical Sketch*, by George Dexter.
(2) Chapter III, supra.

educational standard for lawyers. In 1784, the standard was
still further raised, by the provision, that any gentleman proposed, who had not had a college education, should undergo an
examination by a committee of the Bar, previous to admission
as a student. The examination was apparently thorough, for, in
August, 1784, it appears that:

The report of the committee on the examination of Messrs.
Gardiner and Hill was considered; and it appearing to the gentlemen present that, although those gentlemen were well versed
in the Latin and English classics, yet that a course of study in
the mathematics, in ethics, logic, and metaphysics was necessary
previous to their admission as students of law; therefore *Voted*
unanimously, That such admission be suspended.

also, in 1793:

The committee appointed for the examination of Mr. Joseph
Rowe report that he received an academical education in the
province of Canada; after which, at about seventeen years of
age, he entered the office of the attorney-general for that province as a clerk and student of the law; that he diligently attended
to the business of that office and a suitable course of study the
term of two years; all which the committee conceive is equal
to a collegiate education in this State. That he has resided
more than three years in Boston as a clerk in the office of Mr.
Tudor. The committee, having considered the qualifications of
Mr. Rowe, are of opinion that he may be duly admitted to the
Bar.

and in 1798:

The committee of Suffolk Bar, appointed to examine and
ascertain the literary acquirements of Mr. Holder Slocum, Jr.,
now a student with Judge Minot, have attended that service, and
report that they find Mr. Slocum has so far attended to the
Latin language that a moderate degree of attention and practice
will probably enable him to render it sufficiently familiar for the
purposes of his intended profession. He has paid no attention
to the Greek, and has not been sufficiently instructed in the
opinion of your committee, in logic, metaphysics, and mathematics. He has read some approved writers in history, and has
attended considerably to the French language.
It is the opinion of the committee that on his remaining in an
office three years from the present time, with an attention for
part of the time, under the direction of his instructor, to history
and metaphysics, and occasionally to the Latin language, it will
be proper, at the expiration of that period, if he continues the

assiduity and attention which he has hitherto manifested, to allow of his admission to the Bar.

and, Jan. 18, 1800, a student from the Litchfield Law School was refused:

The committee of Suffolk Bar, appointed on the application of Mr. Samuel Hawkins for admission to the bar in this county report,—that in September last the said Hawkins was admitted as an attorney and counsellor at law at the Court of Common Pleas in the county of Litchfield, in Connecticut, and in October last he was admitted an attorney and counsellor at the Court of Common Pleas in the county of Dutchess, in the State of New York, which admissions appear to be duly certified. He also produces certificates of having studied one year with Tappan Reeve, Esq., in Connecticut, and two years with Jno. ———, Esq., of Troy, in the State of New York. He also states that he studied one year with Mr. Ogden, of which he has no certificate with him. He had not a college education, but studied with a private tutor previous to his living with Mr. Ogden. Mr. Hawkins is a native of the State of New York. The committee are of opinion, under the circumstances above stated (that he) is not now admissible to the Bar of this county.

Often, however, the rules were enforced liberally, owing to special circumstances. Thus, on July 21, 1778, it was voted that Mr. Christopher Gore (later Governor of Massachusetts and a noted lawyer) "be considered as having studied the law according to the rules of the Bar since the month of July 1776, and that he be entitled to the privileges of such a student."

So too, on December 3, 1779:

Upon motion made by Mr. Tudor, that Mr. Fisher Ames might be considered as a student with him from April, 1778, although he had during that time pursued his studies at Dedham, after consideration and debate, *Voted,* That Mr. Ames be considered as a law student from the first day of January, 1779, only (this indulgence allowed from some particular circumstances in his favor), and that at the expiration of three years from that day, he continuing in Mr. Tudor's office for the future, he be recommended to be sworn only on condition that he submit to an examination by the Bar, particularly in the practical business of the profession.

In 1782, John Adams was allowed by vote to take into his office, Jonathan Williams, as a clerk, "Mr. Williams having a fair moral character and a liberal education at Harvard College;" Mr.

Adams also took another clerk having "a fair character," Mr. Edward Hill.

It is interesting to note that the legal reputation of the Suffolk Bar was so high at this time that there were many applications from Southern law students—men who in pre-Revolutionary days would have gone to England to study in the Inns of the Inner or Middle Temple.

Thus, in October 1783, it was voted:

On motion of Mr. Hichborn, that Mr. Richard Brook Roberts be admitted as a student in his office with a deduction of one year from the usual term required by the rules for such students previous to their recommendation for the oath, *Voted,* That Mr. Roberts be admitted accordingly with the proposed allowance, provided he produces a certificate from a gentleman of the profession in Carolina that he has read law under such gentleman's direction for one year at least.

And, in July 1784:

On motion of Mr. Gardiner, to have his son, John Gardiner, admitted into his office as a student of law; and on motion from Mr. Gore to have the liberty of taking into his office Mr. William Hill (a young gentleman from North Carolina), as a student of law, it appearing to the Bar that neither of these young gentlemen had received a college education, *Voted* unanimously, That a committee be appointed to examine the said young gentlemen with respect to their literary qualifications, and to report their opinion thereon to the Bar.

And in April 1781, it was "unanimously assented to that Mr. William Hunter Torrens of Charlestown, South Carolina, be considered as a law student in Mr. Lowell's office from Jan. 1, 1781". On August 21, 1787, there is the record that Mr. Isaac Parker—(afterwards the first Royall Professor of Law at Harvard College, and Chief Justice of Massachusetts) "be considered as a student in Mr. William Tudor's office from August 1, 1787"; and, July 3, 1790, Mr. Tudor received consent to take into his office as a student, Mr. Josiah Quincy (later President of Harvard College).

In 1780, it was voted by the Suffolk Bar, that "no gentleman take a student into his office for a less consideration than one hundred pounds sterling," and in 1783, that "no gentleman should in the future have more than three students in his office."

Of the standard of legal etiquette and morality, the vote of March 20, 1784, is significant:

Voted unanimously that no gentleman of the Bar ought to go out of his office to put himself in the way of applications for drawing of writs nor to employ any other persons to do business for him out of his office.

Other States had similar restrictive provisions as to admission to practice, sometimes formulated by Bar Associations, and sometimes prescribed by rules of Court or by statute. Thus, in New Hampshire, a State Bar Association, as early as 1788, and later in 1805, adopted elaborate *General Regulations for the Gentlemen of the Bar,* providing that:

In case a candidate for admission as a student in an office has not had a degree in the arts he shall, excepting a knowledge of the Greek language, be duly qualified to be admitted to the first class of students of Dartmouth College.

College graduates were required to study in an office three years; non-graduates, five years. No member of the Bar could receive more than three students in his office; nor could he receive any student without the consent of the County Bar. No member of the Bar was allowed to receive less than $250 as a tuition fee for a student. No lawyer was to be admitted to the Bar of the Superior Court, until after two years practice in the Court of Common Pleas.(1)

In Vermont, by statute of 1787, and by Regulations of the Bar, the same conditions prevailed.

In Rhode Island, two years study for college graduates, and three years for non-graduates, were prescribed; and a candidate could not be proposed to the court until he had obtained the approbation and consent of his County Bar.

The same rule prevailed in Connecticut, as early as 1795, either by rule or custom, and after 1807 by rule of the Supreme Court.

In New Jersey, a lawyer had to be recommended by the Justices of the Supreme Court to the Governor for a license to practise, and to receive such recommendation, he must serve as a clerk

---

(1) *Rules of the Court,* by Joseph B. Walker,— *Southern New Hampshire Bar Assn. Proc.,* Vol. IV. See also *Proceedings of Grafton and Coos County Bar Assn.* (1891).

three years if a college graduate, four years if a non-graduate. He must also pass an examination before a committee of three out of the twelve serjeants.

In New York, a Bar Association had existed from about 1745 to 1770; but little is known of it, and its records are not extant. In the middle of the 18th Century, the members of the Bar, to prevent inroads upon their practice, made an agreement not to receive into their offices, as clerks, any young men who intended to pursue the law as a profession. This rule did not long prevail; for it was found that it would tend to cause young men to leave the Colony to study—as for instance, John Jay, whose father had decided to send him to England, but changed his mind when the Bar revoked its rule, and placed him in the office of Benjamin Kissam. In 1799, the Supreme Court of New York adopted rules, requiring a period of seven years study in the office of a practising attorney, before admission to practise; but a period not exceeding four years spent on classical studies might be credited on the seven years.(1)

In Maryland, three years' study under inspection of some practising attorney or judge was required. and also an examination by two gentlemen of the Bar.

In Delaware, three years' study was prescribed.

In Pennsylvania, by rule of the Supreme Court in 1788, the requirements were, four years' study as a clerk and one year's practice in the Court of Common Pleas, or three years' clerkship and two years' practice and examination by two attorneys; or two years' clerkship after 21 years of age and two years' practice, and examination.

In Virginia, only one year's study was required.

In North Carolina and South Carolina, no particular time was prescribed.

In Massachusetts, New York, and New Jersey, the old distinction between attorneys and counsellors existed. In the other States, there were no such separate classes of lawyers; but, in all of them, two year' practice before the inferior court was prescribed, before admission was granted to practice in the higher court.

In two States, law clubs had existed for the promotion of social intercourse in the profession.

(1) For complete account, see *Admission to the Bar in New York, Yale Law Journal,* Vol. XVI. (1906).

Thus, in Massachusetts, "The Sodality" was formed in 1765, with Otis, Gridley, Quincy, and Adams as its leading spirits, of which Otis said:

Let us form our style upon the ancient and best English authorities. I hope, I expect to see at the Bar, in consequence of this Sodality, a purity, an eloquence, and a spirit surpassing anything that has ever appeared in America.

In New York, in 1770, "The Moot" was founded, as a club "to encourage a more profound and ample study of the civil law, historical and political jurisprudence, and the law of nature". Its most active member was William Livingston, and the "father of the bar," Samuel Jones. Other veterans—Kissam, Smith, Scott, and Morris—used to attend, while the junior members of prominence were John Jay, Egbert Benson, Richard Morris Smith, Robert R. Livingston, Stephen DeLancey, and Lindley Murray. Many learned questions were seriously discussed; and it is said that a Chief Justice of the Superior Court once sent an issue of law to the Moot for its advice. Its last meeting was on January 6, 1775(1).

One other feature in the practice of the profession in these early years, which disappeared later, had a marked influence on the lawyer's development—the close, personal relationship which the members of the Bar bore to each other.

This is well described in a letter from John Adams to his nephew William Cranch (the Supreme Court Reporter), of March 14, 1790.

To the original of the bar meetings I was a witness. . . .
They introduced a candor and liberality in the practice of the Bar that was never before known in Mass. Mr. Pratt was so sensible of their utility that when we took leave of him at Dedham, his last words to us were. Brethren, forsake not the assembling of yourselves together. My advice to you and all the young gentlemen coming up, as well as to those now on the stage, is never to suffer such meetings to go into disuse, let who will clamor about them. . . . What? is it unlawful for the gentlemen of the profession to spend an evening together once a week? to converse upon law and upon their practice; to bear complaints of unkind unfair and ungentlemanlike practice; to compare difference; to agree that they will not introduce ignorant, illiterate, or ill bred, or unprincipled students or can-

---

(1) See *The Republican Court,* by Rufus W. Griswold (1855).

didates; that they will not practice any kind of chicanery, or take unmanly disadvantages of one another, to the injury of clients, for accidental or inadvertant slips in pleading or otherwise?

And again he wrote:

Many of these meetings were the most delightful entertainments I ever enjoyed. The spirit that reigned was that of sense, generosity, honor, and integrity; and the consequences were most happy; for the courts and the Bar, instead of scenes of wrangling, chicanery, quibbling and ill manners, were soon converted into order, decency, truth and candor. Mr. Pratt was so delighted with these meetings and other effects, that when we all waited upon him to Dedham on his way to New York to take his seat as Chief Justice of that State, he said to us, Brethren, above all things forsake not the assembling of yourselves together.

The intimacy and gaiety of the intercourse between the Bar and the Bench, is shown in the account of the conditions surrounding James Sullivan's practise in Massachusetts and Maine in the latter part of the 18th Century.(1)

Professional habits were decidedly convivial, and gentlemen thrown together for several weeks, often under the same roof, were quite disposed to be amused. The manners of the judges were not only decorous, and the members of the Bar were courteous and well-bred; but in their familar intercourse there was little formality or restraint and their festivities were seasons of wit and frolic, and often sufficiently uproarious. When the business of the term was nearly completed, it was customary for both Bench and Bar to assemble at the tavern for a social meeting. On these occasions, they constituted a court among themselves, appointing one of their number Chief Justice, for the trial of all breaches of good fellowship during the term. Judge Sewall describes one of these meetings at Biddeford, when the inferior court was sitting at Ladd's Tavern, there being no courthouse in the place. John Lowell had arrived, late on Monday evening, to attend its sessions, and, finding the inn full, sought lodgings elsewhere, probably at his friend Sullivan's, where he was always a welcome guest. He left his horse tied at the inn door, expecting it would be properly cared for; but the landlord never gave it a thought. When, on Friday evening, a court was held for the hearing of all omissions and commissions which had occurred during the week, Ladd was called upon to answer for leaving the horse unattended to, and defended himself on the

---

(1) *Life of James Sullivan,* by R. G. Amory.

plea that he had received no orders to put him up. The case was tried with becoming gravity, and the judge, upon the evidence, sentenced Ladd to pay a single bowl of good punch for his neglect, and Lowell twice as much for not taking care of his own steed.

And the same conviviality existed in the other States, as Kennedy's description of the Virginia Circuits, during the early life of William Wirt, shows(1):

> The riding of the Circuit, which always brought several into company, and the adventures of the wayside, gave to the Bar a sportive and lighthearted love of association which greatly fostered the opportunity and the inclination for convivial pleasure. A day spent upon the road on horseback, the customary visits made to friends upon the way, the jest and the song, the unchecked vivacity inspired by this grouping together of kindred spirits— all had their share in imparting brotherhood. Then the contests of the Bar which followed in the forum, the occasions they afforded for the display of wit and eloquence, and the congratulations of friends were so many additional provocatives to that indulgence which found free scope, when evening brought all together under one roof, to rehearse their pleasant adventures and to set flowing the currents of mirth and good humor, "to make a night of it" as the phrase goes. The Bar yet retains some of these characteristics; but the present generation (1849) may but feebly conceive the prevading and careless joyousness with which in that early time the members of their mirthful craft pursued their business through a country side. . . . The present generation will bear witness to many an ancient green room joke of the circuit.

In fact, many older lawyers have been of the opinion that the largest and best part of the legal education of the past was this mingling of the whole Bar together in travelling from county to county, and from court to court, the enforced personal relations which were brought about, and the presence of the younger members of the Bar during the trials of cases by their seniors.

"An able Bar," said Hugh Blair Grigsby, of Virginia, in his eulogy of L. W. Tazewell, "is the best school of law; for of all lessons for a student, the contests of able men with each other in the practical game of life are the best."

Perhaps nowhere was this side of a lawyer's training better summed up than in the words by Senator George F. Hoar (writing, it is true, of a later period of practice (1845-1855),

---

(1) *Memoirs of William Wirt,* Vol. I, by John P. Kennedy (1849).

but of a period which had not entirely lost the old characteristics) (1) :

The judge and jurymen and the lawyers from out of town used to come into Worcester and stay at the old Sykes or Thomas Tavern.

The court sat till six o'clock and often far into the evening and began at half past eight or nine—so there was no chance for country lawyers to go home at night. There was great fun at these old taverns in the evening and at meal time . . . The whole Bar and the public seemed to take an interest in important trials. People came in from the country round about with their covered wagons, simply for the pleasure of attending court and seeing the champions contend with each other. The lawyers who were not engaged in the case were always ready to help those who were, with advice and suggestion. It used to be expected that members of the Bar would be in the court house hearing the trials, even if they were not engaged in them. . . . I cannot but think that the listening to the trial and argument of causes by skilful advocates was a better law school than any we have now and that our young men especially in the large cities fail to become good advocates and to learn the art of putting on a case and of examining and cross examining for want of a constant and faithful attendance on the courts.

A similar glimpse of the sociability of the judges and the lawyers, written of a later period, but descriptive of the earlier is to be found in the diary of Richard Henry Dana, Jr.(2)

March 10, 1853. Court at Dedham. We have very pleasant times here at the trials. The judge, the sheriff and the members of the Bar from out of town board together at the hotel; the judge sitting at the head of the table, and the sheriff at the foot, the lawyers seating themselves by a tacit understanding according to age and importance, and there is a good deal of pleasant conversation. At dinner there will often be a stray guest from Boston, who has come up to make a motion or look after his docket. Choate, Bartlett and Hallett dropped in on us this week. Here, too, is the remnant of the old style in which the courts used to be received. The sheriff with a long white rod comes to the tavern and stands by the door and precedes the judge on his way to court and into his seat, and in the same way conducts him back at the adjournment each day.

(1) *Autobiography of Seventy Years,* by George F. Hoar, Vol. II.
(2) *Richard Henry Dana,* by C. F. Adams, Vol. I, (1891).

CHAPTER VIII.

Early Law Professorships.

With the close of the Revolutionary War there began a new era in legal education.

The broadening of the field of general education and the development of American Nationality in all branches of arts and sciences, which then took place, were reflected in the plans which were made in various American colleges to introduce the study of the Law into their curriculum. It seems to have escaped the attention of historians, however, that the first move in this direction was at Yale College—and by its President, Ezra Stiles, a man of singularly liberal learning and broad character.(1)

It appears from President Stiles' diary that, at the time of his election in 1777, the Assembly or Legislature of Connecticut proposed to endow three professorships for the College— one of law, one of medicine, and one of oratory, provided the Assembly might have some voice in the appointment of Professors and Government of the College, and provided Stiles should be elected President(2)

The plan was never consummated, as the Corporation of the College declined to yield any of its powers. Pending negotiations, however, President Stiles was actively interested in the project, as appears from his diary Dec. 3, 1777:

---

(1) See *Literary Diary of Ezra Stiles*, Vol. II, p. 209.
"Sept. 19, 1777. My election to the Presidency of Yale College is an unexpected and wonderful ordering of Divine Providence. Not but that it has been talked of for years past; but I knew such reasons in the breasts of the fellows and I tho't such were the sentiments of the Assembly and a plurality of the Pastors respecting my ideas of ecclesiastical polity and doctrinal system of divinity as that it was impossible I should be elected . . . I have no more resolved in my mind whether I am qualified for such an office than for that of a prime minister or a Sultan; or whether I should on the whole be desirous of it; considering the smallness of the salary, and the great and complicated difficulties and labours which attend it, and hundred and fifty or 180 young gentlemen students is a bundle of wild fire not easily controlled and governed—and at best the diadem of a president is a crown of thorns."
(2) See *Literary Diary of Ezra Stiles*, Vol. II, under dates of Sept. 27, 1777, Nov. 13, 1777, Nov. 14, 1777, Dec. 3, 1777, Feb. 12, 1778, Feb. 27, 1778.

I drafted a plan of an University, particularly describing the Law and Medical Lectures, at the desire of the Corporation of Yale, to be by them laid before the Committee of the General Assembly of Connecticut, appointed to consider among other things whether it be expedient to found these two professorships.

This plan for a law professorship—the earliest ever suggested in this country—is well worthy of reproduction in full, as it has never before been published.(1)

The Professorship of Law is equally important with that of Medicine; not indeed towards educating Lawyers or Barristers, but for forming *Civilians*. Fewer than a quarter perhaps of the young gentlemen educated at College, enter into either of the learned professions of Divinity, Law or Physic: The greater part of them after finishing the academic Course return home, mix in with the body of the public, and enter upon *Commerce* or the *cultivation of their Estates*. And yet perhaps the most of them in the Course of their Lifes are called forth by their Country into some or other of the various Branches of civil Inprovement & the public offices in the State. Most certainly it is worthy of great attention, the Discipline and Education of these in that knowledge which shall qualify them to become useful Members of Society, as Selectmen, Justices of Peace, Members of the Legislature, Judges of Courts, & Delegates in Congress. How happy for a community to abound with men well instituted in the knowledge of their Rights & Liberties? This Knowledge is catching, & insinuates [among those] not of liberal Education—to fit them for public service. It is greatly owing to the Seats of Learning among us that the arduous Conflict of the present day has found America abundantly furnished with Men adequate to the great and momentous Work of constructing new Policies or forms of Government and conducting the public arrangements in the military, naval & political Departments & the whole public administration of the *Republic of the United States,* with that Wisdom & Magnanimity which already astonishes Europe and will honor us to late Posterity. We are enlarging into still greater Systems, in which we may transplant the Wisdom of all Countries & Ages. It is in this view chiefly, & principally for this end, that the several States may see the Expediency of endowing Professorships of Law in the Colleges. It is scarce possible to en-

---

(1) From a copy of the original manuscript now in the Yale University Library, furnished to the author by the courtesy of Franklin **B. Dexter,** Assistant Librarian of Yale University.

slave a Republic of Civilians, well instructed in their Laws, Rights & Liberties. The Lectures of a Professorship of Law may be resolved into four series.

I. The *civil Law*. It will be necessary to exhibit an Idea of the antient Roman Law in its purest State under the Senate, before the period of the Cæsars, & previous to the mutations which the Jus civile received by the imperatorial Edicts: then to take a view of the imperatorial Law down to the Times of Justinian. Then instead of attending to the mutations it assumed by being blended with the local Laws of the Roman Conquests, the Provinces—instead of considering how much of it is still preserved in the Jurisprudence of Poland, Germany, Holland, France, Spain or Italy—go directly to England and consider how much of the Jus civile entered into the Jurisprudence of England, for the greatest part of the Jurisprudence of America has been adopted from England. Three Streams of the imperial Law entered England & obtaines there with Efficacy to this day. The first is the canon or ecclesiastical Law, which it is hoped will never enter America; the second testamentary law; the third the maritime Law in Admiralty Courts. This last is of great Importance, for the Laws of Rhodes & Oleron. The whole system of Maritime Law will probably be adopted by these States, under the Improvement of a Jury for Trials in maritime Courts. This is all of the Civil Law which will be ever necessary for Americans to study.

II. The second series of Lectures may be upon the *Common Law* of England. For although neither this nor any other foreign Law will ever be in force in America by any Authority or Jurisdiction on the other side the Atlantic, it will however prevail by derivative Use, Custom & Adoption. It will be of particular Utility to exhibit a Lecture of Negatives, *i. e.,* a number of capital Things of the common Law of England which never could be, nor never was introduced here—& so to draw the Line—leaving all the rest as the common Law System of these States. Connected with this may be a summary Representation of the Statute Law, both those designedly made by Parliament for the Colonies which are henceforth forever abolished, & those adopted by the American Legislatures: and tho' many of these will be repealed, yet the greater part may remain in the Jurisprudence of the United States. As Justinian's Institutes may be the Textual Book for the Civil: so Hale's Analysis &c may be for the common Law.

III. The Subject of the third Series will be the Codes of the thirteen States. The Professor will exhibit the Spirit & Governing Principles of each Code. Connected with this will be a particular Representation of the Jurisprudence of Connecticut, the Courts & their Jurisdictions, and as much of the Course of Practice as is founded in principle, and not merely officinal,

for this is best learned at the Bar & by living with a Lawyer.
Degrees to be taken.

IV.   The last Series may consist of Lectures exhibiting the
Policies and Forms of Government of all the Kingdoms, Em-
pires & Republics in the World, especially those of Europe &
that of China—which last is perhaps the best formed Policy on
Earth, as it alone combines one-third of the whole human race.
The Nature & Wisdom of such a Policy is worthy the peculiar
Attention of the infant Empire in America, growing into a future
Greatness & Glory surpassing perhaps what have ever appeared.
And as we shall transplant all the Improvements in Knowledge,
Manufactures & Commerce from all Countries, so by a thorough
Knowledge of the fundamental Principles of their respective
public Politics, we may learn how to distinguish & avoid Pre-
cedents dangerous to Liberty.   Summary Representations of the
Spirit of the Laws & Jurisprudence of each & all the Kingdoms
& States will shew us what, having endured the Trial of Ages,
will be worthy of Adoption by the American Legislatures.   All
this will lay a Foundation for the accurate Knowledge of the
Laws of Nations—Laws of mutual Intercourse & political Trans-
actions between separate Sovereignties & Independent States, a
Branch of Knowledge necessary to regulate the Intercourse between these States, as well as the negotiations with European &
other foreign Powers.   This will enable such a multitude of
Gentlemen among the body of people at large to judge on political matters, as shall awe those into Fidelity whom the States
may entrust with public & important negotiations.   This political
Knowledge diffused through a State, will establish its Liberty,
Security & Aggrandizement too firmly to be overturned by either
a military power or those insidious Arts & corrupt measures,
which in conjunction with Arms have at length in all countries
prostrated the Rights of mankind, in a general Ruin.   The cultivation of this political Knowledge & Wisdom will transfuse
a spirit among the body of the people in America [which] will
be the only security of their Liberty under Providence, & tend
to effect that public Virtue & produce those wise Institutions
which may advance the United States to the Summit of political Perfection & Honor.

As stated before, this law professorship was never actually
founded; although candidates for the positions were discussed;
and John Adams, writes Stiles, "spoke of Mr. John Trumbull
Treas., of Yale Coll. as qualified for a Professorship in Law."(1)
Notwithstanding the failure of his plan, President Stiles evi-

_____

(1)   John Trumbull was a Yale graduate of 1767, had studied law in
the office of John Adams at Boston, was a practising lawyer in New
Haven and Treasurer of Yale College, 1776-1782.

dently retained his belief in the value of law as a part of an undergraduate education; for July 13, 1781, he notes in his Diary, "I gave an evening lecture on Law and Jurisprudence;" and on March 12, 1789, "This day I introduced for the first time Montesquieux Spirit of Laws as a Classical book into Yale College. The Senior Class began to recite the first Vol. this day. It never was used here before. But it has been recited in Jersey Coll (Princeton) ph. 3 or 4 years;" and on March 8, 1792, he noted that he gave a "Lect. on Law, 1. Law of Nature and Nations, 2 Jus Civile or antient Rom. Law, Pandects, Imperatorial Edicts and Eccl. or Canon Law, 3. Law of Engl. Common Law, Statutes, Courts of Westminster Reports, 4. Laws of the United States."

Although the Bar of Virginia was by no means the most prominent of the Colonial Bars, the first American Law Professorship (and the second in any English speaking country), was founded at the College of William and Mary in 1779—in the year after Blackstone had published the eighth and final edition of his lectures, and a year before his death.

It was to Thomas Jefferson that the science of law owed its first collegiate professor, eighty-seven years after the chartering of the College. In his autobiography he says:

On the first of June 1779, I was appointed Governor of the Commonwealth and retired from the Legislature. Being elected also one of the visitors of William and Mary College, a self electing body, I effected, during my residence in Williamsburg that year, a change in the organization of that institution, by abolishing the Grammar School and the two Professorships of Divinity and Oriental Languages, and substituting a Professorship of Law and Police, one of Anatomy, Medicine and Chemistry, and one of Modern Languages; and, the charter confining us to six Professors, we added the Law of Nature and Nations and the Fine Arts to the duties of the Moral Professor, and Natural History to those of the Professor of Mathematics and Natural Philosophy.

The following regulation was then adopted:

A student on paying annually 1000 pounds of tobacco shall be entitled to attend any two of the following professors, viz: of Law and Police; of Natural History and Mathematics; of Moral Philosophy, the Laws of Nature and of Nations, and of the Fine Arts.

Jefferson's old friend and teacher, George Wythe (then judge in the Court of Chancery), was appointed Law Professor. One of his first pupils, in 1779-1780, was John Marshall; but, the college exercises being interrupted by the occupation of the buildings successively by the British and French, in the summer before Yorktown, Marshall's law studies came to a rapid end, and he was admitted to the Bar, after slight preparation, in the same year, 1780.(1)   Among other of Wythe's students, prior to 1800, who later became distinguished lawyers, were Spencer Roane, Marshall's rival at the Virginia Bar; Benjamin Watkins Leigh, John J. Crittenden, William A. Rives, Alexander Campbell, John Breckenridge, John Wickham, H. St. George Tucker, W. H. Cabell, and L. W. Tazewell.

"Wythe, above all early statesmen, was deeply learned in the law; had traced all its doctrines to their fountain heads, delighted in the year book, from doomsday down; had *Glanville, Bracton, Britton,* and *Fleta* bound in collects; had all the British Statutes at full length, and was writing elaborate decisions every day, in which, to the amazement of county court lawyers, *Horace* and *Aulus Gellius* were sometimes quoted as authorities."(2)

"He carried his love of antiquity rather too far, for he frequently subjected himself to the charge of pedantry; and his admiration of the gigantic writers of Queen Elizabeth's reign had unfortunately betrayed him into an imitation of their quaintness—Yet, he was a man of great capacity, powerful in argument, elegantly keen and sarcastic in repartee—long the rival of Mr. Pendleton at the bar, whom he equalled as a common lawyer and greatly surpassed as a civilian. . . . No man was ever more entirely destitute of art . . . This simplicity and integrity of character sometimes exposed him to the arts and sneers of the less scrupulous—but he was not only pure, but above all suspicion."(3)

(1)   *American Historical Association Papers,* Vol. IV.
(2)   *Discourse on Life and Character of Littleton Waller Tazewell,* by Hon. Hugh Blair Grigsby (1830).
(3)   *Sketches of the Life of Patrick Henry,* by William Wirt (1817). John Randolph said of him, "he lived in the world without being of the world; that he was a mere incarnation of justice—that his judgments were all as between A and B; for he knew nobody; but went into court, as Astraea was supposed to come down from heaven, exempt from all human bias."
See especially *The Supreme Court of Appeals in Virginia, Green Bag.* Vol. V.

GEORGE WYTHE

Nat 1726 - Ob 1806

The quality of Judge Wythe's lectures may be estimated by the following opinion of Judge Roane, expressed regarding a manuscript copy of these lectures, in a letter from Governor John Tyler written to Jefferson, in 1810:

Judge Roane has read them, or most of them, and is highly pleased with them, thinks they will be very valuable, there being so much of his sound reasoning upon great principles, and not a mere servile copy of Blackstone and other British Commentators—a good many of his own thoughts on our constitutions and the necessary changes they have begotten, with that spirit of freedom which always marked his opinions.(1)

The following enteresting sidelight on this Professorship of Law is found in President Stiles' diary, June 8, 1784(2):

His Excellency, Gov. Jefferson of Virginia visited me with a letter from Mr. (Roger) Sherman at Congress. . . . He was educated at and entered Wm. & Mary Coll. 1761, where he studied five years, and left in 1766. Then became a Lawyer. He was one of the 24 visitors of Wm. & Mary Coll. . . . The salaries of the professors were £80 in Tobacco, now worth £150 or £160, the price of tobacco has doubled. The Professors besides their salys. have about £8 in Tobacco, now £12 or £15, from each scholar per ann. for Instruction. There are Eighty Undergraduates Students at present. . . . The Professor is

(1) The rest of the letter is of interest. It is not known if the lectures referred to are in existence now or not.

"Perhaps Mr. Ritchie before this time has informed you of his having possession of Mr. Wythe's MSS. lectures delivered at William and Mary College while he was professor of law and politics at that place. They are highly worthy of publication and but for the delicacy of sentiment and the remarkably modest and unassuming character of that valuable and virtuous citizen they would have made their way in the world before this. It is a pity they should be lost to society and such a monument of his memory be neglected. As you are entitled to it by his will (I am informed) as composing a part of his library, could you not find leisure time enough to examine it and supply some omissions which now and then are met with, I suppose from accident, or from not having time to correct and improve the whole as he intended.

I do not see why an American Aristides should not be known to future ages. Mr. Wm. Crane gave it to Mr. Ritchie who I suppose got it from Mr. Duval who always had access to Mr. Wythe's library and was much in his confidence."

See *Letters and Times of the Tylers*, by Leon G. Tyler, Vol. I.

(2) See *Literary Diary of Ezra Stiles*, Vol. III, p. 124, (1901). Thomas Jefferson had been introduced to Stiles by Roger Sherman in the following letter dated Annapolis, May 11, 1784.

"I take the liberty to introduce to you the Honorable Thomas Jefferson, Esqr. . . . He is a Gentleman of much philosophical as well as political knowledge—and I doubt not you will be very agreeably entertained with his conversation."

the Att. Gen. of the State and he makes more by his Professorship than as Attorney. . . . The Gov. is a most ingenious Naturalist and Philosopher—a truly scientific and learned man —and every way excellent. . . . *Blackston* is the Basis of Law Lect. in Wm. & Mary Coll., Philosophy, Medicine and Law seem to be their object.

Wythe resigned his professorship in 1800, and the chair was filled by St. George Tucker, whose lectures became the basis of his famous edition of *Blackstone,* published in 1803, and containing his commentaries on the Federal Law and Constitution. It was not until 1824, however, that the College conferred any degree of LL.B.

Ten years after the foundation of this Virginia professorship, the College of Philadelphia, on Aug. 17, 1790, formally appointed as Professor of Law, James Wilson, then an Associate Justice of the United States Supreme Court. The idea of this professorship probably originated in a request made to the Trustees by Francis Hopkinson, in 1789, that a number of young lawyers, who had formed themselves into a society for their mutual improvement, might have permission to hold their meetings in a college room. A year later, in August, 1790, the Trustees appointed Edward Shippen, James Wilson and Charles J. Hare, a committee to consider the utility and propriety of a law professorship. Wilson reported a plan embracing Constitutional and International Law, Origin and Rules of Common Law, Civil Law, Law Merchant and Maritime Law, designed "to furnish a rational and useful entertainment to gentlemen of all professions, and in particular to assist in forming the Legislator, the Merchant, and the Lawyer."(1)

Philadelphia, at this time, was the seat of the Federal Government; and the first of the twenty-four lectures which he was to deliver was given by Judge Wilson in the Hall of the Academy, in the presence of President Washington and his Cabinet, the Governor, and Members of Congress and of the Legislature, Mrs. Washington and other ladies, " a polite assembly" as the papers of the day described it.(2) Although he had read law with John Dickinson, and had been one of the signers of the

(1) *Historical Sketch of the Law Department of the University of Pennsylvania,* by Hampton N. Carson (1882).
(2) As to these lectures of Judge Wilson, see *History of Law Schools Amer. Bar Assn. Proc.* Vol. XXIV. See also *American Law Schools,* by W. G. Hammond, *Southern Law Review,* Vol. VII.

Declaration of Independence, and one of the leaders of the Philadelphia Bar, "Mr. Wilson on the bench was not the equal of Mr. Wilson at the bar, nor did his law lectures entirely meet the expectations that had been formed," wrote William Rawle, who practised under him;(1) and another contemporary writer said, "These lectures (since included in his works, published in 1804), have not met with general approbation, nor is their excellence altogether undisputed." It seems that his violent criticisms of Blackstone, and his ultra-Federalist views as to the powers of the National Government, did not commend themselves to the lawyers or to the public.

Of this first lecture, Fisher Ames wrote from Philadelphia to Thomas Dwight, Jan. 6, 1791(2):

I enclose Judge Wilson's introductory law lecture, addressed with a propriety which he says malice cannot question, to Mrs. Washington. . . . The great law learning and eminent station of the writer had raised great expectations of the performance. Whether there are not many parts that discretion and modesty . . . would have expunged you will be at liberty to judge. It will be a frolic for the London Reviewers to make the Judge's feathers fly. He has censured the English form of government and can expect no mercy.

The truth is, Wilson's temper and habits were those of an advocate, rather than of a judge. His style was diffusive; and the lectures, though scholarly and elegant essays on general jurisprudence, embellished with historical allusions, were not useful as practical instruction in Common Law(3) Published in 1804, these lectures are now chiefly of interest for the complete exposition of Wilson's views of the principles of the Constitution and of the Federal Government.

The course was kept up through part of the second winter; but though requiring a third season for its completion, was discontinued, probably because of lack of general interest shown by the students. And although on the consolidation of the College of Philadelphia with the University of Pennsylvania, in 1792, a

---

(1) See *Address of Samuel Dickson, Penn. Bar Assn. Proc.,* Vol. VI.
(2) *Life and Letters of Fisher Ames.*
(3) See *The Study of the Common Law,* by W. D. Lewis, *Penn Bar Assn. Proc.* Vol. IV.
See also comments on these lectures by David Hoffman, in 1823, in his *Lecture introductory to a course of lectures now delivering in the University of Maryland.*

similar law professorship was founded, to which Wilson was appointed, he gave no lectures. He died in 1798. No step was taken to fill his place, until March 20, 1817, when Charles Willing Hare (who had been admitted to the Bar in 1799 with Charles Chauncey, John Sergeant, and John B. Wallace) was elected Professor.

From 1790 to 1824, it is stated that David Howell, a distinguished lawyer of Rhode Island, filled a chair of Law at Brown College, being also Professor of Mathematics and Natural Philosophy; but little is known of his lectures.

There had been a professorship of Natural Law in King's College (Columbia) in New York, as early as 1773; but it does not appear from the records that anything like a system of education in Common Law, or in the preparation of young men for the Bar, was intended. The Professor probably taught political ethics, rather than law. At the disruption of the College, in 1776, when the British occupied New York, the professorship was discontinued. But in 1784, the College voted to establish an elaborate curriculum of sixteen professorships in the Faculty of Arts, eight in the Faculty of Medicine, three in the Faculty of Law and a Faculty of Divinity.(1) No further action was taken as to a Faculty of Law until Dec. 2, 1793, when the Trustees resolved to establish a professorship of law, with a salary of two hundred pounds per annum, to be paid out of the founds allowed to the College by the Legislature; and James Kent was elected to fill the chair.(2)

A graduate of Yale in 1781, Kent had, at the time, a rather small practice in Poughkeepsie, but had "with an intensity of

---

(1) *The College Curriculum in the United States,* by Louis F. Snow (1907).

(2) A Pamphlet entitled *Present State of Learning in Columbia College,* says:
"This Professorship is intended to comprise a brief review of the history, the nature, the several forms and just ends of civil government—a sketch of the origin, progress and final settlement of the government of the United States—a particular detail of the organization and duties of the several departments of the general government, together with an examination of such parts of the civil and criminal codes of the federal jurisprudence as shall be most susceptible of illustrations and most conducive to public utility. The constitutions of the several states and the connections they bear with the general government will then be considered and the more particular examination of the constitution of this state. The whole detail of our municipal law with relation to the rights of property and forms of administrating justice, both civil and criminal will be treated fully and at large."

ardor embarked in Federal politics and quite gained an ascendant in the local proceedings and discussions."

. . It was the character I had insensibly acquired as a scholar, and a Federalist, and a presumed (though it was not true) well read lawyer, that the very first year that I removed to New York, I was appointed a Professor of Law in Columbia College. The influence of Dr. S. Bard, of Judge Hobart (of the Supreme Court), of B. Livingston, Edward Livingston, and probably of Chief Justice Jay procured me the appointment.(1)

Kent wrote regarding his course of lectures which began in Nov., 1794, in the College Hall.

I read that season twenty-six lectures (two a week), and was honored by the attendance, throughout the course, of seven students and thirty-six gentlemen, chiefly lawyers and law students who did not belong to the college. . . . They were very well received; but I have long since discovered them to have been slight and trashy productions. I wanted judicial labors to teach me precision. I soon became considerably involved in business, but was never fond of, nor much distinguished in, the contentions of the Bar.

One of his hearers, however, entertained a different view of the introductory lecture, and described "the views that it unfolds of the true nature and province of the law and of the advantages to be derived from its study" as "judicious, discriminating, and comprehensive." This lecture was privately printed by the Trustees of the College in 1794; and, the next year, the first three lectures, or dissertations, on the *Theory, History and Duties of Civil Government,* the *History of the American Union,* and the *Law of Nations,* were published in book form by the author.

Of these lectures, John Adams wrote, in 1795, to his son, "I am much pleased with the Lecture and esteem the talents and character of the Professor". When he closed his course, in March 1795, Kent wrote that his lectures had extended not only through the Constitution and jurisprudence of the Union, the Constitution of this and the other States, but our doctrine of real property.

My first plan was to examine law of personal property, includ-

----

(1) *Memoirs of Chancellor Kent,* by William Kent (1898).

ing the commercial branches and the system of our criminal code. But I found myself absolutely unable to complete the whole, and was obliged to leave this first course imperfect. It will be an easy thing to make these additions and review and improve the whole by next November.

As a matter of fact, Kent never did completely "make these additions," until his later lectures delivered in 1824, but the earlier lectures, together with the later, formed the nucleus of his famous *Commentaries*.

Of his second course, begun in November 1795, Kent wrote:

I read thirty-one lectures in my office, and had only two students, besides my clerks. The next season I attempted another course; but, no students offering to attend, I dismissed the business, and in May 1797, sent a letter of resignation to the Trustees. This was not accepted; and, in the winter of 1797 and 1798, in my office, I read lectures to six or eight students; and, in April 1798, I finally resigned the office.

In his letter of resignation to the Trustees he expressed the hope

that the general principles of our Constitution and laws may still be academically taught, and that the institution which you have so liberally established may hereafter under abler professors, and in more auspicious times be crowned with happier success.

Though unsuccessful as a professor, Kent's claims as a profound lawyer were recognized, in this same year, by his appointment as a judge of the Supreme Court, by John Jay, Governor of New York. He was, at the time, just thirty-five years of age. It would be unjust, however, to Kent's fame as a jurist to attribute the failure of his law course to any lack of legal ability. Unquestionably, the heated political rancor of the time, the sharp division of parties, and the constant newspaper and pamphlet discussion of Federalist and Anti-Federalist principles caused the students of those days to regard these lectures as more political in their nature than legal. And while the lecturer's views on constitutional law were broad and scientific, they were essentially Federalist,—saturated with Alexander Hamilton, and presenting a view of the power of the courts which was not popular with the rising tide of Republican, anti-John-Adams lawyers and laymen. (1)

In the same year of Kent's resignation at Columbia, 1798, there was founded the first collegiate law professorship intended for other than undergraduates, which had any permanency. It is certainly striking that this event should have occurred in a little frontier town of about 1700 inhabitants—at the University of Transylvania in Lexington, Kentucky. This institution was chartered in 1798, and in the next year the law department was organized, with George Nicholas as Professor of Law and Politics. On his death, the same year, he was succeeded by James Brown, who held the office until 1804. In that year, Henry Clay, a young man of twenty-seven, who had been at the Bar seven years, was appointed, and held the professorship until 1807. He was succeeded by John Monroe, in 1807. Then the office lapsed; but was revived in 1814, when John Pope held it until 1816, succeeded by Joseph Cabell Breckenridge, in 1817.

The University, though small and local, had, by 1802, acquired a library of 1700 volumes and also a separate law library. In 1814, out of a total attendance of 62, nine were law students; and, in 1818, the University had a total of 110 students, or fully half the number then in Harvard College.

Three years after Kent's resignation at Columbia, the Corpo-

---

(1) The high conception of the place of a lawyer and of his duty to know the Constitution in a Republic, is shown in the following extracts from Kent's introductory lecture:

"The importance of a knowledge of our Constitutional principles as a part of the education of an American lawyer arises from the uncommon efficacy of our courts of justice in being authorized to bring the validity of a law to the test of the Constitution . . . I consider then the courts of justice as the proper and intended guardians of our limited constitution against the factions and encroachments of the legislative body.

. . . A lawyer in a free country . . . should be a person of irreproachable virtue and goodness. He should be well read in the whole circle of the arts and sciences. He should be fit for the administration of public affairs and to govern the Commonwealth by his councils, establish it by his laws and correct it by his example. . . .

The people of this country are under singular obligations from the nature of their government to place the study of the law at least on a level with the pursuits of classical learning. The art of maintaining social order and promoting social prosperity is not with us a mystery for only for those who may be distinguished by the adventitious advantages of birth and fortune. . . . A wide field is open to all—all may be summoned into public employment. . . . Extensive legal and political knowledge is requisite to render men competent to administer the government. A general initiation into the elementary learning of our law has a tendency to guard against mischief and at the same time to promote a keen sense of right and warm love of freedom."

ration of Yale College again took up the subject of legal education, and, as a part of President Dwight's efforts to broaden the
scheme of studies, voted to establish a professorship of law:

to furnish lectures on the leading principles of the Law of Nature
and Nations, on the general principles of civil government, particularly of Republican representative government, on the Constitution of the United States and of the State of Connecticut
. . . and on the various obligations and duties resulting
from the social relations, especially those which arise from our
own National and State Governments.

After that date no lectures were given until 1826, when the
Hon. Elizur Goodrich, of the Class of 1779, was appointed to the
Chair, and gave occasional lectures until 1810;(1) after which
date, no regular lectures were given until 1826, when the Kent
Professorship was founded (endowed in 1833) :

for delivering lectures, or otherwise communicating instruction
to the undergraduates in the academic department in natural,
international, constitutional or municipal law, and civil polity,
and such other subjects of jurisprudence as the Faculty or corporation shall from time to time approve.

Princeton College offered instruction in law to undergraduates,
1795-1812, by its President Samuel S. Smith, whose lectures, as
appears from the title page of Vol. 2 of his *Moral and Political
Philosophy* (1812), comprehended "those principles on the subjects of jurisprudence, politics and public law or the law of
nature and nations, with which every man . . . in a free
country ought to be acquainted."(2)

At Dartmouth College, as early as 1808, the Trustees, a large
number of whom were eminent lawyers, planned to establish a
law professorship, and accordingly passed the following vote
Jan. 7, 1808(3) :

Whereas, An establishment of professorships in different
branches of education at universities facilitates improvement;
and as a more general acquaintance with the important science

---

(1) President Dwight, in his *Travels in New England,* published in
1821, says: "The Professor of Law at Yale is required to read 36 lectures
only, to be completed in two years, on the Law of Nations, the American
Constitution, and the Jurisprudence of Connecticut."
(2) See *Collegiate Study of Law,* by James F. Colby, *Amer. Bar Ass.
Proc.,* Vol. XIX (1896).
(3) See *Legal and Political Studies in Dartmouth College,* by James
F. Colby (1896).

of law would be greatly conducive to the welfare and prosperity of the citizens of our country; and as in promoting that end the establishment of a professorship of Law at this university is highly desirable; Therefore,

Resolved, Unanimously that this board will proceed to establish a professorship of Law and appoint a suitable person to the office so soon as adequate means shall be furnished. And as all the present funds are necessarily applied to other objects of education the liberal and patriotic are earnestly solicited to favor and promote by their munificence the early accomplishment of this design.

Voted, that the secretary be requested to cause a suitable number of subscription papers to be printed for the purpose of aiding the object contemplated in the foregoing resolution.

Owing to the factional troubles which prevailed among the governing officials of the College, and which finally culminated in the famous *Dartmouth College Case,* in 1817, no action was taken under this vote for many years.

In 1816, the Regents of the University of Maryland established a professorship of law, and appointed David Hoffman. He however gave no regular course of lectures; but, in his own words:

In America alone, a law student was left to his own insulated and unassisted efforts. In the hope of supplying what I deemed an important deficiency in the education of our country, I have since my appointment to the law Chair devoted myself to performing a course of lectures, and sketched a plan, laid before the Public in my *Syllabus,* (April 1821), embracing every title known to the great body of law, exceeding in variety and extent any scheme of lectures hitherto attempted. I prepared *A Course of Legal Study*—the first manual ever arranged for law students in England or this country (published in 1817).(1)

Later, 1821-1826, Hoffman conducted a struggling "Law Institute," a private affair of his own, to which he proposed to deliver his stupendous course of 301 lectures, combined with a most elaborate system of Moot Courts—his fee being $120. From lack of interest or the expense, the number of students was small, and the school gradually died out.

---

(1) *An Address to Students of Law in the United States,* by David Hoffman, (July, 1824).

For further information as to Hoffman's work, see his *Syllabus* (April, 1821); his First Lecture, on Law Books and Instruction, published in Oct. 1823; his Second Lecture, published in 1825, his Third Lecture on Moot Courts in 1826, and his Ninth Lecture on Civil Law, in 1832.

In 1816, Middlebury College in Vermont established a professorship of law, which attracted considerable attention, because of its incumbent, the noted Nathaniel Chipman, Chief Justice of Vermont.(1)

The system of study advocated was described by Chipman, in his introductory lecture:

> Let the student not content himself with merely learning to recollect or repeat the arguments or reasons which he has met with in reading as the arguments or reasons of others; but let him endeavor so to penetrate, understand and appropriate them that they may appear to his mind to be exclusively his own. The former is mere memory; the latter only is knowledge. . . .
> All this, the attentive student will find in the volumes of Blackstone, which as an elementary treatise, has not been surpassed in any science. The next step proper to be taken by the students is to proceed analytically; to begin with one branch and the minor divisions of that branch, to make himself fully master of it; then and not till then, to proceed to another branch, until he shall have encompassed within his knowledge the whole system complete. In his course of reading it is indispensable for him if he wishes to make proficiency to turn to all the cases and authorities and to examine them for himself.

It will be readily seen that none of these professorships attempted to afford a complete or practical education for law students. Towards the end of the 18th Century, however, several private law schools were founded by individual lawyers, where such an education could be obtained.

Of these, the first and by far the most influential was that founded by Judge Tapping Reeve, and known as the Litchfield Law School. Oddly enough, this School, to which students came from all parts of the Union, grew up, not in any city or seat of learning, but in a little country town of Connecticut, a county seat, having hardly more than 1500 inhabitants, the home of the distinguished Wolcott family, the birthplace of several Governors and Chief Justices of the Colony and of the State. "Here on a broad shaded street, in one of the most beautiful of New England villages, stood (and stands) an old Colonial house, the residence, at the close of the American Revolution, of a Connecticut lawyer. Hard by the house was the owner's law office, a small

---

(1)   See *Life of Nathaniel Chipman*, by Daniel Chipman (1846).

one story wooden building, much resembling the familiar district school."(1)

In this small wooden building, Judge Tapping Reeve began his own School for law students, in 1784,(2) five years after Wythe was made professor of law at William and Mary, five years before the establishment of the United States Supreme Court, and five years before the publication (in Connecticut) of the first volume of American law reports. Judge Reeve was born in Long Island, New York, in 1744, a graduate of Princeton (then the College of New Jersey), in 1763, studied law with Jesse Root(3) at Hartford, and settled in Litchfield in 1772. Five years after he started his School, he was appointed judge of the Superior Court, and he became later Chief Justice.

In 1798, one of his pupils, James Gould, then a practicing lawyer in Litchfield, born in 1770, and a Yale graduate of 1795, became associated with him. Later Jabez W. Huntingdon(4) assisted Judge Gould as an instructor. Judge Reeve died in 1823, and Judge Gould had sole charge until 1833.

Prior to 1798, the School had, in all, about 210 students. From 1798 to its abandonment, in 1833, there were 805 students.

As proof of the national character of the School, it is interesting to note, that from 1798 down to the founding of the Harvard Law School in 1817, the students (other than those from Connecticut), hailed from the following localities:—Massachusetts 72; New York 44; Georgia 35; South Carolina 27; Maryland 25; New Hampshire 15; Vermont and Delaware 14 each; Rhode Island 11; Kentucky 9; Pennsylvania 8; New Jersey and North Carolina 7 each; Virginia 6; Louisiana 3; District of Columbia and Ohio 2 each; Maine and Mississippi 1 each.

---

(1) *Address of Prof. James Barr Ames,* at the Dedication of the New Building of the Law Department of the Univ. of Penn. (1900).

(2) A writer in the Albany *Law Journal,* Vol. XX, in an article on the Litchfield Law School, says that it was established in 1782; and so it appears in the catalogue of the School, published in 1831. Professor Joel Parker, of the Harvard Law School, and other law writers, give the correct date, however, as being 1784. (See *The Law School of Harvard College,* by Joel Parker (1871.)

(3) Jesse Root was graduated at Princeton in 1756, became a preacher, was admitted to the Bar as a lawyer in 1763, and after serving as colonel in the war and a member of the Continental Congress, became a judge of the Superior Court.

(4) Jabez W. Huntingdon graduated at the School in 1808, was later United States Senator, and Judge of the Connecticut Supreme Court.

The founding of the Harvard Law School in 1817 and various private law Schools in Massachusetts (1820-30) largely reduced Litchfield's quota from that State; so that from 1817 to 1833, the graduates (outside of Connecticut), were distributed as follows: from New York 81; Georgia 29; Pennsylvania 21; South Carolina and Massachusetts 16 each; Virginia and North Carolina 13 each; Maryland and Rhode Island 11 each; Vermont 10; New Jersey and New Hampshire 5 each; Louisiana and Delaware 4 each; Maine and Alabama 3 each; Ohio and District of Columbia 2 each; Tennessee and Indiana 1 each.

Of these alumni—16 became United States Senators; 50 Members of Congress; 40 Judges of higher State courts; 8 Chief Justices of State courts; 2 Justices of the United States Supreme Court; 10 Governors of States; 5 members of the Cabinet. And as Professor Joel Parker of the Harvard Law School said in 1871(1):

Probably no law school has had—perhaps I may add never will have—so great a proportion of distinguished men on its catalogue, if for no other reason, because attendance upon a Law School was then the rare exception, an advantage obtained in general only by very ambitious young men, and because there was then much less competition for the office and honors to which they aspired.

The contemporary opinions of the School are interesting. In 1813, it had fifty-four students, the largest in any one year of its history; and about that time, Timothy Dwight wrote(2):

It would not, it is believed, do discredit to any country. Law is here taught as a science, and not merely nor principally as a mechanical business; not as a collection of loose independent fragments, but as a regular well compacted system. At the same time, the students are taught the practice by being actually employed in it. A court is constituted, actions are brought and conducted through a regular process, questions are raised and the students become advocates in form. Students resort to this school from every part of the American Union. The number of them is usually about 40.

Nine years later, one of the first American law periodicals, the *United States Law Journal,* said in 1822:

---

(1) *Litchfield Hill,* by John D. Champlin, quoted in the Catalogue of 1900 prepared by George M. Woodruff and Archibald M. Howe.
The Law School of Harvard College, by Joel Parker (1871).
(2) *Travels in New England,* by Timothy Dwight, Vol. IV.

Law School, Litchfield, Conn.—First Law School in America

It enables the Law Student to acquire more in one year than is gained in three years if not in five in the ordinary method of securing an acquaintance with legal principles. . . . We speak with safety when our humble tribute is subsequent to the eulogium of such men as Chancellor Kent, Justice Spencer, Judge Story, the late C. J. Parsons. The fame of the law School at Litchfield was long since diffused over the nation and the seminary has been viewed for many years by legal tribunals as the fertile source of elemental knowledge and the nursery of eminent men.

Judge Gould was thus portrayed by an early and loyal graduate, Charles G. Loring, of Massachusetts(1):

The recollection is as fresh as the events of yesterday of our passing along the broad shaded streets of one of the most beautiful of the villages of New England with our inkstands in our hands and our portfolios under our arms to the lecture room of Judge Gould—the last of the Romans of Common Law lawyers—the impersonation of its genius and spirit. It was indeed in his eyes the perfection of human reason by which he measured not only every principle and rule of action, but almost every sentiment. . . . His highest visions of poetry seemed to be in the refinements of special pleading and to him a non sequitur in logic was an offence deserving at the least, fine and imprisonment—and a repetition of it, transportation for life.

The plan of instruction pursued is described by Professor Joel Parker, with the following comments:

Judge Gould read from his manuscript, pausing for the students to write out the principle or rule stated; which was very well at that day when there were few elementary treatises, but no one would commend it for adoption at the present time (1871), when text books have multiplied *ad infinitum*. Judge Reeve's lectures were accompanied by more of colloquial explanation.

In a letter written November 17, 1822, Judge Gould thus summed up the object of his system:

Of the objects proposed in my lectures, the first is of course to possess my pupils of all the principal rules or doctrines of the law, to each of which I add a collection of reference. But a higher object, and one which I regard as in some measure peculiar to my plan of instruction, is to teach the law—the common law especially—not as a collection of insulated positive rules as from the exhibition of it in most of our books it would appear

---

(1) See *Biography of Marcus Morton, Law Reporter,* Vol. XXVI. (1863).

to be; but as a system of connected rational principles, for such the common law unquestionably is; not only in its fundamental and more comprehensive doctrines, but also, generally speaking, in its subordinate and more artificial provisions. In this view of the common law, I regard our books in general as extremely defective. They treat it rather as a code of arbitrary but authoritative rules and dogmas than as a science. They are conversant too exclusively about doctrines, to the neglect of principles. They deal much in rules, but little in reasons. In other words, they teach us what the rule is; but seldom why it is. It is therefore one of my primary objects to show the reason of the law by tracing its rules so far as I am able to their proper principles.

Disciples of Professor Langdell and of the modern Harvard Law School System will read, with curiosity, Judge Gould's advice that:

Reports, generally speaking, are to be read, only by way of reference, as a test to the lectures or for the purpose of studying particular questions, given to them by discussion. I always dissuade them from reading reports in course, until they have acquired a pretty thorough knowledge of the outline of the science by studying each principal title separately; being fully convinced that reading in the former mode is of little comparative profit in an early stage of legal studies.

The catalogue of the Litchfield School gave the following detailed account of the schedule of its course and prices(1):

According to the plan pursued by Judge Gould, the Law is divided into forty-eight Titles, which embrace all its important branches, and of which he treats in systematic detail. These titles are the result of thirty years' severe and close application. They comprehend the whole of his legal reading during that period, and continue moreover to be enlarged and improved by modern adjudications.

The Lectures, which are delivered every day, and which usually occupy an hour and a half, embrace every principle and rule falling under the several divisions of the different Titles. These principles and rules are supported by numerous authorities, and generally accompanied with familiar illustrations. Whenever the opinions upon any point are contradictory, the authorities in support of either doctrine are cited, and the arguments, advanced by either side, are presented in a clear and concise manner, together with the lecturer's own views of the question. In fact, every ancient and modern opinion, whether over-ruled, doubted, or in any way qualified, is here systematically digested.

---

(1) See also article on the *Litchfield Law School, Albany Law Journal,* Vol. XX, (1879).

These lectures, thus classified, are taken down in full by the students, and after being compared with each other, are generally transcribed in a more neat and legible hand. The remainder of the day is occupied in examining the authorities cited in support of the several rules, and in reading the most approved authors upon those branches of the law, which are at the time the subject of the lectures.(1)

These notes, thus written out, when complete, are comprised in five large volumes, which constitute books of reference, the great advantages of which must be apparent to every one of the slightest acquaintance with the comprehensive and abstruse science of the Law.

The examinations, which are held every Saturday, upon the lectures of the preceding week, consist of a thorough investigation of the principles of each rule, and not merely of such questions as can be answered from memory without any exercise of the judgment. These examinations are held by Jabez W. Huntington, Esq., a distinguished gentleman of the bar, whose practice enables him to introduce frequent and familiar illustrations, which create an interest, and serve to impress more strongly upon the mind the knowledge acquired during the week.

There is also connected with this institution, a Moot Court for the argument of law questions, at which Judge Gould presides. The questions that are discussed, are prepared by him in the forms in which they generally arise. These courts are held once at least in each week, two students acting as Counsellors, one on each side, and the arguments that are advanced, together with the opinion of the Judge, are carefully recorded in a book kept for that purpose. For the preparation of these questions, access may at all times be had to an extensive library.(2)

Besides these courts, there are societies established for improvement in forensic exercises, which are entirely under the control of the students.

The whole course is completed in fourteen months, including two vacations of four weeks each, one in the spring, the other in the autumn. No student can enter for a shorter period than three months. The terms of instruction are $100 for the first year, and $50 for the second, payable either in advance or at the end of the year.

---

(1) Those interested in this early law school method may find a collection of notes of Judge Gould's lectures now in the Harvard Law School Library, complete in three manuscript volumes, presented by W. S. Andrews of Boston. See *Harv. Coll. Arch. Reports, Report of Law Librarian,* July 12, 1861.

(2) It is said that the Law Library of Judge Gould was then the largest and best in the United States.

CHAPTER IX.

OBSTACLES AND PREJUDICES.

While the American Bar developed great lawyers and great judges in the period from 1789 to 1815, there were three obstacles to its growth and to the study of law as a science. These obstructive factors were: first, the unpopularity of lawyers as a class; second, the bitter feeling against England and English Common Law; third, the lack of any distinct body of American Law, arising from the non-existence of American law reports and law books.

The services rendered by the legal profession in the defence and maintenance of the People's rights and liberties, from the middle of the 18th Century to the adoption of the Constitution, had been well recognized by the People in making a choice of their representatives; for of the 56 signers of the Declaration of Independence, 25 were lawyers; and of the 55 members of the Federal Constitutional Convention, 31 were lawyers, of whom four had studied in the Inner Temple, and one at Oxford, under Blackstone. (1)

Of the First Congress, 10 of the 29 Senators, and 17 of the 65 Representatives were lawyers. After the Revolution, however, the old prejudices and dislike of lawyers again arose in the popular mind. Many things contributed to excite this feeling.

In the first place, a large number of the most eminent and older members of the Bar, being Royalists, had either left the country, (2) or retired from practice. Thus, Maryland was deprived of two of her greatest advocates, Daniel Dulany and George Chalmers; Pennsylvania lost John Galloway; New York lost William Smith Jr., Thomas Barclay, and John Tabor Kempe; New Jersey lost Josiah Ogden. In Massachusetts, the

---

(1) *The Supreme Court of the United States,* by Hampton L. Carson.
(2) See *Loyalists of the American Revolution,* by Lorenzo Sabine, (1864).
It is to be remembered that in the American Colonies 25,000 Loyalists, at the least computation, took up arms for the King. Sabine gives sketches of the lives of at least 130 lawyers who left the country as Tories; and there were several hundred other lawyers whose lives were not of sufficient note to describe, but who also became refugees.

losses to the Bar from this cause were especially heavy. The situation was graphically described in 1824 by William Sullivan, from his personal recollections.(1) "Thirteen of the Bar" he says "were Royalists and left the country; and among them Jonathan Sewall, then Attorney General, a man held in high esteem for professional talent; and Sampson Salter Blowers, who enjoyed an honorable reputation as a lawyer and the esteem of many affectionate friends; Samuel Quincy, Timothy Ruggles, and James Putnam. Some who remained were neutral, so far as they could be, consistently with safety. The Royalists who departed, and those who remained, are not to be censured at this day, for conscientious adherence to the mother country. The former had little reason to rejoice in the course which they adopted. Few received such reward for loyalty as they expected. Some exchanged eminence in the Province for appointments, such as they were, in the Colonies; and some ease and comfort here, for insignificance and obscurity at home. Most of them deeply regretted their abandonment of their native land. Such effect had the Revolution on the members of the Bar, that the list of 1779 comprised only ten barristers, and four attorneys, for the whole State, who were such before the Revolution."(2)

Of the lawyers who remained, many were either actively engaged in politics or in the army; while others had accepted positions on the bench.

This left the practice of the law very largely in the hands of lawyers of a lower grade and inferior ability.

Meanwhile, the social and financial conditions of the country after the Revolution tended to produce great unrest. Interruption of business by the war, and high prices, had brought about embarrassment in all classes, and an inability to meet their debts. Great Britain, in closing her ports by navigation laws and prohibitory duties, had deprived the American industries of employment. Public debts were enormous, necessitating ruinous taxation. The Federal Government owed to its soldiers large sums, and payment in the paper money of the time was farcical. The Tories whose estates had been confiscated were returning and

---

(1) *Address to Suffolk County Bar in March*, 1824, by William Sullivan (1825).
(2) Emory Washburn said that in 1775, when Levi Lincoln (Harvard 1772) settled in Worcester County, only two lawyers remained in the county, the rest having left the country.
See *Mass. Hist. Soc. Proc.*, Vol. XI, (1869).

making strenuous efforts to have their property restored. English creditors were trying to recover their claims, barred by various statutes of confiscation and sequestration.

The chief law business, therefore, was the collection of debts and the enforcement of contracts; and the jails were filled to overflowing with men imprisoned for debt under the rigorous laws of the times.(1)

Irritated by this excessive litigation, by the increase of suits on debts and mortgage foreclosures, and by the system of fees and court costs established by the Bar Associations, the people at large mistook effects for cause; and attributed all their evils to the existence of lawyers in the community. Thus, in the conservative little town of Braintree, close to Boston, the citizens in town meeting, in 1786, and voted that: "We humbly request that there may be such laws compiled as may crush or at least put a proper check or restraint on that order of Gentlemen denominated Lawyers, the completion of whose modern conduct appears to us to tend rather to the destruction than the preservation of the town."(2)

Other communities who were more radical, and demanded the complete abolition of the legal profession.

Such was the popular discontent arising from all these conditions, that, in Massachusetts, an open rebellion broke out, in 1787 (the well known Shays Rebellion), directed largely against the courts and the lawyers, and requiring to be put down by military force.(3)

As McMaster says(4):

The lawyers were overwhelmed with cases. The courts could

---

(1) In the little rural county of Worcester, Massachusetts, having a population of less than 5,000, there were at one time more than 2000 actions on the docket of the Inferior Court of Common Pleas.

See for an excellent account of the condition of affairs at this time, from a lawyer's standpoint, the *Life of James Sullivan,* by T. G. Amory.

(2) *Three Episodes of Massachusetts History,* by Charles Francis Adams. See also Remarks of Charles Francis Adams, in *Proceedings of The American Antiquarian Society* (October, 1902).

(3) It is curious to note that the sentiment of the Massachusetts Bar was, in turn, so aroused by the popular feeling against it, that two of its distinguished anti-Federalist members, James Sullivan (afterwards Attorney General and Governor of Massachusetts) and Levi Lincoln (afterwards Attorney General of the United States), who undertook the defence of four of the ringleaders of the Shays Rebellion, on their trial for treason, were bitterly attacked for this action by their associates of the Massachusetts Bar, most of whom were Federalists.

(4) *History of the United States,* by James B. McMaster, Vol. I.

not try half that came to them. For every man who had an old
debt, a mortgage, or a claim against a Tory or Refugee, hastened
to have it adjusted. While, therefore, everyone else was idle,
the lawyers were busy; and as they always exacted a retainer,
and were sure to obtain their fees, grew rich fast. Every young
man became an attorney, and every attorney did well. Such
prosperity soon marked them as fit subjects for the discontented
to vent their anger on. They were denounced as banditti, as
blood suckers, as pickpockets, as windbags, as smooth tongued
rogues. Those who having no cases, had little cause to complain
of the lawyers, murmured that it was a gross outrage to tax them
to pay for the sittings of courts into which they had never
brought and never would bring an action. . . . The mere
sight of a lawyer . . . was enough to call forth an oath or
a muttered curse from the louts who hung around the tavern.

McRee, in his Life of James Iredell, thus describes conditions
in South Carolina(1):

The return of the Tories, and their strenuous efforts to procure the restoration of their property, the activity of the lawyers,
stimulated by the opening of a lucrative career; the commencement of new, the revival of long dormant suits—all conspired to
foster exasperation, cupidity, avarice, revenge. . . . A very
violent prejudice, at this period, existed in narrow and vulgar
minds against the legal profession. This antipathy was fer-
mented by many persons of more talent and less principle as a
means of destroying those whom they feared as rivals, and as
an instrument by which they might effect their political ends.
The lawyers of the State were generally conservatives; hence it
was that they excited, in addition to other cause, the animosity of
the radicals; and in a signal degree the hatred of those who may
be distinctively and exclusively characterized as demagogues
charlteans and political tricksters.

The *Letters of an American Farmer,* written in 1787, by H. St.
John Crevecoeur, also express the sentiment of the time:

Lawyers are plants that will grow in any soil that is cultivated
by the hands of others and when once they have taken root they
will extinguish every vegetable that grows around them. The
fortune they daily acquire in every province from the misfortunes
of their fellow citizens, are surprising. The most ignorant, the
most bungling member of that profession will, if placed in the
most obscure part of the country, promote litigiousness and
amass more wealth than the most opulent farmer with all his

---

(1) *Life and Times of James Iredell,* by Griffith J. McRee.

toil. . . . What a pity that our forefathers who happily
extinguished so many fatal customs and expunged from their
new government so many errors and abuses both religious and
civil, did not also prevent the introduction of a set of men so
dangerous. . . . The value of our laws and the spirit of
freedom which often tends to make us litigious must necessarily
throw the greatest part of the property of the Colonies into the
hands of these gentlemen. In another century the law will possess in the North what now the church possesses in Peru and
Mexico.

Much the same conditions prevailed in all the States. In New
Hampshire, and in Vermont, there were the same widespread
outcries that the courts should be abolished, that the number of
lawyers was too large, that the profession should be entirely suppressed, that their fees should be cut down, that the payment of
debts and the foreclosure of mortgages should be postponed by
"Stay Acts", until debtors could pay. There were numerous
riots. The debtors of Vermont set fire to their court houses;
those of New Jersey nailed up their doors. Lawyers were mob-
bed in the streets, and judges threatened.

In Rhode Island, an act providing for payment of debts in
paper money was held unconstitutional, in 1786, in the famous
case of *Trevett v. Weeden;* whereupon the Legislature passed
an act prohibiting lawyers from practising unless they took the
Test oath, agreeing to take paper money at par.

When the great debates were going on in the various State
conventions, in 1787-89, regarding the adoption of the Constitution, much of the opposition of the anti-Constitution men, or Anti-
Federalists as they were later called, was due to the fact that the
proposed Constitution "was the work of lawyers". Thus, in the
Massachusetts Convention, "Not a member from the country districts got up without indulging in harsh words about lawyers and
judges", says McMaster. " 'The lawyers and men of learning
and moneyed men that talk so finely', said one delegate, 'expect
to get into Congress. They mean to be managers of the Constitution. They mean to get all the money into their hands and
then they will swallow up us little folk.' "(1)

For nearly thirty years after the Revolution, constant efforts
were made in many States to mitigate the evil of lawyers by

---

(1) See *Elliot's Debates on the Constitution.*
McMaster's *History of the United States,* Vol. I.

abolishing the system of bar-call and fees established by courts or Bar Associations.

In Massachusetts, acts were passed, in 1785 and 1786, authorizing parties to a suit to argue their own causes in court and forbidding the employment of more than two lawyers by either party. Plans for law reform were urged even by prominent members of the Bar, such as John Gardiner(1)—to the disquiet however of most of their fellow members. Through Gardiner's influence, resolutions were introduced into the Legislature, in 1790, to investigate "the present state of the law and its Professors in the Commonwealth." A statute was enacted authorizing parties to empower under seal any person whom they chose, whether regular attorney or not, to manage their causes.

Perhaps the most powerful attacks on the "dangerous" and "pernicious" "order" of lawyers and their "malpractices, delays, and extravagant fees" were the letters of Benjamin Austin, an able pamphleteer and Anti-Federalist politician of Boston, who wrote, in 1786, under the name of "Honestus", and whose letters had a widespread influence:

The distresses of the people are now great, but if we examine particularly we shall find them owing in a great measure to the conduct of some practitioners of law. . . . Why this intervening order? The law and evidence are all the essentials required, and are not the judges with the jury competent for these purposes? . . .

The question is whether we will have this order so far established in this Commonwealth as to rule over us. . . . The order is becoming continually more and more powerful. . . . There is danger of lawyers becoming formidable as a combined body. The people should be guarded against it as it might subvert every principle of law and establish a perfect aristocracy.

The remedies he proposed were (a) an American code of law; (b) parties to appear in person or by any friend whether attorney

(1) John Gardiner was born in Boston in 1731, and removed to England, where he studied law and was called as a barrister at the Inner Temple. He became an intimate acquaintance of Lord Mansfield, appeared as junior counsel for the defendant in the famous John Wilkes case, and also for Beardmore and Meredith, two of the publishers indicted with Wilkes. He removed to the Island of Saint Christopher, where he became Attorney General; thence he came to Boston in 1783.

or not; (c) referees, to take the place of courts; (d) a State advocate general, to appear for all persons indicted.(1)

The situation in Massachusetts was described by John Quincy Adams, when a Senior in College, in 1787, as follows(2):

At a time when the profession of the law is laboring under the heavy weight of popular indignation; when it is upbraided as the original cause of all the evils with which the Commonwealth is distressed; when the Legislature have been publicly exhorted by a popular writer to abolish it entirely, and when the mere title of lawyer is sufficient to deprive a man of the public confidence, it should seem this profession would afford but a poor subject for panegyric; but its real ability is not to be determined by the short lived frenzy of an inconsiderate multitude nor by the artful misrepresentations of an insidious writer.

And further in a letter to his mother, in December, 1787:

The popular odium which has been excited against the practitioners in this Commonwealth prevails to so great a degree that the most innocent and irreproachable life cannot guard a lawyer against the hatred of his fellow citizens. The very despicable writings of Honestus were just calculated to kindle a flame which will subsist long after they are forgotten . . . A thousand lies in addition to these published in the papers have been spread all over the country to prejudice the people against the "order," as it has invidiously been called; and as a free people will not descend to disguise their sentiments, the gentlemen of the profession have been treated with contemptuous neglect and with insulting abuse. Yet notwithstanding all this, the profession is rapidly increasing in numbers, and the little business to be done is divided into so many shares that they are in danger of starving one another; when I consider the disadvantages which are in a degree peculiar to the present time . . . I confess I am sometimes almost discouraged and ready to wish I had engaged in some other line of life.

Even as late as 1803-1806, the public dissatisfaction, in Pennsylvania, against the legal profession and the judicial system generally, culminated in a series of statutes, which, in the language of an old lawyer of that State, "betray a more anxious than

---

(1) See *Observations on The Pernicious Practice of the Law by Honestus (Benjamin Austin) as Published occasionally in the Independence Chronicle in Boston in 1786*, (1819).

(2) *Diary of John Quincy Adams—Mass. Hist. Soc. Proc.*, 2nd Series, Vol. XVI (1902).

wise desire to make every man his own lawyer . . . Then the common law was looked on with jealousy and the profession of the law regarded with distrust."(1)

These statutes provided an elaborate machinery by which a party having a claim or debt might file a statement in court, the other party might file an answer in informal shape and thereupon the case should proceed to judgment without the intervention of counsel.

An interesting reference to the state of affairs is found in a letter of Charles Jared Ingersoll of Philadelphia, in December, 1803(2):

I am jogging on my professional path. My father nudges me along, and the Governor has given me a publick room adjoining the court, where I have established my desk and arm-chair. . . . Our State rulers threaten to lop away that excresence on civilization, the bar; and Counsellor Ingersoll declares he'll go to New York. All the eminent lawyers have their eyes on one city or another, to remove to in case of extremes.

In Virginia, as late as 1816, Thomas Jefferson, writing to Benjamin Austin, of Massachusetts, referred to the popular sentiment towards the profession(3):

Your favor of Dec. 21 has been received and I am first to thank you for the pamphlet it covered. The same description of persons which is the subject of that is so much multiplied here as to be almost a grievance and by their numbers in the public courts have wrested from the public hand the direction of the pruning knife. But with us as a body they are republican and mostly moderate in their views; so far therefore less objects of jealousy than with you.

Parallel with this animosity against lawyers as a class was the prejudice against the system of English Common Law on which the courts based their decisions—a prejudice felt, not only by many intelligent as well as unintelligent laymen, but also by many American lawyers themselves.

After the Revolution, there had been much discussion in the courts as to the extent to which the Common Law of England

(1) *Discourse before the Law Academy*, by R. McCall (1838).
(2) *Life of Charles Jared Ingersoll*, by William M. Meigs.
(3) *Writings of Thomas Jefferson*, Vol. X.

was binding. Some States had expressly adopted, in their Constitutions, such parts of the Common Law as formed the law of the Colonies prior to 1775 or 1776 or to the date of the State Constitution—New York, New Jersey, Delaware, Maryland, Rhode Island, New Hampshire. In other States there had been much feeling of uneasiness until some authoritative declaration should be made.(1)

All parties, of course, agreed that English law, since the Revolution, had no binding force whatever; but many of the Anti-Federalists claimed that the English law prior to the Revolution, had no force in the United States except and by virtue of these express Constitutions and statutes.

They sought to entirely eliminate English law from the United States; and their position is well stated in a letter of Jefferson to John Tyler, Judge of the United States District Court in Virginia, written in 1812(2):

I deride with you the ordinary doctrine that we brought with us from England the Common Law rights. This narrow notion was a favorite in the first moment of rallying to our rights against Great Britain. But it was that of men who felt their rights before they had thought of their explanation. The truth is that we brought with us the rights of men. On our arrival here, the question would at once arise, by what law will we govern ourselves. The resolution seems to have been, by that system with which we are familiar, to be altered by ourselves occasionally and adapted to our new situation . . . The state of the English law at the date of our emigration, consituted the system adopted here. We may doubt, therefore, the propriety of quoting in our courts English authorities subsequent to that adoption, still more the admission of authorities posterior to the Declaration of Independence, or rather to the accession of that King whose reign *ab initio* was that very tissue of wrongs which rendered the Declaration at length necessary . . . This relation to the beginning of his reign would add the advantage of getting us rid of all Mansfield's innovations.

Tyler himself, when Governor of Virgina, in a message to the Legislature, had spoken of

the unfortunate practice of quoting lengthy and numerous Brit-

---

(1) *The Adoption of the Common Law by the American Colonies,* *Amer. Law Register,* Vol. XXI (1882).

As to how far the Common Law has been adopted in the various States, see *Amer. and Eng. Encyl. of Law,* 2nd Ed., Vol. VI, p. 286, note 3.

(2) *Letters and Times of the Tylers,* by Lyon G. Tyler, Vol. I, (1884).

ish cases; the time of the court being taken up in reconciling absurd and contradictory opinions of foreign judges which certainly can be no part of an American Judge's duty . . . Shall we forever administer our free republican government on the principles of a rigid and high toned monarchy?

And when he became a Federal judge he used his utmost endeavor to eradicate the influence of English law, precedents and citations; and he held that:

As soon as we had cut asunder the ligatures that bound us together as parent and children, the Common Law was done away until we saw fit to establish so much of it as did not contravene our republican system.

It was this same spirit which led the New Hampshire Judges of the Supreme Court (1785-1800) to put to rout counsel arguing before them, by declining to listen to citations from "musty, old, worm eaten books," and by stating that "not Common Law —not the quirks of *Coke* and *Blackstone* but common sense" should control their decisions.

"English authority did not stand very high in these early feverish times," wrote James Kent, "and this led me a hundred times to bear down opposition or shame it by exhaustive research and overwhelming authority." It was from this anti-English sentiment in New York that at least one lasting and invaluable addition to American law was made in the introduction by Kent of civil law principles, of which he wrote:

Between 1799 and 1804, I read *Valin* and *Emerigon* and completely abridged the latter . . . I made much use of the *Corpus Juris,* and as the judges (Livingston excepted) knew nothing of French or Civil law I had immense advantage over them. I could generally put my brethren to rout and carry my point by my mysterious wand of French and civil law. The judges were Republicans and very kindly disposed to everything that was French and this enabled me without exciting any alarm or jealousy to make free use of such authorities and thereby enrich our commercial law.

Many lawyers as well as laymen felt that what was needed was a law wholly and strictly American. Thus, wrote Benjamin Austin:

Instead of the numerous codes of British law, we should adopt a concise system, calculated upon the plainest principles and agreeable to our Republican government. This would render useless hundreds of volumes which only serve to make practice mysterious.   .   .   .

One reason of the pernicious practice of the law and what gives great influence to the "order" is that we have introduced the whole body of English laws into our courts.   Why should these States be governed by British laws?   Can the monarchical and aristocratical institutions of England be consistent with the republican principles of our Constitution?   .   .   .   We may as well adopt the laws of the Medes and Persians   .   .   .   The numerous precedents brought from "old English authorities" serve to embarrass all our judiciary causes and answer no other purpose than to increase the influence of lawyers.

Mingled with the antagonism to anything savoring of England and monarchy in our law was another factor, the influence of which was felt in the decisions of the United States Courts for nearly seventy-five years of our early jurisprudence—namely, the jealousy of the individual States at any infringement by the National Government on their State jurisdiction.   In the early cases brought before the Federal Courts, the doctrine was upheld that these Courts were bound by the Common Law of England as the National Common Law of this country.

In 1793, Judges Jay, Wilson, Iredell, and District Judge Peters held all violations of treaties were indictable without a Federal statute; almost at the same time, before Judges Iredell, Wilson and Peters, an American was indicted at Common Law for sending threatening letters to the British Minister(1).   Then came Isaac Williams' case where the same doctrine was held by Chief Justice Ellsworth.   In 1794, it was also laid down as law by Judge Iredell, in a charge to the Grand Jury, on the Southern Circuit.

"Such was the state of the law when Judge Chase, in *U. S. v. Worrall*, (2 Dall), in 1798, (Chief Justice Jay, Judge Wilson and Judge Iredell being no longer on the Bench, and Chief Justice Ellsworth being abroad), without waiting to learn what had been decided by his predecessors, startled both his colleagues and the Bar by announcing that he would entertain no indictments at Common Law.   No reports being then or for a long time afterwards published, of the prior rulings to the contrary, it is not to be wondered that the judges who came on the Bench

---

(1)   See *Henfield's Case in Wharton's State Trials*, p. 49; *Wharton's State Trials*, p. 651.   See also *Federal Common Law* in *Virginia Law Register* (1904).

after Judge Chase supposed that he stated the practice correctly."(1)

This decision, as stated above, caused an immense excitement among lawyers, and many protests were made against it by those of Federalist politics, who lamented this denial of Common Law jurisdiction. Their feeling was expressed, as late as 1820, by John Quincy Adams in his diary, in his view of the life of Samuel Chase(2):

> I considered Mr. Chase as one of the men whose life, conduct, and opinion had been of the most extensive influence upon the Constitution of this country. . . . He himself as a judge had settled other (principles) of the highest importance—one of them in my opinion of very pernicious importance. He decided, as I think, directly in the face of an amendatory article of the Constitution of the United States (the seventh) that the Union in its federative capacity has no common law—a decision which has crippled the powers not only of the judiciary but of all the Departments of the National Government. The reasons upon which he rested that decision are not sound, but, as they flattered the popular prejudices, it has remained unreversed to this day.

Equally strenous, however, were the opponents of such Common Law jurisdiction; and Jefferson wrote to Edmund Randolph, Aug. 18, 1799(3):

> Of all the doctrines which have ever been broached by the federal government the novel one, of the Common Law being in force and cognizable as an existing law in their courts, is to me the most formidable. All their other assumptions of un-given powers have been in the detail. The bank law, the treaty doctrine, the sedition act, the alien act, the undertaking to change the state laws of evidence in the state courts by certain parts of the stamp act, etc., etc., have been solitary inconsequential timid things in comparison with the audacious bare-

---

(1) See Wharton's *Criminal Law*, Vol. I, p. 168.

P. S. Duponceau wrote in 1824 that: "This decision of Judge Chase made a great noise at the time and left vague but strong impressions, the more so as he was known to be a man of deep learning and considerable strength of mind, and more disposed to extend than to limit power."

See also *Review of Duponceau's Dissertation on the Nature and Extent of the Jurisdiction of the Courts of the United States April 22, 1824*, by Charles G. Davies, in *North Amer. Review*, Vol. XXI (1825), in which he says "The opinion of Judge Chase seems to have been reverenced as a sort of perpetual edict."

(2) *Diary of John Quincy Adams*, Vol. V, Dec. 18, 1820.

(3) *Writings of Thomas Jefferson*, Vol. VIII.

faced and sweeping pretension to a system of law for the United States without the adoption of their legislature, and so infinitely beyond their power to adopt. If this assumption be yielded to, the state courts may be shut up as there will then be nothing to hinder citizens of the same state suing each other in the federal courts in every case, as on a bond for instance, because the Common Law obliges the payment of it and the Common Law they say is their law.

And on Oct. 29, 1799, he wrote to Charles Pinckney:

Ellsworth and Iredell have openly recognized it; Washington has squinted at it; and I have no doubt it has been decided to cram it down our throats. In short, it would seem that changes in the principles of our government are to be pushed, until they accomplish a monarchy peaceably, or force a resistance, which with the aid of an army may end in monarchy. Still I hope that this will be peaceably prevented by the eyes of the people being opened and the consequent effect of the elective principle.

In January, 1800, the opposition took the form, in Virginia, of an instruction from the General Assembly to its Senators and Representatives in Congress "to use their best efforts to oppose the passing of any law founded on recognizing the principle lately advanced that the Common Law of England is in force under the Government of the United States:"

The General Assembly of Virginia would consider themselves unfaithful to the trust reposed in them were they to remain silent, whilst a doctrine has been publicly advanced, novel in its principles and tremendous in its consequences: That the Common Law of England is in force under the government of the United States. It is not at this time proposed to expose at large the monstrous pretensions resulting from the adoption of this principle. It ought never, however, to be forgotten, and can never be too often repeated, that it opens a new tribunal for the trial of crimes never contemplated by the federal compact. It opens a new code of sanguinary criminal law, both obsolete and unknown, and either wholly rejected or essentially modified in almost all its parts by State institutions. It arrests or supersedes State jurisdictions, and innovates upon State laws. It subjects the citizens to punishment, according to the judiciary will, when he is left in ignorance of what this law enjoins as a duty or prohibits as a crime. It assumes a range of jurisdiction for the Federal Courts which defies limitation or definition. In short, it is believed that the advocates for the principle would themselves be lost in an attempt to apply it to the existing institution of Federal and State Courts, by separating with precision their judiciary rights, and thus preventing the constant and mischievous interference of rival jurisdictions.

Finally the prejudices of the people crystallized in radical legislation. In 1799, the State of New Jersey actually passed a statute, forbidding the Bar to cite or read in court any decision, opinion, treatise, compilation, or exposition of Common Law made or written in Great Britain since July 1, 1776, and prescribed heavy penalties.

In 1807, the State of Kentucky followed suit with a statute, providing that reports and books of decisions in Great Britain since July 4, 1776 "shall not be read or considered as authority in any of the courts." Under this statute, the court went so far as to stop Henry Clay from reading from 3 East's Reports 200 that portion of an opinion of Lord Ellenborough which stated the ancient law prior to 1776 (See *Hickman v. Boffman*, Hardin's Reports 356).

In Pennsylvania, the feeling against the Common Law took shape, in 1802-1805, in the impeachment trial of the Chief Justice and Judges of the Supreme Court, Edward Shippen, Jasper Yeates, and Thomas Smith, charged with a single "arbitrary and unconstitutional act," that of sentencing Thomas Passmore to jail for 30 days and imposing a $50 fine for a "supposed contempt," the ground of the impeachment being that punishment for contempt of court was a piece of English Common Law barbarism, unsuited to this country and illegal.(1)

---

(1) *The Courts from the Revolution to the Revision of the Civil Code,* by William H. Loyd, Jr., *Univ. of Penn. Law Review*, Vol. LVI (1908).

In this trial, in which Caesar A. Rodney (later United States Attorney General) appeared for the prosecution, and Alexander J. Dallas and Jared Ingersoll for the defendants, occurred one of the finest pleas in behalf of the Common Law, in the annals of American legal history.

The following extract from Dallas' argument, as reproduced in his *Address to the Republicans of Pennsylvania June,* 1805, is well worthy of preservation:

"In depicting the Common Law, they have ransacked the cells of monks; they have pillaged the lumber of colleges; they have revived the follies of a superstitious age; they have brandished the rigors of a military despotism; but in all this rage of research they have forgotten or concealed that such things enter not into the composition of the common law of Pennsylvania; for the Constitution tolerates only that portion of the Common Law which your ancestors brought voluntarily with them to the wilderness as a birthright. Let us not therefore be ensnared by prejudices nor be deceived by mere similitude of names. Every nation has its common law. The Common Law of Pennsylvania is the Common Law of England, as stripped of its feudal trappings, as originally suited to a colonial condition,

The result of the trial being the acquittal of the judges, public sentiment against the English law was still further enflamed in Pennsylvania; and in 1810, a statute was passed (and not repealed until 1836), forbidding the citation of any English decision made since July 4, 1776, except in cases involving the law of nations and maritime law.(1)

The question of the existence of a national Common Law in the criminal jurisdiction of the Federal Courts was finally set at rest by the decision, in 1812, in the case of *U. S. v. Goodwin* (7 Cranch 32), argued by Attorney General Pinkney for the Government, Dana of Connecticut for the defendants declining to argue. Judge Johnson gave the opinion, holding that an indictment for libel on the President could not be sustained without a Federal statute on the subject, and stating that:

Although this question is brought up now for the first time to be decided by this court, we consider it as having long since been settled in public opinion . . . the general acquiescence of legal men shows the prevalence of opinion in favor of the negative of the proposition. . . All exercise of criminal jurisdiction in common law cases is not within their implied powers.(2)

Even after this decision a feeling of unrest at the weight

---

as modified by acts of the General Assembly, and as purified by the principles of the Constitution. For the varying exigencies of social life, for the complicated interests of an enterprising nation, the positive acts of the Legislature can provide little, and, independent of the Common Law, rights would remain forever without remedies and wrongs without address. The law of nations, the law of merchants, the customs and usages of trade, and even the law of every foreign country in relation to transitory contracts originating there but prosecuted here, are parts of the common law of Pennsylvania. It is the Common Law, generally speaking, not an Act of Assembly that assures the title and the possession of your farms and your houses, and protects your persons, your liberty, your reputation, from violence; that defines and punishes offences; that regulates the trial by jury; and that gives efficacy to the fundamental principles of the Constitution—simply because it originated in Europe cannot afford a better reason to abandon it, than to renounce the English or German languages, or to abolish the institutions of property and marriage, of education and religion, since they were too derived from the more ancient civilized nation of the world."

See *Life of Alexander J. Dallas,* by George M. Dallas, (1871).

(1) Henry H. Brackenridge, then Judge of the Supreme Court of Pennsylvania said in his *Law Miscellanies* (1814), that this act ought to be repealed, and he questioned its constitutionality, "as abridging the right of the judiciary to hear all reason on a question before them."

(2) See *U. S. v. Coolidge,* 1 Gallison 488, in 1813, in which Judge Story attempted to make a distinction between power to indict and power to punish. Judge John Davis dissenting, the case was taken to the Supreme Court on a division of opinion; but the Supreme Court refused (1 Wheaton 415), in 1816, to hear an argument on the point.

given to the English Common Law by the courts cropped up through the country; and an excellent description of this condition was given by Peter S. DuPonceau, Provost of the Law Academy of Philadelphia, in an address to the students, as late as 1824(1):

Various circumstances have concurred after the Revolution to create doubts in the public mind respecting the operation of the Common Law in this country as a national system, particularly in criminal cases. The bitter feeling of animosity against England which the revolutionary war produced was not amongst the least of these causes. . . .

. . . . I am well aware that this doctrine of the nationality of the Common Law will meet with many opponents. There is a spirit of hostility abroad against this system which cannot escape the eye of the most superficial observer. It began in Virginia, in the year 1799 or 1800, in consequence of an opposition to the alien and sedition acts; a committee of the legislative body made a report against these laws which was accepted by the House, in which it was broadly laid down that the Common Law is not the law of the United States. Not long afterwards, the flame caught in Pennsylvania; and it was for a time believed that the Legislature would abolish the Common Law altogether. Violent pamphlets were published to instigate them to that measure. The whole, however, ended in a law for determining all suits by arbitration in the first instance, at the will of either party, and another prohibiting the reading and quoting in courts of justice of British authorities of a date posterior to the Revolution.(2)

It was not long before this inimical disposition towards the Common Law made its way into the State of Ohio. In the year 1819, a learned and elaborate work was published in that State(3) in which it was endeavored to prove not only that

(1) See *A Dissertation on the nature and extent of the Jurisdiction of the Courts of the United States, being a valedictory address to the students of the Law Academy of Philadelphia, April 23, 1824*, by Peter S. Duponceau, Provost of the Academy.
Tucker's *Blackstone* Vol. I, App. E.; Kent's *Commentaries*, Vol. I, p. 311; *Rawle on the Constitution*, Chap. 30; *North American Review*, July 1825; Speech of Bayard, in *Debates on the Judiciary*, in 1802, p. 372, Story's *Commentaries on the Constitution*, Vol. I, s. 158.
Federal Common Law, Virginia Law Register, Vol. X (1904). Wharton's *Criminal Law*, Vol. I.
(2) This spirit was considerably checked by a well written pamphlet published at the time by Joseph Hopkinson, Esq. of Philadelphia, in which he demonstrated the absurdity of the project of abolishing the Common Law.
(3) *Historical sketches of the principles and maxims of American Jurisprudence, in contrast with the doctrines of the English common law on the subject of crimes and punishments*, by Milton Goodnow, (Steubenvale, 1819).

the Common Law was not the law of the United States, but that it had no authority in any of the States that had been formed out of the old Northwestern Territory. But few copies of his work have been printed; nevertheless, as it is learnedly and elaborately written, it cannot but have had a considerable degree of influence. In other States, attacks upon the Common Law, more or less direct, have appeared from time to time. Its faults are laid hold of and exhibited in the most glaring light; its ancient abuses, its uncertainty, the immense number of volumes in which its doctrines are to be sought for, . . . and above all the supposed danger to our institutions from its being still the law of a monarchical country, the opinions of whose judges long habit has taught us to respect, which opinions are received from year to year and admitted in our courts of justice if not as rules, at least as guides for their decisions; these are the topics which are in general selected for animadversion.

CHAPTER X.

Early American Law Books.

It has been seen in the preceding chapter how general was the feeling that the law in the United States should be emancipated from its dependence on English decisions. Conditions of life, of commerce, of real estate dealings, and of court practice were essentially different in the United States from those in England; and a distinct body of law was demanded for this country. To supply this demand there arose the body of American law reporters and law writers.

James Sullivan, of Massachusetts, well expressed this general sentiment of those who felt that the country should have a genuine American system of law based on American cases, in his preface to his work on *Land Titles*, in 1801:

> The want of accurate reports necessary to evince what statutes and principles of the English Laws had been adopted, used, and practised upon before the Revolution is very discouraging in this work. . . . It would be well for us to have our own comments, and to reject those of other governments which have been issued since we became an independent nation. . . . We ought to have our own reporters, compilers anl compositors. Everyone who will attempt something in this way ought to be encouraged by the public.
>
> There have been motions in some of the legislatures in the Union to prohibit the reading of English reports in our courts of justice. . . . The judges themselves in several of the States have with great propriety inclined to reject the reports of cases determined by England since the American Revolution. These motions, however crude and undigested they may have been, no doubt had their origin in a strong love to our national independence. And the motive is therefore a laudable rather than a reprehensible one.

And, as Cranch said in the preface to his Supreme Court Reports, in 1804:

> Much of that uncertainty of the law, which is so frequently and perhaps so justly the subject of complaint in this country,

may be attributed to the want of American reports. Many of the causes, which are the subject of litigation in our courts, arise upon circumstances peculiar to our situation and laws, and little information can be derived from English authorities to lead to a correct decision.

But before a body of American Law could be established, there was need of some authoritative method of preserving the decisions of the courts, in order that the judges might have some means of knowing what the American precedents were.

As a reviewer of one of the early volumes of American reports stated(1):

The United States have, until within a few years, trusted to traditions the reasons of their judicial decisions. But with wealth and commerce, and with more enlarged views of jurisprudence, it became obvious that the exposition of our statutes and the validity of our customs should rest upon a more secure basis than the memory of man or the silent influence of unquestioned usage.

An accurate view of the state of the law, resulting from the absence of recorded decisions, was given by John Duer, a contemporary of Kent, in describing the condition of New York courts before the era of law reports(2):

The decisions . . . were not the fruit of that careful and laborious investigation which is essential to the proper discharge of the judicial functions; and the authority they might otherwise have claimed was greatly impaired by these frequent differences of opinion that are the necessary result of imperfect examination and study. It was seldom that the opinions of the judges, even in the most important cases, were reduced to writing; and as no reports were then published, and no records preserved of the grounds on which their decisions were placed, the cases were numerous in which they had no rules to direct, no precedents to govern them. Of this state of things, the inevitable consequences were vacillation, contradictions, confusion, and uncertainty. . . . This defective administration of the law had a most unfavorable influence on the character and pursuits of the Bar; for when cases are slightly examined and rashly decided by the judges, the principal motives for a diligent preparation on the part of counsel cease to exist.

---

(1) Review of Vol. I. of *Tyng's Massachusetts Reports,* quoted in Hall's *American Law Journal,* Vol. I (1808).
(2) *Discourse before the Bar of New York,* by John Duer (1848).

And as a writer in the *North American Review* said, in 1825(1):

The practice of reporting decisions with their grounds and reasons is indeed an insuperable barrier to the corruption of judges; and it is the strongest possible guard against negligent and inconsiderate decrees. . . . The publication of reports again affords the only means of informing the community of the laws by which their conduct is to be governed and their rights to be determined.

To the State of Connecticut is due the credit of making the first move towards the establishment of a record of American Law, by the passage, through the efforts of two of its great lawyers, Roger Sherman and Richard Law, of a statute, in 1785, requiring the judges of the Supreme and Superior Courts to file written opinions, in disposing of cases on points of law, so that they might be properly reported, and "thereby a foundation laid for a more perfect and permanent system of common law in this State."

This statute made possible the first regular printed law reports in America(2); for in 1789, Ephraim Kirby, a country printer at Litchfield, formerly a student at Yale, and a soldier in the Continental Army, made the first collection of cases, and published the volume known as *Kirby's Reports,* in the preface to which he says:

The uncertainty and contradiction attending the judicial decisions in this State have long been subjects of complaint. The source of this complaint is easily discovered. When our ancestors emigrated here, they brought with them the notions of jurisprudence which prevailed in the country from whence they came. The riches, luxury, and extensive commerce of that country, contrasted with the equal distribution of property, simplicity of manners, and agricultural habits and employments of this, rendered a deviation from the English laws, in many instances, highly

---

(1)   Review of *Pickering's Reports Vol. I.,* by Willard Phillips, *North Amer. Rev.,* Vol. XX (1825).

(2)   While Kirby was the first American Law Reporter, in the legal use of the term, he was not the first person to publish reports of cases, for throughout the 18th Century printed reports of famous criminal trials were to be found, and an occasional printed account of a civil action. (See Chapter VI supra.)

Neither does *Kirby's Reports* contain the earliest American cases; for *Harris and McHenry's Reports* published in 1809 contains cases of a date as early as 1658; *Quincy's Reports* (Massachusetts), published in 1865 has cases from 1761-1772; and in 1829, there was published at Charlottesville, Virginia, a book by Thomas Jefferson entitled *Reports of cases determined in the General Court of Virginia from 1730 to 1740 and from 1768 to 1772.* (See *Forgotten Chapters in the Life of Jefferson,* in Green Bag, Vol. VIII.)

necessary. This was observed; and the intricate and prolix practice of the English courts was rejected, and a mode of practice more simple, and better accommodated to an easy and speedy administration of justice, adopted. Our courts were still in a state of embarrassment, sensible that the common law of England, 'though a highly improved system,' was not fully applicable to our situation; but no provision being made to preserve and publish proper histories of their adjudications, every attempt of the judges to run the line of distinction between what was applicable and what was not proved abortive, for the principles of their decisions were soon forgot, or misunderstood, or erroneously reported from memory. Hence arose a confusion in the determination of our courts. The rules of property became uncertain, and litigation proportionably increased.

In this situation, some legislative exertion was found necessary; and in the year 1785 an act passed, requiring the judges of the superior court to render written reasons for their decisions in cases where the pleadings closed in an issue at law. This was a great advance towards improvement. Still it left the business of reformation but half performed; for the arguments of the judges, without a history of the whole case, would not always be intelligible, and they would become known to but few persons, and, being written on loose papers, were exposed to be mislaid, and soon sink into total oblivion.

Hence it became obvious to every one that should histories of important cases be carefully taken and published, in which the whole process should appear, showing the true grounds and principles of the decision, it would in time produce a permanent system of common law.

Alexander J. Dallas followed Kirby, the next year 1790, with his first volume of decisions of Pennsylvania cases dating from 1754, of which Lord Mansfield wrote to Chief Justice McKean of Pennsylvania, in 1791: "They do credit to the court, the bar, and the reporter; they show readiness in practice, liberality in principle, strong reason and legal learning." *Hopkinson's Admiralty Reports* were printed in 1792. *Chipman's Reports* came next in Vermont in 1793. Chancellor Wythe published his *Cases* in 1795—a volume particularly interesting from the fact that Henry Clay, a lad of fifteen, then a poor assistant in the Clerk's office, was picked out by Wythe to write out and record his decisions for this work, and in the copies of these reports sent to Jefferson, John Adams, and Samuel Adams are notes in English and Greek written by Clay at Wythe's dictation.

Martin's Reports in North Carolina followed, in 1797; *Root's,* in Connecticut, and *Washington's,* in Virginia, in 1798; and *Hay-*

wood's, in North Carolina, in 1799; *Addison's,* in Pennsylvania, in 1800; *Call's,* in Virginia, in 1801; *Taylor's,* in North Carolina, in 1802; *Hughes',* in Kentucky, in 1803; *Bay's,* in South Carolina, in 1804; *Pennington's,* in New Jersey, in 1807; *Harris and McHenry's* in Maryland, and *Tyler's,* in Vermont, in 1809; *Hardin's,* in Kentucky, in 1810; *Martin's,* in Louisiana, in 1811; *Overton's,* in Tennessee, in 1813; and *New Hampshire Reports,* in 1816.

The first reports in New York (*Caines*) were not printed until 1804; and it was Kent who introduced in New York the system of filing written opinions, as he writes:

When I came to the bench, in 1798, there were no reports or state precedents. The opinions from the bench were delivered ore tenus. We had no law of our own and nobody knew what it was. I first introduced a thorough examination of cases and written opinions. In Jan. 1799, the second case reported in 1 Johnson of *Ludlow v. Dale* is a sample of the earliest. . . . This was the commencement of a new plan and there was laid the first stone in the subsequently erected temple of our jurisprudence. . . . In 1814 I was appointed Chancellor. The office I took with considerable reluctance. It is a curious fact that, for the nine years I was in that office, there was not a single decision, opinion or dictum of either of my predecessors—Livingston or Lansing—from 1777 to 1814 cited to me or even suggested.

It was six years after Kent began his written opinions, before the Legislature provided (in 1804) for a regular Reporter on a salary—William Johnson being the first to be appointed.

In the same year, Massachusetts established the office of Reporter and initiated the publication of reports, intended at first as an experiment, for the statute was limited in its operation to three years. Ephraim Williams was made Reporter, and his first volume was published in 1806.

The first volume of United Supreme Court reports was published by Dallas in 1798 (2 Dallas); and in 1804, Cranch began the publication of his reports, containing the first of Chief Justice Marshall's opinions.

The American law text book, like the American law report, owed its origin largely to the demand for the creation of a native body of law distinct from the English law.(1)

---

(1) The compilation of books described in these pages has been made largely from the large and comprehensive *Legal Bibliography,* published at Philadelphia in 1846, by James G. Marvin—a student at the Harvard Law School 1842-1846. In his preface he says:

"With regard to the law books of the United States, I trust this volume

The need arose first in the department of Pleading, and was
well expressed in the preface to the first American collection of
forms, published at Salem, Mass., in 1801, entitled *American
Precedents of Declarations*(1) :

The motives which induce this publication after the laboured
books of entries which, under the sanction of *Coke, Rastall, Lilly,
Mallory* and *Raymond,* have received the approbation of the profession, become particularly necessary to be developed.   The
redundances of the English forms, however proper in their
courts, where remuneration is proportionate to literal labour,
have ever been the subjects of complaint among our own lawyers
who have been obliged at a vast expense of time and money to
purchase researches into ponderous volumes where the useful
matter was buried amid heaps of antiquated learning and super-
fluous detail.   This end has indeed been most severely felt in New
England, where juridicial practice, though bottomed on the principles of the Common Law, from the character of the people and
the peculiarity of the laws assumed a more compact and simple
form.   In addition to this, the structure of our government, so
materially variant from European sovereignties, as well as domestic remedies of statutory appointment have created deficiencies
and changes which no foreign works could meet and no personal
industry supply. . . .   They have been almost wholly tran-

---

will be found to contain a tolerably complete list. For this department of
the work, in addition to the resources afforded by the ample library of
the Dane Law School, gentlemen in various states have kindly rendered
me material assistance.

Through the politeness of the Hon. Edward Everett, President of Harvard University, and Dr. Harris, Librarian of the same, the free use of the
college library of this venerable seat of learning has been granted to me
and I should do injustice to my feelings did I not here acknowledge the
indispensable aid derived by this favour. The very liberal manner in which
the use of books is granted at this University the admirable order and
condition in which they are kept and the conveniences for consulting them
are worthy of imitation, and will be fully appreciated by those who have
had occasion to make researches at other libraries where quite a different
regime prevails."

A practically complete list may also be found in the summaries of the law
of the various States contained in the *Annual Law Register,* Vols. III and
IV, published by William Griffiths, at Burlington, New Jersey, in 1822—a
most valuable source of information regarding legal conditions of the early
part of the 19th Century.

(1)   Judge Iredell of the United States Supreme Court left unfinished
at his death, in 1798, a legal treatise entitled *An Essay on Pleading in Suits
at Common Law,* consisting of four volumes folio, 1229 pages of closely
written manuscript—also 365 pages of *Doctrine of the Laws of England
Concerning Real Property so far as it is in use or in force in the State of
North Carolina;* also 12 chapters of 275 pages of an *Appendix to the Law
of Evidence,* a work originally published by an anonymous writer in 1777.

See *Life and Letters of James Iredell,* by Griffith J. McRee, Vol. II
(1857).

scribed from manuscript forms which have been preserved with veneration and collected with fidelity by the first ornaments of the bench and forum in our own and adjacent states. By the offers of celebrated living counsel, the work has been perfected in many valuable forms, which have either received judicial decisions or been approved by unquestionable authority.

In the same year, 1801, Thomas Harris published at Annapolis, Md., *Modern Entries, adapted to the American Courts of Justice, being a complete system of approved precedents.*

Four years later, in 1805, Joseph Story, then only twenty-six years of age, published at Salem his *A Selection of Pleadings in Civil Cases,* of which J. G. Marvin, the author of *Legal Bibliography,* said, in 1847:

> The appearance of the volume was opportune and serviceable to the Profession in this country, who had hitherto been obliged to resort to the voluminous books of *English Entries* for precedents. The notes and references show attainments in the service of special pleading at the early age in which this his first attempt at legal authorship was published. 'The work gave a new impulse to study in this department of professional learning.'

In 1810, John Anthon published, at New York, the second edition of *American Precedents of Declarations collected chiefly from the manuscript of Chief Justice Parsons and other accomplished Pleaders in the State of Massachusetts.*

In 1806, Colinson Read of Philadelphia published *American Pleaders' Assistant;* and in 1811, W. W. Hening of Virginia published his *American Pleader,* in New York.

Although the early reports were largely filled with cases involving real property, the text books in use on that subject were mainly English.

In 1768, however, John Adams had written anonymously the first American book on this branch of the law, *An Essay on Feudal and Common Law,* first published in London, in 1768, but not until 1783 in this country, in Philadelphia.(1)

---

(1) Its authorship was ascribed to Jeremiah Gridley, but a few persons knew its real author as the following letter from Rev. Dr. Chauncey to Rev. Dr. Stiles Dec. 12, 1768, shows:

"He is but a young man not above 33 or 34 but of incomparable sense, a true son of liberty and as well able to write or talk upon it as any one I am acquainted with. I esteem that piece one of the best that has been written. It has done honor to its author; and it is a pity but he should be known." See *Mass. Hist. Coll.,* 1st Series, Vol. X, p. 187.

In 1794, William Wyche published in New York,(1) *An Essay on the Theory and Practice of Fines;* and in 1801, James Sullivan of Massachusetts published in Boston the first really comprehensive work on real estate law, entitled *Land Titles in Massachusetts.*

In 1808, John Kilty of Maryland published his *Landholders' Assistant and Land Office Guide.* In 1810, W. Graydon of Pennsylvania published *Forms of Conveyancing and Practise.* In 1816, Benjamin Lynde Oliver published his *Practical Conveyancing,* which long remained a standard work.

The important part which admiralty and maritime cases played in the courts in the thirty years, 1785-1815, is reflected in a remarkable degree in the number of translations made by American lawyers of the works of foreign writers on maritime, admiralty, civil, and international law.   These translations displayed considerable legal scholarship, and proved the lawyers of this country to be largely in advance of their English brethren, who, in general, took little interest in anything outside of the Common Law of England.   Thus in 1795, William Cobbett published in Philadelphia his translation of Marten's *Law of Nations*   A translation of *Burlamaqui* was published in 1792, in Boston.   In 1802, Francis Xavier Martin published at Newbern, North Carolina, a translation of *Pothier on Contracts;* and in 1806, W. D. Evans published the same work, in Philadelphia.

In 1800, Montesquieu's *Esprit des Lois* was published in Boston ; and in 1802, in Philadelphia.   In 1805, *Vattel* was published, in Boston.

In 1806, *Azuni* was translated and published by William Johnson, in New York.   In 1809, J. R. Ingersoll translated *Roccus.*

In 1808, John E. Hall published, at Baltimore, his translation of *Clerke's Praxis, with notes on American Admiralty Practice;* and in 1811, his translation of Emerigon's *Maritime Loans.*

In 1810, P. S. Du Ponceau, of Philadelphia, translated Bynkershoek's *Laws of War.*   In 1812, Thomas Cooper published in Philadelphia a translation of Justinian's *Institutes.*   In 1809 John E. Hall of Baltimore wrote a treatise on *Admirality Practice;* and in the same year William J. Duane wrote his *Law of Nations* (Phila. 1809).   In 1815, Henry Wheaton wrote his able

---

(1)   See *Modern Law of Real Property, Columbia Law Review,* Vol. I, (1901).

book on *Maritime Captures and Prizes*. In 1818, William Frick of Baltimore translated Jacobsen's, *Laws of the Sea*.

Four general works on the Common Law, written in this period, showed genuine scientific thought and research; and have remained of more or less permanent value in American legal literature. In 1793, Nathaniel Chipman, Chief Justice of Vermont, published his *Dissertations*. In 1804, the lectures delivered before the students of the College of Philadelphia by James Wilson, Judge of the U. S. Supreme Court, were printed. In the year prior, St. George Tucker, Professor of Law, published his famous edition of *Blackstone,* in five volumes (following the 9th English edition of 1783), which work, under the title of *Tucker's Blackstone* had widespread circulation, both as a text-book and otherwise, giving to him the sobriquet of the "American Blackstone", and containing the first legal commentaries on the Federal Constitution which appeared in the United States.

In 1814, Judge H. N. Brackenridge, of Pennsylvania, wrote his *Law Miscellanies containing Introduction to the Study of the Law, Notes on Blackstone's Commentaries, Strictures on decisions of the Supreme Court of the United States with some law cases.*

In 1795-6, Zephaniah Swift published his *System of the Laws of Connecticut,* a keen, scientific work of much more than local interest.

There were a few scattered treatises on special subjects, but they were of little scientific or permanent value. Thus in 1796 John F. Grimke of South Carolina published his *Law of Executors;* in 1801, Thomas Cooper wrote a manual on *The Bankrupt Law of America* (Phil. 1801). In 1803, Francis Xavier Martin published in North Carolina a short treatise on the *Powers and Duties of Executors and Administrators;* and in the same year, Samuel Freeman at Boston, his *Probate Directory. A Treatise on Criminal Law* was published by H. Toulman and James Blair, at Frankfort, Ky., in 1804.

In 1808, James Bradly published, in New York, a *Treatise on the Law of Distress*. In 1810, Zephaniah Swift, of Connecticut, published the first American *Digest of the Law of Evidence* and also a *Treatise on Bills of Exchange and Promissory Notes*. In 1811, Samuel Livermore, of New Orleans, who at his death bequeathed his large library to Harvard College, wrote the first American work on *Principal and Agent and Sale by Auction*.

In the same year, Thomas Sergeant, of Philadelphia, published a treatise on *Foreign Attachment*. In 1816, Judge Tapping Reeve, of the Litchfield Law School, published at New Haven, his work on the *Domestic Relations*.

The greater proportion, however, of the American law books consisted of mere manuals for town officers, Justices of the Peace, and other petty officers—books of ephemeral value.(1)

There were also a number of other makeshift, "handy books for lawyers" such as *The Attorney's Vade Mecum, and Client's Instructor* by John Morgan (published originally in Dublin in 1787) and reprinted in the United States and much used by the profession(2); Joshua Montefiore's *American Trader's Conpendium* (Phil. 1811) and *Commercial Dictionary* (Phil. 1804), and a compilation called *Lex Mercatoria Americana* (N. Y. 1802).

For the most part, however, lawyers still continued to rely on important English text books and English editions of the law reports. A movement now began however towards republishing and re-editing English works; and in this movement Joseph Story became a leader—editing *Chitty on Bills and Notes* in 1809; *Abbott on Shipping,* in 1810, and *Lawes on Pleading in Assumpsit,* in 1811.(3)

---

(1) See James Parker's *Conductor Generalis* (N. Y. 1787); John F. Grimke's *Justices of the Peace* (So. Car. 1796); Francis X. Martin's *Office of Justice of the Peace* (N. C. 1791), *Jurisdiction of Justices of the Peace in Civil Suits* (N. C. 1796), and *Powers and Duties of Sheriff* (N. C. 1806); Ewing's *Justice of Peace* (N. J. 1805); Samuel Freeman's *The Town Officer* (Boston 1799, 1815), and the *Massachusetts Justice* (Boston 1802, 1810); *Justices and Constables Assistant* by W. Graydon (Phil. 1805); R. Bache's *Manual of Pennsylvania Justices of the Peace* (Phil. 1810, 1814); C. Reade's *Precedents in office of Justice of Peace and Short system of Conveyancing* (Phil. 1810); Samuel Whiting's *Connecticut Town Officer* (1814); *The Civil Officer* (Boston 1809, 1814); John Tappan's *County and Town Officers of New York* (Kingston, N. Y. 1816); W. W. Hening's *The Virginia Justice* (Virg. 1811); Rodolphus Dickinson's *Powers of Sheriff* (Mass. 1810); Jonathan Leavitt's *Poor Law of Massachusetts* (Mass. 1810); *Probate Directory* (Mass. 1812); *Overseers Guide* (Mass. 1815).

(2) Termed by Judge Morton in *Whiting v. Smith,* 13 Pick. 364, in 1832, "A Practical work of respectable authority."

(3) Among the more prominent English text books thus republished in America were *Jones on Bailments* (London 1781; Boston 1796)) *Kyd on Bills and Notes* (London 1795, Boston 1798); *Park on Insurance* (Boston 1800); *Burn on Marine Insurance* (N. Y. 1801); *Marshall on Insurance* (Boston 1805; Phil. 1810); *Sullivan's Lectures on The Feudal Law and the Constitution and Law of England* (London 1776; Portland, Maine, 1805); *Runnington on Ejectment* (N. Y. 1806); *Ballantine on Law of Limitations* (London, 1810, N. Y. 1812, containing 71 decisions of American Law); *Woodfall on Landlord and Tenant* (N. Y. 1816).

Perhaps the best illustration of the condition of the times in this respect may be found in the fact that in the library of Theophilus Parsons the great Chief Justice of Massachusetts, which was sold at auction June 2, 1814, the only American law books, out of the whole 282, were the following: *Livermore on Agents and Factors* (Boston 1811); *Lawes on Pleading with Joseph Story's Addition* (Boston 1811); *Story's Pleading* (1805); *Laws of the United States* (10 Vols.); *Laws of Massachusetts; Laws of New Hampshire; Cranch's Reports* (6 Vols.); *Dallas' Reports* (4 Vols.); *Day's Reports* (3 Vols.); *Johnson's Reports* (8 Vols.); *Journal of Congress* (13 Vols.); and *Digest of Massachusetts Law* (1809).

In 1807, John E. Hall of Baltimore announced to the legal profession his intention to publish a legal periodical, in order to make the decided cases more quickly accessible to the Bar and more widely spread.

The first publication of this kind ever printed had been in existence only five years, since 1803, *The Law Journal*, edited in England by John Morgan and Thomas Walter Williams. And in January, 1808, appeared the first number of the *American Law Journal and Miscellaneous Repository*, printed for Hall at Philadelphia. Six volumes were issued between 1808 to 1810 and 1813 to 1817. A review of its first volume in the *Boston Anthology* for June 1809 says:

We agree with the editor in his opinion of the importance of such a work as he has undertaken, and we believe the public voice approves the execution.

Our country is composed of seventeen different communities, each enjoying independent Legislatures, each governed by laws, many of whose provisions, both statute and traditional are very different. A publication like Mr. Hall's seems therefore absolutely necessary to afford information to an inhabitant of this State in the prosecution of his rights in New York, Maryland, or Carolina. It will also afford much assistance in producing uniformity in our decisions on commercial questions which would be so beneficial to the whole community . . . and must be considered by the politician as one of the surest bonds of the federal union.

Two volumes of a law magazine called the *North Carolina Law Repository* were published in 1813.

The first distinct Law Library was founded by Philadelphia

lawyers, who incorporated a Society for that purpose in March 1802, described by John Samuel, in an address on the opening of the Law Library of the Law Association of Philadelphia, March 3, 1898, as follows: "So far as I, after some research have been able to discover, this was the first law library established in the United States, the Social Law Library of Boston, the next oldest, not being formed until two years later in 1804. The oldest law library in New York is that of the New York State Library at Albany founded in 1818.(1) A claim was set up to the establishment of the Kennebec Law Library in Augusta, Maine, as having been founded in 1800, but after inquiry I am convinced that no evidence can be adduced in support of this claim. In 1805 was published the first catalogue of the books of the Law Library Company of the City of Philadelphia. It was prepared by William Rawle, and I believe, was the first printed catalogue of a law library published in the United States. It is a modest booklet of eleven duodecimo pages, containing 249 titles of 375 volumes, whose character is curiously suggestive. Nearly all the books are reports of cases; and of the small remainder, the large majority are books on practice—and treatises on commercial law and maritime insurance; but one digest, *Comyn's* and not over a dozen text books. Of the reports, all are English save three—*Dallas'* (Pennsylvania), *Caine's* (New York), and *Taylor's* (North Carolina) *Reports.*"

---

(1) In the *Life of Charles J. Ingersoll,* by W. M. Meigs (1897), reference is made to a movement for a law library in Washington, in a letter written by Ingersoll to R. Rush.

"Feb. 14, 1823, The Bar had a meeting to-day at which Mr. Wirt presided and Messrs. Clay Harper and Winder were appointed a committee to devise means of procuring law library of which the want is deplorable here (Washington) and also of obtaining if practicable an establishment in which all the lawyers attending the Supreme Court may be accommodated with lodgings together which would be a convenience, I dare say."

CHAPTER XI.

THE BAR AND THE LAW, 1789-1815.

With the year 1789, American Law, as a national system, began; and its early history falls, naturally, into two periods, the one closing in 1801, with the appointment of Chief Justice Marshall, the other with the end of the War of 1812, in 1815.

On September 24, 1789, President Washington approved the great Judiciary Act, which established the judicial system of the Federal Government, and which was framed by Oliver Ellsworth chiefly.(1) On the same day, Washington sent to the Senate, as his nominees to the first United States Supreme Court: for Chief Justice, John Jay of New York, and for Associate Justices, John Rutledge of South Carolina, James Wilson of Pennsylvania, William Cushing of Massachusetts (then Chief Justice of that State), Robert H. Harrison of Maryland, and John Blair of Virginia. Harrison declining, in order to accept the position of Chancellor of Maryland, James Iredell of North Carolina took his place.

The Court was opened in New York Feb. 2, 1790; and the next day, three lawyers were admitted to practice before it as counsellors, Elias Boudinot of New Jersey, Thomas Hartley of Pennsylvania, and Richard Harrison of New York. By rule of Court, (amended in 1801) an attorney or counsellor who had practised as such in the Supreme Court of any State for three years, might be admitted to practise; but he was required to make his election

---

(1) It is interesting to note the adverse contemporary comments made on this act. Thus, August 2, 1791, the great North Carolina lawyer, William R. Davie, wrote to Judge James Iredell:

"I sincerely hope something will be done at the next session of Congress with the Judiciary Act; it is so defective in point of arrangement, and so obscurely drawn or expressed, that, in my opinion, it would disgrace the composition of the meanest legislature of the states. The Attorney General's Report is a type of it—an elegant piece of unmeaning obscurity."

Samuel Dexter in his argument, in 1816, in *Martin v. Hunter's Lessee,* 1 Wheat, p. 305, said: "That great man and those who advised him improvidently assented to a law (the Judiciary Act) which is neither constitutionally nor politically adapted to enforce the power of the National Courts in an amicable and pacific manner."

between the two degrees and could not practise both as counsellor and as attorney.

By the Judiciary Act, three Circuit Courts and thirteen District Courts were established. There being no business ready before the Supreme Court, its judges entered at once upon their duties in the inferior courts, the first Circuit Court being held in the Eastern Circuit, in New York, April 3, 1790, by Chief Justice Jay, Judge Cushing and District Judge Duane.

A contemporary account of the opening of the Circuit Court at New Haven, April 22, 1790, is given by President Stiles as follows(1):

The federal circuit Supreme Court of the United States sat here for the first time since its institution by Congress. Present, 3 Judges, Hon. Ch. Just, Jay, late Ambassador to France, Judge Cushing, and Judge Law. The Ch. Justice sent the Marshall to me this morning to open the court with Prayer; but I was unable to go abroad and Dr. Dana prayed with the court. Then Mr. Jay made a speech to the Grand Jury: all the Attornies of two years' standing present were then admitted and Sworn Barristers, Attorneys and Counsellors of the Supreme Court.

It is interesting to note that in at least one of the United States Circuit Courts (the First), rules of court provided for four degrees at the Bar—attorneys, counsellors, barristers, and sergeants. The latter degree was a distinct innovation in the United States, existing hitherto only in the Colony and State of New Jersey. To qualify as an attorney in the Circuit Court, an applicant must have been either a college graduate who had studied law in the office of an attorney or counsellor of the court for three years (four years if a non-graduate), or admitted to practice in the State court for one year. After two years' practice in the Circuit Court as attorney, he was eligible for admittance as counsellor. Counsellors "of six years' standing in practice" might be "called by the court to the degree of Barrister, and after ten years' standing in practice to the degree of Sergeant at Law."

The conferring of these latter degrees was of rare occurrence, the most notable instance being the order made by Judge Story in 1812, as follows:

_____

(1) *Literary Diary of Ezra Stiles,* Vol. III.

Whereas the court have a full knowledge of the learning, integrity and ability of the Hon. Jeremiah Smith and the Hon. Jeremiah Mason and upon the most entire confidence therein and being willing to express this opinion in the most public manner as well as a testimony to their merits as also a laudable example to the junior members of the Bar; and the court having taken the premises into their mature deliberation of their own mere motion and pleasure, have ordered and do hereby order that the honorable degree of sergeant-at-law be and hereby is conferred upon them. . . .

The court on mature deliberation do order that the degree of barrister at law be and hereby is conferred on the following gentlemen—Oliver Peabody, Daniel Humphreys, George Sullivan and Daniel Webster, esquires; in testimony of the entire respect the court entertains for their learning, integrity and ability.

As there were practically no early cases for the Supreme Court, only five cases being heard up to the February Term of 1793, this Circuit Court work remained for some time the chief occupation of the Judges—a very arduous work in those days, owing to the difficulties of interstate communication—"the life of a Postboy"— so Iredell described it.(1) At first, the judges were divided into pairs, and each assigned to one Circuit permanently. As the Southern Circuit involved a journey of at least 1900 miles from Philadelphia and return, to be covered twice a year, it is no wonder that Iredell, to whom it was assigned, should write to Jay, Feb. 11, 1791, "I will venture to say, no judge can conscientiously undertake to ride the Southern Circuit constantly and perform the other parts of his duty,"—nor that Jay should reply March 16, 1791, "The Circuits press hard upon us all; and your share of the task has hitherto been more than in due proportion." Later the Circuits were changed annually, the judges taking them in turn.

A unique function of the new Supreme Court Justices, (since

---

(1) After the Circuits were annually changed, Judge Cushing's travels on circuit are thus described:

"He travelled over the whole Union, holding courts in Virginia, the Carolinas and Georgia. His travelling equipage was a four-wheeled phaeton, drawn by a pair of horses which he drove. It was remarkable for it's many ingenious arrangements (all of his contrivance), for carrying books, choice groceries, and other comforts. Mrs. Cushing always accompanied him, and generally read aloud while riding. His faithful servant, Prince, a jet-black negro, whose parents had been slaves in the family, and who loved his master with unbounded affection, followed."

Lives of the Chief Justices, by Henry Flanders.

largely discontinued) was the instruction in the elementary principles of law, which they were supposed to lay down in charging the Grand Jury at the opening of each Circuit Court. In
the unsettled state of the law during the early days of the new
Government, these charges to the Grand Jury, published in the
newspapers, had immense influence upon the people at large.(1)

Credit for the formation of our early Federal law, however,
should not be given entirely to the new courts; for on the first
Attorney General of the United States, Edmund Randolph of
Virginia, fell a large part of the burden. He had not only to
create an office, but to adapt the whole judiciary apparatus of
the country to its work. The organizing Judiciary Act of 1789,
drawn by Ellsworth, was still to be tested by experience; and
there had been sufficient friction after a year's experience to
cause the House of Representatives to request its revision by
Randolph, whose training, as the son and grandson of two Royal
Attorney Generals, and whose practice as the first Attorney General of the new State of Virginia, pre-eminently fitted him for
the task.

During the first eleven years, the Supreme Court decided only
55 cases; but two of these, however, were of highest importance. The first,—*Chisholm v. Georgia* (2 Dallas 419),—in 1793,
in which the Court upheld the right of an individual to sue a
State, emphasized the sovereignty of the new United States
over one of its members; but at the same time nearly caused a
disruption of the young nation—owing to the outburst of resentment at the decision, coming from those who had opposed
the Constitution as an infringement on States' Rights. It was
argued by Edmund Randolph for the plaintiff, and a remonstrance was filed by Jared Ingersoll and Alexander J. Dallas
for the State of Georgia, which declined to formally appear.(2)

(1) See the report in the *United States Oracle of the Day*, a Portsmouth, N. H., newspaper, May 24, 1800, of the opening by Judge Patterson
of the first United States Circuit Court in that place.
"After the jury were empanelled, the Judge delivered a most elegant and
appropriate charge. The law was laid down in a masterly manner. Politics were set in their true light, by holding up the Jacobins as the disor-
ganizers of our happy country, and the only instruments of introducing discontent and dissatisfaction among the well-meaning part of the Community.
Religion and Morality were pleasingly inculcated and enforced, as being
necessary to good government, good order and good laws; for 'when the
righteous are in authority, the people rejoice.'" *Green Bag*, Vol. II.
(2) See *Life of Patrick Henry*, by William Wirt (1817). *Georgia as
a Litigant, Georgia Bar Assn. Proc.*, Vol. XIII. *Letters and Times of the
Tylers*, by Leon G. Tyler.

The other—*Ware v. Hylton* (3 Dallas 199), the famous British Debts case—in 1796, involved a question of immense pecuniary importance; namely, whether the State laws, confiscating and sequestrating debts due to a hostile enemy, or allowing their payment in depreciated money, were valid against the provisions of the Treaty with England. In Virginia alone, it was estimated that there were more than $2,000,000 of such debts; and on the decision of this case hung the fortunes of thousands of American citizens. The question had been originally argued, in 1791, in *Jones v. Walker* (2 Paine 688), in the Federal Circuit Court in Virginia, before Judges Johnson and Blair of the Supreme Court, and District Judge Griffin, and again, in 1793, before Chief Justice Jay and Judge Iredell—Ronald, Baker, Starke, and John Wickham, of the Virginia Bar appearing for the British creditors, and Patrick Henry, Alexander Campbell, and Attorney General Innis of Virginia, for the debtors. Of these counsel, Judge Iredell in his opinion, said:

> The cause has been spoken to at the Bar, with a degree of ability equal to any occasion. However painfully I may reflect at any time on the inadequacy of my own talents, I shall, as long as I live, remember with pleasure and respect, the arguments which I have heard in this case. They have discovered an ingenuity, a depth of investigation, and a power of reasoning, fully equal to anything I have ever witnessed, and some of them have been adorned with a splendor of eloquence surpassing what I have ever felt before. Fatigue has given way under its influence and the heart has warmed, while the understanding has been instructed.

In the Supreme Court, the case was argued by Edmund Tilghman and William Lewis, of Philadelphia for the creditors, and John Marshall and Campbell for the debtors, the latter losing their case, and the court holding a treaty to be supreme over State law.(1)

Two other cases in the Supreme Court during this period deserve mention.

One, *Hylton v. United States* (3 Dallas 171), in 1796, was of interest because of the fact that though relied on largely in the great Income Tax cases in 1894(2) it was undoubtedly a fic-

---

(1) For graphic description of this case and its argument see *The Supreme Court of the United States,* by Hampton L. Carson (1891).
(2) *Pollock v. Farmers Loan and Trust Co.,* 158 U. S. 601.

titious case, based on a false statement of fact. It involved the Federal tax on carriages, and the record states:

Parties, waiving the right of trial by jury, mutually submitted the controversy to the court, on a case, which stated "that the defendant, on the 5th of June, 1794 . . . .owned possessed and kept 125 chariots for the conveyance of persons, and no more; that the chariots were kept exclusively for the defendant's own private use, and not let out to hire."

The case is also noteworthy as being the only case ever argued before the United States Supreme Court by Alexander Hamilton. Associated with Hamilton was Charles Lee, United States Attorney General, and opposed to him were Alexander Campbell, United States District Attorney for Virginia and Jared Ingersoll, Attorney General of Pennsylvania.

Of Hamilton's argument, Judge Iredell wrote, Feb. 26, 1796(1):

The day before yesterday Mr. Hamilton spoke in our court attended by the most crowded audience I ever saw there, both Houses of Congress being almost deserted on the occasion. Though he was in very ill health he spoke with astonishing ability, and in a most pleasing manner, and was listened to with the profoundest attention. His speech lasted about three hours.

The other case—*Georgia v. Brailsford* (3 Dallas 1), in 1792, argued by Jared Ingersoll and Alexander J. Dallas, against William Bradford, Edward Tilghman and William Lewis is of interest as one of the very few cases in which a special trial by jury has ever been had in the United States Supreme Court.

As the Supreme Court sat in the City Hall in Philadelphia from 1791 to 1801, the chief practitioners appearing before it were naturally the brilliant members of the Philadelphia Bar, then the ablest in the country—"the eloquent Dallas, the accomplished Rawle, the rough and rugged Lewis, the elder Tilghman, and the elder Ingersoll—the former strong-pointed and logical, the latter a perfect dragnet in the law"(2). Few lawyers ap-

---

(1) *Life and Letters of James Iredell,* by Griffith J. McRee, Vol. II (1857).

(2) *The Supreme Court of the United States,* by Hampton L. Carson (1891).

As to these Pennsylvania lawyers, see further Chapter IV supra.

Sam.ˡ Dexter

peared from other States; the chief ones being Samuel Dexter, from Massachusetts; James Reed and John Julian Pringle from South Carolina; Jeremiah B. Howell(1), and Ashur Robbins(2), from Rhode Island; James Hillhouse(3), from Connecticut; Josiah Ogden Hoffman, from New York; John Thompson Mason(4), from Maryland; James A. Bayard(5), from Delaware; and Charles Lee(6) and those previously named, from Virgina.

Such was the Supreme Court Bar. "During this period," says Kent, "the Federal Courts were chiefly occupied with questions concerning their admiralty jurisdiction, and with political and national questions arising out of the Revolutionary war, and the dangerous influence and action of the war of the French Revolution upon the neutrality and peace of our country—the principles of expatriation, of ex post facto laws, of constitutional taxes."

In these eleven years, the Court suffered many changes. In 1791 Rutledge resigned to become Chancellor of South Carolina.(7) In 1795 Jay resigned, as Chief Justice, to become Governor of New York. Ellsworth, who was appointed Chief Justice, in 1796, resigned in 1800 because of ill health.(8)

---

(1) Born in 1772, Brown 1789, U. S. Senator 1810.

(2) Born in 1757, Yale 1782, U. S. Dist. Atty. 1795, U. S. Senator 1825.

(3) Born in 1754, Yale 1773, U. S. Senator 1796.

(4) Born in 1764, offered the position of U. S. Atty. Gen. by President Jefferson and by President Madison, but declined.

(5) Born in 1767, Princeton 1789, studied with Jared Ingersoll and Joseph Reed.

(6) Born in 1758, studied with Jared Ingersoll, U. S. Atty. Gen. 1795-1801.

(7) Rutledge was appointed Chief Justice, on Jay's resignation, and presided over the Court during the August Term of 1795; but the Senate rejected his nomination.

William Cushing was appointed, but declined.

(8) Ellsworth, during his term as Chief Justice, served as Envoy Extraordinary and Minister Plenipotentiary to France, 1799-1800. At this time, he visited England and was present at the trial of the famous case of *Rex v. Waddington*, 1 East in which Mr. Law (Lord Ellenborough) Mr. Erskine, Mr. Garrow and Mr. Scott (Lord Eldon) were counsel. Wharton in his notes to *American State Trials* thus describes the scene in Westminster Hall:

"Notwithstanding Mr. Jay's previous appearance at the Court of St. James, and the contemporaneous appearance there of Mr. Rufus King, the fame of their accomplishments had not reached the King's Bench, whose precincts they had probably never invaded; and it was consequently with great curiosity that the elder lawyers, whose notions of America had been derived from the kidnapping cases which were the only precipitate cast on the reports of the Privy Council by the current of Colonial litigation, spied

Iredell and Wilson died in 1798. Samuel Chase, of Maryland, became a Justice, in 1796, in place of John Blair (resigned), and William Paterson, of New Jersey, became a Justice, in 1793, in place of Thomas Johnson, who took Rutledge's place, in 1791; Alfred Moore, of North Carolina, became a Justice, in 1799; and Bushrod Washington, of Virginia, in 1798.

As late as 1800, Jay, in declining re-appointment, stated that he "left the bench, perfectly convinced that under a system so defective, it could not obtain the energy, weight and dignity, which were essential to its affording due support to the national government; nor acquire the public confidence and respect, which, as the last resort of the justice of the nation, it should possess."

And the difficult situation in which the Court was placed in these early years was well depicted by Caleb Cushing, writing in 1824(1):

To say that the Supreme Court of the United States was forced to contend with all the prejudices and misconceptions which cast a cloud around the dawning of our national constitution is far short of the reality; for its duties brought it directly in conflict with those prejudices and misconceptions in their worst and most aggravated shapes. As entrusted with the execution of the laws, it was necessarily thrust forward to bear the brunt in the first instance, of all the opposition levelled against the federal head; to enforce the collection of revenue; to punish riots which the pressure of odious taxes had excited; to quell disaffections maddened and enflamed into insurrection by popular clamor; to maintain the neutrality of the nation in spite of the usurpations of foreign armaments, consuls, ministers and directories; to compel obedience to commercial restrictions of which they on whom they fell most heavily, would not acknowledge the utility, efficiency or expediency; to withstand the pretensions of individual States to independent sovereignty; in short to guarantee the integrity of our constitution wherever that instrument opposed the feelings or combatted the claims of constituent members of the union.

---

out the American Chief Justice. Mr. Ellsworth's simple but dignified carriage was in happy contrast to the awkwardness of the English Chief Justice (Kenyon); and as soon as it was discovered that, though his worn and marked features bore a stamp which had not then become familiar to the English eye, he was neither an Indian nor a Jacobin . . . he was surrounded by a knot of lawyers, curious to know how the common law stood transplanting."

(1) Review of *Law Reports*, by Caleb Cushing, *North Amer. Rev.*, Vol. XVIII (1824).

John Adams, however, in the closing days of his administration, placed the Supreme court at one stroke upon the pinnacle which it has ever since held, by his appointment of John Marshall on January 31, 1801, Chief Justice—a man "born," said William Pinkney, "to be the Chief Justice of any country into which Providence should have cast him."(1)

With the installation of Marshall, the Court moved to Washington, and sat in the room which now serves as the law library of Congress.

During the first fifteen years of the 19th Century, the Federal Bar consisted largely of Virginia, Maryland and Pennsylvania lawyers, a fact hardly surprising, in view of the difficulties of access to Washington, and habitation there.

"Washington, in 1800, was regarded as a fever stricken morass. The half finished White House stood in a naked field, overlooking the Potomac, with two awkward Department buildings near it, a single row of brick houses and a few isolated dwellings within sight and nothing more; until across a swamp, a mile and a half away, the shapeless, unfinished capitol was seen, two wings without a body. . . . Discontented men clustered together in eight or ten boarding houses, as near as possible to the capitol."(2)

As late as 1808, Sir James Jackson, the British Minister, described the city as "five miles long, the scattered houses intersected with woods, heaths and gravel pits. I put up a covey of partridges within three hundred yards of the house of Congress, yclept the capitol. It is more like Hampstead Heath than a city." Of the difficulties of a journey to the city, there are many contemporary descriptions. Edmund Quincy writes that his mother (wife of Josiah Quincy, President of Harvard College and previously Congressman) "used to describe the discomforts, and dangers even, of the journeys to Washington from Boston, as things to remember to the end of a long life."(3)

---

(1) Edward C. Marshall, youngest son of the Chief Justice, writing of a visit to John Adams in 1825, said, "He gave me a most cordial reception, and, grasping my hand, told me that his gift of Mr. John Marshall to the people of the United States was the proudest act of his life."
(2) *History of the United States,* by Henry Adams, Vol. I.
(3) *Memoir of Josiah Quincy,* by Edmund Quincy.
Hon. Elijah H. Mills, of Northampton, the leader of the Western Bar in Massachusetts, wrote to his wife from Washington in 1815. (See *Mass. Hist. Soc. Proc.,* Vol. XIX) :
"My anticipations were almost infinitely short of the reality, and I can

Judge Story wrote to his wife, in 1812: "It will probably take me twelve days to reach home after I set out on the journey."

"Between Boston and New York was a tolerable highway, along which, thrice a week, light stage coaches carried passengers and mail, in three days. From New York, a stage coach started for Philadelphia every week day, consuming the greater part of two days, the road between Paulus Hook (now Jersey City) and Hackensack, being exceedingly bad. South of Philadelphia it was tolerable as far as Baltimore, but beyond Baltimore it meandered through forests. Four miles an hour was average speed everywhere. Beyond the Potomac the roads were steadily worse; and south of Petersburg, even the mails were carried on horseback. Except for a stage coach which plied between Charleston and Savannah, no public conveyance of any kind was mentioned in the three Southernmost States. Of eight rivers in the one hundred miles between Monticello and Washington, Jefferson wrote) in 1801, "five have neither bridges nor boats." Six cents a mile was the usual stage fare. The cost of a journey from Baltimore to New York was about $21."(1)

The journey from Charleston South Carolina, was even more of a task, requiring from ten days to three weeks, according to the lightness of the vehicle and swiftness of horse, the state of the rivers and swamps, or, if one went by Philadelphia packet, the fairness of the winds.(2)

For these reasons, the cases before the Supreme Court were as a rule argued by counsel who could make the journey thither with the least difficulty.

Peter S. DuPonceau, of Pennsylvania, thus describes the attendance of lawyers from that State:

---

truly say that the first appearance of this seat of the national government has produced in me nothing but absolute loathing and disgust. . . . From Washington to Baltimore we went in the first day. There we took passage in a packet for French-Town, in the Chesapeake Bay, and were delayed by a dead calm, so that we were twenty-four hours performing a passage usually completed in six. On Wednesday, we left our packet and went overland to Newcastle. There we again took a packet, and arrived in Philadelphia late in the evening. On Thursday, we remained in that city, the stage being too full to receive us that day. . . . This morning we left it at two o'clock, and ought to have arrived in New York this evening. But the excessive badness of the roads has arrested our progress at a distance of about forty miles from it. I shall make no stay in New York, but shall press my journey with all the rapidity in my power, and shall be with you, my dear Harriette, I hope, by the Friday stage."

(1) *History of the United States,* by Henry Adams.
(2) *Life of William Lowndes,* by Mrs. St. J. Ravenel.

The counsel engaged in those causes were in the habit of going together to Washington to argue their cases. These were Mr. Ingersoll, Mr. Dallas, Mr. Lewis, Mr. Edward Tilghman, Mr. Rawle and myself. We hired a stage to ourselves in which we proceeded by easy journies. The court sat then in the month of February, so that we had to travel in the depth of winter through bad roads in no very comfortable way. Nevertheless, as soon as we were out of the city, and felt the flush of air, we were like school boys in the playground on a holiday.

Flashes of wit shot their corruscations on all sides; puns of the genuine Philadelphia stamp were handed about, old college stories were revived, songs were sung— in short, it might have been taken for anything but the grave counsellors of the celebrated bar of Philadelphia—except Mr. Ingersoll, who, sad, serious and composed, rode thinking of his causes and little inclined to mirth.

Our appearance at the bar of the Supreme Court was always a scene of triumph. We entered the hall together, and Judge Washington was heard to say, "This is my bar." Our causes had a preference over all others, in consideration of the distance we had to travel.(1)

Joseph Story gives the following lively description of the Pennsylvania Bar before the Supreme Court in 1808(2):

Duponceau is a Frenchman by birth, and a very ingenious counsellor at Philadelphia. He has the reputation of great subtilty and acuteness, and is excessively minute in the display of his learning. His manner is animated but not impressive, and he betrays at every turn the impatience and the casuistry of his nation. His countenance is striking, his figure rather awkward. A small, sparkling, black eye, and a thin face, satisfy you that he is not without quickness of mind; yet he seemed to me to exhaust himself in petty distinctions, and in a perpetual recurrence to doubtful, if not to inclusive arguments. His reasoning was rather sprightly and plausible, than logical and coercive; in short, he is a French advocate. Tilghman is quite an old man, of an unpromising appearance; his face indicates rather a simplicity and weakness of character. Indeed, when I first saw him, I could not persuade myself that he possessed any talent. I heard his argument, and it was strong, clear, pointed, and logical. Though his manner was bad, and his pronounciation not agreeable, every person listened with attention, and none were disappointed. Rawle is quite a plain but genteel man, and looks like a studious, ingenious, and able lawyer. He argues with a very pleasant voice, and has great neatness, perspicacity,

---

(1) See *Letter of P. S. DuPonceau* in *Penn. Hist. Soc. Coll.*, Vol. IV.
(2) *Life and Letters of Joseph Story*, by W. W. Story (1851).

and even elegance.   He keeps his object steadily in view; he distinguishes with care, enforces with strength, and if he fail to convince he seldom spends his thoughts vainly.   Ingersoll has rather a peculiar face, and yet in person or manner has nothing which interests in a high degree.   He is more animated than Rawle, but has less precision; he is learned, laborious, and minute, not eloquent, not declamatory, but diffuse.   The Pennsylvanians consider him a perfect dragnet, that gathers everything in its course.   Dallas is a book-man, ready, apt, and loquacious, but artificial.   He is of a strong, robust figure, but his voice seems shrill and half obstructed.   He grows warm by method, and cools in the same manner.   He wearies with frequent emphasis on subordinate points, but he cannot be considered as unscientific or wandering.   Lee, of Virginia, is a thin, spare, short man; you cannot believe that he was attorney general of the United States.

Maryland lawyers were especially distinguished for their knowledge of the science, and their skill in the practice, of special pleading.

The acknowledged head of the profession in that State during this period was Luther Martin, Attorney General of the State for many years, a lawyer of great force, of profound learning and memory,(1) powerful in argument but often discursive, slipshod, and sometimes inaccurate.   The rude vigor, pertinacity, and fearless courage of the man made him hated by those whom he opposed—"an unprincipled, impudent, Federal bull dog," so Jefferson called him—though beloved by his friends.

No tribute has ever been paid to a lawyer in the United States so remarkable as the action taken by the Maryland Legislature, in 1822, in passing a Resolve imposing a license tax on every practising attorney, of $5 annually, to be paid to trustees "for the use of Luther Martin", he being at the time broken in health and in fortune.(2)

---

(1)   Born in 1748, a Princeton graduate of 1766, admitted to the Bar in 1771, Atty. Gen. of Maryland 1778-1805, and again in 1818.

(2)   This Resolve of the Legislature of Maryland passed in February 1822, was as follows: "*Resolved* that each and every practitioner of law in this State shall be and he is hereby compelled . . . to obtain from the Clerk of the County Court in which he may practice, a license to authorize him so to practice, for which he shall pay annually . . . the sum of five dollars, which said sum is to be deposited . . . in the treasury—subject to the order of Thomas Hall and William H. Winder, Esquires, who are hereby appointed trustees for the application of the proceeds raised by virtue of this resolution to the use of Luther Martin . . . and provided that this resolution shall cease to be valid at the death of the said Luther Martin."

Story gives this picture of Martin, before the Supreme Court in 1808(2):

Shall I turn you to Luther Martin, that singular compound of strange qualities? With a professional income of $10,000 a year, he is poor and needy; generous and humane, but negligent and profuse. He labors hard to acquire, and yet cannot preserve. Experience, however severe, never corrects a single habit. I have heard anecdotes of his improvidence and thoughtlessness which astonishes me. He is about the middle size, a little bald, with a common forehead, pointed nose, inexpressive eye, large mouth, and well formed chin. His dress is slovenly. You cannot believe him a great man. Nothing in his voice, his action, his language impresses. Of all men he is the most desultory, wandering, and inaccurate. Errors in Grammar, and, indeed, an unexampled laxity of speech, mark him everywhere. . . .
But everyone assures me that he is profoundly learned, and that though he shines not now in the lustre of his former days, yet he is at times very great. He never seems satisfied with a single grasp of his subject; he urges himself to successive efforts, until he moulds and fashions it to his purpose. You should hear of Luther Martin's fame from those who have known him long and intimately, but you should not see him.

After 1810, another Maryland lawyer—William Pinkney—stepped to the front and until his death, in 1822, remained the undisputed head of the American Bar. The comments of his contemporaries are interesting.(1) "He appears to me," wrote Story when a justice of the Supreme Court in 1812, "a man of consummate talents. He seizes his subject with the comprehension and vigor of a giant and he breaks forth with a lustre and a strength that keep the attention forever on the stretch." Chief Justice Marshall stated that he never knew his equal as a reasoner—so clear and luminous was his method of argumentation.

---

(2) *Life and Letters of Joseph Story,* by W. W. Story, Vol. I. See also *Luther Martin, American Law Review,* Vol. I; *Luther Martin,* by Henry P. Goddard, *Proc. Maryland Hist. Soc.* (1887); *Luther Martin as a Lawyer and Lover, Maryland Bar Assn.,* Vol. IV (1899).

(1) Born in 1764, studied with Judge Samuel Chase, admitted to practise in 1786, U. S. Atty. Gen. 1811-1814, U. S. Senator 1820. *William Pinkney,* by Henry Flanders, *Proc. N. Y. State Bar Assn.* (1906). *Lives of the Chief Justices,* by Henry Flanders. *Life and Letters of Joseph Story,* by W. W. Story. *Miscellaneous Works,* by Joseph Story. *Life and Times of Roger B. Taney,* by Samuel Tyler. *Familiar Letters on Public Characters,* by William Sullivan—in which interesting anecdotes are told of Pinkney's appearance before the Massachusetts Supreme Court. *William Pinkney,* by Rev. William Pinkney. *Life, Writings and Speeches of William Pinkney,* by Henry Wheaton (1826). Review of *Wheaton's Life of Pinkney, North Amer. Rev.,* Vol. XXIV (1826).

"Mr. Pinkney was the greatest man I have ever seen in a court of justice".

"He had an oceanic mind", said William Wirt, "he was the most thoroughly equipped lawyer I ever met in the courts."

In manner, Pinkney was a tremendous fop, always wearing doe colored kid gloves in arguing before the Supreme Court. His preparation of his cases and arguments was elaborate to the uttermost degree. He was arrogant, vain, often boisterous. His voice was harsh and feeble. "Yet, notwithstanding these defects," wrote Judge Story, "such is his strong and cogent logic, his elegant and perspicuous language, his flowing graces, and rhetorical touches, his pointed and persevering arguments that he enchants, interests, and almost irresistibly leads away the understanding."

From Maryland also came Robert Goodloe Harper—able in mercantile cases, a thorough lawyer and a felicitous and graceful orator(1); Philip Barton Key(2), Francis Scott Key(3), and W. H. Winder(4).

The lawyers from Virginia who argued the principal cases before the Supreme Court at this time were Edmund J. Lee, John Wickham(5), Thomas Swann, Charles Simms, Walter Jones, and William Wirt.(6)

A brief survey of the volumes of *Cranch's Reports*, through the year 1815, shows a mere handful of counsel from other States. Roger Griswold, of Connecticut(7), appeared in a case in 1801. John Quincy Adams of Massachusetts, William Hunter of Rhode Island,(8) and Luther Martin, appeared in a Rhode Island case, *Head v. Providence Ins. Company* (2 Cranch 127), in 1804-05. A later Massachusetts case in the same volume, *Graves v. Boston Marine Insurance Company*, was argued by Richard Stockton of New Jersey, and Luther Martin of Maryland, against R. G. Harper and F. S. Key of Maryland and Jared Ingersoll of Pennsylvania. In a famous group of cases

---

(1) Born in 1765, Princeton 1785, admitted to the Bar in Charleston, S. Car. 1786, son-in-law of Charles Carroll of Carrollton, U. S. Senator 1816-1821.
(2) Born in 1757.
(3) Born in 1780, nephew of P. B. Key.
(4) Born in 1775.
(5) Born in 1763.
(6) Born in 1772, U. S. Atty Gen. 1817-1829.
(7) Born in 1762, Yale 1780, Judge of Supreme Court of Conn. 1807.
(8) Born in 1774, studied in the Temple in London, admitted to the Bar in 1795 in Rhode Island.

reported under the name of *Rose v. Himely* (4 Cranch), in 1807-08, ten counsel argued—C. Lee, Harper, S. Chase, Jr., Dallas, Rawle, Ingersoll and Drayton against Du Ponceau, E. Tilghman and Luther Martin; of whom John Drayton, from South Carolina(1), was the only one not of the Maryland, Virginia, or Pennsylvania Bar. Henry Clay, then from Kentucky, made his appearance, in 1808, in *Skillem's executors v. May's executors* (4 Cranch). In 1809, Horace Binney, destined to lead the Philadelphia Bar for nearly half a century, made his first argument before the Supreme Court in *Bank of the United States v. Deveaux;*(2) and in the same year he appeared in a case with John Quincy Adams and Ingersoll. Edward Livingston, of New York and Louisiana, appeared also in 1809.

In 7 and 8 Cranch (1812-1814), Samuel Dexter, Daniel Davis and Rufus G. Amory of Massachusetts, and Pitkin and Putnam of Rhode Island, appear in various prize cases. In 1814, the name of Daniel Webster appears, for the first time, he having been admitted to practice before the Supreme Court in the winter of 1813-14. The next year Clay, Charles A. Wickliffe,(3) and George M. Bibb(4) of Kentucky, argued; and for the first time prominent New York counsel appear, when Thomas Addis Emmett and J. Ogden Hoffman argued the famous case of *The Nereide,* (9 Cranch 388) against Dallas and Pinkney.

Such were the lawyers who built up the fabric of early American law. And, as has been justly remarked, "While no judge ever profited more from argument; it is not, perhaps, diverging into the circle of exaggeration to say, that no Bar was ever more capable of aiding the mind of the Bench, than the Bar of the Supreme Court, in the time of Chief Justice Marshall."

The Attorney Generals of the United States during this period were Edmund Randolph, of Virginia, appointed in 1789; William Bradford, of Pennsylvania, in 1794; Charles Lee, of Virginia, in 1795; Theophilus Parsons, of Massachusetts, appointed in 1801, but who never served; Levi Lincoln, of Massa-

---

(1) Born in 1766.
(2) Chief Justice Marshall in this case speaks of the "course of acute, metaphysical and abstruse reasoning employed" by the defendant's counsel, R. G. Harper and P. B. Key, to shake the previous "common understanding of intelligent men in favor of the right of incorporated aliens or citizens of a different state from the defendant, to sue in the national courts."
(3) Born in 1788.
(4) Born in 1772, Princeton 1792, author of *Bibb's Reports* 1808-11, Chief Justice of Kentucky.

chusetts, in 1801; Robert Smith, of Maryland, in 1805; John Breckenridge, of Kentucky, in 1805; Cæsar A. Rodney, of Delaware, in 1807; William Pinkney, of Maryland, in 1811; Richard Rush, of Pennsylvania, in 1814. In the above list of the Bar practising before the Supreme Court, the names of many notable lawyers who practised only in State courts are lacking.

The Bars of New Hampshire, New York and of Massachusetts at this time were of peculiar lustre; but their fame was largely local. Of the great lawyers of the two former States, mention has already been made. A more detailed description of the conditions of the Massachusetts Bar of this time will be given in the following chapter, as illustrating the political aspect of the practise of the law at the beginning of the Century.

The part taken by lawyers in the early years of the political and commercial development of the United States may be gathered from a rapid survey of some of the noted cases connected with its history, prior to 1815, with particular reference to the counsel engaged in them. (1)

Within two years from his appointment, Marshall pronounced the first in the long line of decisions which were to establish the United States Constitution, irrevocably, as the Supreme Law of the Land, and the Supreme Court as the final arbiter of its construction and of the validity of State and Federal statutes. (2)

This was the case of *Marbury v. Madison* (1 Cranch 137),

---

(1) "If then the case is in itself of the utmost importance, its settling might well be a matter of interest as well as of moment. The parties to the action; the lawyers in the case; the judge or judges delivering the judgment of the court—a consideration of these not only lends an interest to the transaction but very often throws a clear and strong light on the case itself, and illuminates, at times, other and unsuspected fields of law.

The very name of the judge means much. The names of the lawyers lend a personal interest to the case. A case in which Hamilton, Pinkney and Wirt, Jeremiah Mason, Webster and Choate appeared is really interesting from that fact alone; this fact of itself means that the case was carefully argued and every aid offered to the court that the wit and ingenuity of man could advance or devise—I would therefore venture to suggest in conclusion that the students and practitioners cannot well afford to neglect the sketches and biographies where they exist of the distinguished lawyers and judges who have honored bench and bar."

See *Letter from James B. Scott* of the Columbia University School of Law in *Green Bag*, Vol. XVI (1904).

(2) In view of Marshall's broad construction of the Constitution, it is interesting to note the fears expressed in a letter from Oliver Wolcott to Fisher Ames, in December 1799. "He is doubtless a man of virtue but he will think too much of the State of Virginia, and is too much disposed to govern the world according to the rules of logic. He will read and expound the Constitution as if it were a penal statute."

in 1803, argued by Levi Lincoln of Massachusetts, Attorney General, against Charles Lee of Virginia, ex-Attorney General. The case has never been better summed up than by Rufus Choate, in his address before the Harvard Law School, July 3, 1845, on *The Position and Functions of the American Bar as an element of Conservatism in the State*:

> I do not know that I can point to one achievement in American statesmanship which can take rank for its consequences of good, above that single decision of the Supreme Court which adjudged that an act of the legislature contrary to the Constitution is void and that the judicial department is clothed with the power to ascertain the repugnancy and pronounce the legal conclusion. That the framers of the Constitution intended this to be so is certain; but to have asserted it against Congress and the executive, to have vindicated it by that easy yet adamantine demonstration than which the reasonings of mathematics show nothing surer, to have inscribed this vast truth of conservatism upon the public mind so that no demagogue, not in the last stages of intoxication, denies it—this is an achievement of statesmanship of which a thousand years may not exhaust or reveal all the good(1).

---

(1) John F. Dillon, in his *Laws and Jurisprudence of England and America* (1895) points out that this power to declare legislative acts void was asserted as early as 1780, by the Supreme Court of New Jersey in *Holmes v. Walton*, a case referred to in *State v. Parkhurst*, 4 Halstead 444. The Virginia Court decided the same way, in *Com. v. Caton*, 4 Call 5, in 1782, and in the *Case of the Judges*, 4 Call 135, in 1788, and in *Kamper v. Hawkins*, 1 Va. Cases 20, in 1793. The Rhode Island Court held the same in *Trevett v. Weeden* in 1786, North Carolina and Massachusetts followed with cases in 1788.

As late as 1825, Judge John B. Gibson (later the great Chief Justice of Pennsylvania) in *Eakin v. Raub*, 12 S and R 330, vigorously denied the existence of the right claimed by the courts to disregard a legislature act because of its conflict with the State Constitution. For interesting discussion of the subject, see *Origin and Scope of the American Doctrine of Constitutional Law*, by Prof. J. B. Thayer, *Harv. Law Rev.* Vol. XII (1893); and J. W. Burrage, in *Political Science Quarterly*, Vol. X (1895).

See also especially Address of James T. Mitchell and Hampton L. Carson in *John Marshall, Life, Character and Judicial Services*, by John F. Dillon (1903).

For many years, however, the authority, as law, of the doctrines announced by Marshall in this case, was bitterly opposed by Jefferson and his adherents; and he wrote to George Hay, during Burr's trial, June 2, 1807:

"I observe that the case of *Marbury v. Madison* has been cited in the Burr case, and I think it material to stop at the threshold the citing that case as authority, and to have it denied to be law . . . I have long wished for a proper occasion to have the gratuitous opinion in *Marbury v. Madison* brought before the public and denounced as not law; and I think the present a fortunate one, because the case occupies such a place in the public attention. I shall be glad, therefore, if in noticing that case, you

In the next year, 1804, the careers of two of the leading lawyers of the country were ended through the fatal duel fought between Hamilton and Burr, on July 7. It is curious however to note that although both were pre-eminent at the New York Bar, one, Burr, had never argued a case, and the other, Hamilton, had argued only one case, before the United States Supreme Court.(2)

Three years later, in May 1807, came the trial of Aaron Burr for treason, held in the Circuit Court for the District of Virginia, before Chief Justice Marshall and District Judge Griffin. No case of the day aroused more intense excitement or enlisted a more brilliant array of counsel. For Burr there appeared, first and foremost, Edmund Randolph, ex-Attorney General of the United States, weighty in counsel, deep in knowledge, but ponderous in style; Charles Lee also ex-Attorney General; John Wickham, the leader of the Virginia Bar, famed for his wit and versatility; Benjamin Botts of Virginia, a lawyer of much tact, local knowledge and common sense; Jack Baker, a local attorney and good fellow; and finally Luther Martin, whose favorite phrase "as great a scoundrel as Tom Jefferson", expressed his fierce hatred of the President. For the Government there appeared Caesar A. Rodney, only recently appointed United States Attorney General, who took part in the preliminaries of the trial; George Hay, United States District Attorney, and son-in-law of James Munroe; William Wirt, then thirty-five years old, and practically at the beginning of his brilliant career and Alexander McRae, Lieutenant Governor of Virginia, a lawyer of

could take occasion to express the determination of the executive that the doctrines of that case were given extra-judicially and against law, and that their reverse will be the rule of action with the Executive." See *Writings of Thomas Jefferson,* Vol. IX.

(1) One of the results of this duel was the passage of statutes in various states, New York, Rhode Island, Massachusetts, and Pennsylvania, forbidding duels; and in New York, by an act of 1816, all attorneys, before being admitted to practice, were required to take an oath of non-participation in a duel.

See *Act of 1804* (Mass.) c. 123; *Commonwealth v. Robert C. Hooper,* Thatcher's Criminal Cases (Mass.) 456, (1834).

See also *In re Attorneys Oaths,* 20 John. 492 (1819). Duels at this time were of common occurrence, both in the United States and England.

See for an interesting account of this condition, *Life of Josiah Quincy,* by Edmund Quincy.

Two years before Hamilton's duel, his own son had been killed in a duel with a lawyer named Eaker.

In 1803, duels had been fought between Col. Sturtevant and DeWitt Clinton, the lawyer; and Robert Sturtevant and Richard Riker, the lawyer.

See *Pleasantries about Courts and Lawyers of New York,* by Charles Edwards (1867).

courage and tenacity but lacking in tact. To these counsel an interesting tribute was paid by the Chief Justice, who said in his opinion:

A degree of eloquence seldom displayed on any occasion has embellished a solidity of argument and a depth of research by which the court has been greatly aided in forming the opinion it is about to deliver. (1)

The definition of the law of treason laid down, with splendid freedom from political considerations, by Marshall saved Burr's life, but gave rise to bitter political attacks upon the Chief Justice, and renewed a popular demand for an elective judiciary or a limited term of office.

Jefferson wrote to James Wilkinson Sept. 20, 1807 (2):

The scenes which have been enacted at Richmond are such as have never before been exhibited in any country where all regard to public character has not yet been thrown off. They are equivalent to a proclamation of impunity to every traitorous combination which may be formed to destroy the Union. . . . However, they will produce an amendment to the Constitution which keeping the judges independent of the executive will not leave them so, of the nation.

And again, on Sept. 26, 1807, to William Thompson:

The scenes which have been acting at Richmond are sufficient

---

(1) John Randolph was foreman of the Grand Jury. On May 22, the trial began, dragging on for five months.

The first fight arose on Burr's move to have a subpoena duces tecum issued to President Jefferson, against whom Martin entered into a violent invective, saying,

"He has let slip the dogs of war, the hell hounds of persecution to hunt down my friend." On June 13, Judge Marshall gave a decision that the subpoena should issue. The President, however, never appeared, and for answer wrote to Hay, suggesting moving to commit Luther Martin as particeps criminis with Burr.

On June 24, the Grand Jury presented indictments against Burr for treason and misdemeanors. On August 17, the jury was impanelled; and on August 19, there began the long ten days of forensic argument, resulting in Marshall's decision that Burr could not be found guilty on the evidence.

Among the many lawyers who attended this trial were Andrew Jackson and Washington Irving.

For the best accounts of this trial, see McMaster's *History of the United States*, Vol. III; and Henry Adams' *History of the United States*, Vol. III. *Trial of Aaron Burr* by James A. Cabell, in *N. Y. State Bar Assn. Proc.*, Vol. XXIII.

Decisive Battles of the Times, by Frederic Trevor Hill (1907).

(2) *Writings of Thomas Jefferson*, Vol. IX.

to fill us with alarm. We had supposed we possessed fixed laws to
guard us equally against treason and oppression. But it now appears
we have no law but the will of the judge. Never will chicanery
have a more difficult task than has been now accomplished to
warp the text of the law to the will of him who is to construe
it.

In 1809, there occurred in the United States Supreme Court
a case famous for its counsel—*Fletcher v. Peck* (6 Cranch 87).
(1) This case arose in the Massachusetts Circuit, and was first
argued by Luther Martin, against John Quincy Adams and
Robert G. Harper.

An entry in J. Q. Adams' diary records that the case was
thought by the court to be a fictitious one—an interesting suggestion in view of the fact that the decision in the great Dartmouth College Case, ten years later, was based partly on this
case.

The court met at the usual hour (11 A. M.) and sat until 12
M. Martin continued his argument until that time, and then
adjourned until two. I went to the capitol and witnessed the
inauguration of Mr. Madison as President of the United States.
The House was very much crowded and its appearance very
magnificent. . . . The court had adjourned until two o'clock.
I therefore returned to them at that hour. Mr. Martin closed
the argument. March 7. In the case of *Fletcher and Peck,* he
(the Chief Justice) mentioned to Mr. Cranch and Judge Livingston, and had done the same to me on Saturday night at the ball,
the reluctance of the court to decide the case at all, as it appeared
manifestly made up for the purpose of getting the court's judgment upon all the points. And although they have given some
decisions in such cases, they appear not disposed to do so now.

The second argument(2) in 1810, was notable for the fact

---

(1) The case involved the famous Yazoo Frauds and the constitutionality
of a statute of the State of Georgia of 1796, voiding certain grants of land
made under a previous Act of 1795 on the ground that the passage of the
Act of 1795 was obtained by fraud and corruption—See *The Yazoo Land
Companies,* by Charles H. Haskins, *Amer. Hist. Ass. Papers,* Vol. V
(1891); and *James Wilson and the so-called Yazoo Frauds,* by M. C.
Klingelsmith, *U. of P. Law Review,* Vol. LVI (1908).
(2) *Fletcher v. Peck* at its first hearing went off on a point of jurisdiction; see the following entry in J. Q. Adams' diary:
"March 11, 1809. This morning the chief justice read a written opinion
on the case of *Fletcher and Peck.* The judgment in the Circuit Court is
reversed for a defect in the pleadings. With regard to the merits of the
case, the Chief Justice added verbally that circumstanced as the court are,
only five judges attending, there were difficulties which would have prevented them from giving any opinion at this term had the pleadings been
correct."

that Joseph Story, one year before his appointment as Supreme Court Judge, appeared as counsel on the winning side, in place of Adams (who had been appointed Minister to Russia). A complimentary comment on the counsel is to be found in Marshall's opinion:

I have been very unwilling to proceed to the decision of this cause at all. It appears to me to bear strong evidence upon the face of it of being a mere feigned case. It is our duty to decide on the rights but not in a speculation of parties. My confidence however in the respectable gentlemen who have been engaged for the parties has induced me to abandon my scruples in the belief that they would never consent to impose a mere feigned case upon this court.

In 1811, occured a case, interesting as being one of the first involving the title to property under the Louisiana Purchase of 1803—*Livingston v. Jefferson* (Federal Cases No. 8411). This was an action known as the "Batture Case", brought by Edward Livingston against Thomas Jefferson for alleged trespass commited while President, in removing Livingston from property made by accretion of soil, known as the "batture," on the river front in New Orleans. A great controversy raged for years over this matter, in the courts, the newspapers and the law magazines. Its permanent effect on the jurisprudence of the country arose, however, from the political complexion of the case.

While it was pending, William Cushing, Judge of the Supreme Court, died. The court was Federalist in its politics; and Jefferson, whose personal fortune was at stake in the Livingston case, urged upon President Madison, with all the energy at his command, the extreme necessity for the appointment of a strong Republican to fill the vacant position. Jefferson's antipathy to Marshall and his distrust of his political motives led him to conceive that Marshall would take revenge by finding against him if the case came before him. Accordingly, he addressed urgent letters to Madison and to all his cabinet, of which the following may be cited.

Writing to Albert Gallatin, Sept. 27, 1810, he said(1):

What the issue of the case ought to be no unbiased man can doubt. What it will be, no one can tell. The judge's inveteracy is profound and his mind of that gloomy malignity which

---

(1) *Writings of Thomas Jefferson*, Vol. IX.

will never let him forego the opportunity of satiating it on a victim.

His decision, his instructions to a jury, his allowances and disallowances and garblings of evidence must all be subjects of appeal. I consider that as my only chance of saving my fortune from entire wreck. And to whom is my appeal? From the judge in Burr's case to himself and his Associate Judges in the case of *Marbury v. Madison*—Not exactly however. I observe old Cushing is dead. At length then we have a chance of getting a Republican majority in the Supreme judiciary. For ten years that branch braved the spirit and will of the nation after the nation has manifested its will by a complete reform in every branch depending on them. The event is a fortunate one and so timed as to be a Godsend to me. I am sure its importance to the Nation will be felt and the occasion employed to complete the great operation they have so long been executing by the appointment of a decided Republican with nothing equivocal about it. But who will it be? The misfortune of [Barnabas] Bidwell removes an able man from the competition. Can any other bring equal qualifications to those of [Levi] Lincoln?

I know he was not deemed a profound common lawyer; but was there ever a profound common lawyer known in one of the eastern states? There never was nor never can be one from these states. The basis of their law is neither common nor civil; it is an original, if any compound can be so called. Its foundation seems to have been laid in the spirit and principles of Jewish law, incorporated with some words and phrases of common law and an abundance of notions of their own. This makes an amalgam sui generis; and it is well known that a man first thoroughly initiated into the principles of one system of law can never become pure and sound in any other. Lord Mansfield was a splendid proof of this. Therefore I say there never was nor never can be a profound common lawyer from those states. [James] Sullivan had the reputation of pre-eminence as a common lawyer—but we have his history of Land Titles which gives us his measure. Mr. Lincoln is, I believe, considered as learned in their laws as any one they have. Federalists say that Parsons is better; but the criticalness of the present nomination puts him out of the question.

To Madison, he wrote, Oct. 10, 1810:

[George] Blake calls himself a republican but never was one at heart. His treachery to us under the embargo should put him by forever. [Joseph] Story and [Ezekiel] Bacon are exactly the men who deserted us on that measure and carried off the majority. The former unquestionably a tory and both are too young. I say nothing of professing federalists. Granger and Morton have both been interested in Yazooism. The former however has been clear of it.

All the lawyers mentioned in these letters were Republicans from Massachusetts (that being the State from which Cushing had been appointed).

Madison was evidently impressed with the appeals; for, after offering the vacant judgeship to Levi Lincoln and to John Quincy Adams, (both of whom declined), he finally appointed Joseph Story, then a young man of thirty-two, and a strong Republican. This appointment in its effect upon the future of American jurisprudence can be reckoned only second in importance to that of John Marshall. The appointment in its political aspect proved, however, a sore disappointment to Jefferson; for Story soon after his accession to the bench, became a staunch supporter of Marshall's strongly Federal doctrines.

When the "Batture Case" was finally argued in the United States District Court in 1811, the plaintiff's counsel was John Wickham, while George Hay, William Wirt, and Littleton Waller Tazewell, appeared for Jefferson; District Judge John Tylor (father of President Tyler) and Chief Justice Marshall presided; and Tyler gave the opinion, finding for Jefferson on a point of jurisdiction.

The following extract throws a quaint light upon the lawyers of the day:

While I freely acknowledge how much I was pleased with the ingenuity and eloquence of the plaintiff's counsel, I cannot do so much injustice to plain truth as to say that any conviction was wrought on my mind of the soundness of the arguments they exhibited, in a legal acceptation. It is the happy talent of some professional gentlemen, and particularly of the plaintiff's counsel, often to make the worse appear the better excuse. . . . These arguments and this eloquence, however, have been met by an Herculean strength of forensic ability which I take pride in saying sheds lustre over the bar of Virginia.(1)

(1) See also *Livingston v. Dorgenois*, 7 Cranch 577 (1813).
Livingston finally lost his case in the Louisiana Supreme Court, see *Morgan v. Livingston*, 6 Martin 19, (1819).
And see Randall's *Life of Jefferson*, Vol. III; *Letters and Times of the Tylers*, by Leon G. Tyler; *Opinions of DuPonceau, Rawle, Ingersoll, E. Tilghman and W. Lewis in behalf of Edward Livingston*, in *Hall's American Law Journal*, Vol. II (1809) ; *Proceedings of the United States Government in maintaining the Public Rights to the Beach of the Mississippi adjacent to New Orleans against the intrusion of Edward Livingston*, by Thomas Jefferson (1812), in *Hall's American Law Journal*, Vol. V (1816).
An answer to Mr. Jefferson's Justification of his conduct in the case of the New Orleans Batture by Edward Livingston (1813), in *Hall's American Law Journal*, Vol. V (1816).

In the same year, 1811, the United States Circuit Court in
New York was called upon, in *Livingston v. Van Ingen* (1 Paine
45),(1) to deal with a new invention—a steamboat patent—
which was, within the next thirty years, to revolutionize the old
law of carriers, to necessitate an elaborate body of new law, and
to produce a tremendous change in the condition of the practise
of law. It was only four years previously that Robert Fulton's
steamboat had made its first successful trip from New York
to Albany, "by fire and steam," 150 miles in 32 hours, on
August 17, 1907, (at the time of Aaron Burr's trial).(2)

THE WAR OF 1812 AND THE DEVELOPMENT OF A BODY OF AMERICAN LAW.

Although the War of 1812 was not an historic event of particular influence on the political growth of the country, its effect

---

On May 25, 1810, Jefferson wrote to Madison:
"In speaking of Livingston's suit I omitted to observe that it is a little
doubted that his knowledge of Marshall's character has induced him to
bring this action. His twistifications in the case of Marbury, in that of
Burr and the late Yazoo case show how dexterously he can reconcile law
to his personal biases; and nobody seems to doubt that he is prepared to
decide that Livingston's right to the batture is unquestionable."
Marshall wrote to Story, July 13, 1821:
"For Mr. Jefferson's opinion as respects this department, it is not difficult to assign the cause. He is among the most ambitious and I suspect
among the most unforgiving of men—That in a free country with a written constitution any intelligent man could wish a dependent judiciary or
should think that the constitution is not a law for the court as well as the
legislature would astonish me if I had not learnt from observation that
with many men the judgment is completely controlled by the passions.
The case of the mandamus (Marbury v. Madison) may be the cloak, but
the batture is recollected with still more resentment."
See *Letters of Marshall* in *Mass. Hist. Soc. Proc., 2nd Series,* Vol. XVI
(1900-1901).
(1) It is interesting to note that the court held in this case that the
United States Courts had no authority to issue injunctions in patent cases.
An Act of Congress, Feb. 15, 1819, gave such authority.
(2) A successful trial trip of the world's first steamboat invented by
John Fitch was made in 1787, in the presence of all the members of the
Federal Convention, except Washington, Oliver Ellsworth being a guest
on the boat. In 1787, Fitch obtained a patent and again in 1791. At this
time he wrote to Gen. Thomas Mifflin of Penn.: "Should I suggest that
the navigation between this country and Europe may be made so easy as
shortly to make us the most popular empire on the earth, it probably at
this time would make the whole very laughable."
Robert Fulton's first, but unsuccessful, steamboat had been tried on the
Seine at Paris in the same month and year (April, 1803) as the sale of
Louisiana to the United States, both the steamboat and the sale being
largely the result of the efforts of Robert R. Livingston.
See *History of American Steam Navigation,* by John H. Morrison
(1903).

was most important on the commercial tendencies and upon the development of the law in the United States. Its impress is markedly seen in legal history—first, in giving rise to a vast number of decisions on Prize and Admiralty Law; second, in the growth of manufacturing corporations and the rise of the important branch of the law relating thereto; third, in turning commercial and industrial efforts from shipping and agriculture to manufactures and inventions, and consequently in establishing a system of patent law; fourth, in necessitating the development of internal means of communication—the coasting trade being ruined by the British blockade—and thus promoting the construction of canals, multiplying turnpikes, and preparing the people to demand the swifter means of transportation by steam railroads; fifth, in shutting off the country from its supply of English law reports and books, and thus throwing the courts upon strictly American resources in the solution of new legal problems.

To the ability of the American judges and lawyers to meet these new contingencies as they arose, the numerous decisions in "cases of new impression", in the early reports of those days, bear ample proof.

Maritime and Admiralty Law was undoubtedly the portion of the law which most immediately affected the citizens of the United States in those days. The troubles with the French Directory, the Mediterranean pirates of Tripoli, the Berlin and Milan Decrees of Napoleon in 1806-07; the retaliatory Orders in Council of the British Ministry, the Embargo and Non-Intercourse Acts of Thomas Jefferson, and finally, the War of 1812,—all created conditions vital to the pockets of the wealthy merchants and ship owners of the United States.

"The Embargo had fallen like a withering curse upon New England. Under its desolating blight, her ships rotted at their wharves, her business stagnated, her industries were paralyzed, and her laboring population was thrown out of work. Ruin confronted her merchants; poverty and starvation stared her workingmen in the face."(1)

At first, shipowners had looked to the courts for relief against the obnoxious laws. But in 1808, Judge John Davis had disappointed their hopes by his decision in the case of *U. S. v.*

---

(1) *Life and Times of George Cabot,* by Henry Cabot Lodge (1877).

Brigantine William, in the United States District Court in Massachusetts, holding the Embargo Act constitutional, notwithstanding the fact that Samuel Dexter, the leader of the Massachusetts Bar, had argued to the contrary, and Theophilus Parsons, the great Chief Justice of Massachusetts had given an extra judicial opinion as to the unconstitutionality of the obnoxious statute.(1)

Despairing of any remedy in the courts, the ship owners adjusted themselves to new conditions, and began to indulge in private warfare, disregarding all the various acts, orders in council and decrees; and privateering became a commercial business. "The merchant became marauder. From every port of the New England States, ships, which had lain rotting and warping in the sun, issued, new rigged as privateers, now returning with prizes, now captured by the enemy."(2)

The early State and Federal Reports are flooded, therefore, with cases not only in the Federal Admiralty courts, but also in the State courts, construing the policies of marine insurance companies, and adjusting the rights of captors, neutrals, belligerents, persons trading under licenses and privateering under letters of marque and reprisal or otherwise. From the large proportion of cases in the law reports involving these marine insurance com-

---

(1)   See Report of the case in Hall's *American Law Journal,* Vol. II, (1809).

John Quincy Adams wrote:

"I wrote to Mr. Bacon that on the question of the Embargo there was in Massachusetts a judiciary of which he must think, what I could not say. It was with a repugnance, I could not express, that I saw a desperate party leader in the Chief Justice of the Commonwealth. It was from him alone that the pretence of the unconstitutionality of the embargo derived any countenance. Even Mr. Pickering had not ventured to start that idea. It was the stimulus to the people of forcible resistance against it. It was a gigantic stride towards a dissolution of the Union. Mr. Parsons not only broached the opinion, but very extra-judicially made no secret of it, upon the exchange and at insurance offices. Even the veneration entertained by the District Judge for his personal fame as a lawyer, was not exempted from the operation of its influence. Mr. Dexter argued against the constitutionality of the embargo, as a lawyer for his client. But there is one decisive proof that Mr. Dexter had no confidence in this argument. The District Judge to whom he addressed it and who decided against him was a Federalist. Four of the six judges of the Supreme Court of the United States Marshall, Cushing, Chase and Washington were Federalists. Yet Mr. Dexter acquiesced in the decision of the District Judge and did not take an appeal to the judge of the Circuit Court, Cushing.

See *Documents Relating to New England Federalism,* by Henry Adams (1870).

(2)   *Life and Letters of Joseph Story,* by W. W. Story.

panies, it would seem that the companies seldom paid a claim, without a contest at law.

The most successful and wealthiest lawyers at this time were those with a maritime practice; and as Horace Binney writes of this period (1807-1817):

> The stoppings, seizures, takings, sequestrations, condemnations, all of a novel kind, unlike anything that had previously occurred in the history of maritime commerce—the consequence of new principles introduced offensively and defensively by the belligerent powers, gave an unparalleled harvest to the Bar of Philadelphia. No persons are bound to speak better of Bonaparte than the Bar of this city.
> He was, it is true, a great buccaneer and the British followed his example with spirit and fidelity; but what distinguished him and his imitators from the pirates of former days was the felicitous manner in which he first, and they afterwards, resolved every piracy into some principle of the laws of nations. Had he stolen and called it a theft, not a single law suit could have grown out of it. The underwriters must have paid. . . . But he stole from neutrals and called it lawful prize. . . . He always gave a reason, and kept the world of law inquiring how one of his acts and his reasons for it bore upon the policy of insurance.

To deal with this sitution, a brand new body of law had to be formulated—and it was the good fortune of the United States that it possessed a judge, capable of performing this task, in Joseph Story, whose decisions practically made the Prize and Admiralty Law for this country, just as the decisions of Sir William Scott [Lord Stowell] were contemporaneously establishing such law for Great Britain.

When Scott was appointed, in 1798, in England, there were no Admiralty Reports; and by 1811, *Robinson's Reports* of Stowell's decisions were practically the sole English authority, the old treatises of *Welwood, Malloy, Malynes* and *Marius* being imperfect and inaccurate. In the United States, all that Story had to go upon, were a few decisions in the first five volumes of *Cranch,* a small volume of *Bee's Reports,* (So. Car.) *Mariott's Admiralty Forms,* and a small collection of precedents accompanying Hall's translation of *Clerke's Praxis;* hence cut off by the war from the benefit of Lord Stowell's contemporary decisions, Story construed Admiralty Law practically unaided and alone.

The first prize case of prime importance in the Supreme Court was *Rose v. Himely* (4 Cranch 241), in 1808, in which ten counsel took part; Charles Lee, R. G. Harper, S. Chase, Jr., A. J. Dallas, W. Rawle, Ingersoll, and Drayton appearing against DuPonceau, E. Tilghman, and Luther Martin. Of this case, Story wrote, February 16, 1808, (before his appointment to the Bench):

Here I am in the wilderness of Washington . . . The scene of my greatest amusement as well as instruction in the Supreme Court. I daily spend several hours there. One cause only has been argued since I came here, and that was concluded today after occupying a space of nine days. Almost all the eminent counsel of the adjoining States were engaged in it.

Seven years later, in 1815, Judge Story delivered his celebrated opinion, in the Circuit Court, in *De Lovio v. Boit* (2 Gall. 398)— one of the most elaborate in the annals of the law, exploring and stating at length the history and extent of admiralty jurisdiction —a treatise in itself—an opinion, which in the words of its opponents, "sucked up jurisdiction like a sponge."

In the same year, the Supreme Court decided the famous case of *The Nereide* (9 Cranch 389), in which Thomas Addis Emmett of New York made his renowned argument, with J. Ogden Hoffman, against Alexander J. Dallas and William Pinkney. The latter though unsuccessful, so dazzled the court with his oratory that Marshall in his opinion felt obliged to advert to it:

With a pencil dipped in the most vivid colors and guided by the hand of a Master, a splendid portrait has been drawn exhibiting the vessel and her freighter, as forming a single figure, composed of the most discordant materials; and so exquisite was the skill of the artist, so dazzling the garb in which the figure was presented, that it required the exercise of the cold, investigating faculty which ought always to belong to those who sit on this bench, to discover its only imperfection—its want of resemblance.

Judge Story, (who dissented from the Marshall's opinion) also wrote of this argument Feb. 22, 1815(1):

----

(1) Thomas Addis Emmett, was at this time the leader of the New York Bar—born in 1765 in Ireland, a student in the Temple in London, he arrived in New York in 1804, and died in 1827.

See especially Story's description of Emmett in Story's *Life and Letters,* Vol. I.

See *Memoirs of Thomas Addis Emmett,* by Charles G. Haines (1829); and *Memoir,* in Story's *Miscellaneous Works.*

Mr. Pinkney and Mr. Emmett have measured swords in a late cause. I am satisfied that Pinkney towers above all his competitors. Mr. Emmett is the favorite counsellor of New York, but Pinkney's superiority to my mind was unquestionable. I was glad, however, to have his emulation excited by a new trial. It invigorated his exertion, and he poured upon us a torrent of splendid eloquence.

To meet the second set of conditions produced by the War— the rapid growth of business and manufacturing corporations —the law had few modern precedents or established rules.

The fundamental distinction between corporations, public and private, had been nowhere mentioned by Blackstone. Kyd's *Corporations,* in 1793, then practically the only book on the subject, related almost entirely to municipal corporations. In the United States, prior to 1800, there had been few cases involving corporations. *Kirby's Reports* (1789) contains only four such cases, one of an ecclesiastical society and three of municipal corporations; *Root's Reports* (1798), containing the earliest Connecticut cases, has one case of a church corporation. *Harris and McHenry's Reports* (Maryland, 1809), containing the earliest American cases, have one church corporation case in 1796, and one private corporation case in 1799.

From 1790 to 1800, the Supreme Court of the United States had only a single corporation case before it—*Bank of North America v. Vardon* (2 Dallas 78), in 1790. During the Colonial Governments before 1776, there were but six corporations of strictly American origin(1). After the Revolution, the first four

Feb. 27, 1829, Story wrote to W. Sampson:
"Mr. Emmett was a new and untried opponent and brought with him the ample honors gained at one of the most distinguished Bars in the Union. His speech was greatly admired for its force and fervor, its variety of research and its touching eloquence. It placed him at once by universal consent in the first rank of American Advocates—but not before Mr. Pinkney."

(1) These were as follows: *The New York Company for Settling a Fishery in these* parts (1675); *The Free Society of Traders,* in Pennsylvania (1682); *The New London Society United for Trade and Commerce,* in Connecticut (1723); *The Union Wharf Company,* in New Haven (1760); *The Philadelphia Contributionship for the Insuring of Houses from Loss by Fire* (1768); *The Proprietors of Boston Pier of the Long Wharf in the Town of Boston in New England* (1772).
Pennsylvania also chartered in 1759 what was in effect a life insurance company, *The Corporation for the Relief of Poor and Distressed Presbyterian Ministers and of the Poor and Distressed Widows and Children of Presbyterian Ministers.*
See also as to early associations in the nature of corporation, *Corporations in the Days of the Colony,* by A. McF. Davis, *Pub. of Colonial Soc. of Mass.* (1892-94).

corporations chartered were the *Bank of North America* in Pennsylvania, in 1780, and by the Congress of the Confederation, in 1781; the *Massachusetts Bank,* in Massachusetts; and the *Mining Company* in Litchfield in Connecticut, in 1789; and the *Agricultural Society of Philadelphia,* in 1785. Prior to 1800, the only States to grant charters to any manufacturing corporations were Massachusetts which incorporated three; New York, two; Connecticut, Kentucky, and New Jersey, each one (1).

The modern law of business corporations may be said to have been brought into being by Jefferson's Embargo Acts—statutes which produced also the insolvency acts which were soon to be the fruitful source of trouble in the courts and especially in interstate relations. Prior to the Embargo Acts (2) and the Declaration of War in 1812, foreign commerce in New York and New England, and the production of food stuffs for export in the Southern States had been the great source of wealth. Both were prostrated by those acts. "The ships rotted in the docks, the crops in the fields and warehouses—a chain of suffering encircled the community." Under these conditions, attention was turned to the development of manufactures. Cotton, woolen, iron, and glass factories sprang up, (3) and with these industries arose the first large business corporations.

One of the first general incorporation acts was passed in New York in 1811, being limited to a few specified industries.

---

(1) See *History of the Law of Business Corporations before* 1800, by Samuel Williston, *Harv. Law Rev.,* Vol. II, (1888).

There had, however, been a considerable development of corporations formed for purposes other than manufacturing. As tabulated by Mr. Simeon E. Baldwin, it appears that in the sixteen states, 5 corporations had been formed for aid of agriculture, 26 for Banking, 36 Bridge, 1 Burying Ground, 21 Canal, 6 Societies of Trade & Commence, 1 Aid of Emigration, 1 Fisheries, 25 Insurance, 2 Logging, 1 Land, 1 Mining, 26 Improving Navigation, 38 Roads and Turnpikes, 21 Waterworks and Aqueducts, and by the United States Government 2 Banks—a total of 213. Of these, Massachusetts had granted 88, or over a third; Connecticut, 37; New York, 21; and Virginia, 20.

See S. E. Baldwin in *Two Centuries Growth of American Law.*

(2) Judicially termed by Judge Sewall, in the first case arising under them in the Massachusetts State Courts in *Baylies v. Fettyplace,* 7 Mass. 325, 1811, "those extraordinary laws."

(3) In 1788, the first cotton factory in this country was started in Beverly, Massachusetts, "regarded as so marvellous and unique an establishment," says Andrew P. Peabody in his *Harvard Graduates,* "that General Washington on his presidential tour in 1789 was taken to visit it." The experiment was a failure and the corporation was dissolved. In 1795 the cotton gin was patented; and at once cotton mills began to revive, the Slater's in Pawtucket, R. I., the Cabots in Beverly, Mass.

Massachusetts however took the lead in number of corporations; and the scheme of the law of business corporations in that State was largely developed on the lines of the charters, statutes, and court decisions relating to the other large corporations of the day—the Turnpike Corporations,(1) the "Proprietors of Bridges" the Banking Corporations, the "Proprietors of Mills" "the Proprietors of Locks and Canals" and "the Proprietors of Log Booms." The first case, however, in which a business corporation appeared as party in Massachusetts, was not decided until 1813, when it was held that a foreign corporation might sue as plaintiff. In the same year, there are court records of cases involving a cotton factory and an iron factory corporation; in 1814, a slate company; and in 1815, a hat corporation.(2)

In New York, the first case involving a business corporation (other than lock, turnpike, or insurance) does not appear until 1817—*Dutchess Cotton Manufacturing v. Davis*, (13 Johnson).

In the Supreme Court of the United States, there had been but two cases involving corporation law between 1800 and 1815. Both, however, had a profound effect upon the development of the law—the one in restricting the growth of corporate liability, the other in emancipating corporate action from old Common Law bonds. In the first, in 1804, *Head v. Providence Ins. Co.* (2 Cranch 600), Marshall laid down the doctrine that "when the charter prescribes to them a mode of contracting, they must observe that mode, or the instrument no more creates a contract than if the body had never been incorporated."

In the other, *Bank of Columbia v. Patterson Admr.* (7 Cranch 299), in 1813, Mr. Justice Story held (largely on the authority of Massachusetts cases) that the old doctrine that a corporation could only act under seal was obsolete, and that "it could answer no salutary purpose, and would almost universally contravene the public convenience."(3) No greater impetus could

---

(1) The Turnpike Corporations had come largely into vogue between 1797 and 1810, and had been the source of much litigation, especially in the matter of assessment on stockholders, and payment of subscriptions to stock.

(2) *Portsmouth Livery Co. v. Wilson*, 10 Mass. 91. *Medway Cotton Manufactory v. Adams*, 10 Mass. 360. *Salem Iron Factory v. Danvers*, 10 Mass. 514. *New York Slate Co. v. Osgood*, 11 Mass. 60. *Emerson v. Providence Hat Mfg. Co.*, 12 Mass. 237.

(3) As an illustration of the difficulties of law practice at this time, arising from the scarcity and infrequency of law reports the court cites in

have been given to business corporations than this decision, which thus allowed them to make parol contracts by authorized agents; and the growth of modern corporation law may be dated from this case.

The rise of corporations was not viewed, however, with equanimity, even in those early days. And many lawyers, as well as laymen, echoed the sentiments of James Sullivan, Attorney General of Massachusetts, who said in 1807 in his argument, in *Ellis v Marshall* (2 Mass. 269), a case in which Theophilus Parsons and Samuel Dexter, also appeared:

The great increase of corporations for almost every purpose is seriously alarming—Interested and corrupt motives are growing daily more prevalent from this source. The independence and integrity of every branch of our government are attempted; and it is full time that a check be put to this spirit. And to an independent and enlightened judiciary can we alone look for its application.

With the development of manufacturing business, came the growth of Insurance Law. The first fire insurance corporation in the United States was *The Philadelphia Contributionship for Insuring houses from Loss by Fire* incorporated on the mutual plan, in 1752. For many years, however, most of the fire insurance companies were unincorporated associations, existing principally in New York.

One of the earliest reported cases of fire insurance was *Stetson v. Mass. Mutual Ins. Co.* (4 Mass. 330), in 1808. There was no text book on the subject however prior to 1815. Marine Insurance was an early and well developed part of the law, although carried on, until after the beginning of the 19th Century, largely by private individuals unincorporated. Life Insurance was, in 1815, hardly known, the earliest case being that of *Lord v. Dall* (12 Mass. 115), in 1809. Accident Insurance was unknown.

In the year 1815, Patent Law in the United States was just beginning to come into existence. In 1790, there had been enacted the first general Patent Act; the first patent being issued

---

Danforth v. Schoharie Turnpike Co., 12 John. 231, decided in May 1815—this case of *Bank of Columbia v. Patterson Admr.* as authority; but the reporter adds in a note "This case was cited and read to the court from a gazette dated March 18, 1815," notwithstanding the case cited was decided in the United States Supreme Court, in 1813.

"for making pot and pearl ashes." In 1792, thirty-three patents had been issued; in 1793, eleven; and in 1794, seventy-three, among which was Eli Whitney's cotton gin. In the whole first ten years, however, there were only 266 patents.

The first book on patents was not written until 1803, when *Collier on Patents* was published in England. It was not until 1819, that cases of infringement of patents were brought under the equity jurisdiction of the United States Circuit Courts. In the Supreme Court prior to 1815 there had been only two patent cases—*Tyler v. Tuel* (6 Cranch 324), in 1810, involving the right of an assignee of part of a patent to maintain an action on the case for infringement, and *Evans v. Jordan* (9 Cranch 199), in 1815; the latter being the first of an interminable series of cases, involving an improved hopper boy for manufacturing flour and meal. In all the Federal Circuit Courts there had only been thirteen patent cases, six of which had been decided by Judge Bushrod Washington, and five by Judge Story.

Perhaps one of the most important effects of the War of 1812 upon American law was the impetus which it gave to the publication of American law reports—first, through the increased spirit of nationality which it promoted; second, through the cutting off of the importation of English books.

It is to be remembered that in 1812, the first American law report was only twenty-three years old; in few of the States had law reports been published for more than six or eight years. In the great State of New York the first report had been published in 1804, and in Massachusetts in 1806.(1)

Judges hitherto had not been in the habit of writing out their decisions; and had they done so, they had no reporter, and no way of making their decisions public, historical, or authoritative as precedent.(2)

With the beginning of printed reports many of the cases were, therefore, so far as they were to be cited in the future, cases "of first impression." Hence it was fortunate for the United States that at the time when American decisions were beginning to be published and the cases so printed were to be used by future generations as establishing the law, there hap-

---

(1) See Chapter X supra, for greater details.
(2) For interesting account of these legal conditions see *Discourse on the Life, Character and Public Services of Ambrose Spencer, Chief Justice of New York,* by Daniel D. Barnard (1849).

pened to be presiding over the courts of many of the States Chief Justices of pre-eminent ability as lawyers. In 1812, in Massachusetts, Theophilus Parsons was Chief Justice; in New Hampshire, Jeremiah Smith; in New York, James Kent, with whom were associated three great lawyers, Ambrose Spencer,(1) Brockholst Livingston and Smith Thompson(2); in Pennsylvania, William Tilghman; in South Carolina, Henry W. De Saussure was Chancellor.

The limited scope of the law of the times is perhaps best illustrated by the fact that the law of torts which makes so large a part of the body of modern law, was, in 1815, practically confined to cases of trespass to person or property, assault, trover, replevin, and slander; actions of deceit and actions for negligence were very few. In Kirby's Reports (Conn.), covering 201 cases from 1785-1788, 52 are actions of tort, of which one half are trespass, and one half actions of disseizin or ejectment. In Harris and McHenry's Reports in Maryland, published in 1809, and covering cases 1658-1775, a large proportion of the cases are actions of ejectment or trespass.(3)

In New York, the first reported negligence case was not until 1810 (*Townsend v. Susquehannah Turnpike Road,* 6 John. 90); the first actions against a common carrier, in 1810 and 1813 (*Schiefflen v. Harvey,* 6 John. 1709), (*Elliott v. Russell,* 10 John. 1); the first negligence case involving a steam carrier, decided in the country, occurred in 1817 (*Foot v. Wiswall* 13 John. 304), in which the conditions to which the law was to be applied were so novel, that the plaintiff argued seriously, that it was negligence, per se, to navigate a steam-boat on a dark night.

As to the field of law outside of torts, covered by the early decisions, a glance at the titles in the indexes of the first half dozen volumes of Massachusetts Reports (1806-1810) shows that Probate, Practice, Real Estate and Mortgage, Highway, Animal, Witness and Evidence, Insurance and Marine Matters, Mills and Fisheries, Sheriffs, Poor and Settlement Law, Turn-

---

(1)　Born in 1765, Harvard 1783, Chief Justice 1819-23.

(2)　Born in 1767, Chief Justice 1814-19.

(3)　Sir Frederick Pollock, writing in 1886, says that the earliest and practically the only English text book on Torts which he could find "was a meagre, unthinking digest of *The Law of Actions on the case for Torts and Wrongs,* published in 1720, remarkable chiefly for the depths of historical ignorance which it occasionally reveals."

pike Corporations, Trespass—practically covered the whole law. The titles of Partnership, Contract, Statute of Frauds, appear for the first time in the index in 1808. The omissions are significant. There are no titles of Equity, Negligence, Bailment, Bank, Carriers, Conflict of Law, Conversion, Easement, Employer and Employee, Estoppel, Landlord and Tenant, Patents, Trust, Railroads, Municipal Corporations, Receiver, or Subrogation.

Similar conditions prevailed in the other States.

CHAPTER XII.

THE MASSACHUSETTS BAR 1785-1815.

While the names of the lawyers of Pennsylvania, Maryland and the Southern States were known through the country, the Bar of New England remained for at least twenty years after the Revolution, isolated and local in character and fame.

Nevertheless, the lawyers practising in this section of the country were men of ability quite equal to those of the better known Bars. Several factors however contributed to this isolation. Previous to 1800, the difficulty of communication between the States was a serious obstacle. After that date, the extreme Federalism of their politics kept the New England lawyers out of touch with the Republican leaders of the Bar at Washington. The length of the journey necessary to attend the Supreme Court was also a serious obstacle.

The influence of the political situation was most marked on the Massachusetts Bar; and for that reason a description of some of its great leaders will throw light upon the legal conditions of the time.

Boston and the large towns of Massachusetts were Federal to the backbone. The clergy, the merchants, and most of the Bar, all united in that political belief. Party lines were rigidly and rancorously drawn, and nowhere more so than at the Bar; so that clients frequently retained counsel because of their political affiliations rather than their legal ability.

"The democrat had no caste, he was not respectable," writes Henry Adams. "When, in 1793, the French nation seemed mad with the frenzy of its recovered liberties, New England looked upon the bloody and blasphemous work with such horror as religious citizens could not but feel. Thenceforward the mark of a wise and good man was that he abhorred the French Revolution and believed democracy to be its cause."(1)

In 1800, when the approaching victory of Jefferson was seen to be inevitable, the clergy and a large proportion of the edu-

---

(1) *History of the United States*, by Henry Adams, Vol. I.

cated citizens of New England began to feel towards the National Government the same distrust which they bore to democracy itself; and they agreed in general with George Cabot, the leader of the Federalists of Massachusetts and head of the so-called "Essex Junto," when he said, "I hold democracy in its natural operation to be the government of the worst.(1)   And when the Democratic (or Republican) electorate was beginning to increase in size and power even in Boston, Fisher Ames wrote to Christopher Gore in 1799:

The Jacobins in the vicinity of Boston are as openly bitter as ever and on the whole the *rabies canina* of Jacobinism has gradually spread of late years from the cities where it was confined to the docks and mob, to the country—all that is base is of course Jacobin and all that is prejudice and jealousy and rancor.

To be an Anti-Federalist or "Jacobin," in Eastern Massachusetts, prior to 1800, meant social and business ostracism.   "In my childhood", wrote Theophilus Parsons, the younger, "Federalists and Jacobins very seldom, I believe, met in society.   I never saw one until I was ten years old, in 1807."(2)   Of the Essex Bar in 1801, Joseph Story wrote: "At the time of my admission, I was the only lawyer within its pale who was either openly or secretly a Democrat.   Essex was at that time almost exclusively Federal, and party politics were inexpressibly violent —all the lawyers and all the judges in the country were Federalists."

The same ostracism of Anti-Federalist lawyers was to be found in other Northern States—notably New York, where a special rule of court, admitting the great lawyer, Thomas Addis Emmet, to practice, after his flight to this country from Ireland, was strongly opposed by James Kent and other Federalists, on the ground that he was a fugitive Jacobin; and his biographer Charles G Haines wrote in 1829:

The great men of the New York Bar were Federalists.   They therefore turned their faces against Mr. Emmet.   They formed a combination and agreed to decline all professional union and consultation with him.   When Mr. Emmet ascertained the exist-

---

(1) Cabot to T. Pickering Feb. 14, 1804, quoted in *Life and Times of George Cabot,* by Henry Cabot Lodge.
(2) *Memoirs of Theophilus Parsons,* by T. Parsons.

ence of the league . . . .he did not wait for an attack. He proved
the assailant. Whenever he met any of the league at the Bar,
he assumed the attitude of professional war, and he lost nothing
by contact. If Mr. Emmet has any one extraordinary power
it is in the ready talent of successful and overaweing reply. The
league was soon dissolved. Business flowed in and not long
after his arrival . . . his profession produced him $10000-
$15000 a year.

This obstinate disbelief in the possibility of any good coming
from the new, democratic, American spirit retarded the intellectual growth of Massachusetts in many directions; and the
conservative, English, anti-American atmosphere greatly influenced the development of the Bar, tending to nurture lawyers steeped in the Common Law, but less in touch with the
growing independence of thought, characteristic of the Bar of
such States as Pennsylvania, Maryland and Virginia.

Nevertheless, the Boston Bar had produced great lawyers
during these years, though its numbers were comparatively small,
there being, in 1800, thirty-three lawyers practising before it, of
whom twenty were attorneys of the Supreme Court, eight attorneys of the Court of Common Pleas, and five barristers,
James Sullivan, Theophilus Parsons, William Tudor, Perez Morton and Shearjashub Bourne(1).

After 1789, no more barristers were called by the court; and
the names given in the note on page 57, supra, are probably
all who were ever called in Massachusetts.

In 1806, the Supreme Judicial Court adopted the following
rule by which counsellors were substituted for barristers:

Ordered—First, no attorney shall do the business of a counsellor unless he shall have been made or admitted as such by
the Court.

Second, all attorneys of this Court who have been admitted
three years before the setting of this court shall be and hereby
are made counsellors and are entitled to all the rights and privileges of such.

Third, no attorney or counsellor shall hereafter be admitted
without a previous examination.

At the same time, examiners were appointed from the various
County Bars.

An introductory view of the older men of the Bar of this
period, may be had from a letter of Fisher Ames to Christopher

(1)   See *Recollections of Judge John Davis, Law Rep.*, Vol. IV (1841).

Gore, who was contemplating resuming practice in Boston, Oct. 5, 1802:

Your share will be made up of insurance cases—questions which our bankrupt law is sowing for the harvest of 1804 . . . Mr. Parsons practises on this large scale, and, I will add, fees are infinitely better than they were in 1786 . . . Who are the rivals for this business with whom you must divide the booty? Parsons stands first, but he is growing older, less industrious, and wealth or the hypo may stop his practice. Otis is eager in the chase of fame and wealth, and with a great deal of eloquence is really a good lawyer and improving. Dexter is very able and will be an Ajax at the bar as long as he stays. You know however that his aversion to reading and to practice is avowed. His head aches on reading a few hours, and if he did not love money very well he would not pursue the law. Sullivan, who seems immortal . . . will not be in our way. John Lowell's health is wretched. A number of eminent lawyers will be wanted in Boston; and though the place is overstocked I think the prospect for 1804 not unhopeful. I know of no very dashing young men coming forward.

Fisher Ames had been born in 1758; a Harvard graduate of 1774, he had studied law in the office of William Tudor, and had early become one of the greatest of the Federalist lawyers, orators and statesmen of the time.

Of him, Theophilus Parsons, the younger, wrote(1):

No man in this community ever won so much admiration and at the same time the warm affection of so wide a circle of friends —He was perhaps our most eloquent man and his eloquence was of a very noble character—formed by an harmonious union of the best and highest moral and intellectual qualities. . . . When we read that, after he closed his great speech in 1796 on Jay's Treaty, his opponents begged delay, that members might have an opportunity to recover their self-possession, we may wonder at this tribute to his power—But when we read the speech itself, we ask "What could delay do for them? What answer to his arguments could time suggest?"(2)

---

(1) *Life of Theophilus Parsons*, by T. Parsons.
(2) April 28, Mr. Ames made his great speech. Vice-President Adams wrote to his wife: "Judge Iredell and I happened to sit together. Our feelings beat in unison. 'My God, how great he is' says Iredell 'How great he has been?'—'Noble!' said I. After some time Iredell breaks out 'Bless my stars—I never heard anything so great since I was born'—'Divine' said I; and thus we went on with our interjections, not to say tears, to the end."

The Sullivan mentioned in Ames' letter was James Sullivan, for years after the Revolution the chief competitor of John Lowell, the elder, and later of Theophilus Parsons. Unlike the others, he was an ardent Anti-Federalist—one of the few prominent lawyers of that political belief. Born at Berwick, Maine, in 1744, he had studied law in the office of his brother General John Sullivan, a leading lawyer, and Governor of New Hampshire. He became a General in the Revolutionary War, and settled later in Boston to practice law. In 1777, he became Judge of the Superior Court. In 1787, he was made Judge of Probate in Suffolk County. From 1790 to 1807, he was Attorney General of Massachusetts, and in 1807, Governor, and died in 1808. The writer of one of his obituaries says that "during a period of nearly forty years his practice at the Bar had been more various and extensive than that of any other man in the State—the court records show that the names of Parsons and Sullivan were entered as opposing counsel." He was also an extremely able pamphleteer, and the newspapers of Boston teemed with political essays from his pen. His interests were broad and varied. He was one of the first members of the American Academy of Arts and Sciences, one of the founders and president of the Massachusetts Historical Society, the originator and head of the great Middlesex Canal Corporation, the author of the first comprehensive American book of Real Estate Law.(1)

The name of Harrison Gray Otis stands well to the front of the brilliant Federalist lawyers and orators.(2)   Born a nephew of James Otis, in 1765, he inherited all his uncle's eloquence.   Graduating from Harvard in 1783, a classmate of the noted lawyers, Ambrose Spencer (later Chief Justice of New York), William Prescott, Artemas Ward, and William King Atkinson of New Hampshire, he studied in the office of Judge John Lowell, became United States District Attorney in 1796, succeeded Fisher Ames in Congress, and later became Mayor of Boston (1829-1831).   In the early Massachusetts Reports his name, with that of Charles Jackson, rivals even Dexter's in number of appearances.   Unlike either Parsons or

---

(1)   *Life of James Sullivan,* by T. G. Armory.
(2)   See *Harrison Gray Otis, Memorial Biographies of N. E. Hist. Gen. Soc.,* Vol. I, (1880).

Dexter, it was on the charm of his manner and the eloquence of his speech that Otis depended for his success.

"From Mr. Dexter, Mr. Otis differed as much as a man could", writes Parsons. "As a book lawyer I suppose he stood on a par with him . . . The winning music of his voice made the hearer reluctant to lose a word, the flow of his language—the persuasive logic—in each and all of these he was unrivalled. And to all these was added their strongest charm perhaps in the apparent spontaneity of it all. . . . He had, if ever man had, the gift of eloquence—grace of delivery, sweetness of tones, beauty of illustration, perfect taste in words, and rapidity and clearness of thought."

On his death in 1848 the *Boston Courier* thus summed up his talents:

Conspicuous for rare intellectual accomplishments, admired for blandness and urbanity of manners,—as an extemporaneous speaker seldom equalled, his mind well stored with the glittering wealth of classical literature. As a lawyer and advocate Mr. Otis made but one step in order to secure an enviable eminence in his profession. His aid as a counsellor was sought at an age when most young lawyers are happy to find employment in the humbler character of juniors.

The three other lawyers mentioned in Fisher Ames' letter were all intimately connected with the history of the Harvard Law School—Theophilus Parsons being the first lawyer to receive an offer of a Law Professorship at Harvard; Samuel Dexter being active in urging the foundation of such a Professorship; and John Lowell the younger being the first elected Professor.

Parsons was born in 1750 and graduated from Harvard in 1769.(1) He studied law at Portland, Maine, (then Falmouth) under Theophilus Bradbury, and was admitted to practice in 1774. Portland being almost totally burned by the British, in 1775 he removed to Essex County, Massachusetts, and soon began to practice in Newburyport. At this time, he had the advantage of the library and company of the aged Judge Edmund Trowbridge, who, being suspected of Toryism, had been driven from Cambridge. Professor Parsons, in his *Memoirs,* speaks of his father's "almost intemperate study" with this "oracle of the common law."(2) An anecdote illustrating how

(1) *Memoirs of Theophilus Parsons,* by T. Parsons.
(2) So Chancellor Kent termed Judge Trowbridge; and see Chapter III supra, for further details regarding him.

complete and exhaustive were his methods and how exact his memory, is told regarding a case in which Parsons was retained in 1797, by the State of Connecticut, to argue against Alexander Hamilton, Ogden Hoffman and Aaron Burr, before Chief Justice Ellsworth in the United States Circuit Court. After the argument, Hamilton said, at dinner: "Mr. Parsons, pray let me ask you one thing. The point I made was suggested to me, only after much study of the case, and then almost by accident; but I thought it very strong. You were fully prepared for it, and gathered and exhibited the authorities at once, and prevailed, and I must submit; but I was a good deal surprised at it, and what I want to know is, whether you had anticipated that point?"—"Not in the least" was the answer "but so long ago as when I was studying with Judge Trowbridge, the question was suggested to me, and I made a brief of the authorities, which I happened to have brought with me."

In 1800, Parsons removed to Boston; but before his removal he was in the habit of practising in all the New England States, though rarely outside.

His early success was as a master of prize and admiralty law, "of which", writes his son, "few lawyers then knew anything. In fact, he had almost the monopoly of it and it was very profitable. The late Governor Sullivan, Judge Lowell, and my father were the only practising lawyers who had much knowledge of it . . . My mother used to speak of the 'prize times' as the most profitable which she had ever known."

He was the most learned lawyer of his time and was called the giant of the law—He comprised in his professional attainments among other things a full and accurate knowledge of the common law, civil, maritime and ecclesiastical law, the law merchant, the statute and common law of his own country, and the law of nations. From the methodical order of his mind, all he knew was ever familiarly at his command. His speeches to juries and judges were neither eloquent nor elegant, in anything but pertinency and argument. They were never long. It is not remembered that he ever used a brief.

Thus wrote Chief Justice Isaac Parker, his successor.

In February 1801 he was nominated as United States Attorney General by President Adams, in place of Charles Lee, but though confirmed by the Senate, he declined the appointment.

Theo^p Parsons

In 1806, he was appointed Chief Justice of Massachusetts; and from that time until his death, in 1813, his judgments laid the foundations for a great portion of the law of Massachusetts. "But few pages of the early reports can be read without finding illustrations of the fact that immemorial usage and early colonial and provincial statutes had upon a vast variety of subjects almost created a law of our own. Judge Parsons was precisely the man to learn, appreciate and apply this local jurisprudence; and his happiest efforts are those in which perhaps by way of reply to learned arguments of counsel founded upon the text of the English law he adduces unanswerable enactments and precedents to disprove its binding authority in the State of Massachusetts. In such cases we see the thoroughly practical man conversant with all sorts of things and familiar with all sorts of people; the man who endowed by nature with extraordinary capacities which study and learning had indefinitely improved and developed allowed none of the innumerable occasions to pass when he was brought into contact with the others without making some important addition to his stock of available knowledge."(1)

Such was the veneration of the bar for him as a lawyer that they exhibited an unusual awe in his presence. There was great neglect (then) in preparing papers for the court and it was several years before it was properly attended to; and I have seen him non-suit our oldest counsellor for that cause very often—He had not much patience to hear an unsound argument nor to hear counsel advance an untenable point; and the lawyers were so poorly versed in legal lore they were not only willing but desirous that he should take the disposal of the whole case into his own hands. I have known him many times to do this.

So said one of his contemporaries.(2)
There is little doubt however that the slack methods of the Bar needed a strong hand to correct them; and probably Parsons' retort to the famous Samuel Dexter was well grounded. Dexter, being stopped in an argument by the judge's remark that he was trying to persuade the jury of that for which there was

---

(1) See *The Jurisprudence of Massachusetts,* Central Law Journal, Vol. I, (1874).
See also *Parsons in Biographical Sketches of Eminent Lawyers,* by S. L. Knapp, (1821).
(2) See Letter of Zachariah Eddy to Professor Emory Washburn, in 1851, in *Memoirs of Theophilus Parsons,* by T. Parsons.

no evidence, replied "Your Honor did not argue your own cases in the way you require us to." "Certainly not," was the reply "but that was the judge's fault, not mine."

"No sooner had he taken his seat upon the bench than the whole air of the court room seemed charged with a terrible energy. No excuse was listened to; no delay was admitted. The dropsical dockets rapidly shrank, when gashed by the unsparing lancet of the new Chief. The lawyers at first grumbled; but suitors were better pleased, and the great improvement effected soon reconciled all persons to the new system."(1)

Much of the difficulty, in which lawyers of the time found themselves, arose from their very general ignorance of pleading. "Only a few of the leading lawyers pretended to be good pleaders", writes Professor Parsons. "My father himself however was a very good pleader, having devoted much time to this subject. When he had students, everyone was expected to write out, in a book prepared for that purpose, declarations, pleas, and forms which my father had prepared or adapted.— And the volumes of precedents afterwards published for the use of the profession by Anthon, Story, Oliver, and others were compiled in a good degree from these books."

Parsons frequently carried his autocratic system too far, and though his perfect honesty and integrity were admitted, his harsh and overbearing treatment of members of the Bar gave him the nickname of "The Awfullest Parsons," just as one of his predecessors on the Bench, Robert Treat Paine, had been called the "Ursa Major."(2) His inflexible spirit, his biting sarcasm, and his reserve of manner made it impossible that he should ever be popular; and he did not know the arts of popularity. But his nature was kindly and all the young lawyers remembered him with affection, as well as awe.

Joseph Story, in describing Parsons to one of his classes at the Law School, said:

The young members of the Bar used to gather around him like the disciples of Socrates. A kind word from him (and he

---

(1) *The Bench and Bar,* by John T. Morse. *Memorial Hist. of Boston,* Vol. IV.

(2) It was said of Lord Kenyon that he would sometimes get excessively angry when on the bench and make a sad exhibition of himself. One day George the Third said to him at court "My Lord, I am told you lost your temper yesterday. I was very glad to hear it; and I hope you will be able to find a better one."

had many of them for young men) went deep into the heart and was never forgotten. . . . When at Salem the Bar usually met at dinner at the same table, but Parsons preferred a private house. He was shy and did not willingly go into crowded company. But he frequently met us in the evening, and we had then an opportunity of enjoying his conversation. He touched upon everything and left us equally astonished and delighted with his wisdom, learning and wit—It was bright and flashing but it never scorched.

Parsons was not merely a lawyer. He read and mastered many branches of science, metaphysics, and classics, and remembered everything which he read. He was himself an inventor and an excellent mathematician.

The sarcastic comment of Sugden on Lord Brougham when he was Chancellor of England that "if he only knew a little law he would know a little of everything" was only a bitter inversion of John Lowell's tribute to Parsons, declaring that Parsons knew more law than anybody else and more of everything else than he did of law.(1)

In politics Parsons was a staunch, even violent, Federalist(2), one of the originators of the "Essex Junto" and called by Jefferson "one of the enemies of the country". A view of his character by a political opponent, John Quincy Adams, is interesting. In his diary, Oct. 8, 1819, Adams writes:

Parsons was an eminent lawyer, a man of extraordinary intellectual powers, of deep research and extensive learning, of brilliant and ever ready though coarse and vulgar wit, and in his domestic and private relations amiable, benevolent and upright. But he was a cunning man. His wisdom was left handed. He was not only addicted to finessing and trick, but he had the weak-

---

(1) See *A Journey with Judge Story*, Josiah Quincy's *Figures of the Past*. The disadvantage of such omniscience was pointed out by William Sullivan (who lived in Parsons' time) as follows:

"By intuition he saw what the end of a case must be and was impatient of the slow process by which inferior minds arrived at it. It is doubtful whether it is best for a judge or for the community that he should know more and discern much more rapidly than any or all around him when engaged in the administration of justice."

Familiar Letters on Public Characters, by William Sullivan (1847).

(2) John Quincy Adams, in his diary, May 10, 1808, says:

"I called on Chief Justice Parsons and had some conversations with him on political subjects—I found him as I expected totally devoted to the British policy—He also thinks the people of this country corrupted, already in a state of voluntary subjugation to France and ready to join an army of Buonaparte if he should send one here, to subdue themselves. The only protection of our liberties, he thinks, is the British navy."

ness to be vain of his artifices. . . . The pride of his heart was to overreach. . . . He was withal a timid man, ready enough to push others into danger, but easily frightened to shrink from it himself. . . . In the career of opposition to the General Government which that of Massachusetts then (1812) pursued, they refused to place the militia under the command of an officer of the United States, upon a construction of the Constitution of the United States by the judges of the Supreme Judicial Court of the Commonwealth, for which nothing but the depravity and stupefying influence of faction can account.

The Governor (Brooks) gave me to understand that he had always disapproved that opinion of the Supreme Court; that there had been almost a misunderstanding on the subject between him and the late Governor Strong who was entirely swayed by the then Chief Justice Parsons, the identical man whom the state of Massachusetts has to thank for being in this trouble. . . .

In this very case after leading the Commonwealth into this quagmire, before his death he disavowed the opinion which had involved the State in this contest and acknowledged that it was erroneous.

In personal appearance the Chief Justice was thus described by Story, in his lecture to his Law School students:

He was about five feet ten inches in height, somewhat corpulent and of heavy appearance. His forehead was high and smooth; he wore a heavy wig (for he was bald at an early age) which was rarely placed upon his head properly. His mind was well adjusted, his wig never. He generally wore a bandanna kerchief about his neck to protect it from cold winds. His eye was clear, sharp, keen and deep set in his head. It looked you through and through. It seemed to me the embodiment of the eye of the law, piercing through you, and seeing and discovering everything with astonishing penetration. It was a glance that few could bear to have steadily fixed upon them.(1)

A description of Parsons would be incomplete without refer-

---

(1) Daniel Webster when a law student in Boston in 1804 in Christopher Gore's office wrote of his personal appearance:

"Theophilus Parsons is now about fifty-five years old; of rather large stature, (six feet) and inclining a little to corpulency. His hair is brown, and his complexion not light. His forehead is low and his eyebrows prominent. He wears a blue coat and breeches worsted hose, a brown wig; with a cocked hat. He has a penetrating eye of an indescribable color. When, couched under a jutting eyebrow, it directs its beams into the face of a witness, he feels as if it looked into the inmost recesses of his soul."

Sullivan describes his "tranquil face amicable and pleasing" and "his habit of drawing his chin towards his breast and looking about through his eyebrows."

ence to his constant fits of hypochondria, which sometimes took the form of an almost insane delusion. These attacks, however, never controlled the vastness of his legal mind.

Samuel Dexter, born in 1761, was eleven years younger than Parsons and died in 1816, three years after Parsons. He graduated from Harvard in 1781, a classmate of John Davis (U. S. District Judge) and studied law under Levi Lincoln (later Attorney General of the United States). In 1799, he was United States Senator; in 1800, Secretary of State and Secretary of the Treasury under President Adams. Of all Massachusetts lawyers of the early 19th Century, with the exception of James Sullivan, Dexter alone could be regarded as the compeer of the Chief Justice; and in most of the important cases in the early Massachusetts Reports, Dexter's name appears.(1)

Of all Massachusetts lawyers, Dexter's services were sought for an argument of cases at Washington, in the early years of the United States Supreme Court. And it was into his place that Daniel Webster may be said to have stepped, on Dexter's death, in 1816.

"For several years," said Joseph Story, "he passed his winters in Washington under engagement in many of the most important cases. Rarely did he speak without attracting an audience composed of the taste, the beauty, the wit and the learning that adorned the city." Just before his death he argued for the State of Virginia, with St. George Tucker, the great case of *Martin v. Hunter's Lessee*, in which Judge Story settled, against Dexter's contention, the power of the Federal Supreme Court to review the decision of a State Court on writ of error. Like John Marshall, Dexter relied on his supreme power of reasoning rather than on precedents and citation of cases. So much was this his habit that William Plumer relates an argument used by him in a case against Parsons which might almost be thought the argument of one of the unlearned lawyers of the times.

"The law in this case is as I have explained it"; said Dexter, "and it lies, as your Honors see, in the compass of a nutshell. My brother Parsons has here a basket full of law books; and he will endeavor to show from them that it is all the other

(1) For the best, though incomplete, sketch of Samuel Dexter, see *Reminiscences of Samuel Dexter,* by Lucius Manlius Sargent ("Sigma") (1857).

way. But one plain dictate of common sense, one clear maxim
of the common law, is worth a cartload of such rubbish."(1)

Says Professor Parsons, "He was not a scientific lawyer—but
he was a great lawyer in rem. . . . As an advocate in cases
which demand a close investigation of complicated facts and rules
and a clear perception and a strong hold of the guiding principle
. . . and in the power to carry the court and jury with him
through the long research or argument I am confident that he
was never surpassed in New England." . . .

"He had a disinclination," said Story, "to blacklettered law,
which he sometimes censured as the scholastic refinements of
monkish ages; and even for the common branches of technical
science, the doctrines of special pleading, and the niceties of
feudal tenure he professed to feel little of love or reverence. .
. . In commercial causes, he shone with peculiar advantage.
. . . Though he might be wrong upon authority and practice, he was rarely wrong upon the principles of international justice. No man was ever more exempt from fineness or cunning
in addressing a jury. He disdained the little arts of sophistry
or popular appeal. It was in his judgment something more
degrading than the sight of Achilles playing with a lady's dis-
taff."

Perhaps the best and liveliest description of his manner as a

---

(1) Daniel Appleton White, who was born in 1776, graduated at Harvard in 1797, a classmate of Horace Binney, Asahel Stearns, and Chief
Justice W. M. Richardson of New Hampshire, and later Judge of Probate for Essex county, wrote May 5, 1804. (See *Mass. Hist. Soc. Proc.*,
Vol. VI [1862].)
"I have passed two days at court and had the satisfaction of hearing
Parsons & Dexter in the Crowningshield case. Each of them delivered
a most learned and ingenious argument. Dexter had the weaker side,
and therefore made greater exertions, and took up more time; but as the
case turned on points of law rather than facts, Parsons appeared more
eminently to advantage as a lawyer. He is indeed a wonderful man. Perfectly
at home in all sorts of law, as well as of other knowledge and learning,
he appears to be incapable of surprise or embarrassment; whereas Dexter for his deficiency in some of the sciences, and perhaps in some
branches of the law is exposed to both; but his astonishing presence of mind
and his intuitive perception and penetration secure him a safe and honorable retreat for every difficulty. These two men I believe to be the
greatest among the lawyers of New England; yet they are very different.
Both are subtle, ingenious, powerful in argument; but, in the one, it
seems to proceed from native strength and quickness of genius; and in
the other from a long and labored culture of his genius and logical powers. On subjects of equity and in addresses to the feelings or discussions
of general policy Dexter may be superior, but nowhere else. Parsons is
the great lawyer—perhaps the greater man. He is certainly the safer
model."

Chas. Jackson

lawyer is found in Story's letter to his wife March 10, 1814, describing the contests between William Pinkney of Maryland and Dexter, in a series of prize cases:

I must, however, after all, give the preference to Mr. Pinkney's oratory. He is more vivacious, sparkling, and glowing; more select and exact in his language, more polished in his style, and more profound and earnest in his judicial learning. Mr. Dexter is calm, collected, and forcible, appealing to the judgment. Mr. Pinkney is vehement, rapid, and alternately delights the fancy and seizes on the understanding. He can be as close in his logic as Mr. Dexter when he chooses; but he can also step aside at will from the path, and strew flowers of rhetoric around him. Dexter is more uniform, and contents himself with keeping you where you are. Pinkney hurries you along with him, and persuades as well as convinces you. You hear Dexter without effort; he is always distinct and perspicuous, and allows you an opportunity to weigh as you proceed. Pinkney is no less luminous, but he keeps the mind on the stretch, and you must move rapidly or you lose the course of his argument.

Besides the above, the following lawyers were distinguished at the Bar during the first quarter of the 19th Century—William Prescott(1); Christopher Gore(2); Charles Jackson(3); Edward St. Loe Livermore(4); William Sullivan(5); Samuel Hoar(6); Artemas Ward(7); and John Phillips(8), all of whom were Federalists.

----

(1) One of Parsons' "most valued friends", and a lawyer of great depth and soundness of learning and exclusive devotion to law was William Prescott of Salem. He was also the friend of young Joseph Story, the father of William H. Prescott the historian, and the father-in-law of Franklin Dexter. Born in 1762, a Harvard graduate in 1783, he was a favorite maritime and insurance lawyer. It was in his office, in 1815, that Theophilus Parsons the younger (later Professor in the Harvard Law School) studied. Of him Story wrote in 1820, in his article on *Chancery Jurisdiction,* "his cautious, well instructed, modest and powerful mind would adorn an equity bench and create an equity bar for Massachusetts, equal to the Chancery Court of James Kent."

(2) Born in 1758, a Harvard graduate of 1776, a student of law in the office of John Lowell, United States District Attorney in 1790, a Commissioner of the United States to London on the British Spoliation Claims, Governor of Massachusetts in 1809, United States Senator in 1814.

(3) Born in 1775, a Harvard graduate of 1795, a student of law in the office of Theophilus Parsons, Judge of the Massachusetts Supreme Court in 1813.

"Of all my pupils," said Parsons, "no one has left my office better fitted for his profession. He will prove himself the American Blackstone." (See *Life of Charles Jackson* in *Law Reporter,* Vol. XIII).

(4) Born in 1762 in Portsmouth, New Hampshire, a student of law in Theophilus Parsons' office, Judge of the New Hampshire Supreme Court in 1799, and afterwards practising law in Boston, especially in maritime cases.

Lined up sharply on the anti-Federalist side of the Bar were Levi Lincoln(1) ; Daniel Davis(2) ; George Blake(3) ; John Quincy Adams(4) ; Perez Morton(5) ; and—greatest of all—Joseph Story(6).

Among the noted lawyers in other parts of the State were Eli P. Ashmun, Elijah H. Mills, Samuel Howe, Caleb Strong, Timothy Bigelow, and Samuel Dana, Jr.; and the offices of these members of the Bar outside of Boston were in fact, in most instances, miniature law schools, as students often came from the surrounding countryside to reside in the towns where these law offices were located.

Among the members of the Bar just coming into practise, in 1815, were Lemuel Shaw(7) ; Marcus Morton(8) ; Charles G. Loring(9) ; Peleg Sprague(10) ; William Minot(11) ; and Franklin Dexter(12).

In 1816, Daniel Webster(13) came to Boston to practise law,

---

(5) Born in 1774, a son of James Sullivan, Harvard graduate 1792, studied law with his father.

(6) Born in 1776, Harvard 1802, a student in the office of Artemas Ward, for many years the leader of the Middlesex County Bar.

(7) Born in 1762, Harvard 1783, brother-in-law of Samuel Dexter, Chief Justice of the Court of Common Pleas in 1821.

(8) Born in 1770, Harvard 1788, Judge of the Court of Common Pleas in 1809, first Mayor of Boston in 1822.

(1) Born in 1781, a Harvard graduate of 1800; his name appears first in 1810 in the case of *Young v. Adams,* 5 Mass. 162, a case involving the sum of $5. He had an office with Thomas O. Selfridge, the defendant in the noted murder trial described infra. In 1820, he took as a partner Sidney Bartlett, and was Chief Justice of Massachusetts 1830-1860.

(2) Born in 1784, a Brown graduate 1804, a student at Litchfield Law School, Judge of the Massachusetts Supreme Court in 1825, Governor in 1840.

(3) Born in 1794, Harvard 1812, a student at the Litchfield Law School and in the office of Charles Jackson.

(4) Born in 1793, Harvard 1812, student at Litchfield Law School.

(5) Born in 1783, Harvard 1802.

(6) Born in 1793, son of Samuel Dexter, Harvard 1812, a student in the office of Samuel Hubbard.

(7) Born in 1749, a Harvard graduate 1772, U. S. Atty. Gen. 1801-1805.

(8) Born in 1762, a student under Shearjashub Bourne, Solicitor General of Massachusetts 1800-1832.

(9) Born in 1769, Harvard 1789, a student under James Sullivan, U. S. Dist. Atty. 1801-1829.

(10) Born in 1762, Harvard 1787, a student under Theophilus Parsons.

(11) Born in 1751, Harvard 1791, Mass. Atty. Gen. 1810-1832.

(12) Born in 1779, Harvard 1798, Judge of United States Supreme Court 1811.

(13) Born in 1782.

having been admitted to the Suffolk Bar in 1805, and before the United States Supreme Court in the winter of 1813-14.

It is curious to note how closely connected with the history of Harvard College were all the leaders of the Bar.

Theophilus Parsons was the first lawyer to receive an offer of a Harvard law professorship, and was a member of the Corporation, from 1806 to 1812. John Lowell the elder was the first lawyer to be a member of the Corporation, from 1784 to 1802. Fisher Ames was tendered the Presidency of the College in 1805. Josiah Quincy was an Overseer from 1810 to 1824 and became President of the College in 1828. Harrison Gray Otis was an Overseer from 1810 to 1825 and a member of the Corporation from 1823 to 1825. Christopher Gore, Governor of the Commonwealth, was an Overseer from 1810 to 1815, a member of the Corporation from 1813 to 1820, and the benefactor who made possible the College Library. William Prescott was an Overseer from 1810 to 1821, and a member of the Corporation from 1820 to 1826. Isaac Parker was an Overseer from 1816 to 1830, and the first Law Professor. Charles Jackson was Overseer from 1816 to 1825 and a member of the Corporation from 1825 to 1834. Joseph Story was an Overseer from 1818 to 1825, a member of the Corporation from 1820 to 1845, the first Dane Professor of the Law School in 1829. Samuel Dexter was an Overseer from 1810 to 1815.

John Quincy Adams was an Overseer from 1830 to 1848, and also Professor in Rhetoric, Oratory and Elocution from 1806 to 1809. John Phillips was an Overseer from 1810 to 1823 and a member of the Corporation from 1812 to 1823.

Daniel Webster was an Overseer from 1822 to 1852. John Lowell the younger was an Overseer from 1823 to 1827, a member of the Corporation 1810 to 1822. Of the later generation Lemuel Shaw and Charles G. Loring were members of the Corporation; the one from 1834 to 1861, the other from 1838 to 1857.

Such was the Bar, by whose influence the early students of the Law School were surrounded, and after a preparatory course in whose offices many students entered the School.

CHAPTER XIII.

JOSEPH STORY.

Joseph Story was born in Marblehead, Mass., on September 18, 1779,—the son of Dr. Elisha Story and Mehitable (Pedrick) Story.(1)

"My father", wrote Story, (in his autobiographical letter) "was a sturdy Whig and took a very early and active part in all the revolutionary movements. He was one of the Indians who helped to destroy the tea in the famous Boston exploit. He did not receive a public education, owing, I believe, to his father's very religious opinions which would not suffer him to go to Harvard College, lest he should there inbibe those heretical tenets which, in the form of Arminianism, were supposed to haunt those venerable shades." . . .

In 1770, Dr. Story removed from Boston to Marblehead. He fought at Concord and Lexington, and beside Warren at Bunker Hill as an army surgeon, and continued in the army until the close of the year 1777, when he retired "being disgusted with the management of the medical department. . . . . To the very close of his life he entertained the highest admiration of General Washington and of John Adams, though in the political controversies between the latter and Mr. Jefferson, he took side with Mr. Jefferson."

The little rock-perched town of Marblehead which was the home of Joseph Story's early years was strongly individual in its character, and nurtured strong men.

Its people were almost wholly engaged in the fisheries or in the navy and privateering; and they had the plain, rugged, hearty natures which belong to seafaring men. As his father was a physician, it was natural that Story should have been brought up in close familiarity with all his fellow townspeople; and it is small wonder that the intimacy with the sailors of Marblehead·

---

(1) This chapter is largely based on the *Life and Letters of Joseph Story,* by William Wetmore Story (1851) ; and wherever, later in this history, letters of Story are quoted they are cited, unless otherwise stated, from the above Life.

turned his thoughts, in later life, with especial love and depth of research to the study of maritime law. To become the great judge of prize and admiralty law was only his birthright.

An amusing anecdote is told of his intimacy, in his practice, with the peculiarities of Marblehead dialect and provincialism:

On one occasion, when some of our fishermen were in court to settle a mutiny, which had taken place on the Grand Bank (of Newfoundland), one, on being called upon to state what he knew, said, that the skipper and one of his shipmates had what he called a "jor of ile". The presiding judge in vain endeavored to get a more intelligible answer, and finally Story was called upon as usual to act as interpreter to his townsman, which he immediately did, telling the Court, that a "jor of ile", in the Marblehead dialect was, a "jaw awhile;" which, being interpreted, meant, that the two men abused each other grossly for sometime.

Of his enormous capacity for absorbing knowledge, Story showed early proof. At the age of fifteen, he presented himself for examination for Harvard College, at the beginning of the six weeks' vacation before the January Term. Learning to his surprise that he would be obliged to qualify, not only on the preparatory studies, but also on all the studies which the freshman class had been pursuing for the past six months, he set to work at this task. In the six weeks he mastered the six months' work, and was admitted into the freshman class in January, 1795. Among his classmates were William Ellery Channing, later the noted Unitarian minister, Sidney Willard, Richard Sullivan, Stephen Longfellow, Joseph Tuckerman, and Samuel P. P. Fay, later Judge of the Probate for Middlesex County.

The scantiness of a college education at that period is well illustrated in Story's account:

In Greek we studied *Xenophon's Anabasis* and a few books of the *Iliad;* in Latin, *Sallust* and a few books of *Livy;* in mathematics, *Saunderson's Algebra,* and a work on arithmetic; in natural philosophy, *Enfield's Natural Philosophy,* and *Ferguson's Astronomy;* in rhetoric, an abridgement of *Blair's Lectures,* and the article on rhetoric in the *Preceptor ;* in metaphysics, *Watt's Logic* and *Locke on the Human Understanding;* in history, *Millot's Elements;* in theology,*Doddridge's Lectures;* in grammatical studies, *Lowth's Grammar.* . . . No modern language was taught, except French, and that only one day in the week by a non-resident instructor. . . . Even in respect to English literature and science, we had little more than a semi-annual importation of the most common works, and a few copies supplied and satisfied the market. The English periodicals were then few in number; and I do not remember any one that was read by the students except the *Monthly Magazine* (the old *Monthly*), and that was read but by a few. I have spoken of our semi-annual importations; and it is literally true, that two ships only plied as regular packets between Boston and London, —one in the spring, and the other in the autumn, and their arrival was an era in our college life. . . . The students had no connection whatever with the inhabitants of Cambridge by private or social visits. There was none between them and the families of the President and Professors of the College. The regime of the old school in manners and habits then prevailed. The President and Professors were never approached except in the most formal way, and upon official occasions; and in the college yard (if I remember right) no student was permitted to keep his hat on if one of the Professors was there. . . . The intercourse between the students and Boston, when my class entered college, was infrequent and casual. West Boston Bridge had been completed but a short period before. The road was then new and not well-settled, the means of communication with Cambridge almost altogether by walking; and the inducements to visit in private circles far less attractive than at present. Social intercourse with the young, and especially with students, was not much cultivated; and invitations to parties in Boston rarely extended to college circles.

It was in his College days that Story developed a strong leaning towards Unitarianism—long before the doctrines were generally preached. He also had a taste for versification, which he cultivated throughout his life, even when on the bench. The College at this time was Federalist, root and branch, and "Adams and Liberty" cockades were everywhere worn by the students, as symbols of loyalty to the government and of hatred to France.(1)

---

(1) J. T. Buckingham in his *Specimens of Newspaper Literature with Memoirs* (1850), writes: "The year 1798 has been signalized by the opponents of Adams' administration as the 'era of the Black Cockade.' . . . Benjamin Russell it has been said was the instigator of the fashion; the first allusion to it that I remember being in the *Centinel* of July 4 as follows—'It has been repeatedly recommended that our citizens wear in their hats on the day of independence the American cockade which is a rose composed of black ribbon with a white button or fastening this symbol of their attachment to the government which cherishes —protects them. The measure is innocent; but the effect will be highly important. It will add cement to the Union.' The next *Centinel* says— 'The Jacobins have the impudence to say that the people of Boston were really divided, and they gave as a proof that not more than half of them wear the American cockade. This being the case, let every Bostonian

Even Story, though son of a Jeffersonian, was drawn into support of Adams in his senior year—a curious memory for him, in his later struggles against Federalist opposition.

In 1798, after graduation, he returned to Marblehead to study law in the office of Samuel Sewall, then a member of Congress, and later Chief Justice of Massachusetts. He embraced the Common Law, however, not without a shudder. "Conceive, my dear fellow," he wrote to his friend Fay, Sept. 6, 1798, "what is my situation, doomed to spend at least ten years, the best of my life, in the study of the law—a profession whose general principles enlighten and enlarge, but whose minutiae contract and distract the mind. Ambition is truly the food of my existence, and for that alone life is desirable". Even in the height of this "ambition" the young law student could hardly have anticipated that in only three years more than the "at least ten", he would be sitting on the bench of the Supreme Court of the United States. Again he writes, "I have begun the study of the law, and shall continue it with unremitting diligence; but a sigh of regret often accompanies my solitary moments—a sigh expressive of my ardent love of literary fame." Again, in 1799, "Law I admire as a science; it becomes tedious and embarrassing only when it degenerates into a trade, I regret the necessity of any profession because it infringes on those studies which a citizen of the world would like to pursue." By 1801, however, this "regret" had changed to a complete love of his profession. "The science claims me as a fixed devotee—it rules me", he wrote.

When he was twenty-one, Story was deputed by the town of Marblehead to deliver the eulogy on the death of Washington, —"an elegant address" so the *Columbian Centinel* called it; "poor and in bad taste", as described by Story himself.

In January, 1801, the month and year of Chief Justice Marshall's appointment, he entered the office of Samuel Putnam (later Judge of the Supreme Court of Massachusetts), in Salem.

As a Republican, he was looked upon by the Federalists, who composed the principal part of the wealth and talent of the town, with doubt and distrust; and as a person entertaining dangerous ideas, and he was, at first, tabooed from society. His Unitarian

---

attached to the constitution and government of the United States immediately mount the cockade and swear that he will not relinquish it until the infamous projects of the external and internal enemies of our country shall be destroyed.' "

views were also considered by many as closely allied to atheism. "Continual reports," he writes, "are being circulated of my being a deist, a defender of suicide, an eccentric phenomenon, a violent Jacobin". Still his devotion to the law and his sweetness of character began to win him friends, and many who objected to his politics could not resist his manners. As a matter of fact, his political biases were of the mildest. "The late Administration (Adams)", he writes, in 1801, "has always been the theme of my praise; though, in some individual measures, my judgment has differed from that of more enlightened statesmen, yet I must also declare that I have never for a moment believed Mr. Jefferson to be an enemy to his country, nor his conduct proved criminal."

In July, 1801, he was admitted to the Essex Bar, and opened an office in Salem.

"All the lawyers and all the judges in the County of Essex were Federalists", he writes, "and I was the first who was obtruded upon it as a political heretic. I was not a little discouraged. . . . For some time I felt the coldness and estrangement resulting from this known diversity of opinion—and was left somewhat solitary at the Bar. I do not mean that I was treated by anyone with harshness or unkindness, but I was in a great measure excluded from those intimacies which warm and cheer the intercourse of the profession."

In the *Salem Gazette* of November 12, 1802, appeared an editorial which illustrates the conditions of the times in Salem. The editor states that on the Saturday evening previous, two gentlemen by the name of Crowningshield, and Mr. Joseph Story, called at his house and requested a private interview. Having been seated, the gentlemen informed him that they had come on unpleasant business, namely, certain publications in his paper abusive of them and their friends. "Mr. Story complained that he had been placed before the public in an injurious point of view—that he was a young man, come into the town to gain a livelihood in an honorable way—that he ought to receive countenance and protection from the community—that his expressing his political sentiments with freedom was perfectly justifiable— that he had no objection to his arguments being fairly combated, but that he would not submit to be arraigned before the public in the manner he had been."(1)

---

(1) See J. T. Buckingham's *Specimens of Newspaper Literature, with Memoirs* (1850).

Such however was Story's evident ability, that even ardent Federalists like William Prescott, one of the leaders of the Bar, and Judge Sewall, were forced to admit that political ostracism could not last long. "It is in vain", said Sewall to Chief Justice Parsons, "to attempt to put down young Story. He will rise, and I defy the whole Bar and Bench to prevent it."

"Gradually business flowed in on me, however," wrote Story in his own memoirs, "and as I was most diligent and laborious in the discharge of my professional duties I began in a year or two to reap the reward of my fidelity to my clients. From that time to the close of my career at the Bar, my business was constantly on the increase; and at the time I left it, my practice was probably as extensive and lucrative as that of any gentleman in the county".

In 1803, he was appointed by Jefferson as Naval Officer of the Port of Salem, which position he declined, in a letter, speaking of "having suffered no small portion of abuse and combated no small portion of oppression", but feeling that "though I may meet with obstacles from political hostility, it would be with real regret that I should quit my profession of the law". Later, in 1805, to a Baltimore friend, who urged him to move to that city, he again wrote of the "petty prejudices and sullen coolness of New England. Bigoted in opinion and satisfied in forms, you well know that in ruling points they too frequently shut the door against liberality and literature."

A single anecdote of this period of life as related by his son W. W. Story, reveals the source of his later greatness as a judge.

In *Rust v. Low* (6 Mass. 90), he was retained as junior counsel with Nathan Dane for the defendants, against William Prescott, for the plaintiff.

When this case was about to come on, Mr. Prescott said to my father, "we shall beat you, Lord Hale is against you," alluding to a note by that great lawyer to *Fitzherbert's Natura Brevium*, (128). This note had not escaped the observation of my father, and satisfied that the passage in Fitzherbert had been misunderstood by Lord Hale, he had explored all the black-letter law on the subject, and had translated nearly thirty cases from the Year Books, to show what the mistake was, and how it arose. At the argument, the note to Fitzherbert having been cited on the other side as clearly expressing the rule of the common law, my father in opening said, "I think I shall satisfy the court that Lord Hale is mistaken." "What, Brother Story," said Chief Justice

Parsons; "you undertake a difficult task." "Nevertheless", was my father's reply, "I hope to satisfy your Honor, that he has really misapprehended the authorities on this point." He then proceeded to explain the mistake, and so strongly fortified his position by the cases from the Year Books as to satisfy even the opposing counsel, that Lord Hale had misconstrued the passage in Fitzherbert. . . . In the judgment of the court, afterwards pronounced in Suffolk, the Chief Justice, without giving the slightest credit to counsel for the argument, or for any suggestion as to Lord Hale's mistake, went through the demonstration of the error, and cited the authorities, as if he had discovered it himself, somewhat to the amusement of those who were in the secret.

At this time, he undertook, but never completed, the task of making a digest, supplementary to *Comyns*. The subjects of Insurance, Admiralty and Prize were among those finished(1).

He also compiled a work on *Pleading* in 1805; and edited *Chitty on Bills and Notes* in 1809, *Abbott on Shipping* in 1810, and *Lawes on Pleading in Assumpsit* in 1811.

By the time he was twenty-six, Story was retained as counsel in cases in adjoining States, and especially in New Hampshire. In this first case in that State, he was opposed to Samuel Dexter of Boston and the great Jeremiah Mason, then the leader of the New Hampshire Bar. "My learned opponents", he wrote, "brought a weight of eloquence and argument which seemed destined to crush me. The jury, rather against the charge of the court, found a verdict in my favor. I have ever thought that the jury felt some sympathy for me in this embarrassed situation, and listened to my appeals, as one strong in faith, however wanting in professional skill."

The case brought him the cordial friendship of Mason, which lasted till his death.

Elected to the legislature in 1805, Story as one of the few Republican lawyers, was pushed forward to prominence in debate. He was especially active in advocating a bill providing more adequate salaries for the Supreme Court Judges, ($2500 instead of $1200 for the Chief Justice); although Chief Justice Parsons being at that time, like all the judges, a Federalist, Story was denounced by his party newspapers for his course.

---

(1) The manuscript of this work in three thick folio volumes, be presented later to the Harvard Law School.

Engraved by J. Cheney from a painting by Chester Harding.

JOSEPH STORY, LL.D.

But though an ardent Republican, Story was, so he writes, "always liberal, a believer in the doctrines of Washington, and little infected with Virginia notions as to men or measures"— one of these Virginia notions being a distrust of the courts and judges.

In 1808, he defended, in the Legislature, Jefferson's embargo policy, against Christopher Gore and the solid "Boston phalanx". In the same year, as chairman of a committee, he wrote an elaborate report in favor of the creation of a Court of Chancery in Massachusetts; but the prejudice in that State against equity jurisdiction was so strong that the report had no effect. The equity powers having been exercised by the old royal governors, were considered as an attribute of royalty, and a means of tyranny, and it was many years before Massachusetts consented to give full chancery jurisdiction to its Supreme Court. Visits to New York and Washington in 1807-1808, enabled Story to see something of the Bar of other States. He visited the New York Supreme Court, sitting at City Hall, and was struck by Chief Justice Kent's celerity and acuteness. "He seems to be a good lawyer and despatches business with promptness. . . . On the whole, if he be not a very great man, I am satisfied he is not humble in his acquirements. He has the confidence of a great lawyer in all his actions, and is self poised on his own resources," he wrote; and he referred to the Bar of New York, as "it is confessed not to be equal to what it has been. Its splendor has been obscured since Burr, Livingston, and Hamilton have departed", and he is satisfied that "Massachusetts has legal talents and juridical learning equal to any of her sisters on this side of the Delaware. What lies beyond is now but speculation." In Baltimore he met all the great lawyers, except Luther Martin. "They do not look like black lettered scholars of the Inns of Court; but are pleasant and frank in their manners, and, as I understand, well versed in the general subjects of juridical consideration." With Robert Goodloe Harper, he visited Judge Samuel Chase, whom he described: "In his person he is tall and not unlike Parsons. I suspect he is the American Thurlow —bold, impetuous, overbearing and decisive."

In 1808, Story was elected to Congress; where one of his first acts was to advocate a modification of the Embargo Act, having become convinced of the evils which it was inflicting on New

England.(1)   Jefferson bitterly resented this move, and wrote
to Henry Dearborn July 16, 1810(2):

The Federalists during their short lived ascendancy have nevertheless by forcing us from the embargo inflicted a wound on
our interests which can never be cured and on our affections
which will require time to cicatrize.   I ascribe all this to one
pseudo-republican, Story.   He came on (in place of Crowninshield, I believe) and staid only a few days, long enough to get
complete hold of Bacon who giving in to his representations
became panic struck and communicated his panick to his colleagues and they to a majority of the sound members of Congress.   They believed in the alternative of repeal or civil war and
produced the fatal measure of repeal.

"The whole influence of the administration", Story wrote to
Edward Everett, "was directly brought to bear upon Mr. Ezekiel
Bacon and myself, to seduce us from what we considered a great
duty to our country, and especially to New England."

Believing that "a continuance in public life was incompatible
with complete success at the Bar," Story was not a candidate for
re-election.   The next year (1810), he went to Washington to

------

(1)   At the same time, Story was convinced of the extreme unwisdom
of the policy of the New England Federalists.   Jan. 3, 1809, he wrote to
Capt. William Story:
"I regret that there are factions in our country that are openly
endeavoring to destroy the confidence of the people in the Constitution.
It seems as if in New England the Federalists were forgetful of all the
motives for union and were ready to destroy the fabric which has been
raised by the wisdom of our fathers.   Have they altogether lost the memory of Washington's farewell address?
The evasions of the embargo and the riotous proceedings in some towns
in your neighborhood are truly distressful.   No doubt they are occasioned
by the instigation of men who keep behind the curtain and yet govern
the wires of the puppet show.
We are diligently employed in amending the Embargo laws; but such
are the perpetual clamors and obstructions interposed by the Federalists
on every occasion that of necessity we move slowly.   You can form no
idea without being here of the continual embarrassments which we
encounter.
Besides it is not easy to devise a system perfectly suited to the object
and yet unobjectionable.   When every motion to amend is by the inflamed
exaggeration of a few men presented to the public as prostrating the liberties of the people and such statements are believed, we must be cautious
or our cause will be permanently injured.   Still the Republicans are aware
of the delay and *regret, deeply regret it.*   They will advance with a firm
step to the object, and if the Embargo should be continued guards
of the strongest nature will encircle it." . . .
See unpublished letter in *Story Papers* in possession of the Massachusetts Historical Society.
(2)   *Writings of Thomas Jefferson*, Vol. IX.

argue the case of *Fletcher v. Peck.*(1) He served, however, once more in the Massachusetts Legislature; and became Speaker of the House, in 1811. In the fall of that year (Nov. 18, 1811), Story, while still Speaker, and at the age of thirty-two years, received the appointment to the seat of Associate Justice of the Supreme Court of the United States. It came as a great surprise, and entirely without solicitation on his part.

The seat had become vacant, in 1810, by the death of William Cushing, who had occupied it since the foundation of the court —twenty-one years. President Madison had offered the position to Levi Lincoln (Attorney General under Jefferson) and to John Quincy Adams (then Minister to Russia), both of whom had declined. Finally, at the suggestion of Ezekiel Bacon, a fellow Congressman from Massachusetts, the tender was made to Story. Though the salary was only $3500, and he had already a professional income of $5000-$6000, Story decided to accept. "The high honor attached to it, the permanence of the tenure, the respectability of the salary, and the opportunity it will allow me to pursue what of all things I admire, juridical studies, have combined to urge me to this result."

The appointment of Story was not received with general enthusiasm. Among his political opponents it was ridiculed and condemned—"that Republican politician, Joe Story", as they called him. Others, by reason of his youth and active political course, augured a host of evil consequences. He was at this time only thirty-two years old—the youngest judge on the bench, and, with the exception of Mr. Justice Buller on the King's Bench in England, the youngest man then ever called to highest judicial station in either country.

Josiah Quincy, Jr. writes in his *Figures of the Past*:

I remember my father's graphic account of the rage of the

---

(1) The following letter from George Cabot to Timothy Pickering, Jan. 28, 1808, is interesting as coming from a vigorous political opponent. The "Georgia claimants" referred to in it were the parties involved in *Fletcher v. Peck.*

"Mr. Joseph Story of Salem goes to Washington as solicitor for the Georgia claimants. Though he is a man whom the Democrats support, I have seldom if ever met with one of sounder mind on the principal points of national policy. He is well worthy the civil attention of the most respectable Federalists; and I wish you to be so good as to say to our friend Mr. Quincy and such other gentlemen as you think will be likely to pay him some attention."

See *Life and Times of George Cabot*, by Henry Cabot Lodge (1870).

Federalists when "Joe Story, that country pettifogger, aged thirty-two," was made a judge of our highest court. He was a bitter Democrat in those days, and had written a Fourth of July oration which was as a red rag to the Federal bull. It was understood that years and responsibilities had greatly modified his opinions, and I happened to be present upon an occasion when the Judge alluded to this early production in a characteristic way. We were dining at Professor Ticknor's, and Mr. Webster was of the party. In a pause of the conversation, Story broke out: "I was looking over some old papers this morning, and found my Fourth of July oration. So I read it through from beginning to end."

"Well, sir", said Webster, in his deep and impressive bass, "now tell us honestly what you thought of it."

"I thought the text very pretty, sir," replied the Judge; "but I looked in vain for the notes. No authorities were stated in the margin."

The Supreme Court, in 1812, was composed of Marshall, Bushrod Washington of Virginia, William Johnson of South Carolina, Brockholst Livingston of New York, Thomas Todd of Kentucky, and Gabriel Duval of Maryland. William Pinkney was Attorney General. In a letter of February 16, 1812, Story wrote that, "the ermine rested upon my shoulders with more ease than I expected"; and on February 24, "My brethren are very interesting men, with whom I live in the most frank and unaffected intimacy. Indeed, we are all united as one with a mutual esteem which makes ever the labors of jurisprudence light"; and on March 5, 1812, "Our intercourse is perfectly familiar and unconstrained, and our social hours are passed in gay and frank conversation."

Story's active mind, however, was not content with the ordinary judicial labors. He at once took up constructive legislation; and in May, 1813, he started a movement towards a Criminal Code for the United States, which finally resulted in the *Federal Criminal Statutes,* of two of which he was the author.

In 1816, he received a tempting offer from William Pinkney (who had been appointed Minister to Russia), to retire from the Bench and take up Pinkney's practice—then worth $21000 per year. Though his salary as a Judge was only $3500, Story declined. At this time, in addition to his other labors, he undertook to assist Henry Wheaton, the Supreme Court Reporter, in his elaborate notes on admiralty and patents, and also in a digest of the Supreme Court decisions.

In 1817, he turned his mind to the great problem of legal education, and wrote his interesting and elaborate essay on the *Growth and Expansion of the Common Law,* as a review of Prof. David Hoffman's *Course of Legal Study,* then just published. And so in this year 1817—the year of the founding of the Harvard Law School—Story's life came in touch with the great subject in connection with which his name is forever noted—the teaching of the law. In 1818, he was elected an Overseer of Harvard College. From that year, his life may be best described in connection with the history of the Law School itself.

CHAPTER XIV.

Isaac Royall and Isaac Parker.

To trace legal education at Harvard University to its earliest source, one must go back to the year 1781, two years after the birth of Story, one year after Marshall was admitted to the Bar, and the year in which Kent began to study law with Egbert Benson.

In this year 1781, at Kensington in England, there died a Loyalist refugee from Massachusetts, one Isaac Royall.

To him belongs the credit of being the founder of the Harvard Law School.

He had been born at Antigua in the West Indies, in 1719; his father, a merchant of great wealth, having emigrated from Boston. In 1738, the family returned to New England, where Isaac Royall fixed his residence in that part of Charlestown now known as Medford. He became a Justice of the Peace in 1753, and a Brigadier General of the Province in 1761. For sixteen years he was chairman of the Board of Selectmen of Medford. He represented the town in the Legislature from 1743 to 1752, regularly returning his salary to the town treasury. In 1752 he was elected a member of the Governor's Council, which honorable office he held until 1774, travelling back and forth from Boston in his coach, the only one in his town. In Medford his father had built the fine old mansion which still stands in that city—a house noted in colonial days for its elegance and richness of furnishing, and built on the model of an English nobleman's house in Antigua.

Isaac Royall appears to have been a man of amiable and mild manners, popular with his neighbors, though a member of what might be termed the aristocracy of the Province. "He loved to give and loved to speak of it and loved the reputation of it," says the historian of Medford.(1) "Hospitality was almost a passion with him. No house in the colony was more open to friends; no gentleman gave better dinners or drank costlier wines. As a

---

(1) *History of Medford*, by Charles Brooks (1886).

Isaac Royall and his Sisters

master, he was kind to his slaves; charitable to the poor and friendly to everybody. He kept a daily journal, minutely descriptive of every visitor, topic and incident, and even described what slippers he wore, how much tar water he drank, and when he went to bed."

Two of his daughters married with distinction, George Erving, and Sir William Pepperell, both of whom became Loyalist refugees. Though declining appointment by the King as a Mandamus Councillor in 1774, in deference to the excited prejudices of the colonists against this usurpation of power by the King, his tendencies were all in favor of a peaceable settlement of the troubles between England and the Colonies. Timid of nature, fearful of the outcome of a Revolution, on the night before the battle of Lexington, without settling his affairs in Medford or taking any of his property with him, he hurried to Boston, and from there sailed for Halifax, and thence to England. His flight appears to have been due to his fears—not that he loved the Colony less, but that he feared England the more; and even at Halifax he wrote home that he hoped to return soon. At first, his popularity saved him from the fate of his sons-in-law, whose property was at once confiscated under the "Conspirator's Act."(1)

Finally his long delay in returning caused even his friends to turn against him. A hearing was held by the Medford Committee of Inspection at which various persons testified as to his Tory sentiments; and as a result, on May 25, 1778, the Selectmen certified to James Winthrop, Judge of Probate that, "Isaac Royall has absented himself for a term of upwards of three months leaving estates behind him to the value of more than

---

(1) It is interesting to note the extreme measures taken by the Colony against the Loyalists, and also the class of men who composed them. Nearly 200 Loyalists were banished by name by the Government of Massachusetts, of whom more than 60 were graduates of Harvard.

Of the five judges of the Superior Court, in 1775, only one (William Cushing) took the American side.

The three statutes passed against the Loyalists were the Act of Sept., 1778, to prevent return of certain persons therein named and others who have left this State or either of the U. S. and joined the enemies thereof; the Act of April 30, 1779, to confiscate the estates of certain notorious conspirators against the government and liberties of the late Province now State of Massachusetts Bay; the Act of Sept. 30, 1779, to confiscate the estates of certain persons commonly called absentees.

twenty pounds within this State, and from the best intelligence we can obtain we verily believe the said Isaac Royall voluntarily went to our enemies and is still absent from his habitation and without the State." "Whereupon Agency was granted to one Simon Tufts, of the estate of Isaac Royall Esquire who was an inhabitant of the Town of Medford but has fled to the enemies of the state for protection."(1)

An inventory of his property on Dec. 15, 1778, (Jan. 13, 1779), appraised his real estate at 50,701 pounds, seven shillings, four pence.(2) It is curious to note, in view of the interest shown by his will in the profession of the law, that only three law books, and several volumes of Journals of the General Assembly appear in this inventory.

Some idea of his wealth may be gained from the fact that, in 1781, the year of his death, his agent's account discloses the item of "Sales of furniture not already accounted for—35,082 pounds, five shillings, ten pence;" and an item by cash further of "Collector Carey for use and damage of furniture—1453 pounds eight shillings nine pence." This sum even in those days of depreciated currency represents personal property of an extraordinary amount for a man who was not in any active business.(3)

For several years, Royall, however, appears to have resented bitterly being classed as a traitor; and in a letter, in 1779, he complained of the interference with his property, declaring that his sailing for Halifax was not voluntary, and that he had been

---

(1) See Probate Records in South Middlesex Registry of Probate.

(2) The "pound" in Massachusetts currency was slightly over a quarter less in value than the English pound.

In January, 1778, the currency of Massachusetts had so depreciated that 100 dollars in coin was worth 325 dollars in bills. In 1779, 100 dollars in coin was worth 742 dollars in bills.

(3) For an interesting account of the legal proceedings taken in reference to Loyalist estates and also for statement as to depreciation of money at the time see

The Confiscation of John Chandler's Estate, by Andrew McFarland. Davis (1903).

As an off set to the depreciation of the currency it is to be noted that as a rule the estates of the Loyalists were greatly undervalued by local appraisers. The author of the note entitled *The Loyalists and Their Fortunes*, in Volume VII of *Narrative and Critical History of America*, Mr. Justin Winsor says in a note (p. 212), "They (the Loyalists) complained of trickery, fraud and gross injustice practiced toward them here. The real value of their property was underestimated in the sworn invoices sent to them."

prevented from returning, solely by ill health. He also wrote at various times, expressing a wish to return to Medford, to marry again, and to be buried by the side of his wife, his father, and his friends. These wishes were never gratified, as he died before the end of the war, in 1781.

His will proved the truth of his assertions, for it contained ample evidence of his retention of affection for his old home. He left legacies to most of his friends in Massachusetts and to the clergymen and church in Medford, a devise to that town of land for school and other public objects, and a devise of land to the town of Worcester.

In his life time, though not a graduate of the College, he had been a liberal contributor towards the restoration of the Harvard College Library, after the burning of Harvard Hall in 1764; and at his death—possibly with the idea of becoming a second Charles Viner, and bringing to light in America another William Blackstone, he made the following bequests to the revered institution of the land of his old home. His will dated May 26, 1778, and codicil of Nov. 31, 1779, read as follows:

Item 12. . . . All the remainder of said tract of land in said Granby containing eight or nine hundred acres more or less, also all my right in a tract of land in the county of Worcester containing in the whole nine hundred and twenty-eight acres which I bought of the Province of Massachusetts Bay on the twenty-eighth day of December 1752 in Company with the Hon. James Otis, Esq., John Chandler, Esq., and Cap. Caleb Dane, I give devise and bequeath to the overseers and corporation of Harvard Colledge Cambridge in the county of Middlesex aforesaid, to be appropriated towards the endowing a Professor of Laws in said College, or a Professor of Physick and Anatomy, whichever the said overseers and Corporation shall judge to be best for the benefit of said Colledge; and they hereby shall have full power to sell said Lands and to put the money out to Interest, the income whereof shall be for the aforesaid purpose.

Codicil Item 6. I give devise and bequeath to the Overseers and Corporation of Harvard College in Cambridge in the County of Middlesex in the Province of Massachusetts Bay in New England, but now by information called the State of Massachusetts Bay, Lott No. 104 containing two hundred acres in the above mentioned Royalston, and all my undivided land not heretofore bequeathed in said Royalston, to be appropriated towards the endowing of a Professor of Laws in said Colledge or a Professor of Physics and Anatomy, whichever the Overseers and Corporation of said College shall choose or judge to be best for the benefit of said College.(1)

This property, so devised, was listed in the inventory of his estate as "a large tract of waste land in Granby and Royalton— value unknown", and of a rentable value of two pounds. No

---

(1) See Probate Records, Suffolk County Registry of Probate (Boston).

The will begins quaintly in the following language: "Kensington in the county of Middlesex in the Kingdom of Great Britain. In the name of God, Amen. I Isaac Royall late of Medford in the county of Middlesex called in the Province of Massachusetts Bay in New England when I left Medford aforesaid on the 16th of April, 1775, but now of Kensington aforesaid having divers estates in said Province of Massachusetts Bay but by information since called the State of Massachusetts Bay—being now weak in body, but of a sound disposing mind and memory thro' the goodness of almighty God I do make and ordain this my last will and testament."

The will is quoted inaccurately in Quincy's *History of Harvard University*, Vol. II, p. 319.

No notice as hitherto been taken of the fact that Royall's will containec' other bequests to the College. Such is the fact however ; and on November 13, 1834, Professor Greenleaf, of the Law School, wrote to T. W. Ward, Treasurer of the College, calling his attention to these bequests, (See *Harvard College Papers*, Vol. VII, 2nd Series, p. 272) as follows:

"In 19th item, he devises bulk of the estate to divers branches of his family in remainder, and on failure of issue, one half to be applied for a hospital in Medford, and the other half to the support of a Professor of Laws in Harvard College.

In item—he provides, that after the line of Harriett Pepperell shall become extinct, no other devisee shall succeed to the estate given to her, till he shall have given bond to the Treasurer of Harvard College for the payment of 10 pounds sterling per annum, to be applied for the support of students.

I suggested to the President the expediency of instituting some inquiry into the condition of these estates at present, and of placing the result on file, as a basis of future measures, if need should require."

The matter was referred to W. I. Bowditch, a distinguished conveyancer, who reported that the testator left a daughter, Mary McIntosh Erving, wife of George Erving, and grandchildren by his son-in-law, Sir Wm. Pepperell, who died in England in 1812, viz. Mary Hurst McIntosh Pepperell, Elizabeth Royall Pepperell, Wm. Pepperell and Harriett Pepperell. Mr. Bowditch further wrote that:

"Isaac Winslow Esq. of this city says that the son died before the father, and that the three daughters are all married, one to Mr. Hutton, one to Sir Charles Palmer, and one not recollected, that it is his strong impression that Mr. Hutton has a large family of children. And he is not certain that the others have not likewise.

Now the College is not to get these 10 pounds a year till all these parties are dead without issue, and in case of all of them are dead with issue, there is still such an endless series of collateral relations, who are named in the will as entitled before the College and hospital, that I think the result amounts to this:

That there can hardly be the remotest possibility that the college can ever get more than the 10 pounds a year ; that the contingency has not occurred when the College is entitled even to that. Nor is there any immediate likelihood that it would happen if Mr. Winslow's impressions are correct." . . .

attention was apparently paid by the College to this bequest, until about 1795, when it engaged counsel to find out where this land was located(1). Then it was discovered, as might have been expected in the long lapse of time, that some of the lands had been sold for taxes, others were occupied by squatters, on others much "strip and waste" had occurred, on others the title of the College was disputed, and the occupiers refused to give up possession. Some of the land was not identified until 1796 and 1797.(2)

The 800 acres in Granby were sold in 1796 for $2000. In 1808, 133 acres in Winchendon were sold for $837.90; in 1809, 250 acres in Westminster were sold for $100. The proceeds were allowed to accumulate at six per cent. interest until in June 1815 the principal fund was $7592.50 and the income, $432.27.(3)

It was at this time, 1815,—twenty-nine years after the probate of Royall's will—that the first move was made to utilize the bequest. An unsuccessful attempt had been made by the College to establish a Professorship of Law within a few years after Royall's death; but this had no connection with the Royall bequest, of the value of which it had, at the time, practically no knowledge. No official record or account of this attempt is

---

(1) See *Harvard College Archives, Miscellaneous Lands* Vol. I.— Letter of Ebenezer Storer, Treasurer, to Daniel Forbes, March 14, 1795; letter from Daniel Forbes from Worcester, March 20, 1795, to Ebenezer Storer stating that "I have found the piece of land willed to the college by Col. Ryol lying in the county of Middlesex" and that it had been partitioned by the Probate Court.

See also letters from Simeon Strong, Dec. 20, 1794, February 22, 1795, March 19, 1795, stating that he has enquired as to values and that the lands might be sold for 10 shillings per acre; letter of Joseph Eastman, August 11, 1795.

(2) See letter of Simon Houghton to Storer, Sept. 3, 1796; letter of William Robins, April 30, 1796; letter of Elisha Tucker, Jan. 23, 1797.

(3) See *Ledger Accounts of the Treasurer of Harvard College*.

Professor Joel Parker in his pamphlet on *The Law School of Harvard College* published in 1871, stated: "In 1815—by some mismanagement, as I have heard, the nature of which I did not learn, the fund amounted to less than $8,000."

This was undoubtedly erroneous; for there appears to have been no evidence of mismanagement.

In *Harvard College Papers* Vol. IV., p. 28, is a letter from President Willard to Treasurer Storer, March 18, 1801, as follows:

"Enclosed is the extract from the will of the late Honorable Theodore Atkinson, Esquire, which you desired. I have also sent an extract from the will of the late Honorable Isaac Royall, Esquire, by which you will see that the money arising from the sale of the lands in Granby ought to be put among the appropriations in your annual accounts and to have interest."

extant; but it is mentioned by Professor Parsons, in his Memoir of his father, Theophilus Parsons(1):

A letter of the late Governor Sullivan, written to a friend, in 1785, says that my father had received an appointment as Professor of Law in Harvard University. Unfortunately there is no evidence of this to be derived from the College records, but from what I am told of the usages of the Corporation at that time, I suppose that the appointment was offered to my father, but not being accepted by him, it did not appear upon the records as a formal vote.

The next suggestion for the study of law at Cambridge came, curiously enough, from a layman, the noted Anti-Federalist pamphleteer, Benjamin Austin, who wrote, in 1786, in one of his series of papers directed against the evils of the legal profession, the following(2):

My principles are to make the study of the law respectable and beneficial. For this purpose we should introduce the study at our University; a professor of law should be established, and the youth should be early taught the fundamental principle of our laws; and from this knowledge, (with small attention) they would become qualified to take the important station of judges.

This answers the question, "If we check the lawyers from whence are to come the judges?"

It is to be noted that if Parsons had accepted the offer in 1785, he would have antedated Wilson, Kent, Clay, and all the others, except Chancellor Wythe, as an American Law Professor.

It is a curious commentary upon the state of the law and the general conditions of education, that thirty years were to elapse after 1785, before Harvard should make the next attempt at legal education. It is also a surprising fact that, though Parsons himself was a Fellow of the Corporation, from 1806 until his resignation in 1812,(3) and, in 1805, extremely active in founding the Professorship of Natural History at Harvard, no effort seems to have been made by him towards promoting legal education.

---

(1) See letter of inquiry from Prof. Parsons to Pres. Walker, March 2, 1858, *Harvard College Papers,* 2nd Series, Vol. XXV.

(2) See Articles in the *Boston Independent Chronicle* for March-April, 1786.

(3) In Parsons' letter of resignation, July 16, 1812—*Harvard College Papers,* Vol. VII, p. 38, he said:

"I resign a connection with the University which is as dear to my heart as it is essential to the best interests of literature, science and religion.

I am happy in knowing that the patronage of the college is now with gentlemen who will endeavor to protect it from the perils to which it is exposed, and to advance its reputation and utility."

Nothing was actually done in this direction until 1815. Possibly the long years of financial embarrassment, due to the Embargo Act, the War of 1812, and the depression in law business in Massachusetts, had seemed to the Corporation an unfavorable time in which to try experiments of this nature in the struggling College. But in the early part of the year 1815, the condition of affairs suddenly changed. Edmund Quincy in his *Memoirs of Josiah Quincy* thus describes the great event with which the year began—the treaty of peace with England:

On Monday, the 13th of February, 1815, an express arrived at the office of the *Columbian Centinel* in the incredibly short space of thirty-two hours from New York bearing a letter—telling of the arrival of the British sloop-of-war Favourite under a flag of truce bearing an English and an American messenger charged with the custody of the treaty. The bells were at once set a-ringing as the readiest way of spreading the joyful news— salutes were fired—the volunteer companies and their bands filled the streets— the schoolboys had a holiday, the whole population was in the streets . . . The wharves so long deserted were thronged and the melancholy ships that rotted along them were once more bright with flags. . . . On Washington's birthday a procession under military escort of which a main feature was a representation of the various trades . . . conducted the authorities of the State and town to the Stone Chapel where fitting religious and musical services were had. A dinner at the Exchange Coffee House, at which Harrison Gray Otis presided, succeeded; and the night was brilliant with fireworks and a general illumination.

And Jared Sparks wrote March 9, 1815, to a friend(1):

I suppose you have been rejoicing with all the rest of the world for peace. We were in as much confusion here for a week or two after the news as we were last fall when it was expected every day the British would make an attempt on Boston. But with this pleasing difference; instead of having our ears stunned with the clangor of drums, bugles, and trumpets, we heard nothing for several days but the ringing of bells and the roar of cannon . . . During one week all business seemed suspended, and everyone joined in a universal shout of joy. All our colleges were splendidly illuminated two nights—Boston was illuminated in the most superb manner, and almost every gentleman's house within ten miles. It is pleasing to see the wonderful change that has already taken place in Boston. Streets which for three years

---

(1) Jared Sparks to Hurd, in *Life of Jared Sparks,* by Herbert C. Adams.

past seem to have been almost entirely deserted are now crowded with merchants and carriers. Vessels are seen sailing out and coming into the harbor and the most cheering prospect appears on every side.

In order to co-relate further the beginning of legal education at Harvard with contemporaneous history, it may be noted that this year 1815 was the year of the battle of New Orleans; James Madison was President; Caleb Strong was Governor of Massachusetts; William Marchant Richardson was Chief Justice of New Hampshire; James Kent was Chancellor and Ambrose Spencer, Chief Justice of New York; William Tilghman was Chief Justice in Pennsylvania. Henry W. DeSaussure was Chancellor in South Carolina; Lord Ellenborough was Chief Justice of King's Bench and Lord Eldon, Lord Chancellor, in England.

It was the year in which Pinkney and Emmet argued the case of *The Nereide,* in the Supreme Court in Washington; it was four years after Judge Story took his seat on the bench, and the year before Daniel Webster settled in Boston to practice law.

It was the year in which the *North American Review* was founded, and Scott published *Guy Mannering,* and two years before Bryant wrote *Thanatopsis.*

It was the year in which Theophilus Parsons Jr. and Jared Sparks graduated from Harvard, and in which Ralph Waldo Emerson was a Freshman.

It was seven years before Boston became a city, two years before the beginning of the Erie Canal, eight years after the voyage of Fulton's Clermont up the Hudson.

It was the year of the Battle of Waterloo, and of the birth of Bismarck.

In Harvard College, in 1815, the lawyers comprised the majority of the Corporation, which then consisted of John Lowell, John Phillips (the first Mayor of Boston in 1822), Christopher Gore (Governor of the Commonwealth in 1809, and United States Senator in 1814), Rev. William Ellery Channing, Rev. John Lathrop, President Kirkland, and the Treasurer, Judge John Davis.(1)

----

(1) In 1806, when Theophilus Parsons was elected a member of the Corporation, that body, for the first time, became composed exclusively of Fellows, all residing out of Cambridge and unconnected with the teaching force of the College.

Of the Board of Overseers, in 1815, a large proportion were lawyers, the fifteen laymen elected under the Statute of 1810, (which first added such laymen to the Board) being Christopher Gore (who resigned that year), Isaac Rand (who resigned that year and was succeeded by Dudley Atkyns Tyng, Reporter of the Supreme Court), William Phillips, Benjamin Pickman, Thomas Dawes, William Spooner, Samuel Dexter (who died the next year and was succeeded by John Brooks, ex-Governor), John Welles, Harrison Gray Otis, William Prescott, Artemas Ward, Isaac Parker, John Phillips, Nathaniel Bowditch and Josiah Quincy.

Such being the conditions in the governing Boards of the College, the lawyers on the Boards and the prominent lawyers in the State, particularly William Prescott, Charles Jackson and John Lowell had discussed, for over a year, the advisability of establishing a Law Professorship at Harvard.

The man to whose active work and enthusiasm the College owed the actual foundation was a lawyer, whom Josiah Quincy later described as "yielding to none in zeal and affection for the university—a man who . . . felt the power and possessed the spirit to attempt to lift the College upwards and to bestow upon it more of the character, as it already had the name, of a University." This was John Lowell, a fellow of the Corporation—the son of Judge John Lowell.(1)   He was born in 1769, at Newburyport, graduated at Harvard in 1786, studied in his father's office and at once sprang into active practise; being associated in many cases with the older leaders of the Bar, like Dexter, H. G. Otis, and Prescott. In 1803, owing to ill health, he had retired from active practise(2). He took an active part in politics, being one of the most Federal of the Federalists; and Edward Everett wrote that "after the death of Fisher Ames, Mr. Lowell possessed a greater ascendency than any other person in New England over the minds of those who were opposed to the Na-

(1) Born in 1743, Harvard 1760, studied with Oxenbridge Thacher, leader of the Bar for several years after the Revolution, Judge of U. S. District Court 1789, Fellow of the Harvard Corporation 1784.

(2) It is a curious fact that, in 1817, after having been fourteen years out of practise of the law, Lowell was persuaded by his old friend and client, Ward Nicholas Boylston, to make a journey to England and try to forward Mr. Boylston's cause in a chancery suit which had been dragging its slow length before Lord Eldon for years. To the surprise of those who were acquainted with the difficulty of the undertaking, Lowell was fully successful.

tional administration." He was a voluminous pamphleteer on political subjects, writing under the pseudonymns of "The Roxbury Farmer" the "Boston Rebel" and others.

In 1814, he was one of the most radical believers in the movement which resulted in the calling of the Hartford Convention; and he lamented the extremely conservative action of that body. He also engaged vigorously in the Unitarian controversy, which was raging fiercely in 1815. But though very severe in tone, his writings were always free from private malice or personal innuendo.

His interests were varied, and of high character. He was one of the founders of the Provident Institution for Savings in Boston, the Massachusetts General Hospital, the Boston Athenaeum, the Botanical Garden at Harvard, and was President of the Massachusetts Agricultural Society. And Edward Everett wrote in 1839 on Lowell's death:

It would not be easy to name an individual in the last generation who either in public or in private life has made himself as extensively felt in the community as Mr. Lowell, and this by the unaided force of personal influence.

He was animated by the loftiest sense of personal honor; his heart was the home of the kindest feelings; and without a shade of selfishness he considered wealth to be no otherwise valuable but as a powerful instrument of doing good. His liberality went to the extent of his means; and when they stopped, he exercised an almost unlimited control over the means of others. It was difficult to resist the contagion of his enthusiasm, for it was the enthusiasm of a strong, cultivated and practical man. He possessed colloquial powers of the highest order and a flow of unstudied eloquence never surpassed, and rarely, as with him, united with command of an accurate, elegant and logical pen.

So too, Rev. F. W. P. Greenwood said in his eulogy(1):

From 1810 to 1822 he was a member of the corporation of Harvard University; and I know not that there is any exaggera-

---

(1) For further details as to Lowell see *Sermon on death of John Lowell L. L. D. March* 22, 1840, by Rev. F. W. P. Greenwood.
Memoir of John A. Lowell, in *Mass. Hist. Soc. Proc.* 2nd Series, Vol. XII (1898).
Memoir of John Lowell in *Mass. Hist. Soc. Proc.* 1st Series, Vol. IX (1840).
Memoir of Mr. John Lowell Junior, delivered on the lectures on his Foundation, in the Odeon, Dec. 31, 1839, *with a note on the death of John Lowell L. L. D.,* by Edward Everett.

John Lowell

tion in saying that during the period of his service he was the soul of that corporation. His time, his acquirements, his exertions and his means were at the call of the best interests of the University; where money was required, he subscribed liberally himself.

Frank and fearless, generous and prompt, and at times even impetuous. This heartiness of disposition was inseparably connected with a keen susceptibility of nature, which was the occasion of a too great quickness and vehemence of language or action, which was the only failing that a friend could ever discover in him or an opponent charge to him.

Reference to Lowell's efforts to persuade the Corporation to constitute a Law Professorship is first found in a letter written by Judge Story from Washington, June 30, 1815, to his friend Charles P. Sumner, who had urged the judge to deliver a course of law lectures in Boston(1):

I have it very much at heart that you should deliver a course of lectures on our Constitution; our Statute Laws; our common law, such as it is—modified by our statutes; and the civil law or such portions thereof as are most worthy the attention of a lawyer in the United States.

You once told me you wanted only the assurance that your expenses should be reimbursed and you would be happy to undertake it. I have revolved the subject in my mind and I think you may at any and all times have as many as twenty auditors who would cheerfully pay 15 to 20 dollars for the course. This would yield 300 or 400 dollars; this would indeed be far short of what it would be worth, but if you should conclude at any time to undertake it, I hope you would consider that you would be thereby rendering a very great and needed service to your country. Law lectures and law treatises are plenty enough for an English student but such as would be entirely useful to an American student are a very great desideratum. Great as may have been our lawyers, they seem to me hitherto to have bent the force of their minds chiefly to benefit themselves; and very few of them seem like you to have considered that there was a great debt due from them to their profession.

Story replied as follows:

Your late letter was very welcome to me. The more so, because it came from a friend whom I had long known, and there-

---

(1) This letter from Sumner was not published in *Life and Letters of Joseph Story* by W. W. Story; but has recently appeared in *Mass. Hist. Society Proc.*, 2nd Series, Vol. XVI (1901-02).

fore could more fully appreciate the value and kindness of his remarks. I will not profess to be insensible to your flattering commendations. They very far exceed my deserts, and I can only regret that I am not worthy of them.

I should have no objection to delivering a course of law lectures in the manner which you suggest. In truth, since our conversation, I had turned the subject several times in my mind; and it was the more agreeable to me, as it would just about fill up the leisure time which I now allot to general reading of the law.

Judge Davis, however, on my last visit at Boston, expressed an opinion, that public law lectures would be delivered at Cambridge, in the course of a year; and that the government had it now in contemplation. Under these circumstances, I should feel it somewhat awkward to announce a determination to pursue a like course; and perhaps it will be best to await the decision of the college.

The College "made its decision," at a meeting of the Corporation on August 18, 1815, at which were present Judge Phillips, Dr. Lathrop, President Kirkland, and the Treasurer, Judge John Davis, and at which the following vote was passed:

Voted: That the corporation are desirous of taking measures to have delivered annually at the University for the benefit of the more advanced students a competent number of lectures on jurisprudence and that $400 of the income of the legacy of the late Isaac Royall Esq., be appropriated each year towards a compensation for such lectures.

Voted: To choose a gentleman to perform this service under such title and regulation as may hereafter be determined.

John Lowell, Esq., was chosen.

President Kirkland thereupon wrote to Lowell, that it was "thought necessary to have in view a proper lecturer before taking steps to complete the institution," and that the Corporation considered him "eminently fitted."(1)

---

(1) Two drafts of President Kirkland's letter, dated August 19 and August 21, 1815, may be found in *Harv. College Papers,* Vol. VII; and *Harv. Coll. Papers,* Vol. VIII. The drafts contain a copy of the votes of the Corporation of August 18, 1815, certified to by President Kirkland and worded as given above in the text. As a matter of fact, however, the wording of the votes as they now appear on the records of the Corporation is slightly different, as follows:

"*Voted* and chose John Lowell Esq. to be Professor of Law under such title and regulations as may hereafter be determined.

Voted that the compensation of the Professor of Law shall be four hundred dollars per year."

Lowell, however, declined to take the position; but, he earnestly urged the appointment of his classmate at Harvard, Isaac Parker, then Chief Justice of Massachusetts, whom the College had recently honored, in 1814, with the degree of LL. D.

Accordingly, in the words of the official record:

At a meeting of the President & Fellows of Harvard College September 4,

Present

The President	Dr. Lathrop
Judge Davis Treas.	Mr. Lowel
Judge Phillips	Mr. Channing

The President prayed.

Mr. Gore came in before the passing of any votes.

(1) *Voted:* That there be established in the University a Professorship of Law agreeably to a provision in the will of the late Hon. Isaac Royall;—that four hundred dollars of the income of the legacy of that Benefactor be annually appropriated towards a compensation for the Professor's services.

(2) *Voted:* To proceed to the choice of a gentleman to be Professor of Law to give lectures on jurisprudence at the University to the members of the Senior Class, to the resident graduates and to others who may be permitted to attend according to such statutes and regulations as may be adopted.

(3) Votes being brought in the Hon. Isaac Parker was chosen.

(4) *Voted:* That Mr. Gore and Mr. Lowell be a committee to devise the rules and statutes for the professorship above named, and report.

At a later meeting of the Corporation on September 14, 1815, it was voted, "that the Professor of Law be called the Royall Professor and that his salary be paid from the fund established by the late Hon. Isaac Royall."

These votes were brought before the Board of Overseers, on Oct. 12, 1815, at a meeting held in the Council Chamber of the State House at Boston, the following gentlemen being present, "Hon. Gen. Cobb, Mr. Tyng, Mr. Quincy, Judge Dawes, Rev. Prest. Kirkland, Rev. Dr. Lathrop, Rev. Dr. Porter, Rev. Dr. Foster, Rev. Mr. Lowell, Rev. Mr. Holley, Rev. Mr. Codman, Rev. Mr. Gray, Rev. Mr. Eliot," (three lawyers, and nine clergymen, it may be noted); and the votes of the Corporation were concurred in, and the statutes of the Professorship adopted by the Corporation on October 11 were referred to a committee consisting of Hon. Judge Dawes, D. A. Tyng and Mr. Quincy.

The statutes having been endorsed by the Committee as, "highly honourable as well as useful to the College," were adopted; and thus Isaac Parker, Chief Justice of Massachusetts, became Harvard's first Law Professor.

ISAAC PARKER.

Of Parker's life only scanty personal records remain, outside of his judicial decisions. He was born in Boston, June 17, 1768—being thus eighteen years younger than Theophilus Parsons, and seven years younger than Samuel Dexter. Graduating from Harvard in 1786, a classmate of John Lowell Jr., he studied law under William Tudor, and was admitted to practice at the Boston Bar in 1789. He soon removed to Castine in the District of Maine, where he acquired a high rank in the profession and a large amount of practice, notwithstanding the great depression in all branches of business and the deep seated prejudice against lawyers. His distinction was undoubtedly partly due to the scarcity of lawyers; for at the end of the 18th Century there had been only 53 lawyers, admitted to practice in Maine, only eight of whom were barristers, John Gardiner, William Cushing, David Sewall, Theophilus Bradbury, David Wyer, William Wetmore.(1)

Parker served in the Legislature in both branches, and was a Member of Congress in 1796. In 1798, he was appointed United States Marshal by President Adams, and removed to Portland— a city which was then the seat of an extensive foreign and domestic commerce, and as Chief Justice Shaw said, "afforded the largest scope in that great section of the Commonwealth for the exercise of forensic talents. From that time, Parker is understood to have taken a high rank and to have been constantly engaged in the active and laborious duty of a counsellor and advocate, and to have enjoyed an extensive and lucrative practice."(2)

On the death of Simeon Strong, Justice of the Supreme Court of Massachusetts, Parker was offered the place but declined be-

---

(1) Prominent at the Bar in Parker's time, in Maine, were Timothy Langdon (Harvard 1768), Roland Cushing (Harvard 1768), John Frothingham (Harvard 1771), Royall Tyler (Harvard 1776) later Chief Justice of Vermont, William Lithgow, George Thacher (Harvard 1776), Daniel Davis (later Solicitor General in Massachusetts), Salmon Chase, William Symmes, Silas Lee (Harvard 1784), Prentiss Mellen (Harvard 1784).

(2) See *Sketch of Life and Character of Hon. Isaac Parker,* by Lemuel Shaw C. J., before the Berkshire Bar, (Sept. 1830), in 9 Pickering 566.

cause the salary ($1,200) was far less than his income at the Bar; but in 1806 he was finally induced to accept. Other reasons, than his conspicuous legal ability undoubtedly led to his appointment—the fact that he was a strong Federalist and the further fact that no other member of that court came from the Maine district of the State. His contemporary William Sullivan says, "he was not supposed to be a learned lawyer when he first took his seat upon the bench . . . but he proved to be one of the ablest judges that ever sat in this court. Probably however he could not number as many hours of study in his whole life, as Parsons could number days."(1)

Almost as soon as he took his seat, in 1806, Parker was called upon to preside over the trial of Thomas O. Selfridge, a well known Federalist lawyer, indicted for shooting the son of Benjamin Austin, the still better known Republican pamphleteer. This case aroused intense political feeling in the community. The press teemed with articles, favorable and otherwise to the defendant. The arguments of counsel at the trial—Attorney General James Sullivan and Solicitor General Daniel Davis for the State, and Samuel Dexter and Christopher Gore for the defendant—contained many allusions to the political significance of the case.(2)

---

(1) *Familiar Letters on Public Characters of the Day,* by William Sullivan.

(2) The facts of the case were as follows: Selfridge, being informed that Benjamin Austin had spoken of "the interference of a damned Federal lawyer," referring to him, had published in the Boston Gazette of Aug. 4, 1806, this remarkable advertisement, peculiarly illustrative of the extreme rancor of the times.

"Benjamin Austin, loan officer, having acknowledged that he has circulated an infamous falsehood concerning my professional conduct in a certain cause, and having refused to give the satisfaction due to a gentleman in similar cases—I hereby publish said Austin as a coward, liar and scoundrel; and if said Austin has the effrontery to deny any part of the charge, he shall be silenced by the most irrefragable proof.

Thomas O. Selfridge.

P. S. The various editors in the United States are requested to insert the above notice in their journals, and their bills shall be paid to their respective agents in this town."

Mr. Austin, having obtained knowledge that this outrageous libel was to be published, had inserted in the *Independent Chronicle* of the same morning, the following:

"Considering it derogatory to enter into a newspaper controversy with one T. O. Selfridge, in reply to his insolent and false publication in the *Gazette* of this day; if any gentleman is desirous to know the facts, on which his impertinence is founded, any information will be given by me on the subject.

Benjamin Austin.

The difficulties of Parker's position as judge at this trial were well described by Chief Justice Shaw in his address, at the time of Parker's death, and Shaw' remarks are the more interesting, by reason of the fact that he himself was a witness for the defendant at this trial(1):

The parties held high positions in society and a prominent rank in the opposite political parties, and the prejudices and passions connected with the prosecution were not a little inflamed by the excited party politics of the day. Yet such was the dignity, the impartiality, the skill and ability with which the newly appointed judge, then comparatively a stranger, conducted this trial that it is believed he gave universal satisfaction and made himself most favorably known—as a jurist of great promise.

In 1814, when the office of Chief Justice became vacant "all eyes", said Story, "were turned towards him as successor;" and

---

Those who publish Selfridge's statement, are requested to insert the above, and they shall be paid on presenting their bills."

Austin, further, on the same day, on meeting a friend of Selfridge said "if Mr. Selfridge attacks me, I hope to have such support from friends at hand as I shall be able to avoid any injury." This remark, being reported to Selfridge, was regarded by him as a threat that Austin proposed to assault him. The fact seems to have been quite the opposite; as Austin only intended to guard himself from any assault by Selfridge.

Unknown, however, to Austin, his son Charles Austin took upon himself the defence of his father's honor. This young man was then a student in Harvard College, of remarkable promise, and a universal favorite, and only eighteen years of age. Chancing to be in Boston that morning, he read the *Gazette* and immediately purchased a long cane. About one o'clock in the afternoon, he was talking with a friend on the sidewalk in front of what is now the Worthington Building on the corner of State and Congress streets. While there, he saw Selfridge coming round the corner of the old State House, Selfridge's law office being in that building. As Selfridge reached a point in State street just opposite what is now the Merchants' Bank Building, Austin stepped out towards him, and raising his cane, dealt him a heavy blow on the head, which cut through his hat and through his scalp. Upon this Selfridge drew a pistol, and shot his assailant through the breast. Austin after dealing him several weaker blows, finally sank on the pavement, and was carried into a shop where he soon died.

(1)   Address before the Berkshire Bar, Sept., 1830.

John Gorham Palfrey in his *Sermon on the Death of Isaac Parker* (1830) spoke of the Selfridge case as "a trial involving questions of the most abstruse, delicate and painful nature, as fresh now in the memory of many of us, as events of yesterday."

Joseph Story, who was of opposite political belief, paid his tribute to Parker's fairness, describing the political condition in which the new judge found himself:

"He lived through times of peculiar delicacy and difficulty, in the midst of great political changes and excitements, when the tribunals of justice were scarcely free from the approaches of the spirit of discord and the appeals of party were almost ready to silence the precept of the law."

he was appointed, said Shaw, "to the universal satisfaction of the community."

It was just one year later that he received the offer of the Professorship of Law.

Parker's personal characteristics were of the pleasantest nature. Story, who knew him well wrote that: "His manners were frank, modest, and winning, without ostentation, and without affectation—a mild temperament, a quiet and moderate cheerfulness, an ingenuous countenance, and social kindness which pleased without effort and was itself easily pleased. His most striking characteristic was sound sense, discretion, patience, judgment."

Palfrey described "his frankness and expression of confidence in his deportment, putting all who approached him at their ease; his habitual gayety of spirit, and power of ready adaptation of others' feelings which only an exhaustless fund of kind and cordial feeling could supply; the honest, equal, friendly, personal regard which he inspired, rarely excited by the most respected and valued publick men."

Sullivan gives an amusing anecdote of his kindly humor, in describing his simple habits of life:

Once a new servant who had left a family where it was the usage to announce visitors, asked two lawyers who came to call for their names. They being amused at the Judge's new style said "John Doe and Richard Roe." The servant threw open the door and announced "Mr. John Doe and Mr. Richard Roe." The Chief Justice came forward with his usual good nature and extending his hand said, "Gentlemen, I have read of you and heard of you all my life, but I have despaired of making a personal acquaintance." The servant however was ordered to forego this gentility in future.

Of his personal appearance, Sullivan writes: "He was a man of middle stature, of full person and face, light or red complexion, blue eyes, and very high forehead, and remarkably bald. His manners were simple and without pretension to polish. He was very affable, amiable, and unpretending, and a most companionable and agreeable associate in private life. Perhaps no man excelled him in kind and friendly feelings. He used snuff immoderately; it affected his voice in his latter years."

Of the legal side of his nature, the most predominant feature was his high quality of common sense. He labored always not to lose sight of the real justice and merits of the case. To

the application of legal acuteness and skill leading towards finding defects in legal process, he had an utter aversion. If he had
a fault it was this very "too ardent desire to reach the equity
of the particular case," said Shaw, and hence he was sometimes
called "The Chancellor of Massachusetts law." His clearness,
his rapidity and readiness in grasping a point, the simplicity and
ease of his opinions, and his patience in listening to explanations
amply made up however for his lack of great learning. "With
all its vivacity I have never known the mind so patient of severe
labor nor the mind which during the period of any observation
has been so heavily tasked. This was no hardship to him. It
never broke his spirit. It never quelled his gayety," said Palfrey.

He was thoroughly interested and conversant with all the varied
interests and passing events of the day. "The interests of our
infant literature were always very near his heart." He was a
vigilant and active Trustee of Bowdoin College, the President for
two years of the Phi Beta Kappa, a Fellow of the American
Academy and later an Overseer of Harvard College.

The law needed at this time a man of just these broad common sense tendencies; and it found him in Isaac Parker. As
Story said:

It was a critical moment in the progress of our jurisprudence.
We wanted a cautious but liberal mind to aid the new growth
of principles to enlarge the old rules, to infuse a vital equity—
we wanted a mind which with sufficient knowledge of the old
law was yet not a slave to its forms, which was bold enough to
invigorate it with new principles—not from the desire of innovation but the love of improvement. We wanted a sobriety of
judgment but at the same time a free spirit. . . . Such a
man was Parker.

This was the man whom Harvard called to be its first Law
Professor.

The principal provisions of the statutes of the new Royall
Professorship were as follows:(1)

_____

(1) The other statutes not quoted in full above were:
"*Statute 2nd.*
The said Professor of Law shall be elected in the same manner
in which other officers •of the College are chosen, and shall hold the
office during good behavior, but the Corporation, with the assent of the
Overseers, may at any time remove him for any cause, which they may
deem just and sufficient.
Statute 4th.
The said Professor shall enjoy all the authority while delivering

Statute 1st. For the present, and so long as the principal support of the Professor shall be derived from the fund bequeathed by the late Hon. Isaac Royall, Esquire, the Professor shall be entitled "Royall Professor of Law;" but the Corporation reserve to themselves the right, with the assent of the Overseers, to change the title of said Professor, whenever and as soon as any such additions shall be made to the aforesaid fund as to render the sum bequeathed by the aforesaid Royall the smaller part of the whole foundation, or for any other good and sufficient reason, not repugnant to the will of the said Royall.

Statute 3rd. The said professor shall enjoy the privileges and rank which appertains of right to the other Professors in the College; but he shall not be obliged to reside in the town of Cambridge, nor shall he be called upon to take any part in the immediate government of the College, unless required so to do by the Corporation and Overseers; he shall, however, when requested by the Corporation, give his opinion on any questions of law immediately affecting the College, provided the delivery of such opinion shall not interfere with the said Professor's other duties.

The Professor was only to be called upon to deliver 15 lectures, which were to be attended by Seniors in the College; though the officers and resident graduates of the College were to be entitled to attend gratis; and the Professor was to be allowed to admit other persons, not resident of the College, on such terms as he should fix.

The scope of the lectures required was most extensive—in fact far greater than any man could give in so short a course.

---

his lectures to the students, as to the preservation of order and decorum and the regulation of the deportment of the students which other professors are entitled to exercise; and for any indecorum during his exercises or insult offered to him, the students shall be subject to such penalties as are provided in like case as to the other officers of the College; which penalties it shall be the duty of the immediate government, after examination, to apply.

Statute 5th.
The said Professor shall before he enters on the duties of his office, subscribe these statutes, as well as the usual declaration prescribed in such cases to the other Professors.

Statute 6th.
The course of lectures shall be delivered in some of the College Publick Rooms and shall consist of not less than fifteen; and until further order, the same shall be attended only by the Senior class among the Undergraduates; but the officers of the College including the Overseers and Corporation together with all the Resident Graduates shall have a right to attend the said Lectures gratis.

It shall be lawful for the said Professor to admit any other persons, not resident at the College, on such terms and conditions as shall to the said Professor seem proper; provided that such arrangements be made as to numbers and seats at the lectures, as may consist with the suitable accommodation of the members of the College who attend."

Statute 7th. It shall be the duty of the said Professor to exhibit in a course of lectures, the theory of law in its most comprehensive sense; the principles and practical operation of the Constitution and Government of the United States and this Commonwealth; a history of the jurisprudence of this State under the Colonial and Provincial as well as under the present government; an explanation of the principles of the Common Law of England, the mode of its introduction into this country, and the sources and reasons of its obligation therein; also the various modifications by usage, judicial decision, and Statute; and, generally those topics connected with law as a science which will best lead the minds of students to such inquiries and researches as will qualify them to become useful and distinguished supporters of our free system of government, as well as able and honorable advocates on the rights of the citizen.

The appointment of Judge Parker was well received by the general public; and the *North American Review* said, in November, 1815 [Vol. II]:

The [Royall] income, although not sufficient for the maintenance of a resident professor, affording a compensation for a competent number of lectures in jurisprudence, considered as a part of general education, the Corporation with the consent of the Overseers have added to the Institution a Professor of Law. The Hon. Isaac Parker is appointed to this office which he has accepted with the view of commencing the lectures next season, it being a part of the year when the official duties of the Chief Justice will not interfere with those of the Professor. We are happy that our educated young men are to be guided to a knowledge of the general principles of law and their application to our forms of civil and ecclesiastical policy under the auspices of a civilian so entirely the object of publick confidence.

Judge Parker was not prepared to enter on his duties at once, and his inauguration did not occur until April 17, 1816. An inauguration of a professor was in those days a solemn and formal affair.

The Overseers met on the day in the Philosophy Chamber in Harvard Hall, the Governor, the Lieutenant Governor, and most of the Board being present. A procession of the officers, Overseers, visitors, trustees, noted guests, the whole preceded by the entire body of resident graduates and undergraduates, then went out of the yard from Harvard Hall "through the north gate and re-entered by the gate fronting University Hall. When the procession arrived at the south steps, it opened to the right

and left, the procession passing between the two lines into the chapel in University Hall, where the ceremonies took place as follows. President Kirkland offered a prayer. He then made an address on the importance of the profession of law, and reciting the acts of the Boards in establishing the new office. The Statutes of the Professorship were then read in full. President Kirkland then called on the new Professor to subscribe and deliver to the Governor his declaration. This being done, the President asked the leave of the Governor to declare the Professor; and this being obtained, he announced him Royall Professor of Law. He then bade him welcome to his place in the University and the Professor replied. Thereupon the President invited him into the desk to deliver his inaugural address. The Professor accordingly pronounced a discourse in English, the Latin language having been used in all the preceding exercises except the prayer. A psalm and anthem were sung by the singing society of the University. The publick exercises and ceremonies being finished, the company dined together in the dining hall No. III, except that the officers and graduates living in commons dined at their respective tables."(1)

Such was the elaborate and classical manner in which a man became Professor of Harvard ninety years ago.

The inaugural address delivered by Parker is of extraordinary interest at the present day, so modern is it in its attitude towards law as a science—and parts of it might indeed be thought to be the words of Langdell himself.(2)

At the outset he explained the reasons for the "publick neglect of so important a branch of education," as follows:

Like all incipient institutions, this must be imperfect in the outset; like them it may, however, be improved in its progress, and *at least* in future time, and in other hands, may grow into a system, honorable to the University and highly useful to the publick.

In the rapid growth of this revered seminary from a school to a college, and from that to an University, keeping pace with the advancement of the Commonwealth, of which it has ever been the favorite child, as well as the faithful nurse, it has been thought difficult to account for so late an introduction of jur-

---

(1) See *Records of the Corporation and of the Overseers—Harvard College Archives.*
(2) See address as published in full in *North American Review*, Vol. III (May 1816).

isprudence among the sister sciences which have long flourished here, under the patronage of the publick. The publick neglect of so important a branch of education may be traced to causes in no way disreputable to the science of jurisprudence in its present improved condition, or to the wisdom and discernment of those who have governed the affairs of the University. The course of education in this country has been wisely adapted to the actual state of things, and until recently has been calculated to give a competent portion of general knowledge, rather than to produce extraordinary instances of wonderful attainment.

Professorships of particular branches of science have therefore been but lately introduced, except in Theology, which in our enlightened Christian country is deservedly the first object of public patronage, and in the demonstrative sciences which are at all times necessary. Our students have been educated for *business,* not for contemplation, and the rare opportunities which have yet occurred of devoting a life to literary or scientific pursuits, have justified the slow advancement of the university to that degree of eminence which the establishments of older countries have so long enjoyed.

But the means of education are multiplying and developing in proportion to the increasing demands of our rapidly improving society.

After showing how early education was concerned with theology, and with matters fitting men for business, he explained how it happened that the teaching of medicine was taken up before that of law:

Next to the care of the soul has been justly estimated the preservation of life and health; professorships for instruction in the various branches of the healing art have therefore succeeded those of Theology, and it ought not to be considered as out of the natural course that thirty years should have intervened between the admission of those necessary sciences into the University and the establishment of jurisprudence as a branch of academick education. Our Commonwealth has now got beyond its infancy, and its institutions are fast advancing to the perfection which accompanies maturity.

He then discussed the low state of the practice of the law and of the legal profession in the early years of the country:

For the first century of our history, we learn little of law and lawyers, but the simplicity of one and the insignificance of the other.

The profession was probably followed by men of low minds and lower reputation, whose efforts were limited to the mechanical drudgery of the craft. . . . The profession of the law was undoubtedly then considered odious, and jurisprudence was probably unknown as a science. . . . In such a state of things, law could not be deemed a science; and a proposition to teach it in a college would probably have been received with as much horror as a scheme to instruct in magick or the black art.—Law was a trade rather than a science; and its professors viewed as cunning artificers, rather than as profound jurists.

He then compared the recent generation of lawyers with the older, stating that Cushing, Dana, Lowell, Strong, Sedgwick, Parsons and Sewall "would have been honored in any country and in any times:"

To a familiar knowledge of our municipal regulations, most of them added an extensive acquaintance with other sciences; and the law as understood and administered by them was a comprehensive system of human wisdom, derived from the nature of man in his social and civil state, and founded on the everlasting basis of natural justice and moral philosophy.

With the development of a Bar consisting of men of such ample learning and character, "Well may the law now be denominated a science and deemed worthy of a place in the University" he said:

A science like this is worthy to be taught, for it cannot be understood without instruction; it should be admitted into fellowship with its fellow sciences, for like them, its ends are noble. Its fundamental and general principles should be a branch of liberal education in every country, but especially in those where freedom prevails and where every citizen has an equal interest in its preservation and improvement. Justice ought therefore to be done to the memory of *Royall,* whose prospective wisdom and judicious liberality provided the means of introducing into the university the study of the law. Let us hope that the practical advantages which he proposed may result from the attempt by this professorship and develop them; so that future benefactors may perceive that an extension of the system, which he could only initiate, is one of the best means of serving their country.

He then pointed out that the course of lectures which he was to give was not, in any sense, a complete legal education:

It is obvious that in the short course of lectures of which the present state of the institution will admit, nothing like a law education can be attempted; and, indeed, I am satisfied, after reflection upon the subject, that such an attempt, if practicable, would not be useful for undergraduates, who cannot devote the time necessary for any tolerable proficiency, without too great an abstraction from other studies, most of which are essential prerequisites to the study of the law.

Exceeding all the rest of his address in importance were his closing sentences. For in these last pregnant words, Parker made the first suggestion ever officially made at Harvard for the founding of a separate school of law:

At some future time, perhaps, a school for the instruction of resident graduates in jurisprudence may be usefully ingrafted on this professorship; and there is no doubt that when that shall happen, one or two years devoted to study only under a capable instructor before they shall enter into the office of a counsellor to obtain a knowledge of practice will tend greatly to improve the character of the Bar of our State. A respectable institution of this sort in a neighboring State, unconnected with any publick seminary has been found highly advantageous in the education of young gentlemen to the law.

The constant engagement of the most eminent counsellors in indispensable business renders difficult for them to devote that portion of their time to instruction which would seem to be necessary for a science which is intricate and abstruse to inexperienced minds. Some improvement, therefore, in professional education, seems to be wanting; and perhaps it can in no better way be obtained, than by establishing a school here under the protection of the University, as preparatory to that acquisition of practical knowledge of business which may always be better learnt in the office of a distinguished counsellor.

Judge Parker's lectures were begun on June 5th, 1816, and were delivered through June and July of that year.(1)

His own report in 1816 gives the best description of them.

The subscribed, Royall Professor of Law at the University of Cambridge, reports that he delivered a course of lectures to

---

(1) See letter from Parker to Kirkland, *University Archives, Loose Letters,* Vol. III.

"I was in hopes to have seen you today and then to have made arrangements about my lectures which I suppose ought to begin tomorrow. I don't know that I can do anything better than to be there ready, in case notice has been given.

Your friend, etc.,

Isaac Parker.

Monday, June 4."

the Senior Class in June and July last, consisting of an introductory lecture recommending the subjects of his course to their attention, four lectures comprising the Juridical History of the Colony, Province and Commonwealth with its various changes —one lecture on the organization of the judicial power of the State, one on the organization and powers of the courts of the United States—one on the Constitution of the Commonwealth and the various historical events which led to its adoption— one on the Constitution of the United States and the several antecedent confederacies—a lecture on Natural Law, one on the history of the common law, one on the civil law, one on ecclesiastical law—a history of the titles to real estate in this Commonwealth—on personal contracts and property—on the domestic relations—with two or three lectures on some of the subjects intended as explanations and illustrations, and a concluding lecture of a monitory nature in relation to the studies, deportment and general principles by which their success in life and usefulness to the public would be covered—On the whole, 17 or 18 lectures.

The young gentlemen were, as far as I could discern, attentive, and their behavior unexceptionable; some of them took minutes and in conversation with them I was satisfied they had comprehended the subjects.

I do not know the number that attended but think from the appearance there were not less than three fourths of the class present at every lecture.

"He brought out in a general way such facts and features of the common and statute law", says Rev. Dr. A. P. Peabody, "as a well educated man ought to know together with an analysis and exposition of the Constitution of the United States. His lectures were clear, strong, and impressive, and were full of materials of practical interest and value. The students, I think, fully appreciated the privilege of having for one of their teachers a man who had no recognized superior at the bar or on the bench."(1)

Such a course, however, good as it might be, did not, in any way furnish an adequate education for a young man intending to take up the profession of the law. No one man saw this more clearly than the Professor himself. The start, however, had been made. The process must be carried to completion.

(1) *Harvard Reminiscences*, by A. P. Peabody (1888).
"His lectures were of an elementary nature adapted to the youthful minds of his audience and were characterized by that free and flowing style which so eminently marks the judicial opinions of this judge."
See Report of the Law School Visiting Committee of the Board of Overseers, Feb. 7, 1849.

CHAPTER XV.

THE FOUNDING.

The experiment of giving law lectures to the undergraduates had proved, after a year's trial, that a more advanced and intimate connection of the University with legal education might be successful.

The founding of a separate School of Law was therefore proposed, described later by Professor Stearns, in his report of 1825, as follows:(1)

> The Law School was established in 1817 by the Govt. of the University, with the advice and under the patronage of some of the most distinguished professional gentlemen and friends of that institution in its vicinity. This measure was adopted with the hope of providing a more systematic and thorough course of legal instruction, and a better preparation for the practice than is generally attainable in the usual way of acquiring a law education.
>
> With a knowledge of the difficulties which students have to encounter at the commencement of their professional studies, they were likewise aware how impossible it is for gentlemen engaged in the duties of a laborious profession to devote so much time as is necessary to the instruction of their pupils.
>
> The advancement of literature and science in our country, and the manifest advantages derived from the establishment of college and other institutions for the education of students in Theology and Medicine, left no room to doubt, whether it was not equally important that similar advantages should be enjoyed by those engaged in the no less difficult study of the Law.
>
> It was thought that the time had arrived, when the demands of the public for the means of thorough and methodical education of all engaged in the study of the liberal professions, should be complied with; especially of those who are to administer the laws, defend the rights of their fellow citizens, and become in no inconsiderable degree the directors of public opinion, and the guardians of the public liberty and welfare.

To Isaac Parker, the credit is due of being the real founder of the School. The idea was really his; and on May 14, 1817, he

---

(1) See Harvard College Papers, Vol. XI.

presented to the Corporation, in writing, a plan for a new Law Professorship, and for the constitution of a separate school or department of the University, which was adopted by the Corporation almost word for word as written by him.

In his letter he said (1) :

The present mode of education is necessarily deficient, as it is obtained principally in the offices of eminent practitioners, who are unable from their constant application to business, to act the part of instructors. It is believed that a school at Cambridge, under the immediate care of a learned lawyer, whose attention would be principally directed to the instruction of his pupils, would afford opportunities for laying a solid foundation of professional knowledge, which would be cheerfully embraced, and would be found highly beneficial. The undersigned proposes that there should be a vote of the Government, establishing such a school, and constituting a department connected with the University.

He proposed that students should be charged $100 a year "the average price of education in the country;" and he further agreed :

to bestow as much of his time upon the school as can be spared from his other public duties, and will, in the intervals of his judicial labours, visit the school as often as possible, converse with the students on the subjects they may be engaged in, examine them occasionally, and as often as possible read to them a prepared lecture upon such subjects as shall be found most conducive to their improvement.

The following is the official record of the birth of the School:

At a meeting of the Corporation of May 14, 1817, present, 1, The President; 2, Mr. Gore; 3, Judge Davis (Treas.); 4, Mr. Lowell; 5, Judge Phillips.

The Royall Professor of Law, having represented to this Board, that, in his opinion and in that of many friends of the University, and of the improvement of our youth, the establishment of a school for the instruction. of students at law, at Cambridge, under the patronage of the University, will tend much to the better education of young men destined to that profession, and will increase the reputation and usefulness of this Seminary; and the Corporation concurring in these views, it was voted, as follows :

1, That some Counsellor, learned in the law, be elected, to be

(1) *Harvard College Papers,* Vol. VIII.

denominated University Professor of Law, who shall reside in Cambridge, and open and keep a school for the instruction of graduates of this or any other university, and of such others as, according to the rules of admission, as attorneys, may be admitted after five years study in the office of some Counsellor.

2, That it shall be the duty of this officer, with the advice of the Royall Professor of Law, to prescribe a course of study, to examine and confer with the students upon the subjects of their studies, and to read lectures to them appropriate to the course of their studies, and their advancement in the science, and generally, to act the part of a tutor to them, in such manner as will improve their minds and assist their acquisitions.

3, The compensation for this instruction is to be derived from the students; and a sum not exceeding one hundred dollars a year shall be paid by each one attaching himself to this school; but this sum shall be subject to be reduced hereafter by the Corporation, if, in their judgment the emoluments of the school shall make such reduction reasonable, and consistent with the interests of the establishment.

4, The students shall have access to the college library on such terms as the Government of the University shall prescribe, and a complete Law Library be obtained for their use as soon as means for that purpose may be found.

5, The students shall be permitted to board in commons on the same terms as the other members of the college; and such accommodation shall be afforded them in respect to lodging rooms, as may consist with the urgent claims of the existing establishment.

6, As an excitement to diligence and good conduct, a degree of bachelor of laws shall be instituted at the University, to be conferred on such students as shall have remained at least eighteen months at the University School, and passed the residue of their noviciate in the office of some counsellor of the Supreme Court of the Commonwealth, or who shall have remained three years in the school, or if not a graduate of any college, five years, provided the Professor having charge of the same shall continue to be a practitioner in the Supreme Judicial Court.

7, The students shall have the privilege of attending the lectures of the Royall Professor of Law, free of expense, and shall have access to the other Lectures of the University usually allowed to be attended by resident graduates, without charge, or for such reasonable compensation, as the Corporation, with the assent of the Overseers, shall determine.

8, The law students shall give bonds for the payment of the college dues, including the charge of the Professor for instruction, which shall be inserted in the quarter bills and collected by the college officer; and the sums received for instruction, shall, when received be paid over by said officer to the Professor.

9, The Law Students shall be on the same footing generally, in respect to privileges, duties and observances of College regulations, as by the laws pertain to resident graduates.

Voted That the foregoing votes constituting a new department at the University be laid before the Overseers that they may approve the same if they see fit.

Agreeably to the statutes relative to a Law School at the University, Ballots being brought in the Hon. Asahel Stearns was chosen.

These votes being laid before the Overseers, on May 15, 1817, referred to a committee consisting of Hon. Timothy Bigelow, Hon. Artemas Ward and Hon. Judge (Charles) Jackson (the latter a judge of the Massachusetts Supreme Court, and elected as Overseer in 1816, on the death of Samuel Dexter). On June 12, 1817, there being present "His Excellency Gov. Brooks and most of the Hon. Council and the Hon. Senate, President Kirkland, Rev. Richard R. Eliot, Rev. Dr. Porter, Rev. Dr. Harris, Rev. Mr. Gray, Rev. Charles Lowell, Rev. John Codman" it was voted to concur with the Corporation and also "to proceed to the choice of a gentleman to reside at Cambridge as Professor of Law."

At a later meeting on June 26, Hon. Asahel Stearns was unanimously elected; and Hon. Charles Jackson, Rev. Mr. Dexter, and Hon. William Prescott were appointed a committee "who with the committee of the Corporation, Hon. John Phillips and the President, were to wait upon Mr. Stearns and request his acceptance."

While the legal conditions of the times may have been ripe for a Law School, the financial and social conditions made it a bold and hazardous experiment.

The War of 1812 had left New England, and especially Massachusetts, in an impoverished condition. Its shipping had been ruined by the war, and the coming of peace wrecked its newly budding manufactures. English goods flooded in from overstocked England and ruinously undersold American manufacturers. Most of the large cotton and woolen factories closed their doors. The population of New England increased slowly; for thousands of its families emigrated to Western New York and the new Middle States—a movement facilitated by the increase of turnpikes and the introduction of the steamboat. The new tariff of 1816 did not give the impetus to manufactures that had been hoped for. To add to the troubles, disorder in the currency set in, caused partly by the fever of Western land speculation, partly by bad banking. The chartering of the United States Bank in 1816 had not materially helped matters. And by 1817, the hard times were seriously felt by the people at large.(1)

It was, therefore, an unfortunate period in which to expect many families to send their sons to a collegiate institution, to acquire a legal education—expensive, as compared to former methods; although, it is true, the expenses of a student in those days do not seem heavy in comparison with those of the present day. Thus, in the President's first Annual Report, of January 1827, the estimate of necessary expenses was as follows: steward and commons, $10; board, 38 weeks, at $1.75, $66.50; instruction, average, $55; rent of study in college, average, $11; library, $3; text books, $12.50; charges for lecture rooms, general repair, care of chamber, catalogue, $14; total, $172.00; wood, commonly about $7; a room in a private house from $30 to $45 a year; washing, $3 to $5 a quarter; board in town, $1.75 to $3 a week.(2)   And a law student's expenses would be about the same, with $100 for tuition.

Nevertheless, that Harvard College was regarded as an expensive place, is illustrated by a letter from John Randolph, of Roanoke, to Josiah Quincy, Dec. 11, 1813, written from Richmond(3):

I had like to have forgotten to tell you that your University is decried in this quarter. The change of Socinianism we once discussed together; but a heavier one is now advanced against

---

(1) See Adams' *History of United States,* Vol. IX, Chapters IV and VII; and McMaster's *History of United States,* Vol. IV.

(2) See Letter of J. Sparks to Davis Hund, May 23, 1812:
"The Quarter bill for board, tuition, room rent, etc., will generally average about $45 a quarter ($180 a year). Some other contingencies will make college expenses about $200 a year, and considering clothes a person may be considered very economical if his yearly expense do not exceed $250. There are more who spend $500 than there are who fall short of $250."

And see letter of Charles Folsom to Sparks, July 17, 1829:
"The steward estimates every necessary expense of a student (supposing him to have a chum) at $190, i. e., exclusive of clothes, washing and pocket money, call it $200. Diminish this by the average of the benefactions stated above (the largest $60, the least $15) and you have what I suppose you want. For a distinguished scholar (not college freshman—five who receive $120 each and four who have charge of recitation rooms, $60 each) I suppose the average to be about $150 per annum."

Life and Writings of Jared Sparks, by Herbert B. Adams (1893).

(3) *Memoir of Josiah Quincy,* by Edmund Quincy (1867).

you—at least, according to the maxims of this calculating age. 'Tis said that your Principal and Professors take a pride in the extravagance of the students, and encourage it, while Yale zealously inculcates the sublime truths of Poor Richard's Almanac. Be this as it may, some of our southern youths have left a great deal of cash at Cambridge, and brought away nothing valuable in return for it. We are so much poorer in this quarter than you wealthy Bostonians, that we smart under an expense that you would scarcely feel. . . . I deemed it proper to apprise you of the fact that such reports are circulated, and with some industry. They have been the means of sending some of our young men to Yale, instead of Cambridge.

The second economic impediment, which must always be borne in mind, was the difficulty of access to Boston, from the States outside of New England. Even at this time (1817), it took two days to go from Boston to New York, two and a half days to go from New York to Washington, four days from New York to Buffalo, five and a half days from Philadelphia to Pittsburg. The mail from Washington to New Orleans, for a long time after 1817, took twenty-four days. On the few routes where steamboats were running the fares were high and the trips infrequent.

One other condition of the times—a social one—undoubtedly kept students away from the Law School. Harvard was regarded as the nest of Unitarianism. And at this time the feud between the Congregationalists and the new Unitarians was bitter. In 1805, Harvard College had appointed Henry Ware, a preacher of Unitarian tendencies, as Hollis Professor of Theology. Many of the prominent men in Boston and especially of the leaders of the Bar and those interested in the College were of the same religious sect. By 1817, there were seven or eight churches, called Unitarian, in and around Boston. In 1819, William Ellery Channing gave the new movement its first definite form. The new Divinity School at Harvard became, at this time, more and more Unitarian.(1)

But outside of Boston the well to do merchants and lawyers

---

(1) In 1820, the noted case of *Baker v. Fales* was decided in the Massachusetts Supreme Court (16 Mass. 488), which resulted in the turning over to the Unitarians of a large amount of the church property of the old orthodox Congregational churches.

In this case, Daniel Davis, Solicitor General, appeared for the plaintiff, and Daniel Webster for the defendants.

were Congregationalists or Presbyterians, and would have nothing to do with those who accepted what they called, "infidel beliefs." An interesting example of this aloofness is to be found at the end of the following letter, written by President Kirkland to Treasurer Davis, Feb. 28, 1819(1):

We left Boston the 13th January, and passed the next Sunday the 17th at Bedford, 14 miles from Stratford, at Mr. Jay's. .
. . We reached New York, Monday night, where I passed the week till Saturday, when I proceeded to Princeton . . .
I had an agreeable time with the gentlemen of Nassau Hall, and heard two orthodox sermons from Dr. Alexander and Dr. Milley (Willey), on Sunday the 24th inst. On Monday I joined Mr. Vaughan in Philadelphia, and I continued there until Thursday 28th, when I went on to Baltimore with Judge Story, Mr. Webster, Mr. Mason and Mr. Ogden. I preached at Baltimore. The next day, Monday, Feb. 1, I went on to Washington, and Tuesday I made calls, accompanied by Mr. Sawyer, of the House, upon the Pres. the heads of departments, the foreign ministers, the senators.
The President was cordial, and asked me to dine every day, and particularly on Friday.
Mr. Clay requested me to preach in the Hall of the House of Representatives the next Sunday, 7 Feb., which I did, to a large and dignified assembly. . . .
Stayed in Washington over 14th, Baltimore, 21, Phila., 23rd.
The beginning of my second week at Washington, i. e., the 7th day—the President requested me to be his guest, i. e., to lodge with him, and mentioned that he had not asked me before, not having a convenient room. Being engaged for every day and evening during my stay, I respectfully declined his kind offer. I dined with him a third time on Sunday, the 14th, when he repeated his invitation, and I therefore accepted it, staying there until Friday morning, i. e., five nights.
. . . I have seen at one dinner the church ministers at N. York, and at another several Presbyterians. But I have not generally found the clergy in my walks. I suppose they purposely often keep out of the way, when they can with decency.

A very moderate statement of the popular views of the College is given in a letter written to President Kirkland, Oct. 26, 1824(2):

---

(1) See letter (hitherto unpublished) in *Harvard College Papers,* Vol. VIII.
(2) See *History of the Harvard Medical School,* by Dr. T. F. Harrington, Vol. II.

In conformity with the letter rec'd from you, I have prepared such a report or answer, as seem'd to become my department.

There is one object involving the interest and prosperity of our College, on which I could not speak in the report; and which, in truth, I must ask leave to confide to you personally.

From many inquiries and much observation, I have come to the conclusion that the popularity and the prosperity of the College is more influenced by religious opinion than any other cause. The difference of political opinion has had comparatively no effect; now, if our College be unpopular, is it to be attributed to its government being in the hands of decided and influential federalists? A large part of this community consists of individuals of religious sentiments opposed to those inculcated at Cambridge. It is thought by some who have studied the matter that two-thirds of the state are strongly opposed to the religious opinions which flow from our alma mater. They complain, with deep feeling, that Cambridge is not merely a literary seminary, but it is a school of sectarian doctrines—doctrines, which they view with alarm and horror. They ask, what necessary connection is there between literature and sectarian religion? Cannot you give us a University, without a school of theology? Cannot our children be permitted to learn the various parts of a scientific education, without imbibing doctrines which we consider poisonous, and which in our view far outweigh the other in importance? Separate the theological school, separate sectarian instruction; give a fair representation to those of different opinions, and we shall no longer hear of new colleges starting up; we shall not be obliged to send our sons 50 or a hundred miles away from us, when the stream of knowledge is floating at our doors.

Such, Sir, is the language which has been held to me repeatedly and earnestly by persons of elevated minds and excellent characters; and I confess, for myself, I am sincerely of opinion that the interest of our University would have them who are anxious for its prosperity and concerned immediately in its welfare, instead of propagating any exclusive sectarianism, rather to build up opportunities for acquiring information from other and opposite denominations of Christians. Sects must exist—they are necessary to the health—to the very life of the Christian religion; but the very necessity of their existence forbids exclusion.

As a rule, much more violent expressions of feeling towards the College were indulged in by those opposed to its religious tenets(1).

---

(1) How unjust was this prejudice against the college for its supposed official Unitarian tendencies, may be seen from the following:
Form of admission to the Church in Harvard University proposed by President Kirkland, Nov. 1, 1814.

These attacks undoubtedly deterred parents from educating their children in the supposedly ungodly institution, and constantly made necessary such explanations as appear in the following letter from Judge Story to his classmate, William Williams, of Tennessee, written Feb. 17, 1823:

You speak of Harvard College. Its prosperity in literature and science is truly great, and in my judgment place it beyond all question, as the first literary institution in America. You have doubtless heard many misrepresentations as to its religious character. I will not disguise that the religious sentiments of its President and Professors are far more liberal than those of our good Doctor Tappan. By liberal, I mean less Calvinistic and more charitable. Unitarian sentiments are certainly prevalent there;— but they are not taught as a part of the studies. . . . I may say, indeed, that by far the most enlightened, learned, and able of our present clergy, as well as laity, in Massachusetts, are Unitarians, and their opinions are manifestly gaining ground. This of course gives much uneasiness to other states, and, as usual, gives rise to many false statements. . . . Our classmate, Dr. Channing is a Unitarian minister of most distinguished talents and character. . . . If you wish to have a child educated at Cambridge, I do not think that you need feel his religious obligations and feelings will be injured. But in making these remarks, I beg you to understand that I myself am a decided Unitarian.

Thus, for religious as well as financial reasons the Law School at Harvard was undoubtedly cut off from the supply of students which it might otherwise have had.

The new professor, Asahel Stearns, was, at that time, a well known lawyer, forty-three years of age, residing in Charlestown.

"We present ourselves for admission to this Church in testimony of our faith in Jesus Christ, our acceptance of his religion, and subjection to his laws. We regard this transaction as an expression of our earnest desire to obtain the salvation proposed in the Gospel, and our serious purpose to endeavour to comply with the terms on which it is offered. We desire to commemorate the author and Finisher of our faith, in the manner established in his church. In a humble and grateful reliance on God for the pardon of sin and assistance in duty, we solemnly take upon ourselves the engagements of the Christian profession. We will, as we shall have opportunity, acknowledge our relations to this Christian community, by attendance on the services of religion, by the office of Christian affection, and by submission to the laws of Christian order, beseeching the God and Father of our Lord, Jesus Christ, that being faithful to each other and to our Common Master, we may enjoy the consolation of our holy religion here, and be accepted to the rewards hereafter, through the riches of divine favour in Jesus Christ. . . . "
See *Harv. Coll. Papers, Supplement,* Vols. V, VI and VII.

He was born in Lunenburg, Massachusetts, June 17, 1774, graduated at Harvard in 1797, and began the practice of the law at Chelmsford. From 1813 to 1832, he served as District Attorney for Middlesex County. In 1817, he had just finished a term at Washington, as a Federalist Congressman, representing the Middlesex District, having been elected for the years 1815-1816. Rev. Dr. Peabody described him as a man "of grave and serious aspect and demeanor, but by no means devoid of humour, and was a favorite in society. . . . He was warmly interested in the public charities of the day, exercised a generous hospitality, and was equally respected and beloved."(1)

A writer in the *Law Reporter* on his death, in 1838, said: "His integrity was not merely that which the world demands and is content with; it was pure, uncompromising, entire. Nor was it mingled with anything of sternness or severity, for his kindness and gentleness were constant and universal."

Mr. Stearns, after taking his election under consideration for about a month, finally accepted, in the following letter, July 5, 1817, characteristically modest(2):

I accept with diffidence the appointment which the corporation and overseers of the University have done me the honor to make.

In taking charge of a new department in this ancient and respectable Institution, I have much reason to fear that I shall be able to fulfill the just expectations of its guardians and friends.

The Corporation had voted, on May 14, 1817, "that the college professors of law be desired to frame a course of instruction for law students, upon which the judges of the Supreme Court are requested to give their advice and opinion"; and that the course proposed be then reported to the Corporation. Professor Stearns at once consulted with the judges, and, within a week after his acceptance, July 11, 1817, he wrote to President Kirkland, the following letter, enclosing a draft for a form of public announcement of the new School:

I have taken the liberty of sketching the outline of a notice, conformable to what I understood to be your views. You will

---

(1) *Old Times at the Law School*, by S. F. Batchelder in *Atlantic Monthly* (Nov., 1902). *Harvard Reminiscences*, by Rev. A. P. Peabody (1888).
(2) See *Harv. Coll. Papers*, Vol. VIII.

please to make such alteration as you deem proper before you add your signature. Not being quite sure that I understood correctly the time you intended the school should open, I have left it blank.

If I have omitted any of the professors who will deliver public lectures, I hope you will be good enough to correct the error.

Perhaps you will think best to omit saying anything about the expense. If you should, you will please to strike it out.

It will be well, I should think, to publish the notices as soon as may be convenient.

I suggested yesterday the propriety of adding, by way of P. S., a request to printers of newspapers in this and adjoining States, to publish the notice. But I submit that to your better judgment.

On Saturday, July 12, 1817, there appeared in the *Boston Daily Advertiser* the following editorial notice:

The Government of Harvard University have lately established under the patronage of the University, a school for the instruction of students at law. . . . The students, besides attending on his lectures and instructions, will have the privilege of attending the lectures of the Royall Professor of Law, and other lectures of the University usually attended by resident graduates . . . will have access to the college library, and a complete Law Library, to be obtained for their use . . . will be permitted to board in commons, on the same terms as other members of the college . . . and on having complied with the regulations of the institution, will receive the degree of bachelor of laws. This school will thus combine advantages for obtaining a complete law education, together with facilities for improvement in the other departments of useful knowledge, never before enjoyed in the country. The school is to go into operation at the commencement of the college term, in October next.

And on July 28, 1817, in the same newspaper, appeared this official notification (which, with a few minor changes in phraseology by President Kirkland, followed Stearns' draft).

Notice is hereby given, that a Law School is established at this University, to commence on the first Wednesday of October, under the superintendance of Hon. Asahel Stearns, University Professor of Law.

Candidates for admission must be graduates of some college, or qualified by the rules of the courts to become students at law, and of good moral character. They will be required to give bond for the payment of the quarterly dues—including the fee for instruction, which is not to exceed $100 annually. Those who desire it will be furnished with commons, upon the same terms as undergraduates, and, as far as possible, with lodging rooms. They will be allowed to attend, free of expense, all the public lectures of the Royall Professor of Law, the private lectures on Intellectual and on Moral and Political Philosophy designed for Graduates, also the publick lectures of the Professors generally, comprising the courses on Theology, Rhetoric and Oratory, Philology, Natural and Experimental Philosophy, Astronomy, Chemistry, and Anatomy and Mineralogy, and other branches relating to Physical Science. The Law Students are to have access to the University Library (consisting of 20000 volumes), upon the same terms as other resident graduates, as well as to the Law Library, which shall be established.

A degree of Bachelor of Laws is instituted in the University, to be conferred upon students as shall have remained at least eighteen months at the University School and passed the residue of their noviciate in a manner approved.

The annual expense of a student, it is believed, will not exceed that of private instruction in any considerable town in New England.

Application in writing, or in person, may be made to the Registrar of the University, or to the President.

John T. Kirkland, President.

Cambridge, July 25.

The following interesting paragraph in Stearns' draft was omitted in the official announcement:

The Corporation has adopted this measure in conformity to the views and wishes of the Judges of the Supreme Court and other distinguished legal characters and with the hope of affording the youth of our country the means of acquiring a more regular and comprehensive law education than is generally attainable in the office of a practising counsellor.

Under the above unpretentious notices, the Harvard Law School opened its doors on the first Wednesday of October, 1817. On November 5, 1817, came the inauguration of Mr. Stearns as University Professor of Law, in the presence of "an unusually large company consisting of strangers of distinction, alumni of the Institution and gentlemen of the first respectability in the higher walks of life . . . with precisely the same forms as customary on such occasions. . . . After the exercises the Corporation, Overseers, and as many as could be accommodated dined together in the Corporation rooms, the rest in the hall below."(1)

---

(1) See *Records of the Board of Overseers.*

CHAPTER XVI.

CAMBRIDGE, AND HARVARD COLLEGE, IN 1817.

Having obtained a professor, the next thing necessary for the new School was a location; and this was provided by a vote of the Corporation, September 5, 1817, as follows:

Voted, that the President may appropriate the lower north room of Mr. Farrar's House to be a Lecture Room and Library for the Professor of Law if it shall appear to be wanted for those purposes.

The "Farrar House," referred to, was a low, two-story, wooden building, situated on the northwest side of what is now Harvard Square, next to the present Lyceum Hall. In this building, two rooms were devoted to the School, one for recitation, the other for a professor's room and library.

Before describing the details of administration of the early years of the School, it may be of interest to give a rough picture of the town of Cambridge and of the College, in 1817.

On the first Wednesday of October, in the year 1817, the Harvard Law School first opened its doors. One lone student registered his name, although five more entered during the year.

The Cambridge, however, to which that solitary student—the predecessor of the 719 law students of to-day—turned his steps, and among whose traditions and conditions the early law students acquired a knowledge of their profession, was a far different place from the city of to-day. It was then a peaceful country town—cut off from Boston by its situation—independent, quiet, and studious.

Perhaps the quaintest contemporary account of it is that given by Timothy Dwight, President of Yale College, in his *Travels in New England*, written in the year 1812(1):

The settlement of Cambridge was begun under the immediate direction of the government, in the year 1631. The town was laid out in squares; one of which was left open for a market,

---

(1)   *Travels in New England*, by Timothy Dwight (1821).

and is now known by the name of Marketplace.(1)   Four of
the streets run from North to South, and three from East to
West.   The houses exhibit every gradation of building, found
in this country, except the log-hut.   Several handsome villas,
and other handsome houses are seen here, a considerable number
of decent ones, and a number, not small, of such as are ordinary
and ill-repaired.   To my eye this last appeared as if inhabited by
Men accustomed to rely on the University for their subsistance;
men, whose wives are the chief support of their families by boarding, washing, mending, and other offices of the like nature.   The
husband, in the mean time, is a kind of gentleman at large; exer-
cising an authoritative control over everything within the purlieus
of the house; reading newspapers, and political pamphlets; deciding on the characters, and measures, of an Administration; and
dictating the policy of his country.   In almost all families of this
class, the mother and her daughters lead a life of meritorious
diligence, and economy: While the husband is merely a bond of
union, and a legal protector of the household.   Accordingly, he
is paid and supported, not for his services, but for his presence.
In every other respect he is merely *nugae canorae;* just such another talking trifle as a parrot; having about as much understanding, and living just about as useful a life; a being, creeping along
the limits of animated and unanimated existence; and serving,
like an oyster, as a middle link between plants and animals.   If
such men are not found here, Harvard College may boast of
exclusive privileges.   This thought struck me irresistibly, as I
was walking in the streets.   How far it is applicable in fact, I am
not informed.

The public buildings in this town, are two churches, a Presbyterian, and an Episcopal; the latter small, and in very bad repair;
a grammar school-house; a court-house; a goal; and an alms-
house.

A more poetic description is given by Lowell, in his memories
of *Cambridge of Thirty Years Ago,* written in 1854:

Approaching it [the town] from the west by what was the
new road(2) you would pause on the brow of Symonds' Hill
to enjoy a view singularly soothing and placid.   In front of
you lay the town, tufted with elms, lindens, and horse-chestnuts,
which had seen Massachusetts a colony and were fortunately
unable to emigrate with the Tories by whom or by whose fathers
they were planted.   Over it rose the noisy belfrey of the College,
the square brown tower of the church, and the slim yellow spire
of the parish meeting-house, by no means ungraceful and the
one invariable characteristic of New England religious archi-

---

(1)   Now (1908) Winthrop Square.
(2)   Now Concord Avenue.

tecture. On your right the Charles slipped smoothly through green and purple salt-meadows, darkened here and there with the blossoming black-grass as with a stranded cloud shadow. Over these marshes, level as water but without its glare, . . . the eye was carried to a horizon of softly rounded hills. To your left hand upon the old road you saw some half-dozen dignified old houses of the colonial time, all comfortably fronting southward. If it were early June the rows of horse-chestnuts along the fronts of these houses showed through every crevice of their heap of foliage and on the end of every drooping limb a cone of pearly flowers . . . Such was the charmingly rural picture which he, who thirty years ago went eastward over Symonds' Hill, had given him for nothing, to hang in the Gallery of Memory. . . . We called it "the Village" then, and it was essentially an English village, quiet, unspeculative, without enterprise, sufficing to itself. A few houses, chiefly old, stood round the bare Common with ample elbow-room.

Up to the beginning of the Nineteenth Century, the two main avenues of the town had been the old highways—the King's Highway, leading from Charlestown to Watertown, and the Turnpike Road to Menotomy, leading from the Great Bridge (built in 1662) along what is now Boylston Street, passing the College buildings, crossing the King's Highway and continuing up Massachusetts Avenue (formerly North Avenue).

In November, 1793, the West Boston Bridge had been built at a cost of $76,000. It was described by the *Independent Chronicle* as "for length, elegance, and grandeur not exceeded by any in the United States, if in any part of the world."(1) The Cambridge and Concord Turnpike was continued a few years later to meet the causeway at the end of the bridge. In 1809, the Canal Bridge (now known as the Craigie or East Cambridge

---

(1) The *Columbian Centinel* of November 27, 1793, in describing the opening of the bridge said: "The elegance of the workmanship and the magnitude of the undertaking, are perhaps unequaled in the history of enterprises. We hope the proprietors will not suffer pecuniary loss from their public spirit."

Judge Iredell of the U. S. Supreme Court, while holding Circuit Court in the Eastern Circuit, wrote to his wife, May 27th, 1795: "The improvements in almost every part of America are wonderful. The bridge between Boston and Cambridge far exceeded my expectations. The causeway leading to Cambridge which is railed in like the bridge is a mile and a quarter long; and the bridge itself three-quarters of a mile, the whole as straight as an arrow; the carriage-way very wide, with passages on each side for foot-passengers, beautifully painted and with an astonishing number of fine lamps all along on each side. The river is very deep and very rapid, notwithstanding which the whole of this bridge was completed, so as to be passable at least, in about six months."

Bridge) was opened; and at the same time Cambridge Street was built, leading from Lechmere Point (East Cambridge) to the Colleges. At this time there was only one dwelling-house on Lechmere Point.

The topography of Cambridge around the College Yard was that of a pleasant country villiage. Near the present corner of Mt. Auburn Street and DeWolfe Street stood, as now, the handsome, square, colonial mansion of Squire William Winthrop, the son of Prof. John Winthrop.

Opposite the College Yard on Braintree Street (later Main Street, now Massachusetts Avenue) was the large estate, and the house (now standing) known as the "Bishop's Palace," built in 1760 by the first Episcopal Rector of Christ Church in Cambridge, Rev. Mr. Apthorp. Farther along to the west on Braintree Street, the other old pre-Revolutionary estates, with their gardens, had only recently been cut up into smaller lots. On the east corner of Braintree Street and Crooked Street, now Holyoke Street (where the Porcellian Club stands), was the store of John Owen, the publisher—the University Bookstore. On the opposite corner of Crooked Street was a dwelling-house. The present site of Sever's Bookstore had been, in the 17th Century, the old village pond, but in 1817 it had long been filled in. Next, on the corner of Dunster Street, stood a house owned by the College, and used as a dormitory (1817-1823), known as College House No. 3. Behind, on Dunster Street, was the old garden of Judge Danforth, and a lot on which stood a printing office, both owned by the College. On the opposite corner of Dunster Street (the home, in 1638, of Stephen Day, the first printer in America) stood Willard's Hotel, where the public booked for places in the hourly stage for Boston, fare twenty-five cents—or for Cambridgeport, fare eighteen and three-quarters cents. "At nine and two o'clock Morse, the stage-driver, drew up in the College Yard and performed upon a tin horn to notify us of his arrival. Those who went to Boston in the evening were generally forced to walk. It was possible, to be sure, to hire a chaise of Jeremy Reed, yet his horses were expensive animals, and he was very particular in satisfying himself of the undoubted credit of those to whom he let them," writes Josiah Quincy, of the Class of 1821, in his *Figures of the Past,* and Dr. A. P. Peabody, of the Class of 1826, speaks of "that dreary walk to Cambridge in dense darkness, with no lights on our way, except dim oil lamps at the toll-houses, over a road believed to be infested with footpads, but on which we neither met nor passed a human being between the bridge and the College Yard. Indeed . . . the road was then so lonely that we used to make up parties of four or five to attend meetings or lectures in Boston."(1)

On the corner of Boylston Street, in 1817, stood Deacon Levi Farwell's country store. Across Harvard Square, on its west side, stood the old Middlesex County Court House (on the present site of the Lyceum Building), a square, wooden building with a cupola, built in 1758, and removed, in 1841, to the corner of Brattle and Palmer Streets (where it now stands). Abandoned for court purposes, when the court moved to East Cambridge, in 1816, it continued to be used for town meetings until 1831; and as Lowell wrote:

The old Court House stood then [1824] upon the Square. It has shrunk back out of sight now; and students box and fence where Parsons once laid down the law, and Ames and Dexter showed their skill in the fence of argument. Times have changed, and manners, since Chief Justice Dana (father of Richard the First and grandfather of Richard the Second) caused to be arrested, for contempt of court, a butcher who had come in without a coat to witness the administration of his country's laws, and who thus had his curiosity exemplarily gratified. Times have changed since the cellar beneath it was tenanted by the twin brothers Snow. Oystermen were they indeed, silent in their subterranean burrow, and taking the ebbs and flows of custom with bivalvian serenity. Careless of the months with an R. in them, the maxim of Snow (for we knew them but as a unit) was "When 'ysters are good, they are good; and when they ain't, they isn't."

For 120 feet north of the Court House, there was a garden, and then an old, two-story, wooden dwelling, with a gambrel roof, much after the style of the present Wadsworth House. It had formerly been occupied by Samuel Webber, President of Harvard College, 1796-1806, at the time when he was Professor of Mathematics and Natural Philosophy. Known at various times as the Williams House, the Russell House, the Farrar

---

(1) It is to be recalled that the first gaslight company in the country—the Boston Gas Light Company—was not incorporated until 1826, and that by 1834 the city of Boston had only 34 gaslights in its streets.

Cambridge Common from the Episcopal Church.

CAMBRIDGE COMMON IN 1805.

From a water-color sketch by D. Bell.

House, and also as College House No. 2—this was the first site of the first Harvard Law School, which occupied two rooms of its lower story. In front was a fence on which the whole Law School of those early days could easily perch. Next to this was a long structure called the Smith House; and on its site a little later, and farther back from the street, was a small one-story building which sheltered the College fire-engine.

About 50 feet north of College House No. 2, and near the location of the present Church Street, was College House No. 1, a wooden three-story building with brick ends, long called by the students "Wiswall's Den." It contained 12 rooms, and these, together with the rooms in College House No. 2, were occupied by law students and undergraduates who could not get rooms in the Yard, and, says Dr. Peabody, "in great part by certain ancient resident graduates who had become water-logged on their life voyage, by preachers who could not find willing listeners, by men lingering on the threshold of professions for which they had neither the courage nor capacity."(1)

In the lower story of this building was Marcus Remy's barber-shop, whose "sunny little room, fronting southwest upon the Common, rang with canaries and Java sparrows," wrote Lowell, and was "a museum of wonders." In it was also a haberdasher's shop, kept by two impoverished ladies of family, who rented to students, at two and three dollars, flimsy gowns for Commencement. Forty-one feet next north, towards the graveyard (where the Unitarian Church now stands), was the Manning House; and next the Deacon Kidder House, both owned and rented by the College.

Cambridge Common then extended from Waterhouse Street to Boylston Street, including the present Harvard Square. It was an unfenced, unimproved, dusty plain,—its grass cut up and scrubby, from the constant passage of herds of cattle driven down the Menotomy and Concord turnpikes on their way to Brighton, Boston, and beyond. On Commencement Days it was used as a great campus for the erection of booths and tents, like a county fair-ground.

In the middle of what is now Harvard Square stood the town pump and scales, and the market-house, a small square one-story

(1) *Sixty Years Ago* in *Harvard Reminiscences,* by A. P. Peabody (1888).

building (removed about 1830). Great elms lined both sides of the Square. In the middle of the Square stood also that old milestone, long located, after 1830, in front of Dane Hall, bearing the apparently lying legend at which so many law students have marveled, "8 miles to Boston A. D. 1737." They forgot that the road to Boston, prior to 1793, was over the Boylston Street Bridge, through Brookline to Roxbury, and over the Neck up Washington Street to the old State House on State Street.

Opposite the College Houses No. 1 and No. 2, in a lot carved out of the College grounds, stood the old meeting-house of the First Church, erected in 1756 on part of the President's orchard. Its north wall occupied the site of the south foundation of the present Dane Hall—"so Law and Divinity rest here on the same base," it has been said. In this building, the Provincial Congress, with John Hancock as its President, had met in 1774. Here, five years later, met the convention which framed the Massachusetts Constitution in 1779. Here, for 70 years, were celebrated all the College Commencement exercises and inauguration ceremonies. Here Lafayette was to be welcomed, seven years later, in 1824. In 1833, the church building was sold to the College and removed.

In the churchyard, near the present corner of Matthews Hall, was the College fire-engine house, before it was moved across the Square. Back of the church was the President's orchard. Next to the church, and standing where it now stands, was the President's, or Wadsworth House, erected in 1726. Sixty feet to the east, in what is now the College grounds, was an old house owned by the College, and rented in 1811 to Professor Ware. One hundred and twenty feet further east, about on the site of the present Boylston Hall, was another old house rented to Professor Hedge. Where the Gate of the Class of '76 now is, and extending back to the present site of Gore Hall, was the lot known as the "Tutor's Lot," or "Tutor's Orchard." East of this was the "ancient and unsightly" parsonage of the First Church, occupied up to 1807 by Rev. Abiel Holmes, the father of Oliver Wendell Holmes.(1) The house on the corner of Quincy Street (now known as the Peabody House) had just been built, in 1811, and was occupied in 1817 by members of the family of Chief Justice Francis Dana.

---

(1) Built in 1670, partly rebuilt in 1790, occupied after 1807 by Prof. Henry Ware, removed in 1843.

In the College Yard, Stoughton Hall, "a neat building," wrote President Dwight, had been built only thirteen years (1804); Holworthy Hall, five years (1812) (1). University Hall, called the "handsomest building in the State," had just been built, (1815), its architect being the famous Charles Bulfinch. In its basement was the College Kitchen. The ground floor had two dining-rooms, one used by seniors and sophomores, the other by freshmen and juniors. In the second and third stories was the College Chapel, with seats on one side for the seniors and sophomores and on the other for the juniors and freshmen, and with different entrance doors, "so that there might be no hostile collision on the stairs," says Dr. Peabody. "In front of the pulpit was a stage for public declamations and exhibitions and on each side of it a raised sentry-box occupied at daily prayers by a professor or tutor on the watch for misdemeanors. Opposite the pulpit was the organ with a double row of raised seats on each side—one for the choir, the other for parietal officers and graduates. There were two side galleries for families of the professors." In the second story of the southern end were two rooms for the use of the Corporation; and at the northern end and in the third story were six recitation rooms. Originally there was a roofed piazza on the front of the building, which was later removed to check the "grouping" of students, then a penal offence.

Just south of where the old College pump so long stood were the College wood-yard, and the College brewery, until it was burned by students in 1814. Massachusetts and Hollis Halls were the other dormitories, having 32 rooms each, the lower floors being reserved for freshmen. Harvard Hall contained the College Library in its second story; and in the lower story were the philosophical and physical chamber and apparatus, and the mineralogical cabinet. Holden Chapel, then divided into two stories, contained in its lower floor the chemical laboratory and lecture-room, and above a lecture-room. "The plan for

---

(1) The following curious letter is to be found in *Harvard College Papers*, Vol. VII, p. 10, written by President Kirkland to Treasurer Davis in 1812: "I find some gentlemen are sorry to have our new college receive so hard a name—Holworthy Hall—has two aspirates besides the W. & the T. H.—which twist and squeeze the organs not a little. Is there any other better or more suitable—or will you reconsider on account of the objection—which is of some consequence."

locating these buildings, if any such plan existed, was certainly unfortunate," wrote Timothy Dwight in 1812.

On Holyoke Street, not far down from the corner of Mt. Auburn Street, lived Professor Willard, in the former home of Dr. Holyoke, President of the College. A house where the Roman Catholic Church stands, on the corner of Holyoke and Mt. Auburn Streets, had been the home of the famous Judge Edmund Trowbridge; and was in 1817 the home of the children of Chief Justice Dana. On Dunster Street, near the corner of Winthrop Street, was the site of the first tavern of the town, inhabited in 1817 by Thaddeus W. Harris, later the College Librarian. Between Dunster and Boylston Streets lived the postmaster, Joseph S. Read, with whom many early law students lodged. On the corner of Boylston Street and Winthrop Square was the house of Judge James Winthrop, the Register of Probate, and not far off on Winthrop Street was the Jail. Opposite Judge Winthrop's, on the corner of Mt. Auburn and Boylston Streets, was the famous Blue Anchor Tavern, or Porter's, as it was known in 1817—the great resort for students, and famous for its punch on Commencement Days.

West of Brattle Square (where Brattle Hall now is) was the town spring, and a good-sized pond with an island, and handsome grounds extending to the river. On this estate stood the Brattle House, in which Margaret Fuller lived in 1833, and which was long used as a student's lodging-house in the 20's and 30's. In the 50's the pond was filled up; and a large, square, ugly hotel, known as Brattle House, was built on its site, later purchased by the Law School for a dormitory, and still later sold to John Wilson's University Press. Windmill or Bath Lane (Ash Street) led to a bathing-place for students on the river.

In the Craigie House, in 1815, was living Dr. Andrew Craigie, who built the Lechmere Point or East Cambridge Bridge. Seven years later, in 1822, Edward Everett, then Professor of Greek, boarded there for a few years; and in 1837 Professor Henry W. Longfellow took rooms in this house, which he bought later. Farther to the west on Brattle Street was "Tory Row"—the estates of many Royalists whose property had been confiscated. The estate now known as "Elmwood" had been owned by Elbridge Gerry, until his death, in 1812, while Vice-President of the United States; six years later, in 1818, Rev. Charles Lowell, son of Judge John Lowell, bought it; and on Feb. 22, 1819, James Russell Lowell was born there.(1)

In the house on the corner of Garden and Mason Streets (now Radcliffe College), in 1817, lived Joseph McKean, Professor of Rhetoric and Oratory. In the northwest room, in 1836, Rev. Samuel Gilman, of Charleston, while a guest at the celebration of the 200th Anniversary, wrote *Fair Harvard*. On Waterhouse Street, facing the Common, William Ware, the author of *Zenobia*, was living in 1817. On Holmes Place, near the site of the present Austin Hall of the Law School, there were four houses, in the second of which lived Rev. Caleb Gannett. Here later was the station of the Harvard Branch of the Fitchburg Railroad, and still later the College eating-house for students, known as Thayer Commons. Nearer the present Gymnasium was the old Holmes House, from which Gen. Joseph Warren went to the Battle of Bunker Hill. In 1807, Judge Oliver Wendell purchased it; and there Oliver Wendell Holmes was born, in 1809. The first house on Kirkland Street was the home of Stephen Higginson, Jr., the College Steward, where, in 1823, Thomas Wentworth Higginson was born. Beyond this, extending to the Charlestown line, were the 120 acres of the Foxcroft Estate, on which stood the house of James Hayward, later Professor of Mathematics; the house near the corner of Oxford Street, in which Asahel Stearns, first professor of the Law School, lived; the house of John Farrar, Professor of Mathematics and Natural Philosophy; and that of Rev. Henry Ware, Hollis Professor of Divinity, in which Charles Eliot Norton now lives. This was the so-called "Professors' Row."

In 1817, that part of Cambridge east of Quincy Street and extending to the Neck, including Cambridgeport, was mostly pastures, woodland, salt marsh and flats, formerly owned by the Goffe and Inman families. As late as 1793, there were only four houses on this great tract—the principal one being near Dana Street, formerly owned by Judge Edmund Trowbridge

---

(1) Judge Iredell wrote to Mrs. Iredell Oct. 7, 1792, from Boston: "I persuaded our driver to go a little out of his usual route that I might see Cambridge, the seat of the University of this State, and about 3½ miles from town across the famous Charlestown Bridge. I had great reason to be satisfied, for it is a most beautiful place and contains many very elegant houses. Mr. Gerry among others has a delightful one in a most beautiful situation. . . . The bridge fully equaled my expectations; it is indeed a very noble one."

and occupied by Chief Justice Dana till his death in 1811. Here
Rev. William Ellery Channing had his home during his college
course, up to 1798. The only other house of importance was the
Inman House, a little south of the site of the present City Hall.

After the building of the West Boston Bridge, in 1793, land
speculators put up several brick buildings; a store and a dwelling-house were built on the causeway near the corner of Main
and Front Streets, in 1793 and 1795; and several taverns and
a scattered group of houses were built a few years later; so
that in 1806 there were about 100 families living in the Port.
The Cambridge and Concord Turnpike Corporation, chartered
in 1803, had extended its turnpike to the West Boston Bridge
in 1805. But, in general, Cambridgeport was not a place of much
size or prosperity. "In January, 1805, an act of Congress made
this place a Port of Delivery, and from which it derived the
name of Cambridgeport. Anticipation looked forward to its
becoming a commercial place, and the borders of Charles River
the depot of its active operation. Roads and canals were formed
for its accommodation at great expense, and wharves to some
extent were actually constructed. An earthquake could have
been but little less destructive to these enterprises than was the
embargo." So writes an old resident. "This horned calamity
(the Embargo Acts 1807-1809) palsied the energies of this
thrifty village, and produced a torpor and protracted debility
which all her efforts could never shake off."[1]

President Dwight wrote of it in 1812:

Since the building of West Boston Bridge, the current of
travelling from the interiour country to the Capital has extensively passed through this town. Under the influence of speculation, a village has been raised up at the Western End of the
bridge, called Cambridge Port. Here, it was supposed, trade
might be made to flourish, and mechanical business be extensively
done. It is doubtful whether the golden expectations, cherished
by the proprietors of the ground, will be speedily realized. The
neighborhood of the capital, and the superiour facilities which
it furnishes for commercial enterprise, will probably be a lasting
hindrance to all considerable mercantile efforts, on this spot.

And Lowell wrote:

---

(1) See letter in *An Account of Some of the Bridges over Charles
River*, by Isaac Livermore (1858).

Cambridge has long had its Port, but the greater part of its maritime trade was, thirty years ago, intrusted to a single Argo, the sloop Harvard, which belonged to the College and made annual voyages to that vague Orient known as Down East, to bring back the wood that in those days gave to winter life at Harvard, a crackle and cheerfulness, for the loss of which the greater warmth of anthracite hardly compensates. . . . The greater part of what is now Cambridgeport was then a "huckleberry pasture." The chief feature of the place was its inns of which there were five with vast barns and courtyards. . . . There were, besides the taverns, some huge square stores where groceries were sold, some houses by whom or why inhabited was to us boys a problem, and, on the edge of the marsh, a currier's shop. . . . The marshes also had been bought, canals were dug, ample for the commerce of both Indies; and four or five rows of brick houses were built to meet the first wants of the wading settlers who were expected to rush in— whence?

Such was the Cambridge of early Law School days(1).

Of Harvard College a quaint general description is given in the *Massachusetts Magazine* for June, 1790:

The seat of this University is a dry, healthy plain, four miles westward of Boston. It enjoys a fine air and commands an agreeable prospect. It has a spacious area in which the students divert themselves in their hours of relaxation with various manly and athletic exercises. They have four vacations in the year which altogether take up three months. The other nine are divided into four terms during which their absence is not permitted without special cause and express license from their governor. All possible care is taken of their morals as well as of their studies; and they have every generous inducement to be diligent and improve it—There is an impartial execu- meeting of the Overseers May 3, 1814, as follows:

For years, it had been the custom for the Board of Overseers to appoint a Committee "to visit the University and inquire into the state of it and consider what may be done to increase its usefulness and respectability." Such a Committee consisting of Hon. Benjamin Pickman, Jr., Hon. William Prescott, Rev. W. W. Eliot, Rev. Mr. Walley and Rev. Mr. Lowell, reported at a meetieng of the Overseers May 3, 1814, as follows:

---

(1) In the preparation of this chapter the author has been much assisted by the admirable *Historic Guide to Cambridge*, issued by the Hannah A. Winthrop Chapter of the Daughters of the American Revolution.

That the number of undergraduates is about 290,(1) that large as the number is, no serious disturbances have taken place since the last report on the subject: On the contrary, that the deportment of the scholars has been quite as correct and their attention to their studies as great if not greater than usual; that the performances of the young gentlemen who had parts alotted to them at the late exhibition did honor to the college and must have been highly gratifying to their friends who attended it. . . .

The Professor of Rhetorick complained of the highly indecorous and injurious habit of expressing approbation at the publick declamations by clapping their hands and sometimes stamping their feet—also of the exercises of the college military company in the vicinity of his dwelling house. . . . The Professor of Mathematics and the Tutors in Geography & Natural Philosophy observed that their exercises had been better attended to than usual. The adjunct Professor of Chemistry desired a complete chemical apparatus. . . .

The committee have only to express their full belief that the college was never in a more flourishing state than it is at present, whether regard be had to the respectability of its Instructors, to the number and character of the students, or the many and great advantages placed in their hands.(1)

The well known lawyer William Tudor, in his *Letters on the Eastern States,* written in 1820, gives the following suggestive account of the College:

The number of students is commonly about 250. The resident graduates have increased of late years, and are now 50 or 60. The expense of an education at this seminary, for lodging and instruction, is about one thousand dollars for the whole term of four years. The private expenses will be according to the discretion of the parent or guardian. There are several little aids given to poor scholars, to assist them in their necessary disbursements.

There are some improvements to be made, which will tend to

---

(1) In 1819, the number of Undergraduates was 272; Medical students, 58; Divinity School students, 30; Resident Graduates, 12.

The first annual catalogue of Harvard College issued in book or octavo form with 16 pages was in 1819. Prior to that, annual catalogues had been issued on broadsides. The first printed annual catalogue was that of October, 1803. In 1825, the first annual catalogue in duodecimo form was issued. Prior to 1803, triennial catalogues containing lists of graduates had been issued from a very early date, the first known printed one being in 1674. The first printed triennial catalogue in book of octavo form was in 1776.

See *Triennial and Annual Catalogues of Harvard University,* by J. L. Sibley, *Mass. Hist. Soc. Proc.* Vol. VIII.

(1) See *Records of the Board of Overseers,* in the *Harvard College Archives.*

raise the character and enlarge the utility of this establishment
. . . One of these is to multiply the number of resident graduates. This will enlarge the society, and excite
sympathy and emulation among young men whose minds are
matured, and who can attend the lectures and pursue the particular studies they prefer, without the restrictions necessarily
imposed on undergraduates. The standard of education will
become higher, if the three years between the two degrees are
devoted to a course of liberal study, to accomplishing the mind
with general knowledge, before it is exclusively given up to one
particular profession. The students in divinity and law, as
well as all young men whose fortune prevents the necessity of
their choosing a profession, would be greatly benefited by a
studious residence here of two or three years. The students
in medicine are more desirous of being in a large town, as their
studies are so closely connected with practice. The greatest
number of resident graduates at present are divinity students;—
the law school is of recent foundation; but it will add very much
to the character of young men, if they pass two or three years
at Cambridge in the study of polite literature, philosophy, and
the elementary parts of law, before they plunge into the narrow
details of an attorney's practice.

Another improvement would be, a strict examination of the
students, before receiving their degrees, and making honorary
distinctions among them, according to their merits, as is done
in the English universities. (1)

It will be noted that in the official announcement of the founding of Law School, in 1817, much stress was laid upon the advantage to be enjoyed by law students, through the privilege
extended to them of attending the lectures of the College pro-

(1) So far as its methods of instruction were concerned, the College
was decidedly retrograde. They are best described in a letter from George
Ticknor to President Hill, Feb. 4, 1863:

"When I was a teacher from 1819 to 1821, the College was in a low state.
The classes were not divided into sections and no class received a lesson
above half an hour long. Lectures were very few, and, except Prof.
Farrar's, purely formal. From 1821 to 1825, some improvements were
introduced. The classes were divided—the recitations were lengthened,
and free lecturing was begun. This imperfect state of things before 1825,
you will find tenderly explained and a good deal smoothed over in the
pamphlet entitled *Remarks on Changes, etc.*, pp. 3-11. The improvements
that it was then thought might be ventured, but by no means all that had
been suggested or were deemed advisable you will find set forth at pp.
32-46. These improvements, however, though they were carried out without difficulty in the Department of Modern Languages (Ticknor's own
department) were opposed by the other teachers, and failed; and in consequence of which, seeing no hope of changing the College into an open
University I resigned in the winter of 1834-5."

See *Harv. Coll. Papers*, 2d Series, Vol. XXX.

fessors. And it cannot be doubted that this privilege formed a considerable inducement and attraction to those who joined the School. In fact, as will be seen in later chapters, many law students have testified to the great and enjoyable extent to which they availed themselves of this opportunity of combining a legal education with a liberal education in other subjects.

Of the Professors of the College at this time, it has been said that they formed "a group of men unequalled in America in varied cultivation and the literary spirit."

John Quincy Adams had been appointed Boylston Professor of Rhetoric and Oratory, in 1806, a distinctly advanced step in intellectual training, of which his two volumes of lectures still give proof. He was succeeded, in 1809, by Joseph McKean, whose place in turn was taken, in 1819, by Edward T. Channing, of whom it has been said "no American professor ever exercised so prolonged and unquestionable a literary influence or trained so many distinguished authors."

Levi Hedge had been appointed Professor of Logic and Metaphysics, in 1810. Rev. Henry Ware had been Hollis Professor of Divinity, since 1805; Sidney Willard, Hancock Professor of Hebrew and Oriental languages, since 1807; Levi Frisbie, Professor of Latin, since 1811; Edward Everett, Eliot Professor of Greek Literature, since 1815; John Farrar, Professor of Mathematics and Natural Philosophy, since 1807; John S. Popkin, Professor of Greek, since 1815; William D. Peck, Professor of Natural History, since 1805. In 1816, George Ticknor became Smith Professor of French and Spanish languages. In 1816, Jacob Bigelow became Rumford Professor on the Application of Science to the Useful Arts, and John Gorham became Erving Professor of Chemistry and Materia Medica. In 1817, Jared Sparks was Tutor of History.(1)

The College Treasurer was Hon. John Davis; the College Librarian, Andrews Norton; the College Steward, Caleb Gannett.

No less important in his influence on the students—undergraduates, and students of the professional schools—was the President of the College.

---

(1) In 1825, Charles Folsom became Instructor in Italian. In 1822, George Bancroft became Tutor in Greek. In 1825, Charles Follen became Instructor in German; and in 1826, Pietro Bachi, Instructor in Italian, Spanish and Portugese. Francis Sales had been Instructor in French and Spanish, since 1816.

HARVARD COLLEGE IN 1805.

Cambridge Common from the west. Caleb Gannett, Esq.

Comp. Steward & Ster. of Harvard University

In 1810, Rev. John Thornton Kirkland, for sixteen years pastor of the New South Church in Boston, had been inaugurated President of Harvard College. Commanding as he did the support, confidence and enthusiasm of the most intellectual, cultivated, public spirited, and wealthy men of Boston, he had raised the College to the rank of a true University.

Of his personal characteristics, James Russell Lowell gives a vivid description:

There was in the soft and rounded (I almost said melting) outlines of his face which reminded me of Chaucer—He was an anachronism, fitter to have been an Abbot of Fountains or Bishop Golias, courtier and priest, humorist, lord spiritual all in one, than for the mastership of a provincial college, which combined with its purely scholastic functions, those of accountant and chief of police. For keeping books he was incompetent (unless it were those he borrowed) and the only discipline he exercised was by the unobtrusive pressure of a gentlemanliness, which rendered insubordination to him impossible.

Possibly his sense of discipline was a trifle lax, as Lowell wrote:

Under him flourished the Harvard Washington Corps, whose gyrating banner on the evening of training days was an accurate dynamometer of Williard's punch or Porter's flip.(1) Under him the Med Facs took their equal place among the learned societies of Europe, numbering among their grateful honorary members, Alexander, Emperor of all the Russias. Under him the College fire engine was vigilant and active in suppressing any tendency to spontaneous combustion among the freshmen, or rushed wildly to imaginary conflagrations, generally in a direction where punch was to be had.

He knew human nature, however, and above all, student nature.

To the Harvard Washington Corps which applied for leave to go into Boston to a collation offered to them, he replied, "Certainly, young gentlemen, but have you engaged anyone to bring home your muskets" (the College being responsible for the weapons belonging to the State). Again, when a student armed with a physician's certificate asked for leave of absence, Presi-

(1) The Harvard Washington Corps had been organized in 1811, George Thacher of the class of 1812 being its first captain. See for an interesting account of this corps *A Collection of College Words and Customs,* by Benjamin H. Hall (1851); also see *The Harvard Book.*

dent Kirkland granted it, but added, "By the way, Mr. ———, persons interested in the relation which exists between states of the atmosphere and health, have noticed a curious fact in regard to the climate of Cambridge, especially within the College limits —the very small number of deaths in proportion to the cases of dangerous illness."

And Dr. Peabody wrote:

Probably no man ever held office in a literary institution with so entirely unanimous respect, admiration and love on the part of his pupils. He knew them all; and with few exceptions he knew all about them and about their parents . . . .He examined the successive classes on their admission, in Virgil's Georgics; but his scrutiny was directed much more to the countenance, the family traits and the indications of character, than to the token of scholarship; and a face thus seen was never forgotten; so that he always addressed students by name. . . .
With all his kindness he had a marvellously quick and sharp eye for trickery and falsity. . . . His personal presence, always dignified and graceful, became on important occasions absolutely august and majestic. No one that witnessed it could ever forget his reception of Lafayette in front of University Hall and his presentation of the students to the illustrious guest.

Such was the President, under whom the Law School was founded.

CHAPTER XVII.

The First Decade.

So far as is known the Law School started with one student —Charles Moody Dustin; and the number entering during the first year was six.

The principal instruction was of course given by Professor Stearns, although the fifteen lectures of Judge Parker as Royall Professor were considered a branch of the Law Department and were attended by the law students, during May and June in the Third Term, when they were given three or four times a week, at ten o'clock in the morning.(1)

No record is extant showing the exact course of study in the early years of the School; but it probably followed along the same general lines as that described in the report made by Professor Stearns to the Board of Overseers, in 1825:

A course of study has been drawn up with much care, under the advice of the judges of the Supreme Court and other distinguished jurists, and with reference to a term of 3 years within which period it can be established. . . .

In the first place a reading of *Blackstone,* more or less particular, of the whole work. This practise has been found by experience to be highly useful. It aids the student in fixing his attention, enables him more readily to acquaintance with the technical terms and language of the law, and at the same time to obtain a more distinct view of that admirable outline of the science. . . . For those gentlemen who do not pursue the study of the law as a Profession, the plan of instruction is varied by substituting for what relates to the practice, a more extended course of reading on the Civil Law, the Law of Nations, Constitutional Law and Political Economy.

---

(1) See letter of Judge Parker to President Kirkland of May 9, 1818, stating that he had heretofore occupied 5 days in the week for lectures, and "calculating upon the same course I have entered into official engagements which required my attendance as early as the 27th June; of course if I should be restricted to 3 days in the week after the 6th of June, I shall not have time to finish. It so happens that the doctor (Bigelow) wishes a dispensation for a week or two in the early part of June and thinks it will be convenient that I should have his days during that time.

If this arrangement cannot be made I must beg to be allowed to begin on Monday the 22nd of this month."

See *Harvard College Archives, Harvard College Papers,* Vol. VIII.

The first description of the method of instruction is contained in Professor Stearns' report to the Overseers, Jan. 9, 1826:

The experience of eight years since the Law School was established has led to several considerable improvements upon its original plan; and the utility of the present system of instruction seems to be fully evinced by the industry, limitation, and rapid improvement of the student.

The regular exercises of the School are the following, viz.:

1. *Recitations and Examinations* in several of the most important text books, such as *Blackstone's Commentaries Cruise on Real Property, Saunders on Uses, Fearne on Remainders,* etc.

In these exercises the points of difference between the law of England and of our own country are carefully distinguished and the grounds and occasions of the difference are fully explained to the students.

2. *Written lectures* embracing a general course of legal instruction, in which those parts of our system of jurisprudence in which we do not adopt the law of England are particularly noticed, and the grounds of our departure from it are explained and illustrated by the decisions and practice of our own courts.

3. *A Moot Court* in which questions are regularly argued (often at considerable length) before the Professor, who pronounces an opinion. In these fictitious actions the pleadings, bills of exceptions, demurrers to evidence, special verdicts and motions in arrest of judgment or for a new trial are drawn up in form by the students.—During the argument those students who are not of counsel are employed in taking minutes, with a view to the acquisition of facility and accuracy preparatory to practice. The cases to be argued are, of course, adapted to the progress of the respective students in their professional studies. But they are strongly urged to engage in them very soon after their commencement; it having been found by experience that no other exercise is so powerful an excitement to industry and emulation or so strongly interests the students in their professional pursuits.

4. *Debating Clubs* including all the members of the Law School in which some question (generally in moral philosophy, political economy, or civil polity) which admits an extended and free discussion, is debated once a week with a view to improvement in extempore elocution.

5. *Written dissertations* by the student upon some title or branch of the law or the history of some department of legal or political science.

Most of the students at this time, as appears from the *First Record Book of the Law School (1817-1840),* had had nearly two years study in a law office prior to entering the School, and were thus supposed to be grounded on the technical details of practice.

In the academic year 1818-19, eight students entered the School, the most prominent of whom was Caleb Cushing of Newburyport, Mass., (later judge of the Massachusetts Supreme Court and Attorney General of the United States under President Peirce).

THE DARTMOUTH COLLEGE CASE.

These first two years of the Law School were years of great anxiety to all educational institutions; for during them, the great case of *Trustees of Dartmouth College v. Woodward* was argued in New Hampshire, and on appeal in the United States Supreme Court. The immediate question involved was the right of the State Legislature to amend the charter of Dartmouth College without the assent of its governing officials. The broad question involved was whether a legislative charter was a contract, which, under the Constitution of the United States, a State was forbidden to impair.

Harvard College had a very lively and serious interest in the outcome of this case; for the Legislature of Massachusetts, only five years before the founding of the Law School, had done exactly what the Legislature of New Hampshire had attempted in the Dartmouth College case. The facts had been as follows:

In 1806, the workings of the old Board of Overseers of Harvard College having become inconvenient, Chief Justice Theophilus Parsons (then a Fellow of the Corporation) framed an act which passed the Legislature, March 6, 1810, changing the constitution of the Board; but Parsons had inserted a clause that the act should be subject to acceptance by the Corporation and the Board of Overseers. This acceptance was given. In 1812, however, the Republicans being in office in Massachusetts, a new act was passed Feb. 29, 1812, without any such clause, taking effect without the requirement of any such acceptance, repealing the act of 1810 and re-establishing the old Board. The validity of this act was at once denied, and two Boards of Overseers organized. The old Board for various reasons however had thought best to submit after protest, and the question had been solved without litigation by another change in the State administration in 1814, when the Legislature repealed the Act of 1812, and restored the provisions of the Act of 1810, calling for 30 elective Overseers, (15 laymen and 15 clergymen) and adding the members of the State Senate.

Thus the legal status of Harvard College had never been settled by judicial decision at the time when this Dartmouth College case was instituted. The case was argued in the fall of 1817, before the Superior Court of New Hampshire, at that time consisting of Chief Justice William Marchant Richardson, (a Harvard graduate of 1797, classmate of Professor Asahel Stearns, and Horace Binney) and of Associate Judges Samuel Bell and Levi Woodbury (both Dartmouth graduates). The counsel were Jeremiah Mason, Jeremiah Smith, Daniel Webster, and Timothy Farrar for the Trustees; and Ichabod Bartlett and George Sullivan for the defendant.

On Nov. 6, 1817, the Court, after brilliantly able arguments, decided the case against the contention of the old Trustees.

Arrangements were at once made for an appeal to Washington; and Daniel Webster took up a heavy collection among Boston merchants and others interested in the cause of education. President Francis Brown of Dartmouth wrote to President Kirkland of Harvard, Nov. 15, 1817(1):

The suit instituted by the charter Trustees of this College against Judge Woodward, their late Secretary and Treasurer, and which was designed to try the validity of certain acts of the Legislature of N. H. virtually revoking the charter issued in a decision by our Sup. Court unfavorable to the Trustees. In this case a writ of error lies to the Sup. Court of the United States, and to that court they have already taken measures to transfer the action.

The prosecution of it to a final decision at Washington will of course require a considerable expense. This expense from our limited means we are unable to meet without calling on the benevolent and wealthy for pecuniary aid.

Our friends in N. H. have already taxed themselves somewhat severely for paying the salaries of officers and for other purposes during the continuance of the struggle.

In this state of things we have thought it right to make an appeal by private communication to the friends of literature and religion abroad. Our cause, we think, has now become substantially the cause of every literary establishment in the country; for it is to be decided by the highest of our judicial tribunals whether charter rights are to be held sacred or whether they may

---

(1)   See letter, (hitherto unpublished) in *Harv. Coll. Papers,* Vol. VIII.

be infringed at pleasure, accordingly as legislative caprice, or party violence shall dictate. And we believe that the friends of other colleges will feel that they shall be contributing to the general interests of religion and learning by affording us help in the present exigency. It is this belief which encourages me now to address you and to request that you will employ what influence you may think proper with the opulent in Boston and its vicinity to aid in procuring funds for prosecuting the cause in the ablest manner through the Sup. Court of U. S.

We expect Mr. Webster to take charge of the action and should feel perfectly safe to entrust it wholly to his management. But possibly he may request an associate; or not improbably it may be thought expedient by our friends abroad, that another able lawyer should join him. In this case we should apply to some southern gentleman, perhaps Mr. L. Martin of Baltimore.

I have written to no other gentleman connected with Harvard except Judge White of Salem.

It is a curious fact that no history, so far as is known, has ever mentioned the intention to secure the services of Luther Martin in the case, as referred to in the above letter. Martin however was not employed; and Webster retained Joseph Hopkinson of Pennsylvania; while William Wirt of Maryland and John Holmes of Maine appeared for Woodward. On March 10-12, 1818, the case was argued before the United States Supreme Court. The counsel for the Trustees however so far over-matched their opponents that the argument was regarded as a legal fiasco for the appellees; and with a view to re-argument they sought to bring into the case the leader of the American Bar—William Pinkney—as the only man who could meet Webster on anything like equal ground.

After the argument, the judges being apparently in hopeless disagreement, the case was continued for a year—to the February term of 1819. Meanwhile the parties interested set actively to work to influence public sentiment. Copies of Webster's argument were sent broadcast throughout New England, and by Webster himself to Judge Story for the other judges(1). The

(1) See Webster to Story, Sept. 9, 1818.

"I send you 5 copies of our argument. If you send one to each of such of the judges as you think proper, you will of course do it in the manner least likely to lead to a feeling that any indecorum has been committed by the plaintiff. The truth is the N. H. opinion is able, ingenious and plausible. It has been widely circulated and something was necessary to exhibit the other side of the question."

Webster's Correspondence, Vol. I.

extent to which the attempt to influence the Court was pushed—
a proceeding of somewhat doubtful character, to the eyes of
lawyers of today—may be seen from the following letter written by Chief Justice Isaac Parker, then Royall Professor of Law,
to Daniel Webster, April 28, 1818:

The effect produced upon my mind by the argument you were
good enough to send me is such as to induce me most earnestly
to wish that it may not only be printed but published and extensively circulated. Public sentiment has a great deal to do in
affairs of this sort, and it ought to be well founded. That
sentiment may even reach and affect a court; at least if there
be any members who wish to do right, but are a little afraid, it
will be a great help to know that all the world expects they will
do right. Besides, there is a natural leaning in favor of legislative power, for it is the power of the people, when constitutionally exercised; but the people ought to be made to know that in
certain cases their rights are above the reach of the Legislature,
and thus popularity may be given to a denial of legislative power.
. . . It is of importance to enlist all enlightened men on
your side of the question, not merely on account of Dartmouth College. Every institution in the country is liable to the
same attack and must be defended on the same principles.
. . I think also that every judge of the Supreme Court of
United States ought to have a copy of this argument.

The decision in the case was rendered by the Supreme Court
Feb. 2, 1819—an opinion in favor of the College, described by
Joseph Hopkinson, one of the counsel, as based "upon principles
broad and deep, and which secure corporations of this description
from legisislative despotism and party violence for the future."

THE FIRST LAW DEGREE.

In the first annual Catalogue of Harvard University, issued in
October, 1819, appear the names of eleven law students, room-
ing in 2 College House, 3 College House and at Prof. Willard's,
Mrs. Gilman's, Mr. Read's and Mrs. Porter's.

Of these students three attained some degree of distinction—
Benjamin F. Hallett, whose name became widely known in the
1850's, because of his connection as United States District
Attorney with the Fugitive Slave Cases in Boston; Joseph Willard; and Samuel E. Sewall, noted later as a prominent abolition-
ist lawyer.

It is interesting to note that the students of the first ten years of the Law School were obliged to undergo a written examination in order to qualify for the degree—although when Professor Langdell introduced written examinations for a degree in 1871, none had been given for forty years previously.

As early as November 16, 1819, the matter of degrees had received the attention of the Corporation, who voted:

that Mr. Lowell, Judge Jackson and Judge Story be a Committee to examine in such way as they may think most suitable, the candidates for the Degree of Bachelor of Laws at the next Commencement and report upon their qualifications to this Board.

On August 29, 1820, the Corporation accepted a report of John Lowell, Chairman of a Committee appointed June 12, 1820, to examine candidates, as follows:

At a meeting of the Faculty of Law at the College Aug. 28, 1820, the board proceeded to the examination of the candidates for the degree of Bachelor of Laws; and the following gentlemen having given satisfactory evidence of their having complied with the statutes on this subject and having read Dissertations on questions previously proposed to them by the Board, in which they evinced their diligence, learning and accuracy, it was unanimously agreed to recommend them to the Rev. Overseers and Corporation as duly qualified.

SUBJECTS ASSIGNED FOR THE DISSERTATIONS.

1—*The Rules of Descent and Distribution of Real and Per sonal Property by the Civil Law, the Law of England and the Law of Massachusetts.*
2—*The several injuries to which the Heir is liable in relation to his right of succession to Real Property, and the several remedies by Entry or Action which are furnished by the Laws of England and of Massachusetts.*

This report was accompanied by the certificate of Asahel Stearns, University Professor of Law, as follows(1):

I certify that Messrs. Charles F. Gore, Wyllis Lyman, John W. Porter, Samuel Edmund Sewall, William R. P. Washburn and Joseph Willard, all of whom are graduates have been members of the University Law School one year and a half or more, during all which time each of them has pursued his legal studies with diligence and success.

---

(1) See *Harv. Coll. Papers*, Vol. IX.

I further certify that each has produced to me satisfactory evidence of having completed the period of his noviciate as required by the statutes of the University to entitle them to be candidates for the degree of Bachelor of Laws. Messrs. Proctor, Washburn and Willard have been duly admitted to practice more than six months.

Thereupon the Corporation voted "that the degree of LL.B. be conferred on each of the said candidates"; and accordingly on Commencement Day, August 30, 1820, the following gentlemen, none of whom were Harvard College graduates, and three of whom had already been admitted to practice in the courts, became the first Harvard Bachelors of Law, and received the first Harvard degrees entitling them to write LL.B. after their names— Charles E. Gore, a Dartmouth graduate; and five Yale graduates—Wyllys Lyman, John W. Proctor, Samuel E. Sewall, William R. R. Washburn, and Joseph Willard.

In the year 1820-21, the Law School after three years of existence, appeared to the Corporation to have justified itself; and it seemed wise to enlarge its teaching force. The eyes of the Corporation naturally turned to the Massachusetts lawyer, who, excepting Webster, had the greatest national reputation as a jurist. Through his opinion in the great case of *Dartmouth College v. Woodward,* which had been decided in the Supreme Court at Washington only five months previously, and through his decisions in the prize, admiralty and patent cases in the Circuit Court, Judge Story's legal fame had been steadily growing brighter. In 1818, he had become connected with the College, through his election as an Overseer. Accordingly, the Corporation, on August 10, 1820, requested the President and Mr. Lowell "to consider the expediency of adding another Professor to the Law Faculty and consulting with the present Professors."

The project met with hearty co-operation from Professors Stearns and Parker; and on Commencement Day in 1820, the Corporation voted to ask the President and Mr. Lowell:

to communicate with Justice Story respecting the office of a Professor of maritime, commercial and publick law,—it having appeared to the Corporation that such a professorship would be an important and useful addition to the Law School and the University. They have thought that it might consist with the views and disposition of Judge Story to occupy such a chair, or, at least, that he might think a proposal of this nature worthy of his attention and consideration; not that it would be necessary to confine his lectures to the branches mentioned, but convenient to have them constitute the designation of the professorship and its principal objects.

Sensible of the benefits and reputation which would accrue to the University and the Law School from his connexion with the Seminary in this department, the Corporation are in hopes that he may regard the subject in a favorable light.

Judge Story considered the offer carefully; but owing to the importance of his work on the Supreme Bench, he felt that he could not combine the two positions, and he therefore declined.

In 1820-21, according to the College Catalogue, the number of law students had increased to thirteen, two of whom are especially to be noted; one, Emory Washburn, later Governor of Massachusetts, and Professor in the Law School from 1856 to 1876; the other, Rufus Choate. While at Dartmouth College, Choate had been advised by his brother-in-law Dr. Thomas Sewall of Washington to enter Mr. Webster's office.

I am aware, Rufus, that you have too much independence to be greatly influenced in your future course by the advice of any one, yet you have, I am persuaded, too much candor to be offended if I tell you what my feelings and opinions are on this subject,— a subject deeply interesting to me as well as to your other friends. . . . I doubt whether there is any place where you would pursue your studies to greater advantage than at Washington. . . . Taking these and many other things into view, I must advise that you commence your course with Webster. Him you will find a different man from what you can have an idea of without a more intimate acquaintance, a friend, a companion, and equal. I am fully satisfied that you will find his office a better place to become an active lawyer, politician, and man of usefulness, than at Cambridge.(1)

But having decided to first take a course at the Harvard Law School, Choate entered in the summer of 1820, induced undoubtedly by the superior advantages which the College could hold out. "I was accustomed to meet him more frequently than other persons of his standing in the library of the University," said Edward Everett who was then Professor of Greek Literature.(2)

In 1821, however, Choate left Cambridge to enter the office of

(1) *Life of Rufus Choate*, by Samuel G. Brown (1878).
(2) *Address on Death of Rufus Choate*, at Faneuil Hall, July 22, 1859, by Edward Everett.

William Wirt, then Attorney General of the United States; and as his biographer wrote:

The year at Washington, although he did not see so much as he wished of Mr. Wirt, who was confined for a considerable portion of the time by indisposition, was not without considerable advantage. It enlarged his knowledge of public men and of affairs. He became familiar with the public administration. He spent some hours almost daily in the library of Congress. He began to comprehend still more fully the dignity of his chosen profession. He saw Marshall upon the bench, and heard Pinkney in the Senate, and in his last speech in court, and thenceforth became more than ever the admirer of the genius of those eminent men. Pinkney he thought the most consummate master of a manly and exuberant spoken English that he ever heard, and he always kept him in view as a sort of model advocate.

This year (1820) was especially interesting to the law students because of the sitting of the Massachusetts Constitutional Convention, over which Chief Justice Isaac Parker was chosen to preside, and the roll of which read almost like a list of the Massachusetts Bar.(1)

It was also the year in which Webster delivered his great oration at Plymouth, on the two hundredth anniversary of the Landing of the Pilgrims, an oration, the effect of which on its hearers may be judged by the remark of John Adams, who was present at the trial of Warren Hastings and who had heard Pitt, Fox and Sheridan, and who wrote to Webster, after reading his Plymouth oration, "Mr. Burke is no longer entitled to the praise—the most consummate orator of modern times."(2)

In April, 1821, a trial occurred in Boston which was of great interest to the lawyers of Massachusetts, and in the excitement over which, the undergraduates and law students of Harvard College shared. No better conception can be had of the influence of the great lawyers of the day over the minds of men,

---

(1) Among the noted lawyers of the period who were members were Joseph Story, Daniel Webster, Charles Jackson, William Prescott, Artemas Ward, John Davis, Josiah Quincy, Daniel Davis, William Sullivan, George Blake, Warren Dutton, Lemuel Shaw, Samuel Hubbard, Nathan Dane, Samuel S. Wilde, Leverett Saltonstall, Samuel P. P. Fay, Samuel Hoar, Luther Lawrence, Samuel Dana, Levi Lincoln, Joseph Lyman, George Bliss, Ephraim Williams, Richard Sullivan, James Richardson, and Perez Morton.

(2) *History of the United States*, by James F. Rhodes, Vol. I.

than by the account given by an Harvard undergraduate of the Class of 1821—Josiah Quincy, Jr.(1):

James Prescott, judge of the probate of wills, was impeached before the Senate of Massachusetts, sitting as a high court of judicature. The trial was conducted under forms similar to those used in the famous prosecution of Warren Hastings. . . .
Daniel Webster, Samuel Hoar, William Prescott, Samuel Hubbard,—the flower of the Boston Bar,—appeared in behalf of Prescott.(2) Articles of impeachment had been found by the House of Representatives, which adjourned to be present at the case. . . . When Webster was to make his final plea, the galleries were crowded with ladies, the floor was packed by such fragment of the crowd as could again admission, and it might almost be said that the pulse of the community stopped, from the excitement of the moment.
By some extraordinary good fortune, or perhaps favoritism, I found myself in one of the best seats in that thronged assembly. On either side of me were personages of no less importance than President Kirkland and Harrison Gray Otis. . . .
Webster spoke for nearly four hours, and held the great assembly breathless under his spell. . . . It is, undoubtedly, to the credit of the independence of the court that Judge Prescott was not acquitted on all the counts of the indictment; but to have heard the noble effort made in his behalf by Daniel Webster marked an epoch in the lives of those present. It gave me my first idea of the electric force that might be wielded by a master of human speech.

On Commencement Day, August 24, 1821, Joseph Story was made an LL.D., together with Charles Jackson, Judge of the Massachusetts Supreme Court and Ambrose Spencer, the great Chief Justice of New York. No students received an LL.B.

In the year 1821-22, the Catalogue shows thirteen law students—the same number as in 1820-21.

In the next year on Commencement Day, August 28, 1822, two law students received the degree of LL.B. in accordance with the usual certificate then given by the Law Professor as follows:

I certify that Messrs. Oliver W. B. Peabody and Ira Barton have been members of the Law School of the University more than one year and a half during all of which time they pursued their studies with great assiduity and success and performed the regular literary exercises in the most satisfactory manner and I

(1) *Figures of the Past,* by Josiah Quincy Jr. (1883).
(2) The case for the prosecution was conducted by Lemuel Shaw (later Chief Justice) and Warren Dutton.

further certify that each of them has pursued his legal studies for the residue of the period of three years in the manner prescribed by the Rules of the Supreme Judicial Court of Massachusetts.

They are both gentlemen of unexceptionable character.

Asahel Stearns.(1)

In this year, 1822, Daniel Webster became an Overseer of the College, and John Lowell, to whose interest the Law School owed so much, resigned from the Corporation.

In 1822-23, there were ten law students, most of whom roomed in private houses and outside the College House or Law School building.

On Commencement Day, August 27, 1823, two law students received an LL.B. in accordance with the certificate of the Law Professor; one of them (Andrew L. Emerson) being given his degree on the strength of a certificate to Stearns from Simon Greenleaf and Isaac Lyman, attorneys in Maine, that Emerson had studied with them one and a half years (less four weeks) since leaving the School in February, 1822.(1)

This is interesting as an example of the manner in which degrees were conferred on men after they had severed all connection with the School, and simply on the ground of completion of a three years' study of the law.

In 1823-24, the number of law students fell to eight, most of them rooming in private houses, and two in the home of Professor Stearns on Kirkland Street.

In August and September 1823, the law students were given the privilege of meeting the great Chancellor Kent, who, having just retired from the Bench, was making a round of visits in Boston, Cambridge and the vicinity. Of his visit and his attendance at the Phi Beta Kappa dinner, on the day after Commencement, August 28, 1823, a lively account is given in two letters from George Ticknor, then Professor of French and Spanish, and Belles Lettres at Harvard, the first written to S. A. Eliot:

---

(1) One student apparently failed to be given a degree because of the insufficiency of the following certificate:

"William Henry Roy certified as of Virginia pursued his legal studies with diligence and success. After he left the University I have understood that he pursued his studies one year with great assiduity at Williamsburg. But I have heard nothing from him for about 6 months past. . . . Mr. Roy's character during his residence at the University, was highly respectable and his deportment unexceptionable."

See *Harvard College Papers*, Vol. X.

(1) *Harv. Coll. Papers*, Vol. X.

A. Stearns

Among the strangers who have been here this season, by far the most desirable is Chancellor Kent, now superannuated by the Constitution of the State of New York, because he is above sixty years old, and yet, de facto, in the very flush and vigor of his extraordinary faculties.(1)   He was received with a more cordial and flattering attention than I ever knew a stranger to be in Boston, and had not a moment of his time left unoccupied. He enjoyed it all extremely, and is of such transparent simplicity of character that he did not at all conceal the pleasure he received from the respect paid him during the ten days he was with us. What pleased him most, I suspect, was the Phi Beta dinner.   All the old members attended it on his account, so that nearly a hundred sat down to table, among whom were Chief Justice Parker, Judge Davis, Judge Story, Mr. Prescott, Sen., Mr. Webster, etc.   The whole was carried through, with extemporaneous spirit, in the finest style, and nothing faltered, up to the last moment.

The best toasts we ever had in this part of the country were given, on requisition from the chair, at an instant's warning, and the succession was uninterrupted.   Judge Parker gave, "The happy climate of New York, where the moral sensibilities and intellectual energies are preserved long after constitutional decay has taken place;" and Judge Story gave, "The State of New York, where the law of the land has been so ably administered that it has become the land of the law;" to which the Chancellor instantly replied, "The State of Massachusetts, the land of Story as well as of song;" and so it was kept up for three or four hours, not a soul leaving the table.   At last the Chancellor rose, and the whole company rose with him, and clapped him as far as he could hear it, and then all quietly separated.   It was the

(1)   The origin of the sixty year limit imposed on judicial tenure of office is amusingly described in *Administration of Justice in New York*, by Giulian C. Verplanck, *Law Reporter*, Vol. II (1839):
"We were plagued before the Revolution with one or two good-for-nothing old barristers sent out from England to be provided for who never were fit for judges and who of course grew stupider as they grew older.   One judge, Horsmanden, who presided in our colonial court just before the revolution was of this cast; and our new constitution was framed by young lawyers (for such then were John Jay and Robert R. Livingston) who had groaned under his venerable dullness. This was the history of the adoption of the constitutional incapacity of our judges at the age of sixty."
And in a *Review of Kent's Commentaries*, by George Bancroft in *American Quarterly Review*, Vol. I (March 1827), it is stated that the New York law as to age "was adopted in consequence of disgust occasioned by one Daniel Horsmanden who under the royal government was Chief Justice of the Province of New York.   He was, and it appears justly, too, a most unpopular judge, tenacious of his will and arbitrary in decisions. He lived to a very advanced age and the Revolution found him on the bench when he was in his dotage.   To prevent a similar occurrence the provision was introduced into the first constitution of the new State," and again into the constitution of 1822.

finest literary festival I ever witnessed, and I never saw anybody who I thought would enjoy it more than the Chancellor did.

I was with him a great deal while he was in Boston; he dined with us the day before he left; and I really think he is not only one of the most powerful, but one of the most interesting men I ever saw.(1)

The second, to Charles S. Daveis of Portland:

Your very gay and happy letter of the 23rd of August came in one morning just as the Chancellor was with me, and we were setting off for Nahant. I had the pleasure, too, that day of taking him to Salem, to Judge Story, and making them acquainted; after which we all came to the new hotel, and with Mr. Otis had a very merry time indeed.

He is, in his conversation, extremely active, simple, entertaining, and I know not when we have had among us a man so much to my mind in all things. I dined with him five or six times, and he dined with us the last day, and a rare display of fine talk we had at table, between him, Mr. Prescott, Mr. Lowell, and Mr. Webster. . . . Everybody was delighted with him. His whole visit among us was an unbroken triumph, which he enjoyed with the greatest openness. . . .

I carried him to Quincy to see President Adams and Mr. J. Q. Adams, . . . and we met them afterwards at table at Mr. Quincy's. Mr. J. Q. Adams made a most extraordinary attack on the character of Chancellor Bacon, saying that his Essays give proof of a greater corruption of heart, of a more total wickedness, than any book he ever saw. Our New York Chancellor expressed the most simple and natural astonishment at this, and we got over the matter the next day, at dinner, by drinking to the "Memory of Chancellor Bacon, *with all his faults,*" a toast which Mr. Prescott evidently gave with the greatest satisfaction. Mr. Quincy gave a beautiful toast at his own table, which I suspect was not the least pleasant to the Chancellor, among all the delicate and indirect compliments that were offered to him among us, and which was very appropriate at a table where were Mr. J. Q. Adams, Mr. Prescott, etc.

(1) See Letter to S. A. Eliot, Sept. 13, 1823, in *Life and Letters of George Ticknor* (1876).

On the day after this dinner, Aug. 29, 1823, Kent wrote to Story, having heard of the news of the sudden death of Story's brother: "This melancholy event has broken the enchantment of my visit to Boston. Your place as a companion cannot be supplied. The charm of your society, your frankness, your benevolence, your vivacity, and your matchless genius cannot be supplied. Be assured of my firm and unalterable esteem and reverence." See unpublished letter in *Story Papers, Mass. Hist. Soc. Collection.*

This was certainly a remarkable tribute from the Senior to the Junior Judge.

It was, "Nature, who repeals all political Constitutions by the great Constitution of mind". And Webster, on the same occasion, made a pleasant repartee in compliment to Mr. Quincy. Mr. Adams, being called on for a toast, said to Mr. Quincy, "I will give you, Sir, the good city of Boston". "That", said Mr. Webster, "we gave Mr. Quincy long ago, ourselves, with the greatest pleasure."

Indeed, the Chancellor seemed to give an uncommon stir and brightness to men's faculties, while he was with us, . . . there seemed to be a happy and healthy excitement of the intellectual powers and social feelings of all with whom he came in contact, that was the evident result of his rich talents and transparent simplicity of character, and which I have never known to be produced among us in the same degree by any other individual.(1)

On Commencement Day, August 25, 1824, no degrees of LL.B. were conferred, but the day was made brilliant for all students of Harvard, by the presence of General Lafayette who had recently landed in the United States. His visit is thus described in the records of the Corporation:

"By reason of the ceremonial for the Reception of General Lafayette, the exercises of the day were delayed beyond the ordinary time. On his arrival, escorted by a volunteer troop of horse accompanied by his Excellency the Governor, His Honor the Lieut. Governor, the Honorable Council, the Mayor and Municipality of Boston, the Sheriffs of Suffolk and Middlesex— the Reverend and Honorable Board of Overseers, strangers of distinction and a large number of most respectable citizens, he was received at the Portico of University Hall by the Corporation, the students being assembled in their classes on the college ground in front.

He received a cordial welcome to . . . this University in a short and appropriate address by the President of the University to which he returned an affectionate, well adapted answer. After introducing him to the officers of the Institution and those citizens who had attended for that purpose, the procession was formed to the meeting house."

After the usual exercises and performances, honorary degrees of LL.D. were conferred on William Wirt, Josiah Quincy, and Daniel Webster.

---

(1) See Letter to Charles S. Daveis, of Portland, Me., Sept. 19, 1833, in *Life and Letters of George Ticknor.*

It is interesting to note that, while Josiah Quincy received his degree of LL.D., his son, Josiah Quincy, Jr., delivered the Latin valedictory for the undergraduates; and, he writes:

To describe the enthusiasm that greeted the guest of the day is simply impossible . . . never was harmony so unbounded, so heartfelt, so spontaneous. It was as if one of the great heroes of history had been permitted to return to earth. . . . The first part of my performance consisted of mere phrases of rhetorical compliment thrown out at creation in general. . . .
But the inevitable allusion came at last. I had drifted among the heroes of the Revolution, and suddenly turned to the General with my 'In te quoque, Lafayette'—and then what an uproar drowned the rest of the sentence! 'Why sir, do you know, the pit rose at me,' said Edmund Kean. The expression of the player is perhaps as good as any I can borrow.

The degree of LL.D. conferred on Webster and Wirt were richly merited at this time; for, in the preceding March, they had argued the great steamboat case—*Gibbons v. Ogden* in the United States Supreme Court. (See Chapter XIX, infra).

The year 1824-25 opened with an increase of law students to twelve in number; and in the spring of 1825, Professor Stearns earnestly tried to get the Corporation to erect a new building for the Law School, in place of the small, dingy, inconvenient rooms in College House No. 2 then occupied by it. The College Treasurer, Stephen Higginson, estimated that the expense of a building "to accommodate twenty law students with the same number of rooms, 16 feet each, together with a library of about 30 feet, to be used also for a lecture room and also an office for the professor, will cost $7500, built of brick and furnished plain with stone door casings and windows like Holworthy."(2)

---

(1) *Figures of the Past,* by J. Quincy, Jr. (1883).
(2) See letter of Stephen Higginson June 18, 1825. *Harv. Coll. Papers,* Vol. XI.
In a previous letter of May 14, 1825, Mr. Higginson had estimated the income then arising from the College property between the court house and the graveyard on the northwest side of Harvard Square as follows:

Income Kidder House & shop	$120
Manning House & stables	180
Lee shop	80
Coll. House No. 1 J. Dana	120
" 6 rooms for students	60
" House No. 2, 6 rooms	150
Janitor's House	35
	$745

And in July, 1825, Mr. Higginson wrote to the Corporation:

In considering the subject of building on the College land near the Court House, the question naturally arises, whether any of the departments of the College can be better accommodated by building thereon.

The law professor is very desirous that his students should be provided with rooms near to their library and lecture room. The rooms now used for the purposes of the law school in Coll. House No. 2 would answer the purpose for the shops of the mechanics who have requested to be admitted as tenants of the College, and there is room to accommodate all their families under the same roof. . . . The rooms for students would rent for $30. The building would be set back from road about 20 ft. Professor Stearns is of opinion it would not be difficult to effect an arrangement with the town, which would admit of building nearer the Court House than 50 ft.(1)

The Corporation decided to look into the matter; and on August 16, 1825, the President having laid before the Board Professor Stearns' proposal, together with a plan and estimates, voted, that the President, Judge Charles Jackson, and William Prescott should be a committee to ascertain on what terms such a building could be built, and how the funds could be raised.

At the same meeting the Corporation, in spite of its previous failure, in 1820, to persuade Judge Story to accept a Professorship, decided to broach the question again; and the same committee was requested to "take into consideration such measures as may be proper to be adopted for enlarging the means of instruction in the Law School."

In this year 1825 occurred also the settlement of a controversy which had lasted for two years, and in which Joseph Story and John Lowell had taken active part in the Board of Overseers, and in which, incidentally, Professor Stearns was involved.

In 1806, the Corporation of Harvard College was composed exclusively of Fellows non-resident in Cambridge; and succeed-

---

To which may be added 3 rooms Coll. House No. 2 used for
    Law Library etc., and not charged......................$ 75
Carpenter's shop and yard north........................... 60
Wood yard and shed 60
Manning House may bring more rent........................ 60

                                         $1000
Deduct for repairs 200

                                         $800

(1) See *Harv. Coll. Papers,* Vol. XI.

ing vacancies in the Corporation had been filled by the election of non-residents. Considerable feeling had arisen among the resident instructors which came to a head in 1823, when, upon the death of Judge John Phillips, a Memorial signed by six of the resident instructors was presented to the Corporation, asking that the vacancy be not filled until they could have an opportunity to be heard. On April 2, 1824, a Memorial was presented signed by eleven instructors claiming that, as a matter of charter right, residence was a qualification for Fellowship.(1)

The Memorial was not acted upon by the Corporation; but the Overseers referred it to a committee which reported on Jan. 6, 1825, against the contention of the resident instructors. In the words of George Ticknor, then a professor in the College(2):

It may be added that, as a legal question, few have ever been examined among us with more laborious care, or by persons better qualified to decide as to what is the law. In the Corporation at the time were Mr. W. Prescott, Mr. H. G. Otis, and Mr. J. Davis, District Judge of the United States. In the Board of Overseers, Mr. Justice Story of the Supreme Court of the United States delivered his opinion against the memorial in a long argument. He was succeeded on the same side by Chief Justice Parker of the Supreme Court of Massachusetts, Mr. Justice Jackson, Mr. F. C. Gray, and some other persons of distinguished talent. On the final question not a voice was raised in the Board or elsewhere, I believe, in favor of the memorial. The profession, in particular, seemed unanimous on all points; and many years will probably elapse before any important question will be decided with such a great weight of legal talent and learning after so long, so patient and so interesting a discussion.

In behalf of the instructors, the main argument was made by Edward Everett, Professor of Greek Literature and Andrews Norton, Professor of Sacred Literature.

---

(1) The earlier memorial contained among the other names that of Asahel Stearns; but it appears that he signed owing to a mistake as to its contents, according to a letter from him in the *Harvard Archives.*

The Records of the Corporation of May 10, 1824, contain the following entry:

"The President communicated a letter of Asahel Stearns University Professor of Law relating to his agency in regard to the memorial of the resident Instructors, etc."

(2) *Remarks on Changes Lately Proposed or Adopted in Harvard University,* by George Ticknor (1829); *Miscellaneous Writings,* by Joseph Story, 1835; *American Jurist,* Vol. I, April 1829.

And see for full account and collection of authorities *History of Harvard Medical School,* by Dr. T. F. Harrington, Vol. II.

The debate lasted three days and the question was finally settled by a vote of the Corporation, "that it does not appear to the Board that the resident instructors in Harvard University have any exclusive right to be elected members of the Corporation." Thereupon Judge Charles Jackson was elected a Fellow on Feb. 8, 1825. Opposition developed in the Overseers at the election of another lawyer, it being felt that there should be another clergyman on the Board. This opposition died down, however, and after first non-concurring, the Overseers at a later meeting elected Jackson. This action was followed on June 2, 1825, by the unanimous election to the Corporation by both Corporation and Overseers of still another lawyer—Joseph Story, in place of Harrison Gray Otis, who resigned.

On Commencement Day, August 31, 1825, Professor Stearns was given the degree of LL. D. in distinguished company with Henry Clay, John Wickham of Virginia, and Judge Samuel Putnam of Massachusetts; and the very large number of ten degrees of LL.B. were conferred.

The College Catalogue for 1825-26 shows the names of ten law students (a later edition reporting thirteen); and contained for the first time the following announcement:

Persons qualified by the rules of the courts in any of the United States to become students of law may be received in the Law School for a period of not less than one term.

Of these students, the most prominent were Seth Ames, later a judge of the Massachusetts Supreme Court; Francis Hilliard, later author of many well known legal text books; and Luther S. Cushing, later Reporter of the Massachusetts Supreme Court, and Instructor in the Law School.

That the Harvard Law School was not securing many of the brilliant young men of the day is shown by the fact that two well known young Bostonians, who, it might be supposed, would have naturally gone into the School, received their legal instruction in the office of Daniel Webster. These two were Charles Francis Adams, and Robert C. Winthrop. Of the latter's study it is related that, Webster being then a United States Senator and being much in Washington:

His local business was attended to by his junior partners. Even when at home he was generally too busy to give much attention to his students, whose duties were to copy papers, look up cases and prepare briefs. . . .

At very long intervals he discoursed a little on the great principles of jurisprudence and more often favored them with a passing insight into contemporary politics.(1)

In 1825, Levi Lincoln, Judge of the Supreme Court of Massachusetts, and son of Jefferson's Attorney General Levi Lincoln, became Governor of Massachusetts. In the same year John Quincy Adams, one of the leaders of the Republican Bar of Massachusetts, was inaugurated as President; and a noted New York lawyer, Governor DeWitt Clinton saw the completion of his great work—in the opening of the Erie Canal. On June 17, 1825, General Lafayette laid the cornerstone of Bunker Hill Monument; and Daniel Webster delivered his famous oration.(2)

This year, 1825, had also been notable for an important upheaval in the methods of administration of Harvard College— a long step towards the transformation of the old College into a real University.

A Committee of the Overseers (appointed in July, 1823), of which Joseph Story was chairman, had drafted an elaborate plan containing important changes in the system of instruction, government and discipline of the College, establishing separate departments, relieving the President of many of his ministerial duties, and providing for frequent examinations and for an increase of elective studies. Their report made on January 25, 1825, had been concurred in by the Corporation on September 28; and these "Statutes and Laws of the University in Cambridge, Massachusetts," as they were entitled, comprising 153 separate laws or regulations, mark the beginning of the modern Harvard University.(3) The only Statutes referring to students in the professional Schools were as follows:

No. 152. Graduates and Students in the Theological and Law Schools and matriculated Medical Students living in Cambridge are admitted to the Lectures and Library of the University.

No. 153. If any Graduate or professional Student residing in Cambridge shall be chargeable with idleness, extravagance or any vice; or shall allow disorder within his room or fail to show

(1) *Memoir of Robert C. Winthrop*, by Robert C. Winthrop, Jr.
(2) For one of the best accounts of this by a contemporary, see *Figures of the Past*, by Josiah Quincy, Jr., of the Class of 1821.
(3) There had been previous printed editions or revisions of the Statutes and Laws in 1790, 1798, 1807 and 1814.

respect to the laws and governors of the University, and, after admonition by the President, shall not reform; all his privileges as a Resident Graduate shall be withdrawn.

No. 149. Candidates for the . . . Degree of Bachelor of Laws shall join the public procession on Commencement Day.

No. 144. Every Bachelor of Arts, having preserved a good character during the three years subsequent to his taking his degree, shall upon his complying with the requisitions hereinafter stated be entitled to the degree of Master of Arts.(1)

Among the changes brought about by these new Statutes had been a new requirement (Statute No. 60) that the heads of the newly constituted departments should make reports to the President on the condition of their respective departments at the end of each of the three terms.(2)

Beginning with 1825, therefore, detailed accounts of the administration of the Law School are in existence in the College Records, for nearly every term of each year, up to 1870. From these reports, it is possible to ascertain the number of students in the School during each term, while the College Catalogue gives the attendance only during the first or fall term. As a rule, it appears that the number of students fell off during the winter terms.

Professor Stearns' second Report, Jan. 9, 1826, notes the presence of 12 students, of whom 7 were from Massachusetts, 3 from Virginia, 1 from New Hampshire, 1 from Louisiana; and, he continues:

It is highly satisfactory to the undersigned to be able to state that the industry, emulation and regular deportment of the student since the commencement of the present academic year with a single exception has not been surpassed at any period since the establishment of the school.

---

(1) The only requirements were the payment of $5.00 for the public dinner and other Commencement charges.

(2) "The Professors in each department where there are more than one, shall constitute a board, at which the Senior Professor shall preside. They shall have charge of the Instruction, in their respective departments, see that it be conducted in an effectual manner, and recommend such Instructors as may be wanted, who shall receive the aid, countenance direction and supervision of the Professors in the department.

The Professors shall make personal examination and critical inquiries into the conduct and attainments of the students in their respective departments.

Reports relating to each department with such observations and recommendations as to studies and discipline as may appear useful shall be made at the end of each term by the Boards respectively to the President to be laid before the Corporation and a similar report shall be made twice a year to be laid before the Overseers."

There was, however, great difficulty in maintaining regular courses of instruction, or accurate classification of the students, at this time, because of the freedom with which entrance to the school was allowed at all times during term; for a student could be admitted whenever he chose to come, and he picked up the courses just where he found them.(1)

The method of instruction at this time was as follows: Professor Parker delivered 18 lectures to the law students and to members of the Senior class; Professor Stearns gave 38 written lectures,(1) held 67 reviews of one hour each, and gave examinations on the text books required to be studied, lasting two or three hours each. The students were required to write 30 dissertations. And there were 37 Moot Courts held, lasting from two to three hours each, and 36 exercises in disputation lasting from two to three hours each.(2)

For purpose of weekly recitation and examination, the students were divided into two classes or divisions according to advancement in studies. And, says Stearns, Aug. 29, 1826, "there were a few individuals whose standing by reason of their having commenced their studies at different periods rendered it inexpedient, if not impracticable, to write them with either class."

This irregularity in the time of beginning their studies had its influence on the part which the students could take in the moot court work; and in his report of April 2, 1828, Stearns notes that the number of Moot Courts was "much less than usual owing to the circumstances that 8 (of the 11 students) began the study of the law since the commencement of the present academic year" and hence "not being sufficiently advanced in their studies to take part in them."

The examination consisted of from twenty to thirty questions

---

(1) As an example of the confusion into which this threw the statistics of the School, it appears from the Catalogue of October, 1825, that there were then ten students in the School, Professor Stearns' Report for the first term shows 12, for the second term 10, and yet in his Report of August 29, 1826, for the whole year 1825-26, "No. first term 12, second term 14, third term 11, the whole number of individuals in the course of the year being 15 of whom 11 were graduates."

(2) In 1826-1827, 39 lectures; 69 reviews and examination by classes; 35 Moot Courts; 34 disputations; 29 dissertations (See *Stearns' Report* of September 24, 1827).

In 1827-1828, 37 lectures; 67 examinations and reviews in class besides separate examinations to individuals; 25 Moot Courts exercises; 31 meetings for extempore discussion (See *Stearns' Report*, Sept. 1828.)

In 1828-1829, 1st term ending Dec. 24, 1828 (See *Stearns' Report*) 15 lectures; 46 examinations and reviews; 3 Moot Courts.

put to each student, on the subjects of the lectures and text books assigned to them.

The course of study was as follows:

In 1825-26, the beginners, or Second Class, were required to read the following elementary text-books—*Sullivan's Lectures, Blackstone's Commentaries, Wooddeson's Lectures, Cruise on Real Property, Sugden on Law of Vendors and Purchasers;* in 1826-27, were added *Littleton's Tenures, Coke on Littleton, Burlemaqui,* Select titles on *Personal Remedies and Pleading,* from *Bacon's Abridgment, Lawes on Pleading, Stephens on Pleading,* and above all, the first volume of *Kent's Commentaries* which had just been published in 1826.(1)

In 1827-28, the new book which Professor Stearns had just written, based on his law lectures,—*Stearns on Real Actions* was added to the course.(2)

For the more advanced students, or First Class, the scope of study, as given in the President's Annual Report for 1825-26 was rather narrow: Law of Real Property—*Littleton's Tenures, Coke on Littleton, Sugden on Law of Vendors and Purchasers;* Personal Relations and Rights—*Reeve on Domestic Relations,* Select titles from *Bacon's Abridgment, Toller on Executors and Administrators, Jones on Bailments, Comyn on Contracts;* Courts of Jurisdiction, etc., Officers of Courts, Process and Autohrity, Personal Remedies—Select titles from *Bacon's Abridgment;*

---

(1) Stearns, in his Report of this year, said: "Some of the Second Class have read (preparatory to commencing the study of law), *Hume's History, Robertson's Charles the Fifth, Mitford's Greece* and part of *Gibbon's Roman Empire.*"

(2) "In the Winter of 1824, during the session of the Court at Cambridge, and when the Bar were accustomed more than at present to spend their evenings together, and when their habits of social intercourse did much to soften the asperities which the practice of the law seems calculated to call forth and strengthen, Mr. Stearns was one evening lamenting that he had so little to do. It was then vacation in the University; he had but few actions in the court; and his time seemed likely to hang heavy on his hands for several weeks. 'I will tell you what to do,' was the answer of Mr. Samuel Hoar, who was a very intimate friend, 'You shall write a work on real actions.' The advice was received with acclamation by all present; and Mr. Stearns immediately commenced the work, which he had more than half completed before the close of the vacation, and which was published in less than six months and passed to a second edition in 1831. . . . It was universally regarded as learned, accurate and useful; and, we may say, without fear of contradiction, that it supplied a desideratum, the want of which, all in any way conversant with the law had acknowledged, and which students and the younger members of the Bar had especially felt."

See *Law Reporter,* Vol. I (April 1839).

Pleadings and Practice—*Lawes on Pleading, Stephens on Pleading, Chitty on Pleading Tidd's Practice.*

The next year 1826-27, a much broader line of work was taken up. The study of Equity was introduced with *Barton's History of a Suit in Equity, Blake on Chancery, Fonblanque on Equity, Mitford on Pleading, Newland on Contracts.* Evidence was introduced with *Phillips* and *Starkie on Evidence;* Merchantile Law came in with *Chitty on Bills; Bailey on Bills; Abbott on Shipping;* and *Marshall on Insurance.* Newer books on pleading and realty law were used—*Selwyn on Nisi Prius; Stearns on Real Actions; Booth on Real Actions; Saunders on Uses;* and *Reeve on Domestic Relations, Toller on Law of Executors, Jones on Bailments* and *Comyn on Contracts* were dropped.

In 1827-28, the courses remained without change.

Combined with recitations from these text books were the lectures, containing "frequent references to reported cases and other text books for illustration and further satisfaction;" and the Professor reported, May 20, 1826, that these exercises were "attended with punctuality and have evinced great industry and thoroughness of study and research."

One other feature of the law course of those days must be especially noticed, as it was, for many years, one of the great attractions of the School—the opportunity to attend the lectures of the distinguished College professors outside the School.

"Most of the law students", says Stearns in May, 1826, "have been lately employed for a considerable time during five days in the week in their attendance on the public lectures of several of the Professors of the University."

So satisfactory, however, had the course of instruction apparently proved that at the end of ten years from the founding of the School, Stearns reported (May, 1827):

As the advantage of the present system of law instruction in the University appears to be most satisfactorily evinced by the industry and emulation of the students, their progression, learning and correct deportment, the professor does not deem it expedient to propose any alteration in the course of instruction.

And again on April 2, 1828:

The students have been generally punctual at the exercises, have manifested a laudable spirit of industry, attention and decorum, and most of them have made a gratifying progress in legal learning.

No change in the course of Instruction or discipline in this department has occurred to the Instructor as requiring the interference or attention of the Overseers.

Two matters appear to have troubled Stearns, however,—the pressure of work on the single professor—and the expense to the students of attendance at the School. As to the first, he reports in August, 1826:

A large portion of the Professor's time is employed in selecting and preparing suitable questions and cases for argument at the moot court, and in assisting the students to put them into this form of judicious action, examining their declarations, pleas, replications, demurrers, bills of exceptions, motions, etc., and directing them in the course of their investigations and researches. But of the amount of time thus employed, and of that also which is devoted to answering the numerous questions, and solving the doubts which occur to the students, (and which they are encouraged and desired to suggest with freedom when they occur), it is impossible to make any correct estimate.

As to the second, he states in May, 1827:

If means could be found to diminish the necessary expenses attending the study of law at the University, so that it should not exceed the expense of private establishments of a similar character in the country, the number of students would unquestionably increase. Without such a change, there is great reason to believe the number will continue (notwithstanding the great advantages arising from the valuable lectures of the other professors of the University to which the law students have gratuitous access) to be small, and perhaps less than heretofore.

Notwithstanding the hard work of Professor Stearns, and the attention paid to the struggling School by the governing bodies of the College, the number of students did not increase, but gradually fell off.

In the year 1826-27, the College Catalogue shows eight law students; Professor Stearns' Report of Sept. 24, 1827, gives 10, first term; 5, second; 3, third; whole number during the course of the year only 10, of whom 7 were college graduates.

In the year 1827-28, the College Catalogue shows eight law students; and Professor Stearns' Report of Sept. 1828 gives the number as 11, first term; 7, second; 8, third; whole number during the year 13, of whom 7 were graduates.

It may be noted that in this year the use of the term "Law School" and a list of the names of the Law Faculty appears in the College Catalogue for the first time.

It has been customary among writers on this subject to attribute the failure of the School to Professor Stearns—either his neglect or his ineptitude; but a careful study of the conditions of the times proves that the School's decline was unquestionably due to other causes. Certain it is, at all events, that Stearns himself was conscious of no neglect on his part; for in his Report of Sept. 24, 1827, he says:

Though the number of students has been greatly diminished in the course of the year, no circumstance has occurred tending to show that this extraordinary change has arisen from any dissatisfaction on the part of the students, their friends, or the public with regard to the administration and conduct of this department—and no change in instruction or discipline of the department has occurred to the Instructor as deserving the attention or requiring the interference of the Overseers.

At this point in the history of the School, Judge Parker resigned his Royall Professorship, Nov. 6, 1827. While no reason for his action is now known, it is evident from the terms and curtness of his letter of resignation that it was not voluntary:

To the President and Fellows of Harvard University.

Having understood from one of your body that it is desirable that the office of Royall Professor of Law now held by me should be vacated, I hereby resign the same.

Respectfully your
obedient servant.
Isaac Parker.

This resignation was accepted by the following not overeffusive vote of the Corporation, Nov. 15, 1827:

The resignation of Chief Justice Parker, Royall Professor of Law, being laid before the Corporation, it was thereupon, voted that in accepting the same, this Board express their full sense of the benefits which the Chief Justice has conferred on the University and on the public by the lectures which he has delivered at Cambridge, and that the Treasurer pay his salary as Professor till next Commencement.

It is probable that this resignation was due to the fact that the Corporation was extremely anxious to obtain as Professor, some lawyer of distinction who would reside in Cambridge, for it appears that a second attempt was made, early in 1828, to secure Judge Story; but Story again declined.

On Feb. 9, 1828, he wrote to a friend:

I am at this moment a good deal perplexed by an application to me to accept the Royall Professorship of Law at Harvard University, and to remove to Cambridge and devote my leisure to the advancement of the Law School there. The offer is made unofficially, but in terms of considerable earnestness, and in a pecuniary point of view it is eligible. What to do puzzles me exceedingly. . . . What to decide, I hardly know, there are so many pros and cons.

And on March 1, he wrote:

I have made up my mind to decline . . . it would require my removal to Cambridge, and such an increase of duties as at my age and with my present labors, I fear might seriously interfere with my health.

Again, on March 6, he wrote to Professor George Ticknor:

I have fears that my health would not hold out against the inroads of such additional labors. If I were there, I should be obliged to devote *all* my leisure time to drilling, and lectures, and judicial conversation. The School cannot flourish except by such constant efforts; and I should not willingly see it wither under my hands.

The delivery of public lectures might not be oppressive but success in a law school must be obtained by private lectures. I have yielded reluctantly to what seems to me on the whole the dictates of duty.

It was especially desirable, however, during this formative period of American Law, that there should be on the Faculty of the School, some lawyer of a national practise, or some presiding judge, through whom the students could be thus brought into contact with the creative legal forces. Such a personal influence was certain to be powerful. As an illustration, it may be noted that Judge Parker, during his professorship, delivered opinions in a number of cases of new impression in Massachusetts, which have since become landmarks in legal history:—thus, in 1818, he decided the first reported case of breach of promise of marriage(1); in 1820, the first case on the rights of parties receiving counterfeit bank notes, involving the doctrine of *Price v. Neal*(2); in 1821, a leading case on the Statute of Frauds(3; in 1822, the famous case as to the completion of a contract on mailing of acceptance(4); in 1823, the first case in the country raising the question of the constitutionality of the Fugitive Slave Act(5); in 1824, the first case of the application of the doctrine of contributory negligence in a personal injury case(6).

The year, 1828, was noted in the legal annals of Boston for the trial of a case over which Judge Parker presided, and which caused the greatest excitement in Harvard College circles.(7) This was the indictment of Theodore Lyman (later Mayor of Boston and uncle of President Charles William Eliot) for criminal libel, at the instance of Daniel Webster. At this time, a heated controversy had arisen between John Quincy Adams and thirteen prominent representative Federalists of Boston over certain charges which Adams had made against the Federalist leaders of New England, of having conspired in 1807-1808 to break up the Union and re-annex New England to Great Britain. Adams had mentioned no names; but Lyman had published, in the *Jackson Republican* (an anti-Adams newspaper), the charges made, and had included Webster, with Samuel Dexter, Josiah Quincy, William Prescott and H. G. Otis, as one of the conspirators intended. In this noted case, James T. Austin (the State Attorney General) and Richard Fletcher (a Dartmouth

---

(1) *Wightman v. Coates,* 15 Mass. 1.
(2) *Gloucester Bank v. Salem Bank,* 17 Mass. 33, argued by W. Prescott and L. Saltonstall against Webster.
(3) *Packard v. Richardson,* 17 Mass. 122, argued by Webster and Morey against Increase Sumner.
(4) *McCulloch v. Eagle Insurance Co.,* 1 Pick. 278, argued by W. Prescott against L. Saltonstall.
(5) *Com. v. Griffith,* 2 Peck. 11, argued by Marcus Morton, W. Baylies and Theophilus Parsons against Pliny Merrick.
(6) *Smith v. Smith,* 2 Pick. 626.
(7) See *A Notable Libel Case,* by Josiah H. Benton, Jr., (1904).
Diary of John Quincy Adams. Papers relating to New England Federalism, by Henry Adams.
It may be noted that this case occurred a year and a half after Webster's famous *Eulogy on Adams and Jefferson,* (both of whom had died July 4, 1826), delivered August 2, 1826, in the presence of President John Quincy Adams in Faneuil Hall.
On Sept. 22, 1826, Webster declined to deliver the Phi Beta Kappa oration at Harvard, writing "I have recently had occasion to appear so often before the public that I feel entirely unwilling soon again to undertake a public performance."
See *Harv. Coll. Papers,* Vol. I, 2nd Series.

graduate and a former student in Webster's office) appeared for the prosecution; and Samuel Hubbard (later Judge of the Massachusetts Supreme Court) and Franklin Dexter (son of Samuel Dexter, later United States District Attorney and Instructor in the Law School) appeared for the defendant. The trial resulted in a disagreement of the jury.

It is stated that but for this case, which aroused so many antagonisms, Webster would have been offered the vacant Royall Professorship in the Law School.

This year, 1828, is marked also, as that in which Rufus Choate removed to Salem, taking his place at once, at the head of the Essex Bar; (1) and as the year in which the famous case of *Charles River Bridge v. Warren Bridge* (described in detail in Chapter XXIV infra) was begun—a case which was to have great effect upon the financial condition of Harvard College, and upon the commercial development of the whole country.

For many years the College had been receiving an annuity from the Charles River Bridge Corporation, the plaintiff in this case; but owing to the incorporation of the defendant Bridge, in 1828, this annuity was about to cease—a serious financial loss. For the last three years, the state of the College finances had been weighing on the minds of the Corporation and of the Overseers. The annual appropriation of $10,000 which had been made by the Legislature of Massachusetts for a period of ten years, had been discontinued in 1825. The number of students had fallen from 302 in 1822 to 199 in 1826. The expenses had exceeded income for the year 1824-25 by $5,000. The unappropriated funds had been greatly reduced and the College accounts were in considerable disorder. It was evident that a rigid system of economy in administration must be put in force.(2) The condition of affairs has been thus described(3):

"Dr. Kirkland, the model of a dignified clergyman, an accomplished scholar, a polished gentleman, bland and courteous in

---

(1) "The Essex Bar was then and it had long been distinguished for learning and skill. The memory of Dane, Parsons, Story and Putnam was fresh and fragrant; John Pickering, Leverett Saltonstall, Eben Mosely, David Cummins and John Varnum were still in full practice; Caleb Cushing, Robert Rantoul, Jr. and others like them were making their influence felt as young men of ability and ambition."
Life of Rufus Choate, by Samuel G. Brown.

(2) See *Overseers Records* of Jan. 17, 1828, and statement of Corporation to Overseers, as to expenses.

(3) *Memoirs of Josiah Quincy*, by Edmund Quincy.

his intercourse with the students, by whom he was greatly beloved, and universally popular in society for his genial graces, was not a man of business, and had no natural or acquired talent for the management of money. Judge John Davis, of the United States District Court, who was Treasurer of the College during the whole of Dr. Kirkland's Presidency, unfortunately was not fitted to make good his deficiencies in this particular. A learned lawyer, and a man of great general erudition, he had rather the tastes and habits of a retired scholar, than those of a man of affairs. Between them both, without the slightest impeachment of their personal integrity, the college finances had fallen into almost inextricable confusion."

Finally President Kirkland, partly because he felt keenly the criticism made by certain members of the Corporation, and partly because of his continued ill health, resigned his position; and the Corporation accepted his resignation on April 2, 1828.(1)   At once an active struggle ensued over the election of his successor. One faction of those interested in the College thought that the time had come when a business man or man of affairs should be placed at its head(2); the other faction vigorously upheld the old, hitherto-unshaken custom of appointing a clergyman. Religious questions also entered into the selection of the new president. The Congregationalists decided to try to stem the tide of Unitarianism which seemed to be sweeping the College from all its ancient moorings.

The community have been slumbering whilst a dereliction of religious and moral principle has been exemplified in the management of Harvard College to which our country furnishes no parallel. . . . It is confidently hoped that the triple chains of Unitarianism, Universalism and Infidelity under which the college of our fathers is now oppressed and sends up her sighs and groans to Heaven, will not be of long endurance.

(1) See *Memoir of John T. Kirkland*, by Rev. Dr. John Pierce, *Mass. Hist. Soc. Proc.,* 2nd Series, Vol. IX (1894-95).
"This event produced at the time a high excitement among many devoted friends of Harvard. The students almost universally bewailed the measure and were for a season for venting their resentment against the supposed authors."
(2) "Though the financial experience and skill of the Corporation, and especially of Dr. Bowditch and Mr. Francis, had already placed the funds on a sage basis, it was thought important that a man of the world, accustomed to business, should be placed at the head of the University. Mr. Quincy was very generally allowed to be the man to satisfy this necessity."
See *Memoirs of Josiah Quincy,* by Edmund Quincy.

So wrote the editor of the *Boston Recorder*. "The religious
system introduced is dishonorable to God, and ruinous to the
souls of men" said another newspaper writer; and an alumnus of
the College wrote in May, 1828:

The present reign of error dates from 1808. Unitarianism
has engulfed in its dark flood nearly all the sons of Harvard.
Can I place my son during four of the most valuable years of
his life for the establishment of principles and character, at
Cambrige College? writes "Hollis." The election of Quincy
will be a "deep laid plot of Unitarians, they dare not elect a
Unitarian minister" writes another.(1)

The fight resolved itself into a struggle between the Congre-
gationalist party; the party favoring the Unitarian minister
Rev. Edward Everett, who had been, up to 1826, Professor of
Greek Literature, and who represented the side of the Resident
Instructors in the effort to obtain representation in the Corporation; and the party favoring George Ticknor, then Professor of
French and Spanish Literature and Belles Lettres, and the representative of the progressive and university spirit. When feelings ran so high that it was evident that no one of these parties
could succeed, Samuel A. Eliot and John G. Palfrey brought
forward Rev. Jared Sparks, a Unitarian clergyman, who had
just done brilliant work as the editor of the *North American
Review* and of the *Washington Letters*(2). Others favored Harrison Gray Otis.

Finally Josiah Quincy's name was proposed, he having just
failed of re-election as mayor of Boston in December, 1828, after
five years of brilliant and able administration. The best friends
of the Institution, and especially the Fellows constituting the
Corporation, from whom the nomination was originally to proceed, were very soon of one mind as to his peculiar fitness for
the place at that particular juncture. The Corporation then
consisted of Rev. Dr. Eliphalet Porter; ex-Judge Charles Jack-

---

(1) For interesting evidence of this controversy, see the *Quincy Papers* in the *Harvard College Archives,* and *Facts and Documents in relation to Harvard College,* by Hollis and others. (1829).

(2) Jared Sparks was in Europe at this time; and his friend, W. H.
Eliot, wrote to him Jan. 26, 1829:
"If you had been in the country you would have been chosen. This and
the unquestionable fact that if Quincy had not lost his election as mayor
he would never have been thought of for the office shows upon what tri-
fles great events sometimes hinge in the world."
See *Life and Writings of Jared Sparks,* by Herbert B. Adams.

son, late of the Massachusetts Supreme Court; Judge Story; Nathaniel Bowditch, the author of the *Navigator*, and the translator of *Laplace;* Francis Calley Gray; and Ebenezer Francis, the Treasurer. And at its meeting of Jan. 10, 1829, (Story being absent) it elected Quincy unanimously.(1)

The Overseers confirmed this action Jan. 29, 1829, although the opposition showed itself to be strong, the vote standing 46 to 42.

Meanwhile the Law School situation was becoming desperate. In the year 1828-29, the College Catalogue gives the number of law students as six; but according to Stearns' Report of Dec. 24, 1828:

The number of students attending the Law School during the greater part of this time was only four. Near the close of the term, the number was increased to five—they have been generally attended to separately in their examinations and reviews though two of them have occasionly been heard together in their exercises. . . . It is due to the students to state that, while all of them have manifested a laudable spirit of industry, two in particular have pursued their studies with great ardor and perseverance and have made very gratifying progress.

By the spring of 1829, though no official report is in existence, it is stated that the number was reduced to one lone law student.

While the Law School was not a matter of great expense so far as present salaries were concerned, the need of a new building, urged as early as 1825 by Professor Stearns, was apparent if the School was to be a success. Furthermore if new professors were to be appointed, some provision must be made for more adequate salaries. The receipt of $100 per student by the University Professor was ridiculously insufficient con-

---

(1) In January, 1829, Story wrote to Mr. Bowditch:
"Since we last met Mr. Quincy has been named as a candidate. If our friend Mr. Ticknor is to be passed by, I am ready to vote for Mr. Quincy. I think he has more qualifications than any other candidate. If you should come to a choice, I authorize you to give my vote for Mr. Quincy, if the Board will allow my vote when I am absent."

See *Harv. Coll. Papers,* Vol. III, 2nd Series. On the Corporation Records of Jan. 15, 1829, is the following:

"Mem. A letter was read from Judge Story proposing Mr. Quincy as a candidate and stating his readiness to vote for him . . . But it was considered that absent members do not vote by proxy."

Josiah Quincy

pensation for the time spent; and the salary of the Royall Professor ($400) was hardly more than a nominal sum.(1)

The Corporation felt that the one thing needful was to bring to the School as a permanent professor some lawyer with a national reputation. But no such man could be found who would accept the small salary of the Royall Professorship. The only other alternative seemed to be to displace Professor Stearns. It would appear from the College Records that some friction had arisen between the Corporation and Stearns as early as 1827, for in December of that year the Corporation had voted that:

the Treasurer and Mr. Gray be a committee to settle all accounts between the College and Professor Stearns and also all demands which have been put into his hands for collection.(2)

A year later, on June 19, 1828, the Corporation voted:

It having been represented to the Corporation that Professor Stearns had accepted the office of County Attorney of the County of Middlesex, Judge Jackson and Mr. Gray were appointed a committee to inquire into the subject and report to the Board thereon(3).

No action, however, was taken as to the Law School until after the election of the new President. Then the Corporation took the bull by the horns; and before President Quincy was fairly in office, it voted on March 19, 1829, that "Dr. Porter, Judge Jackson and Mr. Gray be a committee to consider the state of the Law School and to make report thereon."

No report was ever made by this Committee; for Professor Stearns, after a conference with it, decided to resign voluntarily, and accordingly, on April 7, 1829, he addressed the following

---

(1) In the *First Annual Report of the President* dated January 1, 1827, the salaries paid to the Law Professors for the year 1825-26 are set down as—Professor Parker $400—Professor Stearns $1270. In the *Second Annual Report,* Jan. 1, 1828, it is stated "Professor Stearns receives the amount paid by the students (supposed amount $700)."

(2) On April 10, 1828, the Committee reported to the Corporation that they had made a settlement of all accounts.

(3) Professor Stearns sent a letter (not now extant) to the Corporation Oct. 16, 1828, in reply, which from the records of the Corporation appears to have been referred to Judge Jackson and Mr. Gray.

It is somewhat difficult to understand this vote of the Corporation, for Professor Stearns had been District Attorney for Middlesex County ever since 1813.

interesting, and decidedly pungent letter to "Rev. Dr. Porter, Senior Member of the Corporation of Harvard College"(1):

In the interview which I had with you in relation to the dissolution of my connection with the college, my feelings were expressed without reserve and I am anxious that they should not be misunderstood.

You will readily believe that if I could have foreseen this result at the time I was solicited to accept the appointment of Professor of Law, I should have declined the proffered honor. The failure of the experiment, as you were pleased to call it, must doubtless have been a severer disappointment to me, than to any other person, however anxious he may have been for the interest and honour of the College. And I must say that it was equally unexpected and painful to me to find that I was considered answerable for this failure.

You will readily believe that my interest in the success of the Law School must have led me to watch the progress of events with solicitude; and so far as I was capable of judging, it may be supposed that I possessed the means of tracing effects to their causes. I trust, therefore, that I shall be pardoned for alluding to some of the chief causes which have operated to the injury of that institution; and these appear to me sufficient to account for what I have so long witnessed with regret, while it could not be prevented, but by the fostering aid of the Corporation.

1. I may mention in the first place the great diminution in the number of law students in the State, which, I understand, in the country (however it may be in the city) is but about half as large as formerly.(1)

2. The establishment of similar institutions elsewhere, particularly in Virginia (which for some years furnished full one third of our number) and at Northampton where the saving of expenses in board and especially in room rent, fuel, etc. (which are understood to have been furnished gratuitously to those who were poor) have held out powerful inducements in addition to

---

(1) See letter (hitherto unpublished) in *Harv. Coll. Papers,* Vol. III, 2nd Series.

(1) See an interesting letter from Rufus Choate, in Salem, to Edmund Carleton (who was practising law in New Hampshire), June 1, 1823:

"I really do not think Massachusetts at all a promising stand for a young practitioner. As inevitably happens in every old community and in all kinds of business, the profession is full to overflowing and starvation, and in this country particularly the complaint is general and earnest. The amount of professional business varies very much with the condition of our foreign commerce and lawyers and merchants grow rich or poor together. The latter are becoming insolvent, and looking to a war in Europe as a last and only chance of relieving their fallen fortunes; the former lounge in their offices, pick clean teeth, and talk of the scarcity of clients and the still greater scarcity of fees and neglect of merit."

local advantages. To this I may add, that several gentlemen who sent their sons there, have assured me that they should have preferred Cambridge but for their desire to separate their sons from particular associates.

3. The great convenience to professional gentlemen, especially in the country, of having a law student in their offices has induced them to give gratuitous instruction in many more cases than formerly.

In many instances, this circumstance has induced young gentlemen to change their determination to study at Cambridge, and to leave the place sooner than they had intended.

4. Perhaps the want of a convenient and respectable building for the Law School has had quite as much influence as any of the circumstances alluded to, since the erection of the theological college has led the law students to contrast their situation with that of the students of theology.

In making these remarks, I hope I shall not be misunderstood. This is not offered as an apology; for I am not conscious of needing one. My only desire is to have facts known that correct inferences may be drawn. I wish to have it distinctly understood that I claim to have discharged my official duty faithfully and conscientiously and to have conducted the business of instruction in my department in as acceptable and satisfactory a manner both to my pupils and their friends as any department of the College. I have therefore only to request (what certainly will not be refused by my judges) that the case shall be examined and understood before any censure is cast upon me.

You did not intimate, sir, that any complaint had been made, or any unfavorable representation presented to the Corporation. But as it has been stated to me that a report has been circulated by one person that two or three students from Virginia had expressed some dissatisfaction with regard to the Law School, it is possible that report may have come to the knowledge of the Corporation or some of the members. I therefore beg leave to state that I have in my possession letters from those gentlemen, introducing their friends to the Law School, and containing such expressions as render it in my view utterly incredible that they can have made the statements imputed to them.

Though this letter has extended so much beyond the limits to which I intended to confine myself, I must still beg your indulgence for one further remark. From something you let fall I was led to suppose that some of the gentlemen of the Corporation regarded the money expended upon the Law School, as an appropriation which had produced little or no public benefit. A different opinion must, I think, be entertained by the professional gentlemen of that body. I am sure they cannot but be aware, that the effect which the Law School has had in raising the general standard of professional education, by introducing a more methodical and thorough course of instruction, has of itself (if no other benefit had resulted) more than compensated for the expenditure. The course of instruction pursued here, which was drawn up under the eye of some of the present members of the Corporation, has not only been adopted in other law schools, but more than 60 professional gentlemen in this and adjoining States have applied for copies for the use of their students. And what is still more important, students in law offices have been more attended to and better instructed in consequence of the establishment of the School.

I cannot but hope, sir, that these suggestions will be received in the spirit of candour, and that however they may fail to establish any claim to the respectful consideration of the Corporation, they may at least shelter me from censure, and that I may still indulge the belief that the respect and attachment manifested by my pupils was in their opinion not wholly undeserved. This is the first occasion which I have had to speak in my own vindication; perhaps you may think I should rather say my own commendation. If the occasion cannot excuse it, it must go unexcused.

You will please to consider me, sir, as hereby tendering my resignation of the chair of University Professor of Law which I shall not consider myself as holding after this day.

I shall rejoice at all times in the respectability and welfare of the University and especially to see the Law Department revive and flourish in more competent and more favored hands, however keenly I may feel the unkindness I have experienced.

You will please to accept my acknowledgment for the personal courtesy I have experienced in my interviews with you, and to be assured I am, as ever,

Your obedient servant,
Asahel Stearns.

Professor Stearns' resignation was promptly accepted by the Corporation by vote of April 16, 1829:

Voted. That the Corporation accept his resignation entertaining a respectful sense of his distinguished attainments in legal science and of his diligence and fidelity in performing the duties of his office and a sincere wish for his future happiness.

Voted. That the Treasurer in settling his account with Professor Stearns allow him usual tutition fees up to close of the present College year for the students in the Law School at the time of his resignation.

Voted. That Dr. Stearns be requested to retain the use of the rooms now occupied by him and of the Law Library in his possession till the end of the present term, if this be any accommodation to him.

Professor Stearns was undoubtedly correct in attributing the failure of the School to causes outside of the School itself.

In the first place, the difficulty of access to Cambridge from other parts of the United States was a great obstacle; for it is to be borne in mind that it was not until 1829 that the first railroad corporations were chartered.

Thus, the noted Philadelphia lawyer, Peter S. DuPonceau, in his *Address delivered before the Trustees and members of the Society for the Promotion of Legal Knowledge,* in Philadelphia, Feb. 21, 1821, said in urging the founding of a national school of law:

If that justly celebrated Seminary (Harvard Law School) were situated elsewhere than in one of the most remote parts of our Union, there would be no need perhaps of looking to this city for the completion of the object which we have in view. Their own sagacity would suggest to them the necessity of appointing additional professors for each important branch of our legal system and thus under their hand would gradually rise a noble temple dedicated to the study of our national jurisprudence. But their local situation and that alone precludes every such hope; for otherwise the world well knows that they are neither wanting in inclination or ability to pursue any great object that may redound to their fame and the benefit of their country.

The expenses of life at Harvard, the lack of a proper building for the School, the prejudice in States outside of New England, as well as within, against the supposedly ultra-Unitarian proclivities of Harvard, the depressed conditions of the national finances during many of the years 1817-1829, and especially the rise of other law schools more conveniently located(1)—all these

---

(1) At New Haven, Conn., the law school kept by Seth R. Staples and Samuel J. Hitchcock was in thriving existence from about 1800 to 1824, at which latter date the noted Judge David Daggett became its head. In 1826, Judge Daggett was appointed to fill the vacant professorship of law in the academic department of Yale College (previously held by Elizur Goodrich 1801 to 1810). The school was not however recognized as the Yale Law School for some years later, (no degrees being conferred on its graduates until 1843.) See *Yale in its Relation to Law* in *Yale Law Journal,* Vol. XI (1901).

In Philadelphia, the "Law Academy" founded by Peter S. DuPonceau in 1821 afforded an opportunity for students of law to attend lectures by the eminent practitioners of that city, and in his address to the students, April 22, 1824, DuPonceau said, "Law Schools within these 2 or 3 years have been increasing in this country to an astonishing degree and the most exalted characters do not disdain to fill professors' chairs."

In Virginia, Dr. Thomas Cooper had been elected temporary Professor of Law in the University of Virginia, in 1817; and, after declinations by

factors—combined with the fact that the legal profession had not yet fully accepted the idea that law could be learned better in a school than in an office—prevented any great growth of the School.

And hence, with no blame to be attached to the devoted, industrious and genial professor, the first period of the Harvard Law School ended in complete failure .

Francis W. Gilmer and his brother-in-law William Wirt, John Taylor Lomax had been appointed permanent professor in 1826. See *Jefferson, Cabell, and the University of Virginia,* by John S. Patton. (1906).

The College of William and Mary continued to furnish an ample course of legal education. There were also in Virginia several local private law schools, the most noted being that founded by Judge Creed Taylor in 1821 at Needham, Va., the average attendance of students at which was twenty. See *Journal of the Law School and of the Moot Courts attached to it at Needham in Virginia,* by Creed Taylor (1822.)

In Massachusetts, the noted private school at Northampton founded by Judge Samuel Howe and Hon. Elijah H. Mills, assisted by John Hooker Ashmun flourished from 1823 to 1829 with a yearly average attendance of ten students. In October, 1828, the eminent Theron Metcalf (later Reporter of Decisions and Judge of the Massachusetts Supreme Court) opened a law school at Dedham; see *American Jurist,* Vol. VIII (1829); and *Theron Metcalf,* by George S. Hale, *Mass. Hist. Soc. Proc.* (1876.)

In June, 1829, a law school was opened at Amherst by Samuel F. Dickinson referring to which the *American Jurist,* Vol. VIII (1829), said editorially "We are glad to witness the efforts which are making to render law education in this country thorough and systematic."

CHAPTER XVIII.

The Law Library—1817-1829.

One of the features of the new School, on which Professor Stearns had been most insistent in drawing up his prospectus, was the institution of a law library; for the few hundred volumes of law books then contained in the general College Library constituted a very incomplete and insufficient collection for educational purposes. Most of them had been the gift of Thomas Hollis—to whom is due the credit of being the father of the Law Library; for after the burning of the College Library in 1764, he presented to the College a number of rare and valuable books of law. These were mainly, however, works on the Civil Law such as *Corpus Juris Civilis, Codex Theodosianus, Brissonius, Voet, Zoesius, Domat, Meerman's Thesaurus, Lindenbrogius* on *Codex Legum Antiquarum;* there were few books on the Common Law—*Bracton, Glanville's Tractatus de Legibus, Horne's Mirror, Barnington's Observations on the Statutes,* and *Bacon's Historical Discourses* being practically the only works of this description. In addition there were *Burn's Ecclesiastical Law, Carpenter's Glossarium, Prynne's Sovereigne Power of Parliaments* and his *Chronological Vindication of the King's Supreme Ecclesiastical Jurisdiction.*

In 1779, two years before Royall's death, a bequest had been made to the College to lay the foundations of a law library, by Theodore Atkinson (Harvard 1718, Chief Justice of New Hampshire 1754-75), who by his will left one hundred pounds for the purchase of "such books as may be thought useful in the study of Civil, Statute, and Common Law of England, the books so purchased to be placed in that part of the College library assigned for the donations made by the Province of New Hampshire, the gilded letter T. A. to be impressed upon one of the covers of each volume."(1)

In 1787, John Gardiner, one of the few native lawyers of

---

(1) See *Mass. Hist. Soc. Coll.*, 1st Series, Vol. VII; Vol. IX; Vol. X. *History of Harvard University,* by Josiah Quincy, Vol. II.

Massachusetts who received an education in the English Inns of Court, and who was the leader in the movement to reform the methods of the Bar, 1785-1787, gave to the College a number of choice law books including *Registrum Brevium, Retorna Brevium, Britton* and *Taylor's Civil Law.*(1)

On Feb. 21, 1814, the Corporation appointed a Committee with authority "to expend $300 in the purchase of books at the sale of the library of the late Chief Justice Parsons"; and it is probable that most of the books so bought were law books.

With these exceptions little is to be ascertained of the acquirement by the College of any books on law.

Hence when the Law School was founded the Corporation saw clearly that one of the first needs to be supplied was a working law library. Accordingly at the same meeting, Sept. 5, 1817, when it voted rooms for the new Law Department, the Corporation passed a vote that "$500 be expended for purchasing law books by the Treasurer joined to the Professor of Law".

A year later, Nov. 17, 1818, Professor Stearns reported to the Corporation that he had purchased books to "the amount of $681.74, exceeding the appropriation of $500 and also a donation made by Mr. John How of $100." His account was approved; and at the same time it was voted that:

The University Professor of Law be authorized from time to time to receive from the College Library into his custody such law books as a committee of the Corporation appointed for the purpose shall think proper, said Professor to give a receipt and be accountable for the same and to return them when required.

Voted that the said books shall be subject to the claims of all persons who have the use of the Library by the Standing laws of the College.

Voted that it shall be the duty of the Corporation to examine the State of the said books annually.

On Oct. 26, 1819, the Committee of the Overseers to visit the Library made a report as to the condition of affairs saying:

By finding so very large a number of Law Books removed from the Library, the Committee with great deference would inquire whether this accommodation granted to a particular department may not establish a precedent which shall lead Professors in

(1) See Preface by Charles Sumner to the *Catalogue of the Library of the Harvard Law School* (1834); and *American Jurist*, Vol. XI (Jan. 1834).

other branches, not merely to solicit, but with the greatest propriety to expect, a like indulgence, and thus be the means of parcelling out the Library into private houses, beyond the care of the College Librarian and the use of those who apply for books, of which he is expected to keep a record and take a receipt.

and on November 6, 1819, a Committee of the Corporation also made a Report recommending that new Alcove Catalogues should be made, and inquiring whether "the removal of a large number of Law Books which have been transferred to the Law Library may not establish a precedent which shall lead Professors in other branches to expect a like indulgence."

In 1822, the Law Library received an interesting accession from Hon. Christopher Gore who in a letter to Pres. Kirkland, of June 4, wrote(1):

I take the liberty to send you for the Law Library of the University a copy of some opinions and judgments of the Board of Commissioners under the 7th Article of the Treaty of 1794 between the U. S. and Great Britain.

It is possible that some future occurrences may excite a desire to know the Principles and Grounds which influenced the Construction of that article and the Decisions of the Board.

From a Report made the last winter by a Committee of the House of Representatives of the United States there is reason to conclude that a similar copy which was in the office of the Department of State & Treasury was destroyed in the conflagration of Public Buildings at Washington in the last war.

Mr. Pinkney had a copy which excepting this one herewith sent is all that I believe to be in existence in this country.

Between 1817 and 1826, Mr. Gore gave to the College for the use of the law students the greater part of his valuable law library, comprising several very rare old books, many of which formerly belonged to R. Auchmuty, James Otis, Jeremiah Gridley, and Samuel Sewall and contained their autographs. In the Catalogue of 1826, 119 volumes are marked as presented by him.

And in 1823, it is apparent that interest from outside was beginning to be taken in the new Law Institution, for the records of the Corporation on June 3, show the acceptance, from Hon. Daniel Chipman, of Vermont, of his *Essay on Law of Contracts for the Payment of Specific Articles.*

---

(1)   See *Harv. Coll. Papers*, Vol. X.

On September 28, 1825, the Corporation voted that:

The following works at the request of the Law School be allowed to be removed to the Law School Library and placed therein the usual receipts being given by Professor Stearns. *Viner's Abridgment* 24 Vols. folio, *Bacon's Abridgment* 5 Vols. folio, *Modern Reports*, 10 Vols. folio, *Raymond's Reports* 2 Vols. folio *Strange's Reports* 2 Vols. folio. And that the President and Librarian shall report rules for the regular examination of books in the Law Library; also that proper care be taken that the College seals be in the books.

On June 12, 1826, the Library Committee of the Overseers reported:

Having found that during the last year a considerable number of volumes had been removed to the office of the Professor of Law, in addition to the former deposits there, your Committee suggests the propriety of having a catalogue of what is now called the "Law Library", and that the books should be annually inspected by the Visiting Committee.

June 18, 1827, the same Committee reported that "no examinations were had of the Law Library and no catalogue of it was furnished." The condition of the Law Library had by this time become inextricably confused, owing to the fact that it was composed not only of books purchased especially for it, but of books transferred from the College Library, and of the private books belonging to Professor Stearns and loaned by him for the use of the law students.

Besides the $500 originally given by it and the $100 donated by John How, the Corporation had voted, in 1825, to appropriate the proceeds of a note from one Royal Makepeace, towards the purchase of books for the Law Library.

This vote had been secured through the efforts of Professor Stearns, into whose hands the collection of the claim of the College against Makepeace had been placed; and on Nov. 2, 1825, he wrote:

---

(1) See Vote of Corporation of June 22, 1821, empowering Stearns "to take measures to secure the debt due to the College from the Cambridge & Concord Turnpike Associates" for land belonging to the College taken by the Turnpike. Also letter of Stearns to Makepeace as to $4,293 due to the College, August 9, 1823, *Harv. Coll. Papers,* Vol. X.

The claim was settled by taking Makepeace's note for $4,310 on which $3,200 was allowed for a conveyance of 1-5 part of 4 lots Easterly of the triangular lot, between the Charlestown and Lechmere Point Roads (the Delta) and 3 acres of marsh near Lechmere Point (East Cambridge).

See letter of Stearns to J. Davis, May, 1827, *Harv. Coll. Papers,* 2nd Series, Vol. II. See also *Harv. Coll. Papers,* Vol. XI.

It will probably be recollected by Judge Davis and Mr. Prescott that, when I was endeavouring to bring about this arrangement, they individually gave me encouragement that, if it could be effected, they should be willing to appropriate a part of the sum to the purchase of Books for the Law Library.

Under that expectation, I have put into the Library a complete set of *Johnson's Reports* and others necessary, to the amount of near $300 purchased with my own money. But we are still without *Wheaton's Reports* published 1816-1828, and many other books which are much needed.

In May 1827, he wrote:

The Corporation having appropriated the proceeds of the debt due from Mr. Makepeace to the purchase of books for the Law Library, we were in great want of them and I expected the money would be received soon. I advanced my own money for that purpose nearly two years ago, and having made several purchases, before I had added together the amount of the bills, I found the sum I had laid out much larger than I had supposed, being nearly $700.

In 1826, a pamphlet catalogue of the Law Library was published, which, not being issued by the official authorities, was prepared and sold among the students, at their request, by John B. Hill and William G. Stearns (son of the Professor) then students in the School. On the flyleaf of the copy now (1908) in the Law School, is an explanation of the various marks set against the books—marks which illustrate the confused condition and sources of the Library, and denote respectively—"Books presented by Mr. Gore"—"Books removed from the College Library" —"Books remaining in the College Library"—"——— belong to the University Professor"(1).

---

(1) The following letter from Stearns to Quincy July 8, 1829, illustrates the loose practice in making purchases for the Library and also shows Stearns' wounded feelings at his compulsory resignation.

"I am sorry to have occasion to trouble you upon a subject of little importance, tho' of considerable interest to myself. Sometime ago I was authorized to purchase books for the Law Library of the University. And among other purchases I bought at auction a number of old German books on the Civil, Common and Federal Law. A few of these old books were originally purchased for my own use but most of them were intended for the Law Library of the College.

About two years ago, supposing that if my life should be spared I should remain in the office I then held, I was induced by that consideration to place in the Law Library the above mentioned books, which were purchased for my own Library. And when I settled with the Treasurer of the College, April 7, 1829, for the books I had purchased, I also received from him the price I had paid for the books in question.

"Purchased by the Professor to be paid for out of the Make-peace debt"—"Purchased in 1817 and 1819 with funds furnished by the College and donation of $100 from the late John Howe of Boston"—"Given by a Resolve of the Legislature obtained by the Professor in 1818"—"Books missing".

This catalogue contains 736 titles, comprising a little over 1752 volumes. Deducting the books belonging to the College Library and to Professor Stearns (afterwards withdrawn by him when he resigned), there remain about 1326 volumes in the actual possession of the Law Library at this early date.(1)

I have now Sir to beg the favour of your laying before the Corporation my request that they will allow me to take back those old books (only 11 volumes) repaying to the College the price I received for them with interest. I trust this request will not be refused by the Corporation when I assure them that these books would certainly have been retained in my library, if at the time I placed them in the Law Library I had even sus-pected that I should be so soon expected to surrender the office I then held."

List of Books	$11.40
Interest 15 months	.85
	$12.26

See *Harv. Coll. Papers, 3rd Series*, Vol. III.

(1) *The Harvard Law Library*, by J. H. Arnold. *Harvard Graduatets Magazine*, Vol. XVI (1907).

See also Preface to First Edition of the *Law Library Catalogue* (1834), by Charles Sumner; and the Report of the Law School Visiting Com-mittee of the Board of Overseers, Feb. 1st, 1849, written by Sumner.

CHAPTER XIX.

THE BAR AND THE LAW, 1815-1830.

The years 1815-1830 were an era of great cases and great lawyers.

At the beginning of this period it is to be noted that the Federal Bar was still almost entirely Eastern in its composition(1)—a fact well illustrated by an entry by John Quincy Adams in his diary, Oct. 30, 1817:

> The President said . . . he had written this morning Mr. Wirt of Richmond, Virginia, offering him the office of Attorney General; but it was very doubtful whether he would accept it. The President said that he should have been very desirous of having a western gentleman in the cabinet but he could not see his way clear. He had taken great pains to inform himself but he could not learn that there was any one lawyer in the western country suitably qualified for the office. He had particularly inquired of Judge Todd who had assured him there was no such suitably qualified person. Graham said that he had inquired this morning of Mr. Clay who told him also confidentially the same thing—that there was no lawyer in that country fit for the office of Attorney General.

William Wirt succeeded Richard Rush as Attorney General,

---

(1)   Ten new States had been admitted into the Union prior to 1830.

Kentucky was admitted in 1792. Its first law reports were Hughes Reports in 1803, the next, Kentucky Decisions in 1810.

Tennessee was admitted in 1796. Its first law reports were Overton's in 1813.

Ohio was admitted in 1802. Its first law reports were Hammond's in 1823.

Louisiana admitted in 1812. Its first law reports were Martin's, published in 1811 for the Territorial decisions and in 1812 for the State Court decisions.

Indiana was admitted in 1816. Its first law reports were Isaac Blackford's in 1830.

Mississippi was admitted in 1817. Its first law reports were Robert J. Walker's in 1834.

Illinois was admitted in 1818. Its first law reports were Sidney Breese's in 1831.

Alabama was admitted in 1819. Its first law reports were Henry Minor's in 1829.

Maine was admitted in 1820. Its first law reports were Simon Greenleaf's in 1822.

Missouri was admitted in 1820. Its first law reports were in 1827.

accepting the position because it facilitated his private practice in the Supreme Court; and held the office until 1829.(1)

During this period, the Bar of the United States Supreme Court showed a marked change in composition; the lawyers of Pennsylvania and Maryland no longer held undivided sway; and the Bars of the other States contributed many eminent counsel, especially after 1825, when the city of Washington became easier of access, through the advent of steamboats in the West and East.

William Pinkney remained the undisputed head of the Bar, until his death, in 1822(2). Thereafter, Daniel Webster over-shadowed all others in the number and importance of cases argued, and in the mastery of the great principles of constitutional law; although he had close rivals in Wirt, and Littleton Waller Tazewell, of Virginia. In a letter of May 9, 1822, Wirt writes to his brother-in-law:

Tazewell and Webster have been reaping laurels in the Supreme Court, and I have been—sighing. North of the Potomac, I believe to a man, they yield the palm to Webster; South, to Tazewell. So, you see, there is section in Everything. Time will set all these matters right.

The difficulties attendant on travelling to Washington in those ante-railroad days were reflected by the immense number of cases argued by eminent counsel residing in the District of Columbia. Probably from one-fifth to one-fourth of all the cases, appearing in the volumes of the reporters, Henry Wheaton and Richard Peters, during this period, were argued by Francis Scott Key, Thomas Swann, Walter Jones, or Coxe—all local counsel residing in or about Washington. From Massachusetts, the chief counsel

---

(1) Prior to the passage of the Act of 1814 requiring the Attorney General to reside in Washington, such residence had not been necessary; and William Pinkney resigned the office in 1814, because of the injury to his immense private practice in Baltimore which would be caused by his compliance with the statute.

(2) Wirt wrote, May 9, 1822:
"Poor Pinkney! He died opportunely for his fame. It could not have risen higher. He was a great man. On a set occasion, the greatest, I think at our bar. I never heard Emmett nor Wells, and therefore, I do not say the American bar. He was an excellent lawyer; had very great force of mind, great compass, nice discrimination, strong and accurate judgment; and for copiousness and beauty of diction was unrivalled. He is a real loss to the bar. No man dared to grapple with him without the most perfect preparation and the full possession of all his strength."
See *Memoirs of William Wirt,* by John P. Kennedy, Vol. II.

who argued before the Court were Webster and George Blake; from Rhode Island, Ashur Robbins and William Hunter; none of the other New England States were represented by counsel in more than two or three cases. From New York, David B. Ogden(1) appeared in a large number of cases; Henry Wheaton and Thomas Addis Emmett were almost equally prominent; and Ogden Hoffman(2), Samuel A. Foot(3), T. J. Oakley(4), J. Prescott Hall(5), and C. G. Haines(6) argued a few notable cases. From Pennsylvania, the names of John Sergeant, Joseph R. Ingersoll and Charles J. Ingersoll were the most prominent. Of the New Jersey Bar, George Wood(7) was the leading representative. The lawyers of Maryland naturally appeared in a large number of cases—William Pinkney, W. H. Winder, R. G. Harper, David Hoffman(8), and (beginning about 1824-1825) Roger B. Taney(9); Virginia sent L. W. Tazewell(10), Edmund J. Lee, Benjamin Watkins Leigh(11), Philip N. Nicholas(12), and Charles C. Lee.

The unsettled condition of the finances, of real estate titles, and of the law in general, in a new frontier State, having somewhat crude courts, is shown in the undue proportion of cases coming from Kentucky and argued by Kentucky lawyers,—

---

(1) Born in 1769.

(2) Born in 1793, son of Josiah Ogden Hoffman, Columbia graduate of 1812. District Atty. of N. Y., 1829-35, for twenty-five years counsel in almost every notable criminal trial, 1840-45, U. S. Dist. Atty., 1853-55, Atty. Gen. of N. Y.

(3) Born in 1790, Union Coll. 1811, Judge of Court of Appeals 1851.

(4) Born in 1783, Yale 1801, Atty. Gen. 1819, Judge of the Superior Court 1828, Chief Justice 1846.

(5) Born in 1796, Yale 1817.

(6) Born in 1793, Middlebury Coll. 1816.

(7) Born in 1789, Princeton 1808, studied with Richard Stockton; admitted 1812; in 1837 removed to N. Y.

(8) Born in 1787, Professor of Law in University of Maryland 1817-36.

(9) Born in 1777, Dickinson College 1795, studied with Judge Samuel Chase, admitted 1799, brother-in-law of Frances Scott Key, U. S. Atty Gen. 1831-1833, C. J. of U. S. Supreme Court 1837-1864.
In March, 1826, Story wrote:
"A cause is just rising which bids fair to engage us all in the best manner. It is a great question of legal morality, which, after all, is being sound morality. Webster, Wirt, Taney (a man of fine talents, whom you have not probably heard of) and Emmet are the combatants."
This case was probably *Cassell v. Carroll*, 11 Wheaton 184.

(10) Born in 1777, William and Mary Coll. 1792; admitted 1796, U. S. Senator 1824.

(11) Born in 1781, William and Mary Coll. 1802, U. S. Senator 1834.

(12) Born in 1773, Atty. Gen. 1793, Judge of Court of Appeals 1823.

Henry Clay, Benjamin Hardin(1), Charles A. Wickliffe, George M. Bibb(2), and Isham Talbot(3).

Of lawyers from other Southern and Western States—from Tennessee, came James K. Polk(4), and John H. Eaton(5); from Missouri, Thomas H. Benton(6); from Ohio, Charles Hammond(7) and Thomas Ewing(8); from Georgia, John McPherson Berrien(9); and from South Carolina, Robert Y. Haynes(10), and Hugh S. Légaré(11).

During these years, 1815 to 1830, the changes in the United States Supreme Bench were few. In 1823, Brockholst Livingston, of New York, died, and a strong effort was made to secure the appointment of Chancellor James Kent in his place; but Kent's political Federalist views were too bitter to be acceptable to President Monroe, and Smith Thompson, one of Kent's associates when on the New York Supreme Court, was appointed. In 1825, Thomas Todd of Kentucky died, and was succeeded by Robert Trimble of Kentucky. In 1829, Trimble died, and John McLean of Ohio, took his place. In the same year, Bushrod Washington's death led to the appointment of Henry Baldwin of Pennsylvania.

An average of less than forty cases a year were decided by the Court during this period; and the comparatively small practise of lawyers in the Federal Courts is marked by the lack of reports of cases in the Circuit and District Courts, and the small sales of Supreme Court Reports.

Peter's Admiralty Reports (covering cases beginning in 1792) was published in 1807; *Gallison's Reports* (First Circuit, cover-

---

(1) Born in 1784, admitted in 1806.
(2) Born in 1772, Princeton 1792, U. S. Senator 1811-14, 1829-35, Sec. of Treasury 1844.
(3) Born in 1773, studied with George Nicholas the first Atty. General of Kentucky, U. S. Senator 1815-19.
(4) Born in 1795, Univ. of No. Car., studied with Felix Grundy the head of the Tennessee Bar, admitted 1820.
(5) Born in 1790.
(6) Born in 1782, Univ. of No. Car., admitted in 1811 under patronage of Andrew Jackson then judge of Supreme Court of Tennessee, in 1815 went to Missouri.
(7) Born in 1779, admitted 1801, went from Maryland to Cincinnati in 1822, author of Reports 1821-39.
(8) Born in 1789, admitted in 1816, U. S. Senator 1831-7.
(9) Born in 1781, Princeton 1796, Judge U. S. Dist. Ct. 1810-21, U. S. Senator 1825-29, 1840-52; U. S. Atty. Gen. 1829-31.
(10) Born in 1791, Atty. Gen. of So. Car. 1818-22, U. S. Senator 1823.
(11) Born in 1797, Atty. Gen. of So. Car. 1824-30, U. S. Atty. Gen. 1841.

ing cases 1812-1813) was first published in 1815; *Peter's Reports*
(Third Circuit, covering cases in New Jersey 1803-1818 and
Pennsylvania 1815-1818) was first published in 1819; *Washington's Circuit Court Reports* (Third Circuit, covering cases in New
Jersey and Pennsylvania from 1803) was first published in 1826;
Paine's Reports (Second Circuit, covering cases in New York
and Connecticut from 1810) was first published in 1827.

Of the sale of Supreme Court reports, Daniel Webster wrote
in 1818, reviewing volume three of *Wheaton's Reports*, "it is not
very rapid. The number of law libraries which contain a complete set is comparatively small."(1)

And as late as 1830, Joseph Hopkinson, reviewing the *Condensed Reports of the United States Supreme Court by R. Peters,*
wrote(2) :

The editor goes on to inform us that the reports of the cases
argued and determined in the Supreme Court are contained in 24
volumes which are so costly that there are found but few copies
. . . in many large districts of our country in which there
are federal and state judicial tribunals. In some of those districts, not a single copy of the *Reports* is in the possession of
anyone. . . . An important result of an extended circulation
. . . will be found in the dissemination of the knowledge
of the labours and usefulness of this tribunal, and a corresponding increase with the people of the United States of their attachment and veneration for this department of their government.
Few of our citizens know what this court has done for them.

This period nevertheless was one of tremendous effect upon
the future of American law, and especially of that branch known
as Constitutional Law—the distinctive creation of the great
American judges and lawyers.

In 1816, the great question of States' Rights was presented in
Martin v. Hunter's Lessee (1 Wheaton 305), by the refusal of
the Virginia Court of Appeals to obey the mandate of the United
States Supreme Court, issued in 1813 (*Fairfax v. Hunter, 7*
Cranch 608) on the ground that the appellate power of the
Supreme Court did not extend to revise a decision of the highest
court of a State. The case was argued by Walter Jones, of Virginia, again Samuel Dexter, of Massachusetts,(3) and St. George

---

(1) See *North American Review*, Vol. VIII (Dec. 1818).
(2) See *American Quarterly Review*, Vol. VII (March 1830).
(3) Judge Story writing to Henry Wheaton, Jan. 8, 1817, in praise of
the first volume of *Wheaton's Reports* refers to Dexter's eloquent argument :

Tucker of Virginia. As the case involved his native State, Marshall left the writing of the opinion of the Court to Story. This being the first great constitutional case which had arisen since Story had come upon the Bench, and as he had given little study to this department of the law during his practise at the Bar, and the views of the Republican party to which he belonged were widely different from those entertained by the Chief Justice in his broad construction of the constitution, no small curiosity was felt by his friends as to the determination his mind should take on these constitutional questions.

When the opinion of the Court was read, it became evident that Story had turned a complete convert to Marshall's views, and no more vigorous decision upholding the fullest powers of the Federal judiciary had yet been made.(1)

"I received yesterday your obliging favor, accompanied with a copy of your Reports. I have read the whole volume through hastily, but *con amore*. I am extremely pleased with the execution of the work. The arguments are reported with brevity, force, and accuracy, and the notes have all your clever discriminations and pointed learning. They are truly a most valuable addition to the text, and at once illustrate and improve it. I particularly admire those notes which bring into view the Civil and Continental Law; a path as yet but little explored by our lawyers. They are full of excellent sense, and juridical acuteness. In my judgment, there is no more fair or honorable road to permanent fame, than by thus breathing over our municipal code the spirit of other ages. . . . The kind notice of our friend Dexter in the preface, is delightful to us all. And turning to the case of *Martin v. Hunter,* I perceive the splendid paragraph with which he closed a most excellent argument preserved in its original brightness."

(1) "Mr. Justice Story was of the democratic party, and shared the general views of that party on questions of constitutional politics; but with a mind of too legal a cast to run into wild revolutionary extremes. Coming upon the bench with prepossessions of the character intimated, Mr. Justice Story rose immediately above the sphere of party; and with the ermine of office put on the sacred robe of the constitution and the law. Henceforward it became his duty, his desire, his effort, neither to strain the constitution, nor to travel round it, on the loose popular maxims which guide the partisans; but to interpret it with impartiality and administer it with firmness."

See review of *Story's Commentaries on the Constitution,* by Edward Everett, in *North Amer. Review,* Vol. XXXVIII (Jan. 1834).

The broad Federal powers in which Story had come to believe were stated by him in a letter to Henry Wheaton, Dec. 13, 1815:

"I was much pleased, on reading in a newspaper this morning, that you had published an essay on the necessity of a navigation act; most cordially do I subscribe to your opinion on this subject. I am truly rejoiced that there are found public spirited young men, who are willing to devote their time and talents to the establishment of a great national policy on all subjects. I hope you will follow up the blow by vindicating the necessity of establishing other great national institutions; the extension of the jurisdiction of the Courts of the United States over the whole extent contemplated in the Constitution; the appointment of national notaries public, and national

The year 1818 was marked by the first important argument before the Court, by Daniel Webster, in a case involving the jurisdiction of the United States courts over a murder committed on a ship of war lying in Boston Harbor—*United States v. Bevans* (3 Wheaton 336).

On Dec. 9, 1818, Judge Story wrote, "The next term will probably be the most interesting ever known"; and this comment was certainly justified, for in the year 1819 the Court decided the three great cases of *Dartmouth College v. Woodward, Sturgis v. Crowninshield,* and *McCulloch v. Maryland.*

The *Dartmouth College Case* was argued March 10-12, 1818, by Daniel Webster of Massachusetts, and Joseph Hopkinson of Pennsylvania, against William Wirt of Maryland, and John Holmes of Maine. It is graphically depicted in the following letters from Webster. On Feb. 17, 1818, he wrote to William Sullivan:

Brother (R. G.) Amory and I are all the brethren of the Boston Bar here—I forgot (George) Blake—Ogden and a Mr. Baldwin from New York; Hopkins, Sergeant, and C. J. Ingersoll, Philadelphia; Harper, Winder, Baltimore; Wickham, Leigh and Nicholas from Virginia; Berrien from Georgia, and the gentlemen of this District. Court meets at eleven, hears long speeches till four and adjourns.

On March 13, he wrote to President Brown, of Dartmouth College:

The argument in the cause of the College was finished yesterday. It occupied nearly three days. Mr. Holmes ventured to ask the Court whether it was probable a decision would be made at this term.

The Chief Justice in answer said, that the Court would pay to the subject the consideration due to an act of the legislature of a State and a decision of a State court, and that it was hardly probable a judgment would be pronounced at this term. . . .
Mr. Wirt said all that the case admitted. He was replied to in a manner very gratifying and satisfactory to me by Mr. Hopkinson. Mr. Hopkinson understood every part of our cause, and in his argument did it great justice. No new view was suggested on either side. I am informed that the Bar here are decidedly

justices of the peace; national port wardens and pilots for all the ports of the United States; a national bank, and national bankrupt laws. I have meditated much on all these subjects, and have the details in a considerable degree arranged in my mind."

with us in opinion. On the whole, we have reason to keep up
our courage.

On the same day writing to Jeremiah Mason, he said:

The case was opened on our side by me. Mr. Holmes followed. . . . Upon the whole he gave us three hours of the
merest stuff that was ever uttered in a county court. Wirt followed. He is a good deal of a lawyer, and has very quick per-
ceptions, and handsome power of argument, but he seemed to
treat this case as if his side could furnish nothing but declamation.
. . . Mr. Hopkinson made a most satisfactory reply keeping to the law, and not following Holmes and Wirt into the
fields of declamation and fine speaking. . . . I may say that
nearly or quite all the Bar are with us. How the court will
be I have no means of knowing.

Of Webster's great argument, many accounts have been given,
but none more vivid than that of Rufus Choate in his eulogy in
1852 before the Bar of the United States Circuit Court, in Boston:

Some scenes there are—some Alpine eminences rising above
the high tableland of such a professional life, to which, in the
briefest tribute we should love to follow him. We recall that day,
for instance, when he first announced, with decisive display, what
manner of man he was, to the Supreme Court of the Nation. It
was in 1818, and it was in the argument of the case of Dartmouth College. William Pinkney was recruiting his great faculties and replenishing that reservoir of professional and elegant
acquisition in Europe. Samuel Dexter, "the honorable man and
counsellor and the eloquent orator," was in his grave. The bound-
less old school learning of Luther Martin; the silver voice, and
infinite analytical ingenuity and resource of Jones; the fervid
genius of Emmett, pouring itself along *immenso ore;* the ripe
and beautiful culture of Wirt and Hopkinson—the steel point
unseen, not unfelt, beneath the foliage; Harper himself, statesman as well as lawyer— these and such as these were left of that
noble Bar.
That day, Mr. Webster opened the cause of Dartmouth College to a tribunal unsurpassed on earth in all that gives illustration to a bench of law.
One would love to linger on the scene—when, after a masterly
argument of the law, carrying, as we may now know, conviction
to the general mind of the court, and vindicating and settling for
his life time his place in that forum, he paused to enter, with an
altered feeling, tone and manner, with these words on his peroration— "I have conducted my alma mater to this presence,

that if she must fall, she may fall in her robes, and with dignity",
and he broke forth in that strain of sublime and pathetic eloquence, of which we know not much more than that, in its progress, Marshall the intellectual—the self-controlled—the unemo-
tional, announced visibly the presence of the unaccustomed
enchantment.

The judges being greatly divided in opinion, no decision was
rendered at this term; and the defendants decided to retain
William Pinkney and to ask for a re-argument.   Hopkinson
wrote to Webster, Nov. 17, 1818:

In my passage through Baltimore I fell in with Pinkney who
told me he was engaged in the cause by the present University,
and that he is desirous to argue it if the court will let him.   I
suppose he expects to do something very extraordinary in it, as he
says Mr. Wirt "was not strong enough for it, has not back
enough."   There is a wonderful degree of harmony and mutual
respect among our opponents in this case.   You may remember
how Wirt and Holmes thought and spoke of each other.   .   .   .
I think if the court consents to hear Mr. Pinkney it will be a
great stretch of complaisance, and that we should not give our
consent to any such proceeding.

No re-argument was had however, and on Feb. 2, 1819, the
Court rendered its decision, of which Hopkinson wrote Brown on
the same day:

Our triumph in the college cause has been complete.   Five
judges, only six attending, concur not only in a decision in our
favor, but in placing it upon principles broad and deep, and
which secure corporations of this description from legislative
despotism and party violence for the future.   The court goes
all lengths with us, and whatever trouble these gentlemen may
give us in the future, in their great and pious zeal for the interests
of learning, they cannot shake those principles which must and
will restore Dartmouth College to its true and original owners.
I would have an inscription over the door of your building,
"Founded by Eleazor Wheelock, Refounded by Daniel Webster."

A contemporary opinion of this case is found in a review of
volume four of *Wheaton's Reports* in 1820(1):

Perhaps no judicial proceeding in this country ever involved
more important consequences or excited a deeper interest in the
public mind than the case of Dartmouth College recently deter-

---

(1)   See *North American Review,* Vol. X (Jan. 1820).

mined. While the cause was pending, there was much anxiety
felt for its final result by the friends of our literary institutions;
for it was early perceived that they stood on no surer foundations
than Dartmouth College. . . . The gentlemen engaged in it
had long been trained in the habits of forensic discussion; and
deeply feeling their responsibility to their task, all that ever
makes men eloquent or convincing, reasoning and authority
seemed to be exhausted, and the cause of Dartmouth College
and of all literary corporations appeared to be fixed immovably
on both.

A few days later, on Feb. 17, 1819, the Supreme Court decided
the case of *Sturgis v. Crowninshield,* declaring the insolvency
act of New York unconstitutional and establishing the power
of the States to pass such bankrupt laws, if confined to contracts
made after the passage of the law. In view of the depressed
condition of business affairs in the country this decision was of
immense importance.(1)
The case had arisen in the Circuit Court in Massachusetts in 1811,
being one of the earliest cases over which Judge Story had presided. In the Supreme Court, Joseph Hopkinson and David
Daggett argued for the plaintiff, and D. B. Ogden and William
Hunter for the defendant.

Webster, writing to Jeremiah Mason, Feb. 15, 1819, two days
before the opinion of the Court was rendered, said(2):

(1) The scope of the decision was not wholly understood at the time;
and in 1828 we find the following amusing plaint of Chief Justice Isaac
Parker in *Hall v. Williams,* 6 Pick. 243:
"This is not the first occasion we have had to regret a too prompt submission to the decision of the Supreme Court of the United States; not, however, from any diminution of respect for that eminent tribunal but because
we have found that further consideration has brought about a qualification
of the doctrine which seemed to have been definitely settled, or that some
qualifying principle in the case itself has been overlooked by us in our
readiness to yield supremacy to that court on all questions in which by the
Constitution their judgment is paramount. I allude to the decision of that
court on State insolvent laws in the case of *Sturgis v. Crowninshield,* 4
Wheat. 722, the effect of which we understand to be to overrule the decision
of this court in the case of *Blanchard v. Russell;* in consequence of which
we dismissed several cases which might have been maintained on the
grounds of that decision. We have since learned by the case of *Ogden v.
Saunders,* 12 Wheat. 213, that there is no decision of the Supreme Court
of the United States militating with our decision and feel ourselves
justified in recurring to the principle there decided on the law of this
Commonwealth. . . .
Held until further decided by the United States Supreme Court we construe *Mills v. Duryee,* 7 Cranch 481, as meaning only that judgments of
foreign States are binding, only if service had been obtained on defendant
and jurisdiction."
(2) *The Writings and Speeches of Daniel Webster,* Vol. XVI (1903).

Nothing has been as yet done with the Bankruptcy (Bill), and it seems too late to do anything. The question is before the court whether the State Bankrupt Laws are valid. The general opinion is that the six judges now here will be equally divided on the point. I confess, however, I have a strong suspicion there will be an opinion, and that that opinion will be against the State laws. If there were time remaining, the decision, should it happen, might help through the bill.

The question between Maryland and the Bank is to be argued this day week. I have no doubt of the result.

The reference at the end of Webster's letter was to the third great case decided at this session of the court—*McCulloch v. Maryland,* which upheld the power of a State to tax a National Agency, and also the constitutionality of the Act of Congress chartering the Bank of the United States. This case arose out of the unpopularity of the new Bank of the United States, and the attempt of Maryland to tax its branch out of business, Mc-Culloch being its cashier(1). The arguments of Pinkney, Wirt and Webster for the Bank, and of Martin, Hopkinson and Jones for the State had extended over a week; and of Pinkney's great effort, Judge Story wrote March 3, 1819:

Mr. Pinkney rose on Monday to conclude the argument; he spoke all that day and yesterday, and will probably conclude to-day. I never, in my whole life, heard a greater speech; it was worth a journey from Salem to hear it; his elocution was excessively vehement, but his eloquence was overwhelming. His language, his style, his figures, his arguments, were most brilliant and sparkling. He spoke like a great statesman and patriot, and a sound constitutional lawyer. All the cobwebs of sophistry and metaphysics about State rights and State sovereignty he brushed away with a mighty besom. We have had a crowded audience of ladies and gentlemen; the hall was full almost to suffocation, and many went away for want of room.

Of the opinion he wrote, March 7, "that it excites great interest and in a political view is of the deepest consequence to the nation. It goes to establish the Constitution upon its great original principle." And so great a blow to State sovereignty was this decision felt to be that Marshall wrote to Story, May 27, 1819:

(1) The Bank of the United States was the chief litigant in the Supreme Court, 1815-1830, being involved in 23 cases. Its regular counsel was John Sergeant of Pennsylvania; but Daniel Webster and Henry Clay were retained in a large number of its important cases.

The opinion in the Bank case continues to be denounced by the democracy in Virginia. An effort is certainly making to induce the legislature which will meet in December, to take up the subject and to pass resolutions very like those which were called forth by the alien and sedition laws in 1799. . . . If the principles which have been advanced on this occasion were to prevail, the constitution would be converted into the old confederation.(2)

The decision of the Supreme Court was handed down on March 6, 1819, but was at once defied by the State of Ohio, whose auditor, Osborn, attempted to collect a tax from the Chillicothe Branch of the United States Bank, under a statute of that State. The Bank obtained an injunction in the United States Circuit Court, in September 1819, which was violated by the State officers, and contempt process was issued.(2) Meanwhile the Ohio Legislature met and withdrew the protection of its laws from the Bank. The Circuit Court decided against Osborn; and the case came to the Supreme Court in 1824, where it was argued twice, first by Charles Hammond and John C. Wright(3) of Ohio, against Clay; the second time by Harper of Maryland,

---

(1)   Samuel Tyler in his *Life and Times of Roger B. Taney,* says:
"In the case of *McCulloch v. the State of Maryland,* Chief Justice Marshall was made to swerve from his earlier strictness of construction by the moulding and transforming logical power, aided by the delusive light of the seductive fancy, of Pinkney. The great orator put his own thoughts into the mind of the Chief Justice without his knowing it, until he made him see in the auxiliary provision of the Constitution to make all laws which shall be necessary and proper for carrying into execution the specific power granted, powers as original as those they are to carry into execution. And the Chief Justice never afterwards freed himself from this persuasive coercion of that master of the forum."
See also letters of Marshall, *Mass. Hist. Soc. Proc.,* 2nd Series, Vol. XIV (1900-1901).

(2)   Story wrote to Stephen White, Feb. 27, 1820:
"The Ohio controversy respecting the Bank of the United States, is kept up with unabated vigor, and there is no probability that the case will come before us until next year. It is indispensable that I should not have any real, or imagined interest in the Bank; as it is not improbable that I shall have causes before me in the Circuit Court, raising some of the questions. I wish you, therefore, to understand that I do not wish, under any circumstances, to have the shares which I transferred to you, kept by you with any view to accommodate me, if I should wish to re-purchase them in future. It is indispensable that I should not hold any shares, at any time hereafter, as the Bank will commence its future suits in the Circuit Court; if therefore you do not wish to hold the shares for yourself, pray sell them immediately at their current price, and if they should not bring what you allowed me, I shall feel bound to refund the difference, as I know you took them merely for my accommodation."

(3)   Born in 1783, 1831 Judge of Supreme Court, author of Reports 1831-34.

Ethan Allen Brown(1) and Wright of Ohio for Osborn, and Clay(2), Webster and Sergeant for the Bank. Decision was affirmed for the Bank (*Osborn v. U. S. Bank*, 9 Wheaton 738).

These cases not only mark the growth of the control by the Supreme Court over State legislation, but also emphasize the disordered condition of the country's finances, and the extreme action which the States were willing to take in order to break down the supremacy of the United States Bank in its control of the currency.

In this year, 1819, the United States Circuit Courts were busy with a branch of law which has now become almost extinct—the law of piracy, incidentally involving illegal slave trade. For several years, the Government had been much embarrassed in its dealings with foreign nations, by the crowd of piratical privateers which sailed, largely from Southern ports of the United States, under flags of the infant, mushroomlike South American Republics. France and Spain had protested violently. Finally John Quincy Adams, as Secretary of State, adopted a vigorous policy, and prevailed on William Wirt, as Attorney General, to prosecute the pirates. At first the courts were inclined to rule the law in favor of the pirates. The following extracts from Adams' diary are illuminating on the situation (allowing for his well known bitter personal prejudices) :

May 26, 1817: I spoke to Wirt about the acquittal at Baltimore of the pirate Daniels. The case went off upon a legal quibble. Wirt says it is because the judges are two weak but very good old men who suffer themselves to be bullied and browbeaten by Pinkney.(3)

---

(1) Born in 1776, Judge of Ohio Supreme Court 1810-18, Governor 1818-22, U. S. Senator 1822-25.

(2) Story wrote to Judge Todd, March 14, 1823:
"Your friend Clay has argued before us with a good deal of ability; and if he were not a candidate for higher offices, I should think he might attain great eminence at this Bar. But he prefers the fame of popular talents to the steady fame of the Bar."

(3) See *Diary of John Quincy Adams*, Vol. IV, in which Adams continued with his reflections on law as follows:
"I told him that I thought it was law logic—an artificial system of reasoning exclusively used in courts of justice, but good for nothing anywhere else. . . . The source of all this pettifogging is, that out of judicial courts the end of human reasoning is truth or justice, but in them it is law. "Ita lex scripta est", and there is no reply. Hence it is my firm belief that, if instead of the long robes of judges and the long speeches of lawyers, the suitors of every question debated in the courts between individuals were led blindfolded up to a lottery wheel and there bidden to draw, each of them one of two tickets, one marked Right and the other

August 21, 1819: Pinkney is the standing counsel for all pirates who, by browbeating and domineering over the courts and by paltry pettifogging law-quibbles, has saved all their necks from the richly merited halter. . . . . Baltimore upon privateering and banking is rotten to the heart.

March 29, 1819: The misfortune is not only that this abomination has spread over a large portion of the merchants and of the population of Baltimore, but that it has infected almost every officer of the United States in the place. . . . The District Judge Houston and the Circuit Judge Duval are both feeble, inefficient men, over whom William Pinkney, employed by all the pirates as their counsel, domineers like a slave driver over his negroes.

Finally, however, the conviction and sentence to death of about fifty persons were secured at Boston, Baltimore, and Richmond.(1)   Many of these cases, as well as cases on the illegal slave trading, came before Judge Story in the United States Circuit Court in Maine and Massachusetts; and the following extracts from his charge to the first Grand Jury in the Maine District, May 8, 1820, illustrate the conditions of the time:

And first, Gentlemen, let me call your attention to the crime of Piracy. This offence has in former times crimsoned the ocean with much innocent blood, and in its present alarming progress threatens the most serious mischiefs to our peaceful commerce. It cannot be disguised, that at the present times there are hordes of needy adventurers prowling upon the ocean, who, under the specious pretext of being in the service of the Patriot Governments of South America commit the foulest outrages. Being united together by no common tie but the love of plunder, they assume from time to time the flag of any nation, which may best favor their immediate projects; and depredate, with indiscriminate ferocity, upon the commerce of the neutral world, regardless of the principles of law and the dictates of justice.

And on the slave trade, after citing the Federal statutes against it, he said:

We have but too many melancholy proofs, from unquestioned sources, that it is still carried on with all the implacable ferocity

Wrong, and execution should issue according to the sentence of the whole, more substantial justice would be done than is now dispensed by courts of law. In criminal cases, by the humanity of the law, which is indeed its best and most amiable feature, the chances in favor of the culprit are multiplied; and when the subtilty and the passions of the judges combine in their favor, no criminal can be brought to justice and punishment."

(1) See *Diary of John Quincy Adams*, Vol. IV.

and insatiable rapacity of former times. Avarice has grown more subtle in its evasions; and watches and seizes its prey with an appetite, quickened, rather than suppressed, by its guilty vigils. American citizens are steeped up to their very mouths (I scarcely use too bold a figure) in this stream of iniquity. They throng to the coasts of Africa under the stained flags of Spain and Portugal, sometimes selling abroad "their cargoes of despair", and sometimes bringing them into some of our Southern ports, and there, under the forms of the law, defeating the purposes of the law itself, and legalizing their inhuman, but profitable, adventures. I wish I could say, that New England and New England men were free from this deep pollution. But there is reason to believe, that they, who drive a loathsome traffic, "and buy the muscles and the bones of men", are to be found here also.

The law was finally settled in a series of nine piracy cases, decided in the United States Supreme Court by Judge Story (*U. S. v. Klintock* and *U. S. v. Smith,* 5 Wheaton), in 1820, against the strong arguments urged in behalf of the pirates by Daniel Webster, and by W. H. Winder of Maryland.

In 1821, the great subject of State Sovereignty again arose in the case of *Cohens v. Virginia* (6 Wheaton 264). Marshall's opinion re-affirmed Judge Story's declaration, in *Martin v. Hunter,* of the full power of the Supreme Court to review the decision of the State courts. Philip P. Barbour, later Judge of the United States Supreme Court(1), and Alexander Smyth(2) appeared for the State of Virginia, and William Pinkney and D. B. Ogden for the plaintiff.

The decision was regarded with grave concern by the upholders of States' Rights, and was bitterly attacked in letters and speeches. Jefferson wrote to Judge William Johnson, June 12, 1823:

On the decision of *Cohens v. State of Virginia* in the Supreme Court of the United States in March, 1821, Judge Roane (presiding judge of the Court of Appeals of Virginia) under the signature of Algernon Sidney wrote for the *Enquirer* a series of papers on the law of that case. I considered these papers maturely as they came out, and confess that they appeared to me to pulverize every word that had been delivered by Judge Marshall of the extra-judicial part of his opinion, and all was extra-judicial, except the decision that the act of Congress had

---

(1) Born in 1783, William and Mary Coll., offered Professorship of Law in Univ. of Va. in 1825, U. S. Dist. Judge 1830, U. S. Supreme Court 1836.
(2) Born in 1765.

not purported to give to the corporation of Washington the
authority claimed by their lottery of controlling the laws of the
States within the States themselves.

The practice of Judge Marshall of travelling out of his case
to prescribe what the law would be in a moot case not before the
court is very irregular and very censurable.

On Jan. 19, 1821, he wrote:

I am sensible of the inroads daily making by the federal into
the jurisdiction of its co-ordinate associates, the state governments. Its legislative and executive branches may sometimes err,
but elections and dependence will bring them to rights. The
judiciary branch is the instrument, which, working like gravity,
without intermission, is to press us at last into one consolidated
mass.

And again, on March 4, 1823, he wrote: "There is no danger
I apprehend so much as the consolidation of our government, by
the noiseless and therefore unalarming instrumentality of the Supreme Court."(1)

Of the criticism on the case, Marshall wrote to Story, June
15, 1821(2):

The opinion of the Supreme Court in the lottery case has
been assailed with a degree of virulence transcending what has
appeared on former occasions . . . I think for coarseness and malignity of invention Algernon Sidney (Spencer Roane, Judge of
the Virginia Court of Errors and Appeals) surpasses all party
writers who have ever made pretensions to any decency of character.

Story writing to Jeremiah Mason, Jan. 10, 1822, said of these
attacks on the Court:

---

(1)   On Dec. 25, 1820, Jefferson had written to Thomas Ritchie:
"The judiciary of the United States is the subtle corps of sappers and
miners constantly working underground to undermine the foundations of
our confederated fabric. They are construing our constitution from a co-
ordination of a general and special government to a general and supreme
one alone. . . . Having found from experience that impeachment is an
impracticable thing, a mere scare-crow, they consider themselves secure
for life; they sculk from responsibility to public opinion, the only remaining
hold on them, under a practice first introduced into England by Lord Mansfield. An opinion is huddled up in conclave, perhaps by a majority of one,
delivered as if unanimous, and with the silent acquiescence of lazy or timid
associates, by a crafty chief judge who sophisticates the law to his mind by
the turn of his own reasoning.
A judiciary independent of a king or executive alone is a good thing;
but independence of the will of the nation is a solecism, at least in a republican government."
See *Writings of Thomas Jefferson,* Vol. X, pp. 169, 184, 197, 246.
(2)   See Mass. Hist. Soc. Proc., 2nd Series, Vol. XIV (1900-1901).

I am glad you write somewhat encouragingly respecting the Judiciary. My only hope is in the discordant views of the various interested factions and philosophists. Mr. Jefferson stands at the head of the enemies of the Judiciary, and I doubt not will leave behind him a numerous progeny bred in the same school. The truth is and cannot be disguised, even from vulgar observation, that the Judiciary in our country is essentially feeble, and must always be open to attack from all quarters. It will perpetually thwart the wishes and views of demagogues, and it can have no places to give and no patronage to draw around it close defenders. Its only support is the wise and the good and the elevated in society; and these, as we all know, must ever remain in a discouraging minority in all Governments. If, indeed, the Judiciary is to be destroyed, I should be glad to have the decisive blow now struck, while I am young, and can return to the profession and earn an honest livelihood. If it comes in my old age, it may find me less able to bear the blow, though I hope not less firm to meet it. For the Judges of the Supreme Court there is but one course to pursue. That is, to do their duty firmly and honestly, according to their best judgments.

Opposition to the Supreme Court took shape in many legislative efforts to change its powers and tenure.

Soon after the Burr trial, in 1807-1808, motions had been made in each branch of Congress to amend the Constitution so that all judges should hold office for a term of years and be removable by the President on address by two-thirds of bouth Houses. This proposition was supported by Resolves of the Legislatures of Pennsylvania and Vermont, as well as by action of the House of Delegates in Virginia and one branch of the Legislature in Tennessee.

In 1822, soon after the decision in *Cohens v. Virginia,* Richard M. Johnson of Kentucky proposed in Congress an amendment to the Constitution giving appellate jurisdiction to the Senate in any case in which a State was party. Later, in 1830, an attempt was made to repeal the 25th Section of the Judiciary Act giving the Supreme Court appellate jurisdiction with reference to the State courts; and in 1831, an attempt was made in Congress to change the tenure of office of Federal Judges, from life to a term of years.

In 1822, the case of *Ricard v. Williams* (6 Wheaton 59) is of interest as being the last case argued by William Pinkney,(1)

(1) Pinkney died Feb. 25, 1822.
Of his funeral, Judge Story wrote, Feb. 28, 1822:
"The concourse was immense; the day was uncommonly fine and bright,

Webster and D. B. Ogden being the opposing counsel. It was vividly described by Professor Theophilus Parsons in an address to the Harvard Law School, in 1859:

Pinkney I had known intimately, having passed some months in his family; and during his last winter in Washington I saw him perhaps every day, from the meeting of the Senate of which he was a member, to the hour when I stood by his deathbed. I was a young man then, and I have thought that it was perhaps because I was young that Mr. Pinkney excited my admiration as he did. He certainly seemed to me the most brilliant person I had ever known; and if I did not call him the greatest advocate in the country, it was because Mr. Webster had begun to dispute the supremacy which until then had not been questioned. Well do I remember the last case in which these giants encountered— the last in which Pinkney appeared. Almost immediately after it, he died of apoplexy, caused, as some supposed, by his great efforts to preserve that sovereignty which had been unchallenged so long.   .   .   .

During all his long argument, the room was crowded—no one seemed to leave but upon compulsion. All, all alike sat or stood, fascinated and charmed. As I listened, I thought then,—and, as I remember it, I think now,—that the effort of that day presented to us all that learning could give, and all that the severest logic could do,—and all of this, used and wielded with perfect skill, and the most consummate rhetoric. That impression is vivid to this day. So long after it was made, as when I first knew Rufus Choate (1834) it was uneffaced and clear; and when I left the court house at the close of the case which he (Choate) conducted, my first remark to a friend was "I have heard the man who is to replace William Pinkney."

In 1823, a case in the United States Circuit Court in South Carolina aroused great interest, as involving in one action the four momentous questions upon which most of the great cases of the first half of the 19th Century turned—States' Rights, Slavery,

---

but a settled gloom was over the countenances of all. Labor was generally suspended. To give you some idea of the length of the procession, I state that there were from one hundred and fifty to two hundred carriages attending in regular succession.

I return from this truly depressing scene in deep affliction. It is impossible to contemplate the death of such a man without the most painful emotions. His genius and eloquence were so lofty, I might almost say so unrivalled, his learning so extensive, his ambition so elevated, his political and constitutional principles so truly just and pure, his weight in the public councils so decisive, his character at the Bar so peerless and commanding, that there seems now left a dismal and perplexing vacancy. His foibles and faults were so trifling or excusable, in comparison with his greatness, that they are at once forgotten and forgiven with his deposit in the grave. His great talents are now universally acknowledged."

Interstate Commerce, and Common Law Jurisdiction of the Federal Courts. The case—*Elkinson v. Deliesseline* (Fed. Cases, 4366)—was an application for a writ of habeas corpus and also for a writ de homine replegiando by a British seaman, imprisoned under the statute of South Carolina of 1822, authorizing the detention of free negroes arriving on any vessel, until the vessel was ready to sail. Judge William Johnson decided: first, that "the right of the general government to regulate commerce with sister States and foreign nations is a paramount and exclusive right."—thus anticipating, by a year, Chief Justice Marshall's decision in *Gibbons v. Ogden* (1); second, the doctrine of State Sovereignty was denied, and the statute was held unconstitutional:

The plea of necessity is urged, and of the existence of that necessity, we are told, the State alone is to judge. Where is this to land us. Is it not asserting the right in each State to throw off the federal constitution at its will and pleasure? If it can be done as to any particular article, it can be done as to all; and like the old confederation, the Union becomes a mere rope of land.

third, the right of the State to legislate as to slavery did not extend to imprisoning free negroes; fourth, the writ de homine replegiando was ingrafted into the jurisprudence of South Carolina, as a part of its Common Law.

The following interesting letter from Marshall to Story, Sept. 26, 1823, clearly shows the spirit of the time, regarding the subjects covered by this decision:

Our brother Johnson, I perceive, has hung himself on a democratic snag, in a hedge composed entirely of thorny State Rights in South Carolina, and will find some difficulty, I fear, in getting off into smooth, open ground.

You have, I presume, seen his opinion in the *National Intelligencer*, and could scarcely have supposed that it would have excited so much irritation as it seems to have produced. The subject is one of much feeling in the South. Of this I was apprized, but did not think it would have shown itself in such strength as it has. The decision has been considered as another act of judicial usurpation; but the sentiment has been avowed

(1) "In the Constitution of the United States" said Johnson "the most wonderful instrument ever drawn by the hand of man, there is comprehension and precision unparalleled; and I can truly say that after spending my life in studying it, I still daily find in it some new excellence."

that, if this be the constitution, it is better to break that instrument than submit to the principle. Reference has been made to the massacres of St. Domingo, and the people have been reminded that those massacres also originated "in the theories of a distant government, insensible of and not participating in the dangers their systems produced." It is suggested that the point will be brought before the Supreme Court, but the writer seems to despair of a more favorable decision from that tribunal, since they are deserted by the friend in whom their confidence was placed.

Thus you see fuel is continually added to the fire at which the exaltées are about to roast the judicial department. You have, it is said, some laws in Massachusetts, not very unlike in principles to that which our brother has declared unconstitutional. We have its twin brother in Virginia, a case has been brought before me in which I might have considered its constitutionality had I chosen to do so; but it was not absolutely necessary, and as I am not fond of butting against a wall in sport, I escaped on the construction of the act.(1)

In 1824, the constitutionality of a statute of one of the Northern States was involved in a case which has played a larger part in determining the economic, social and political conditions of the country, than any case ever decided by the Supreme Court,—the great Steamboat Case, *Gibbons v. Ogden* (9 Wheat. 1). For twenty-six years, Ex-Chancellor Robert R. Livingston and Robert Fulton and their assigns had enjoyed, under grant from the New York Legislature, an exclusive right to run steamboats in the waters of New York. Efforts in the courts to break this monopoly had been frequent but unavailing. A case in the United States Circuit Court, *Livingston v. Van Ingen,* in 1811, had been dismissed for want of jurisdiction. A case in the New York State Court between the same parties had resulted in a decree upholding the power of the State to grant such exclusive rights. Pending this case, the State had passed a further statute authorizing the seizure of any steam vessel found in New York waters in violation of the Livingston grant, thus practically making it impossible for any person to try his rights in court, without first forfeiting his vessel. Retaliatory statutes were passed in New Jersey and Connecticut forbidding boats "operated by fire or steam" under the license granted by the New York Legislature from plying in the waters of New Jersey, or of Connecticut; and so

(1) Unpublished Letter in the *Story Papers* in possession of the Massachusetts Historical Society.

bitter were the feelings aroused by the monopoly that, as William Wirt said in his final argument before the Supreme Court the three States "were almost on the eve of civil war." Finally, a test case was brought in New York by Ex-Governor Aaron Ogden, of New Jersey, who, having established a steamboat line between New York and Elizabethport in defiance of the monopoly, had been enjoined by John R. Livingston and had accepted a license from the latter. The defendant was Thomas Gibbons, of Georgia, a former partner of Ogden, but who had refused to act under the Livingston license, and had started an opposition line in 1818. A motion to dissolve the injunction issued was heard by Chancellor Kent and denied in 1819; and the Court of Errors sustained Kent in 1820.(1) Thereupon an appeal was taken to the United States Supreme Court, an interesting reference to which is found in a letter of Judge Story, Feb. 28, 1821:

We are to take up, in a few days, another question, whether a State can give to any person an exclusive right to navigate its waters with steamboats, against the right of a patentee, claiming under the laws of the United States. The case comes from New York, and Mr. Emmett of New York, and Mr. Pinkney are on one side; and Mr. Webster, Mr. Ogden, of New York, and Mr. Wirt, the Attorney-General, on the other. The arguments will be very splendid. . . .

The case was dismissed, however, on a point of practice(2).

Meanwhile other suits had been brought in the United States Circuit Court to test the question—one of which—*Livingston v. Fulton Steamboat Company* (6 Wheat. 450) in which Daniel Webster and Roger Minott Sherman were counsel reached the Supreme Court, but was dismissed for want of jurisdiction(3).

Before *Gibbons v. Ogden* came up in the Supreme Court again, William Pinkney, one of the chief counsel for Ogden died, and Thomas J. Oakley, of New York, was engaged in his place.

On February 4-7, 1824, the case was argued at Washington. "Tomorrow week," wrote William Wirt, "will come on the great steamboat question from New York. (T. A.) Emmett and (T.

(1) See *Livingston v. Van Ingen*, 9. Johnson 807 (1812).
Livingston v. Van Ingen, 1 Paine 45 (1811).
Livingston v. Ogden and Gibbons, 4 John Ch. 150 (1819).
Gibbons v. Ogden, 17 John. 488 (1820).
Steamboat Co. v. Livingston, 3 Cowen 741; 1 Wend. 560.
(2) *Gibbons v. Ogden*, 6 Wheat. 450.
(3) See *Life of Roger Minott Sherman*, by W. A. Beers (1882).

J.) Oakley on one side, Webster and myself on the other. Come down and hear it. Emmett's whole soul is in the case and he will stretch all his powers. Oakley is said to be one of the first logicians of the age; as much a Phocion as Emmett is a Themistocles, and Webster is as ambitious as Caesar. He will not be outdone by any man if it is within the compass of his power to avoid it. It will be a combat worth witnessing."(1)

When Wirt and Webster met for consultation as to the argument, it was found that Wirt, who was senior counsel differed wholly from the position which Webster stated he intended to take; and it was agreed that each should argue on his own lines.

Wirt urged as his main point the conflict between the State statute and the patent laws of the United States. Both counsel urged the conflict between the State statute and the coasting license issued to Gibbons under the Federal statute. But Webster alone took the broader ground, as stated by himself later (1847):

It is true that . . . I declined to argue this cause on any other ground than that of the great commercial question presented by it—the then novel question of the constitutional authority of Congress exclusively to regulate commerce in all its forms on all navigable waters of the United States. . . . without any monopoly, restraint, or interference created by State legislation.

And he maintained that the State statute was void, irrespective of the existence of any conflicting Federal legislation.

It is related that when Webster stated his position to the

---

(1) *Memoirs of W. Wirt,* by John P. Kennedy, Vol. II.
Daniel Lord, at the New York Bar meeting on the death of T. J. Oakley, said:
"Judge Oakley represented the mighty sovereignty of the State of New York. His associate was Thomas Addis Emmett, and by whom were they met? By Daniel Webster and William Wirt. These four men debated that question before Marshall, Story, Washington, Todd, and Thompson. This, I conceive, to have been the culmination of professional eminence. What court could have so great a question? What court could be so greatly constituted? What court had the power of bringing private men to sit in judgment upon sovereign States? What court could feel the capacity to arbitrate among arguments of such talent, power and learning?"
See *Law Reporter,* Vol. XX. (1857).
In the *Passenger Cases,* 7 Howard, p. 437, in 1849, Mr. Justice Wayne says, "The case of *Gibbons v. Ogden* in the extent and variety of learning, and in the acuteness of distinction with which it was argued by counsel is not surpassed by any other case in the reports of courts. The case will always be a high and honorable proof of the eminence of the American Bar of that day".

court, "Judge Marshall laid down his pen, turned up his coat cuffs, dropped back upon his chair, and looked sharply upon him; Mr. Webster continued to state his propositions in varied terms, until he saw his eyes sparkle and his doubts giving way; he then gave full scope to his argument."(1)

In his decision announced on March 2, 1824, only three weeks after the argument, Marshall made slight reference to Wirt's argument, and followed Webster's almost in his very language. Though the precise point decided was that the State statute was in conflict with the Federal coasting license, the opinion of the Chief Justice went far beyond this, and expressed clearly his adoption of Webster's broader view.(2)

The immediate result of the decision was the destruction of the Livingston monopoly,(3) which otherwise would have lasted until 1838. Its secondary results were far-reaching.

It opened the Hudson River and Long Island Sound to the free passage of steamboats, thus tremendously increasing the freight and passenger traffic on those great waterways, and proving a potent factor in the building up of New York as a commercial centre. It promoted interstate communication by steam throughout the country, by removing the danger of similar grants of monopolies in other States(4). It was of immense importance

(1) See *Reminiscences of Daniel Webster,* by Peter Harvey.
Daniel Webster as a Jurist, by Joel Parker.
(2) Webster himself states Marshall's indebtedness in a letter to Edward Everett, Oct. 30, 1851:
"I presume the argument in *Gibbons v. Ogden* was written by me and given to Mr. Wheaton. The argument is a pretty good one, and was on a new question. It has been often observed that the opinion of the court delivered by Chief Justice Marshall follows closely the track of the argument. He adopts the idea which I remember struck him at the time that by the constitution, the commerce of the several States has become a unit."
(3) On March 5, 1824, the *New York Evening Post* said:
"This opinion, drawn up by Justice Marshall presents one of the most powerful efforts of the human mind that has ever been displayed from the bench of any court. Many passages indicated a profoundedness and forecast in relation to the destinies of our Confederacy, peculiar to the great man who acted as the organ of the court. The Steamboat Grant is at an end."
For detailed account of *Gibbons v. Ogden,* presented with many interesting sidelights, see *The Federal Power over Carriers and Corporations,* by E. Parmalee Prentice (1907).
(4) New York had not been the only State to grant a steamboat monopoly; Pennsylvania in 1813, and Georgia in 1814, had granted such monopolies; Massachusetts, in 1815, had given an exclusive license to John L. Sullivan for steam tow-boats on the Connecticut River; and New Hampshire had granted a similar license in 1816. Louisiana in 1811, had granted a monopoly, similar to that in New York, to Fulton and Livingston.

in developing the coal industry, then largely an experiment; for it produced a great demand for coal as a fuel on the steamboats. It was largely responsible for the sudden growth of the New England manufacturing industries, by making possible the cheap transportation of coal to New England by water. It is to be noted that the lack of coal had been a serious obstacle to the use of the steam engine in factories, as William Tudor, writing in 1820, in his *Letters from the Eastern States,* said:

> It seems, then, that there can be no doubt of the practicability of our becoming manufacturers, and the expediency is I presume growing daily more evident. . . .
> The want of coal will prevent our making use of steam engines of large dimensions, until it shall be discovered, which it probably will be at no remote period, between the Connecticut and the Hudson, if not in other parts of this district.

In the consideration of the influence of *Gibbons v. Ogden* upon the commercial prosperity of the country another leading case of the period, *Rogers v. Bradshaw* (20 Johns on 735), decided in the preceding year, 1823, may be incidentally noticed. This case sustained the constitutionality of the Erie Canal statute, a work begun July 4, 1817, the court applying broad rules of statutory construction, for the promotion of so great a project(1):

> A statute vesting large powers resting very much for their exercise in undefined discretion and checked only by the gentle admonition of doing "no unnecessary damage" ought to be construed more benignly and more liberally. Especially ought this to be the case when the powers are to be applied to a great public object calculated to intimidate by its novelty, its expense, its magnitude and which depended for its successful results upon decision of character as well as upon maturity of judgment.
> We give to the expressions the sense most suitable to the subject and best adapted to the facility and success of a great and generous scheme of public policy.

The year after *Gibbons v. Ogden,* in 1825, Judge Story delivered an opinion in another steamboat case which, if it had not been overruled, twenty-six years later, would have very substantially narrowed the powers of the Federal Courts and the development of American commerce. This was the case of *The Steamboat Thomas Jefferson* (10 Wheaton 428), in which the

---

(1) The Erie Canal was opened in October, 1825, having cost $10,-000,000.

Court ruled that a vessel making a voyage from a Kentucky port up the Mississippi and Missouri Rivers was not on navigable waters, so as to bring it within admiralty jurisdiction:

Whether under the power to regulate commerce between the States, Congress may not extend the remedy by the summary process of admiralty to the case of voyages on the Western waters, it is unnecessary for us to consider. If the public inconvenience . . . shall be extensively felt, the attention of the legislature will doubtless be drawn to the subject.

It was the "public inconvenience" arising from such a doctrine, and the immense commercial development of the West and its rivers between 1825 and 1851, which largely influenced the Court to reverse this ruling, when a case arose again—*The Genesee Chief* (12 Howard 443).

In 1827, three years after the Steamboat Case, came another great case of economic as well as legal importance—*Brown v. Maryland* (12 Wheaton 419)—the first case announcing the "original package" doctrine, and the first case in which the phrase "police power" was used. It was argued by Meredith and Attorney General Wirt.(1)

In the same year (1827), the constitutionality of the State Bankruptcy statutes was further established by *Ogden v. Saunders* (12 Wheaton 215)—a case which had been first argued in 1824 by a remarkable array of counsel—Henry Clay, D. B. Ogden and Charles G. Haines for the debtor, and by Daniel Webster and H. Wheaton for the creditor—and reargued, in 1827, by Wirt, Edward Livingston, D. B. Ogden, Samuel Jones (2) and William Sampson for the debtor, and by Webster and Wheaton for the creditor—resulting in a victory for Webster's client. The Court, however, divided in great confusion on the constitutional question—Marshall, Story and Duvall dissenting.(3)

---

(1) The beginning of the "original package" rule may be traced to State statutes adopted under the Articles of Confederation, in Maryland and Pennsylvania.

See interesting historical discussion of this case in *The Federal Power over Carriers and Corporation*, by E. Parmalee Prentice (1907).

(2) Born in 1769, Columbia 1790, Chancellor of N. Y. 1821-8. Chief Justice of Superior Court 1828-47, Judge of Supreme Court 1847-49.

(3) The decision, owing to the strength of the dissenting opinions, was an unsatisfactory one; see *Braynard v. Marshall*, 8 Pick 194, in which Chief Justice Parker says, in 1829:

"The questions which arise out of the subject of state insolvent laws and the effect of the discharges under them have been so long unsettled

Of the intricate opinions rendered in this case, Webster wrote to Nicholas Biddle, Feb. 20, 1827:

> You see what a fire the judges have made on the question of State Bankrupt laws. No two of those who are for the validity of such laws agree in their *reasons*. Those who are *against* their validity concur entirely. Is there not an old saying—if there be not let it go for a new one—that truth is one; but error various.

The pendency of this case denying the validity of a State law granting a discharge in bankruptcy, so far as a creditor, citizen of another State, was concerned, was expected by some to give an impetus to the passage of a National Bankruptcy Act, a measure in which Judge Story was immensely interested. The bill failed, however, and as Story wrote Feb. 4, 1827:

> It was lost under circumstances which will forbid any attempt to revive it for many years. It has had much of the talent, eloquence, and influence of the Senate to support it, but it has failed from causes not likely to be overcome in future times. It interferes with State policy, pride, and prejudice; with the political expectations of others; with the Anti-Federalism of others; and above all, with that mass of public opinion, which, in different States of the Union, floats in opposite directions, even when apparently impelled by the same common cause.

In this same year, Judge Story gave a decision, (Marshall dissenting) in *Bank of U. S. v. Dandridge* (12 Wheaton 64), which settled for all time the doctrine, that approval of acts of its agents by a corporation may be shown by presumptive testimony, as well as by written record and vote. This case was a victory for Webster and Wirt arguing against L. W. Tazewell of Virginia.

Two letters from Webster to Nicholas Biddle, President of the Bank, relating to this case, are of extreme interest. In the first, March 21, 1826, he said(1):

> Dandridge's case was not reached until almost the last day

---

in this commonwealth owing to the unsatisfactory character of the decisions of the Supreme Court by the United States which ought to govern cases of this nature, that we have waited with anxiety for a revision of all the cases by that higher court and a final adjudication upon a subject so universally interesting and hitherto involved in so much perplexity. The case of *Ogden v. Saunders* seemed in its progress to promise such a result but unhappily on some of the points which the case presented the law is left as uncertain as it was before."

(1) See *The Writings and Speeches of Daniel Webster*, Vol. XVI (1903).

of the court, and until the court had intimated that they should not take up another long or important cause. It was ready for argument and printed cases are prepared for the use of the court. In this case, according to your request, I engaged Mr. Wirt on the part of the Bank, as I have already advised you. I wish it to be understood in regard to this cause that I consider myself as only filling Mr. Sergeant's place temporarily. If he should be here at the next term he will conduct the case with Mr. Wirt.

On Feb. 20, 1827, he wrote:

As to Dandridge, we hear nothing from the court yet. The Ch. Jus. I fear will die hard. Yet I hope, that as to this question, he is moribundus.

In everything else, I cheerfully give him the Spanish Benediction. "May he live a thousand years!" I feel a good deal of concern about this; first, because of the amount in this case; second, because of its bearing on other important questions, now pending or arising, as I have understood; and last, because I have some little spice of professional feeling in the case, having spoken somewhat more freely than usually befits the mouth of an humble attorney at law, like myself, of the "manifest errors" in the opinion of the great Chief. I suppose we shall have a decision in a few days.

The slavery question first came prominently before the Supreme Court, in 1825, in the great case of *The Antelope* (10 Wheaton 66), argued by Key, Berrien, Charles J. Ingersoll and Wirt, in which Chief Justice Marshall held that the slave trade was not piracy or contrary to the law of nations, unless prohibited by statute law or treaty.

Another noted case involving the slave trade was decided by Judge Story, in 1826—*The Marianna Flora* (11 Wheaton 1)— John Knapp of Boston and T. A. Emmett of New York arguing against George Blake and Daniel Webster.(1)

---

(1) In 1827, the case of *Armstrong v. Lear* (12 Wheaton 169) throws an interesting light on the growing feeling on the slavery question. It involved the will of the famous Polish patriot, Thaddeus Kosciuszko, who died in 1817, directing in his will that: "Should I make no other testamentary disposition of my property in the United States, I hereby authorize my friend Thomas Jefferson to employ the whole thereof in purchasing negroes from among his own or any others and giving them their liberty in my name, in giving them an education in trade or otherwise, and in having them instructed for their new condition in the duties of morality which may make them good neighbors, good fathers or mothers, husbands or wives, in their duties as citizens, teaching them to be defenders of their liberty and country, and of the good order of Society and in whatsoever

In 1829, another case involving a further phase of the slavery question arose, in *Boyce v. Anderson* (2 Peters 150), in which Chief Justice Marshall was called upon to decide whether a Steamboat Company was liable for loss of slaves drowned in an accident—the question being whether slaves were passengers or merchandise freight, and the decision being that the Company was only to be fixed with a common carrier liability for passengers.(1)

This period in American jurisprudence, 1815-1830, may be justly characterized as the reign of Marshall; for in these fifteen years the great doctrines of American Constitutional Law were firmly established by him; and the supremacy of the power of the Federal Government forever secured against successful attack. "Marshall found the Constitution paper; and he made it power," said James A. Garfield. "He found a skeleton, and he clothed it with flesh and blood." "He was not the commentator upon American Constitutional Law; he was not the expounder of it; he was the author, the creator of it. . . .

The field was absolutely untried. Never before had there been such a science in the world as the law of a written constitution of government. There were no precedents. . . . An original field of judicial exertion very rarely offers itself. To no other judge, has it ever been presented, except to Mansfield, in the establishment of the commercial law; unless perhaps the remark may be extended to the labors of Lord Stowell, in the department of English consistorial law, and to those of Lord Hardwicke in equity."(2)

---

may make them happy and useful. And I make the said Thomas Jefferson my executor."

Edward Livingston and Henry Wheaton argued that this provision was invalid as being immoral and contrary to the public policy of Virginia and Maryland. Attorney General Wirt and Benjamin Lear appeared on the other side.

(1) Marshall's opinion was in part as follows:

"A slave has volition and has feelings which cannot be entirely disregarded. These properties cannot be overlooked in conveying him from place to place. He cannot be stored away as a package. Not only does humanity forbid this proceeding, but it might endanger his life or health— Being left at liberty he may escape. The carrier has not and cannot have the same absolute control over him that he has over inanimate matter. In the nature of things and in his character, he resembles a passenger, not a package of goods. Responsibility should be measured by the law which is applicable to passengers, rather than by that which is applicable to the carriage of common goods."

(2) See address of Edward J. Phelps before the American Bar Association (1879).

In his five great cases—the Marbury case, the Cohens case, the McCulloch case, the Dartmouth College case, and the Sturgis case—Marshall did not cite a single decision as authority. "His only light was the inward light of reason. He had 'no guides but the primal principles of truth and justice' "(1) "The decisions of no other eminent judges have so few citations of authorities. It used to be said of him that, when he had formed his conclusions, he would say to one of his colleagues, 'There, Story, is the law. Now you must find the authorities'. Story himself said, 'When I examine a question, I go from headland to headland, from case to case; Marshall has a compass, puts out to sea, and goes directly to the result'."(2)

In thirty years, Marshall had transformed the Supreme Court, from a weak and uncertain body, hesitating to measure its strength against the prevailing jealousy of the Federal power, into an acknowledged supreme authority.

As early as 1820, a writer in the *North American Review* (Vol. X,) in a review of volume four of *Wheaton's Reports* spoke of the increasing weight of the decisions on constitutional questions:

This part of the law of the land is daily becoming more interesting, and exerting a wider influence upon the affairs of our country, from the respect that is generally felt for judicial decisions, from the intelligible forms in which principles are exhibited, and from the gradual formation of a body of constitutional exposition which will furnish precedents and analogies to future times.

And a review of Kent's *Commentaries* by the able Massachusetts lawyer, Willard Phillips, in 1827, expresses the same view(3):

The decision in *Weymouth v. Southard* (10 Wheaton 1) on one of the Kentucky "stop laws" in relief of debtors,(4) and some other decisions of the Supreme Court have given great dissatisfaction to some of the people of Kentucky and provoked much virulent declamation against the court itself. During the late session

(1) Address of Le Baron Colt before the Rhode Island State Bar Association, February 5, 1901.
(2) Professor Theophilus Parsons in *American Law Review*, Vol. I.
(3) See North American Review, Vol. XXIV (1827).
(4) This case involved the Kentucky statutes requiring judgment creditors to indorse on their executions that bank notes of the Bank of Kentucky or of the Bank of the Commonwealth of Kentucky would be taken in payment. This law arose out of the antagonism to the Bank of the United States. Chief Justice Marshall held that the statute did not apply to executions issued in the Federal courts.

of Congress, some member intimated that a judicial tyranny was
secretly creeping in upon us.   .   .   .   But notwithstanding all
that has been said to the contrary, we verily believe that the citizens . . . feel their persons and rights almost as safe in the hands
of the Supreme Court of the United States as in those of some of
the States.

One of the most interesting contemporary views of the position
of the Supreme Court and its relation to the subject of States'
Rights is found in a letter of Attorney General Wirt to President Munroe, May 5, 1823, relative to the filling of the vacancy
caused by the death of Judge Brockholst Livingston:

Can you make an appointment more acceptable to the nation
than that of Judge Kent? I know that one of the factions in New
York would take it in high dudgeon at first. Probably, too, some
of the most heated republicans and interested radicals who seize
every topic for cavil, might, in every quarter of the Union, harp
a little, for a time on the same string. But Kent holds so lofty a
stand everywhere for almost matchless intellect and learning, as
well as for spotless purity and high-minded honor and patriot-
ism, that I firmly believe the nation at large would approve and
applaud the appointment.   .   .   .   The appointment of a judge
of the Supreme Court is a national and not a local concern. The
importance of that court in the administration of the Federal
Government, begins to be generally understood and acknowledged.
The local irritations at some of their decisions in particular
quarters (as in Virginia and Kentucky for instance) are greatly
overbalanced by the general approbation with which those same
decisions have been received throughout the Union. If there are
a few exasperated portions of our people who would be for nar-
rowing the sphere of action of that court and subduing its energies to gratify popular clamor, there is a far greater number of
our countrymen who would wish to see it in the free and independent exercise of its constitutional powers, as the best means of
preserving the Constitution itself.   .   .   .   It is now seen on
every hand, that the functions to be performed by the Supreme
Court of the United States are among the most difficult and peril-
ous which are to be performed under the Constitution. They
demand the loftiest range of talents and learning and a soul of
Roman purity and firmness. The questions which come before
them frequently involve the fate of the Constitution, the happiness of the whole nation, and even its peace as it concerns other
nations.   .   .   .
With regard to the great subject of state rights, which has
produced so much excitement in Virginia and Kentucky, it
happens that, if he (Kent) has any leaning, it is rather in favor
of state rights. This has been shown by his decisions in the

steamboat cases, where he has uniformly upheld the state laws of New York against all the objections which could be raised of their repugnance to the Constitution and laws of the United States.

Three decades later, Edward Everett paid to the Supreme Court of this period the following eloquent tribute(1) :

I do not know what others may think on the subject, but for myself, sir, I will say, that if all the labors, the sacrifices, and the waste of treasure and blood, from the first landing at James-town or Plymouth, were to give us nothing else than the Su-preme Court of the United States, this revered tribunal for the settlement of international disputes (for such it may be called), I should say the sacrifice was well made. I have trodden with emotion the threshold of Westminster Hall and of the Palace of Justice in France; I thought with respect of a long line of illustrious chancellors and judges surrounded with the insignia of office, clothed in scarlet and ermine, who within these ancient halls have without fear or favor administered justice between powerful litigants. But it is with deeper emotions of reverence, it is with something like awe, that I have entered the Supreme Court at Washington. Not that I have there heard strains of forensic eloquence, rarely equalled, never surpassed, from the Wirts, the Pinkneys, and the Websters; but because I have seen a bright display of the moral sublime in human affairs. I have witnessed from the low dark bench destitute of the emblems of power, from the lips of some grave and venerable magistrate, to whom years and gray hairs could add no new titles to respect (I need write no name under that portrait), the voice of equity and justice has gone forth to the most powerful State of the Union, administering the law between citizens of independent States, settling dangerous controversies, adjusting disputed boundaries, annulling unconstitutional laws, reversing erroneous decisions, and with a few mild words of judicial wisdom dispos-ing of questions a hundred fold more important than those which, within the past year, from the plans of Holstein, have shaken the pillars of continental Europe, and all but brought a million of men into deadly conflict with one another.

LEGAL LITERATURE.

American legal literature during these years made a slight advance.(2)

(1) See address, February 22, 1851, delivered in New York, *Everetts Orations,* Vol. III.

(2) No attempt is made here to give a complete list of law books published between 1815 and 1830; but the main works of importance are noted.

Between 1822 and 1826, the *United States Law Journal,* edited by members of the Connecticut and New York Bars, had been published; in 1829, the *United States Law Intelligencer and Review* had been started at Providence, R. I., lasting for three years; and in the same year the noted *American Jurist,* in Boston, which lasted until 1842 and to which Story, Charles Sumner, Asahel Stearns, Charles G. Loring Luther S. Cushing, George S. Hillard, and many of the ablest lawyers of Massachusetts were contributors.(2)

Of law books, Hoffman's *Course of Legal Study* had appeared in 1817.

In 1820, Nathan Dane published the first volume of his *Abridgment of American Law*—the profits from which were to be the means of the re-creation of the Harvard Law School. In 1821, Caleb Cushing edited the first American Translation of Pothier's *Maritime Contracts*(1).

In 1822, came the first American book on Patent Law—Fessenden's *Law of Patents for New Inventions;* in 1823, the first American book on Insurance Law, by Willard Phillips.

In 1824, came *Angell on Watercourses,* in the preface to which is found the following interesting comment—showing the book to have really been the first American Case-Book:

The plan of putting adjudged cases into an appendix . . . was recommended, by one whose distinguished talents and profound knowledge of the law have made him an ornament and blessing to his country—Mr. Justice Story.

The book contained 96 pages of text and 246 pages of cases.

In this connection it is of interest to note that the value of the study of cases as a means of legal education was well recognized even in those early days of law schools.

---

(2)   See article on *American Law Journals* in *Law Reporter,* Vol. VII.
(1)   *Kent's Commentaries,* Vol. III, p. 201, Note (1st Ed.):
"The translation of Pothier's *Treatise on Maritime Contracts* by Mr. C. Cushing and published at Boston in 1821 is neat and accurate and the notes which are added to this volume are highly creditable to the industry and learning of the author. . . . It would contribute greatly to the circulation and cultivation of maritime law in this country if some other treatise of Pothier and also the commentaries of Valin could appear in an English dress."
In the third edition, Kent said, "Mr. L. S. Cushing has published at Boston a translation of Pothier's *Treatise on the Contract of Sale;* and if duly encouraged as we hope and trust he will be, he promises a translation of the other excellent treatises of Pothier on the various commercial contracts."

In a review of *Elijah Paine's Circuit Court Cases*, written in 1828, the writer said(1):

We wish also to see some books of reports put earlier into the hands of youth for their legal education than they have been hitherto.

If we are not greatly mistaken they would, with proper facilities for their explanation find them far more interesting and instructive to read and infinitely more easy to remember than codes, or digests, or elementary treatises. We believe these last to be commonly too abstract and general, and best suited to the minds of those who are somewhat advanced in the science of the law. . . . The facts in cases serve as bonds of association by which the principle interwoven with them are held together and kept long and strongly fastened in the mind. . . . The student so far as he can read reported decisions intelligently is sure of learning his law more accurately, as well as more pleasantly than he can in any other way.

In the years 1822 and 1825 a new department of legal literature was opened by the publication in Philadelphia of Thomas Sergeant's *Constitutional Law* and William Rawle's *A View of the Constitution of the United States*.

In the same years, another subject was treated for the first time in the United States—that of contracts—in Daniel Chipman's *Essay on the Law of Contracts for payment of Specific Articles* (Middlebury Vt, 1822)(2), and Gulian C. Verplanck's *Essay on Doctrine of Contracts; being an Inquiry how contracts are affected in Law and Morals by Concealment, Error, or Inadequate Price*. (N. Y., 1825).

In a review of this latter work by Joseph Hopkinson, a noted lawyer, of Philadelphia, the state of American legal writing is thus depicted in 1827(3):

The learning and industry of the American lawyer have been repeatedly exercised in the republication of professional works, with such additions as were proper to render them more useful to the American student; but an original treatise on the science of jurisprudence is a rare occurrence with us.

In 1824, Asahel Stearns published his *Summary of the Laws and Practice of Real Actions,* in the preface of which he states

---

(1) See *North American Review*, Vol. XXVII (1828).
(2) See Review by Nathan Dane in *North American Review*, Vol. XVII (1823).
(3) See Review in *American Quarterly Review*, Vol. I (March 1827).

that the treatise is the "substance of his course of lectures at the Law Department in the University."

The year 1826 was a landmark in American legal literature for in the spring of that year Chancellor Kent, at the age of sixty-three, undertook the task of embodying in a book, the mass of American Common Law, using as a basis his lectures delivered 1823-1824 at Columbia College(1) ; and in the fall, Volume I of his *Commentaries* was published.

In April 1830, Volume IV was published; and the work meeting with instant and enthusiastic success, a second edition was printed as early as 1832.

In a review of this work, George Bancroft said in 1827(2) :

Now we know what American law is; we know it is a science which indeed has not reached its utmost degree of perfection, but is fast advancing towards it. We know it is a science which in the course of another fifty years will by its own force, *vi propria,* expel from our shelves the ponderous mass of foreign lore by which they are still encumbered, and perhaps (the idea is not at all wild or extravagant) and perhaps, we venture to say, make the works of our writers on jurisprudence the ornament of the libraries of foreign jurists.

In the same year, Chief Justice Isaac Parker referred to it as one of his judicial opinions, as "a recently published book which I trust from the eminence of its author and the merits of the work will soon become of common reference in our courts."(3)

In 1828, Charles Jackson, Judge of the Supreme Court of Massachusetts, published his well known, much needed, and much used *Treatise on the Pleadings and Practice in Real Actions,* in the preface of which he refers to Professor Stearns' book as composed on a different plan, saying, "an inconvenience has attended

---

(1)   See letter of Kent to Story, Dec. 18, 1824, *Mass. Hist. Soc. Proc.,* 2nd Series, Vol. XVI (1902).

"I sent a day or two ago by the mail, the summary of the first 20 lectures of my present or 2nd course. I know you are so kind as to take some interest in my pursuits, and this emboldened me to trouble you with such an uninteresting paper. . . . You need not be apprehensive that the topics I am discussing will lead to commence a crusading war on your judicial opinions. . . . I almost uniformly agree with you and in every case in which due opportunity offers I speak of you and of your court as you desire in the height of your ambition. I shall find some fault with the Steamboat Case, but most decorously."

(2)   See *Kent on American Law,* by George Bancroft, in *American Quarterly Review,* Vol. I (March 1827).

(3)   *Dean v. Richmond,* 5 Pick. 466.

the use of real actions in this country from the want of some digest of this branch of the law and of a manual of pleadings adapted to our jurisprudence and modes of proceeding."

An interesting sidelight on the learning of the American lawyer of this period is found in Kent's comments, in 1829, on Jackson's book(1):

I think it must somewhat startle and surprise the learned sergeants at Westminster Hall if they should perchance look into the above treatise of Judge Jackson on *Pleadings and Practice in Real Actions* or into the work of Professor Stearns on the *Law and Practice of Real Actions* to find American lawyers much more accurate and familiar than, judging from some of the late reports, they themselves appear to be with the learning of the Year Books, Fitzherbert, Rastel and Coke on the doctrine and pleadings in real actions. Until the late work of Mr. Roscoe on *Law of Actions relating to Real Property* which was subsequent to that of Professor Stearns . . . there was no modern work in England on real actions to be compared with those I have mentioned. Those abstruse subjects are digested and handled by Judge Jackson with a research, judgment, precision and perspicacity that reflect lustre on the profession in this country.

The scope of the American law books above enumerated, however, shows the limited field of the law of this period(2).

During these years, only five copyright cases had been decided in the United States Circuit Courts, and only three in the State courts. It was not until 1819, that the Circuit Courts obtained jurisdiction in equity in copyright matters; and as late as 1827, Kent wrote in his *Commentaries* (Vol. II): "There are no decisions in print on the subject and we must recur for instruction to principles settled by the English decisions under the statute of Anne and which are no doubt essentially applicable to the rights of authors under the acts of Congress".

Charles J. Ingersoll, the noted Philadelphia lawyer, wrote in 1823(3):

---

(1) The need of settled forms in real estate matters was interestingly set forth in Chief Justice Parker's remarks in *Phillips v. Stevens,* 16 Mass. 238, in 1819.

(2) In addition to the books given above, the following are the only law works of importance written by Americans at this period:
Angell on Adverse Possession, in 1827, and *Angell on Assignments* in 1825; John Anthon's *Law of Nisi Prius* in 1820; Blake's *New York Chancery Practice* in 1818; Dunlap's *New York Supreme Court Practice* in 1821; Daniel Davis *Justices of the Peace* in 1828; Reeve's *Law of Descent* in 1825.

(3) See review of *A Discourse concerning the Influence of America on the Mind,* Oct. 18, 1823, *by C. J. Ingersoll,* by Jared Sparks, *North Amer. Rev.,* Vol. XVII, (1824).

It is to be regretted that literary property here is held by an imperfect tenure, there being no other protection for it than the provisions of an inefficient act of Congress, the impotent offspring of an obsolete English statute.   The inducement to take copyrights is therefore inadequate and a large proportion of the most valuable American books are published without any legal title. Yet there were 135 copyrights purchased from January, 1822, to April, 1823.(2)

---

(2)   The condition of the law of copyright fairly illustrates the general conditions of literature in the United States at the time.   Thus, prior to 1830, the only works of American literature of any considerable fame published were: *Webster's Dictionary,* in 1806, Washington Irving's *Knickerbocker History of New York,* in 1809, his *Sketch Book* in 1819, his *Life of Columbus,* in 1820, and his *Conquest of Granada* in 1829.   In 1817, Bryant's *Thanatopsis* had appeared, and in the same year Wirt's *Life of Patrick Henry.*   In 1821, Fenimore Cooper wrote *The Spy,* and in 1826, *The Last of the Mohicans.*   In 1827, Poe's *Tamerlane* and Goodrich's *Peter Parley's Tales* were published.   In 1828, came Hawthorne's first book, *Fanshawe.*

CHAPTER XX.

NATHAN DANE AND THE NEW RÉGIME.

Just at this stage, when the project of a school of law at Harvard seemed to have resulted in utter failure, a new benefactor of the College stepped forth in the person of an oldtime, staunchly Federalist statesman, seventy-seven years of age,—a lawyer of the Essex Bar, and the author of the most important American digest then published—Nathan Dane.

Born in 1752, a Harvard graduate of 1778, he had studied law in Beverly, Massachusetts, with William Wetmore. From 1785 to 1787, he had been a delegate to the Congress of the old Confederation, in the same delegation with John Hancock, Rufus King, Theodore Sedgwick and Nathaniel Gorham; and the crowning glory of his political life was the fact that he was the draftsman of the celebrated *Ordinance for the Government of the Territory of the United States Northwest of the River Ohio,* and particularly of that provision which excluded "Slavery or involuntary servitude"—"A political measure", said Daniel Webster, "of large and enduring consequences which impressed on the soil itself, while it was yet a wilderness, an incapacity to bear any other than free men, and laid an interdict against personal servitude, in original compact, not only deeper than all local law, but deeper also than all local constitutions."

Returning to his native State, Dane served three years in the Massachusetts Senate. In 1795 and 1811, he was a member of the Commissions to revise the laws of the State. In 1814, he was a member of the Hartford Convention, and was then described by John Lowell as "a man of great firmness, approaching to obstinacy, singular, impracticable, and of course it must be uncertain what course he will take. Honestly, however, inclined."(1)

In 1816, he was on a Committee to report on the proposed revision of the Probate law of the State; and in 1820, he had been

(1) Letter of John Lowell to Timothy Pickering, Dec. 3, 1814, in *Documents relating to New England Federalism,* by Henry Adams (1877).

a member of the Constitution Convention, although then too deaf to be able to attend.

His law practice was largely an office practice; and he devoted all his extra time to study, so that Judge Story stated:

Lord Coke, that prodigy of professional learning, in laying down for the benefit of his students the various employments of every day, assigned six hours for the pursuit of the law. . . . I feel justified in saying that for more than fifty years our generous patron has daily devoted to his favorite studies of politics and jurisprudence more than double that number of hours(1).

President Quincy described Dane as follows:

The manners and address of Mr. Dane were mild and simple, indicating goodness of heart and uprightness of purpose. Calm, even, and serene, not easily disturbed, never violently agitated, systematically industrious, punctual and prompt in the duties of his profession . . . the relations of law, morals, politics and religion, the almost exclusive objects of his intense and assiduous studies.

From his experience in making, compiling and revising laws at this formative period of American jurisprudence, and from the special study which he had made, from his youth, of the development of law in America, no man was so well qualified as he to construct the first great digest of our statutes and decisions. And his *General Abridgment and Digest of American Law,* known as *Dane's Abridgment,* which, begun in 1820 and finished in 1829 in nine volumes, at once took rank as a standard work. Practically the only work which could then compare with it was Zephaniah Swift's *System of the Laws of Connecticut,* published in 1795-96 and *Digest of the Laws of Connecticut,* published in 1822-23—works of far more than local interest, and frequently termed by writers, an American Blackstone(2). Dane's work became a necessary adjunct to the library of every American lawyer of distinction, and his profits from its sale were large.

While the criticisms which appeared in the press and in the magazines were everywhere eulogistic, no such masterly, scholarly, and discriminating review had appeared as that written by Judge Story in the *North American Review* in 1826, in which the work was thus summed up:

(1) *Discourse pronounced on the Inauguration of the Author as Dane Professor of Law in Harvard University,* by Joseph Story, 1829.
(2) See *Yale Writers on Law and Government,* by S. E. Baldwin; *Yale Law Journal,* Vol. XI.

Nathan Dane

The learned author has executed his task with becoming diligence and ability. He has bestowed forty years of a most studious life on the labor; and has here given the results of all the juridical learning in a compendious and accurate form. His comments exhibit various learning and close reflection; and his illustrations cannot fail. to assist such as seek for aid in those obscurer parts of the law.(1)

In the latter part of 1828, this deaf old man of seventy-six years, this old man who was still studying twelve hours a day, and up to midnight, as he had done for years in the past, conceived the idea that the profits from his great work could not be better applied than in the manner in which Charles Viner had applied the profits from his *Abridgment,* seventy-five years previously in England. Dane had no children. He was a loyal son of Harvard, and could find no better object for his beneficence.

And no part of the work of the University interested him more than that of the Law School. To found a Professorship which should redound to the glory of the University and which should be filled by some man of pre-eminent ability, was the plan he proposed to himself. One man in the country in his opinion, and one alone, could fill the proposed position—Joseph Story. Story had at this time been Justice of the United States Supreme Court for nearly eighteen years and was at the height of his judicial fame. His opinions, not only in the Supreme Court but in the Circuit Courts, had taken rank as standard authority. His literary labors, legal and otherwise, had been immense, and of the fullest scholarship. He was the author of the valuable notes on prize, admiralty, maritime and patent law contained in the Appendices to *Wheatons Reports;* his reviews in the *North American Review* on *Hoffman's Course of Legal Study* (1817); *Johnson's Chancery Cases or Chancery Jurisdiction* (1820); *Phillips on Insurance* (1825); *Dane's Abridgment* (1826); his *Address to the Suffolk Bar,* in 1821, on *The Progress of the Com-*

---

(1) Review of *Dane's Abridgment,* in *Story's Miscellaneous Works.*

In a review of *General Laws of Massachusetts,* published in 1823, by Asahel Stearns and Lemuel Shaw, Caleb Cushing wrote in *North American Review,* Vol. XVII (1823).

"*Dane's Digest* will go far towards creating a new era in our judicial history. He is one of the few surviving luminaries of that constellation of legal sages who illustrated the bar and bench of Massachusetts in the periods immediately succeeding the Revolution. Who, then, so able to combine and digest the elements of our law as he beneath whose eye it has grown up into the complete proportions of its present maturity?"

mon Law—all had been complete, masterly treatises on the various branches of the law.

His constructive work in legislation had been of important service—on the bill to extend the Jurisdiction of the Circuit Courts (1816); on the bill to reform the Criminal Code of the United States (1825), enacted through the joint efforts of Webster and Story; and on the many United States Bankruptcy bills unsuccessfully urged on Congress for nearly twenty years. He had been a delegate to the Massachusetts Constitutional Convention in 1820; and had been considered by President John Quincy Adams, for appointment as Secretary of State, in the event of Clay's declination.

In 1827, he had prepared and superintended the publication of the three volume edition of the *Laws of the United States*. His active work as a member of the Board of Overseers and of the Corporation of Harvard has already been noticed. He was the Phi Beta Kappa orator in 1826. For ten years he had carried on a steady correspondence with Sir William Scott, (Lord Stowell), his great English compeer in Admiralty Law, then (1829) an old man of eighty-three. Sir James Mackintosh and J. Evelyn Denison, Esq., M. P., also were two of his constant English correspondents; and his great interest in English law was kept alive through their letters, as well as in his assiduous reading of all the English law reports, magazines and newspapers. In this country, his closest friends and freest correspondents were the greatest legal minds of the day, Pinkney, Webster, Jeremiah Mason and James Kent.

Furthermore, Story was an Essex County man, a fellow member of the Essex Bar. Though Dane was twenty-seven years old when Story was born, and had been over twenty years at the Bar when Story was admitted to practice, he had recognized, in common with the whole Essex Bar, the exceeding ability of the talented young Republican lawyer. There was also a close connection between the two men, from the fact that Dane had studied law in the office of Story's father-in-law, William Wetmore.

With all these things in view, early in 1829, shortly after President Quincy's inauguration, Dane wrote to Story requesting an interview at his house in Beverly, and at this meeting, he unfolded his plan. He stated that, in his belief, the establishment of a Law School at which the principles of jurisprudence should be taught systematically as a science, would not only extend the influence of the College but would render effectual service to the country and the profession; that he was willing to devote $10,000 of the profits of his *Abridgment* for this purpose, but upon the sole condition that Story should accept the professorship.

Story was at first unwilling to listen to the plan, having already declined the Royall Professorship, but finally after several interviews he yielded—chiefly because he felt deeply that his refusal would deprive his beloved College of a useful and honorable foundation.

At this point, Dane for the first time made known his intention to President Quincy. The news came as a grateful surprise; for it was one of Quincy's ambitions to rehabilitate the Law School. Of his conference with Dane, Quincy said later:

He expressly stated to me that one of his chief inducements to apply his funds to the establishment of a Law Professorship was his opinion concerning the wonderful adaptation of your father's (Story's) talents and acquirements to give his foundation depth, celebrity and usefulness; and when, in a degree astonished at the work he was about to require of his first professor, I asked him if he thought it possible that Judge Story would fill out that extensive outline, Mr. Dane replied "Yes Sir, I know the man, he will do this and more; for uncommon as are his talents, his industry is still more extraordinary."(1)

Story, having conferred with the other members of the Corporation, and with President Quincy, and having found that this announcement of his willingness to serve as Professor on certain conditions was received with the greatest enthusiasm, he addressed to the Corporation, May 19, 1829, a formal letter which was laid before that body, May 23.(2)

(1) Letter from Josiah Quincy to W. W. Story, Aug. 20, 1851, see *Life and Letters of Joseph Story,* Vol. II, p. 564.

(2) See *Harvard College Papers,* 2nd Series, Vol. III, p. 239. This letter, of great interest, is as follows:

"Mr. Dane proposes to establish a new Law Professorship in Harvard University for the delivery of lectures on the subjects of Natural Law, Commercial and Maritime Law and Constitutional Law. He proposes to give as a foundation $10,000, the income of which is to be applied to the maintenance of the Professor. He wishes me to take the professorship, and wishes that it should be a fundamental statute of his foundation that residence at Cambridge should not be required of the Professor; but that it should depend upon his own choice. As an inducement to my accepting this professorship, he expresses a willingness to have the other statutes of the foundation framed according to my wishes; and he also expresses

In it he stated his conditions, the chief of which was that another professor should be appointed who should take upon himself the detailed superintendence of the School and the "drill duty and a constant attention to the students."

On June 2, 1829, at a special meeting of the Corporation held immediately prior to the inauguration exercises of President Quincy, the following letter from Nathan Dane was laid before the Board by Judge Story and was referred to the Committee on the Law School:

As I have a long time wished to aid and promote the law branch in the said University, and, now, by the profits of my law work, can conveniently do it, I proceed to lay the foundation of a professorship of law therein, and to provide for the appointment of a professor, and to aid in his support, in the manner following, and submit the same to your consideration.

In the first place, it shall be his duty to prepare and deliver,

---

a contingent determination to add $5,000 more to the foundation to be applied in the same way. I am given to understand that the Corporation wish to ascertain under these circumstances whether I will accept the professorship, and upon what further terms I am willing to remove to Cambridge. I have thought much upon the subject and have great reluctance in quitting Salem. I cannot do so without a considerable sacrifice of property. I have stated to Mr. Dane that I will accept his Professorship, if non-residence is allowable, the statutes of his foundation are satisfactory to me, and the duties thereof are so arranged as not to interfere with my judicial duties, which are and ever must be with me of paramount obligation and interest. I shall deem it indispensable, therefore, to my acceptance of the office, that it shall be explicitly understood that I shall not be bound to perform any duties incompatible with my judicial duties, and that my leisure only, allowing reasonable periods for recreation and health, shall be devoted to the professorship. I have no objection to the delivery of oral or written lectures or both, as from time to time may be thought most advisable by the Corporation. My written lectures I should ultimately propose to have published, which indeed the founder explicitly wishes me to understand is his principal object.

I should be willing to remove to Cambridge, if the Corporation deemed it advisable, if the following terms could be complied with.

(1) That the Corporation should guarantee to me an annual income of $1,000, including in this sum whatever I might receive from the Dane Professorship.

(2) That I can sell my real estate in Salem (which has cost me at least $8,000 and is now in perfect repair and the best order) for $7,000. A greater sacrifice than this difference, I could not consent to make, as the estate is now well suited to my wants and conditions.

(3) That the Corporation erect a suitable house on land owned by the College at Cambridge for my residence, at an expense in the whole not exceeding $7,000, in such form and with such accommodations as might be mutually agreed on. That I should take a lease of the same for five or seven years, and pay an annual rent equal to six per cent per annum upon the amount expended, with a clause that upon my removal from Cambridge or resignation of all duties excepting the Dane Professorship or the Professorship itself, I should be at liberty to surrender the lease. My

and to revise for publication, a course of lectures on the five following branches of Law and Equity, equally in force in all parts of our Federal Republic, namely: The law of nature, the law of nations, commercial and maritime law, federal law and federal equity, in such wide extent as the same branches now are, and from time to time shall be administered in the Courts of the United States, but in such compressed form as the professor shall deem proper; and to prepare, deliver, and revise lectures thereon as often as the said Corporation shall think proper. But as the Corporation may, after one course of lectures shall have been prepared, delivered and revised, on these branches, think it best to include in his lectures other branches of Law and Equity, that shall from time to time be in force in Massachusetts, I authorize the said Corporation so to do; ever confiding in the discretion thereof, to select the state branches, the most important and the most national, that is, as much as may be branches the same in other States of the Union as in this; making lectures on this state law useful in more states than one, law clearly distinguished from that state law which is in force, and of use, in a single state only.

2d. I now appropriate ten thousand dollars, to be by me placed in the possession of the said Corporation, on or before

---

object in this clause is to provide against the possibility of the office interfering in the future with my judicial duties or my health, so that I could not or ought not to retain it.

(4) That at least one permanent University Professor shall be appointed with a constant residence at Cambridge, whose duty it should be to perform, throughout the year, the common duties of Professor and Instructor. He ought to receive a larger compensation than myself, because he will be called to perform duties throughout the year, whereas mine can be occasional only. I think he ought to receive $1,500 per year; if I receive $1,000. If the Law School should succeed, so that the income should be more than sufficient to pay both our salaries, the residue to be divided equally between him and myself, unless the Corporation should think it better to establish a third professorship. In that event, the surplus income, to an amount not exceeding $1,500, might be devoted to such third professorship. The surplus, if any, to be divided between the second professor and myself. But in no event, should I desire, as my services cannot be constant, more than an annual income of $1,500, whatever might be the success of the School. Situated as I am, and must be, I should not choose to be deemed by the public to seek a compensation beyond the reasonable value of my services.

(5) I should be willing to take a general superintendence of the Law School, that is to visit it and examine the students occasionally, and to direct their studies, and to lecture to them orally on the topics connected with the Dane Professorship from time to time in a familiar way. But I should rely on the permanent Professor, for what I may call the drill duty and a constant attention to the students, giving them my advice and assistance as far as I could. I could not undertake to be with them in their ordinary studies, but rather to aid them by occasional explanations and excitements. In short, to put them upon the means of instruction, rather than to see that they only get them. This is a sketch of my views and I put them on paper, that my objects may be distinctly understood; and that my promise may not exceed my performance."

the first day of September next, as a fund forever, towards the support of the said professor, all the income whereof, and of such other moneys and funds as I may hereafter add, shall be paid over, annually or semi-annually, as the Corporation may direct, to the professor for the time being; each year beginning on the first day of September.

3d. In conformity to the constitutions of the United States, of Massachusetts, and of most of the other states, I declare that no religious test shall ever be required as a qualification of this professorship, but each person who shall be appointed professor, shall, before entering on the duties of his office, make and subscribe a declaration in the words following: "I do solemnly declare that I will, to the best of my ability, perform the duties required of me, by the statutes under which I am now appointed ———— Professor of Law in Harvard University;" and that no oath or other declaration shall ever be required.

4th. It is my object that a professor shall always be appointed who shall be a counsellor at law, at least of seven years' standing at the bar, and to insure a suitable appointment, from time to time, of a professor learned in the branches of law and equity aforesaid, and especially in the said five branches, I do declare that his residence at Cambridge shall never be required as a condition of his holding the office; believing the best professors will generally be found among Judges and lawyers, eminent in practice in other places conveniently situated, and who, while professors, may continue their offices and practice generally; also thinking law lectures ought to increase no faster than there is a demand for them. Clearly, their great benefit will be in publishing them.

5th. As the honorable Joseph Story is, by study and practice, eminently qualified to teach the said branches both in law and equity, it is my request that he may be appointed the first professor on this foundation, if he will accept the office, and in case he shall accept the same, it is to be understood that the course of his lectures will be made to conform to his duties as one of the Justices of the Supreme Court of the United States; and further, that time shall be allowed him to complete, in manner aforesaid, a course of lectures on the said five branches, probably making four or more octavo volumes; and that all the lectures and teachings of him, and of every professor so to be appointed, shall be calculated to assist and serve in a special manner, law students and lawyers in practice, sound and useful law being the object.

6th. The number of lectures, and the manner of delivering them, I leave to the discretion of the Corporation, as I do all other matters and things not contravening the rules or statutes herein contained, placing full confidence in its wisdom and judgment.

But as the present state of the law branch in the said university, and the times of meeting of the overseers thereof, allow less time to prepare statutes and system than is desirable, I reserve, so far as may be consistently done, liberty to put, before the first of September next, the proper rules and statutes in the case into a more technical and intelligible form, strictly preserving the substance and principles herein contained. The name of the professorship I leave to the Corporation.

Such good news was not to be kept private; and hence, at the dinner served at the end of the inauguration exercises of the new President, announcement was made of Mr. Dane's generosity. The *Boston Courier* of June 5 gave the following interesting account: "More than 600 persons sat down to dinner. We did not hear the toasts, but we cannot omit a sentiment given by Hon. Mr. Otis which was very happily and very elegantly turned. When it was announced that the Hon. Mr. Dane had given funds for a Law Professorship, he rose and after a short preface said "Non timeo Danaos et dona ferentes."

June 3, 1829, on the report from Committee, the Corporation voted to accept the donation and proceeded to elect Hon. Joseph Story, LL.D., as Dane Professor, as follows:

Voted That the Board accept the donation of the Hon. Nathan Dane for founding a professorship of law on the terms and conditions set forth in his communication to the Corporation dated 2nd June, 1829.

Voted That the Professor on this foundation shall be styled the Dane Professor of Law in Harvard University.

Voted That the Professor shall be elected in the same manner in which other officers of the College are chosen, and shall hold his office by the same tenure as the Professors on other foundations, and shall be subject to removal by the President and Fellows for any cause by them deemed just and sufficient, the Overseers consenting thereto.

Voted To proceed to the election of a Dane Professor of law. Ballots being given it appeared that the Hon. Joseph Story LLD was chosen.

Voted that the above proceedings be laid before the Overseers that they may approve the same if they see fit.

Voted That the President be requested to communicate these proceedings to Mr. Dane and to express to him the grateful sense which is entertained by this Board of his enlightened and timely liberality.

At a meeting of the Board of Overseers on June 12, 1829,

these votes as well as Story's election were unanimously concurred in.(1)

The next step to be taken was the filling of the Royall Professorship, which had been vacant since Judge Parker's resignation in 1827. It was obvious that as Story's duties would keep him in Washington a large part of the time, there must be a resident professor to take charge of the School. Story also had made this one of his conditions. Accordingly, it was decided, after much consideration, to appoint John Hooker Ashmun, a young lawyer of distinction, lately associated with Judge Howe and Senator Mills in the Northampton Law School, as Royall Professor. And as it was desirable that the Harvard Law School, thus revivified, should start at once in the fall term of 1829, action was taken at the meeting of the Corporation on June 11, 1829, at which the following report of the Committee on the Law School was presented by Hon. Charles Jackson and Francis C. Gray:

The liberal donation of Mr. Dane and the appointment of Judge Story as Dane Professor, if it shall be approved by the Overseers, encourages the hope that a Law School may be established in Cambridge, highly honorable to the University and useful to the Publick. It is obvious, however, that even if Judge Story shall reside in Cambridge, as, we trust he will do, his duties, as one of the justices of the Supreme Court of the United States will require his absence during so large a portion of the year, that such an Institution cannot be properly established without the appointment of another Instructor. The Committee therefore recommend the election of a Professor on the foundation of Mr. Royall. It is highly important that this Seminary should have a prosperous beginning; and, to this end, it is desirable that it should be opened immediately after Commencement. In every class, there are many who study law and most of the graduates of this year who do so will undoubtedly enter a school estab-

---

(1) The following members of the Board of Overseers were present:
"His Excellency the Governor (Levi Lincoln).
His Honor the Lieutenant Governor.
The Honorable Council and a principal part of the Honorable Senate with the following elected members:

Hon. Judge Davis	President Quincy
Hon. John Wells	Rev. Dr. Porter
Hon. John Pickering	Rev. Dr. Holmes
Hon. Richard Sullivan	Rev. Dr. Gray
Hon. Daniel Webster	Rev. The Secretary
	Rev. Dr. Lowell
	Rev. Dr. Codman
	Rev. T. M. Gannett
	Rev. Francis Parkman
	Rev. N. L. Frothingham."

lished at that time under such favorable auspices. But if it should be delayed, they may make other engagements which it will not be easy or convenient for them to relinquish.

The Committee greatly regret that it was not in the power of the Corporation to present a nomination of a Royall Professor to the Overseers at their last meeting; for it is not probable that the Legislature will remain another week in session; and there is a rule of that Board which provides that no election of a Fellow or Professor shall be approved excepting during a session of the Legislature, and another rule providing that no election shall be approved until 7 days after it has been communicated. But the records of the Overseers show that the latter rule has sometimes been dispensed with and a nomination concurred in at the same meeting to which it was presented. Whether a similar course may be pursued on the present occasion or whether any other course can be adopted by the Overseers for accomplishing the same object, so that this Law School may be opened immediately after Commencement, are questions which it belongs exclusively to that Board to decide. It is the opinion of your Committee that there ought to be no delay on the part of the Corporation and that a nomination should be presented to the Overseers at their next meeting, that they may take such order thereon as shall seem to them expedient under all the circumstances of the case.

The following votes were passed:

Voted that this report be accepted.

Voted that this Board will now proceed to the election of a Royall Professor.

Ballots being given it appeared that John H. Ashmun Esq. of Northampton was chosen.

Voted that the above proceedings be laid before the Overseers that they may approve the same if they see fit.

Voted that if the Overseers approve the election of the Dane Professor and the Royall Professor or either of them. Judge Jackson and Mr. Gray be a Committee to join such Committee as may be appointed by the Overseers to communicate the election and request the acceptance of the officers."

On June 12, 1829, the Overseers voted to concur with the Corporation in the above proceedings and also "to add Chief Justice Parker, Hon. Daniel Webster and Hon. James T. Austin to the Committee of Notification."

On June 15, 1819, the Committee addressed the following letter to the two new Professors (1):

---

(1) See *Corporation Records,* Meeting of August 20, 1829.

We are instructed by the President and Fellows to give you notice of your election as   Professor of Law and we accordingly enclose our official certificate of your appointment. We take the occasion to state distinctly in writing the views which we understood the Corporation to have adopted in regard to the Law School.

It is to be for the present under the care of the two Professors, the Dane Professor being the head of the Department. The annual charge to students constantly attending for instruction is to be fixed at a sum not exceeding $100. What charge shall be made to persons attending a single course of lectures will be a subject of future consideration.

Each Professor will receive the income of his own foundation which will probably amount to about $500 or $600 for the Dane Professor and for the Royall Professor $400 per annum.

The amount received for instruction is to be equally divided between the two Professors until the sum received by the Dane Professor shall amount in the whole to $1000 per annum, the surplus to be paid to the Royall Professor till his whole compensation shall be made up to $1500 per annum. Whatever may remain beyond this shall be appropriated exclusively to the benefit of the Law School, in such manner as may be hereafter determined. The Corporation will engage that each Professor shall receive at least $1000 for the term of 3 years.

The arrangement of the salaries is made on the assumption that both Professors will reside in Cambridge. Such residence will be required of the Royall Professor.(1)

JOHN HOOKER ASHMUN.

John Hooker Ashmun, the new Royall Professor, was at this time only twenty-nine years old, but already marked by lawyers as possessing great legal knowledge and the keenest of legal minds. He was born in Blandford, Massachusetts, July 3, 1800. His father was Hon. Eli P. Ashmun, a distinguished lawyer of the Hampshire County Bar, for several years a State Senator, and, from 1816 to 1818, United States Senator, with Harrison Gray Otis as his colleague. At the early age of twelve, he was deemed qualified to enter college, but was kept back for a year, entering Williams College in 1813, and the junior class of Harvard College in 1816, graduating from Harvard in 1818. He studied law in his father's office, until the death of the latter in 1819, when he entered the office of Hon. Lewis Strong of Northampton. From the time of his admission to the Bar, "he

(1) The letter of acceptance received from Professor Ashmun was presented at the meeting of the Corporation July 16, 1829.

devoted himself", says Story, in his eulogy, "with intense zeal and strenuous industry to the science of the law. . . . His career was soon marked by deserved success and before he left the Bar . . . he stood in the very first rank of his profession without any acknowledged superior. . . . It has been said . . . that in the three interior counties of the State he was, during his last years of professional residence, engaged on one side of every important cause. Certain it is that no man of his years was ever listened to with more undivided attention by the Court and Bar or received from them more unsolicited approbation."

His success was the more marvellous because of the fact that he was slightly deaf, and that for eight years before his death he suffered intensely and continuously from the tubercular trouble of which he died. By reason of this ill health he had few graces of person; his voice was feeble and his utterance labored. He had none of the attributes of oratory. "Yet", says Story, "he was always listened to with the most profound respect and attention. He convinced where others sought but to persuade; he bore along the court and jury by the force of his argument. He was particularly a master of the law of real property and of special pleading."

About 1825, he became associated with Judge Howe and Hon. Elijah H. Mills in the conduct of the Northampton Law School. "From the ill health of Mr. Mills, the principal instruction of the school devolved almost entirely on Mr. Ashmun; and with his characteristic vigor, he rose in energy as the pressure demanded more various and exhausting labors". During this time he was the law partner of Mr. Mills, and on him rested the entire labor of preparing all the cases for trial, both on the law and the facts.(1)

The offer of the Royall Professorship came to him as a spontaneous movement of the Harvard Corporation, upon a de-

(1) On Judge Howe's death in 1828 Ashmun undertook the work of preparing for the press Howe's unpublished book on Practice. But even with the assistance of others, writes Sumner, "he was unable to bring a single title to what he thought the proper degree of perfection and he thereupon, a short time before his own death (in 1833) relinquished his whole design in despair. Upon his death Chapman and Fay purchased the copyright. . . . There is one short essay, an amendment written by Ashmun himself, which is so admirably characteristic of his peculiar mind."
See unpublished letter of Sumner to J. H. Ward, Sept. 30, 1839, *Sumner Papers* in Harvard College Library.

liberate review of his qualifications, and entirely unsought by him.

Of his personal characteristics, Story says: "He was a man of most inflexible honor and integrity, a devout lover of truth, conscientiously scrupulous in the discharge of his duties and constantly elevating the standard of his own virtue. His candor was as marked as his sense of honor was acute and vivid. . . . The most characteristic features of his mind were sagacity, perspicacity, and strength. His mind was rather solid than brilliant; rather acute in comparing than fertile in imagination. He was not a rapid but a close thinker; not an ardent but an exact reasoner. . . . Few persons have left upon the minds of those who have heard them so many striking thoughts uttered with so much proverbial point and such winning simplicity."

One of his pupils, George S. Hillard (L. S. 1830-32) said of him:

No man had a clearer and more piercing intellectual sight; he saw all things in their true form and exact proportion. . . . He was a man cast in a peculiar mould. His mind had been developed and his character formed each by its own unassisted energies and with very few external influences. He was highly independent in opinions and conduct. He made up his mind deliberately, and acted and spoke resolutely according to the conviction.

His bodily infirmities prevented him from reading or talking much, but gave him the greater opportunity for original and deep thinking. And while these infirmities made him reserved and retiring, he was not as often supposed cold, or indifferent to social life.

"Among those with whom he was intimate," says Story, "no man was more social in his temper, more indulgent in playful and delicate humour or more familiar in easy conversation."

It was felt to be highly desirable that the new Professors should take charge at the opening of the fall term. Accordingly Story prepared at once to sell his house in Salem; but some difficulty was met in finding a suitable house in Cambridge; and on July 10, he wrote to Ebenezer Francis, the College Treasurer(1):

I shall be glad to know as early as practicable what you con-

---

(1) See *Harvard College Archives, Letters to the Treasurer,* Vol. I: Letters of Quincy to Francis, June 25, 1829; Letters of Story to Quincy, June 25, 1829; Letter of Story to Francis, July 10, 1829.

clude on, because every hour is now important to me, if I am to remove, to prepare for that and also to prepare for the commencement of lectures. There is hardly now time to prepare even an outline for a course, and I am anxious that when we start there shall be a favorable beginning.

By vote of the Corporation, July 16, 1829, the Treasurer was authorized "to erect a house forthwith on some land now belonging to the college for the accommodation of the Dane Professor in Cambridge, consulting the Professor in relation to the Plan of the House."(1)

Finally however the square brick house on the corner of Hilliard and Brattle Streets, owned by Deacon Hilliard, was rented; and in this house Story lived until his death.

On July 23, the President, Story and the Treasurer were "authorized to prepare such rooms as they shall see fit for the accommodations of the professors and students of the Law School, and Judge Jackson and Mr. Gray together with the Law Professors were appointed a committee to prepare statutes for the Royall Professorship."

And on August 20, 1829, these statutes were changed by votes of the Corporation and of the Overseers, so as to provide that the Professor should reside in Cambridge, and that the Dane Professor should be head of the Law Department as follows:

Voted 1—The third article of the said former statutes so far as it respects the residences of the Professors, is repealed and he is required to reside hereafter in the town of Cambridge.

2—The sixth and seventh articles of said statutes shall be and hereby are repealed.

3—The Dane Professor of Law is considered for the present and until the further order of the Government as the head of this Department in the University. It shall be the duty of the Royall Professor in conjunction with the Dane Professor, to devise and propose from time to time to the Corporation such a course of instruction in the Law School as may best promote the design of that institution and honour of the University, and to do all in his power

---

(1) This vote was due to the refusal of several Cambridge house owners to lease on reasonable terms; see letter of Story to Francis, July 17, 1829:

"On the whole, I am glad that the Corporation have concluded to build, as it will operate very usefully upon the Cambridge people, and teach them to their cost that they may be too sharp for their interest."

to promote these objects. He shall have the immediate charge and oversight of the students, meeting them frequently at stated periods to ascertain their progress, to assist and stimulate their studies and to explain and remove such doubts and embarrassments as may occur in the course of their reading.

In addition to the familiar lectures and conversations at his above mentioned meetings with the students, the Royall Professor will, if it should be deemed expedient by the Corporation, prepare and deliver written lectures on such branches of the law as are not included in the department of the Dane Professor, and in all his instructions whether oral or written, he will not only endeavor to explain the principles of the English Common Law; but will show its various modifications in this country by the principles of our Constitutions of Government, and by statutes, judicial decisions and usage; and generally he will strive to lead the minds of the students to such inquiries and researches as will qualify them to become useful and distinguished supporters of our free system of government as well as able and honorable advocates of the rights of the citizens. And it shall be in the power of the Corporation with the assent of the Overseers to vary, modify, enlarge, or wholly change the above course and to prescribe any other duties not inconsistent with the general principles on which the Professorship is founded.(1)

On August 25, 1829, on the day before Commencement, the inaugural ceremonies of the two new Professors took place in the old Meeting House (near the present site of Dane Hall), the exercises being described in the Overseers' Records as follows: "I A Prayer by Dr. Ware. II Address in Latin by the President. III The Statutes of the two Professorships were read by Professor Hedge. IV The Dane and Royall Professors elect replied in Latin to the President's address and signed the statutes. V The President announced the two Professors. VI Judge Story, Dane Professor, then delivered an Inaugural Discourse in English."

After the exercises a dinner was given in Porter's Hotel, at which Daniel Webster presided.(2)

---

(1) A letter from Nathan Dane dated August 29, 1829, was presented to the Corporation at the meeting of Sept. 17, 1829:

"Being informed that it is your practice to apply the income of donations and to pay salaries quarterly, I agree that the same may be done in my case.

As to the power of the Corporation to remove Professors from office, I think it has it of course in my case as I have declared nothing to the contrary."

(2) A dinner was given to Story at Salem Sept. 3, 1829, on his removal

Story's inaugural discourse was one of his most finished literary productions, as it treated of the value and importance of the study of the law, and unfolded the elaborate nature and objects of the Professorship.

An unpublished letter from Story to Bushrod Washington August 13, 1829, shows his appreciation of the labors he had undertaken(1):

to Cambridge, regarding which Webster, who was one of the speakers, wrote to Story September 5, 1829:

"I find it quite impossible to recall the recollections of my observations— Besides 'enough is as good as a feast'. The provision for the day was with you and you did your duty. While the sun shines we need no little twinklers in the sky. Your discourse was the intellectual feast of the occasion. The rest was talk, talk, talk: and at least my part of it may as well be forgotten as not. At any rate I cannot recall it and I remember a mass of things but nothing distinctly; a speech but nothing wherefore. The Daily of this morning speaks the exact feeling which we all brought away of your admirable discourse. Sic itur ad astra." See *Mass. Hist. Soc. Proc.* 2nd Series, Vol. XVI (1902).

The other speakers were President Quincy, Harrison Gray Otis, then Mayor of Boston, Jeremiah Mason, Governor Coles of Illinois, Judge John Davis, Judge Samuel P. P. Fay, John Pickering, Nathaniel Bowditch, George Ticknor, Daniel A. White. The *Boston Daily Advertiser* of Sept. 5, quoting the *Salem Gazette,* said: "The honored guest on this occasion made a most eloquent and feeling address to his fellow citizens from whom he was about to separate and dwelt on the circumstance of his residence among them for thirty years and his emotion on parting from his early and fast friends."

(1) See *Story Papers* in possession of the Massachusettts Historical Society.

See also letter of Story to Richard Peters of Aug. 1, 1829:

"I have been driven to accept the Dane Professorship of Law in Harvard University, and am now just beginning to write my inaugural discourse, which is to be delivered on the twenty-fifth of August. It is truly a formidable task. On the first of September, I am to remove to Cambridge, to take up my permanent residence there. The Law School opens on that day. If you read the third number of the *American Jurist,* you will see the objects and nature of the foundation. They show a liberal mind. I mean to lend all my leisure to accomplish this noble design."

In a letter to the Dublin Law Institute, (quoted in *Law Reporter,* Vol. IX in 1846), Story said on the subject of the reasons which impelled him to accept Mr. Dane's offer:

"I have been long persuaded that a more scientific system of legal education than that which has hitherto been pursued is demanded by the wants of the age and the progress of jurisprudence. The old mode of solitary unassisted studies in the Inns of Court or in the dry and uninviting drudging of an office is utterly inadequate to lay a just foundation for accurate knowledge in the learning of the law.

It is for most part a waste of time and effort at once discouraging and repulsive. It was, however, the system in which I was myself bred; and so thoroughly convinced was I of its worthlessness that I then resolved if I ever had students I would pursue an opposite course. It was my earnest desire to assist in the establishment of another system which induced me to accept my present professorship in Harv. Univ., thereby burthening myself with duties and labors which otherwise I would gladly have declined."

I have accepted the Dane Professorship of Law in Harvard College and shall remove to Cambridge in September. I am now preparing an inaugural discourse which I find a work of great labor. Mr. Dane expects my commentaries on public, maritime and commercial law to fill when published *four goodly volumes*. What think you of my courage to undertake such a task?

And that his friends were highly impressed with the arduous course which Story had laid out for himself, is seen from three letters received by him about this time.

Marshall wrote Sept. 30, 1829:

I have read with great pleasure your discourse . . . It is in your best style of composition.

You have marked out for yourself a course of labour which is sufficiently arduous; but I believe you love to struggle with difficulty and you have generally the good fortune or merit to overcome it.

At seventy-five, you will find indolence creeping over you. But we will not anticipate evil. You have not spared the students of law more than the Professor. You have prescribed for them an appalling course. Our southern youth would stumble at the threshold and I think such a task too formidable for even a commencement. You Yankees have more perseverance or think more justly on the proposition that he who attempts much may accomplish something valuable, should his success not be complete. I hope I shall live to read your lectures.(1)

Kent wrote, Sept. 17, 1829(2):

I have just been reading twice over your excellent inaugural discourse. It is masterly in matter and style, in eloquence and taste, and you cannot but display in every production of

---

(1) Marshall had already written to Story as to these labors, July 3, 1829:

"Directly after writing my last letter I saw your appointment to the Dane Professorship and anticipated your acceptance of it. The situation imposes duties which I am sure you will discharge in a manner useful to others and conducive to your own fame I did not however anticipate that the labour would immediately press so heavily on you as your letter indicates.

Four octavo volumes in five years is a heavy requisition on a gentleman whose time is occupied by duties which cannot be neglected.

I am confident that no person is more equal to the task than yourself, but I cannot help thinking that the publication may be postponed with advantage. I presume the work will be in the form of lectures. I suspect you will find it advisable to postpone the publication of them till they have been revised for a second course. Precipitation ought to be carefully avoided."

(2) This letter and the preceding one from Marshall were published in *Mass. Hist. Soc. Proc.*, 2nd Series, Vol. XVI (1902).

your pen how richly and extensively your mind is endowed with every accomplishment. Your plan is magnificent
and I am satisfied you will fill up the outline with pre-eminent
learning and the noblest doctrines and with the profoundest views
of morals and government and all the various classes of national,
political and social obligations and duties. Your professor's chair
will be of itself (without the aid of Cranch and Gallison and
Mason and Wheaton and Peters) a vehicle to conduct you to
immortality.

A year later, Daniel Webster wrote to Story, Sept. 18, 1830:

You must allow me to repeat what I have said to you *ore tenus*,
that I have felt great concern about you ever since I saw what
degree of labor you were bestowing on this Law School. There
is a limit to what the strongest can do. I pray you be persuaded
to diminish your labors. I beg this of you out of the depths
of my regard and affection. For all our sakes spare yourself.

Story, however, did not at all foresee the instant influx of students who would be attracted by his fame.

Immediately after the opening of the School, applications came
from large numbers of persons in and about Boston asking on
what terms they might attend Judge Story's lectures. And on
September 29, 1829, the Corporation voted that the Law Faculty
"be authorized to admit persons not members of the School, to
attend the Law Lectures or any of them, upon the payment of
such sum as the Faculty may see fit, not less in any case than
$50."

Meanwhile the School had opened promptly on September 7,
1829, under Story's immediate supervision; and, a week before,
wrote to President Quincy(1):

I have seen several of the law students and arranged their
studies. But it is very probable that some will not arrive until
after I have left Cambridge I wish notice to be given to any
who may come that I shall be at Cambridge again on Monday
next and shall be glad to meet all etc. law students at the Law
Library Room in the Russell House on that day at eleven o'clock
A. M.

In the meantime, it is very desirable to have a number of
Blackstone's Commentaries purchased (as the Corporation proposed) for the use of the students, and either to be sold to the
students if they wished, or delivered to them for use. It will be

(1) *Harvard College Archives, Letters to the Treasurer,* Vol. I.

indispensable that we should have some copies by Monday and also some copies of *Kent's Commentaries,* say a half dozen.

The *Boston Daily Advertiser* of September 12 thus reported the new birth of the School: "The exercises of this School commenced on Monday last under highly favorable circumstances. Eighteen young gentlemen were present. These with those expected from the School at Northampton will form a department worthy of the ancient university."

On October 20, less than two months after the opening of the School, Story wrote to Simon Greenleaf(1): "We have at present twenty-seven law students at Cambridge, with a prospect of more. I perceive that there is a vast labor before me."

As the Corporation had never seen its way clear to providing more adequate quarters, the School still remained in the small rooms in the lower story of the building known as College House No. 2 or Russell House(2) and into one of these rooms Story moved the large law library which he had accumulated during his service on the Supreme Bench.(3)

---

(1) The *American Jurist,* Vol. VIII, (1829), in its account of the inauguration of the Dane and Royall Professors, states editorially:
"It will be gratifying to our readers to learn that the course of instruction under Professors Story and Ashmun has commenced, under the most favorable auspices. The number of students already entered amounts to 27."

(2) By a vote of the Corporation of Sept. 29, 1829, the President was "requested to procure for the use of the Law School the room now occupied by Mr. Dabney."

(3) The conditions of the day are illustrated in a letter written by Story to President Quincy, Nov. 14, 1829, in which he states that the lecture room in Russell House "is very cold and a Lehigh Grate would be a great advantage—also in the other room which contains my law library and to which the law students make constant resort." In response to this, Nov. 19, 1829, the Corporation authorized Quincy to "have such stoves erected if he sees fit"—a curious example of the extent to which the President was then burdened with petty details.

Joseph Story, Dane Professor 1829-1845

CHAPTER XXI.

The Ashmun Period—1829-1833.

The steady growth and evident assured prosperity of the School gave infinite delight to both Professors during the first four critical years of the new experiment.

For the year 1828-29 the President's 4th Annual Report gives the number of students, December, 1829, as 27. Professor Ashmun's first Report of Oct. 18, 1830, shows the number then as 35, and states:

From the limited experience we have had, we think it probable the average number in future will not fall short of this.

We are very happy to state that the situation of the School, as regards the attention, capacity, and progress of the students, and their general conduct, so far as it falls without our observation, is highly satisfactory—that those who have left us to pursue their studies elsewhere, or enter into the profession, have appeared convinced of the advantages of a systematic legal education and of a public institution for that purpose.

The President's 5th Annual Report for 1829-30, gives the number of law students resident in the University as 31, and states that "the number of students during the past year has never fallen short of thirty, and during the last term has been 37." Then follows this stereotyped expression which appears with a slight amendment in every President's Report, until the 22nd Annual Report:

Their attendance upon the exercises has been hitherto wholly voluntary; and has been marked by a punctuality and degree of advancement highly satisfactory. The opportunity of pursuing the study of the profession at the School is considered a privilege, and the students themselves are understood to have been well satisfied with the arrangements.

For the year 1830-31, the President's 6th Annual Report gives the number during the year as 41 and the number then resident as

41. The College Catalogue reports the number as 31, (25 Seniors 6 Juniors).(1)

For the year 1831-32, Professor Ashmun reports the number on November 24, 1831, to be 42 (so also in the President's 7th Annual Report for this year) ; and he notes "their general character and conduct and the attention bestowed by them on the exercises of the School such as he has never known excelled by any class of equal size."

For the year 1832-1833, Professor Ashmun reports, Oct. 16, 1832 :

The condition of the Law School continues to be satisfactory. The number of students is usually about 40 and is at present 42. The course of study and other exercises are the same as heretofore. There is no subject on which the undersigned finds room for any particular remark.

The President's 8th Annual Report for this year says, "the number of students during the past year has varied from 42 to 53, the number now in attendance." The number resident is given as 42.

April 29, 1833, after the death of Professor Ashmun and the completion of the new Law School building, Judge Story reported that the number of students had dropped to 31, but that "the students are diligently and successfully engaged in their studies, so as fully to justify the public confidence in the value of the Institution."

METHODS AND COURSE OF INSTRUCTION.

During the first few years of the new régime, the principal instruction was, of course, given by Professor Ashmun, whose methods did not vary greatly from those employed by Professor Stearns, consisting largely of written lectures by the Professor and recitations by the students. The latter were arranged in two classes, according to their extent of preparation, it being still usual for many to enter the School after a year or more of study in a law office.

Professor Ashmun in his Report of Oct. 18, 1830, says:

(1) *The American Jurist,* Vol. IV, said in July 1830: "The Law School is in a florishing state. The present number of students 30, having increased from 27 at which it stood at the time of our former notice of the school in October last (1829) ; and there is as we understand, a fair prospect of a still more rapid gain in the autumn."

The course of instruction is principally by recitations from the text books. Each of the classes usually recited every other day to each Professor, making while the Dane Professor is in Cambridge one recitation on an average every day.

During his absence, which is for the whole middle term, the students recite three times a week. Once a week regularly, and sometimes oftener, they have Moot Courts, at which in rotation they argue questions of law before one of the Professors. They occasionally write disputations and opinions on subjects connected with their course of study.

Judge Story's method of instruction was rather by informal lectures, sometimes written out beforehand, but more often extempore, and branching into byways, as the various subjects suggested themselves to him, during the lecture.

Charles Sumner thus described the two Professors(1):

Professor Ashmun by his exactness of learning, his acuteness of mind and untiring perseverance co-operated powerfully with his associate. Their manner of teaching was different; and that of each peculiar. Judge Story was always ready and profuse in his instructions, anxiously seeking out all the difficulties which perplexed the students and anticipating his wants, leaving no stone unturned by which the rugged paths of the law might be made smoother, and the steep ascents be more easily passed. Professor Ashmun with the same elevated object in view left the student more to himself, throwing out hints which might excite his attention, cheering as the glimpses of a distant light to a benighted traveller, but which nevertheless did not supersede labor on his part. Whoever would prepare himself to make an enquiry of Professor Ashmun must already have applied his mind so strongly to the subject matter as to have obtained a good conception of it; in short he must have understood where the difficulty was.

As stated in the President's Annual Report of January 1, 1830, Story's lectures were "on the Law of Nature and Nations, and on Chancery, Commercial, Civil and Constitutional Law." Ashmun's were "on Miscellaneous branches of the Common Law".

Reviews and examinations in the text books were had on four days in the week, lasting from one to two hours for each class. The Moot Courts were held once a week, one of the Professors presiding, and two students, members of the two classes, arguing on each side.

---

(1) *American Jurist*, Vol. XIII, (Jan. 1835).

The course of study was intended to be completed in three years; but in 1832-33 a two years' course was adopted, with extra books suggested for those who desired the full three years. It embraced "a selection from the best elementary works in each branch of the law." . . . "The students are referred to series of leading cases in the English and American Reports and to a parallel course of reading", in addition to the prescribed list of text books.

"The students are also instructed in the practice of the courts, in the making of writs, preparation of pleadings, and other legal instruments. An opportunity is afforded for acquiring the routine of office practice."

It was in the vastly more elaborate list of text books that the instruction differed from that given by Professor Stearns. (1)

---

(1) This list as it appeared in the President's 8th Annual Report for the year 1832-33 was as follows, and was prefixed by a note stating that, "The books marked thus (*) compose the course which is completed in two years. The studies of gentlemen who remain longer in the School are pursued in the remaining books in the regular course, to which others are added from time to time, as far as the leisure and progress of the students may permit. The parallel course is prescribed chiefly for private reading."

Regular Course.	Parallel Course.
*Blackstone's Commentaries.	Sullivan's Lectures.
*Kent's Commentaries.	Hale's History of the Common Law.
Wooddeson's Lectures.	Reeves's History of the English Law.
	Hoffman's Legal Outlines.

Law of Personal Property.

*Chitty on Pleading.	Select titles in the Abridgments of
*Stephen on Pleading.	Dane and Bacon.
*Chitty on Contracts.	Collinson on Idiots and Lunatics.
*Starkie on Evidence.	Shelford on Lunatics, etc.
*Long on Sales.	Hammond's Nisi Prius.
Bingham on Infancy.	Kyd on Awards.
Angell and Ames on Corporations.	Reeve's Domestic Relations.
Williams on Executors.	Roberts on the Statute of Frauds.
Hammond on Parties.	Roper on Legacies.
Angell on Limitations.	Gould's System of Pleading.
Roper on Husband and Wife.	Starkie on Slander.
	Saunders' Reports, (Williams' Edit.)
	Select cases in the Reports.

Commercial and Maritime Law.

*Abbott on Shipping.	Phillips on Insurance.
*Bayley on Bills.	Benecke on Insurance.
*Paley on Agency.	Stevens on Average.
*Marshall on Insurance.	Livermore on Agency.
*Story on Bailments.	Azuni's Maritime Law.

A description of the conditions of life at the Harvard Law School and of the legal influences brought to bear upon the students during these years, would be incomplete without some

*Gow on Partnership.
Theobald on Principal and Surety.
Brown's Admiralty Law.

Fell on Guarantee.
Bacon's Abridgment, tit. Merchant.
Dane's Abridgment, select titles.
Pothier on Maritime Contracts.
Collier on Partnership.
Select cases in the United States Courts.

Law of Real Property.

*Cruise's Digest.
Fearne on Remainders.
Powell on Mortgages, (Rand's ed.)
Sanders on Uses and Trusts.
*Stearns on Real Actions.
Adams on Ejectment, by Tillinghast.
Sugden's Vendors.
Jackson on Real Actions.

Preston on Estates.
Runnington on Ejectment.
Powell on Devises.
Angell on Water Courses.
Woodfall's Landlord and Tenant.
Roscoe on Actions respecting Real Property.
Coke upon Littleton.
Dane's Abridgment, select titles.
Hayes on Limitations in Devises.
Select cases in the Reports.

Equity.

Barton's Suit in Equity.
*Maddock's Chancery.
*Cooper's Pleadings.
Jeremy's Equity Jurisdiction.
Newland on Contracts in Equity.
Eden on Injunctions.

Fonblanque's Equity.
Redesdale's Pleadings in Equity.
Beame's Pleas in Equity.
Hoffman's Master in Chancery.
Blake's Chancery.
Select cases in the Reports.

Criminal Law.

East's Pleas of the Crown.
Russell on Crimes.

Chitty's Criminal Law.
Archbold's Pleading and Evidence.
Select cases in the Reports.

Civil Law.

Gibbon's Roman Empire, Ch. 44.
Justinian's Institutes.

Pothier on Obligations.
Domat's Civil Law, select titles.
Brown's Civil Law.
Butler's Horae Juridicae.
Ayliff's Roman Law.

Law of Nations.

Martens's Law of Nations.
Rutherforth's Institutes.
Wheaton on Captures.

Ward's Law of Nations.
Vattel's do.
Bynkershoek's Law of War.

Constitutional Law.

American Constitutions.
*Story's Commentaries on the Constitution.

The Federalist.
Rawle on the Constitution.
Select cases and speeches.

knowledge of the contemporaneous events in legal history and of the great lawyers among whom the young law students were growing up.

These considerations are especially to be borne in mind during Judge Story's professorship; for his judicial life was very closely associated with his Law School labors. Through him, the students and Professors were constantly kept in touch with the noted cases occurring in Washington and in Boston, in the United States Supreme Court and Circuit Courts. And a very considerable part of the value of the education received at the Law School has been attributed by its graduates, dead and living, to the vivid impressions which they gained of the actual legal events of the day, through the personal connection of Judge Story with the great cases and the great men who were then making legal history.

The year 1829, at the very beginning of the new régime in the Law School, was notable in the legal annals of Boston for the first visit of William Wirt to that city. He had just ended ten years of service as United States Attorney General, and with Webster, headed the Federal Bar. The case in which he was retained was that of *Henry Farnum, Administrator v. Peter C. Brooks* (9 Pick. 212), which was a bill in equity to set aside a settlement of insurance accounts from 1785 to 1803, made in 1808, and involving over $60,000. Associated with Wirt for the plaintiff were B. R. Nichols and Benjamin Rand of Boston, and opposed to him were Daniel Webster, Benjamin Gorham and Charles H. Warren. Wirt's letters give an interesting picture of the times; on June 14, 1829, he wrote:

I walked through town last night with Webster by moonlight and was quite overwhelmed with the air of wealth exhibited in the vast number of granite and brick palaces which abound through the place . . . This is certainly the most hospitable place in the world . . . . I am brought here to combat Webster in his own arena, and I think I shall gain the day, which will be a great triumph. Having grappled with my adversary before, I know his strength and all his trips.

On June 15 and 28, he wrote:

Webster receives and treats me with a kindness and cordiality that cannot be exceeded . . . Otis has been twice with me, pressing me to dine. Judge Story insists that I must go to Salem to see him. . . . I have told you how kind Webster has been to me . . . He praises my speech. "Our people thought highly of you," he told me, "but they had no idea of your strength. The judges have spoken on the subject and expressed their gratification." . . . When I had finished (my argument) Mr. Brooks, who was the defendant against whom I had been trying the cause, came to me at the Bar and, taking my hand, spoke to me in the kindest terms, expressing his high satisfaction at my demeanour towards him during the trial.(1)

Though Wirt failed to win his case, the court for the first time applying the statute of limitations to an action in equity, he returned to Maryland with the liveliest satisfaction in his trip, and on August 3, he wrote:

I think the people of Boston amongst the most agreeable in the United States . . . I say they are as warm hearted, as kind, as frank, as truly hospitable as the Virginians themselves. In truth they are Virginians in all the essentials of character . . . I expected to find them cold, shy, suspicious; I found them on the contrary, open, playful and generous . . . Would to Heaven the people of Virginia and Massachusetts knew each other better.

He also wrote to Daniel Webster, after his return, July 8, 1829(2):

All figures and brevity apart, my visit to Boston comes back to me at times, more like a delightful dream than a reality, so far did it surpass all other comparatively "dull realities of civil life." . . . By the way of secret and in your ear, I am unaffectedly surprised that such a speech as I made in one cause should have been thought worthy of so much newspaper notice. I am not conscious and cannot see at this moment that it was at all beyond an every day speaking in the Supreme Court, and yet one who did not know me would suppose from these eulogies that the people of Boston had caught a *hippopotamus at the Court*. . . . If you should meet with our friend, Mr. Justice Story, assure him of my constant and grateful remembrance of his kindness—would to Heaven that I had such a

---

(1) Chief Justice Parker in the opinion rendered in this case said:
"For the eloquent and accomplished lawyer who closed this cause for the plaintiff in a manner so true to his client and yet so courteous to the defendant, explicitly and repeatedly disavowed the intention to charge the defendant with anything beyond constructive fraud. We have taken this view of the case, prolix perhaps but after all not minute, because the nature of the demand, the circumstances under which it is brought forward and the powerful manner in which it has been supported in the previous preparation, as well as in the skillful but honorable manner in which it has been conducted in court, seemed to demand an examination of the general merits of the bill.
(2) *The Letters of Daniel Webster* (1902).

oracle of the law in my neighborhood in the form of a Judge of the Supreme Court. How does he contrive to carry such a load of law with such buoyancy of spirits. I do not observe that his ability to enjoy sinks the thousandth part of an inch the deeper, with all her load, but makes her way as gaily and sportively as if she were a mere gondoler for pleasure. Such is the effect of a happy constitution, and there is no builder, at least, like nature.

Of the Class which first enjoyed Story's instruction and which entered in September, 1829, the most noted member was Benjamin R. Curtis, later Judge of the United States Supreme Court and head of the Bar of the Country. Of his career at the School, his brother, George Ticknor Curtis (who was in the Law School in 1833-34), wrote:

Judge Story had come there with his affluence of learning, his power of satisfying young men who had a real thirst for knowledge, and his magnetic activity . . . There too had come . . . John Hooker Ashmun . . . who was as winning in his intercourse with young men as he was capable of instructing them in his particular department . . . Among the studious young men of talent who first gathered about Judge Story . . . Curtis was regarded as one of whose future the most confident hopes might be entertained, because he had given and was constantly giving, proofs of his peculiar adaptation to the profession of the law . . . His commonplace book kept at this time, and long afterwards continued, shows with what diligence he read, and with what system he digested his reading. Its titles and references exhibit a remarkable sagacity in selecting and preserving the learning that would be useful in practice.

Benjamin R. Curtis left the School after one year, but returned, however, for the summer term of 1832, for reasons explained in the following interesting letter written to his uncle, George Ticknor, Jan. 22, 1832:

I write to ask your advice relative to a plan I have been for some time deliberating on—of coming to Cambridge in the spring, and spending the summer term there in the Law School. There is one branch of the law, viz: the doctrines and practice of courts of equity, which I have no means of studying here. Both books and instruction are wanting; the former being of course indispensable, and the latter even more necessary in this department than any other of my profession, on account of the want of elementary treatises, and, indeed, of any means of gaining an entrance to its most simple and often-recurring principles. The jurisdiction of our Supreme Judicial Court is now such that this knowledge is important and there is every reason to believe that that jurisdiction will be extended to meet the increasing wants of the community. In the meantime, there is almost an entire ignorance on the subject in the Bar of Massachusetts, out of Boston; and the younger part of the profession do not seem to be making more progress in it than their fathers have done. I have also thought that it was well to get an early start in this branch of learning; for it must be difficult for one bred up in the rigid rules of the Common Law to imbibe the more liberal principles of Equity. If I can get this start, and make some little progress under an instructor, I can then go on by myself.

In addition to this, I have heard that it was proposed by the students to get a course of lectures on the Civil Law from Dr. Follen in the summer term, either at the expense of the Institution or at their own expense; and this would of course be an additional inducement, for though I may find little opportunity to commence chancery suits, or apply the doctrines of the Civil Law in the remote town of Northfield, I know you would not have me form my plan of studies in reference to the narrow arena in which I now stand, or limit my requirements to the humble demands which are made upon me here.

Later, in 1832, he wrote: "I still think there is no place in this country for getting the theory of the law like the Cambridge Law School." In 1833, he wrote to Mr. Ticknor:

While I have acquired considerable knowledge of practice, and some facility and dexterity in the art, I have not been gaining ground as I wished in the science of the law. The course of study which Mr. Ashmun was so kind as to lay out for me when I left his care has been broken in upon and irregularly pursued; and I feel every day as if I were losing my hold upon the roots and groundwork of the science which I had so painfully and laboriously laid. I feel the force of a remark which I once heard Mr. Ashmun make; when asked if some person "was a good lawyer", he answered, "No, he has always had too much business to be a good lawyer."

At the same time, I feel that I was never so well prepared for the study of law as I am now; and that, if I could have leisure and books and advice, I could go on with an ease and freedom to which I was a stranger before my mind had become habituated to think upon and decide questions of law, and when I was at almost every step checked and embarrassed by forms and modes of proceeding of which I was ignorant.(1)

---

(1) Curtis' great knowledge of pleading was largely gained from Professor Ashmun and his training in the country office at Northfield, and he once stated that he knew by heart "the whole series of declarations,

Among the other law students in 1829-1830, attracted by Judge Story's fame, were Oliver Prescott, later Judge of Probate; and Timothy Walker, the founder of the Cincinnati Law School, and author of *American Law*. But of all the noted men who were students in this opening year, the best known later in life, though not as a lawyer, was Oliver Wendell Holmes—a recent graduate of Harvard in 1829. His letters contain frequent references to his short Law School life. In September, 1829, he wrote to his classmate Phineas Barnes:

I am settled once more at home in the midst of those miscellaneous articles which always cluster around me wherever I can do just as I please—*Blackstone* and boots, law and lathe, *Rawle* and rasps, all intermingled in exquisite confusion when you were here I thought of going away to study my profession; but since Judge Story and Mr. Ashmun have come, the Law School is so flourishing that I have thought it best to stay where I am.

On January 13, 1830, he wrote (1):

I will tell you honestly that I am sick at heart of this place and almost everything connected with it. I know not what the temple of law may be to those who have entered it, but to me it seems very cold and cheerless about the threshold. . . . I will give you a chronicle in rhyme now if I can, and go back to prose if I can't:

> The Praeses has a weekly row
>   I think they call it a levee
> And people say it's very fine
>   I'm sure it's flat enough to me.
> Judge Story's bought a horse in town,
>   The Law School every day grows bigger,
> And Sukey Lennox—I forgot
>   I've told you all about the nigger.

In December, 1829, at the end of the first term, Judge Story returned to Washington, leaving the School for the first time in the sole charge of Professor Ashmun.

Early in January of the next year, 1830, occurred Webster's memorable speech in reply to Hayne, of which Story wrote back to Cambridge, on January 29:

---

pleas, replications, rebutters, sur-rebutters, etc., as given by Chitty; that he had sometimes walked the floor of his nursery for hours in the night, with a sick child in his arms, repeating to it these forms; and that he found them as good a lullabye as anything in Mother Goose, and much more of a relief to his own mind."

(1) For these and succeeding letters of Holmes, see *Life and Letters of Oliver Wendell Holmes,* by John T. Morse, Jr.

Nothing new has occurred since I last wrote you, excepting a very vivid controversy in the Senate between Mr. Webster and Mr. Hayne of South Carolina. . . . Mr. Webster occupied two days in a second reply. The last speech, in the opinion of friends and foes, was the ablest he ever delivered at any time in Congress. He subdued Mr. Hayne who concluded the debate in a mild and amiable tone.

Story might have added that he had called on Webster, on the evening previous to his speech, and, expressing some anxiety as to the result of the debate, had offered to look up material to be used in his reply. Mr. Webster thanked him and said, "Give yourself no uneasiness, Judge Story, I will grind him as fine as a pinch of snuff."(1)

At this term of the Supreme Court, 1830, Judge Marshall gave one of his great constitutional decisions, in which Story concurred, *Craig v. Missouri* (4 Peters 410). The case involved a State statute under which Missouri was held to be issuing bills of credit in contravention of the United States Constitution, and was one of the earliest in which Thomas H. Benton appeared before the Supreme Court.

The close of Marshall's opinion gives a vivid idea of how urgently the vexed political question of States' rights was pressed upon the courts of the period, and of the dignity with which the great Chief Justice dealt with it:

In the arguments we have been reminded by one side of the dignity of a sovereign state; of the humiliation of her submitting herself to this tribunal; of the dangers which may result from inflicting a wound on that dignity; by the other, of the still superior dignity of the people of the United States who have spoken their will in terms which we cannot misunderstand.

To these admonitions we can only answer, that if the exercise of that jurisdiction which has been imposed upon us by the Constitution and law of the United States shall be calculated to bring on these dangers which have been indicated; or if it shall be indispensable to the preservation of the Union, and consequently of the independence and liberty of these states, these are consider-

---

(1) A similar feeling of confidence is related in a reply of Webster made on the morning of his speech to a fellow senator who had said, "It is a critical moment, and it is time, it is high time that the people of this country should know what the Constitution is."—"Then," Webster had answered, "by the blessing of Heaven they shall learn this day before the sun goes down what I understand it to be." *Reminiscences of Daniel Webster,* by Peter Harvey. *History of the United States,* by James F. Rhodes, Vol. I.

ations which address themselves to those departments which may with perfect propriety be influenced by them. This department can listen only to the mandates of law, and can tread only that path which is marked out by duty.

His judicial labors did not lessen Story's interest in his new duties as Professor; and on March 10, 1830, he is found writing to Professor Ticknor: "I shall be glad to return home and work with the Law Students. I am impatient for leisure to prepare some written lectures, for there is a terrible deficiency of good elementary books."

No sooner had Story returned to Cambridge in the spring of 1830, than a case arose which excited the greatest alarm and horror through the whole community—the trial of the four men indicted for the murder of Joseph White, an aged and wealthy citizen of Salem, killed while asleep in his bed at night.

A letter of Story to Webster, written from Cambridge, April 17, 1830, described his personal interest in the case, and the general panic which prevailed in the community:

An entire new direction was given to my thoughts by the horrible murder of Captain White at Salem. You are aware that he died childless and that his principal heirs are Mr. Stephen White and my sister's children. It is altogether the most mysterious and dreadful affair that I ever heard of . . . Not the slightest trace has been found by which to detect the assassins . . . I never knew such a universal panic. It is not confined to Boston or Salem, but seems to pervade the whole community. We are all astounded and looking to know from what quarter the next blow will come. There is a universal dread and sense of calamity, as if we lived in the midst of a banditti. . . . The bulk of his fortune goes to Mr. Stephen White, who will get from $150,000 to $200,000. My nieces will receive about $25,000 each.

As is well known, four men were arrested, Joseph J. and J. Francis Knapp, and George and Richard Crowninshield, charged as the murderers and accessories. Owing to the tremendous public excitement, a special session of the Supreme Court was held; and Daniel Webster was retained to aid Attorney General Marcus Morton and Solicitor General Daniel Davis for the State, and for the defendant J. Francis Knapp, appeared Franklin Dexter (son of Samuel Dexter) and William H. Gardiner, assisted by Robert Rantoul Jr., then a young man just admitted to practice in the lower court; and Samuel Hoar appeared for the defendant, George Crowinshield.

Webster's famous argument, his "peroration of surpassing pathos", as the newspapers described it, and the strenuous legal fight of the defendants' counsel are familiar to all(1); but by reason of Webster's constant correspondence with Story and reliance on him for legal advice throughout the case, and Story's own personal and local connection with the murdered man, and because of the noted counsel engaged, the case was of peculiar interest to the Harvard Law School students.

A classmate of Charles Sumner writes:

The trial attracted many from the neighboring towns—law students and young lawyers. Among them Sumner was present. I recollect how delighted he was with the keenness of Dexter in worming the truth out of witnesses on cross examination, and especially in summing up the evidence in the prisoner's behalf. I met him at the trial several times, and he seemed to take as much interest in it as if he were one of the lawyers. He was not a member of the Law School at the time; and I could not help thinking that if he had not decided what profession to study, the dignity and even solemnity of that trial conducted by the ablest counsel to be found, must have decided him to study law.(2)

Another sidelight on this trial is thrown by a letter of Oliver Wendell Holmes who was still in the Law School, May 8, 1830:

I will just tell you that I have been very busy for some time with one kind of nonsense and another, and you know the laxity that always follows the tension of a man's sinews. In the first place I have been writing poetry like a madman. . . . The collegers got up a little monthly concern called *The Collegian,* and I wrote poetry fiercely for the four numbers which have been published. . . . The people are crowding in so to the Law School that we begin to apprehend a famine. . . . Nothing is going on but murder and robbery; we have to look in our closets and under our beds, and strut about with sword canes and pistols. The first thing a fellow knows is that he has a rap over his head and a genteel young man fragrant with essences is

(1) See *Commonwealth v. Knapp,* 10 Pick. 477; *Commonwealth v. Crowninshield,* 10 Pick. 497; and *Webster's Works,* Vol. II., and for an interesting and complete account of the case, see *Life of Webster,* by George T. Curtis, Vol. I; and *Autobiography of Seventy Years,* by George F. Hoar, Vol. I. *Retrospect of Western Travel,* by Harriet Martineau (1838).
See *Webster's Private Correspondence,* Vol. I; and letters in the *Story Papers,* in the Massachusetts Historical Society Library.
(2) This letter and the many letters of Sumner quoted in this work are taken from the *Memoirs and Letters of Charles Sumner,* by Edward L. Pierce, Vol. I. (1878).

fumbling with white gloved fingers in his pockets and concludes
his operations with kicking him into a gully or dropping him over
a bridge. Poor old Mr. White was "stabbed in the dark" and
since that the very air has been redolent of assassination. The
women have exhausted their intellect in epithets and exclamations,
the newspapers have declared it atrocious, and worst of all the
little poets have been pelting the villain or villains with verses.

Holmes, while still a law student, was destined to make at
least one permanent mark on the history of the nation.

On Sept. 14, 1830, an item appeared in the *Boston Daily Advertiser* which was read by the young law student, with the result
that he contributed to the issue of Sept. 16, a poem entitled *Old
Ironsides*—the effect of which is graphically described by Holmes'
biographer, John T. Morse, Jr:

One genuine lyric outburst, however, done in this year of the
law almost made him in a way actually famous. The frigate
Constitution, historic indeed, but old and unseaworthy, then lying
in the navy yard at Charlestown, was condemned by the Navy
Department to be destroyed. Holmes read this in a newspaper
paragraph and it stirred him. On a scrap of paper with a lead
pencil he rapidly shaped tthe impetuous stanzas of "Old Ironsides" and sent them to the *Daily Advertiser* of Boston. Fast
and far they travelled through the newspaper press of the country; they were even printed in handbills and circulated about the
streets of Washington. An occurrence, which otherwise would
probably have passed unnoticed, now stirred a national indignation. The astonished Secretary made haste to retrace a step
which he had taken quite innocently in the way of business. The
Constitution's tattered ensign was *not* torn down. The ringing
spirited verses gave the gallant ship a reprieve, which satisfied
sentimentality, and a large part of the people of the United States
had heard of O. W. Holmes, law student at Cambridge, who had
only come of age a month ago.

It was to this fatal gift of verse writing that the early abridgment of Holmes' legal career is attributed. An undergraduate
paper, the *Collegian,* edited by John O. Sargent of the Class of
1830, was "alluringly ready" to receive contributions from him;
and Holmes himself thus described the results in his farewell
address to the Medical School in 1882:

Let me begin with my first experience as a medical student. I
had come from the lessons of Judge Story and Mr. Ashmun in
the Law School at Cambridge. I had been busy more or less with

I hereby certify that Mr Edward S. Rand has been a member of the Law School in Harvard University for one year commencing Sept 1. 1829. & has pursued his studies in connexion with my office with great diligence & proficiency and sustained an unreproachable moral character

John H. Ashmun
Counsellor practising in the
Sup. Jud. Court &
Professor of Law in
Harv? Univ?.

Cambridge
Aug. 1830

I entirely concur in the foregoing certificate.

Joseph Story Dane Professor of Law in Harv University

the pages of *Blackstone* and *Chitty,* and other text books of the first year of legal study. More or less, I say; but I am afraid it was less rather than more. For during that year I first tasted the intoxicating pleasure of authorship. A college periodical conducted by friends of mine, still undergraduates, tempted me into print, and there is no form of lead-poisoning which more rapidly and thoroughly pervades the blood and bones and marrow than that which reaches the young author through mental contact with type metal. . . . In that fatal year I had my first attack of author's lead poisoning and I have never got quite rid of it from that day to this. But for that, I might have applied myself more diligently to my legal studies and carried a green bag in place of a stethoscope and a thermometer up to the present day.

The description of his transition from Law to Medicine had also been written by him to his classmate Barnes:

I suppose now that whenever you take the trouble to think about me your fancy sketches a twofold picture. In the front ground stands myself, on one side sparkle the fountains of Castalia, and on the other stand open the portals of Nemesis (if that be the name of Law). My most excellent romancer, it is not so! I must announce to you that I have been a medical student for more than six months. I do not know what you will say—but I cannot help it. . . . I know I might have made an indifferent lawyer—I think I may make a tolerable physician—I did not like the one, and I do like the other.

In the fall of 1830, just at the end of the Knapp murder trials, there occurred an event which was to have tremendous effect upon the legal history of Massachusetts and indeed upon that of the Nation—the appointment of Lemuel Shaw as Chief Justice of the Supreme Court of Massachusetts, August 23, 1830.

Chief Justice Isaac Parker had died at the opening of the Knapp trials, July 25, 1830, three years after his resignation as Royall Professor of Law at Harvard.

Judge Story had been strongly urged for the place, but he had declined.

I was strongly assailed from several quarters to resign my seat in the Supreme Court and become Chief Justice, and I had no small difficulty in escaping from the attack. The appointment which has been made of Lemuel Shaw Esq. is highly respectable, and the profession is generally satisfied.

So he wrote to Richard Peters, Oct. 25, 1830, and Marshall wrote to Story, Oct. 15, 1830:

My regret for the loss of this estimable gentleman (Chief Justice Parker) was much enhanced by the fear that Massachusetts might be able to supply his place by seducing from the Federal bench a gentleman whose loss would be irreparable. I felicitate myself and my country on the disappointment of this apprehension.

The lawyer on whom Governor Levi Lincoln's choice fell was a young man, thirty-nine years of age, an Overseer of Harvard College, and then in receipt of the very large annual fees of $15,000 to $20,000.(1)

For thirty years (1830-1860) Lemuel Shaw, as Chief Justice, was one of the chief constructive jurists of the country, and for twenty-seven years (1834-1861) he was, as a member of the Harvard Corporation, one of the most active and zealous workers in behalf of the Harvard Law School.

The years 1831 and 1832 were notable in the field of Federal law, as well as in politics, for a determined attack on Federal sovereignty. Jan. 28, 1831, Story wrote:

A most important and alarming measure . . . to repeal the 25th section of the Judiciary Act. If it should prevail, (of which I have not any expectation), it would deprive the Supreme Court of the power to revise the decisions of the State Courts and State Legislature in all cases in which they were repugnant to the Constitution of the United States, so that all laws passed and all decisions made, however destructive to the National Government would have no power of redress. The introduction of it shows the spirit of the times.

This bill was strongly urged by the upholders of the States' rights

---

(1) Webster said in later years, "Massachusetts is indebted to me for having Judge Shaw at the head of her judiciary for thirty years; for he never would have taken the lead had it not been for me. Gov. Levi Lincoln consulted me and I said 'Appoint Lemuel Shaw by all means' . . . I plied him (Shaw) in every way possible and had interview after interview with him . . . I guess he smoked a thousand cigars while settling the point" See *Reminiscences of Daniel Webster*, by Peter Harvey.

Benjamin R. Curtis, when a student at the Law School, wrote, August 4, 1830:

"I am sorry to learn that it is probable that (John) Davis of Worcester will be placed on the Bench: I hoped it might be one of the Boston Bar— The appointment of Mr. (Samuel) Hubbard or Mr. (Lemuel) Shaw would leave a fine practise to be distributed among the remaining lawyers; and would be a good example to teach young men that, though the number of lawyers does increase, still from time to time an old gray beard makes way and leaves room for others."

It is to be noticed that the "old graybeard" in Shaw's case was 39 years old.

doctrine, and was the result of the bitter feeling created by Judge Story's powerful opinion in *Martin v. Hunter,* and Marshall's in *Cohens v Virginia,* and in the long line of opinions in which the Supreme Court had now definitely established its right to review the decisions of State courts. The bill was defeated by a vote of 137 to 51; all but 6 of the 51 votes coming from Southern States.(1)

In the same year occurred the case of the *Cherokee Nation v. Georgia* (5 Peters 17) involving the constitutionality of a Georgia statute dealing with the Cherokee Indian lands, in countervention of a United States Treaty.

In this case, William Wirt and John Sergeant appeared for the Cherokee Chiefs, and Horace Binney, James Kent, Ambrose Spencer and Daniel Webster were their advisers out of court,— a remarkable array of legal talent. The State of Georgia declining to recognize the jurisdiction of the United States Supreme Court refused to appear; the Court, however, (Story and Thompson dissenting) decided the case on a technical point in favor of the State,(2) although the Chief Justice stated in his opinion: "If courts were permitted to indulge their sympathies, a case better calculated to excite them can scarcely be imagined." "The great interest excited throughout the Union by this controversy", said the *North American Review* of that period, "was naturally to be expected from the novelty of the case, the dignity of the parties and the question, and the high importance of the principles involved."(3) Story's views of the legal and political situation at this time became very despondent, and his letters show his constant desire to return to his Law School labors, in which he now took an increasingly active interest.

On Jan. 20, 1831, he wrote to Professor Ashmun:

There is nothing here worthy of drawing aside one's atten-

---

(1) See McMaster's *History of the United States,* Vol. VI.
(2) Story wrote to his wife from Washington Jan. 13, 1832:
"At Philadelphia, I was introduced to two of the Chiefs of the Cherokee Nation, so sadly dealt with by the State of Georgia. They are both educated men and conversed with singular force and propriety of language upon their own case, the law of which they perfectly understood and reasoned upon. I never in my whole life was more affected by the consideration that they and all their race are destined to destruction. And I feel, as an American, disgraced by our gross violation of the public faith towards them. I fear and greatly fear that in the course of Providence there will be dealt to us a heavy retributive justice."
(3) See also review of *The Cherokee Case,* by Joseph Hopkinson, in *Amer. Quart. Rev.,* Vol. X (March 1832); also, *Amer. Jurist,* Vol. VI (1831).

tion, unless.it be to lament over the state of our public affairs, and that is by no means an agreeable topic. I have for a long time known that the present rulers and their friends were hostile to the judiciary, and have been expecting some more decisive demonstrations than had yet been given out. The recent attacks in Georgia and the recent nullification doctrine in South Carolina are but parts of the same general scheme, the object of which is to elevate an exclusive state sovereignty upon the ruins of the general government. . . . As to the Law School, though I am sorry to have lost some of our best students, I have never thought we could safely calculate on more than thirty students at a time. I am ready to do what I can to deserve as many, and I wish no better coadjutor for the law, or in the law, than now fills the chair. May God grant you, my dear sir, all the success you are entitled to.

This complimentary and affectionate letter indicates the warm and intimate friendship which existed between the two Professors. No less close also were Ashmun's relations with his students, by whom he was not only respected but loved. As Story said, in his eulogy at the time of Ashmun's death:

There is not and there cannot be, a higher tribute to his memory than this, that, while his scrutiny was severely close he was most cordially beloved by all his pupils. He lived with them upon terms of the most familiar intimacy; and he has sometimes with a delightful modesty and eloquence, said to me, "I am but the eldest boy upon the forms."

And George S. Hillard, who was in the Law School 1830-32, said(1) :

His bodily infirmities made him appear sometimes austere and irritable, but no man had a warmer heart or deeper sensibility. If he had ever given pain, he felt it no less himself, and always made up for it by some marked kindness in tone, looks, or manner. He associated with his pupils on terms of perfect equality, and gained their attachment while he preserved their respect, and parted with none of the dignity of his station and character. He delighted to mingle with them and to be surrounded with the fresh and buoyant spirits which are the natural heritage of youth and health; but to which he, alas! had been long a stranger. Though his heart was heavy, he loved the sunshine of happy faces. We felt it a privilege to be in his society and that we had done a good deed, if we had by tasking our faculties of entertain-

(1) See Obituary Notice of Ashmun, by G. S. Hillard in *Boston Daily Advertiser,* April, 1833.

ment made him forget for an hour the pain and languor of disease.

During 1831, Professor Ashmun had almost entire charge of the School; for Story was busily engaged, when in Cambridge, in writing the first of his great series of law books—his *Commentaries on the Law of Bailments,* which was published in the spring of 1832.

Mr. Dane had prescribed that the Dane Professor should deliver and revise for publication a course of lectures on five specified branches of law. This scheme was modified by Story, owing to the fact that the method of teaching adopted by him in the School was by familiar and conversational expositions, and not by written lectures. As adequate modern text books were sorely needed, he determined, instead of reducing his lectures to writing, to prepare a series of systematic treatises to serve as text books, covering even more than Dane had proposed—all branches of Commercial Law, Federal Law, Equity, and the Law of Nature and Nations.

His work on *Bailments* was dedicated:

To the Honorable Nathan Dane, LL.D., distinguished alike for purity, simplicity, and dignity in his private life, for talents, learning, and fidelity in his profession, and for public labors in the State and national councils, which have conferred on him an imperishable fame as a statesman and patriot, this work, the first fruits of the professorship founded by his bounty, is respectfully dedicated, by his obliged friend and servant, the author.

The only previous English treatise on the subject had been that of Sir William Jones, published in England in 1781; and the lapse of fifty years and the progress of modern civilization had made a new work absolutely necessary. Perhaps, however, the most important feature of the book was the extent to which Story utilized the doctrines of civil law and foreign law writers—an innovation in American law works. Of this he says in his preface:

My reasons are as follows:—In the first place, the learned founder of the Dane Professorship, with that spirit of professional liberality which has always characterized him, suggested to me at an early period the propriety of my presenting, in all my labors upon commercial law, some view of the corresponding portions of commercial jurisprudence of Continental Europe. To advice so given it was impossible not to listen with the utmost respect; and the wisdom of it has appeared more and more strongly to my mind, as it has been contemplated in all its bearings.   In the next place, I have long entertained the belief, that an enlarged acquaintance with the Continental jurisprudence, and especially with that of France, would furnish the most solid means of improvement of commercial law, as it now is, or hereafter may be, administered in America.   Mr. Chancellor Kent has already led the way in this noble career; and has, by an incorporation of some of the best principles of the foreign law into ours, infused into it a more benign equity, as well as a more persuasive cogency and spirit.   The English common lawyers (it must be acknowledged with deep regret) have hitherto generally exhibited an extraordinary indifference to the study of foreign jurisprudence.

There is a remarkable difference, in the manner of treating juridical subjects, between the foreign and the English jurists. The former almost universally discuss every subject with an elaborate, theoretical fulness and accuracy, and ascend to the elementary principles of each particular branch of the science. The latter, with few exceptions, write Practical Treatises, which contain little more than a collection of the principles laid down in the adjudged cases, with scarcely an attempt to illustrate them by any general reasoning, or even to follow them out into collateral consequences.   It appears to me, that the union of the two plans would be a great improvement in our law treatises; and would afford no inconsiderable assistance to students in mastering the higher branches of their profession.

Among the students during these years, 1830-1833, the most prominent was Charles Sumner, who entered the School in 1831; and his letters give an instructive view of the law student's life of that period.   In May, 1831, he wrote to Charlemagne Tower in Albany:

Your method and application are to me an assurance that the studies of the law office will be fruitful; but excuse the impertinence of a friend.   I fear that Blackstone and his train will usurp your mind too much, to the exclusion of all cultivation of polite letters.   The more I think of this last point, the more important it seems to me in the education of a lawyer. "Study Law hard" said Pinkney "but study polite letters as hard."   So also says Story. The fact is, I look upon a *mere* lawyer, a reader of cases and cases alone, as one of the veriest wretches in the world. Dry items and facts, argumentative reports, and details of pleading must incrust the mind with somewhat of their own rust.   A lawyer must be a man of polish with an omnium gatherum of knowledge.   There is no branch of study or thought but what he can betimes summon to his aid if his resources allow it.

Later he wrote:

Give me my first year and a half in the entirely theoretical studies of a law school, and my remainder in a thronged business office, where I can see the law in those shapes in which a young lawyer can alone see and practice it. It is years which makes the counsellor.

Again just before entering the School he wrote:

I shall go to Cambridge with a cartload of resolves. . . . Law, classics, history and literature; all of them shall meet my encounter.(1)

Because of his studious habits, Sumner at once became a favorite of the Professors. Story had long been a friend of his father, Charles P. Sumner, who had graduated from Harvard in 1796, when Story was a sophomore. A close intimacy with the son now sprang up, of which Sumner's biographer says: "Biography gives no instance of a more beautiful relation between teacher and pupil. The judge admired Sumner's zeal in study, enjoyed his society, and regarded him like a son. . . . This friendship entered very largely into Sumner's life, and for many years gave direction to his thoughts and ambition."

An example of this friendship is seen in a letter of Story from Washington, February 3, 1833, asking Sumner to help him in forwarding books: "There are not many of whom I would venture to ask the favor of troubling themselves in my affairs; but I feel proud to think that you are among the number, and I have, in some sort, as the Scotch would say, a heritable right to your friendship."

On July 12, 1833, Story wrote to Sumner who was then proposing to leave the School at the end of the two years' course:

I am very glad that you have concluded to remain at the Law School another term. It will, I think, be very profitable to you, and not in the slightest degree affect your means of practical

---

(1) To this, his correspondent made answer, not without reason:
"I cannot altogether applaud your resolution to include so much in your system of study for the coming year. 'Law, classics, history and literature' is certainly too wide a range for any common mind to spread over at any one time. Better follow Captain Boabdil's example; take them man by man and kill them all up by computation."

knowledge. Let nothing induce you to quit the law. You will, as sure as you live, possess a high rank in it, and need not fear the frowns of fortune or of power.

While in the Law School, Sumner roomed, as did many of the law students, in Divinity Hall. He was a member of a debating society connected with the School, and in 1833 was the first president of the Temperance Society just organized in the College, on the executive committee of which was another famous lawyer, Richard H. Dana Jr., then a sophomore in College.

Among Sumner's fellow students were Benjamin F. Thomas, later Judge of the Massachusetts Supreme Court, who graduated in 1831; Wendell Phillips, against whom he argued in a Moot Court case, and who graduated in 1832; Henry W. Paine, long one of the leading lawyers of Boston, famed for his wit; George C. Shattuck of Boston; George Gibbs, author of *Judicial Chronicle* and of the *Memoirs of the Administration of Washington and John Adams,* a nephew of Rev. William Ellery Channing; Charles C. Converse, later Judge of the Supreme Court of Ohio; and George S. Hillard of Boston, the noted author,—all of whom graduated in 1832.

In the fall term of 1831, owing to Story's illness, Ashmun continued his sole charge of the School; and Story wrote to him, December 2, 1831:

I feel great discontent and impatience in not being about my accustomed duties, especially in the Law School. I long for recitations and Moot Courts, and in short, for disputation and action. I regret that you have "the cold." Pray, in mercy to us all, do not get sick until I am better and can relieve you.

Shortly after this Story returned to Washington, and of his absence and his manner of teaching, the following letter from Sumner to Charlemagne Tower, January 31, 1832, gives a striking account:

Judge Story is at Washington with the Supreme Court for the winter. Of course the School misses him. . . . Our Class, as yet, has had nothing to do with him. Those who do recite to him love him more than any instructor they ever had before. He treats them all as gentlemen, and is full of willingness to instruct. He gives to every line of the recited lessons a running commentary, and omits nothing which can throw light upon the path of the student. The good scholars like him for the knowledge he distributes; the poor (if any there be) for the amenity with which he treats them and their faults.

Of the principal case in which Story sat this winter, *Worcester v. Georgia* (6 Peters 515), another case involving the Cherokee lands statute of Georgia, he wrote to his wife February 26, 1832:

We have had from Mr. Wirt and Mr. Sergeant in the past week some fine arguments in the Cherokee case, brought before us in a new form. . . . Both of the speeches were very able, and Mr. Wirt's in particular was uncommonly eloquent, forcible and finished. . . . No person appeared for the State of Georgia.

And he wrote to Professor Ticknor, March 8, 1832:

We have just decided the Cherokee case, and reversed the decisions of the State Court of Georgia, and declared her laws unconstitutional. The decision produced a very strong sensation in both houses; Georgia is full of anger and violence. . . . Probably she will resist the execution of our judgment, and if she does I do not believe the President will interfere(1). . . . The Court has done its duty. Let the Nation do theirs.

On March 4, 1832, he wrote to his wife:

Yesterday morning the Chief Justice delivered the opinion of the court in the Cherokee case, in favor of the missionaries. It was a very able opinion in his best manner. Thanks be to God the Court can wash their hands clean of the iniquity of oppressing the Indians and disregarding their rights. . . . We shall adjourn about the sixteenth of the month, and I shall move towards Cambridge with all the rapidity with which steam and coaches can carry me.

A letter from Story of March 1, 1832, written to Professor Ashmun, well expresses his devotion to his Law School work:

I have never known a winter pass away with so few refreshing cases—except the Cherokee Missionary case, and scarcely remember one which it was not irksome to go over and that was an

---

(1) Story was correct in this. President Jackson having already one struggle on his hands in the South Carolina Nullification matters, took no action. The Georgia Court refused to obey the mandate issued by the United States Supreme Court; and the missionary plaintiffs ordered to be released, remained in prison for a year, when they were voluntarily released by the State.

oasis in the desert. . . . We shall rise about the middle of March and I shall find my way home as soon as possible afterwards, so that I may relieve you from some extra duty. I would rather work in the Law School than here.

Returning to Cambridge, Story embodied in his lectures many comments on the constitutional and political questions arising in Washington. He was in constant touch with legislation, through Webster and Edward Everett; and the information obtained from these authoritative sources was imparted to his students. At the same time he was always in receipt, through his correspondents in London, of the latest news of English Parliamentary Law and judicial decisions.

In a letter to James J. Wilkinson of London, August 25, 1832, he says:

Forty young gentlemen are now at the Law School in this place, and I may add, that they know what is passing in Westminster Hall almost as well as what is passing in our own courts. Your publications of all sorts reach us in a short period.

In September of this year, 1832, Story and Ashmun had the great joy of seeing the completion of the new building for the Law School—Dane Hall (described in the following chapter).

Towards the close of the year, Story was finishing his *Commentaries on the Constitution of the United States,* (published in 1833) on which he had been engaged for eighteen months, and most of which had already been delivered in the form of lectures to the students. In its dedication to Chief Justice Marshall, he said:

I know not to whom it could with so much propriety be dedicated as to one whose youth was engaged in the arduous enterprises of the Revolution; whose manhood assisted in framing and supporting the national Constitution; and whose maturer years have been devoted to the task of unfolding its powers and illustrating its principles. When, indeed, I look back upon your judicial labors during a period of thirty-two years, it is difficult to suppress astonishment at their extent and variety, and at the exact learning, the profound reasoning and the solid principles which they everywhere display. Your expositions of Constitutional law . . . constitute a monument of fame far beyond the ordinary memorial of political and military glory. They are destined to enlighten, instruct and convince future generations;

and can scarcely perish but with the memory of the Constitution itself, . . . Allow me to add that I have a desire—to record upon these pages the memory of a friendship which has for so many years been to me a source of inexpressible satisfaction.

It will be noticed that in this year, 1832, on November 24, came the Nullification Ordinance of South Carolina and on December 10, President Jackson's proclamation. Story was so strongly impressed with the constitutional principles announced by the President, that, though detesting the latter's politics, he introduced his argument into his new *Commentaries;* and he wrote, Jan. 27, 1833, regarding a dinner to which the President had invited him:

Notwithstanding I am "the most dangerous man in America," the President especially invited me to drink a glass of wine with him. But what is more remarkable, since his last proclamation and message the Chief Justice and myself have become his warmest supporters, and shall continue so just as long as he maintains the principles contained in them. Who would have dreamed of such an occurrence?

The especial value and appropriateness of the appearance of Story's book at this particular crisis in national politics (1833) was noticed in the *Reviews*.

Thus Edward Everett wrote in the *North American Review* (January 1837):

Its peculiar seasonableness at the present time gives Mr. Justice Story's work a value, which no work could have possessed under different circumstances. Constitutional law in our day, instead of being the calm occupation of the schools or the curous pursuit of the professional student, has become,—as it were —an element of real life. The Constitution has been obliged to leaves its temple, and come down into the forum and traverse the streets.

And a reviewer in the *American Quarterly Review* wrote, in December 1833:

We know not that we could point to an individual better qual-

---

(1) Sumner wrote December 17: "Civil war in a portentous cloud hangs over us. South Carolina though the sorest part of our system, is not the only part that is galled. Georgia cannot, Virginia cannot, stomach the high Federal doctrines which the President has set forth in his proclamation . . . Judge Story speaks much of its value; and so striking did its argument appear to him that he has introduced it into a note to his work on the Constitution."

ified for this task than the author of these *Commentaries*. His habits of severe study and accurate investigation and comparison of written instruments, and his long official experience in the examination of legal and constitutional questions, with a powerful and penetrating mind, give a value to his labours upon this subject which few commentators could receive or claim. The researches of the Judge are peculiarly acceptable at this time, when many of the questions he has discussed have an interest from the movements which they lately excited in the South.

The personal attachment which Story felt for the School was shown, not only in his affectionate relations with the students while at Cambridge, but also in the manner in which his thoughts turned toward the School when he was in Washington. The three following letters show his feelings, better than any mere words of description.

Henry Moore (L. S. 1830-32) writing to "Charles Sumner, Librarian, No. 4 Dane Hall" Jan. 7, 1833, said(1):

On Wednesday afternoon I called upon Judge Story to take leave of him. I spent nearly an hour with him very pleasantly as you may well suppose, but when I came away I betrayed a weakness of which I was myself ashamed. In speaking of his regard for the Law School, the Judge said that "next his own children were his foster children," and I really believe that he spoke as he felt. He gave me full liberty to call on him for advice whenever I wanted it, a privilege for which I surely feel grateful.

On March 3, 1833, Moore wrote to Sumner from Washington:

I have seen Judge Story frequently and he seems never to have been happier except when at the Law School and I do think that he likes the Law School better than he does anything else. . . . I have met near a dozen law students here with many of whom you are acquainted . . . and the Judge says he must have a recitation.

To Sumner, Judge Story wrote, Feb. 6, 1833:

I thank you most sincerely for your kind letter, bringing, as it does to me, of Cambridge, news of home and of friends, of pursuits which I love, and interests which I am tied to by professional ties. I rejoice that Mr. Ashmun is well, and that the School goes on with its accustomed zeal. I would to God, that

---

(1)   Unpublished letters in *Sumner Papers* in *Harv. Coll. Library.*

I might be able to permanently associate my name with it as a perpetuity not forbidden by the law. . . . Pray give my kindest regards to Mr. Ashmun and remember me to all the School, as like Plowden, "apprentices in the law."

Affectionately your friend

Joseph Story.

To the amplitude with which Story's wish contained in this letter was fulfilled, the future history of the School bore and still bears witness.

Story's connection with the School in the spring of 1833 became immediately closer than he anticipated through the sad and sudden death of Professor Ashmun, on April 1, 1833, at the age of thirty-two. As already described, Ashmun had long been in ill health, and his brave success in doing his legal and Law School work in spite of his physical disabilities may be said to have resembled greatly Robert Louis Stevenson's masterful struggle to live.

Of his end, Sumner, one of his most devoted pupils, wrote May 5, 1833:

His death, though for a long time anticipated, yet had a degree of suddenness about it. All deemed his days numbered; but few were prepared to hear that they were cut short when they were. I was with him, and was the only one with him, at his death. It was the first deathbed, not to say sickbed, I ever stood by. If death comes as it came to him, surely in it there is nothing to fear, except in the thoughts of going we know not where.(1)

Ashmun's funeral was attended by the students in a body; and on April 5, 1833, Story delivered in the University Chapel a eulogy which is among the most tender and beautiful of all his writings, in which he paid this tribute to his friend:

My own acquaintance with him commenced only with his residence in Cambridge. But ever since that period, I have counted it among my chief pleasures to cultivate his friendship,

---

(1) Of the close relations between Professor Ashmun and his pupil Sumner, the following unpublished letter in the *Sumner Papers* in the Harvard College Library is a sign. It was written by Ashmun, Jan. 12, 1833:

"Will you have the goodness to ask Mr. Stimson to send in to the Tremont House tomorrow at about 4 o'clock for my horse and chaise.

If you would like to come into town yourself either in the morning or afternoon, I would be glad to have you bring in the aforesaid animal and we will go out together; as we should not get out in season for your commons, I will furnish you with some refreshing tea. Will you replenish my fire so as I may find it warm?"

and justify his confidence. Engaged as we have been, in kindred pursuits and duties, it has been almost of course that our intercourse should be frank as well as frequent; and I feel a pride in declaring that we have worked hand in hand with the most cordial fellowship and with a union of opinion which nothing but the strongest mutual attachment could have successfully cherished. . . . If he had lived longer, he might have reared more enduring monuments of fame for posterity; but his virtues would not have been more mature or more endeared. . . . He lived as a wise man would desire to live. He died as a good man would desire to die. Well may we exclaim "How beautiful is death when earned by virtue."

Largely by the efforts of James C. Alvord and Sumner, a monument was erected to Ashmun in Mount Auburn(1), on which was enscribed a loving epitaph written by Charles C. Emerson (L. S. 1829-31), E. Rockwood Hoar (L. S. 1837-39), in his speech on the Law School Day at the celebration of the 250th Anniversary of Harvard College in 1886, said of Ashmun and of this epitaph:

I have personally known every instructor in the law at this University from the beginning . I knew as a boy Chief Justice Parker. I knew Professor Stearns very well, as a boy and as a young man. I had the pleasure of some acquaintance with that model teacher, whose light went out too early for this institution and for the society around him—John Hooker Ashmun, whose epitaph at Mt. Auburn contains that summary of the character of a great lawyer: "He had the beauty of accuracy in his understanding, and the beauty of uprightness in his character."

There being no portrait in existence so far as is known,(2) the

---

(1) See unpublished letter of Alvord to Sumner, Aug. 7, 1834, *Sumner Papers*, Harv. Coll. Library.

(2) Reference is made, in a letter from Professor Greenleaf to Sumner, July 22, 1845, of a cast taken from Ashmun's face after death; but no trace of this cast can be found. (See unpublished letter in *Sumner Papers* in Harv. Coll. Library.)

"You are aware that by the care of Judge Story a cast in plaster was taken from the face of Professor Ashmun after his death. From this cast, aided by the recollections and advice of Mr. Ashmun's friends, Mr. Dexter, the sculptor, will make a bust representing the living subject, and has no doubt it can be successfully done. His price will be $100 for the first cast, after which he will deliver copies for $10 each. I am desirous to place this bust in our Law Library, as a tribute due to that eminently sound and learned lawyer and professor; and it seems to me that among his pupils the requisite sum would, upon this intimation, be readily subscribed. If you concur in this view, will you take the trouble to write a brief subscription paper and circulate it among his pupils in this city? I also will subscribe."

Harvard Square in 1831

only tangible relics of the loved Professor are the manuscripts of his lectures on Medical Jurisprudence, and on Equity, presented to the School, in 1860-61, by Sumner, and now in the Library of the Harvard Law School, (1)

(1) See Law Librarian's Report July 12, 1861, *Harv. Coll. Archives—Reports.* Charles Sumner attempted to collect Ashmun's manuscripts in 1834, in order to publish selections in the press; and George Ashmun, the Professor's brother, wrote that he had the lectures on Equity, Limitations, Assumpsit and Medical Jurisprudence complete. (See letter unpublished and to be found in the *Sumner Paper*):

"In the handwriting of your letter I think I see an identity with that of a statement in my possession of the events of the last night of my late brother's life, and my first impulse as well of feeling as of duty is to say to you how highly I appreciate the kind feelings which your attentions to him on that occasion, as well as the expression in the letter before me indicates."

Sumner replied Dec. 5, 1834 (See letter in possession of Giles Taintor Esq.), stating that he would "feel gratified by the opportunity you offer me of reading the manuscript of your lamented brother and making selections for the press. Be assured it will be to me a labor of love." He also speaks of a missing lecture on Wills as "a valuable one, being prepared with care by your brother and delivered in a course before the professors' families, etc., by gentlemen connected with the college."

CHAPTER XXII.

DANE HALL AND THE LAW LIBRARY

THE LIBRARY.

One of the first matters to which the Corporation turned its attention under the new régime which was the condition of the Law Library, and on September 29, 1829, it was voted: "That the Law Faculty be requested to recommend a fit person for Librarian in that Department and to consider and report to this Board what ought to be his duties and compensation."

Under this vote, no person seems to have been appointed for a year; but beginning in 1830-31 the practice prevailed of appointing one of the students. The first three Librarians were George Thomas Davis (1830-31); Wheelock Samuel Upton (1831-32); Charles Sumner (1832-34).

On November 3, 1829, Story wrote to Quincy, saying that there were then 28 students, and calling urgent attention to the deplorable state of the Library and the need of developing this part of the School as a special attraction and inducement to new students(1):

One of the most important objects is to give it (the School) at once, in the view of every student a decided superiority over every other institution of the like nature. It will therefore obtain a fixed reputation with the Public and give some confidence to parents that neither the time of their children nor their own money will be expended without an adequate return. It is important too, that the first class which leaves us, which will probably be a large one, as many of the students are in the 2nd and 3rd years of their studies, should enjoy the fullest benefits of the Institution, and carry with them in their own attainment and testimony the just proofs of the success of our course of instruction.

To accomplish this end it is indispensable that students should have a ready access to an ample Law Library which shall of

---

(1) *Harv. Coll. Papers*, 2nd Series, Vol. IV.

itself afford a complete apparatus for study and consultation. I need not say that no such library now belongs to the College. At present the students are compelled to resort to my own private library. . . .

In a practical sense, the present Law Library is of very little value or importance. We have very few of the best elementary books, and of those we have, most are of poor editions. . . . The text-books of study required by the students may be obtained without much difficulty; but those which are required for occasional consultation are very deficient. . . . The primary want is . . . the entire circle of Reports, English as well as American. . . . The English Reports, of which we have a considerable number, are principally the old reporters and rarely of the best editions. . . . But of modern reports we have few —a single copy only of *Burrow, Douglas, Cowper, Durnford and East, East, H. Blackstone, Bosanquet and Puller,* and *Taunton.*

Of *Massachusetts Reports* we have three copies, 1 copy *Johnson, Hare* (none of his *Chancery Reports*), 1 of *Cranch, Pickering, Binney, Dallas,* and *Yeates,* and an incomplete copy of *Wheaton.*

Our deficiency in American Reports is scarcely less than 150 volumes, but we ought to have duplicates of principal reports such as *Pickering, Johnson, Binney, Cranch* and *Wheaton.*

Of Equity Reports, in a practical sense we have none. We have ordered *Atkyns, Cases tempore Talbot, Brown's Ch. Rep.* . . . We not only propose to teach Equity law, but many of our students are from States where Equity Jurisprudence is of primary importance. . . .

I have no desire to part with any portion of my own library which has been the gradual collection of many years and cannot be easily if at all replaced. But as at a moderate calculation it would take a year to collect the body of common reports. And as both Mr. Ashmun and myself deem it vital to our success to begin with ample means, I have concluded, therefore, to offer my series of Reports to the Corporation if they choose to take them. . . . I am willing to have them appraised by any two gentlemen.

Professor Ashmun also wrote on November 4, 1829, to the same effect:

I do not suppose there can be any doubt of the necessity that the student should at once be furnished with an extensive library. It is not only in fact indispensable, but what is not to be overlooked, it is by them so considered. Much of the success of the School must depend upon first impressions and upon the mere impressions, right or wrong, of the students themselves.

Story's private library was at this time a very select and extensive one(1).

"It had been collected with great care at large expense and was
precisely adapted to his wants," says his son. "To surrender it
to the use of the students was exceedingly inconvenient and
annoying. To sell it to the College involved the purchase of a
new one for himself, which would be difficult and in many cases,
from the rarity of the books, impossible". While his limited
means did not warrant him in presenting his library to the College,
Story was unwilling to accept from the College, in its straightened financial condition, its full value. He therefore offered his
collection of 553 volumes of law reports at $4 per volume—
$2212,(2) and the Corporation, by vote of Dec. 17, 1829, thankfully accepted his generous offer, "being satisfied by the information obtained from Judge Jackson and Professor Ashmun, that
the price is very low."

In reality the price was less than one half the cost of replacing them; and on Dec. 17, 1829, the Corporation voted to
insure them for $4000. The liberality of the gift was increased
by the fact that Story's salary was only $1000, out of which $400
was paid to the College for the rent of his house.

Meanwhile Story had written to Dane requesting him to give
to the new School six to ten copies of his *Abridgment;* and
Dane replied December 8, 1829, presenting ten copies, (90
volumes), saying: "I find the School prosperous, much beyond

---

(1)   Story had written to Treasurer Francis, on August 19, 1829:
"Have you ascertained whether I can have a room in the chapel for my
library? I am now preparing to put it up and know not where I can put
it in Cambridge."
See *Harv. Coll. Archives, Letters to the Treasurer,* Vol. I.
(2)   Letter of Story to Quincy, Dec. 9, 1829, *Harv. Coll. Archives,
Letters to the Treasurer,* Vol. I.
"I herewith send you enclosed a catalogue of my books of Reports
amounting in all to 553 volumes. I have made an estimate of their present
value and I believe the estimate is very low—350 volumes of these Reports have been published since 1800.
I offer the whole Reports to the Corporation at the average price of $4
per volume, that is, at the sum of $2,212 for the whole. I would not sell
them to any private person for a very much larger sum; but I take into
consideration that I shall still have constant access to them so as to supersede the necessity of repurchasing them for my private use. I am confident I could not replace them for less than $3,500 to $4,000. I have
consulted Professor Ashmun on the subject, and he authorizes me to state
to you and the Corporation that he considers the estimate very low.
If the Corporation should not incline to purchase the whole at this
price, I wish you to consider my offer for a sale of them altogether withdrawn—."

my expectations, which were high. . . . The manner of instruction I think will increase the number of students; and I trust, if any course of studies will make good lawyers, the one adopted in the School will".(1)

The Treasurer was authorized by vote of the Corporation, January 21, 1830, to have a catalogue of the Law Library made, and in April 23, 1830, the finances of the School appeared so prosperous that Professor Ashmun was asked "to keep up the series of law reports, as they are published".

There was one peculiar feature of the Library which was a relic of the system instituted by Professor Stearns—a feature which, though a great attraction to the students of moderate means, constituted a heavy tax upon the finances of the School. This was the custom of supplying text books to the students, free of charge—a custom explained by Professor Ashmun, in a letter to the new College Treasurer, T. W. Ward, Sept. 12, 1831, as follows :(2)

The books, of which a considerable number have been purchased, are those which the students study in classes. Each member of the class is furnished with one copy which is returned when it is finished. They are allowed, if they please, to purchase them—in which case, or if for any reason they do not return them, notice is regularly given to the Steward that they may be charged in the term bills.

Our supply of these books is now not far from complete, and the orders for books which I am authorized to give, will probably be few and rare.

The system established for the delivery and reception of books is not so secure as I could wish, but the best I have been able to devise. Such books as will admit of it, including all the class books, are kept locked up and in the Librarian's custody. If the whole library should ever be brought into one room, it may be advisable to have some person constantly in it, to see that none are taken out without being charged. At present there is no guard against fraud, which we do not, however, fear,—and none against gross carelessness.

I had a satisfactory examination of the Library made a year ago, and another at the close of the last term. The books are in as good order as could be expected—a few have been missed, but I trust will be found. . . .

Of the amount of books purchased for this purpose, Ashmun's

(1)   *Harv. Coll. Papers*, 2nd Series, Vol. IV.
(2)   See *Harv. Coll. Archives, Letters to the Treasurer*, Vol. I.

letters to the Treasurer give ample proof. Thus in January, 1830(1) he asked for three copies of *Bacon's Abridgment*, 12 of *Wooddeson's Lectures*, 14 of *Chitty on Contracts*, 6 of *Stephens on Pleading*, 3 of *Saunders' Reports*, 14 of *Long on Sales* and 14 of *Bailey on Bills*, 2 of *Hoffman's Legal Outlines*. In August, 1830, he wished bought for the ensuing term 9 copies of *Chitty on Pleading*, 9 or more copies of *Abbott on Shipping*.

There was still a great lack of American reports,(2) and a report to the Overseers from the Library Visiting Committee, February 4, 1830, demanded with vigor that the Law Library should be made "a complete, American Library".

In January, 1831, Story offered to the Corporation the residue of his law library of 384 English books and 123 foreign law books, miscellaneous, and elementary works for the very moderate sum of $1400—a price less than one half their cost(3) ; and on July 21, 1831, the Corporation voted to make the purchase(4).

Any very large increase in the Library during these early years of the new régime was of course rendered impossible by the

---

(1)   See letter of Ashmun to Francis, Jan. 23, 1830, *Harv. Coll. Arch- Letters to the Treasurer*, Vol. I.

"I send you herewith a letter I received in answer to my inquiries for the prices of Law Books to be delivered in Boston for cash, and a memorandum below of the books that I think it would be well to purchase. We are in want of *Wooddeson's Lectures*, and I believe it is not to be had in this country. I should be glad to have a dozen copies imported and beg leave to suggest it to you. *Bacon's Abridgment* also is much needed. Mr. Halsted says it is soon to be published but I have heard the same story for years and cannot depend at all upon it. If half a dozen copies could be obtained in England at a reasonable price, I should think it advisable; indeed, unless they are high there, I think we ought to have them and if they are cheap, as many more. *Hoffman's Legal Outlines* is marked by Mr. Halsted at a very high price, and at that price I should wish but 2 or 3 copies. If it could be obtained more reasonably, 6 copies would be useful."

(2)   A letter from Ashmun to the Treasurer, Aug. 2, 1830, notes his order to purchase the *Connecticut Reports* from Thomas Day.

(3)   See letter of Story to Quincy, July 16, 1831, *Harv. Coll. Arch., Letters to the Treasurer*, Vol. II:

"I have made an estimate in a general way of their present value. It exceeds by some hundreds of dollars that at which I propose to offer it to the Corporation. I am very certain that these volumes cost me more than double the price I have affixed to them. The books are in good preservation and I offer them to the Corporation at the sum of $1,400. Mr. Ashmun went away to New York on Friday and so unexpectedly that I had not completed the catalogue at the time. He desired me to say that he was entirely satisfied with the above stated price of them."

(4)   There continued also to be a transfer of books from the College Library to the Law Library. See *Corporation Records*, Nov. 15, 1832, containing reference to a letter from Prof. Ashmun requesting such transfer. No copy of this letter appears to be preserved in the Harvard College Archives.

financial condition of the School. This condition was, however, only temporary, for Story's fame was attracting more students each year.

In the President's 6th Annual Report for 1830-31, the Treasurer presents in his Report, for the first time, a separate "Law School and Library Account", which is of interest as showing the slender resources of the School(1).

That this account made a favorable showing for the new School is seen from the Treasurer's statement:

There is a balance against the Law School of $3485.01 but upwards of $6000 has been expended on the Law Library which

---

(1) LAW SCHOOL AND LIBRARY.

DR.

For balance debt against this account August 31, 1830.........		$2,152 44
Of interest due to Aug. 31, 1831, at 5 per cent.....		169 95
Paid during the year for Books bought in U. S..... $1,900 94		
Invoice of Books per Coliseum from Havre, by Baring Brothers & Co... $176 28		
Hilliard & Brown for Law Books, May, 1830, transferred from account of Text Books, to which it was charged 535 75		
	$712 03	
		$2,612 97
Wood from College Yard, $112.50; Wood and Coal, otherwise $31.25	$143 75	
Paid Fire Insurance on $4,000 on Library, $32; other Insurance, $2.33	34 33	
Book Case and covering Books $45 00		
Printing, $5; Advertising, $7.25; Cleaning, $3 .... 15 25		
	$60 25	
		$238 33
Paid salaries to Professor Ashmun	$1,500 00	
to Judge Story	1,000 00	
		$2,500 00
		$7,673 69

CR.

By received amount of Term Bills for—		
Instruction, etc.	$3,233 00	
Books sold	52 50	
	$3,285 50	
Do. for use of Books during vacation.............	$6 00	
		$3,291 50
Income for the year on Isaac Royal's Legacy....	$397 18	
Nathan Dane's Donation	500 00	
	$897 18	
Balance debt against this account August 31, 1831		3,485 01
		$7,673 69

is charged against this account, so that there has been a gain of between two and three thousand dollars, and it is expected the Law School will gradually pay its debt and leave the library clear without cost to the College.

The Treasurer's account of August 31, 1832, showed that during the preceding year $321.04 was spent for books, that the amount received from Term Bills was $3,507, and that the deficit had been decreased to $2,352.51; and the Treasurer stated that the income "is gradually extinguishing the balance against that account and will leave that department in possession of a valuable library without cost to the College."

The amount spent for books during the year ending August 31, 1833, was $1,383.29; and the deficit showed a slight increase to $2,686.50.

One factor which strengthened the financial condition of the School was undoubtedly the ridiculously small salary paid to the Professors, Story receiving only $1000 and Ashmun $1500. The inadequacy was so evident that the Corporation, on August 31, 1831, voted to pay Ashmun, in addition to his salary, 15 per cent. of the tuition fees, after deducting annual expenses of $2200 ($196.05 in 1831-1832). The Committee, consisting of the President, Judge Jackson and Mr. Gray, appointed July 31, 1831, to investigate further compensation for Professors which recommended this vote, reported that the "Dane Professor at present wholly refuses any increase."

DANE LAW SCHOOL BUILDING.

As the students increased, and the Library became more complete, the smallness and inconvenience of the rooms in College House No. 2 proved unbearable.

As early as February 4, 1830, the Library Visiting Committee urged the Overseers to provide new quarters for the Law Library. At Story's urgent suggestion, the Corporation voted on July 15, 1830, that the Treasurer should consider the expediency of a new building for the School; and on August 19, 1830, the President and Treasurer were directed to cause a plan and estimate to be prepared and a location selected, for consideration of the Board.

The general funds of the College were, however, too small to carry out such a project. There were no available Law School funds, as the incomes from the Dane and Royall foundations were insufficient to pay even the small salaries allowed to the Professors.

Story accordingly wrote to Ashmun from Washington, Jan. 11, 1831:

> In respect to a Law Building at Cambridge, I expressed to President Quincy, a few days before I left home, some doubt whether it was not a premature project. I would not have a dollar expended on our account, which would ultimately prove a loss. It would mortify me beyond measure. I would rather live in the old house, and work our way there through its dark lecture-rooms. It is perhaps yet uncertain how far our success may be permanent, and there is some danger, at least, that some of the profession, as well as other dignitaries, may not take a liberal interest in our success. At all events, it will be well to resist, rather than to invite expenses, until we find assurance doubly sure. As a temporary arrangement, I should not object to remain as we are, or to take a part of Massachusetts Hall, though I feel a good deal of repugnance to the latter course.

Though this project was temporarily abandoned, the Corporation took up an analogous subject on July 2, 1831, when it appointed a committee, consisting of the President, Treasurer and Mr. Francis C. Gray, "to consider the expediency of making further provisions for accommodations of the law students residing in Cambridge."

But President Quincy was a man of most tenacious character, and, urged by Story with whom he had formed the closest intimacy, he determined to seek aid for the erection of a new Law School building from outside sources. The most natural person to whom to turn was the old man who was so largely interested in the success of the School—Nathan Dane. Accordingly, Quincy addressed a letter to him on September 12, 1831—which, as an example of artfulness and tact, could not be excelled. He pointed out the need of the new building, the lack of funds, the likelihood that the Corporation would be compelled to erect a cheap, temporary, wooden structure, unworthy of the character of the School. He skilfully suggested that of course the building, whether of wood or brick, must bear Dane's name. He set forth that the Corporation thought it unwise to call for a general public subscription; and he concluded by saying that he thought it his duty, before taking any steps, to apprise Mr. Dane of the facts, so that if he had any views he might state them. (1)

The answer from Dane was exactly what Quincy had hoped for and had framed his letter to obtain. For, September 13, 1831,

---

(1) This masterly letter in full was as follows: (See *Harvard College Archives, Quincy Papers*).

"The Law School in Harvard University in its present flourishing state is justly considered a creation of your own. As its founder, I deem it my duty to keep you apprised of any intentions concerning it, which may have a tendency to affect its prosperity and usefulness, to the end that any views you may entertain in relation to it may not be counteracted by any acts done without your knowledge; or that should they differ from your plans or be less adequate or appropriate than your anticipation, you may know our reasons, before they take the form of acts, and be varied or abandoned by any wishes you may have or may see fit to indicate.

The School is flourishing beyond all expectation. It already consists of thirty-five members. Five or six more are anticipated. We think ourselves justified in calculating with certainty on 40 members, and I have reason to think it will exceed that number; in this state of things a serious question is pressed upon us. The Corporation have completed the purchase of the whole of Judge Story's Library. The cost of it, with books previously purchased, have stood the College in stead the sum of $8000. The Library is too large for any single room we can appropriate for it, and is consequently distributed into two or three, and is consequently very inconvenient for arrangement or research, and extremely exposed to injury and dilapidation.

Besides which, none of the rooms at present possessed by the College are suitable for public lectures, moot courts and occasional meetings of the students and professors.

The circumstances are so imperious, and the professors are so urgent upon the subject, that I have determined at our next meeting (Thursday the 15th instant) to submit a proposition to the Corporation for the building a Law College, having mainly in view security and convenience as it respects the library and the accommodations for the professors and students above alluded to. Something must be done. But what I shall be able to induce the Corporation to do is a matter of great uncertainty. In conversation with influential individuals of that body, I find that they are opposed to meeting the necessary expenditures. They say the general funds of the College do not justify a further advance out of them in favor of that School. That these funds have already incurred a debt of $4000 on account of that School, and, however flourishing, they are not disposed to incur a greater debt on that account. Having caused an estimate to be made, I find that a brick college, suitable to contain a library, professors' rooms, lecture rooms and every convenience the institution now demands, will cost and can be finished complete, for $7000. Nothing short of this in my opinion ought to be done. It is, however, out of the question for me to induce the Corporation to create on this account so considerable a debt. The result I fear will be that they will agree, urged on one hand by a sense of the necessities of the School and restrained on the other by the apprehension of debt, to erect a temporary wooden building barely sufficient to answer our immediate necessities; but not at all predicated upon the great increase of the numbers of the students which from its past success, present popularity and the natural growth of our country, we have every reason to expect.

Such a building it is found can be built for $2000, and this sum is the extent of the appropriations I anticipate.

Now, it neither suits my sense of the interests of the institution nor my feelings of gratitude to its distinguished founder, that a building of the

Dane wrote: "I should be unwilling to have a mean building erected or to have the Law School ultimately any charge on the funds of the Corporation or aided by a subscription. As things are at present, I see no need of it." He then suggested that perhaps he might be willing to erect a building at a cost of $7000, the property to remain at his disposal.(1)

---

last mentioned description should be erected. It must unquestionably bear your name. If not given to it by the Corporation as it would be, it would be done by the public voice. Now such a building, if erected, ought to be fully adequate to our wants, and to have some feature of permanence, and bear some affinity in material and effect to our benefactor's distinguished bounty. Now a building of wood to cost $2000 would do neither the one nor the other. My opinion of the inadequacy and inexpediency of erecting such a building is so strong that I have contemplated attempting a subscription for the difference between the sum I deem adequate and the sum I find these influential individuals of the Corporation with whom I have conversed are alone willing to appropriate. I am deterred from this measure from considerations of a general character, which in the judgment of the friends of the University render an application of this kind to the generosity of the community at this time peculiarly inexpedient. I have thus taken the liberty, sir, to present to you a simple statement of the prosperity, the prospects and the exigencies of the School your liberality has founded. My purpose has been simply to make a distinguished benefactor know precisely the relations of the object of his bounty. I consider the moment to be somewhat in the nature of a crisis in respect of the progress of the School. If nothing is done by the Corporation, the tendency to check the growth to which it seems destined is unquestionable. A temporary wooden building seems to me neither suited to our exigencies, nor yet worthy of the Institution or its founder.

Before taking any step, therefore, I have thought that my duty required I should apprise you of facts, that if any views or wishes exist in your mind on the subject, they may be known, should you see fit to communicate them; and that should you have any reason to be dissatisfied with any of our proceedings, you should have no occasion to complain of our intentions not having been previously communicated. This communication you will consider confidential, or otherwise, at your pleasure, and should you see fit to make any reply to it, any restriction you may choose to impose on the subject matter of it it shall scrupulously be observed."

(1) See letter in *Harv. Coll. Papers*, 2nd Series, Vol. V, as follows:

"I have just received your letter of the 12th inst., and am much obliged to you for your information. It is of some importance, I have a correct understanding of the situation of the Law School. I now understand, if correct, a library has been purchased for the School which has cost $8,000, that this Library is the property of the Corporation, which has received two years income from the School, say $4000, hence the Corporation has contracted a debt on account of that School to the amount of $4000. That if a brick building shall be erected that shall cost $7000 it will be the property of the Corporation in fee simple. That though the building will be the property when erected of the Corporation, the members of it do not find it convenient to advance towards it more than $2000.

It has never been my wish the Law School should be a charge on the funds of the Corporation or on public charity. In my donation I allude to an addition. This I have put into a paper I always have by me. It is no present aid—as your meeting will be as soon as this letter can reach you, I write in a hurry. I can only say at present, I should be unwilling to have a mean building erected or have the Law School ultimately any charge on the funds of the Corporation or aided by a subscription. As

To this, Quincy replied, September 16, that he had communicated Dane's letter to the Corporation, who had received the unexpected news with "a grateful sense of obligation, feeling that it gave them a hope of relief from the dilemma either of being obliged to do something which would be unworthy of Dane's noble spirit, or else injure other departments of the University by using the general funds to a degree unwarranted."(1)

Dane's response to Quincy, Oct. 13, stated that he had intended to leave to the Law School $5000 at the time of his death, but that he would now lend it, interest to be paid during his life, and at his death the principal to be added to the Dane Professorship foundation. This offer amounted therefore to a loan to the Cor-

---

things appear at present, I see no need of it. Perhaps I shall be willing to erect the building at an expense of $7000, provided it can be at my disposal when erected. To advance $7000 and make the building the property of the Corporation would be going beyond my present means. At the same time, I want the affairs of the School so conducted that it shall not be felt as a burden by any Corporation or the public. Probably if you build, you will not begin before next spring. Perhaps in season a plan may be adopted to have the building you propose."

(1) See letter in *Harvard College Archives—Quincy Papers,* as follows:

"I have the honor to acknowledge your favor of the 13th inst., and had the happiness to communicate its interesting intimations to the Corporation of Harvard University.

The suggestions were received by that body with all the respect and grateful sense of obligation which they were so well calculated to excite. No vote was taken on its contents, because, it being a letter to me personally, it was not deemed proper to predicate upon it an official act.

I am, however, authorized to say that should your judgment result in a determination to aid in the erection of the contemplated building, the Corporation will be happy to accede to any conditions you may be disposed to prescribe; and, as it must be erected upon land the fee simple of which is in the University, the Corporation will readily enter into stipulations which will place the whole at your disposal, with the single provision that they shall have the right to take the building, paying the cost whenever you shall notify that such is your wish. Indeed the Corporation cannot fail to accede to any terms you can prescribe.

The tenor of your letter was to me and to them as unanticipated as it was gratifying. It gave them hope of relief from a dilemma in which they were involved—on the one hand being pressed with the desire to do nothing on their part which should seem unworthy of the noble spirit which had laid the foundation of one of the most important and successful institutions of our University, and on the other being embarrassed by the many claims on the funds of the seminary which precluded them from the power of applying what was necessary for the erection of a building in some degree worthy of the name it must bear. The hopes which your letter has raised will be submitted entirely to be fulfilled according to your own discretion and liberal views. The Corporation are well aware how adequate and well directed these are to advance in the truest and readiest mode this great and flourishing branch of their seminary, and they will not so much co-operate in your designs as yield the whole subject to be conducted by your own wisdom."

poration which must be paid back on Mr. Dane's death out of the general funds of the College, although such payment was to be simply as a transfer of funds from the Law School account to the Dane Professorship account.(1)

Quincy replied, Oct. 17, in an interesting letter pointing out that as the general funds were already inadequate, there might be criticism from the friends of the other departments of the College, if the general funds were thus to be eventually used for the Law School.(2)

---

(1) See letter in *Harv. Coll. Papers,* 2nd Series, Vol. V., as follows:

"I received your letter of the 16th, 1831, stating (among other things) you are authorized by the Corporation to say, should my judgment persist in the determination to aid in the erection of contemplated building, the Corporation will accede, etc. I refer you to my letter of Sept. 13th for my views on the subject. I have, since receiving yours of the 16th, thought much on it; and have reviewed what I have done.

In my letter to the Corporation of June the 2nd, 1829, you will observe I proposed $10,000 as a fund forever towards the support of a law professor, "all the income whereof and of such other monies and funds as I may hereafter add, shall be paid over annually," etc.

In my letter of the 13th ultimo, I mention I have put into a paper, I always have by me (my will), an addition alluded to as above. Before I knew such a building would be necessary, I had fixed in my mind five thousand dollars addition; making my whole permanent fund fifteen thousand dollars. This is my present intention and to add in this manner. As it appears probable the Law School will ultimately be no charge to the Corporation but requires present funds, the question seems to be how can these be provided to the amount of $7000? I have now monies nearly to that amount deposited in two banks not engaged. I propose to lend to the Corporation $5000 at 5 per cent. interest. Interest to be paid to me yearly during my life, with an understanding to be expressed in writing that the principal of $5000 shall at my decease be so added as to increase my permanent fund to $15000.

As to the $2000, I will lend it to the Corporation in common form at 5 per cent., interest payable annually, with a general understanding the principal $2000 will not be paid for several years. This appears to me the most simple and best way to aid the plan contemplated.

I prefer pursuing my original plan; as the proposed building must be erected on the land of the Corporation, it must be, and as I think it ought to be, the property of the Corporation unembarrassed by our special agreement. I therefore conclude it will not be best for me or for the Corporation for me to have any interest in the building. You will observe the business is not in a state for me to write to the Corporation in form. I am willing however you shall lay this letter before it.

If it shall deem my proposition admissible, it can pass a vote accordingly and authorize the treasurer to contract for the Corporation and receive the monies. As far as I propose, I shall aid with pleasure. The $15000 is return of books."

(2) See letter in *Harvard Coll. Archives, Quincy Papers,* as follows:

"Your favor of the 13th has been received and will be laid before the Corporation on Thursday. The exceeding liberality and kindness of your views in relation to the University, will receive the gratitude of that body which it manifestly deserves. At the same time, I will not conceal from you confidentially the embarrassment in which the mode of a loan places

This objection was partially obviated by an agreement by Dane, that the interest on the $5000 should be paid only out of the surplus income arising from the tuition fees of the Law School, after payment therefrom of the Professors' full salaries. The proposition, as finally submitted to the Corporation Oct. 27, 1831, was, that Dane should loan $5000, on which 5 per cent. interest should be paid as above stipulated for six years, at the end of which time the principal should be added to the Dane Professorship fund.

He was also to loan a further $2000 for six years at 3 per cent. Quincy in communicating this offer said:

The Corporation cannot fail to recognize the continuance of that liberal and enlightened spirit which has heretofore character-

the Corporation, from circumstances not known to you and which could not have been anticipated by you.

One of the great difficulties with which the Corporation have to contend arises from the zeal with which the friends of the respective schools press for assistance out of the general funds of the College. Now, as the Corporation have in fact no, or very limited, general funds so applicable, any assistance of this kind is equivalent to a tax upon the undergraduates for the support of such a school. Divinity School is frequent in such applications. There is now before us an application from the medical professors for an extension of the building used by the Medical School to an amount of $3000 or $4000. All these applications we are compelled to resist, and the general ground of inability and inexpediency is that on which we have to depend for resisting these applications, without offending the applicants.

The extraordinary success of the Law School and in the manner in which it has reimbursed the College for its advances, seemed to place that school on a more advantageous ground than the others could take. Yet the Corporation in all their discussions on the subject of a Law Building have been careful to do nothing which should give the friends of the other schools claims which it could not answer. And the determination to limit our advances to $2000 for the Law School was predicated upon the idea that, as the new building would relieve us from the occupation of buildings which would rent for the interest of that sum, it was in fact no advance for that School, and could not be urged as such by the friends of the other Schools.

My fear is that, as the funds of the University are pledged for the payment of the loan, and as the capital is at all events to be ultimately placed to the credit of the professors fund, that the form of a loan will be considered an erecting of a Law Building out of the general funds of the University, and may place us in a predicament somewhat difficult in relation to the friends of the other schools. I entirely approve of all your views in relation to your application of the $5000, and I do not know that other gentlemen will feel the embarrassment which I have intimated. I have, however, thought that this communication, as it respects the only difficulty I anticipate, due to you. I do not know that it will be possible for you, by any arrangement consistent with your general views, to relieve us from the embarrassment. If not, we must meet it in the spirit which the extreme liberality of your general purpose will, I trust, justify.

P. S. You will consider this as wholly confidential and written without authority."

ized this distinguished benefactor to the University. Being predicated upon a principle of relieving the general funds of the University from all charge on account of the interest of the said principal sum of $5000, all objections arising from the circumstances that the donation of six years takes the form of a loan, which the donor has deemed proper to adopt, will be obviated. The Corporation will also perceive that as it respects the remaining sum of $2000, which is to be repaid at the end of six years, so far from being any additional charge upon the general funds of the University, it will be in effect an aid and enlargement of those funds, inasmuch as the building proposed to be erected will place at the disposal of the Corporation the buildings which are now and have been for 15 years past occupied by the Law School. The income of these buildings cannot be less than $200 annually, leaving the difference between that amount and the amount ($100) of interest on the said sum of $2000, a clear annual gain to the general funds of the University.(1)

---

(1) The exact wording of the proposition as it appears on the *Corporation Records* was as follows:

"The President informs the Board that he is authorized by the Hon. Nathan Dane to offer to the Corporation of Harvard College a loan of $7000 at the rate of 5 per cent., payable annually, to be applied to the erection of a building for the accommodation of the Law School, on the following conditions.

1. The interest upon $5000 ($250) to be paid annually during the six years out of the surplus incomes of the Law School, which surplus income Mr. Dane is willing to consider as the sole fund out of which the said interest is to be paid.

2. That the interest of the remaining $2000 ($100) the Corporation will pay annually to the said Dane, his executors or administrators, during the said six years, and that at the expiration thereof they will pay over the said sum of $2000 to the said Dane, his executors, or administrators.

3. That after the expiration of the said six years, the Corporation will transfer the remaining sum of $5000 to the credit of the Dane Professorship on the books of the Treasurer of the said College; and that such transfer shall be a full discharge to the said President and Fellows of Harvard College from all claims of said Dane, his executors and administrators, on account of such loan; it being understood that the above sum of $5000 is to be added to the amount ($10000) heretofore given by the said Dane to such College, to constitute a permanent fund of $15000 for the said Dane Professor, and the interest of the said $5000 to be paid to him thereafter, accordingly.

4. In order that the payment of the interest upon the last mentioned sum of $5000 may in no case be a charge upon the general funds of said College, the said Dane consents that the same shall be forever a charge upon the surplus income of the Law School, and that the said surplus incomes shall be the sole fund out of which the same shall be paid. It being understood, that any deficiency of the incomes of the funds applicable for the payment of the salaries of the law professors, to the amount of $2500, shall alone be first deducted from the annual receipts of the Law School: And the payment of said interest shall always next be provided for and have priority to all other charges and expenditures on account of said Law School. And it being also understood, that in case by donation or otherwise funds shall hereafter come to the hands of the Corporation for the Law School generally, or which shall be applicable to the

The following votes were passed:

That this Corporation receive with great respect and gratitude the very liberal proposition of this distinguished benefactor contained in the above communication, and accept the same upon the terms and conditions therein specified; and that the President address a letter to the Hon. Nathan Dane expressive of their sense of this additional evidence of his generous and effective disposition to aid in the advancement of that great branch of learning which he has by his foundation already so munificently patronized.

Voted that the President, Judge Story, and the Treasurer be a Committee, to cause a plan of the said Law College to be forthwith obtained, together with the estimates of the expense, both in brick and stone . . . and that they also select the place they may deem most suitable for the location of the building.

The Committee went to work enthusiastically, and quickly, Feb. 16, 1832, reported the estimated cost of the new building to be $10,000, and suggested the location, "north of the Meeting House". Accordingly the Corporation voted that the Treasurer should "cause the same to be built", and should make contracts "for the erection of the Dane Law College". He was also authorized to erect a block of three buildings adjoining the court house, on the site of the old Law School, College House No. 2. This new block, when built later, was known as Graduates Hall (the present College House).

On September 24, 1832, the Dane Law College was dedicated with impressive ceremony. Prayer was offered in the new building by the Reverend John G. Palfrey, Professor of Sacred Literature in the Divinity School. After this service, the President, officers and Professors of the University, together with ex-President John Quincy Adams, Daniel Webster, Jeremiah Mason, Edward Everett and others, attended by the undergraduates and the law and divinity students, walked in procession to the College Chapel, where President Quincy delivered an oration on *Legal Education*, marked by "his usually original and striking thought, forcible expression and animated and glowing style."(1)

---

payment of the debt accruing from the erection of the said proposed building, that thereafter the surplus funds of the Law School shall be relieved from this incumbrance."

(1) See *American Jurist*, Vol. VIII.

Chief Justice Marshall wrote to Quincy acknowledging a copy of this oration, December 10, 1832:

"I am much indebted to you for the renewed proof of your recollection given by sending me a copy of your address at the dedication of Dane Law

Dane Hall, 1832-1845

Charles Sumner, writing to his friend Tower, Oct. 22, 1832, thus described the day:

Yesterday, Dane Law College (situated just north of Rev. Mr. Newell's church), a beautiful Grecian temple, with four Ionic pillars in front,—the most architectural and the best-built edifice belonging to the college,—was dedicated to the law. Quincy delivered a most proper address of an hour, full of his strong sense and strong language. Webster, J. Q. Adams, Dr. Bowditch, Edward Everett, Jeremiah Mason, Judge Story, Ticknor, leaders in the eloquence, statesmanship, mathematics, scholarship, and law of our good land, were all present,—a glorious company. The Law School have requested a copy for the press. It will of a certainty be given. I shall send you the address when published.

When you again visit Cambridge you will be astonished at the changes that have been wrought,—trees planted, common fenced, new buildings raised, and others designed. Quincy is a man of life, and infuses a vigor into all that he touches.

The new building was forty feet in frontage with a depth of sixty feet. It contained two rooms for the Professors, a library and reading room on the lower floor, and a large lecture room and two other small rooms on the upper floor, one of the small rooms fronting on what is now Harvard Square, being termed by Sumner "the pleasantest room in Cambridge."

Into these commodious quarters the Library, which had then grown to three thousand volumes, was at once moved, and early in the following year, 1833, Charles Sumner was made Librarian. This proved to be a most fortunate appointment; for no one ever in the School had proved to be so indefatigable a student or omnivorous a reader. Of him, W. W. Story wrote:

I think there was scarcely a text book in the Library, of the contents of which he had not some knowledge. Nor was this a

College. You have added to my respect for that estimable gentleman, who has bestowed a large portion of the acquisition of a valuable life on an institution which promises to be so advantageous to the profession he had adopted. I had not supposed that law was so negligently studied in your country, whatever it may be in the South, as you represented. But, however this may be, you satisfy me entirely that it may be read with greatly increased benefit in an institution connected with your University. I can very readily believe that 'to disincorporate this particular science from general knowledge is one great impediment to its advancement.' The vast influence which the members of the profession exercise in all popular governments, especially in ours, is perceived by all; and whatever tends to their improvement benefits the nation."

See *Memoir of Josiah Quincy*, by Edmund Quincy.

superficial knowledge, considering its extent and his youth.   He
had acquainted himself also with the lives and character of most
of the authors, and could give a fair résumé of the contents of
most of their works.   His room was piled with books; the
shelves overflowed and the floor was littered with them.(1)

By vote of the Corporation of April 3, 1832, the new Law
School building was to be termed "The Dane Law College."(2)
Naturally the term soon began to be applied to the Law School
itself, and the following letter written from Cincinnati, December
13, 1832, by Uriah Tracy Howe (L. S. 1831-32), to Charles
Sumner, is of interest as showing the feeling of a then recent
student of the School, as to this change(3) :

My thanks to you for your kindness in sending Mr. Quincy's
address. . . . I think it does honor to the illustrious author,
the university and last not least, the Law College.   I had no idea
that Josiah was capable of perpetrating so good a thing—he has
not yet lost all his power, though some have been ready to believe
and propagate this doctrine.   This address, I think, shows a
freshness and playfulness of thought which mind us of the efforts
of his younger days, before his mind had become steeped in the
lethargy which has seized upon his body.

How high sounding you have become—Dane Law College!
This produces a powerful sensation abroad—there is a potent
charm in names and the word College conjures up images of awe,
respect and distant admiration which were never destined to
cluster around the plain unvarnished simplicity of the word,
school, and the idea attached to it.   Although as Mr. Quincy
says, "it was not necessary in order to preserve the name of
Nathan Dane and transmit it with honor to posterity, that it
should be associated with the great design and useful improvement", yet I think Nathan has made assurance doubly sure by
inscribing his name upon a monument which shall endure so long

---

(1) *Memoir and Letters of Charles Sumner*, by Edward L. Pierce,
Vol. I.

(2) A mistake in the public mind as to the form of this vote caused
the Law School itself, rather than the building, to be called for many
years almost universally the "Dane Law College" or the "Dane Law
School." This mistake was countenanced even in official College publications. Finally, in 1859, as President Walker stated in his report to the
Overseers.

"The Corporation have passed a declaratory vote in order to correct a
prevalent error respecting the name by which this department of the
University is known . . .

The true and legal name of the School is not, as many will have it, the
'Dane Law School' but 'The Law School of Harvard College.'"

(3) Unpublished letter in the *Sumner Papers* in Harvard College Library.

as the noblest of sciences shall continue to hold its place among the institution of man. Success to the institution; long may Dane Law College continue to send forth lights to the profession and the world, and may its illustrious professors live to see some of the scions of the law who were reared and fostered by their watchful care grow up into mighty trees whose strength and beauty shall reflect honor upon them and the institution. . . . There is a specimen of 4th of July oration for you, which I assure you nothing but the hallowed recollections of old Harvard which this memento calls up would have induced me to use; especially to a man of your chastened imagination. There is very little legal acquirement among the younger members of the profession here. . . . You and Browne had better transfer some of the old black letter from Harvard to the new western world; I assure you it would find a good market, and no doubt would be properly appreciated. I should be glad to welcome a portion of the information and legal lore which may be obtained in the new College in the shape of Charles Sumner and John W. Browne, of pleasant memory, to the green shores of the fair Ohio. . . . How comes on the Judge and the Professor Royall (Give my respects to them).

CHAPTER XXIII.

THE STORY—GREENLEAF PERIOD—1833-1836.

"The lamented death of Professor Ashmun has deprived the School of one of its highest ornaments and most successful teachers", wrote Story in his Report to the Overseers of April 29, 1833. "It is indispensable to the success of the Institution that another Professor should as soon as may be, with a due regard to the public convenience, be appointed and inaugurated. In the meantime the duties of Prof. Ashmun will continue to be punctiliously performed by the Dane Professor in addition to his own appropriate duties."

The Corporation had already, at Story's suggestion, elected Simon Greenleaf of Portland, Maine, as Royall Professor, on April 23, 1833(1); and Story wrote to Greenleaf, April 24, announcing the Corporation vote, and saying:

I congratulate you, but more the institution, on this choice. To me, it will be an inexpressible gratification to be hereafter associated with you in the labors for the improvement of your favorite science.

Very truly and affectionately yours, Joseph Story.

SIMON GREENLEAF.

Simon Greenleaf was born in Newburyport, Massachusetts, on December 5, 1783, four years after the birth of Story and twenty years after the birth of Kent. He was the son of Moses and Lydia (Parsons) Greenleaf and the grandson of Hon. Jonathan Greenleaf, who had been prominent before the Revolution as a member of the Provincial Legislature, the Provincial Congress and the Governor's Council.

Having received an academic education in the Latin school at Newburyport, he entered upon the study of law in 1801, in the office of Ezekiel Whitman, at New Gloucester, Maine, to which place his family had moved. He was admitted to the Bar of Cumberland County four years later; and after practising in several small towns, he removed to Portland in 1808. He soon took high

---

(1) The Overseers concurred in this vote, Jan. 23, 1834.

rank at the Bar, and his contemporary, Hon. William Willis, says in his *History of the Courts and Lawyers of Maine* that "by his winning manners and persuasive style of speaking and address, accompanied by the skill and ingenuity of his arguments, he established his reputation on a firm basis."

In 1820, when Maine became a State, the act establishing the Supreme Judicial Court provided that the Governor and Council should "appoint some suitable person learned in the law to be a reporter of the decisions." The Court, consisting of Prentiss Mellen, Chief Justice, Nathan Weston, Jr., and William P. Preble, at once suggested Greenleaf, who received the appointment, and entered on his duties at York, at the August term of 1820. He was elected, the same year, and again in 1821, to the Legislature from Portland, and shared in the responsibilities of putting into operation the initial government of the new State and of establishing for it a code of law.

For twelve years (1820-1832) he held the office of Reporter, his labors during that period comprising nine volumes of reports, which, distinguished for their clear and concise statements of the points of law and arguments of counsel, at once took high rank as a standard authority throughout the United States. During his time of service as Reporter, he continued to practice law with high success. In 1821, he published the unique work entitled *Collection of Cases Doubted and Overruled;* and it was during the preparation of this book that an intimacy of correspondence sprang up between him and Judge Story, early signs of which may be seen in a letter from the latter, Sept. 5, 1819:

I rejoice that there are gentlemen of the Bar who are willing to devote their leisure to the correction and ministration of the noble science of the law. It is redeeming the pledge which Lord Coke seems to think every man implicitly grants to his profession on entering it. It is eminently useful because it accustoms lawyers to reason upon principle and to pass beyond the narrow boundary of authority.

On Nov. 11, 1819, Story sent for Greenleaf's use a list of overruled cases prepared by himself; and on Dec. 11, 1821, he wrote:

I am glad to hear that your overruled cases are printed. I want to get a copy and interleave it. . . . You must not feel too anxious about your Reports. A young author is apt to be unduly sensitive as to the fate of his productions. I have no doubt as to the success of yours, and I am sure that the profession will join heartily in your favor.   . . I wish you to consider me as a subscriber to your Reports. Your compensation is not such as ought to induce you to give away a single copy; and by subscribing for the work I believe I shall do some good in the way of aiding its circulation.

. . . Pray do not think that anything in which I can aid you will be a labor to me. I shall cheerfully do what you may wish at any time.

It was not, however, from his books only that Greenleaf was known to Story. The Judge's attention had been called to him first in the United States Circuit Court in Portland, where Greenleaf's surprising acquaintance with the facts, and the peculiar doctrines of law applicable in the cases in the Admiralty Court, made him eminent among the practitioners. Admiralty was a branch of law of particular importance in the seafaring state of Maine; and from his father, who was a ship carpenter, Greenleaf had learned many of the nautical details especially serviceable in his maritime practice. In view of Story's predilection for Admiralty Law and his belief in the increasing value of instruction in this branch of the Law School, and in view, further, of his close epistolary and personal relations with Greenleaf, it is not surprising that the latter's name was the first to occur to him when the filling of the vacant Professorship at the School was under consideration.

The personality of Greenleaf was interesting in its contrast to his colleague. He is described as a "grave, sedate looking man, very quiet in his movements. He was about five feet, ten inches in height, rather stoutly built, full face, with a small sharp eye, nearly black. His hair was a very dark brown; his posture, a little stooping, with his head projecting forward; his countenance expressive of benignity and intelligence."

Sumner, in a letter to Story, Dec. 5, 1838, written from London, likened him to Lord Denman, then Chief Justice of England(1):

---

(1) See also letter of Sumner to Story, July 12, 1838:
"I have recently breakfasted with Lord Denman—Bland, noble Denman! On the bench he is the perfect model of a judge—full of dignity and decision and yet with mildness and suavity which cannot fail to charm. His high personal character and his unbending morals have given an elevated tone to the bar . . . In conversation he is plain, unaffected and amiable."

You know Lord Denman intellectually better than I; but you do not his person, his voice, his manner, his tone—all every inch a judge. He sits the admired personation of the law. He is tall and well made, with a justice-like countenance; his voice and the gravity of his manner and the generous feeling with' which he castigates everything departing from the strictest line of right conduct, remind me of Greenleaf more than any man I have ever known. He is honest as the stars. . . . In conversation he is gentle and bland; I have never seen him excited.

Professor Parsons in his eulogy said(1):

Judge Story and Professor Greenleaf worked together harmoniously and successfully, and perhaps the more harmoniously because they were so entirely different. With much in common, for they were both able, learned, and of the most devoted industry, there were other traits that belonged to one or the other of them exclusively. Greenleaf was singularly calm, finding strength in his very stillness. Always cautious, and therefore always exact, Story was as vivid and impulsive as man could be. His words flowed like a flood, but it was because his emotion and his thoughts demanded a flood as their exponent. And Story's manner was most peculiar. Everybody listened when he spoke, for he carried one away with the irresistible attraction of his own swift emotion, and Greenleaf, somewhat slow and measured in his enunciation, by the charm of his silver voice, the singular felicity of his expression, and the smooth flow of his untroubled stream of thought, caught and held the attention of every listener as few men can. . . . No wonder that such a man as either of these succeeded; no wonder that a School, in which were two such men, succeeded. And their success was so great, and so large a portion was due to each, that it is not worth while to apportion it exactly. But if I were to endeavor to do this, I should say that Story prepared the soil, and Greenleaf sowed the seed. Not that Story failed to impart much and very valuable instruction; but when we remember that his official engagements, while they gave him very peculiar opportunities for advancing the interests and swelling the numbers of the School, compelled his absence for the larger part of every term, and exposed him while here to interruptions which must have interfered very seriously with regular instruction; and that he frequently indulged himself and his hearers with interesting biographical sketches of learned lawyers and eminent statesmen whom he had known, and with his own personal reminiscences of the growth and development of the law and jurisprudence of this country; and that his lectures were employed in the exposition of the general principles of the law, rather than

---

(1) *Address to Students of Harvard Law School,* by Professor Theophilus Parsons, Oct. 20, 1853.

in its details; when we know this, and remember also his fervid utterance, and the vivid interest in his topics which he felt and imparted, we may perhaps say, that Story quickened and stirred the minds of his hearers, awoke in them that love of the law, as a science, which he felt so strongly, and made them ready for the lectures by which Greenleaf satisfied that appetite for instruction which Story had awakened; and thus, what each did derived value and efficacy from what the other did.

A letter written at the time of Greenleaf's death, describes his personal traits as follows: "Affable, polite, courteous, frank, liberal minded, he secured the confidence of his fellow citizens and neighbors . . . Combined with varied and learned attainments, he possessed great simplicity of character. . . . To all other attainments were added those of a mind eminently benevolent and devout."

A letter from Charles Sumner to Tower, May 5, 1833, shows how well the new appointment was received in the School itself:

A successor has been appointed to Mr. Ashmun, who will commence his duties here in July, or next September. You have seen him announced in the papers,—Mr. Greenleaf, of Maine,—a fine man, learned lawyer, good scholar, ardent student, of high professional character, taking a great interest in his profession; and to this, a gentleman, a man of manners, affability, and enthusiasm, nearly fifty years old; now has a very extensive practice in Maine, which he will wind up before he starts upon his new line of duties. It were worth your coming from New York to study under Judge Story and Greenleaf next term.

Of Greenleaf's first year in the School, Professor Parsons said:

It was not without much misgiving and many fears that Mr. Greenleaf accepted the position, and his new duties pressed upon him at first and for a considerable time, as a painful burthen, filling him with the constant dread that he had assumed a duty too large for his fulfilment.

As Greenleaf did not finally settle in Cambridge until August, 1833, (when he moved into a house on Hilliard Street, not far from Story's residence), a part of the burden of teaching during these five months, from April to August, was taken from Story by the appointment, as Instructor, of James C. Alvord,—then regarded as probably the most brilliant of the younger lawyers of the Commonwealth.(1)

---

(1) He was born in 1808 at Greenfield, Mass., graduated from Dartmouth in 1827, and studied law at the Law School in New Haven, and

Simon Greenleaf

There were at this time, April, 1833, 31 students in the School, of whom Story reported that they were "diligently and successfully engaged in their studies so as to justify the public confidence in the value of the Institution."

Among them may be mentioned Thomas Gold Appleton, Wendell Phillips, Francis Boott, Charles Sumner, and John Holmes. The spring of 1833 was made memorable by the visit to Cambridge of President Andrew Jackson, and the heated controversy which arose over the conferring upon him of the honorary degree of LL.D. Nowhere had there been more bitter opposition to Jackson than in Massachusetts. His defeat of John Quincy

---

in the Harvard Law School in 1830. He became a member of the Legislature in 1837, and was elected to Congress in 1838, but died before taking his seat. He was also one of the Commissioners appointed in 1837 to revise the criminal statutes of the Commonwealth.

Benjamin R. Curtis thus described him after his early and lamented death in 1839:

"With an ardent love for the noble science he professed, he withdrew himself from practice, and entered the Law School at Cambridge, then conducted by Mr. Justice Story and the late Mr. Ashmun. There he pursued his studies with a breadth of views, a lively interest and strength of purpose, which are rare indeed in one of his years. His progress was truly great; and when, in the autumn of 1830, he returned again to the bar, he carried with him a depth of learning and habits of thought and investigation which were a broad and deep foundation for future eminence.

The numerous and great obstacles which beset the path of a young lawyer everywhere, especially at the crowded bar of our Commonwealth, he cleared at a bound, and almost at once stood in the front rank of the distinguished lawyers whom the valley of the Connecticut River for several generations has continued to produce. Within the short period of a little more than ten years, that valley has seen three of its great lights of the law sink in early night. Howe, that bright example of a Christian judge; Ashmun, of whom it was beautifully said that he was fit to teach when most men are beginning to learn; and now Alvord, of whom it is not too much to say that he was worthy to stand side by side with them.

At the decease of Mr. Ashmun, Mr. Alvord, though scarcely older than the majority of the pupils at the Law School, was called to supply his place until a permanent professor could be appointed. The young men who were under his care, as well as the eminent judge, who then, as now was at the head of the school, will bear witness how faithfully and well he discharged his duties.

His was truly a remarkable mind. With a quickness of intellect which travelled to conclusions with the rapidity of light, he united habits of the most patient investigation. Searching always for principles, he had yet as much deference for authority as a vigorous mind can feel. Though capable of long-continued labor, his power of concentration was so great as almost to dispense with it.

Though exceedingly zealous in action and of an ardent temperament, his opinions, even on the most exciting subjects of the day, were uniformly the result of a nicely balanced judgment. United with these intellectual qualities was a character from which they borrowed new vigor. Courage which always arose with the occasion, until it became perfectly indomitable; firmness of purpose which no opposition could shake; a generous self-devotion, easily excited; an entire frankness and openness."

Adams for the presidency and his war on the United States Bank, had aroused intense feelings, which are well shown by Adams, in his diary, June 18:

Called from my nursery and garden by a visit from Mr. Quincy, President of Harvard University. He told me that as President Jackson is about visiting Boston the Corporation of the University had thought it necessary to invite him to visit the colleges; that he (Mr. Quincy) should address him in a Latin discourse and confer upon him the degree of Doctor of Laws, and he intimated that I should receive an invitation to be present at these ceremonies.

I said that the personal relations in which President Jackson had chosen to place himself with me were such that I could hold no intercourse of a friendly character with him. . . . I could therefore not accept an invitation to attend on this occasion. And, independent of that, as myself an affectionate child of our Alma Mater, I would not be present to witness her disgrace in conferring her highest literary honors upon a barbarian who could not write a sentence of grammar and hardly could spell his own name.

Mr. Quincy said he was sensible how utterly unworthy of literary honors Jackson was, but the Corporation thought it was necessary to follow the precedent and treat him precisely as Mr. Munroe, his predecessor, had been treated. As the people of the United States had seen fit to make him their President, the Corporation thought the honor which they conferred upon him were compliments due to the station, by whomsoever it was occupied. Mr. Quincy said it was thought also that the omission to show the same respect to President Jackson which had been shown to Mr. Munroe would be imputed to party spirit—which they were anxious to avoid.

I was not satisfied with these reasons; but it is College ratiocination and College sentiment.

Time-serving and sycophancy are qualities of all learned and scientific institutions.

The degree was finally voted by the Corporation, and also by the Overseers (although the action of the latter board was questioned later as illegal, because of irregularities in giving notice of the meeting).

An interesting account of the occasion is found in the official records of the Corporation of June 26, 1833.

"The President, attended by Vice-President Van Buren, Lewis Cass, Secretary of War, Levi Woodbury, Secretary of the Navy and others, was received on the steps of University Hall and conducted to the Corporation Room, where they were introduced to the College Professors and instructors by President Quincy.

At a quarter before 10 o'clock the students had been collected by tolling the bell in the chapel of the University, and were concentrated in close order upon the front seats so as to have as much space in the rear as possible for strangers and visitors; the galleries having been opened at 9 o'clock for ladies, they were filled by them, and the students in their seats, with the members of the Divinity and Law School immediately behind them, ready for the reception of the President.

Accordingly, after the ceremony of introduction had terminated, the President of the United States entered the chapel with the President of the University, the Governor and Lieutenant Governor of the Commonwealth, the suite of the President, the Corporation, Faculty, and immediate instructors, Overseers, and strangers; no persons having been as yet admitted on the floor of the chapel except the members of the schools and the undergraduates. On the entry of the President into the Chapel, the students and members of the schools rose and continued standing until he was seated.

President Quincy then made an address in which he said:

Permit us, Sir, on this occasion, to congratulate you on the happy auspices under which your present term of administration has commenced, on the disappearance of those clouds which of late hung so heavily over the prospects of our Union, which your firmness and prudence contributed so largely to dissipate.

President Jackson made a short and appropriate reply, reciprocating the kind wishes of the President of the University, expressing his gratification at its flourishing state and his admiration of the system of public education established in New England. An oration in Latin by Francis Bowen of the Senior Class then succeeded."

After the degree was conferred, the Presidential party passed between the lines of the law and divinity students and undergraduates, and visited the Library and the other rooms in Harvard Hall, and were then escorted to Wadsworth House where a collation was served.

Edmund Quincy, in his life of his father, Josiah Quincy, makes the following comment on the episode:

Nothing could be more soldierly and gentlemanlike than the

bearing and manners of General Jackson, when he was upon his
good behaviour; and much of the prejudice which had raged
against him, and which soon revived with the war he declared
against the United States Bank, disappeared before the charm of
his personal presence.   This academic action was made the occasion of much ridicule and of many virulent attacks upon my
father.   Party spirit, which had slept for a moment, soon awoke
again, and the same outside influence which the next year
fostered the intestine disturbances of the college, seized on this
occasion to cast odium upon him.   At the next regular meeting
of the Overseers, whose consent was necessary to confirm the
degree, but which could not be had in proper form for want of
time at the moment, there was an attempt to invalidate the transaction, or at least to censure it.   But precedent, common sense,
and the custom of learned bodies in the Old World, overbore the
attempt, and General Jackson lived and died a Doctor of Laws,
entitled to all the privileges and pre-eminences thereunto appertaining.

The reputation of the new Professor, Greenleaf, attracted students at once, and the year 1833-34 showed a gratifying increase
in numbers.   Sumner wrote in September:

Our Law School has begun to fill with students.   Already is
gathered together, I believe, the largest collection of young men
that ever met at one place in America for the study of the law.
There are now upwards of fifty who have joined the School.   So
we expect the ensuing term will be a driving one.

And Greenleaf, in his first semi-annual Report to the Overseers,
Oct. 12, 1833, was able to say that the number of students by the
Catalogue was 54, "of whom 51 are present and in the diligent,
zealous and successful prosecution of their studies".   He reported
the attendance as satisfactory, and their moral conduct believed
to be irreproachable:

Though these characteristics may not apply with equal just-
ness and in equal degree to each member of the School, yet the
Professors are happy in being able to state that they know of no
individual who ought to be regarded as forming an exception.(1)

The President's 9th Annual Report for the year 1833-34 stated
that during the year the number in the School varied from 32 to
53.   Owing to the increase in students, they were for the first time

---

(1)   See Report for April 1833, in *Harvard College Archives, Reports
to Overseers,* Vol. II.

divided into three classes according to seniority and advancement. And when Story left for Washington in December, 1833, he felt amply satisfied that the School had suffered no irreparable blow in the death of his talented colleague, Ashmun, and that the new Professor was fully qualified for the position.

An interesting account written by Sumner to Greenleaf, Feb. 19, 1834, of his then recent visit to ex-Chancellor Kent, shows that great jurist's estimate of Greenleaf:

"That Mr. Greenleaf is a civil sort of a man," said Chancellor Kent this afternoon to me, after he had finished and fully read your kind letter of introduction. "He was a great loss to the profession at Portland; makes a fine professor, I have no doubt," he continued. To all of which I, of course, sincerely responded. . . . He received me cordially; talked fast and instructively, but without elegance or grammar (however, *falsa grammatica non vitiat*); praised the civil law highly; thought Livermore's bequest a splendid one; liked the civil law, all but that relating to husband and wife,—he would stick to the common law on that subject; spoke with warmth of the present politics; thought Jackson would ruin us; wanted to go to Washington, but if he went should be obliged to see much company, call upon Jackson and dine with him perhaps, all of which he could not consent to do; were he there, he should associate with such men as Webster; . . . showed me also "Greenleaf's Reports"; said he set much by that man . . . he had wafered into the first volume your letter to him presenting the book, which he said he had done to preserve how you had honored him. . . . Kent has great simplicity and freedom of manners; he opens himself like a child. This, though, I attributed to a harmless vanity. He undoubtedly knows that he is a lion, and he therefore offers himself readily for exhibition. Indeed, he seemed to me to be unfolding his character and studies, etc., to me, as if purposely to let me know the whole bent and scope of his mind. I thought more than once that he was sitting for his picture.

The winter of 1833-34 in Washington was marked in legal annals by the death of William Wirt, on February 18, 1834, and by the appointment of Roger B. Taney of Baltimore (Wirt's successor at Attorney General of the United States under Jackson, and at that time Secretary of the Treasury) to the Supreme Bench, in place of Gabriel Duval who had resigned. The appointment, however, was refused confirmation by the Senate.(1)

(1) It is not generally noted that Marshall himself favored Taney's appointment to fill the vacancy caused by the resignation of Judge Duval. See *Life and Times of Roger B. Taney,* by Samuel Tyler.

Charles Sumner, having resigned his position as Librarian and left the Law School, Story wrote to him Feb. 4, 1834:

Professor Greenleaf has written me a letter full of lamentation at your departure and he complains of being now left alone, and I grieve also, but not as those who are without hope, for if the Law School succeeds, I am sure you will be with us again at no distant period. The number for the winter term exceeds all my expectations. I had not dreamed of more than 35. Mr. Livermore's is a noble bequest and contains works which I should have gladly consulted if they had been within my reach.

The latter reference was to the recent bequest made by Samuel Livermore to the School of his splendid collection of books on French, Spanish, Civil and Roman Law (referred to in Chapter XXVIII infra).

In March, Sumner went to Washington, and while there saw much of Judge Story(1). In a letter from him to Greenleaf, March 3, 1834, a vivid glimpse is afforded of the Supreme Court of that day:

Mr. Francis Scott Key is now speaking in the Supreme Court where I write these lines. The case before the court is an important one, between Amos Binney and the Chesapeake Canal (8 Peters 201)—Key, Walter Jones and Webster on one side, and Coxe and Swann on the other. Key has not prepared himself, and now speaks from his preparation on the trial below, relying upon a quickness and facility of language, rather than upon research. Walter Jones—a man of acknowledged powers in the law, unsurpassed, if not unequalled by any lawyers in the country—is in the same plight. He is now conning his papers and maturing his points—a labor which of course he should have gone through before he entered the court room. And our Webster fills up the remiss triumvirate. He, like Jones, is doing the labor in court which should have been done out of court. In fact, politics has entirely swamped his whole time and talents. All here declare that he has neglected his cases this term in a remarkable manner. It is now whispered in the room that he has not looked at the present case, though the amount at stake is estimated at half a million of dollars.

The insurance case (*Hazard v. N. E. Mar. Ins. Co.*, 8 Peters 555, 1 Sumner 218) argued by Selden of New York, at Boston last year before Judge Story, has been argued here, since my

(1) Writing to his parents, Sumner said:
"I called first upon Judge Story; found him boarding with the rest of the court, in a house near the capitol; was most kindly received by him. He wished me to tell you that he should take good care of me."

being in town, by Selden on one side and Charles G. Loring and Webster on the other side. It was Loring's first appearance in the Supreme Court, and he acquitted himself honorably . . . was very clear and full, delivering his arguments in a calm, undisturbed manner, which was a beautiful contrast to the rhetorical, excited, disturbed, tinselled manner of Selden, who spoke as if addressing his constituents at the Park or at Tammany Hall. .

. . We expect a very interesting case. *Wheaton v. Peters* —an action brought by Wheaton (the old reporter) against Peters for publishing in his *Condensed Reports* the twelve volumes of *Wheaton*. . . . John Sergeant is Peters' counsel, and Webster, Wheaton's. Franklin Dexter made an argument here a few days before I came, which gained him a good reputation (*Carrington v. Merchants Ins. Co.*, 8 Peters 495). . . . Judge Story has shown me immense kindness.

To this Greenleaf replied, March 8(1):

Your letter from New York was "a great medicine". Not in the Indian sense of that term, a powerful and terrific agent of unknown force; but the true cordial of good fellowship, of kindly feeling, "not the less interesting", as was said of a certain preface, "for the vein of sly humor".

I hope you have not lost yourself in the city of "magnificent distances". . . . You must be in the enjoyment of all that the mightiest efforts of intellect and the kindlings of the loftiest feeling and the sources of the highest interest, can afford. I wish I could share them with you, but you must give me a whole day on your return, for the double pleasure of your society and an account of all you have seen. Meanwhile, the course of my daily round is as readily told as was the inventory of Poins' stocking, viz, "these and those that were the peach colored ones". Kent, I am more and more delighted with. Starkie vexes me by his frequent obscurity, diffuseness and want of method; and I sometimes resolve to write a compendium of the law of evidence myself. We are putting Mr. Livermore's bequest in separate alcoves at each end of the library over which his name is to be inscribed— "*Sic volvere Parcae*" that is, the President—and I like the sentiment of honor to the donor as well as the motive of sound policy which dictates this arrangement.

. . . The inauguration is reprieved till some convenient time next summer, but I understand that an address will be expected from the new professors unless they "get a lawyer to speak for them."

I call on Bro. Rand when I go into the city and we are growing quite "budge". "Equity" brings us together at any time and the hope brightens that this jurisdiction may be enlarged during the

---

(1) Unpublished letter in *Sumner Papers,* Harvard College Library.

present session. I love the honest common law, with all its severe justice,—its just severity—but in my judgment the preservation of that system in the integrity and symmetry of its fair proportions depends much on placing by its side an ample equity jurisdiction as a safety valve, through which that "intemperate love of justice" which makes shipwreck of legal principles on the occurrence of every hard case, may escape.

. . . But adieu for there is no end to these topics.

Yours affectionately, S. Greenleaf.

In the spring of 1834, Story published "another portion of the labors appertaining to the Dane Professorship," on a new branch of the law, *Commentaries on the Conflict of Laws,* of which the *London Law Review* stated: "No work on National jurisprudence merited or ever received greater praise from the jurists of Europe". It is not too much to say that its publication constituted an epoch in the law; for it at once became the standard and almost the sole authority. As was said in its preface:

There exists no treatise upon it in the English language, and not the slightest effort has been made, except by Mr. Chancellor Kent, to arrange in any general order even the more familiar maxims of the common law in regard to it.

It was reprinted almost immediately in England, France and Germany, and received the honor of being practically the first American law book to be cited as authority in English Courts.(1)

---

(1) Sir N. C. Tindal, Chief Justice of Common Pleas in *Huber v. Steiner, 2 Bing.* New Cases 211, said, "It would be unjust to mention it without at the same time paying a tribute to the learning, acuteness and sagacity of its author."

And Daniel Webster in his argument before the Supreme Court in *New Jersey Steam Navigation Company v. Merchants Bank,* 6 Howard 92 (1848), paid this splendid tribute:

"It is a great truth that England has never produced any eminent writer on national or general public law,—no elementary writer who has made the subject his own, who has breathed his own breath into it, and made it live. In English judicature Sir William Scott has, it is true, done much to enlighten the public mind on the subject of prize causes, and in our day Mackintosh has written a paper of some merit. But where is your English Grotius? Where is your English Barbeyrac? Has England produced one? Not one. The English mind has never been turned to the discussion of general public law. We must go to the continent for the display of genius in this department of human knowledge. What have the Courts of Westminster Hall done to illustrate the principles of public law? With the exception of a tract by Mansfield, of considerable merit, more great principles of public law have been discussed and settled by this Court within the last twenty years, than in all the common law Courts of England for the last hundred years. Nay, more important subjects of law have been examined and passed upon by this bench in a series of twenty years, than

Story's keen interest in foreign law was displayed, not only in this book, but in the urgent efforts which he had for several years been making to secure the consent of the Corporation to the delivery in the School of a course of lectures on the Civil Law by Charles Follen, the talented young Professor of German in the College(1). Finally, on April 17, 1834, the Corporation voted:

(1) The Instructor, Dr. Follen, shall give instruction during the spring term to such of the law students as may desire it, in the civil law, by semi-weekly recitations in Cooper's *Justinian's Institutes,* with such oral illustration and exposition thereof as he may deem useful, at such hours and on such days as the Law Faculty may from time to time prescribe.

(2) The Instructor shall receive for his services the sum of $200 to be paid out of the proceeds of the Law School.

This arrangement is to be deemed temporary and for one term only, in order to ascertain how far the civil law may be advantageously studied in the Law School.

Of the 44 students registered in the Spring Term, according to Greenleaf's report of April 28, 1834, a class of 9 took Dr. Follen's course.

In the summer of 1834, great excitement was caused throughout Boston and Cambridge, on account of the burning of the Catholic Ursuline Convent at Charlestown by a mob of rioters, August 11, 1834. Fears were entertained of retaliation by the Catholics, and reports were prevalent that the center of attack was to be Harvard College and especially its library. Most of the undergraduates were absent on vacation, but a number of the law students were still in Cambridge, including Sumner. These law students, with a volunteer guard of recent graduates called together by Rev. J. G. Palfrey, Dean of the Divinity School, formed two companies, one seventy in number, commanded by Franklin Dexter and Robert C. Winthrop, the distinguished Boston lawyers, and another of about the same number, commanded by David Lee Child and George W. Phillips. They were on duty, armed with muskets, for two nights.(2)

---

in all Europe for a century past. And I cannot forbear to add, that one in the midst of you has favored the world with a treatise on public law, fit to stand by the side of Grotius, to be the companion of the Institutes, a work that is now regarded by the judicature of the world, as the great book of the age,—*Story's Conflict of Laws.*"

(1) Professor Follen resigned in 1835, and lost his life in the burning of the steamboat Lexington on Long Island Sound, in 1840. See *New Jersey Steam Navigation Co. v. Merchants Bank,* 6 Howard 92 (1848).

(2) See account by Robert C. Winthrop in *Mass. Hist. Soc. Proc.,* 2nd Series, Vol. III (1886-88):

Greenleaf was inaugurated as Royall Professor in the College Chapel, in University Hall, on August 26, 1834, at the same time, with the new College Professors, Cornelius C. Felton, Charles Beck and Benjamin Pierce.

The Overseers' records gives the following account: "Rev. Henry Ware Jr. prayed. Pres. Quincy delivered an address in Latin on the foundation and purposes of the several professorships. Prof. Peck made a brief reply in Latin. The above professors were then severally announced pro more universitatis. Professor Felton then delivered an Inaugural address on the subject of his professorship. Professor Greenleaf then closed with an Inaugural address on Law."

The next day, August 27, was notable for being the first Commencement Day on which the exercises were held in the new Unitarian Church, opposite Dane Hall(1).

"I am sorry to remember that little or no effort was made by the civil authorities to arrest such atrocious proceedings. I was one of a committee of investigation of thirty members, of which Charles G. Loring was Chairman. . . .

Rumors that some act of vengeance would be perpetrated were soon rife. . . .

Among the earliest of these rumors was one that the Library of Harvard College was doomed to assault and destruction by the Irish Roman Catholics. An early night was named for this act of vengeance, and measures were at once quietly taken to guard against its success. Some 40 or 50 graduates of Harvard were hastily summoned to the rescue. It was arranged that they should repair separately to the Library at Cambridge each one with a musket and ball cartridges at sundown of the appointed day. . . . Franklin Dexter was agreed upon as the commander of the party and I was selected as his first lieutenant. . . .

The Library was in old Harvard Hall; and there we assembled at early dusk and remained all night. Sentinels were stationed at the doors and windows, patrols were sent out on the streets and roads, and every preparation was made for defending the building and books at all hazards. More than once during the night rumors reached us of a mob approaching. At one time there a came a man on horseback at full speed announcing that a thousand infuriated Irishmen were coming along the Charlestown road and were hardly more than a mile off."

See also Austin's *History of Massachusetts,* p. 422, and *Memoir and Letters of Charles Sumner,* by Edward L. Pierce, Vol. I.

Attempts at legislation to indemnify the Catholic owners of the destroyed property were made in the Massachusetts Legislature, but they were not successful. See *Law Reporter,* Vol. V. (Feb. 1843), as to the Report to the Legislature for the winter session of 1842.

A general statute was passed, however, covering future cases; see Acts of 1839 c 54, imposing a liability on towns and cities for property destroyed by rioters.

Those engaged in the riot were indicted and an interesting report of their case is to be found in *Com. v. Buzzell,* 16 Pick. 153 (1834), showing the extreme religious prejudices which were aroused at the time.

(1) The first Commencement held in the old Church (situated on the site of Dane Hall) was in 1758. No Commencement was held in 1764, be-

Degrees of LL.B. were conferred on eight law students, of whom Charles Sumner was one; and honorary degrees of LL.D. were given to Professor Greenleaf, John Davis of Massachusetts, and Edward Livingston of Louisiana.

The year 1834-5 was again a prosperous one for the School; and the President's 10th Annual Report states that the number of students varied from 30 to 52; the number generally fell off during the spring term, and Greenleaf in April 26, 1835, reports 31 students registered, of whom 29 were present. Prominent among them were Otis P. Lord, later Judge of the Massachusetts Supreme Court, and Charles A. Welch of Boston. As the School had now increased so far beyond expectation, the Professors found their labors greater than they had anticipated, and a suggestion was now made for an additional instructor, Greenleaf writing to Story, Nov. 28, 1834(1):

On the subject of an assistant instructor of which we have so frequently conversed, it struck me last winter that as long as we were obliged to use English text books, the labor of ascertaining and pointing out the differences between English and American Law on each topic studied, in addition to the other duties of the School, was rather more than one man could discharge towards two classes at a time, so thoroughly as it ought to be done; and that the general interests of the School would be promoted by some aid in the business of daily instructions, not, however, to absolve the Professor from any active duties which he, better than any other, can perform. I need not remind you how unpropitious it is to any successful research into a subject requiring long continued study and careful comparison or general survey, to be subjected necessarily to frequent interruptions in a day, by the recurrence of other duties, and oftentimes to quit the subject by the time the mind has become sufficiently excited to renew the grasp. On such occasions, though not of very frequent occurrence, the aid of an intelligent instructor to attend the recitations of the day, or to solve some minor doubt for the student, would be invaluable; as well as to attend to the care of the School when the Professors are absent on official or professional duties.

As a result, Charles Sumner was appointed an Instructor in January, 1835, during Story's absence in Washington; and Story wrote to him, Feb. 9:

---

cause of small pox, nor in 1773 to 1781, because of the Revolutionary War, but in all other years the exercises had been in the old Church.

See Note in *Overseers Records,* Aug. 27, 1834.

(1) *Harv. Coll. Papers,* 2nd Series, Vol. VI, p. 280.

I rejoice that you have gone through the ordeal of your inauguration and fairly through, and are now acclimated in the Law School. I never had any doubt upon the subject. Your success (for I learn from Mr. Greenleaf) has been complete and every way gratifying. I hope this is but the beginning, and that one day you may fill the chair which he or I occupy, if he or I, like autocrats, can hope to appoint our successors.

Of Sumner's work as an Instructor, his biographer says:

Like the two professors, Sumner taught by oral examinations, also by formal lectures. He used as text books, *Kent's Commentaries* and *Starkie's Evidence.* . . . He had a difficult place to fill in the School—one always suggesting a comparison with Story and Greenleaf. Few recall his method as a teacher; and while he did not leave a strong impression of any kind on the students, he appears to have realized a fair measure of success for so young a lawyer.(1)

The winter was an uneventful one in the Supreme Court at Washington, owing to Chief Justice Marshall's failing health and to the further fact that there was an unfilled vacancy due to Judge Duval's resignation. Judge James M. Wayne of Georgia had just been appointed to take the place of William Johnson of South Carolina, who died in 1834(2). It was of the Supreme Court room at this period that Harriet Martineau gave her well known account in her *Retrospect of Western Travel*:

I have watched the assemblage when the Chief Justice was delivering a judgment, the three judges on either hand gazing at him more like learners than associates; Webster standing firm as a rock, his large, deep set eyes wide awake, his lips compressed, and his whole countenance in that intent stillness which easily fixes the eye of the stranger. Clay leaning against the desk in an attitude whose grace contrasts strangely with the slovenly make of his dress, his snuff box for the moment unopened in his hand, his small grey eye, and placid half-smile conveying an expression of pleasure, which redeems his face from its usual unaccountable commonness. The Attorney General (Benjamin F. Butler) his fingers playing among his papers, his quick black eye and thin tremulous lips for once fixed, his small face, pale with thought, contrasting remarkably with the other two; these

---

(1) *Memoir and Letters of Charles Sumner,* by Edward L. Peirce, Vol. I.

(2) There were at this time two other new judges, appointed by Jackson, in 1829, John McLean of Ohio, and Henry Baldwin of Pennsylvania, in the places of Judges Trimble and Bushrod Washington, deceased.

men absorbed in what they are listening to, thinking neither of themselves nor of each other, while they are watched by the groups of idlers and listeners around them; the newspaper corps, the dark Cherokee chiefs, the stragglers from the far West, the gay ladies in their waving plumes, and the members of either House that have stepped in to listen; all these I have seen constitute one silent assemblage, while the mild voice of the aged Chief Justice sounded through the court. . . . How delighted we were to see Judge Story bring in the tall, majestic, bright-eyed, old man (the Chief Justice), old by chronology by the lines on his composed face, and by his services to the republic; but so dignified, so fresh, so present to the time, that no feeling of compassionate consideration forage dared to mix with contemplation of him.

The illness of his friend, the Chief Justice, the realization of the fact that he himself was the only survivor of those who comprised the Court when he was appointed, and the immense pressure of business in the Circuit Court produced in Story a great depression at this time; and he seriously contemplated resigning from the bench, in order that he might devote his whole time to his beloved Law School; and he wrote June 19, 1835:

The Law School, as to my department, also stands suspended until my return, and as it happens to be the most busy and important part of the term, and many students close their studies at the end of it, every day lost is to them irreparable.

On July 6, 1835, at the age of eighty, Chief Justice Marshall died, and the profession generally looked forward to Story's appointment as his successor. But "the school of Story and Kent," to use Jackson's phrase, could expect no favors at the hands of the President, for their political and constitutional views differed far too widely; and as Story wrote: "Whoever succeeds Marshall will have a most painful and discouraging duty. He will follow a man who cannot be equalled, and all the public will see or think they see the difference.
. . . I take it for granted that all of us who are on the bench are hors de combat."

John Quincy Adams, in his diary, July 10, 1835, thus described the situation:

John Marshall died at Philadelphia last Monday. He was one of the most eminent men that this country has ever produced— a Federalist of the Washington School. The Associate Judges from the time of his appointment have generally been taken from the Democratic or Jeffersonian party. Not one of them excepting Story has been a man of great ability. Several of them have been men of strong prejudices, warm passions, and contracted minds; one of them occasionally insane. Marshall, by the ascendency of his genius, by the amenity of his deportment, and by the imperturbable command of his temper, has given a permanent and systematic character to the decisions of the court and settled many great constitutional questions favorably to the continuance of the Union. Marshall has cemented the Union which the crafty and quixotic democracy of Jefferson had a perpetual tendency to dissolve. Jefferson hated and dreaded him. It is much to be feared that a successor will be appointed of a very different character. The President of the United States now in office, has already appointed three judges of the Supreme Court; with the next appointment he will have constituted the chief justice and a majority of the court. He has not yet made one good appointment. His chief justice will be no better than the rest.

President Jackson waited six months, and then, to the surprise of most of the Bar, appointed Roger B. Taney, of Maryland (1), as Marshall's successor, in December, 1835.

This year, 1835, was notable in the legal annals of Massachusetts for being that in which Rufus Choate removed from Salem to practice in Boston, where he, together with Jeremiah Mason(2), who had come there from New Hampshire in 1832,

---

(1) Benjamin R. Curtis, in his Eulogy on Taney, before the Bar of the First Circuit Court of the United States, in Boston, Oct. 17, 1864, said:

"I have been long enough at the Bar to remember Mr. Taney's appointment; and I believe it was then a general impression in this part of the country that he was neither a learned nor a profound lawyer. This was certainly a mistake. His mind was thoroughly imbued with the rules of the common law and of equity law; and when I first knew him he was master of all that peculiar jurisprudence which it is the special province of the courts of the United States to administer and apply. His skill in applying it was of the highest order. His power of subtle analysis exceeded that of any man I ever knew . . . in his case balanced and checked by excellent common sense and by great experience in practical business, both public and private.

It is certainly true, and I am happy to be able to bear direct testimony to it, that the surpassing ability of the chief justice and all the great qualities of character and mind, were more fully and constantly exhibited in the consultation room while presiding over and assisting the deliberation of his brethren than the public knew or can ever justly estimate . . . There his dignity, his love of order, his gentleness, his discrimination, were of incalculable importance. The real intrinsic character of the tribunal was greatly influenced by them, and always for the better."

(2) Jeremiah Mason was born in 1768, and died in 1848. Before he came to Boston he had served with distinction as United States Senator from New Hampshire. His practice had carried him not only all over New England but often to Washington.

In 1833, all Massachusetts rang with the account of his famous successful

and Daniel Webster, formed a trio of lawyers, unequalled in the country. At the Boston Bar at this time there were many other great lawyers,—Charles G. Loring, counsel for Harvard College,(1) Sidney Bartlett, George F. Farley, Samuel Hoar, Charles Levi Woodbury, Theron Metcalf, Charles P. Curtis, Richard Fletcher and William C. Aylwin.

Of the younger men at the Bar, probably the most prominent was Benjamin R. Curtis, who had just come to Boston to practice, and of one of whose first cases in the Supreme Court the following story is told: "It is said that an old Deputy Sheriff who had just heard Curtis' opening argument was met in the street, and was asked if anything was going on in court. 'Going on'? was the reply, 'There's a young chap named Curtis up there has just opened a case so all Hell can't close it.' "(2)

In this year also, George S. Hillard and Charles Sumner began practice, in No. 4, Court Street—a building famed for its legal

---

defense of Rev. Ephraim K. Avery, tried for the murder of Sarah M. Cornell.

Webster, who was sixteen years his junior and who had been much under his influence in his early years at the Portsmouth Bar, and who later had been his chief rival, said of him to Choate, "I regard Jeremiah Mason as eminently superior to any other lawyer whom I have ever met. I would rather, with my own experience (and I have had some pretty tough experiences with him) meet them all combined in a case than to meet him alone and single handed. He was the keenest lawyer I have ever met or read about."

"Mr. Mason was a man of strongly marked individuality, with great independence and courage, a clear, strong and keen mind, a trenchant wit and a brusque manner, and famed for his shrewd, witty, often sarcastic, frequently rough, retorts in the trial of his cases.

Probably the best and most familiar is that of his remark to a judge who insisted on questioning himself an important witness. Mr. Mason checked the witness's reply by saying, 'May it please your Honor, I should like to inquire on whose side you ask that question. If it is on our side we do not want it, and if it is on the other side it is inadmissible.'

He was above all else a "cause getting" man, of immense influence with juries, whom he addressed from their own level in an irresistible way— with no rhetoric, no polish, or artificiality of manner, but in words full of rugged force and with a logical clearness that was just as effective before the court as before the jury".

See *Bench and Bar of Boston,* by John T. Morse, in *Memorial History of Boston,* Vol. IV ; and *Life of Jeremiah Mason,* by George S. Hillard.

(1) Of Charles G. Loring, Professor Theophilus Parsons later said, that "from 1825 to 1855, the published reports of decisions will show that no other man had so large a number of cases in court; and of the cases of no other, was the proportion so large of those which by the novelty of the questions they raised or the peculiar circumstances to which they required the application of acknowledged principles, may be considered as establishing new law or giving scope and meaning to recognized law."

(2) *Autobiography of Seventy Years,* by George F. Hoar, Vol. I.

associations (the present site of Young's Hotel).(1)   Here
were the offices of Choate, Theophilus Parsons, Peleg W. Chandler, John A. Andrew, Horace Mann, Edward G. Loring, and
Luther S. Cushing.

The culture and friendliness of Hillard and Sumner attracted
many callers—not only the other tenants of Number 4, but besides them Judge Story, Greenleaf, Cleveland, Cornelius C. Felton, Park Benjamin and George Bancroft.   Greenleaf deposited
his writing desk, table and chair in the office, calling it "our
office".   Here, when he came to the city, he usually called upon his
two friends and met the clients whom he served while he was professor.(2)

It is to be noted that Professor Greenleaf continued in active
practice during his professorship, and was counsel in many cases
of great magnitude and importance, one of which, tried in 1835,
was the case of the *Boston Water Power Company v. Boston
and Worcester Railroad Company* (16 Pick. 512), in which
Greenleaf, Richard Fletcher and Franklin Dexter appeared for
the defendant, against Jeremiah Mason and Charles G. Loring.
This case is notable as being the first case in the Massachusetts
Supreme Court involving a steam railroad.   In the previous year,
Greenleaf had argued *Wellington Petitioner* (16 Pick. 82), against

---

(1)   See *Farewell to Number Four*, a poem by George S. Hillard, *Law
Reporter*, Vol XVIII (1856).
(2)   The affectionate and playful relations between Greenleaf and his
young colleague were very marked.   See unpublished letter from Greenleaf to Sumner, Nov. 14, 1834, in *Sumner Papers* in Harvard College
Library.
"To Charles Sumner, Esquire, one of the Keepers of 'our' office in
      Boston, Greeting:
"Whereas a certain writing desk, table and armed chair stand charged
under lawful affirmation with being the goods and chattels of one Simon
Greenleaf, and are therefore adjudged and ordered to be taken to Boston
for trial—You are hereby requested to receive the same into your custody
in our said office and then there detain them, that they may be held to
answer the said charge and be *further dealt with* as to law and justice may
appertain.   And for so doing this shall be your sufficient warrant.   Given
under our hand and seal at Cambridge this 14th day of November in the
first year of our domicil in *two places at the same time!*
                                          S. Greenleaf."
   See also unpublished letter of July 15, 1835:
"July 15, 1835, Dane Hall, Therm circ 82 degrees,
      Dearly Beloved——
   It is theological examination in University Hall—cloudy—hot—damp—I
am trying to study law—interrupted every five minutes—but patient as a
lamb—The Divines have begun with an onslaught on the Pentateuch.
                     Yours as aforesaid,
                                          S. G."

Jeremiah Mason and A. Peabody, the case being interesting from the fact that it involved the right to the laying out of a highway over Cambridge Common on the line of the old Cambridge and Concord Turnpike—a proceeding vigorously opposed by a committee of Cambridge citizens headed by Joseph Story.

In the year 1835-1836, the Law School opened with students from many distant States, 21 from Massachusetts, 11 from Maine, 3 each from New Hampshire and Connecticut, 2 each from Rhode Island, Virginia, South Carolina and Ohio, 1 each from Vermont, Georgia, Kentucky, Alabama and Indiana,—52 in all—so Greenleaf reported Oct. 20, 1835, and the 11th Annual Report of the President reported attendance during the year, from 40 to 54.

Story left for Washington in December; and shortly afterwards Sumner again took his place as Instructor in the School; Story in a letter to him, Feb. 10, 1836, saying(1):

I am glad that our good Professor Greenleaf has called you to his aid for you are "William of Doleraine—good at need". By the bye, he has had tempting offers to remove into Boston. I am *totis viribus* against this step, and I trust to you to aid me in disenchanting the enemy of this spell. . . . If I do not live otherwise to posterity, I shall at all events live in my children in the law. While that endures I am content to be known through my pupils.

In the spring of 1836, Story published the first volume of his *Commentaries on Equity Jurisprudence*—dedicated to the old friend of his youth, William Prescott of Salem, who had then just retired from the Bar. Regarding this book, his friend, Mr. Justice Vaughan of the Court of King's Bench, wrote to him from London:

If the founder of the Dane Professorship of Law in Harvard University had lived to witness the rich harvest which has been reaped by the sweat of your brow from his liberal endowments, he must have reflected with the sweetest satisfaction on having been the instrument, under Divine Providence, of improving the condition of Society, by maturing the growth and diffusion of so much valuable knowledge amidst the civilized portion of the Globe.

_____

(1) See unpublished letter in *Sumner Papers* in Harvard College Library.

As Chief Justice Taney and Judge Barbour, the newly appointed members of the Supreme Court, did not take their seats until March 1836, Judge Story, being the Senior Justice, presided over the Court. He felt keenly the loneliness of his position, and although only fifty-seven years of age he wrote in February: "I miss the Chief Justice at every turn . . . I am the last of the judges who were on the Bench when I took my seat there. I seem a monument of the past age and a mere record of the dead."

Shortly after Story's return to the Law School, a case was argued in the Massachusetts Supreme Court which aroused the attention of the whole community; for it settled the attitude of the courts and law of that State towards the great question of slavery which was then looming dark on the political horizon. The American Anti-slavery Society had been in existence two years. The previous year had witnessed the mobbing of William Lloyd Garrison in Boston, and the publication by Rev. William Ellery Channing of his noted book on *Slavery*.

In *Commonwealth v. Aves* (18 Pick. 211), at the Spring Term of 1836, Chief Justice Shaw was called upon to decide the question whether a slave child brought into this State by a slave owner from Louisiana temporarily on a visit, could be kept in custody as slave. Benjamin R. Curtis and Charles P. Curtis represented the slave owner, Rufus Choate and Ellis Gray Loring, the slave; and Shaw, in one of his great decisions, laid down the doctrine that slavery was contrary to natural right and to the principles of justice, humanity and sound policy, and could not exist in Massachusetts.

Of this case, Story wrote to Loring: "I have rarely seen so thorough and exact arguments as those made by Mr. B. R. Curtis and yourself. They exhibit learning, research and ability, of which any man may be proud."

The case is interesting in connection with the Law School from the fact that only eighteen years later, a prominent judge, Edward G. Loring, was refused confirmation by the Board of Overseers of Harvard, as Lecturer, in the School, because of his action in a Fugitive Slave case.

At this time, another question was greatly agitating the public mind—that of law reform and codification. Popular interest demanded radical changes in the administration of law.(1) This demand in Massachusetts was partially met in 1836 by the passage of the act abolishing special pleading, and the appointment of a Commission "to take into consideration the practicability and expediency of reducing in a written and systematic code the Common Law of Massachusetts or any part thereof." Governor Everett appointed as its members—Story, Greenleaf, Theron Metcalf, Charles E. Forbes and Luther S. Cushing(2). The

---

(1) The following are samples of the varying opinions prevalent:
Governor Edward Everett, in his message to the Legislature, Jan. 15, 1836, said:
"The opinion that it would be expedient to incorporate into a uniform code with the statute legislation of the State, those numerous principles of the common law which are definitely settled and well known, is gaining prevalence and on good grounds."
Robert Rantoul Jr., in his noted Fourth of July oration at Scituate, Mass., in 1836 said, advocating a code:
"Judge-made law is ex post facto law and therefore unjust. . . . The common law sprung from the dark ages. . . . Judge-made law is special legislation. The judge is human and feels the bias which the coloring of the particular case gives. . . . The law should be a positive and unbending text. The Revised Statutes are the most important act of our Legislature since the Revolution."
On the other hand, James C. Alvord wrote to Sumner, May 3, 1836, (see unpublished letter in *Sumner Papers* in Harvard College Library) referring to "the spirit of radicalism which has been fanned by the breath of his Excellency", and stating that while he (Alvord) was not in sympathy with codification, Story and Cushing, because of their civil law predilections, and other members of the Commission, had probably been appointed with this in view.
(2) The following letter written in April, 1836, by Theophilus Parsons to Charles Sumner, is of interest in this connection:
"My dear friend:
I do not want you to mistake my views about your appointment on the Code Commission, and so I put them down in black and white.
It seems to me doubtful whether it will benefit you to be on the preliminary commission. They who envy and malign you now attribute your success to life, (which, whatever you may think of it, is great) to Judge Story's friendship and favours. No one ever accused him, within my knowledge, of wrongful favoring of anyone—but the idea is that his influence in Society could have raised you without corresponding superiority in personal merit.
Now you and I know this to be a lie; but it is still a fact that such a lie is told by those who love to lie, and the fact cannot be wholly disregarded with prudence. Besides, you have now distinguished enough and employment for the present and you must in common prudence seem to hold back rather than press forward, and you may rest assured neither your friends nor our own powers will allow of your being kept back.
The Report must be a single work, and you will I am sure pardon my saying that if Judge Story be on the Commission, and of course at its head, the work must be substantially his work. Whatever aid other commissioners bring, he will accept and use, but he cannot if he would, and ought not if he could, prevent their contributions from being fused down into strict unity with his own views.
. . . . You know codification is a matter which I have much at

Commission made a report to the Legislature, in 1837, favoring codification of certain parts of the law relating to civil rights and duties and implied contracts, and especially evidence and crimes. Of this, Judge Story wrote to a friend, Dec. 26, 1836:

A commission has been appointed by the State of Massachusetts to report to the Legislature on the practicability and expediency of codifying the common law or any part thereof. Much against my will I was placed at the head of the commission. We shall report favorably to the codification of some branches of the commercial law. But the report will be very qualified and limited in its objects. We have not yet become votaries to the notions of Jeremy Bentham. But the present state of popular opinion here makes it necessary to do something on the subject.

The beginning of the year 1836-37 was made notable by the 200th celebration of the Foundation of Harvard College, held on September 8, 1836, Judge Story, President Quincy and James Walker being the Committee of the Corporation in charge—together with a Committee of the Alumni, of which Governor Everett was chairman. In this celebration the law students participated, marching in the procession from University Hall to the exercises in the Congregational Church. Here was sung, for the first time, the ode composed by Rev. Samuel Gilman of Charleston, South Carolina—*Fair Harvard*. "The touching allusions of this beautiful ode excited a deep and solemn enthusiasm," wrote President Quincy. After an address by the President, the procession numbering over 1500 marched around the College buildings to a pavilion, erected near the site of the present Gore Hall, where a dinner was served, at which Governor Everett presided. President Kirkland, Rev. Dr. Palfrey, Dr. John C. Warren, Chief Justice Shaw, ex-Governor Levi Lincoln, ex-Governor John Davis, H. S. Legaré, a distinguished lawyer from South Carolina, Daniel Webster, Samuel T. Armstrong, Mayor of Boston, Samuel Jones, Chancellor of New York, William Plumer, a distinguished lawyer of New Hampshire, William Sullivan of Boston, Loammi Baldwin, Leverett Saltonstall, Mayor of Salem, Peleg Sprague, Judge of the United States District Court, Alden Bradford, Franklin Dexter, United States

---

heart, and I hope you know I have your interests there too, and I cannot but think you will consult both by staying off the preliminary commission." (See unpublished letter in *Sumner Papers* in Harv. Coll. Library.)

District Attorney, William H. Gardner, Josiah Quincy Jr., Robert C. Winthrop, Chief Marshal of the day, and William Elliott of South Carolina, were the speakers; as well as Judge Story, who responded to the toast of "Nathan Dane"—"The memory of him who added a seminary of law to the School of the Prophets. A structure of immortal fame has been reared on his foundation."

In his speech, he said of Dane, who had died, Feb. 15, 1835, six months previously (1):

No one can hold in more reverence than myself the memory of that excellent man, the founder of the professorship which I have now the honor to hold, whose bounty is worthy of all praise; for its noble object is to inculcate through all generations the doctrines of the supremacy of the constitution and laws. But, although I am conscious of my own inability to carry into full effect his admirable design, I trust that it will not be thought presumptuous in me to indulge the hope, that there may hereafter be found among the pupils of this school of jurisprudence some master spirit who will task himself to its accomplishment, and thereby secure to himself and it an enviable immortality.

In the evening, the Dane Law College was brilliantly illuminated by the law students, in the same manner as the other College buildings.

The number of students in the School had now grown to 54; and the increase may be attributed, in part, to the policy of advertising, initiated by Judge Story, and explained in his letter to the College Treasurer, Sept. 24, 1836(2):

The expense of advertising of the Law School seems very large, but it occurred to us that it was important to the prosperity of the Law School that its course of instruction and arrangements should be known throughout the United States. For this purpose Professor Greenleaf directed a programme of the studies, etc., to be published in one or more of the principal newspapers in the leading States in the Union.

The expense of so full an advertisement in so many papers was necessarily great. But it has been amply repaid by an increase of the School by students from various parts of the Union.

In the future we suppose we may confine our annual adver-

---

(1) Story wrote to Sumner, Feb. 22, 1835: "I feel melancholy at the death of Mr. Dane. He has gone to his grave, full of honors as well as years."

(2) *Letters to the Treasurer, Harv. Coll. Archives.*

tisement to a very few papers, including one at Washington, which will greatly diminish the charge.

In January 1837, Judge Story went to Washington, as usual; and at this term of the Supreme Court there were decided three cases of more than ordinary interest—one of which—the famous Charles River Bridge case—so deeply involved the national interests of Harvard College, and was so closely connected with the Harvard Law School, through the fact that Professor Greenleaf was one of the counsel engaged, that it deserves a full description, which will be given in the following chapter.

CHAPTER XXIV.

The Charles River Bridge Case.

In a lecture delivered to the students of the Law School, in 1838, Greenleaf, speaking of the proper attitude in which a case in the law reports should be studied, made the following suggestive comments:

Judges and lawyers, like other classes of men, become interested in the absorbing topics of the day, and subjected to their magnetic influences; and some passages in the history of the times, or some glimpses of their temper and fashion may be seen in the most dispassionate legal judgments. . . . The manner of the decision, the reasons on which it is professedly founded, and even the decision itself, may receive some coloring and impress from the position of the judges, and their political principles, their habits of life, their physical temperament, their intellectual, moral and religious character. . . . Thus we should hardly expect to find any gratuitous presumption in favor of innocence or any leanings *in mitiori sensu* in the bloodthirsty and infamous Jeffries; nor could we, while reading and considering their legal opinions, forget either the low breeding and meanness of Saunders, the ardent temperament of Buller, the dissolute habits, ferocity and profaneness of Thurlow; or the intellectual greatness and integrity of Hobart, the sublimated piety and enlightened conscience of Hale, the originality and genius of Holt, the elegant manners and varied learning of Mansfield, or the conservative principles, the lofty tone of morals, and vast comprehension of Marshall.

Neither should we expect a decision leaning in favor of the liberty of the subject from the Star Chamber; nor against the King's prerogative among the judges in the reigns of the Tudors or of James the First; nor should we on this side of the water, resort to the decisions in Westminster Hall to learn the true extent of the Admiralty jurisdiction which the English Common Law Courts have been always disposed to curtail and in many points to deny; while it is so clearly expounded in the masterly judgments of Lord Stowell, and of his no less distinguished and yet living American contemporary (Story).

Just one year before Greenleaf made the above remarks, he himself had argued, and the United States Supreme Court had decided, in 1837, one of the most noted and historic cases ever argued before that tribunal—*Charles River Bridge v. Warren Bridge.* (11 Peters 420).

A close study of the facts of the case, of the counsel engaged, and of the judges who heard it, is of great interest in making clear the influence which the social and economic conditions of the times had upon its decision; for this case, begun in 1828, and the noted case of *Gibbons v. Ogden,* decided in 1824, were the great Anti-Trust cases of the early 19th Century.

If the Charles River Bridge Proprietors had not been regarded as the "grasping monopoly" of Boston, and as the "octopus corporation" of its time, it is highly probable that the court would have reached a different conclusion; and it is certain that the fact that railroads were just starting as struggling enterprises, needing protection against possible claims for damages which might be set up by rich turnpike corporations, had a very marked influence upon the final decision.

The roots of the case went back to the early date of October 17, 1640 (ten years after the founding of Boston) when at the General Court of Massachusetts Bay Colony it was resolved that "the ferry between Boston and Charlestown is granted to the College"—this vote being one of the many measures by which the early colonists set out to encourage liberal education. For forty years after 1672, various statutes recognized that the profits and revenues of the ferry belonged exclusively to Harvard College. In 1701, appeared the first entry on the College books showing the lease of the ferry by the College. During the 18th Century, the ferry was not a great source of revenue, owing to the cost of maintenance. Between 1775 and 1781, it had been supported at an actual loss. In 1785, however, when the College had just expended 300 pounds in repairing the ferry ways, and when it was beginning to receive 200 pounds annual rent, with an apparent certainty of a steady increase, the Commonwealth of Massachusetts took action gravely affecting the interests of the College. For on March 9, 1785, John Hancock, Thomas Russell and others, were incorporated by the Legislature as the "Proprietors of Charles River Bridge," to build a bridge in place of the ferry, the charter providing that the grantees should pay the College 200 pounds a year for forty years, at the end of which time the bridge was to become the property of the Commonwealth: "saving to the said College a reasonable and annual compensation for the annual income of the ferry which they might have received had not said bridge been erected."

To the inexact and careless wording of this charter—"an act not drawn with any commendable accuracy," as Judge Story mildly said(1)—was due the long legislative and legal fight which ensued for sixty years after its date, and which resulted in one of the great cases in American legal history.

The bridge itself, the first one connecting Boston with the mainland, was opened June 17, 1786, and was considered, at the time, one of the marvels of the United States, attracting many persons from other parts of the country to view it(2).

Of the hazards of its construction, mention was made in the argument at Washington, fifty-one years later:

> It was hazardous, for no attempt at that time had been made to carry a bridge over tide water; and so doubtful were the subscribers of its stability that a number of them insured their interest in it. The hazard was all their own; and so great was it thought to be, upon the breaking up of the ice, persons assembled on the shore to see it carried away. It has stood, however, against the time and the elements; it has stood against everything except legislation. It was opened with processions and every demonstration of a general rejoicing, and was considered, at the time, as an enterprise of great patriotism as well as of utility.(3)

The *Independent Chronicle*, in June, 1786, referred to the opening day as a "day of rejoicing"; and thus described the bridge itself:

> This commodious and handsome structure is 1470 feet in length, and 42 feet within the paling. This bridge has been completed in 13 months, and while it exhibits the greatest effect of private interprise within the United States, is a most pleasing proof how certain objects of magnitude may be attained by spirited exertions.(4)

---

(1) See Story's dissenting opinion in 11 Peters (1837).

(2) President Ezra Stiles of Yale College wrote in his diary, Oct. 10, 1787, "Left Cambr. Crossed Charlesto. Bridge—a grand work!"

(3) See argument of Warren Dutton, counsel for the Charles River Bridge, in 11 Peters (1837).

(4) *The Ferry, the Charles River Bridge and the Charlestown Bridge. Historical comment prepared for the Boston Transit Commission by its Chairman, November 27, 1899.*

"This was first effort to erect a bridge over a broad river in the American states. A brief account of its origin will not be destitute of interest.

Judge Russell, the gentleman whom I have mentioned in an earlier chapter, was long and ardently desirous that a bridge should be erected between these towns. As he advanced in years he became more and more solicitous

The capital stock of the bridge was 150 shares of a par value of $333.33.

Six years later, in 1792, a petition came before the Legislature to incorporate the Proprietors of the West Boston Bridge, to build a bridge between Boston and Cambridge. Harvard College objected strongly, on the ground that it would reduce the revenues of the Charles River Bridge. The Charles River Bridge urged that it had spent for the erection of its bridge $51,000, that the cost of support was $18,000, and that its profits had not amounted to 11 per cent. A joint committee of the Legislature, however, reported that Charles River Bridge had no exclusive rights, and the Legislature granted the West Boston

---

to see the work accomplished. His son, the late Hon. Thomas Russell, and his son-in-law, the late Hon. John Lowell, district judge of Massachusetts, together with several other gentlemen connected with them, were earnestly desirous to see the wishes of this venerable man realized. At that time it was universally believed that for a river so wide, and a current so strong a floating bridge was the only practicable structure of this nature. They, therefore, engaged a gentleman to obtain for them a correct account of the construction, expense, convenience, and security of the floating bridge then lying on the Schuylkill at Philadelphia. Several other persons at that time bound to Europe they requested, also, to furnish them with similar information concerning bridges in that quarter of the globe. While this business was in agitation, both the gentlemen being on a visit at Cambridge, during the session of the Supreme Judicial Court, they made the projected bridge a subject of conversation with the Hon. David Sewall, one of the judges. In the course of this conversation the designs mentioned above were particularly stated. On his return to York, the place of his residence, Judge Sewall communicated this information to his brother, Major Sewall, a gentleman distinguished for peculiar mechanical talents. After being informed that the difficulties presented by the stream furnished the only reason for erecting a floating bridge, Major Sewall observed that a fixed bridge might be so constructed as easily, and certainly to be secure from the dangers of the current. His brother requested him to state his views to the gentlemen concerned. Accordingly, he formed and communicated a scheme for the intended structure. After this scheme had been thoroughly examined, the original design was relinquished, and the present bridge begun. At the request of the undertakers Major Sewall came to Boston, and continued to superintend the work until he had completely possessed the builders of the principles on which it was to be accomplished.

The facts I had from Judge Lowell himself. I have recited them merely to do justice to merit to which justice has not hitherto been publicly done. Major Sewall I never saw; but I think him deserving of a high tribute of respect from every American, as a source of those vast improvements which have been made throughout the United States in this interesting branch of architecture.

Charlestown bridge was finished in 1786. It is built on seventy-five wooden piers, and is forty-two feet in breadth and one thousand five hundred and three in length, the river being here two hundred and eighty feet wider than the Thames at Westminster Bridge, and six hundred and three feet wider than the same river at London Bridge. It is also deeper. Footways are formed on each side. The centre rises insensibly two feet higher than the ends. The bridge was built by two able and ingenious American

Bridge charter (St. 1791 c. 62); but at the same time it recognized the interests of the College and of the old bridge, by providing that, "Whereas the erection of the Charles River Bridge was a work of hazard and public utility, and another bridge in the place proposed for the West Boston bridge may diminish the emoluments of the Charles River Bridge, therefore for the encouragement of the enterprize", an annuity of 300 (reduced by an Act passed the same year to 200), pounds should be paid to the College, and the rights and privileges of the Charles River Bridge and the annuity payable by it to the College should be extended from 40 to 70 years.(1)

The West Boston Bridge was opened November 23, 1793, Elbridge Gerry, who then resided in "Elmwood," being the first person allowed to pass over it. It was described as a "magnificent structure"; and the *Independent Chronicle* said, "for length, elegance and grandeur, not exceeded by any in the United States, if in any part of the world."

For many years these two toll bridges played an important

---

artists, Messrs. Cox and Stone, and cost $50,000. About forty large bridges have been built in the United States in consequence of the erection of this structure.

West Boston bridge is a more expensive and a more interesting object. It is made up of four parts:—

	Feet.
The abutment on the Boston side in length	87½
Principal bridge	3,483
Second bridge	275
Causeys	3,344
Total	7,189½

This bridge is forty feet wide, and is executed in the same manner. The principal bridge stands on one hundred and eighty piers, the second on fourteen. The sides of the causeys are stoned, capstained, and railed, and accompanied by a canal thirty feet wide. The whole work was accomplished under the direction of Major Whiting, of Norwich (Connecticut), at the expense of $76,700, about £17,250 sterling. It was begun July 15, 1792, and was opened November 23, 1793. It is finished with more neatness than the Charlestown bridge."

See *Travels in New England*, by Timothy Dwight (1821).

(1) Two other bridge charters were granted, affecting Cambridge and the College—one, the Act of February 27, 1807, incorporated Christopher Gore and others, as Proprietors of the Canal Bridge, to build from the Northwest end of Leverett Street in Boston to the east end of Lechmere's Point (now Craigie or East Cambridge Bridge), payment to be made to the West Boston Bridge of an annuity of $333.33, and the West Boston Bridge to be continued a corporation for seventy years from completion of Canal Bridge, and to pay to the College an annuity of $666.66 during that term. The other was the Act of June 21, 1806, chartering the Proprietors of Prison Point Dam Corporation, under which, in 1815-16, a bridge was built from Cambridge to Charlestown.

part in the life of the community. The amount of money invested in them was large. Many noted citizens of Boston and of Charlestown were involved in the enterprises. All residents of the towns and counties north of Boston were vitally interested in their maintenance.

By 1805, the traffic over the Charles River Bridge and its consequent income had so increased that the value of its shares had risen to $1650. In 1814, Harvard College bought two shares at $2080 per share.

Naturally the large profits accruing from tolls produced at last a feeling of unrest in the public, and cries of "grinding monopoly" were heard on all sides.

Webster, in his argument in 1837, thus described the local conditions:

The history of the Warren Bridge began with a clamor about monopoly. It was asserted that the public had a right to break up the monopoly which was held by the Charles River Bridge Company; that they had a right to have a free bridge. Application was frequently made to the Legislature on those principles and for that purpose, during five years without success, and the bill authorizing the bridge, when it was first passed by the Legislature, was rejected by the veto of the governor. When the charter was granted it passed by a very small majority, the Boston representatives voting against it.

While the profits from the old bridge had undoubtedly been very large(1) those who indulged in the outcry against this monopoly ignored other features of the situation, described later by Peter C. Brooks, in a letter of Josiah Quincy(2):

I might instance the cost of your relative Lieutenant Governor Phillips' estate in Tremont street, which cost, if I mistake not, $9500 in 1807, and has since been sold for about $80,000. I mention this to show the value of money when the bridge was built, and to do way the senseless clamor about the inordinate gain to the proprietors from being the owners of the stock. The same sum laid out in real estate over the city would have been in many instances quite as profitable. All this nonsensical noise had nothing on earth to do with the merits of the question. And so as to income it was great, after a few years, to those who held shares from the beginning; but to those who become

(1) The total tolls from June, 1786, to January, 1827, were $824,498, an average of $20,000 a year.
(2) See *Harv. Coll. Archives, Quincy Papers,* unpublished letters to Peter C. Brooks, September, 1840.

owners after 1805—comprising about three-fourths of the 150 shares, it was not so good as 6 per cent., and more especially if you consider that the principal was sinking fast and would be wholly lost in about 20-30 years. At the time when Warren Bridge was thought of in 1827, there was but one share held by an original subscriber.

The legislative contest, which was to last five years, began with the petition of John Skinner and other citizens of Charlestown for a charter to build a bridge which should be "toll free for foot passengers," introduced in the Senate May 30, 1823.(1) Many remonstrances were filed against this petition by wharf owners in Cambridge, Charlestown, and Boston, claiming that an obstruction to navigation would be caused by the new bridge. The Charles River Bridge Proprietors objected, denying any public necessity for another bridge, and setting forth the injury to their own property, then valued by them at $280,000: "by far the greater part of which is holden by persons who have purchased the stock within the last ten or fifteen years—by widows, by orphans, by literary and charitable institutions. The erection of another bridge from Charlestown to Boston would annihilate at once two-thirds of this property."

In February, 1824, the Legislature gave the petitioners leave to bring in a bill, and they were ordered to give notice to parties interested. The Charles River Bridge thereupon, by formal vote of February 25, 1825, offered to make any addition or alteration in its structure that the Legislature might desire; and the Legislature postponed action on the Skinner petition. In June, 1825, a new petition was filed, offering to build either a free bridge to be maintained by the counties of Suffolk and Middlesex, or a toll bridge to become free after its cost with interest should be reimbursed.

In January, 1826, the petition came up again; and there were many memorials in its favor from inhabitants of towns in Essex and Middlesex counties, objecting to the payment of the high tolls, demanded by the Charles River Bridge, and urging their right to a free bridge. The joint legislative committee headed by the great lawyer, Samuel Hoar, a senator from Middlesex, made an adverse report on the bill; and it was referred to the next Legislature. This report was of interest as containing in concise form the grounds on which the case was later argued

(1) See manuscript *Legislative Records of Massachusetts.*

before the courts. It found that there was no "public necessity" for the new bridge, that the question of toll had no bearing on the determination of the general public necessity, that
the Charles River Bridge charter was "a contract," which under
the doctrine of *Fletcher v. Peck*,(1) the Legislature could not
impair, and that a new bridge would be a nuisance as against
the rights of the old bridge.(2)

Meanwhile the Bridge Proprietors consulted Daniel Webster on
the question whether the proposed State statute authorizing a
new bridge over a navigable river might not be unconstitutional,
as an interference with interstate or foreign commerce, under
the recent doctrine of *Gibbons v. Ogden*. They received little
encouragement from Webster, however, on this point.(3)

---

(1) *Fletcher v. Peck* (6 Cranch 87) had been decided by the United
States Supreme Court in 1810, having been argued by Luther Martin of
Maryland, against Robert G. Harper of Maryland and Joseph Story of
Massachusetts, the latter prevailing. As is well known this case was the
precursor of the decision nine years later, in the Dartmouth College Case,
in 1819 (4 Wheaton) in which Story sat as one of the Justices of the
Court.

(2) In an elaborate pamphlet published in 1825, entitled *Reasons,
Principally of a Public Nature, against a New Bridge from Charlestown to
Boston*, it is said: "The present bridge was not granted as a favour to the
stockholders, but because the legislature perceived that the whole community were to be benefitted, and the terms on which the proprietors were
willing to undertake this novel and hazardous enterprise gave an advantageous bargain to the public. The object in view in obtaining this projected bridge is merely local and personal, so entirely a project to get rid
of paying foot toll at the present bridge, that scarcely a man in Charlestown would be in favour of a new bridge if the charter contained a provision for taking a foot toll."

(3) Webster wrote, March 20, 1826, See *Letters of Daniel Webster*
(1902) the following opinion:

"I have been favored with yours of the 14th instant relative to the proposed new Bridge, and another also from Mr. Webbs, accompanied by a
Report, made to the Senate, by a committee of which Mr. Hoar is chairman.

In a question, at once so important and so difficult, I feel extremely un-
willingly to say more than the emergent occasion requires. Whether the
State Legislature can authorize an obstruction in an arm of the sea, on
which a Port of delivery is established, by the laws of the United States,
and, if it cannot, whether a Bridge, built for public convenience, and having suitable draws for the passage of vessels is to be deemed an unlawful
obstruction, are questions depending on very general considerations and
are of great moment. Very little has been decided, or discussed, on such
questions, except what transpired in the New York Steam Boat cause, with
which you are probably acquainted. On the other hand, the rest of the
Bridges about Boston and especially Craigie's, seem to stand only on the
supposition that the Legislature may exercise such a power. There is a
Bridge, also, over Piscataqua River at Portsmouth, fifteen or twenty miles
below the head of the tide. There are other similar cases. It is difficult
to draw a line between Rivers, below the head of the tide, and arms of the
Sea. If the commerce of the United States, for its substantial interest

In June, 1826, a new petition was filed, in which the claim was advanced that Charles River Bridge had obtained the extension of its charter in 1792 by fraudulent representations as to its profits. The petition contained a long, plausible legal argument, evidently drafted by eminent counsel. Up to this time, the case for the petitioners had been urged solely on grounds of the public need of a new bridge. In this petition, however, the popular prejudice against the old bridge, which in reality formed the basis for the desired legislation, was made clear:

It is plain that most of the remonstrants must resort to the ambuscade of vested rights in Charles River Bridge in order even to make out a plausible case. And upon this point your petitioners are free to say that if vested rights of the kind insisted upon actually exist, they will never ask for their violation. But if they do not, from what we know of the history of Charles River Bridge, we are equally free to say that that corporation is, under all circumstances, one of the last which demands the sympathy of the Legislature.

Harvard College had early foreseen the injury to its interests, in case the petition for the new bridge should be granted; and, June 27, 1824, the Corporation voted that the President and Treasurer should "attend to the College interests relating to an application for a bridge from Charlestown to Boston, and make such Memorial and Remonstrance as they may deem proper." During all the succeeding legislative struggle the interests of

---

and convenience, require a port of delivery at Roxbury, and if a Bridge, with suitable draws ought to be considered as a real and substantial obstruction, in the way of such commerce, then it would seem to follow that such Bridge could not be lawfully erected. But I do not feel prepared at present, to express an opinion on either of these questions. I might mislead you by doing so, and they are, indeed, questions of nature as fit to be considered by yourselves as by me. The courts of U. S. could not regard the injury to private property.

I am the more willing to be spared from giving an opinion on these points at present, because I do not see how the question can be raised till the Bridge shall be built or begun. The courts of the U. S. cannot interfere, till some one lawfully navigating, meets with an unlawful obstruction. He can then sue and try the right. There must be some actual conflicts between a right exercised under the U. S. and a right exercised under the State before a ground of action can be laid.

In this view of the case, it is perhaps not expedient that I should do more than indicate the general nature of the questions, which would come, in my opinion to be discussed, should the occasion be furnished."

In connection with this letter it is interesting to note that within three years, the United States Supreme Court upheld a Maryland statute which interfered with navigation on certain small navigable creeks, *Wilson v. Blackbird Creek Marsh Co.*, 2 Peters 245, in 1829.

the College were vigorously defended in the debates. For the first three years, however, no attention to its rights had been paid by the adherents of the bill; but in the new petition of June 8, 1826, the College rights were thus mentioned:

The Interest of Harvard College in this matter is too trifling to intercept the progress of the petition. At most it cannot exceed, now, or hereafter, $700 a year, and a way can be easily found to obviate the ground of complaint without any injustice to the University.

No action was taken by the Legislature in 1826; and in June, 1827, for the fourth time, a new petition was filed, asking for a toll bridge, which should become free after reinbursement of the proprietors. By this time the public were greatly aroused. Over one thousand citizens of Charlestown signed the petition, and the matter had become a political issue on which the Democrats and country legislators were lined up largely in favor of the new bridge,—the Whigs, the lawyers, the merchants with the old Federalist affiliations, and the city legislators supporting the old bridge.

The sharp drawing of political lines gradually made it evident to the Charles River Bridge faction that their previous feeling of confidence was now no longer warranted.

In the Senate, an attempt was made at a compromise, and a committee was appointed to report at what date the present stockholders of Charles River Bridge would realize the amount paid by them for their stock, and six per cent. interest. The committee reported such reimbursement would be effected through accrued profits by the year 1859.(1)

This was felt by the Senate to be too long a period to continue the rights of the old bridge; and notwithstanding generous offers on the part of the old bridge proprietors to build a new draw, to repair or reconstruct their bridge or to build a spur bridge, and to make a reduction of 50 per cent. on all tolls except foot passengers, or a 50 per cent. reduction on foot tolls and a reduction of over one-third on all other tolls, a bill passed both House and Senate, granting a charter for the new bridge,

(1) The Committee reported that it found that 82 shares had been bought by stockholders, 1812 to 1823, at prices varying from $1800 to $2200. That between October, 1823, and April, 1824, the stock sold for from $1270 to $1550; and that $1600 was a fair market value, October 1, 1820. The dividends for 1821 were $129; for 1826, $138.

but postponing its construction for four years provided the old bridge Proprietors should within 60 days agree to convey their property to the State on December 31, 1831.

So intense, however, were the feelings created by the passage of this bill, that fourteen senators, among whom were Caleb Cushing, James T. Austin (later Massachusetts Attorney General), David Sears, the noted Boston merchant, and Nymphas Marston, the eminent lawyer of Barnstable, signed a formal protest, filed on the Senate records March 9, 1827.(1)

On March 10, 1827, Governor Levi Lincoln vetoed the bill, which passed over his veto in the House, but was lost in the Senate, by a vote of 16 to 12. After speaking of the violation of contract and of vested rights caused by the new charter, he thus mentioned the College interests:

Further, the obligation to keep up and repair the bridges and pay the College ought not to be continued if they are not to receive tolls. It is not equitable or good faith.

The money pledged to the College must also be paid from the Treasury or lost to science and the faith of the government here again violated.

Further, Governor Lincoln, bearing in mind that the State was being agitated from one end to the other by various schemes for new canals, and that the Commission on Internal Improvement was making a report advocating the construction of the then novel system of railroads and providing for surveys from Boston to the Rhode Island and New York boundaries, was profoundly impressed with the serious effect which this legislative act would have in unsettling the confidence of financial men, and dampening their ardor for embarking in new enterprises.

In one other point of view the bill is regarded as unsalutary. Great improvements of the country have, with us, been the

___

(1) "The undersigned, members of the Senate of the Commonwealth of Massachusetts, hereby protest against the enactment of a bill to establish the Warren Bridge Corporation for the erection of a free bridge over Charles River between Boston and Charlestown, for the following reasons, viz:

Because the erection of the contemplated bridge in the manner authorized in and by said bill would destroy the franchise which the proprietors of Charles River Bridge hold under a grant of this Commonwealth having all the force of a contract; and

Because the grant contemplated by said bill would be in violation of the public faith and of the constitutional rights of the proprietors of said Charles River Bridge, and would tend to unsettle the security of private property."

work of private interprises and responsibility. To the interest and confidence of private associations we must look for investments of funds in the prosecution of valuable and useful objects, and it is only from a firm reliance on the most scrupulous regard to rights under acts of incorporation that they will be encouraged to action. Let distrust of the good faith of the government, nay of its most careful and jealous protection of corporate interests, once be entertained, and there is an end to the labors of associations of individuals in great and noble undertakings. The worst policy will be introduced and the greatest prejudice to country suffered.

It is to be recalled that only six months previous, in October, 1826, George Stephenson had demonstrated in England the success of his steam locomotive "The Rocket." A full description of this had appeared for the first time in the *Boston Daily Advertiser,* November 23, 1826. On November 25, that newspaper stated: "These experiments constitute a new era in the history of railroads. They prove conclusively that they are adapted in the most perfect manner for rapid traveling—whatever power may be used." Earlier, in 1826, the first railway corporation was chartered in Massachusetts—the "Granite Railway Corporation," a tramroad for horse power from the Quincy quarries to the Neponset River. In the same year, New York had chartered the Mohawk and Hudson Railroad Company.

Undiscouraged by their fourth failure, the Warren Bridge petitioners appeared in the Legislature with a new bill early in 1828; and on January 12, 1828, the Charles River Bridge filed a memorial: "We do hereby most respectfully but earnestly and for the fifth time remonstrate, . . ." A remonstrance of the great Middlesex Canal corporation was also filed.

Compromise suggestions were made by the Proprietors of the old bridge to surrender their property to the State at once, for a sum to be fixed by impartial commissioners, or as an alternative to surrender without any payment at the end of eight years. They also expressed, through a committee consisting of Warren Dutton, Richard Sullivan, and Peter C. Brooks, their willingness to reduce tolls, and stated that:

We can discern nothing in the facts or the law of the case or in the present state of public opinion, which should impair their confidence or discourage their hopes. They rely with confidence on the intelligence, wisdom and good faith of the Government for a reasonable protection.

At the same time they are ready to admit that they are desirous of being relieved from the very great burden of making a defence before successive committees of the Legislature, or ultimately, if it should become necessary, which they do not believe, before other tribunals.

By this time, however, the new bridge party in the Legislature was in no mood to accept any offers, however generous or adequate to meet the public needs. The fight had now become one of the country against the city—the country members insisting on the right of their constituents to enter Boston without payment of toll; the city members, having a large financial and commercial constituency, insisting that the State should keep faith and observe its solemn contract. There was also prevalent in the State at this time, a very violent anti-corporation feeling, and the Charles River Bridge corporation was held up as the shining example of a grasping monopoly.(1)

The joint committee reported in favor of the bill, which was ordered to a first reading in the House, February 5, 1828, by a large majority. The Charles River Bridge Proprietors were now thoroughly alarmed; and they again, by vote of February 25, 1828, offered to alter their present bridge, and even to build a new bridge in any manner the Legislature might desire, stating that they made

an earnest appeal to the enlightened wisdom of the Legislature to decide whether the Public Good or Public Policy, without reference to the equity, justice, or legality of such a measure, can require the absolute sacrifice of the great amount of property which they have innocently purchased, and now hold upon the faith of the government.

The Legislature paid no attention to the offer, and on March 12, 1828, the bill passed, granting a charter to the "Proprietors of Warren Bridge," with a right to take toll until the cost of construction with 5 per cent. interest should be reimbursed, the bridge to then revert to the State and to become a free bridge, the term of toll, however, not to exceed six years, and until the

---

(1) The Free Bridge question had become a political issue to such an extent that in the state election of 1827, in April, a candidate was put into the field in opposition to Gov. Levi Lincoln, who based his campaign on this issue—William C. Jarvis, Speaker of the House of Representatives. Owing to Lincoln's personal popularity, Jarvis received only 7130 votes to 29029 for Lincoln.

reversion of the bridge, the Proprietors to pay one-half of the annuity of $666.66 required to be paid to the College by the Charles River Bridge, the latter being relieved from paying this one-half. (See c 127 of the acts of 1827).

Before the bill was signed by the Governor a protest was filed in the House on March 11, 1828, signed by 70 members, among whom were the following prominent lawyers:—Rufus Choate, Emory Washburn, Leverett Saltonstall, Asahel Huntington, Joseph Willard—and also noted men like Horace Mann and James Savage.(1)

Construction of this new bridge was at once begun; and it was so located that on the Charlestown end, the distance between the two bridges was only 260 feet, and on the Boston end 916 feet, the roads leading from the two bridges converging to within a distance of 26 feet. The distance to Charlestown by the old bridge was 3134 feet, by the new, 3243 feet.

The new bridge was opened December 25, 1828; and the effect was seen at once in the alarmingly rapid diminution of traffic over the old bridge, whose toll fell, in the first six months of 1829, from $15,000 to $6,500, as compared with the same period in 1828.

It was quite apparent, therefore, that when the Warren Bridge should become a free bridge in 1834, the Charles River Bridge stock would be worth practically nothing. The damage to the interests of Harvard College would also be severe—first, by its loss of an annuity of $666.66 which had nearly 23 years more to run; second, by the decrease in the value of the Bridge stock owned by it; third, by the loss of the reversionary right which was to remain in the College after the expiration of the old bridge charter, but which would become valuless when the Warren Bridge became a free bridge.

The Charles River Bridge did not wait for the completion of

---

(1) The protest was based on the following grounds—
"First, because neither the public convenience nor necessity require it.
Second, because evidence of amount of tolls was one of the ingredients of public conveniences and necessity on which the committee founded this report.
Third, the granting of another bridge so near as to essentially injure value of property without providing any indemnity, is a violation of existing right, a breach of public faith, and tends to diminish the confidence in and lessen the security of the right of property.
Fourth, because the Legislature have no right to obstruct an important navigable river by another bridge when the same is not required by public convenience and necessity, "apart from any consideration of tolls."

the new bridge before taking action in the courts, but at once engaged as counsel, Daniel Webster and Lemuel Shaw, who proceeded to file a bill in equity June 17, 1828, in the Massachusetts Supreme Court, setting forth the new bridge as a nuisance and an injury to the exclusive rights of the old bridge, and asking for a preliminary injunction.

It is interesting to note that this was one of the first equity suits in the State, based on nuisance; for the statute giving equity jurisdiction in such cases had only recently been passed (St. 1827 c 88). Up to that time, the only matters in equity cognizable by the Massachusetts Courts had been, mortgages and forfeitures under St. 1785 c 22; trusts arising under deeds, wills or in the settlements of estates, and contracts in writing where specific performance was claimed, under St. 1817, c. 87; redemption of lands, under St. 1818, c 98 and St. 1821, c 85; bills for discovery and adjustments between freighters and other parties interested in the same subject matter, under St. 1818, c 122; bills for discovery and delivery and delivery of goods, etc. secreted, and bills of account between partners, etc., under St. 1823, c 140.

Richard Fletcher and William C. Aylwin, who appeared for the Warren Bridge, vigorously opposed the issuance of any preliminary injunction and denied the court's jurisdiction.

Chief Justice Isaac Parker (who had resigned as Professor in the Harvard Law School only a year and a half before) gave the opinion of the court (6 Pickering 376), holding that the Court had jurisdiction, but refusing to issue a preliminary injunction, and—what is surprising to modern lawyers—stating that the plaintiff's request for such an injunction prior to filing of an answer, was something "novel," and almost as "startling" as the first application for this kind of injunction in 1752 seemed to Lord Hardwicke.(1) The Chief Justice said that this kind of injunction was "but sparingly exercised, and only in cases which hardly admit of controversy"; and such conditions he did not find in this case. In order, however, to make it plain that the court had not considered the merits of the case, he began his opinion by warning counsel:

---

(1) In 1752, in an anonymous case, 2 Vesey 414, Lord Hardwicke summarily dismissed such an application for a preliminary injunction, "saying this was a most extraordinary attempt of which he never knew an instance before."

We think it will be unsafe for either party to found any hope or expectation of the final result of this bill upon the failure of the present motion, for it will be seen that there was no occasion to go into the general merits of the case in order to discharge our present duty, and we have not thought ourselves authorized in the actual state of the proceedings, when only one party is formally before the court (the time for answer not having arrived), to decide or even deliberate upon a question on all hands deemed to be of magnitude and importance.

Meanwhile, pending the decision, there had been much speculation in the Charles River Bridge Stock. This was the period when the first railroad enterprises were being discussed and plans for railroad charters made throughout the State. It was foreseen that the final decision of this case would vastly effect the respective rights of such railroads and of the old and powerful turnpike corporations which, it was then apparent, the railroads were likely to supplant. There was consequently immense excitement over the question in all business and financial circles. This fact the Chief Justice recognized, for he closed his opinion as he had begun, by giving

a caution to the parties and to others interested in the question, to all who may wish to speculate on the result, whose projects and schemes are connected with the maintenance or overthrow of the bridge, that we consider the question of the validity of the grant and charter of the new bridge as open and undecided as it was before this motion was made.

Before the Warren Bridge was in actual receipt of tolls, a supplemental bill was filed, and later an amendment (the Warren Bridge then being in receipt of tolls), claiming that the charter under which the Proprietors acted was a violation of the contract of the State with the Proprietors of the Charles River Bridge, and was therefore repugnant to the Constitution of the United States, and claiming further that it was a taking of property without compensation, and thus in violation of the Massachusetts Constitution.

On December 2, 1828, the defendants filed their answer, and both parties proceeded to take depositions. In June, 1829, the defendants asked for delay, claiming insufficient time to gather evidence, but in fact seeking delay until the bridge should be completed and public sentiment created in their favor. This motion being denied, on June 15, the defendants claimed a right under the Constitution to a trial by jury. In deciding this point, Judge Parker spoke of the limited time and opportunity given the court to consider it, as one of the obvious disadvantages of the method of administering equity; and said that the incessant engagements on the common law side of the court unfitted the judges to give the proper amount of attention to its equity cases. He held, however, that no rights of the defendants were infringed if the court should decide which facts, if any, were proper to be left to the jury. The defendants thereupon waived the point, and in October, 1829, the case was argued on its merits by the same counsel as at the previous hearing.

Opinions were given in the case, January 12, 1830 (7 Pick. 344). The court divided evenly, two judges,—Chief Justice Isaac Parker and Judge Samuel Putnam, denying the constitutionality of the statute; two upholding it—Judge Samuel Sumner Wilde and Judge Marcus Morton.(1)

Judge Parker upheld fully the plaintiff's contention that the statute was an impairment of contract and also a taking of property without compensation, saying:

I think this question of the necessity of indemnifying the Proprietors of the Charles River Bridge has been prejudiced by the well known fact that the profits of the bridge have been great beyond the example of any similar institutions in this country. It seems to me that if the legislature of 1787, which is one year after the building of the bridge, when its success could be only conjectural and the experiment of its durability was scarcely tried, had incorporated this company to build the Warren bridge without indemnifying the Proprietors of the old bridge, the opinion of the injustice would have been universal.

Judge Morton (a robust Democrat of the radical type), took the position that to hold the statute unconstitutional would retard all progress, that such a construction as the plaintiffs claimed was not to be placed on a charter for a great public work, and that the grant was to be construed rigidly in favor of the State and against the grantee. The extent to which the economic and social conditions of the day entered into the decision is well illustrated by his remarks:

(1) Robert Rantoul, in his noted Fourth of July oration at Scituate in 1836, spoke of the tendency among corporation advocates to hold an "obnoxious statute unconstitutional, as would have happened in the case of the Warren Bridge, but for the firmness of Judge Morton." See *Memoirs of Robert Rantoul, Jr.,* by Luther Hamilton (1854).

Scarcely a turnpike has been established in the state which has not diverted more or less travel from the former ones. If, therefore, the different private charters in the Commonwealth, granted for that purpose of improving the state of the country and bettering the condition of the people, are to receive the extensive construction contended for, they amount to an entire prohibition of all further internal improvement during their continuance. No improved road, no new bridge, no canal, no railroad, can be constitutionally established. For I think, in the present state of our country, no such improved channel of communication can be opened without diminishing the profits of some old corporation.

Meanwhile, the pendency of this case had already had a serious effect in retarding the development of railroads in Massachusetts. South Carolina, Maryland, New Jersey and New York had already chartered and operated railroads; but Massachusetts financiers had hesitated to embark in such doubtful enterprises, fearing future action of the Legislature which might destroy the value of their charters, similar to that which had wrecked the Charles River Bridge. Finally, however, in 1830, a charter was obtained for the Boston and Lowell Railroad, though with the protection of the express grant of an exclusive right for thirty years. Other charters were granted in the same year without such right; but the difficulties of obtaining stock subscriptions were so great that no railroad was opened for operation until 1834. And even as late as 1835, the effect of the Bridge case was felt when attempts were made to finance the Western Railroad (chartered in March, 1833), which was to connect Boston with Albany. Thus, Josiah Quincy, Jr., its treasurer, noted in his diary, November 25, 1835:

Went round with Mr. Edmund Dwight to obtain subscribers for the Western Railroad and they all with one accord began to make excuses. Some think the city is large enough and do not want to increase it. Some have no faith in legislative grants of charters since the fate of Charlestown Bridge. . . . It is the most unpleasant business I ever engaged in.

An appeal was taken at an early date from the decision of the Massachusetts Court; and the case was entered in the United States Supreme Court, March 19, 1830, to be argued in the January term of 1831. At this point, the great case becomes intimately and interestingly connected with the history of the Harvard Law School,—then an institution only fourteen years old.

Judge Story had been appointed Dane Professor in the School in 1829. Two weeks before the argument, Feb. 24, 1831, he wrote to his colleague, Professor Ashmun:

We are not yet at the Charlestown Bridge case, though it has been staring us in the face for a week past. I think it will be reached next week and then comes the tug of war. We have already a deputation from Charlestown to take care of the court and report progress, and the address of Mr. (Marcus) Morton's constituents has taken some pains to prevent our falling into great errors without all proper admonitions. I want no better gauge of the man than that as a judge he is willing to be the candidate of such people with such avowed opinions.(1)

The first argument took place, March 7-11, 1831, before Chief Justice Marshall and Justices Joseph Story, Smith, Thompson, John McLean, and Henry Baldwin, Justices Gabriel Duvall and William Johnson, being absent. For the Charles River Bridge, Daniel Webster appeared as counsel with Warren Dutton, the latter being one of the most prominent of the Bridge Proprietors. For the Warren Bridge were Walter Jones, the noted lawyer of the District of Columbia, and William Wirt of Maryland, who had recently resigned as Attorney General of the United States. Judge Story wrote to Professor Ashmun March 10:

We are now upon the Charlestown Bridge case and have heard the opening counsel on each side in three days. Dutton for the plaintiffs made a capital argument in point of matter and manner, lawyerlike, close, searching and exact; Jones on the other side was ingenious, metaphysical, and occasionally strong and striking. Wirt goes on to-day and Webster will follow to-morrow. Six Judges only are present which I regret, Duvall having been called suddenly away.

No more important constitutional question had come before the Supreme Court than that involved in this case, since the famous Steamboat Case of *Gibbons v. Ogden,* in 1824. Not only was the fate of this particular corporation involved, but the whole

---

(1) *The Boston Daily Advertiser,* of February 7, 1831, quoting from the *Bunker Hill Aurora,* said, "agents for the parties in the case have repaired to Washington to conduct the cause to its final issue before the Supreme Court now in session. General Austin left town on Thursday."

The reference in Story's letter to Morton is to the fact that Marcus Morton, while still a Justice of the Massachusetts Supreme Court, was the Democratic candidate for Governor in each year from 1828 to 1834 inclusive, the Democrats being largely Warren Bridge men.

trend of future railroad and other corporate development was to hang upon the decision.

After the arguments, it was at once evident that no agreement could be reached by the judges at the current term, and the case was taken under advisement until the January term of 1832, at which time, March 1, 1832, Story wrote to Ashmun:

> The Charlestown Bridge cases not yet decided. Some of the judges had not prepared their opinions when we met; and Judge Johnson has been absent the whole term from indisposition. . . . I may tell you, confidentially, that we are greatly divided in opinion, and it is not certain what the finale may be. Perhaps it may not be decided this term. We shall rise about the middle of March, and I shall find my way home as soon as possible afterwards, so that I may relieve you from some extra duty. I would rather work in the Law School than here.

Though no definite knowledge has ever been had of the decision reached by the Court at this time, it seems probable that Marshall, Story, and a majority of the judges who had heard the argument, had arrived at a conclusion in favor of Charles River Bridge and contrary to that reached by Chief Justice Taney and the Court at the final decision of the case made in 1837.(1) At all events, Story had written out his opinion as early as November 19, 1831, for he wrote to Jeremiah Mason:

> I am now engaged on the Charles River Bridge case. After it is finished I should be glad to have you read it over if I thought it might not give you too much trouble. It is so important a constitutional question that I am anxious that some other mind should see, what the writer rarely can in his zeal, whether there is any weak point which can be fortified or ought to be abandoned. The general structure of the argument, I hope, is sound, but all the details may not be.

To this Mason replied, November 24, stating that he would most willingly examine the opinion and give the result of his reflections on it. Story wrote, December 23, that illness had delayed the completion of his opinion, but that he would send it soon, and he continued:

> I wish to make some remarks to explain the great length and

---

(1) In fact it would appear from the statement made by Judge Baldwin in his *General View,* 11 Peters, App. that he was the only judge in 1831 who held the view taken by the court in 1837.

the repetition of the same suggestions in different parts of the same opinion. I have written my opinion in the hope of meeting the doubts of some of the brethren, which are various and apply to different aspects of the case. To accomplish my object, I felt compelled to deal with each argument separately and answer it in every form, since the objections of one mind were different from those of another. One of the most formidable objections is the rule that royal grants, etc. ,are to be strictly construed; another is against implications in legislative grants; another is against monopolies; another is that franchises of this sort are bounded by local limits; another, that the construction contended for will bar all public improvements. I have been compelled, therefore, to restate the arguments in different connections. I have done so, hoping in this way to gain allies. I should otherwise have compressed my opinion within half the limits.

The opinion thus referred to became the dissenting opinion delivered by Judge Story, when the case was finally decided six years later.

A long delay now ensued, owing to illness and death of several members of the Court, and to the disinclination of the Court to hear or decide so important a case involving a state statute, unless the full Court should be present. By January, 1832, the Court had come to no conclusion; and owing to the illness of Judge Johnson, the case was again held under advisement until the January term of 1833, when, on February 26, 1833, it was ordered for re-argument. Owing to the illness of Judge Baldwin, no argument was had at that term. In 1834, Judge Johnson died, and Judge Duvall was ill. During the next year, 1835, came the death of Chief Justice Marshall and the resignation of Judge Duvall.(1)

Meanwhile William Wirt, then one of the leaders of the United States Bar and chief counsel for the Warren Bridge had died on February 14, 1834; and after much consideration, the Proprietors decided to retain in Wirt's place Professor Simon Greenleaf.

---

(1) In Massachusetts, Lieutenant-Governor S. T. Armstrong sent the following special message to the Legislature, March 20, 1835:

"It appears that at the term of the Court which has just closed there being a vacancy on the bench, the cause was again continued and now stands for argument at the next term in January, 1836; and that it is understood that the Supreme Court of the United States will not usually hear a cause involving the validity of a *State* law unless all the Judges by law to be appointed are commissioned and present on the Bench; so that it is not to be expected that this cause will be again argued without a full court."

Although Greenleaf would be obliged, as counsel in this case, to act in a capacity adverse to Harvard College, no question seems to have been raised by the College as to the propriety of his action. The only official reference to the case is to be found in a letter in the Harvard Archives from Greenleaf to the Corporation, November 27, 1834(1):

Having been requested to argue a cause before the Supreme Court at Washington some time in the ensuing winter, I deem this a proper occasion respectfully to ask whether in your opinion the statutes of the Law Department militate with the practice of law by the Royall Professor, and if not entirely so, then to what extent you should consider him at liberty to accept professional engagements; or by what rule is he to govern himself in such cases. I have hitherto followed the course I understand to have been pursued by my predecessor, accepting only such engagements as I thought would not injuriously interfere with the duties of the Professorship; but the present application inviting me beyond the limits of any former precedent, I feel some difficulty in deciding how to dispose of it. I would request the favor of your opinion as early as convenient, it being for the interest of all parties that no time be lost in preparing the cause.

And in a vote of the Corporation in response to this letter, November 29, 1834:

Voted that the request of Professor Greenleaf for the permission to be absent during the ensuing term one fortnight, for the purpose of arguing an important cause before the Supreme Court of the United States be granted under the Circumstances stated by him,—such absence not being likely to be injurious to the Law School in the opinion of the Law Faculty.

Thus it was that when this great case was argued and decided, nearly three years later (in 1837), it was won by one Harvard Law School Professor, arguing directly contrary to the interests of Harvard College, and with the other Professor delivering from the Bench a dissenting opinion, denying the validity of his Law School colleague's argument.

Chief Justice Taney (appointed in December, 1835), and Judge Barbour (Duvall's successor), did not take their seats until the end of the term in 1836; so that it was not until 1837, six years

---

(1) See *Harv. Coll. Papers,* 2d Series, Vol. VI.

Simon Greenleaf

after the first argument, that a full Court assembled to hear the famous case.(1)

Meanwhile the earnings of the new Warren Bridge had been so large that early in 1832, within about two years after its construction, the bridge had paid for itself, and therefore should under its charter become a free bridge. As, however, an adverse court decision might impose large damages on the corporation, it was deemed by the Legislature advisable to continue the tolls. Accordingly by act of March 24, 1832, (c 170), the tolls were extended until the last day of the first session of the next Legislature. No decision having been rendered by the Supreme Court, the Legislature by act of March 28, 1833 (c 219), again extended the tolls, and provided that unless the Warren Bridge should give a suitable bond, the State should itself collect the tolls and assume the defence of the suit. The Warren Bridge gave its bond, and continued to collect the tolls, and to pay to Harvard College the money required by its charter.

The year 1833 passed without any decision from the Supreme Court. Meanwhile the same popular feeling was now growing against the Warren Bridge as had risen against the Charles River Bridge. The public demanded that the bridge should become free. Nevertheless, Governor John Davis sent a special message to the Legislature, February 12, 1834, stating that he was informed the case was to stand over until 1835, and that in order to do justice to all parties this would probably render further legislation necessary. Hence, by act of March 28, 1834 (c 131), the tolls were for a third time continued. The same action was attempted in the spring of 1835; but the opposition of the town of Charlestown and of signers of 60 other petitions, demanding the abolition of tolls, was so strong that the two branches of the Legislature could not agree on a bill. At the first session of the Legislature,(2) by act of November 4, 1835, (c 155), the tolls were continued until March, 1836, with the following proviso:

----

(1) Professor Greenleaf had written to Treasurer Ward, Jan. 9, 1835:
"My journey to Washington will depend on the contingency of President Jackson's filling the present vacancy on the Bench, and of the new judge taking his seat this term; as the case of the Warren Bridge will not be argued but to a full Bench. Should I go, I shall be happy to be of service to you."—See *Letters to the Treasurers, Harvard College Archives.*
(2) Lieutenant-Governor, S. T. Armstrong, on September 2, 1835, sent a special message to the Legislature saying:
"Many well disposed persons expressed doubts as to legality of longer demanding tolls, strenuously contended that Act of 1834, c. 131, had ex-

That the tolls already collected and such as may hereafter be collected shall be exclusively appropriated to the repairs and maintenance of such bridge, and other purposes relating thereto, and to the payment of all such sums of money as may be recovered by the proprietors of Charles River Bridge in any suit in law or equity.

On March 2, 1836, the bridge became free; and a resolve of the Legislature of April 16, 1836, directed the Governor to appoint a State agent to take charge of it. A famous celebration was held in Charlestown in honor of the event; and the noted lawyer and democrat, Robert Rantoul, was formally thanked for his "indefatigable exertions" in behalf of a free bridge.

The event, however, was a serious one for Harvard College; for when the Warren Bridge became free, it discontinued payment of all annuities to the College.(1) On April 21, 1836, the College Treasurer informed the Corporation that the Charles River Bridge also declined to make any further payment, and on September 19, 1836, he reported that "the bridge shares are at present valueless."(2)

---

pired, and that there was no authority anywhere conferred by virtue of which tolls could be lawfully demanded, and that the Bridge had become a free public highway. . . . Our fellow citizens who are to be so much affected by the eventual decision of this protracted controversy wait with patience and confidence for the removal of the burden of which they complain. . . . Will it not be best to consider and decide the question early and declare what is intended as our settled policy?"

(1) See the following interesting letter from N. I. Bowditch of this Corporation, to Treasurer T. W. Ward, November 24, 1835, *Harv. Coll. Papers*, 2nd Series, Vol. vii.

"I have conferred with Mr. (William) Prescott upon the subject of the rights of the College in the annuity payable by Charles River Bridge. He says that it is possible in case the College have accepted from Warren Bridge the half of said annuity which by their charter they were bound to pay, that act may have operated as an extinguishment of one-half of the annuity in favor of Charles River Bridge, leaving the College to look solely to Warren Bridge for that half—and when that is made free, to the Legislature who made it so. It is clear that nothing can be done by the College until a failure of payment of the annuity occurs. And then Mr. Prescott thinks that the first step should be a petition or memorial to the Legislature reciting the original rights of the College and the subsequent arrangements by which the same became converted into an annuity—and the final act by which the franchise of the corporation chargeable with payment of it has become worthless and their property destroyed, and praying for relief. If this is refused, a suit must be commenced against Charles River Bridge, and perhaps in the new aspect presented by Warren Bridge being made free, a decision of our courts may be obtained which could not be while it continued a toll bridge. Mr. Prescott says that he is happy to be of any service to the College, and makes no charge for his trouble."

(2) See Reports of the Treasurer, April 21, 1836, *Harv. Coll. Papers*, 2nd Series, Vol. VII, and September 12, 1836; *Harv. Coll. Papers*, 2nd Series, Vol. VIII.

The Charles River Bridge received from 1828 to 1836 about one-third of the tolls collected on the two bridges. It was kept open for about one year after the Warren Bridge became free, but was discontinued as a public highway, May 5, 1837, the Legislature having refused its petition for compensation.

The loss to the College was therefore figured as follows: On the two shares purchased by it in 1814 at $2,080—$4,160 loss. The annuity of $666.66 represented a capital of $11,111.11 and the loss of interest on the shares for nine years figured $8,246.40—a total loss of $23,517.71.(1)

Such was the situation when Daniel Webster and Warren Dutton for the Charles River Bridge; and Professor Greenleaf and John Davis (then Senator from Massachusetts), for the Warren Bridge, went to Washington in January, 1837, to argue the great case. Owing to the absence of Judge James M. Wayne, Greenleaf was compelled to wait in Washington for over two weeks, the re-argument of the case not being heard until January 19, and ending January 26.

The following correspondence between Greenleaf and Charles Sumner, who was supplying his place as Instructor at the Harvard Law School during his absence, is full of interest.(2) On January 11, 1837, Greenleaf wrote from Washington:

This is indeed the city of magnificent distances, not only in its own arrangements but in its distance from good New England, especially from that most desirable of all places, the very oculus Novangliae and therefore oculus mundi—need I say, Dane Hall? What is this mighty mass of marble called the Capitol compared with that little edifice of brick which honest Mr. Dane (may he rest in peace) so eloquently remarked to the President was "worth the money it cost?" And what is this mighty realm of Mephistopheles, this, his very headquarters, in comparison with the circle of choice and cultivated spirits, and above all the moral atmos-

---

(1) See estimate made for President Quincy in *Harvard College Archives—Quincy Papers*. In the *History of Harvard University*, Vol. II, App. LIII, Quincy figures the loss at $35,401.16.

(2) The letters from Greenleaf of January 11, 1837, and January 24, 1837, never before published, are to be found in the *Sumner Papers* in the Harvard College Library. The letter from Sumner is contained in *Memoirs and Letter of Charles Sumner* by Edward L. Pierce Vol. II. The letters from Story unless otherwise stated may be found in his *Life and Letters*, by W. W. Story.

Greenleaf also wrote to Sumner, Jan. 11, 1837, that on his way to Washington he paid a visit to Ex-Chancellor Kent "who made very affectionate inquiries after you. I have ordered his portrait to Boston by the first packet and hope soon to see it in the Law Library."

phere, of our own Cambridge? Away with the pitable race of cringing colored menials whose very demeanour speaks slavery, and let me once again be served by Jonathan at the top of his stature for twelve dollars a month, and Betty in pink ribbons Sundays, "only till spring," when she is to be married perchance, or go to Lowell.

You perceive that I am ready to return home so far as the disposition is concerned, but when that blessed day will dawn is deplorably uncertain. Judge Wayne is not arrived. He usually comes to New York in a packet. . . . The Court has as yet done nothing but meet and adjourn, in the hope that by to-morrow he may be here, when our cause will be taken up, it being the first for argument. As soon as the argument is closed I shall start for home on the wings of steam.

I am with you daily in imagination and trust that you are by this time fairly at work. Give my affectionate regards to the members of the School, one and all, for they are capital fellows and I love them as my own brothers.

On January 24, 1837, Greenleaf wrote:

For a week I have had scarcely a thought that was not upon Warren Bridge. The argument was begun Thursday by Mr. Dutton, who concluded Saturday morning. I spoke about two hours on Saturday and nearly three on Monday, and yet merely went straight over my brief, answering, by the way, a few objections on the other side. Mr. Davis followed me yesterday and concluded in three hours to-day, in a most cogent, close, clear and convincing argument. Peters the Supreme Court Reporter says the cause was not nearly as well argued before as now; and in proof of it says that his own opinion is changed by it and that he now goes for the Def'ts! Mr. Webster spoke about an hour this afternoon on general and miscellaneous topics in the cause, and will probably occupy all day to-morrow, as he said he should consume considerable time. He told us he should "tear our arguments to pieces," and abuse me. The former will puzzle him; the latter I doubt not he will do, as he was observed to be very uneasy and moody during the whole defense. Both Mr. Davis and I avoided everything "peoplish" in our remarks, confining ourselves closely to legal views alone. But we expect a great effort from Mr. W to-morrow.

It causes me much uneasiness to be absent from the Law School so long; but I was delighted to learn from your letter to the Judge that things go on so well. They are capital fellows, and possess a large share of my affections.

Present to them my hearty love and good will, and tell them I hope to see them all next week. . . . Had Judge Wayne been here at the opening of the Court, I should have been on my return as early within a day as I anticipated before I left home.

But it is now well understood that he and Cuthbert staid at home to work at the election of a member of Congress.

It has given me a fortnight's residence in Washington and the opportunity to see a little of this great world. Most of the great men, as usually happens on a near view, appear smaller than before, and some who were scarcely seen in the distance, appear greater. The newspapers, as you know by similar experience, give us a very imperfect and often erroneous view of things here. . . . My present judgment is that political life is not to be coveted; that at the present day and in this country, whatever it may have been in the proud days of the old school, the corruptions of public places are great and that it requires no small degree of virtue to withstand them.

I think that many a man used to the world comes here in his complete simplicity and is mortally polluted in a single session—thought here are any others who may remain for years unscathed. After all, give me New England and her sons. There is, to be sure, excellent pluck in the south—men of worth and of valor too—but I cannot sigh with the poet for "a beaker full of the warm south," nor, on the other hand should I prefer our land, for the same reason given by him who "longed to see white women and yellow butter" once more. . . . Heaven bless you.

Sumner wrote on January 25, 1837:

Many thanks for your cordial letter of the 11th from Washington; . . . Pray stay as long as your affection requires, with your daughter, and banish all thought of the Law School. All are cheerful, respectful and contented, and seem to receive the law with perfect faith from their pro tem professor. A murmur, slight as that of a distant brook, has reached me from a counsel against whom I decided in a moot-court case, with an expression of an intention to appeal to Caesar on his return. The parties were, however, entirely respectful, and none have given me any reason to be uneasy. Starkie I hear three days in the week, while Kent I encounter every day. This week I have held two courts, and decided the questions of our partnership and statute of limitations; and also that of the Hindu witness.

The students inquire of me daily when you will be back, and enter earnestly into forensic contest. I have explained again and again the nature of the question you have argued, and endeavoured to enforce and illustrate your views; in short, to make the School "Warren-Bridge men." I have been with you in your labors, and have hung with anxious confidence upon the accents of your lips. I have hoped that some of your points might reach our dear judge's prejudices and bear them away. If such be the case I shall have great joy with you. To convince him would be a greater triumph than to storm a citadel.

Two days after the close of the argument Judge Story wrote to
his son W. W. Story, January 28, 1837(1):

I am glad to learn the localities and gossip and news of Cambridge. To me these have more interest than many topics of
great stirring moment to the public, and especially to public men,
for I have long seen and known that it is scarce worth while to
be worried about public affairs, since they are rarely such as are
controllable by any appeals to wisdom or experience or patriot-
ism, and mainly go just as the headlong, headstrong zeal and discipline of party directs. We have been for a week engaged in
hearing the Charles River Bridge cause. It was a glorious argument on all sides, strong and powerful and apt. Mr. Greenleaf
spoke with great ability and honored Dane College. . . . Mr.
Webster pronounced one of his greatest speeches. Mr. Dutton
was full of learning and acute remarks, and so was Governor
Davis. . . . "Greek met Greek."

Of the arguments of counsel, Judge Story said afterwards, in
his dissenting opinion:

The arguments at the former term were conducted with great
learning, research and ability, and have been renewed at the present term with equal learning, research and ability. But the
grounds have been in some respects varied and new grounds.

Of Greenleaf's argument, his colleague, John Davis said, in
opening his own argument:

If others had not exhausted the subject my worthy and learned
associate has brought such untiring industry into the case that
nothing remains to me but a method of my own, less perfect than
his, and a mere revision of the subject under that arrangement.

Story wrote regarding the argument to Sumner January 25,
1837:

I thank you truly and heartily for your kind letter. It was like
a warm spring breeze, after a cold, wintry, northern blast which
had frozen up all one's feelings and sensations. It was not the
less comforting, that it was dated from Dane College, and told
of all that was thought and done there, and of the law, and the
learned in the law, sojourning there in literary ease, and not dis-
quieted with the turmoils of Washington.
The Charles River Bridge case has been under argument ever

---

(1) See unpublished letter in *Story Papers* in Massachusetts Historical
Society Library.

since last Wednesday, and is just concluded. Every argument was very good, above and beyond expectation, and that is truly no slight praise, considering all circumstances. Our friend Greenleaf's argument was excellent,—full of ability, point, learning, condensed thought, and strong illustration,—delivered with great presence of mind, modestly, calmly, and resolutely. It was every way worthy of him and the cause. It has given him a high character with the Bench and with the Bar, and placed him in public opinion exactly where you and I could wish him to be, among the most honored of the profession. He has given Dane College new *éclat,* sounding and resounding fame; I speak this unhesitatingly. But at the same time I do not say that he will win the cause. That is uncertain yet, will not probably be decided under weeks to come. I say so the more resolutely because on some points he did not convince me; but I felt the force of his argument. Governor Davis made a sound argument, exhibiting a great deal of acuteness and power of thinking. Dutton's argument was strong, clear, pointed, and replete with learning. Webster's closing reply was in his best manner, but with a little too much of *fierté* here and there. He had manifestly studied it with great care and sobriety of spirit. On the whole it was a glorious exhibition for old Massachusetts; four of her leading men brought out in the same cause, and none of them inferior to those who are accustomed to the lead here. The audience was very large, especially as the cause advanced;—a large circle of ladies, of the highest fashion, and taste, and intelligence, numerous lawyers, and gentlemen of both houses of Congress, and towards the close, the foreign ministers, or at least some two or three of them.

The Judges go on quite harmoniously. The new Chief Justice conducts himself with great urbanity and propriety. Judge Barbour is a very conscientious and painstaking Judge, and I think will improve as he goes on. . . . Greenleaf departs to-morrow morning, but he leaves a high repute behind. I feel a sort of homesickness in parting with him, though I have seen less of him here than I should at home.

Later, Story wrote to Professor Greenleaf, on February 11, 1837, just before the announcement of the decision of the case:

I have the pleasure of your letter from Dane College, and I rejoice at it because you are safe and sound at home and in "good fame" abroad. . . . The Court will adjourn on Tuesday or Wednesday next. I shall then go on the speed of high pressure to Cambridge, the first and last in all my thoughts. To-morrow (Monday) the opinion of the Court will be delivered on the Bridge Case. You have triumphed.

On February 14, Story wrote to his wife:

Mr. Greenleaf has gained the cause, and I am sorry for it.
. . . A case of grosser injustice or more oppressive legislation never existed. I feel humiliated, as I think every one is here, by the act which has now been confirmed.

The decision of the court, as is well known, was that public grants are to be construed strictly, and that in the absence of express words in a charter, giving exclusive privileges, no such grant can be inferred. While the legal grounds of the opinion were strong, it is strikingly clear that the Court was powerfully influenced in its decision by the economic conditions of the times and especially by the effect which, it was supposed, a contrary decision would have upon the development of the young railroads of the country.

On this latter point, Dutton for the plaintiff argued:

But the principles to be established by the judgment of the court, in this case, will decide the title to more than ten millions of dollars in the State of Massachusetts alone. If that judgment shall decide that the legislature of Massachusetts has the constitutional power to pass the act in question, what and where is the security for other corporate property? More than four millions of dollars have been invested in three railroads leading from Boston, under charters granted by the Legislature. The title to these franchises is no other and no better than that of the plaintiffs. The same means may be employed to accomplish the same ends, and who can say that the same results will not follow? Popular prejudice may be again appealed to; and popular passions excited by passionate declamations against tribute money, exclusive privileges, and odious monopolies; and these, under skilful management, may be combined, and brought to bear upon all chartered rights, with a resistless and crushing power. Are we to be told that these dangers are imaginary? That all these interests may be safely confided to the equity and justice of the Legislature? That a just and paternal regard for the rights of property and the obligations of good faith, will always afford a reasonable protection against oppression or injustice? I answer all such fine sentiments by holding up the charter of Charles River Bridge, once worth half a million of dollars, and now not worth the parchment it is written upon.

To this, Davis for the defendant replied:

The counsel are mistaken when they say that a decision in favor of the defendants will be fatal to future enterprises. This case has stood decided in their court for several years, and the history of Massachusetts can exhibit no period that will compare with it in investments for internal improvements; confidence in the integrity and good faith of the state never stood higher, nor did capitalists ever go forward with greater resolution and courage.

Chief Justice Taney in his opinion dealt at length and very powerfully with this argument:—[11 Peters 551-552].

Indeed, the practice and usage of almost every State in the Union old enough to have commenced the work of internal improvement, is opposed to the doctrine contended for on the part of the plaintiffs in error. Turnpike roads have been made in succession on the same line of travel; the latter ones interfering materially with the profits of the first. These corporations have, in some instances, been utterly ruined by the introduction of newer and better modes of transportation and traveling. In some cases railroads have rendered the turnpike roads on the same line of travel so entirely useless that the franchise of the turnpike corporation is not worth preserving. Yet in none of these cases have the corporations supposed that their privileges were invaded, or any contract violated on the part of the State. Amid the multitude of cases which have occurred, and have been daily occurring for the last forty or fifty years, this is the first instance in which such an implied contract has been contended for, and this court called upon to infer it from an ordinary act of incorporation, containing nothing more than the usual stipulations and provisions to be found in every such law. . . . We cannot deal thus with the rights reserved to the States; and by legal intendments and mere technical reasoning, take away from them any portion of that power over their own internal police and improvements which is so necessary to their well being and prosperity. . . . Let it once be understood that such charters carry with them these implied contracts, and give this unknown and undefined property in a line of traveling, and you will soon find the old turnpike corporations awakening from their sleep, and calling upon this court to put down the improvements which have taken their place. The millions of property which have been invested in railroads and canals, upon lines of travel which had been before occupied by turnpike corporations, will be put in jeopardy. We shall be thrown back to the improvements of the last century, and obliged to stand still, until the claims of the old turnpike corporations shall be satisfied, and they shall consent to permit these States to avail themselves of the lights of modern science, and to partake of the benefit of those improvements which are now adding to the wealth and prosperity and the convenience and comfort of every other part of the civilized world. Nor is this all. This court will find itself compelled to fix, by some arbitrary rule, the width of this new kind of property in a line of travel; for if such a right of property exists, we have no lights to guide us in marking out its extent, unless, indeed, we resort to the old feudal grants, and to the exclusive rights of ferries, by prescription, between towns; and are prepared to decide that when a turnpike road from one town to another had been made, no railroad or canal, between these two points, could afterwards be established. This court is not prepared to sanction principles which must lead to such results.

Judge Story and Judge Thompson dissented from this decision, Story's opinion being undoubtedly one of the ablest efforts of his life. In it he said:

I have examined the case with the most anxious care and deliberation and with all the lights which the researches of the years intervening between the first and last argument have enabled me to obtain, and I am free to confess that the opinion which I originally formed after the first argument is that which now has my most firm and unhesitating conviction. The argument at the present term, so far from shaking my confidence in it, has, every step, served to confirm it. . . . In now delivering the results of that opinion I shall be compelled to notice the principal arguments urged the other way. My great respect for the counsel who have pressed them and the importance of the cause will, I trust, be thought a sufficient apology for the course which I have, with great reluctance thought it necessary to pursue.

The interest taken at the Law School in the case is well shown in a letter from Sumner to Story, March 25, 1837, after the decision had been announced:

I have read most deliberately all the opinions of the judges in the Warren Bridge case. I have studied them and pondered them, and feel unable to restrain the expression of my highest admiration for the learning the argument, the ardour and the style in which you have put your views. If I had not been magnetized by many conversations with Mr. Greenleaf and Mr. Fletcher, and by the deep interest which I was induced, from my friendly intercourse with them, to take in favor of the Warren Bridge, I should feel irresistibly carried away by the rushing current of your opinion. Reading it with a mind already preengaged to the other side, I feel my faith shaken, nevertheless, and cannot but say, "Thou almost persuadest me." . . . As I read Taney's before I read yours, I felt agreeably surprised by the clearness and distinction with which he had expressed himself and the analysis by which he appeared to have been able to avoid the consideration of many of the topics introduced into the argument. But on reverting to his opinion again after a thorough study of yours, it seemed meagre indeed. Your richness of learning and argument was wanting. I thought of Wilke's exclamation on hearing the opinion of Lord Mansfield and his associates in his famous case—that listening to the latter after the former was taking hog wash after champagne. Your opinion is a wonderful monument of juridical learning and science. Indeed, I do not know where to turn for its match in all the books. . . At present it will suffice for me to say that you have made a skeptic, even if you have not gained a convert.

Nobody in our country, or in the world, could have written your opinion but yourself. . . . *Aut Morus, aut Diabolus.* It will stand in our books as an overtopping landmark of professional learning and science.

Ex-Chancellor James Kent wrote to Story, April 18, 1837:

The Bridge case I read as soon as I received it, to the end of the opinion of the Chief Justice, and I then dropped the pamphlet in disgust and read no more. I have just now finished your masterly and exhausting argument.

Later he wrote to Story, June 23, 1837:

I have re-perused the Charles River Bridge case, and with increased disgust. It abandons, or overthrows, a great principle of constitutional morality, and I think goes to destroy the security and value of legislative franchises. It injures the moral sense of the community, and destroys the sanctity of contracts. If the Legislature can quibble away, or whittle away its contracts with impunity, the people will be sure to follow. *Quidquid delirant reges plectuntur Achivi.* I abhor the doctrine that the legislature is not bound by every thing that is necessarily implied in a contract, in order to give it effect and value, and by nothing that is not expressed *in hæc verba,* that one rule of interpretation is to be applied to their engagements, and another rule to the contracts of individuals. . . . But I had the consolation, in reading the case, to know that you have vindicated the principles and authority of the old settled law, with your accustomed learning, vigor, and warmth, and force.

Story's dissenting opinion was also approved by such eminent Massachusetts lawyers as Webster, William Prescott and Jeremiah Mason. Webster wrote, shortly after the decision:

I lost the first five minutes of your opinion, but I heard enough to satisfy me that the opposite opinion had not a foot, nor an inch, of ground to stand on.

I say, in all candor, that it is the ablest, and best written opinion, I ever heard you deliver. It is close, searching, and scrutinizing; and at the same time full of strong and rather popular illustrations.

The intelligent part of the profession will all be with you. There is no doubt of that; but then the decision of the Court will have completely overturned, in my judgment, one great provision of the Constitution.

Later, Webster said, in an argument in behalf of the Lowell & Boston Railroad Company made in January, 1845, before a committee of the Massachusetts Legislature:

When I look back now after a long lapse of years and read the judgments of those judges. . . . I must say that I see, or think I see, all the difference between a manly, honest, and just maintenance of the right, and an ingenious, elaborate, and sometimes half shamefaced apology for what is wrong. Now I am willing to stake what belongs to me as a lawyer, and I have nothing else, and to place on record my decision that that decision cannot stand; that it does not now enjoy the general confidence of the profession; that there is not a head, with common sense in it, whether learned or unlearned, that does not think, not a breast that does not feel, that, in this case, the right has quailed before the concurrence of unfortunate circumstances.

As a summary of the whole case, perhaps the following statement by George W. Biddle is among the best of the many favorable comments upon it(1):

Story's dissenting opinion in the bridge case is a wonderful combination of great learning, and, if the phrase may be permitted, of judicial oratory, in defense of a cause in which he thought the principles of morality and public integrity were involved and about to be successfully overthrown in the person of a valuable corporation which had been a pioneer in the cause of internal improvements. It was lighted up with the fires, not yet cooled, of the rulings in the Dartmouth College case, and was something like a protest against an assault supposed to be about to be committed upon the doctrine solemnly announced by that important decision.

In truth, the principle of the Dartmouth College case perhaps correct enough, when limited as it was, applied to a private grant, had been pushed by its advocates to an extreme that would have left our State governments in possession of little more than the shell of legislative power. If the liberality of construction

---

(1) *Contitutional Developments in the United States as Influenced by Chief Justice Taney,* by George W. Biddle.

contended for had been permitted, all its essential attributes would have been parcelled out without possibility of reclamation, through recklessness or something worse, among the greedy applicants for monopolistic privileges.

. . . Unless the luxuriant growth, the result of the decision in 4 Wheaton, had been lopped and cut away by the somewhat trenchant reasoning of the Chief Justice, the whole field of legislation would have been choked and rendered useless in time to come for the production of any laws that would have met the needs of the increasing and highly developed energies of a steadily advancing community.

Whether the above tribute to the decision has been justified may well be doubted.

In view of the expansion of railroads, the unnecessary parallelling of lines and the recklessness of legislatures in granting charters, in subsequent years, a very strong argument could be made that the prosperity of the country would have been better promoted had the court followed Judge Story's decision on the law and the arguments urged by Mr. Dutton and Mr. Webster.

The subsequent course of State statutory law in the United States would seem to show that the legislatures needed no encouragement from the bench towards a relaxation of the policy of maintaining complete faith as to past grants.

The sequel to this case may be briefly summed up.

At the session of the Massachusetts Legislature of 1837, the Charles River Bridge applied for compensation but without success, although by resolve of April 20, 1837, a joint committee was appointed: "to consider and report: 1. What is the value of Charles River Bridge? 2. What would have been the value of the franchise of the Corporation if the Warren Bridge charter had not been granted? What would have been its value if the Warren Bridge had remained a toll bridge and what is its value as it is now situated? 3. To inquire whether any arrangement can be made with any cities, towns or counties, for contributing to supporting said bridge as a free public avenue."

In 1838, notwithstanding Governor Edward Everett, in his message of January 9, recommended "a final adjustment on liberal and equitable principles," nothing was done for the Charles River Bridge. In 1839, in his message of June 10, Governor Everett said, "Public convenience and private seem to call loudly for some definite arrangement as to the Warren Bridge," but again nothing was done. In 1840, Marcus Morton was elected

Governor as a Democrat, by one vote over Edward Everett. As, however, he had been the judge who had prevented a decision in favor of the Charles River Bridge in the Massachusetts Supreme Court, and as he was strongly opposed to all corporations, it was not to be expected that the Legislature would do anything for the Bridge.

In 1841, however, when John Davis, a Whig, was elected Governor, the long drawn controversy which had now lasted for eighteen years, was finally settled so far as the Bridge was concerned by the passage of an act, March 17, 1841 (c 88) providing for the payment of the meagre sum of $25,000 for a surrender of the title to the Charles River Bridge and of its rights and charter. The long fight, however, came to a most impotent and unsatisfactory conclusion as regarded the general public; for notwithstanding the determined struggles of the public for a free bridge, the statute provided that while Charles River Bridge should be opened again for travel (it having been closed for nearly four years), toll should again be collected, and further that the Warren Bridge should again become a toll bridge.

Thus at a cost of only $25,000, plus the amount spent by the State in maintaining the Warren Bridge for the previous five years, the State came into possession of two fine bridges, and the public was still obliged to pay toll.

No action, however, was taken towards compensation to Harvard College for its losses until 1847 when its claims received recognition and justice was at last accorded.

By resolve of April 26, 1847 (c 98), the Legislature appropriated the sum of $3333.30 in compensation for the loss of the annuity from Charles River Bridge during the five preceding years the Bridge had been in the possession of the Commonwealth; and it revived the right to receive the original annuity during the succeeding nine years, the remainder of the term of the Bridge Corporation had it continued to exist. In the words of the Treasurer of Harvard College in his Annual Report for 1846-47:

This is a partial revival of one of the first legislative grants to the College, one which bears date more than two centuries ago (1640); and although it by no means compensates the loss of the College, yet it is agreeable to see the disposition manifested by the State, once more to do something for education at Cambridge after the lapse of so long an interval in her patronage;

and it encourages the hope that her ability may provide for some of those wants which are heavily fclt there, and which by limiting the education of her sons, limit also her own prosperity.

So ended the Charles River Bridge Chapter on the legislative and judicial records of the State and Nation.